A HANDBOOK
on
THE GOSPEL OF MARK

The Handbooks in the **UBS Handbook Series** are detailed commentaries providing valuable exegetical, historical, cultural, and linguistic information on the books of the Bible. They are prepared primarily to assist practicing Bible translators as they carry out the important task of putting God's Word into the many languages spoken in the world today. The text is discussed verse by verse and is accompanied by running text in at least one modern English translation.

Over the years church leaders and Bible readers have found the UBS Handbooks to be useful for their own study of the Scriptures. Many of the issues Bible translators must address when trying to communicate the Bible's message to modern readers are the ones Bible students must address when approaching the Bible text as part of their own private study and devotions.

The Handbooks will continue to be prepared primarily for translators, but we are confident that they will be useful to a wider audience, helping all who use them to gain a better understanding of the Bible message.

P9-ASJ-723

Helps for Translators

UBS Handbook Series:

A Handbook on . . .

Guides:

A Translator's Guide to . . .

Technical Helps:

A HANDBOOK ON

The Gospel of Mark

by Robert G. Bratcher
and Eugene A. Nida

UBS Handbook Series

United Bible Societies
New York

Books in the series of Helps for Translators may be ordered from a national Bible Society or from either of the following centers:

United Bible Societies
European Production Fund
PO Box 81 03 40
70520 Stuttgart
Germany

United Bible Societies
1865 Broadway
New York, New York 10023
U.S.A.

L.C. Cataloging-in-Publication Data:

Bratcher, Robert G.
      [Translator's handbook on the Gospel of Mark]
      A handbook on the Gospel of Mark / by Robert G. Bratcher and Eugene A. Nida.
            p.   cm. — (UBS handbook series) (Helps for translators)
      Originally published: A translator's handbook on the Gospel of Mark, 1961.
      Includes bibliographical references and index.
      ISBN 0-8267-0156-6
      1. Bible. N.T. Mark—Translating. I. Nida, Eugene Albert, 1914-   . II. Title. III. Title: Gospel of Mark. IV. Series. V. Series: Helps for translators.
BS2585.5.B7 1993
226.3'077—dc20   92-40062
                                                                                     CIP

ABS-11/94-350-4,850-CM-10-102666

CONTENTS

INTRODUCTION

The reader may rightly wonder why the United Bible Societies should publish a "Translator's Handbook," when there are so many excellent commentaries available on all the books of the Bible. Why are these commentaries not sufficient? How can a "Translator's Handbook" possibly differ sufficiently from them so as to warrant an additional publication of this nature?

In the first place we must emphasize the fact that the present volume is not designed to take the place of commentaries, not even for the translator. Commentaries are indispensable for any translator who is going to do justice to his work. There are, however, some essential differences between this volume and commentaries, and in order that the special relevance of this and the volumes of the Handbook series which are to follow may be more fully understood, we need to examine briefly some of these differences.

For the average translator commentaries tend to present something of a problem, for they often contain a great deal of material which seems irrelevant to his task, such as expository insights, homiletical suggestions, and historical developments in theology and doctrine. At times it is difficult to see the exegetical trees because of the homiletical forest. Many of these matters, of course, which may at first appear somewhat marginal to the translator's immediate task, are nevertheless important to his ultimate work, but if he is to appreciate them fully they need to be presented in such a way as to indicate clearly their particular significance to the task of translating. At the same time, not only do writers of commentaries present a vast variety of information, since they are attempting to write for an audience of widely different backgrounds and interests, but more often than not they tend to have certain special points of view which they try to promulgate or defend, sometimes to the neglect of other orientations or possibilities of interpretation. If the translator, however, is to do his work well, he must have guidance as to the relevance of the background data, and he needs to be shown the entire range of possible interpretations and, whenever possible, the particular exegesis which reflects the majority view of scholarly opinion.

In addition, however, to an introduction to the problem of the meaning of the Greek, any translator who is working in a language which is outside the Indo-European family of languages will need to have help on just how the various interpretations, as may exist in the Greek, can be adequately rendered in some other language. For these problems the commentaries are relatively useless, for there is no real need and, consequently, little attempt to explore these difficulties. In English, for example, the explanation that the Greek term for "repent" means "to change the mind" offers little difficulty to the reader. In many languages, however, "to change the mind" means merely "to change one's opinion," which is a far cry from the radical change envisaged by the original Greek term. It is necessary, therefore, to add that the meaning of "repent" in Kekchi, a language of Guatemala, is brought out by the phrase "it pains my heart;" in Baouli, of the Ivory Coast, "it hurts so much I want to quit" is the proper equivalent; in Northern Sotho, of South Africa, one must say "it becomes untwisted," and in Tzeltal, of Mexico, the correct expression is "my heart returns because of my sin." The idiom "to beat the breast" needs no explanation for English readers, but translators working in many of the languages of Africa need to be warned that this idiom, when literally translated, may mean "to congratulate oneself" (the equivalent to the English "pat oneself on the back"). Similarly, there are problems of cultural contrasts which need to be brought to a translator's attention, or the resulting translation may be utterly meaningless or entirely misleading.

Perhaps the most serious obvious problem for translators is the fact that many languages have obligatory categories which simply do not exist in Greek. For example, there may be two types of first person plural pronouns, inclusive and exclusive, resulting in a number of translation problems. Even more frustrating are the honorifics which exist in many languages of India and other countries of Southeast Asia, where in both the choice of words and grammatical forms one must attempt to indicate the relative social position of the participants in any communicative event.

On the other hand, these difficulties of lexicon, involving the meanings of words, idioms, and categories, though very striking are not so complex as those which involve syntax. For example, many of the long sentences of Greek must be broken up into more understandable units, the involved Greek hypotaxis must be rendered into the parataxis of many indigenous tongues, and the numerous transitional particles, which are the symbol of Greek grammatical elegance, must be radically altered if an equivalent message is to be communicated in another language.

It is quite understandable why such problems are not treated in commentaries, for many of these lexical and syntactic difficulties do not occur in translating Greek into English and other European languages. With respect to syntax and accidence these modern languages are quite similar to Koiné Greek, and a commentary written in one of these languages will not deal with problems which appear at every step to a translator working in another language. Some problems, of course, do appear even in modern European languages, such as the precise equivalent of the Greek aorist; and an exegetical commentary will deal adequately with these problems. It is only when we confront the problems of interpretation in quite different languages spoken by people having very diverse cultures that we come face to face with many and unusually acute difficulties.

In order to meet the particular needs of the average Bible translator working in any one of the hundreds of tongues in which work is now in process, this volume has been specially designed in what are essentially two parts: the first, dealing with textual notes, punctuation, and exegesis, written by Robert G. Bratcher, and the second, treating the ways in which the various meanings may be translated into other languages, prepared by Eugene A. Nida. Though it has been quite impossible to be exhaustive in the handling of either the exegetical or translational phase, the authors, with the generous help of many translators and colleagues, have endeavored at least to suggest something of the range of difficulties and the nature of some of the more satisfactory solutions.

Though textual problems cannot, of course, be treated in anything like a comprehensive manner, it is felt that the translator should be aware of some of the textual problems in connection with the Greek text he is translating. The textual notes, however, make reference only to the most important printed editions of the Greek text, and very rarely to the original manuscripts and early versions of the New Testament.

Due to the still widespread use of the *Textus Receptus* (the text underlying the King James version, 1611, and many other major versions), it was felt that the translator should see for himself, in a convenient form, the *Textus Receptus* readings which are today rejected by most, if not by all, major critical Greek texts. Accordingly, where significant meaning is involved, most variants of the *Textus Receptus* have been duly noted. [1]

---

[1] It may be useful to notice here, briefly, the genesis and nature of the *Textus Receptus*. The first printed Greek New Testament to be published was edited by Erasmus in 1516. At the instigation of Froben, a Basle publisher, Erasmus hurriedly prepared a text in order to get it published before the publication of the Greek text of the Complutensian Polyglot. Erasmus used very few Greek manu-

It is clear that the brief textual notes given in this Handbook are designed simply to inform the translator concerning textual problems and allow him to ascertain the position of the most important modern critical Greek texts with regard to disputed readings.

---

scripts in preparing his text, none of which was older than the 10th century and some of which were as late as the 16th century. His principal manuscript for the Gospels was from the 15th century; for the Acts and Epistles, the 13th or 14th century; and for Revelation he had only one manuscript, of the 12th century. Since this manuscript lacked the last six verses Erasmus translated these verses from the Latin into Greek and incorporated them into his text. Further editions of his New Testament were published in 1519, 1522, 1527 and 1535.

The Parisian publisher Robert Estienne (latinized as Stephanus), and his son Henri, in 1546 published the Greek New Testament, largely reproducing Erasmus' text; further editions followed in 1549, 1550, and 1551. This last edition, published in Paris, was the one into which Estienne introduced the verse division of the text, followed to this day.

Theodore Beza, of Geneva, from 1565 to 1611 published several editions of the Greek New Testament, based mainly on the 4th edition of Stephanus.

The Elzevir brothers of Leyden, Bonaventure and Abraham, in 1624 published their first edition, following closely Beza's text. Their second edition of 1633 had a typical publisher's "blurb" which, however, had effects far more widespread and deleterious than most advertisements. The editors said of their edition: *Textum ergo habes nunc ab omnibus receptum, in quo nihil immutatum aut corruptum damus* ("The text, therefore, you now have is accepted by all, in which we give nothing changed or corrupt"). This edition was to become the famous *Textus Receptus*, the basis of nearly all major translations of the New Testament through the 19th century. (In England the *Textus Receptus* is Stephanus' 3rd edition of 1550, practically identical with the Elzevir edition of 1633; according to one calculation there are only 287 differences between them).

The *Textus Receptus*, then, is a late and corrupt edition of the Greek New Testament, based on inferior manuscripts. It contains many changes that scribes introduced into the text throughout the centuries in which manuscripts were copied by hand, changes which are now known to be spurious as we compare the late manuscripts with earlier ones. Although some older and more reliable manuscripts were available at that time, most editors were content simply to reproduce Erasmus' work, with minor alterations based on the Complutensian edition and some other Greek manuscripts.

Following the work of Mill, Bentley, Bengel, Griesbach, Lachmann, Tregelles, Tischendorf, Hort, Westcott, Weiss, and other scholars, the present editions of the Greek New Testament—of which the most widely used are the Nestle editions—are based upon much older and much more reliable Greek manuscripts, such as the uncials Vaticanus, Sinaiticus, and Alexandrinus, and the papyri manuscripts such as the Chester Beatty and Bodmer collections, to name only a few. These date from the 5th back to the 2nd centuries, and enable the modern editor of the Greek New Testament to prepare a text much older and more accurate than the *Textus Receptus*. The early versions and patristic citations also provide a wealth of evidence for the reconstruction of the original text.

Translations of these Greek New Testaments, therefore, are in fact much "older" New Testaments than the translations of the *Textus Receptus*, such as the King James Version of 1611.

As is well known, all punctuation is the work of editors, since the Greek manuscripts themselves are devoid of punctuation. In most cases editors are agreed; where, however, differences of opinion arise affecting the meaning of the Greek text, notice is taken of the various ways in which the text is punctuated (cf. 1:1, 8:18).

The exegetical notes are meant to make clear the meaning of the text, in terms of the translator's problems and needs. Consequently, as noted above, matters of derived theological or doctrinal import are rarely, if ever, touched upon. Abundant use is made of grammars, lexicons, and commentaries. The Lexicon of Bauer, as translated by Arndt and Gingrich, is quoted at almost every step, in the hope that every translator will constantly avail himself of this invaluable tool or its equivalent in other languages.

Where there are grounds for different meanings in a given verse or sentence, the attempt is made to set forth these different valid interpretations; sometimes preference is given to one over other interpretations, and at times no preference is expressed. Ancient versions and major modern translations in European languages have been consulted at every step.

Commentaries are referred to by the name of the author alone, as well as grammars and lexicons (cf. Bibliography); Greek texts are cited by the name of their editor (cf. Bibliography), while translations are referred to either by conventional abbreviations (AV, *Authorized Version*, 1611; ERV, *English Revised Version*, 1881; ASV, *American Standard Version*, 1901; RSV, *Revised Standard Version*, 1946), or by the name of the translator. The English text quoted in this commentary is that of the Revised Standard Version (1946) [1] used by permission of the Division of Christian Education of the National Council of the Churches of Christ in the United States of America. Though the RSV is employed as a "running text" preceding the discussion of each section (usually individual verses), the exegetical section is not based on the RSV, but on the Greek text itself, usually the Nestle 24th edition. The Greek is given, however, in transliterated form, for it is recognized that many Bible translators, especially those working in so-called "primitive languages," do not have a ready working knowledge of Greek. On the other hand, the citation of the Greek forms provides a much more satisfactory basis for explanation and can be of real usefulness to translators who may wish to use concordances or wordbooks having transliterated forms. At the same time, translators who are familiar with Greek can readily adjust

---

[1] Edition of 1960.

themselves to the use of transliteration, even though this may seem somewhat awkward at first.

The Greek expressions are cited in terms of primary and secondary levels of comments, with two steps of indentation. The primary level, which often includes an entire phrase, is given in the grammatical forms of the Greek text, while the secondary comments, which are largely lexical, are cited in their traditional lexical forms so as to facilitate use of lexicons.

One important feature of the lexical discussions is the fact that except for very common terms, each word is followed at its first point of occurrence by a list of all passages in which it is to be found in the book of Mark. This provides the translator with a kind of built-in concordance for these key words.

No attempt has been made to cite the full range of scholarly works which might be noted as supporting or opposing certain interpretations. However, in most instances of significant differences of opinion a number of authorities are noted, not only as means of indicating to the reader the extent of the scholarly support for the position in question, but also as a way of guiding the translator to sources of fuller information on such points.

There are, of course, numerous interesting lexical and grammatical points which are not touched, simply because they do not seem to be specifically related to serious translational problems.

In the sections of the Handbook identified as *Translation*, there are essentially two different types of problems: lexical and syntactic, but these are not treated separately since so often they are interrelated. For example, an equivalent expression for "love" may involve not only the mention of a psychological focus of the personality, e.g. the liver, spleen, abdomen, throat, etc., but also the fact that such an expression must be cast as a verbal, rather than as a nominal phrase. The range of translation difficulties for any given passage is only illustrative, for one simply could not, nor need not, introduce constantly all the types of problems that would occur where languages differ radically in such categories as aspect, voice, number, gender, distance, participation, viewpoint, source of information, etc. We have, however, tried to cite a sufficient range of difficulties as to warn the translator of the problems which he is likely to encounter.

The selection of problems for the translational section has not depended, however, upon our having had some illustrative data on the problem in question. Rather, these difficulties are treated because they are recognized as involving (1) features of grammar which are known to require reorganization of form because of the structural complexities involved or the lack of ready correspondences between languages, and (2) features of meaning which tend not to have direct equivalents in other languages due to differences of word classes, cultural backgrounds, figurative extensions of meaning, and/or levels of generic or abstract usage. The citations of renderings in various languages are incorporated in order to illustrate the diversity of usage and to suggest possible alternatives. They are certainly not to be conceived as prescriptive models, nor do they delimit the range of the problems considered. In other words, the analysis of the semantic problems is not restricted to available illustrations.

The data which are cited in the section under *Translation* are drawn from a number of sources, including principally: (1) *The Bible Translator*, which during the last ten years has included a wide variety of translational problems and solutions; (2) the field notes of Eugene A. Nida and his colleagues, who have checked translations in over one hundred and fifty languages; (3) correspondence from translators in the field, who have sent in their difficulties and solutions; (4) results of translators' conferences (including especially the Djakarta Translators' Conference in 1952, sponsored by the Netherlands Bible Society and the Indonesian Bible Society, and the yearly Translators' Conference in Guatemala); and (5) the generous assistance of Dr. van der Veen, of the Netherlands Bible Society, who supplied a number of examples of translations in various Indonesian languages.

Despite, however, a file of some 25,000 different translational problems and solutions, which constituted the major source of the data cited in the translation section, it is fully recognized that this is by no means exhaustive. It is hoped, however, that this source will grow as more translators are willing to share their problems and solutions with others.

When citing a rendering which is misleading or incorrect, we have purposely not indicated the language. There is no need to engage in such unnecessary criticism, since the name of the language is not essential to an understanding of the problem. Where there are commendable translations, however, we have consistently tried to indicate the language, wherever this is known to us, for it is felt that credit should go where credit is due. In a number of instances, however, the notes which we have made of translation problems and solutions reflect not a final but an evolving stage of the work, and hence the translators working in these languages may have in the meantime modified their renderings or

XIII

adopted quite different forms of expression. It has not been possible, of course, to revalidate all of these details, but the authors will certainly welcome correspondence from translators whose data are cited here and who may have now found still more satisfactory solutions.

Though the major thrust of this Handbook is admittedly in the direction of Bible translators working in languages which are outside of the Indo-European family and which reflect very different cultural backgrounds, nevertheless, translators working in Indo-European languages and in those with a long literary heritage will find much that is very useful for their study, since the basic principles and procedures of effective communication, which underlie good translation work in whatever language, have been carefully followed and generously illustrated.

No attempt has been made in this volume to provide an introduction to the theory of Bible translating. These problems have been fully dealt with from time to time in *The Bible Translator*, and are discussed in a general handbook, *Bible Translating* by Eugene A. Nida. One useful tool, referred to frequently in this volume, is *Mark, a Greek-English Diglot For the Use of Translators* (1958), published by the British and Foreign Bible Society, the Greek text of which has been edited by Prof. G. D. Kilpatrick, and the English text translated by a highly competent committee. For translators familiar with various languages in India, Hooper's *Indian Wordbook* is an important tool, though it does not contain discussions of the meaning of various words as they are used in different Indian languages.

In a very real sense it must be recognized that this volume is a "dependent" one, for it does not attempt any novel exegetical solutions nor does it presume to suggest translational equivalents which have not already been proven by experience. In this sense, therefore, it is a volume which must be dedicated to those who as scholars of the Greek text or as translators of it into other languages have provided the basic data of which the authors have only been collators. It is hoped, therefore, that the results may prove useful to the student who is seeking a useful guide to the exegesis of the Greek text, and most especially to the translator who can profit from the wide variety of solutions found by his fellow workers facing similar problems in other parts of the world.

United Bible Societies
Sub-Committee on Translation

BIBLIOGRAPHY

1. Greek Texts

Kilpatrick, G. D., *Mark, A Greek-English Diglot for the use of Translators*. London, 1958.

Lagrange, M.-J., *Évangile selon Saint Marc*. Paris, 1947.

Legg, S. C. E., *Novum Testamentum Graece. Secundum Marcum*. Oxford, 1935.

Merk, Augustinus, *Novum Testamentum Graece et Latine (editio septima)*. Rome, 1951.

Nestle, Erwin, *Novum Testamentum Graece (editio vicesima prima)*. Stuttgart, 1952.

Soden, H. F. von, *Die Schriften des Neuen Testaments (Teil II, Text und Apparat)*. Göttingen, 1913.

Souter, Alexander, *Novum Testamentum Graece*. Oxford, 1910.

Taylor, Vincent, *The Gospel According to St. Mark*. London, 1952.

Textus Receptus: F. H. A. Scrivener, *Novum Testamentum, Textus Stephanici A. D. 1550*. Cambridge, 1877.

Tischendorf, Constantinus, *Novum Testamentum Graece (editio octava critica maior)*. Leipzig, 1869.

Turner, C. H., "A Textual Commentary on Mark I," *Journal of Theological Studies*, xxviii, 1926-7, 145-58.

Vogels, H. J., *Novum Testamentum Graece et Latine (editio quarta)*. Barcelona, 1955.

Westcott, B. F., and Hort, F. J. A., *The New Testament in the Original Greek*. London, 1890.

LXX: *Septuaginta (editio quarta)*, ed. Alfred Rahlfs. Stuttgart, 1950.

2. Translations

AV: *The New Testament of our Lord and Saviour Jesus Christ. Authorized Version*, 1611.

ASV: *The New Covenant, commonly called The New Testament of our Lord and Saviour Jesus Christ. American Standard Edition of the Revised Bible*. New York, 1901.

Berkeley: *Berkeley Version of the New Testament* (6th edition), by Gerrit Verkuyl. Grand Rapids, 1945.

BFBS: *Mark, A Greek-English Diglot for the Use of Translators*. London, 1958.

Brazilian: *O Novo Testamento de Nosso Senhor Jesus Cristo. Revisão Autorizada*. Rio de Janeiro, 1955.

Goodspeed: *The New Testament. An American Translation*, by Edgar J. Goodspeed. Chicago, 1923.

Knox: *The New Testament of our Lord and Saviour Jesus Christ. A New Translation*, by Ronald P. Knox. New York, 1952.

Manson: *The Beginning of the Gospel*, by T. W. Manson. London, 1950.

Moffatt: *New Testament. A New Translation* (new edition, revised), by James Moffatt. New York, 1934.

Montgomery: *The New Testament in Modern English*, by Helen B. Montgomery. Philadelphia, 1924.

RSV: *The New Testament of our Lord and Savior Jesus Christ. Revised Standard Version.* New York, 1946.

Synodale: *Le Nouveau Testament. Version Synodale* (7e édition entièrement revisée). Paris, 1952.

Vulgate: *Novum Testamentum Latine secundum editionem Sancti Hieronymi* (editio minor), ed. by J. Wordsworth and H. J. White. Oxford, 1950.

Weymouth: *The New Testament in Modern Speech*, by R. F. Weymouth. *Newly Revised*, by J. A. Robertson (5th edition). London, 1929.

Williams: *The New Testament. A Translation in the Language of the People*, by Charles B. Williams. Chicago, 1950.

Zürich: *Das Neue Testament, Verlag der Zwingli-Bibel.* Zürich, 1954.

3. Commentaries on Mark[1]

Bengel, J. A., *Gnomon of the New Testament: Notes on St. Mark* [E. T. by A. R. Fausset] (6th edition). Edinburgh, 1866.

Branscomb, B. H., *The Gospel of Mark (Moffatt New Testament Commentary).* New York, n.d.

Bruce, A. B., *The Synoptic Gospels (The Expositor's Greek Testament).* Grand Rapids, n.d.

Gould, E. P., *The Gospel According to St. Mark (International Critical Commentary).* Edinburgh, 1896.

Grant, F. C., *The Gospel According to St. Mark. Introduction and Exegesis (The Interpreter's Bible*, vol. VII). New York, 1951.

Lagrange, M.-J., *Évangile selon Saint Marc* (édition corrigée et augmentée). Paris, 1947.

Rawlinson, A. E. J., *St. Mark (Westminster Commentaries Series)* (7th edition). London, 1953.

Swete, H. B., *The Gospel According to St. Mark.* London, 1905.

Taylor, Vincent, *The Gospel According to St. Mark.* London, 1952.

Turner, C. H., *The Gospel According to St. Mark (A New Commentary on Holy Scripture*, ed. by C. Gore, H. L. Goudge, A. Guillaume). New York, 1928.

4. Lexicons

Arndt, W. F. and Gingrich, F. W., *A Greek-English Lexicon of the New Testament and Other Early Christian Literature.* Chicago, 1957.

Abbott-Smith, G., *A Manual Greek Lexicon of the New Testament* (3rd edition). Edinburgh, 1944.

Brown, F., Driver, S. R. and Briggs, C. A., *A Hebrew and English Lexicon of the Old Testament.* New York, 1907.

Koehler, Ludwig and Baumgartner, Walter, *Lexicon in Veteris Testamenti Libros.* Leiden, 1953.

Liddell, H. G. and Scott, Robert, *A Greek-English Lexicon. A New Edition revised and augmented throughout*, by H. S. Jones. Oxford, 1948.

Moulton, J. H. and Milligan, George, *The Vocabulary of the Greek Testament illustrated from the Papyri and other non-literary sources.* London, 1914-1929.

Souter, Alexander, *A Pocket Lexicon to the Greek New Testament.* Oxford, 1916.

Thayer, J. H., *A Greek-English Lexicon of the New Testament* (corrected edition). New York, 1889.

---

[1] Cited by name of author, alone.

5. Other Literature

Allen, W. C., *A Critical and Exegetical Commentary on the Gospel According to St. Matthew* (3rd edition). Edinburgh, 1947.

Bernard, J. H., *A Critical and Exegetical Commentary on the Gospel According to St. John*. Edinburgh, 1942.

Black, Matthew, *An Aramaic Approach to the Gospels and Acts* (2nd edition). Oxford, 1954.

Bouquet, A. C., *Everyday Life in New Testament Times*. New York, 1954.

Burton, E. D., *Syntax of the Moods and Tenses in New Testament Greek* (3rd edition). Chicago, 1923.

Creed, J. M., *The Gospel According to St. Luke*. London, 1953.

Dalman, Gustaf, *The Words of Jesus* [E. T. by D. M. Kay]. Edinburgh, 1902.

——— , ——— , *Sacred Sites and Ways* [E. T. by P. P. Levertoff]. London, 1935.

Daube, David, *The New Testament and Rabbinic Judaism*. London, 1956.

Deissmann, G. Adolf, *Bible Studies* [E. T. by Alexander Grieve]. Edinburgh, 1923.

——— , ——— , *Light from the Ancient East* [E. T. by L. R. M. Strachan]. New York, 1927.

Dodd, C. H., *The Parables of the Kingdom*. London, 1946.

Edersheim, Alfred, *The Life and Times of Jesus the Messiah*. Grand Rapids, 1940.

——— , ——— , *The Temple*. New York, n.d.

Farrer, Austin, *A Study in St. Mark*. Westminster, 1951.

Field, F., *Notes on the Translation of the New Testament*. Cambridge, 1899.

Fuller, R. H., *The Mission and Achievement of Jesus*. London, 1954.

Goodspeed, E. J., *Problems of New Testament Translation*. Chicago, 1945.

Hatch, Edwin, *Essays in Biblical Greek*. Oxford, 1889.

Howard, W. F., *A Grammar of New Testament Greek*, vol. II. Edinburgh, 1924.

Jackson, F. J. and Lake, K. (edd.), *The Beginnings of Christianity. Part I: The Acts of the Apostles*, vol. V, *Additional Notes*. London, 1933.

Jeremias, Joachim. *The Eucharistic Words of Jesus* [E. T. by A. Ehrhardt]. Oxford, 1955.

——— , ——— , *The Parables of Jesus* [E. T. by S. H. Hooke]. New York, 1955.

Kennedy, H. A. A., *Sources of New Testament Greek*. Edinburgh, 1895.

Kümmel, W. G., *Promise and Fulfilment* [E. T. by D. M. Barton]. London, 1957.

Lightfoot, J. B., *Saint Paul's Epistle to the Philippians* (6th edition). London, 1881.

——— , — , *Saint Paul's Epistles to the Colossians and to Philemon*. London, 1892.

Lightfoot, R. H., *The Gospel Message of St. Mark*. Oxford, 1950.

Major, H. D. A., Manson, T. W. and Wright, C. J., *The Mission and Message of Jesus*. New York, 1947.

Manson, T. W. (ed.), *A Companion to the Bible*. Edinburgh, 1946.

——— , ——— , *The Teaching of Jesus*. Cambridge, 1945.

McNeile, A. H., *The Gospel According to St. Matthew*. London, 1915.

Milligan, George, *The New Testament Documents*. London, 1913.

Moule, C. F. D., *An Idiom Book of New Testament Greek*. Cambridge, 1953.

Moulton, J. H., *A Grammar of New Testament Greek*. Vol. I, *Prolegomena* (3rd edition). Edinburgh, 1920.

Nineham, D. E. (ed.) *Studies in the Gospels. Essays in Memory of R. H. Lightfoot*. Oxford, 1955.

Richardson, Alan (ed.) *A Theological Word Book of the Bible*. New York, 1950.

Robertson, A. and Plummer, A., *A Critical and Exegetical Commentary on the First Epistle of St. Paul to the Corinthians* (2nd edition). New York, n.d.

Robertson, A. T., *A Grammar of the Greek New Testament in the Light of Historical Research* (5th edition). New York, 1931.

Robinson, J. Armitage, *St. Paul's Epistle to the Ephesians*. London, 1903.

Robinson, J. M. *The Problem of History in Mark*. London, 1957.

Simpson, E. K., *Words Worth Weighing in the Greek New Testament*. London, 1946.

Smith, Morton, *Tannaitic Parallels to the Gospels*. Philadelphia, 1951.

Streeter, B. H., *The Four Gospels*. New York, 1925.

Taylor, Vincent, *Jesus and His Sacrifice*. London, 1948.

Vincent, M. R., *Word Studies in the New Testament*. New York, 1914.

Warfield, B. B., *An Introduction to the Textual Criticism of the New Testament*. London, 1886.

Westcott, B. F., *The Epistle to the Hebrews* (3rd edition). London, 1909.

Westcott, B. F. and Hort, F. J. A., *The New Testament in the Original Greek*. Vol. II, *Introduction, Appendix*. London, 1881.

Williams, C. S. C., *Alterations to the Text of the Synoptic Gospels and Acts*. Oxford, 1951.

TREATMENT OF THE TEXT

Title: *The Gospel according to Mark.*

The Greek text has only 'according to Mark', but it has been traditional in most translations to expand this title to 'The Good News according to Mark' or 'The Gospel according to Mark' (or 'Saint Mark'). In some publications designed especially for distribution to people who are not already familiar with the Scriptures, and to whom 'the Good News according to Mark' might mean little or nothing, there has been a tendency to employ certain supplementary titles which might be more attractive to the eye and to some extent indicative of the theme of the book. For example, in the Illustrated series, published by certain Bible Societies, this volume has been called "The Field is the World," with an appropriate picture of the Sower on the cover.

Even though for some particular publication a translator may wish to employ a supplementary title (this should be worked out in close consultation with the Bible Society), he must nevertheless solve the basic problem of the conventional title. The choice of the portion 'the Good News' or 'the Gospel' will depend of course on what expression is used in the first verse (see below), but there are two other problems: (1) the syntactic form of the title and (2) a title used with the name Mark.

In some languages an expression such as 'Good News according to Mark' would not be meaningful, since all such expressions must be complete sentences. This usually requires the addition of a verb, as for example, in the Tzeltal language of Mexico, where the title reads, 'the Good News written by San Marcos'. (A verb of 'writing' or 'reporting' is usually adequate). Note, however, that in this Tzeltal form of the title the word *San* (Spanish 'saint') has been added. In many regions which have had some familiarity with Christendom Mark may be known only as 'Saint Mark', and to say anything less than this would be completely confusing, since the name of the person in question is a kind of fused title-name combination (something which happened historically in Spanish with *Santo Jacobo* 'Saint James', a phrase which ultimately became *Santiago*, a single word). The employment of the title 'saint' is therefore not necessarily a matter of theologically dictated accretion but of employing a term already intimately associated with the name and without which not only would misunderstanding be likely to arise, but there might be a genuine feeling of offense to deep religious sentiments.

I

CHAPTER ONE

1 *The beginning of the gospel of Jesus Christ, the Son of God.*

Text: *huiou theou* 'the Son of God' is missing in some important mss. and some of the early Fathers, and so is omitted by Tischendorf, Nestle, Westcott and Hort, Kilpatrick; its presence is attested by most of the external evidence, however, and the phrase is included by *Textus Receptus*, Soden (in brackets), Vogels, Souter, Lagrange, Taylor, Merk, Turner (see the evidence set forth by C. H. Turner, *Journal of Theological Studies* 28. 150, 1926-7).

Punctuation: The verse is not a complete sentence, and its relation to the verses which follow has been proposed in three ways: (1) the verse is taken to be a title, with a full stop placed at the end: so Nestle, Westcott and Hort, Vogels, Merk, Soden, Tischendorf, AV, ASV, RSV, other translations and commentators (Gould, Taylor, Grant); (2) verses 2-3 are treated parenthetically, and v. 1 is connected to v. 4: "The beginning ...was John...": so Rawlinson, Branscomb, Turner (*Journal of Theological Studies* 26.146, 1924-5); (3) the verse is connected directly to v. 2: "The beginning... (was) as it stands written in Isaiah": so BFBS. For a discussion of the question see Goodspeed *Problems*, 47-48. The overwhelming majority of translations and commentators favor the first solution.

Exegesis: *archē* (10:6, 13:8, 19) 'beginning' has several possible meanings, but its sense here is simply temporal, 'the starting-point', 'the beginning'. The absence of the article does not necessarily make the word indefinite, and it has been suggested that such absence favors understanding the verse as a title. Modern languages, as required, may or may not use the definite article: cf. Zürich *Anfang*, Synodale *Commencement*, Brazilian *Princípio*.

euaggeliou (1:14, 15, 8:35, 10:29, 13:10, 14:9, 16:15) 'of the gospel'. From the earlier meaning of 'reward for good news' and 'good news' the word developed into a technical Christian term, i.e. the content of the Christian faith, the good tidings of God's redemptive act in Jesus Christ. Lagrange: "It is the proclamation of salvation in Jesus... the announcement of the salvation contained in the words and acts of Jesus." Only after N.T. times did the word take on the further specialized meaning of 'a book relating the words and deeds of Jesus' (cf. Arndt & Gingrich 3, 4 and literature referred to).

Iēsou Christou (only here in Mark) 'of Jesus Christ'. The genitive may mean: (1) the gospel *about* Jesus Christ, or (2) the gospel that *comes from* Jesus Christ. Almost without exception the translations and commentators prefer the first interpretation.

Christos is no longer a title 'The Anointed One': it is a proper name, just as Jesus is a proper name. As a title, 'Messiah' (or 'The Anointed') has its origins in the O.T. concept of God anointing the individual or people of his choice with his Spirit and power. In the case of Jesus, however, the title becomes a proper name.

huiou (tou) theou (3:11, 5:7, 15:39; cf. 14:61; cf. 1:11, 9:7) '(the) Son of God'. Though there is no article with *huiou* 'son' it is nevertheless definite, '*the* Son of God' or (what amounts to the same thing) '*Son* of God'.

huios 'son': wherever the word refers to Jesus, in Mark, it is always followed by a qualifying genitive, with the single exception of 13:32 where *ho huios* 'the Son' is used absolutely.

Translation: The translator is faced with two principal types of problems in this verse: (1) lexical, involving the words for *gospel* and *God*; and (2) syntactic: (a) how to relate the four principal lexical units: *beginning, gospel, Jesus Christ,* and *Son of God*; and (b) how to relate this verse to the following verses.

In choosing a word for *gospel* there are two principal alternatives: (1) borrowing a term from a more dominant language, e.g. the use of Spanish *evangelio* in some Indian language translations in Latin America, or (2) constructing a phrase meaning 'good news', 'joyful report' or 'happiness-bringing words'. The latter method is almost always preferable. In some instances such a phrase may be slightly expanded in order to convey the proper meaning, e.g. 'new good word' (Tzotzil), or it may involve some special local usage, e.g. 'good message' (Mazatec) or 'good story' (Navajo, Ifugao), or 'joyful telling' (Joloano); 'joyful message' (South Toradja).

An adequate term for *God* is one of the major problems for any translator and its full exposition is beyond the limits of this volume. See, therefore, *The Bible Translator* (hereafter abbreviated as *TBT*), 1.86-87, 1950; 2.36, 1951; 3.173-74, 193-94, 1952; 5.87, 96, 1954; 6.24-28, 110-19, 174-75, 1955, also *Bible Translating* (hereafter abbreviated as *BT*) pp. 204-9, and *God's Word in Man's Language* (hereafter abbreviated as *GWIML*), pp. 160-61. Cf. also Hooper's *Indian Word List*, pp. 86-87.

Wherever, of course, there is a generic term used to designate 'a god' or 'gods' this should be used, and the context must be counted on to make the reference definite and unique, while at the same time permitting the radical contrast of the Bible between "the God of the believer" and "the gods of the heathen." One must not, however, imagine that a "high-god concept" (which is relatively widespread throughout the world) is the same as Biblical monotheism, for the high god may have few if any of the moral qualifications of the God of the Scriptures. Moreover, his name may not permit generic extension or pluralization. In such instances one may be forced to use a more generic term for 'spirit' and add a qualifier, e.g. 'the Great Spirit' (Mazahua) and 'the Eternal Spirit' (Navajo, which, however, also employs the English borrowing *God*). In other instances one may take an indigenous phrase and

"Christianize" its meaning by context, e.g. 'the great Father' (San Blas) or *Nhialich* 'one in the above' (Ngok Dinka), or *camaq* 'he who is sufficient' (Chanca Quechua), or *Jehoba* (which accidentally resembles *Jehovah*) 'the great ruler', a kind of generic descriptive term used among the Kipsigis.

In trying to discover an adequate word for *God* one must recognize that there is little or no likelihood that one will encounter a fully adequate term within the indigenous language, for the very significance of the revelation of God in Jesus Christ is that He is radically different from what men have devised. This means that an indigenous term will be considerably less than perfect, even at best. But this should not, however, lead one to resort automatically to a borrowed term, with its essentially zero meaning. Such a word is likely to imply only 'the white man's God' or be equated, as a proper name, with an already known high god. Accordingly, wherever at all possible one should employ some indigenous equivalent, even though it is a descriptive title. However, the particular form which this expression must take within any given situation must be determined by a very careful, exhaustive study of all the religious beliefs and practices of the people; otherwise there is entirely too much chance of having the message distorted by an unfortunately chosen key term.

If we assume that this first verse is in the nature of a title (which is by far the most widely accepted interpretation—see above), the principal syntactic problems involve the internal arrangements of the principal constituent parts. The first of these is the relationship between 'beginning' and 'good news'. What makes this combination somewhat of a problem, however, is the fact that in most languages 'beginning' (which is essentially a process and not an object) is a verb-like word, not a noun. That is to say, in most languages one may say 'something begins' but one cannot talk about 'the beginning of something'. This means that the expression must often be recast so as to read, 'the good news about . . . began this way', or '. . . begins thus' (Cakchiquel, Bolivian Quechua). In Maninka one may translate 'here begins the good news . . .'

In relating the constituents 'good news' and 'Jesus Christ' one should be sure that this is the 'good news about Jesus Christ', not the 'good news that Jesus Christ announced'. This, of course, does not deny the fact that Jesus announced good news, but the viewpoint of the Gospel writers was that Jesus Christ was in himself the good news, hence this must be a so-called objective, rather than subjective construction.

The expression *the Son of God* is in apposition with *Jesus Christ*. In some languages, however, one cannot express such identity merely by juxtaposing expressions. One must use more specific relators, e.g. 'Jesus Christ, he is the Son of God' or 'Jesus Christ, who is the Son of God'.

If verse 1 is to be interpreted as a title and if in the language in question the title needs to be a complete sentence, as is often the case, one can render this verse as 'the good news about Jesus Christ, God's Son, began thus' (or '. . . in this way', or '. . . here'). If, on the other hand, one relates the first verse to what follows (alternatives 2 and 3 under *Punctation*,

4

above,) one may translate either: '...began as it is written in...' (alternative 3) or '...began (As it is written in...) when John the baptizer..'. (alternative 2).

Compare the following renderings, retranslated more or less literally from the languages in question: 'Here begins the good word, the good word regarding God's child Jesus Christ' (Shipibo, in which 'good word' must be repeated because of syntactic requirements and 'child' is the appropriate generic term for such a context), 'This is the beginning of the good news about the Lord Jesus Christ, the Son of God' (Balinese, in which an obligatory honorific pattern requires the addition of 'Lord'), and 'The good news' beginning is this, about Jesus Christ God's Son' (Kpelle).

2 *As it is written in Isaiah the prophet, "Behold, I send my messenger before thy face, who shall prepare thy way;*

Text: Instead of *tō Ēsaia tō prophētē* 'Isaiah the prophet' of all modern editions of the Greek text, *Textus Receptus* has *tois prophētais* 'the prophets': this late reading is an obvious correction which a scribe introduced into the original text because the first O.T. passage quoted by Mark is not from Isaiah but from Malachi 3:1.

After *tēn hodon sou* 'your (sg.) way' *Textus Receptus* adds *emprosthen sou* 'before you (sg.)' in harmonizing the quotation with Mt. 11:10 and Lk. 7:27. This addition, supported only by later mss., is rejected by the modern editions of the Greek text.

Exegesis: *kathōs* (4:33, 9:13, 11:6, 14:16, 21, 15:8, 16:7) 'according as', 'even as': this adverb of manner begins a new sentence whose conclusion is v. 4 (the quotations from the O.T. in vv. 2-3 being parenthetical): 'As it is written... John the Baptizer appeared...' (see Goodspeed *Problems*, 48).

gegraptai (7:6, 9:12, 13, 10:4, 5, 11:17, 12:19, 14:21, 27) '(it) has been written': the perfect tense expresses permanent Scriptural authority. In the proclamation of the Christian message the O.T. Scriptures were often quoted, not simply as an illustration, but as cause and origin of the events proclaimed. Where indicated, full force must be given to this expression of the early Christian preaching: these things came to pass and happened thus and so *because* it was on record in the O.T. The meaning of the Greek perfect is perhaps best represented in English by the present tense: 'it is written', 'it stands on (Scriptural) record'.

en tō Ēsaia tō prophētē 'in (the roll of) Isaiah the prophet' (for this use of *en* 'in' see Arndt & Gingrich I.1.d).

tō prophētē (6:4, 15, 8:28, 11:32) 'the prophet': the words, in this position, limit or define the individual called Isaiah: 'Isaiah the prophet'. He is quoted by name once more (7:6-7) and without being identified in 11:17.

idou (3:32, 4:3, 10:28, 33, 13:23, 14:41, 42) 'see!', 'behold!', 'look!' As an imperative of *eidein* 'to see' the word is used as a demon-

5

strative particle, especially in the LXX and N.T., calling attention to what follows.

apostellō (3:14, 31, 4:29, 5:10, 6:7, 17, 27, 8:26, 9:37, 11:1, 3, 12:2, 3, 4, 5, 6, 13, 13:27, 14:13) 'I send': the present tense of the verb is essentially timeless in this context, a declaration rather than a promise, though in the original context in the LXX it had the force of a future. Though here simply in a quotation, this is an extremely significant verb in the N.T., conveying a sense of commission, authority and responsibility in the transmission of God's word to man (cf. Moulton & Milligan for papyri examples illustrating "the frequent N.T. sense of 'commissioning'"). The subject of the verb, of course, is God.

ton aggelon mou 'my (i.e. God's) messenger' (further use of the word *aggelos* in Mark is restricted to 'angels' as such: 1:13, 8:38, 12:25, 13:27, 32). The figure, that of an oriental monarch or conqueror who sends heralds ahead of him to announce his imminent arrival, here applies to John in his specific task of Forerunner.

pro prosōpou sou literally 'before your face'. The Semitic phrase means 'ahead of you', 'in front of you', 'in your presence'. For an example of its use in the LXX see Micah 6:4, and for further examples in the N.T. see Mt. 11:10, Lk. 7:27 (see further Lk. 9:52, 10:1, Acts 13:24). 'Your' refers to Jesus Christ, ahead of whom John goes as herald of his coming.

hos kataskeuasei tēn hodon sou 'who will prepare your road'. The relative clause expresses purpose, a common Attic idiom. The relative *hos* 'who' has for its antecedent *aggelos* 'messenger'.

kataskeuazō (only here in Mark) 'make ready', 'prepare'. Moulton & Milligan quote a passage in which the verb is used with *hodoi* 'roads' along which the procession of devotees of Zeus and Dionysus was to pass. The sense in a passage such as this is not simply that of building or repairing the road, but that of making all necessary arrangements to insure a fitting welcome and reception for the heralded king or conqueror.

Translation: The following expressions tend to cause lexical difficulty for the translator: *in Isaiah, prophet, behold, before thy face,* and *prepare.* In a high percentage of languages it is necessary to add 'roll' or 'book' to the expression 'in Isaiah' or the expression becomes ludicrous. For example, in some of the Mayan languages the equivalent of *in* is 'stomach', and when speaking of a house it is quite obvious that one is speaking of the inside of a house, but when a person is referred to, the meaning of 'stomach' may be readily understood. Hence, one often needs to say, 'written in the book of Isaiah' or 'Isaiah wrote in a book' (where the active form may be required).

Discovering an adequate term for *prophet* is not easy (see *BT* p. 234 and *GWIML* p. 20). In general there are two types of alternatives: (1) an expression which specifies foretelling the future, and which, as such, is often equivalent to soothsayer, fortune-teller, and clairvoyant, and (2) a phrase which describes the prophet's function as one who speaks out on behalf of God, a particularly important aspect of the New Testament usage of this term. Though words of the first type are usually readily available, the connotations are often undesirable, and hence most translators have chosen the latter emphasis, without of course implying any denial of the foretelling function. The following expressions are typical: 'interpreter for God' (Pame, Vai), 'one who speaks the voice of God' (San Blas), 'one who speaks for God' (Cakchiquel, Navajo, Yaka), 'God's town crier' (Gbeapo), 'one who causes them to know', in the sense of 'revealer' (Totonac), 'foreteller' (Toba Batak), 'God's sent-word person' (Putu), 'one who speaks God's word' (Shipibo, Valiente), 'one who speaks-opens', a compound meaning 'one who discloses or reveals' (Zoque). Cf. Hooper's *Indian Word List*, pp. 194-95.

Too often translators have rendered *Behold* by a verb which means only 'to look', but obviously the context does not refer to literal viewing of an object, but the need of paying close attention to God's promise. Accordingly, one should employ an expression which can also include the ideas of 'pay attention', or 'listen' (somewhat like the archaic English expression *harken*).

The phrase *before thy face* is a Semitism which means simply 'in front of one', (see above) but translated literally it may mean, as in some languages, 'to be face to face with', and in this context the resultant meaning is rather ridiculous, for it implies that the viewer had to back up as the messenger went forth.

The preparation of the way is not constructing the road, but getting it ready to receive a dignitary. In Pame the equivalent is 'to clear the way', implying in the local culture cutting down trees and bushes which may have grown in the path, and which must always be removed when a visiting government official is to be received in a town. In many parts of Africa the equivalent would be sweeping and cleaning the path (see *TBT*, 1.32-33, 1950).

The syntactic constructions in this verse are often complex because of the numerous explicit and implicit relationships. In the first place, the whole of verses 2 and 3 should be combined in such a way as to form a kind of introduction to verse 4 (see above). This cannot be done easily in some languages because of the included direct discourse and the quadruple shift of subjects: 'Isaiah writes', 'God sends', 'the voice cries', and 'you (subject of the imperative) prepare'. The difficulties are made even greater by the fact that after an introductory expression such as, 'Isaiah wrote...' a following 'I' in direct discourse would seem to refer to Isaiah, rather than to God. Because of the high probability of misunderstanding at this point, some translators have added 'God' in apposition with 'I', e.g. 'I God send my messenger...'

Because of the problems involved in relating the whole of verses 2 and 3 to verse 4, some translators have made declarative statements of 2 and 3, and then shown the relationship in the beginning of 4, e.g. 'It says in the book of Isaiah...So, too, came John...' (Balinese), and 'God's spokesman Isaiah wrote...So the baptizer John came...'

The combination *Isaiah the prophet* should be treated as any appositive expression, e.g. 'Isaiah, who was a prophet' or 'Isaiah, he was a prophet' or 'the prophet Isaiah' (by reversing the order in some languages, 'prophet' may serve as a kind of title). In all such expressions one must discover the closest syntactic equivalent in the receptor (or target) language.

3 *The voice of one crying in the wilderness: Prepare the way of the Lord, make his paths straight —"*

The quotation, from Isa. 40:3, does not reproduce the Hebrew text word for word.

Exegesis: *phōnē boōntos* '(the) voice of one shouting'. There is no article before *phōnē* 'voice': the participle *boōntos* 'shouting', however, makes 'voice' definite. The sense, however, can be expressed in English by the absence of any article, definite or indefinite: 'Voice of one who shouts...'

phōnē (1:11, 26, 5:7, 9:7, 15:34, 37) 'sound', 'voice', 'cry', 'call' (see Arndt & Gingrich).

boaō (15:34) 'cry aloud', 'shout'. The present participle here could be masculine or neuter; the context clearly shows it to be masculine, i.e. 'someone (is) shouting', 'someone is calling in the desert!' (see Arndt & Gingrich). The RSV *crying* should not be understood in the sense of 'weeping'.

en tē erēmō 'in the desert': this clause is connected in the LXX with the preceding phrase, although the Hebrew text connects it to the following verb 'prepare'. If necessary, a complete sentence may be constructed: 'It is the voice of one who in the wilderness shouts...'

erēmos (1:4, 12, 13, 35, 45, 6:31, 32, 35) 'wilderness', 'wild country'. The word does not necessarily stand for an arid desert, such as exists in Africa or Asia: it means an uninhabited territory, 'wild open country' (Grant), in contrast with the cultivated and inhabited sections of the land: cf. American "Bad Lands."

hetoimasate (10:40, 14:12, 15, 16, 15:1) 'prepare', 'keep in readiness'. Moulton & Milligan give examples of the word used almost as a technical term for preparations in view of an approaching visit. The aorist imperative of the verb carries overtones of urgency: 'Prepare now!' The plural shows that the order is directed not to an individual but to a group, to the people or nation to whom the Lord is about to come.

tēn hodon kuriou 'the road of the Lord', i.e. 'the road over which the Lord shall come'.

kurios 'Lord': the word appears 18 times in Mark, with the following meanings: (1) 'the Lord' meaning 'God' in 5:19, 13:20 and in the quotations from the O.T. in 11:9, 12:11, 12:29-30 and 12:36-37 (in the last passage there are two different "Lords", one of whom is God and the other the Messiah—cf. *Exegesis* of the passage); (2) 'master', 'owner' in 2:28, 11:3, 12:9, 13:35; (3) in the vocative, 'sir' in 7:28; and (4) 'the Lord' referring to Jesus in 16:19-20. In the present instance, in the original O.T. passage 'the Lord' refers, of course, to Yahweh: here in Mark, however, the term probably refers to (the Lord) Jesus (cf. Lagrange who points out that in the next clause the LXX 'of our

God' has been substituted, in Mark, by 'his'—i.e. the Lord's; cf. also Rawlinson, Gould, Taylor; Arndt & Gingrich II. 2. c.α; Black (*Aramaic*, 73): "The Lord is Jesus, announced as Christ, the Son of God, and it is *His* paths that John the Forerunner summons men to make straight").

eutheias poieite tas tribous autou 'make ye his paths straight'.

eutheias 'straight': the thought is not simply that of eliminating curves, but of doing everything necessary to make travel easy and rapid (cf. Lk. 3: 4-5 where the quotation from Isaiah is continued). Cf. Synodale *aplanissez*.

tribos (only here in Mark) 'a beaten track', 'path': from the verb *tribō* 'to beat'.

Translation: Perhaps the most difficult problem in this verse is the use of the expression 'voice of one crying...', introducing direct discourse. In most languages it is quite easy to say, 'a man cries out with his voice...' (note this is the 'crying out' of shouting, not the 'crying' of weeping), but to say that 'a voice cries out...' may involve complications for the reader. Where, of course, one can reproduce the Semitic expression intact, one should do so; if not, one may employ a kind of indirect equivalent 'there is the voice of a man crying in...' (Balinese) or 'he is the person whose voice is rising in...' (Kpelle); 'the voice of a man (someone), who cries' (South Toradja, Bare'e, Indonesian).

The *wilderness* was essentially an uninhabited place. It is also true that it was lacking in vegetation, but this was a secondary feature and in many instances must not be introduced if one is to make sense. For example, if in some languages spoken in tropical areas of the world one translates 'a place without vegetation', almost the only meaning it can have is 'a recently prepared field' or 'the open space in the middle of the village'. In Shipibo the equivalent of *wilderness* is 'where no house is', in Bandi the term is literally 'grasslands' (no one lives there), in Indonesian 'the uninhabited land in between the inhabited areas', and in Kpelle it is 'rocky region'. One must, however, be sure not to introduce some contradictory term at this point. For example, one can often use 'where no one is' (or 'exists') as an equivalent of *wilderness* (Mark 1:12), but in this verse 'to shout where there was no one' would not make much sense.

In Greek the terms translated 'prepare' in verses 2 and 3 are different, but the meaning is essentially the same: 'to make ready', 'fix up' (not 'to construct a new road').

The expression *way of the Lord* involves a subtle ambiguity, for if translated literally into some languages, e.g. Ponape, it would mean 'the path on his land', obviously not what the prophet was talking about. This must be the 'path which the Lord is to use' or 'the way for the Lord'.

Though *Lord* in the O.T. source of this verse refers to Jehovah (Yahweh), it is necessary here to use a term which identifies the Lord Jesus Christ. N. T. translations should preserve a calculated ambiguity at this point, for this was precisely what the N. T. writers did.

There are few terms any more difficult to render adequately than *Lord*;

see *TBT*, 1.87, 106-9, 1950; 2.165, 1951; 3.173, 176, 179-80, 1952; 4. 135-36, 1953; *BT*, pp. 182, 210, and *GWIML*, p. 159. The Greek term *kurios* had a range of meaning in secular usage all the way from a title for the emperor to a polite 'sir', used in speaking to one of higher social rank. In the LXX *kurios* translates Hebrew *Adonai* and *Yahweh*, and this same usage comes into the N. T., with additional specific application of *kurios* to Jesus Christ. In translating into another language it is generally quite impossible to find an exact equivalent for this entire range of meaning. The alternatives are usually (1) a term which is an honorific title of respect for a high-ranking person and (2) a word meaning 'boss', 'master', or 'chief'. There are certain inherent dangers in either of these types of terms. In the first place, a word which is primarily a title for a highly prestigeful person will deprive the Scriptures of the emphasis on a man's immediate loyalty to and dependence upon a 'master' or 'chief'; and as a result the 'Lord' will imply a distant, impersonal relationship. On the other hand, a word which denotes essentially a 'boss' or 'chief' may have connotations of resistance and disfavor. On the whole, however, it has generally seemed better to employ a word of the second category, in order to emphasize the immediate personal relationship, and then by context to build into the word the prestigeful character, since its very association with Jesus Christ will tend to accomplish this purpose. If, however, a word of the first category is employed, it is sometimes impossible to teach the personal relationship, for the cultural overtones of the word place too much distance between the 'lord' and the people. The following terms, as indicated in the literal translations (and explanations where necessary) indicate certain of the major types of solutions to this problem of finding an adequate term for *Lord*: 'the one who has charge' (Navajo), 'person-owner', a term which may be applied to a chief (Kpelle), 'the one who commands' (Amuzgo), 'the big one', used commonly of one in authority (Piro), 'the one who has the head' in other words, 'the leader' (Moré), 'chief' (Uduk), 'the one who owns us' (or 'commands us') (Pame), and 'the great one over all' (San Blas).

One additional problem is involved in the choice of a term for *Lord*, namely the fact that in many languages it is always possessed. That is to say, a person who is a chief or leader is always related to a particular group, and hence in speaking of such an individual, the grammatical structure requires that one specify whether this person is 'our chief', 'their chief', 'his chief', etc. In this particular context one would need to use 'our chief' (inclusive, if the inclusive-exclusive contrast should exist in the language [1]), but in each context the appropriate form would need to be selected.

---

[1] Many languages possess for the first person plural two forms: (1) the inclusive 'we' meaning the speaker and those spoken to, and (2) the exclusive 'we' identifying only the speaker and certain others, but specifically excluding the audience. Failure to recognize these problems adequately has lead to numerous serious mistakes in translating (see *BT*, p. 256).

4 *John the baptizer appeared in the wilderness, preaching a baptism of repentance for the forgiveness of sins.*

Text: Instead of *egeneto Iōannēs ho baptizōn en tē erēmō kērussōn* 'John the Baptizer appeared in the wilderness preaching' of the majority of editions of the Greek text, *Textus Receptus* and Soden have *egeneto Iōannēs baptizōn en tē erēmō kai kērussōn* 'John was baptizing in the wilderness and preaching' (for a discussion of the problem see Goodspeed *Problems*, 50-52).

Punctuation : This verse stands as the conclusion of v. 1 : 'As it is written ... John the Baptizer appeared...' (cf. v. 1).

Exegesis: *ho baptizōn* (6:14,24) 'the one baptizing': this is a title, 'the Baptizer', equal in meaning to *ho baptistēs* 'the Baptist' in 6:25, 8:28 (and in Matthew and Luke). For a discussion of the verb *baptizō* 'baptize' see v. 5.

egeneto 'appeared': the verb *ginomai* has several shades of meaning, including that of 'come', 'go', 'appear' (cf. Jn. 1:6, 2 Pe. 2:1, 1 Jn. 2:18; cf. Arndt & Gingrich II.5). The phrase *egeneto en tē erēmō* could conceivably mean 'was in the wilderness' or 'came into the wilderness' (for this use of *en* see 1:16, *en tē thalassē* 'into the sea'). In keeping with the O.T. passages being quoted, however, John, as a *voice*, appears, rather than comes, for nothing is said about his previous history (cf. Taylor). *egeneto* could be taken with *kērussōn* 'came...preaching'. It is more probable, however, that *egeneto* functions as the principal verb, while *kērussōn* is an independent participle which modifies 'John'.

erēmos 'wilderness' (cf. v. 3): here refers to the wild uncultivated country west of the Dead Sea (cf. Taylor).

kērussōn (1:7,14,38,39,45, 3:14, 5:20, 6:12, 7:36, 13:10, 14:9, 16:15,20) 'announcing', 'proclaiming'. The word has an official, authoritative sense: it is not simply a shouting, as such, but the public announcement or proclamation by an authorized herald (*kērux*) who is, in this case, God's own messenger.

baptisma metanoias eis aphesin hamartiōn 'a baptism of repentance for remission of sins': the whole phrase is the direct object of the participle *kērussōn* 'preaching', and as such describes the content of John's proclamation.

baptisma metanoias (cf. Lk. 3:3, Acts 13:24, 19:4 for the same phrase) 'a baptism of repentance'. The genitive *metanoias* 'of repentance' qualifies and defines the baptism John proclaimed: the rite was characterized by repentance. Grant: "a Semitism, meaning 'a baptism which symbolized or expressed repentance'."

baptisma (10:38,39, 11:30) 'baptism': a noun with the ending *-ma* ordinarily expresses the result of the action contained in the verb. In the N.T., however, *baptisma* is the rite itself, not the result of the practice of the rite (see v. 5 for *baptizō*).

metanoia (here only in Mark) 'change of mind', 'repentance'. The word indicates more than an intellectual process: it involves a deliberate 'turning' (cf. O. T. *shubh*, and see Taylor, 167, on 1:15), involving heart and will, as well as mind. Moulton & Milligan: "a coming to one's sense, resulting in a change of conduct." The implication is that of turning *from* (*apo* Acts 8:22, Heb. 6:1) sin and *to* (*eis* Acts 20:21, *epi* Acts 26:20) God. The rite John proclaimed was qualified by *metanoia* 'repentance': as the next verse shows, the performance of the rite, by John, included the open confession of sin, by the candidate, as an expression of his repentance. Cf. the following translations: "a baptism based on repentance" (Manson); *auf Grund der Busse* (Zürich).

eis aphesin hamartiōn 'for (leading to, pointing toward) remission of sins'.

eis 'to', 'into' may indicate, in this context, either purpose or result. Moule *Idiom Book*, 70, prefers the former: "with a view to." What is the exact shade or significance of *eis* in this passage is determined not by grammar alone, but by the context as well. The English preposition *for* with its various shades of possible meanings, and its equivalent in other languages, is the best translation (AV, RSV, Weymouth, Moffatt; Manson "leading to"; Synodale *pour*; Zürich *zu*; Brazilian *para*).

aphesis (3:29) 'remission', 'passing over', 'forgiveness' (from *aphiēmi* 'send away', 'drive out'). The word corresponds to the O.T. *nasa'* 'lift up', 'carry away'. The Biblical meaning of the word is that of the act of God whereby sin, as a debt, is cancelled, or, as a transgression of the Law, is pardoned or remitted (Moulton & Milligan give examples from the papyri of this use of the word in connection with remission from debt or punishment). N. H. Snaith ("Forgiveness," Richardson *Word Book*) connects the word with the rites of the Hebrew sacrificial system, "by which the taking away of sins involved in the forgiveness which follows repentance was symbolically set forth."

hamartia (1:5, 2:5,7,9,10) 'sin': this is the common N.T. word for sin, conceived of, fundamentally, as disobedience to the revealed will of God. The verb from which it is derived, *hamartanō* means "to miss the mark" (cf. O. T. *hata'*).

On the whole phrase Grant comments: "a baptism of immersion, undertaken at John's direction and in response to his preaching, preceded by repentance... and followed by the divine forgiveness."

Translation: This verse may seem to be simple, but it is probably the most difficult verse in the entire Gospel of Mark, not only because of some of the difficult terms, but because of the unsuspected complication in the syntax (see *TBT*, 3.97-102, 1952).

For a discussion of 'baptize' see verse 5, but in this verse there is a problem of relating the participial form of Greek *baptizōn* to the proper name 'John'. If, of course, the language in question has a regular means of designating a person who habitually or professionally does a particular type of work, such a form may be used in this context (such formations occur in a number of Bantu languages).

In order to obtain an adequate equivalent for *preaching* one needs to discover the way in which so-called "official pronouncements" are made within a particular society, for this is essentially the meaning of the Greek term. It is unfortunate that in English *preach* has acquired such a specialized meaning that it is understood almost entirely as a religious activity. This was not true of the Greek word *kērussō*. Accordingly, one should not attempt to import religious connotations (these will come soon enough); what is more important is the emphasis upon the authoritative character of the pronouncement. This means that one will want a term more equivalent to 'declare', 'announce', or 'proclaim'. In Tzeltal there is a fascinating kind of compound meaning 'he explains ,they hear' (the goal of all preachers) and in Zoque a preacher is 'one who speaks-scatters' (a figure based on the scattering of seed in the process of sowing).

Forgiveness is a concept, which though it exists in all languages, is expressed in quite varied ways (see *TBT*, 1.26-27, 1950; 2.57, 1951; 4.25, 136, 185-86, 1953; 5.95, 1954; and *GWIML*, pp. 60, 141-42). Perhaps the most common figures of speech involved in describing forgiveness are (1) 'forgetting about' (Tswa, Barrow Eskimo, Huanuco Quechua), (2) 'to give back', based on the idea that sin produces an indebtedness, which only the one who has been sinned against can restore (Navajo), (3) 'erase', 'wipe out', 'blot out' (Huastec, Yaka, San Blas, Huichol, Shipibo, Eastern Otomí, Uduk), (4) 'to lose', 'cause to be lost', 'to make lacking' (Totonac, Mazatec) and 'to lose another's sin out of one's heart' (Tzeltal), (5) 'to be released' or 'to be freed' (Lahu, Burmese), (6) 'to level off' (Chanca Quechua), (7) 'to cast away' (Villa Alta Zapotec), (8) 'to pass by' (Chol) or 'to make pass' (Goajira), (9) 'to turn one's back on' (Kpelle), (10) 'to cover over' (Trique), a figure of speech which is also employed in Hebrew, but which in many languages is not acceptable, because it implies 'hiding' or 'concealment', (11) 'to take away sins' (Chontal of Tabasco, Huichol), and (12) 'to do away with sins' (South Toradja, Javanese).

In some instances figures of speech conveying the meaning of forgiveness are highly specialized in form and cultural significance. In both the San Blas ('to erase the bad heart') and in Juárez Zapotec ('to repair the peace of heart') the emphasis is upon the guilt felt by the sinner rather than upon the sins, certainly a perfectly valid viewpoint. In the Shilluk language forgiveness is expressed as 'spit is returned to the ground for us by God' or more idiomatically 'God spit on the ground in front of us'. This is an expression arising from the requirement that the plaintiff and the defendant, upon the conclusion of a trial and the termination of punishment or the payments of fines, spit on the ground in front of each other to signify that the case is finished, forgiveness has been accomplished, and the accusations can never come into court again—a very apt analogy to God's forgiveness.

In Kipsigis forgiveness is expressed as 'healing the neck', for since sin is spoken of as causing a mortal wound in the neck of the offender, so forgiveness is the healing of this wound.

It is generally not too difficult to find a word meaning 'forgiveness', but what may be more of a problem is choosing between two or three alternative forms, which may have slightly different connotations and which may be required in different types of context. For example, in Huichol there are three expressions: (1) 'to pass over' (meaning essentially 'to excuse'), (2) 'to rub out', 'sweep out', 'wipe off', and (3) 'to take away'. All of these expressions are useful in particular contexts. On the other hand, one may find that some expression may be widely used, but not fully adequate, at least in some contexts, as for example in Palau in the use of 'to throw away', for which 'to erase' would be in most instances a better substitute. In some languages it is wise to choose the more intensive of any alternative expressions. For example, in Conob one could say 'to erase', but the more adequate equivalent is a rather full, descriptive phrase, 'to erase and make fall', implying that the sin has been made to disappear completely.

The difficulties encountered in discovering an adequate term for *sin* (see *TBT*, 1.21, 1950; 1.88-89, 1950; 2.57-58, 1951; 4.73, 138-40, 149-52, 1953; *BT*, pp. 219-20; and *GWIML*, pp. 37, 148-49) are not the result of the scarcity of the phenomenon, but the utterly diverse ways in which people regard it. In general the translator's problems are of five types: (1) classifying words according to the various grades and types of transgressions, (2) distinguishing between words indicating acts and those implying guilt, (3) eliminating terms which apply almost exclusively to certain special sins or which may have ranges of meaning quite different from the Biblical expressions, (4) determining the degree of moral responsibility which is involved in the use of any one word, and (5) discovering a sufficient number of expressions, so that if possible, one may be able to parallel such Biblical distinctions as are implied in such words as *sin, transgression, trespass, evil, wickedness,* and *iniquity* (this last problem is beyond the immediate scope of this volume, but needs to be taken into consideration by any translator right from the beginning of his work).

It is quite common for languages to have several words for sins, ranging from terms which designate very mild kinds of 'mistakes' to words used almost exclusively of 'horrible crimes'. The tendency in such languages is usually to play down the extent of a person's sins (especially in speaking of one's own) by using as the most common term one which tends to excuse the offender. As the result such a word may mean little more than 'error'. For example, a word which may be said to be equivalent to English *sin* may actually be restricted in most contexts to the meaning of 'adultery', which in some societies is the one sin which acquires the greatest social significance, but its very frequency may seem to make it more excusable. Such a term is unlikely therefore to imply much guilt. On the other hand, one does not wish to use a term for 'sin' which means only 'guilt', even though the implication of guilt should not be missing in the expression chosen. In Valiente the transgression and the guilt are rather neatly linked in the phrase 'that which makes one guilty', implying not only a transgression of an established norm (i.e. violation of the law and will of God) but the resultant guilt which inevitably follows.

14

One of the more serious problems in analyzing the meanings of words for sin is the tendency for terms to be too specific in their significance or to include areas of meaning quite outside the Biblical range. For example, in Huichol it was found that the term *xuriki*, which at first seemed to be quite acceptable because it included stealing, murder, and adultery, was not correct, for it also meant getting married and harvesting a cornfield. The underlying meaning was 'destroying the value or character of something', and in the latter two instances *xuriki* referred to destroying the virginity of the bride and ruining the cornfield by gathering the ears of corn. As a result, in Huichol, there are now in use two expressions, (1) meaning 'bad action', used to denote the act of sin and (2) describing a 'bad heart', employed to designate the sinner.

Quite frequently one finds that where there are several words for sin, some may be almost totally lacking in the connotation of moral responsibility. That is to say, people speak of sins as happening, but do not always assign a factor of choice or decision to such an act. This is overcome to some extent in Conob by designating sinners as 'people with bad hearts' (not just people who do bad things). The fact of decision is expressed in Loma by describing certain types of sin as 'leaving the road', an expression which also implies a definite standard, the transgression of which is sin. This same concept of violation of standard is contained in the Navajo expression for sin: 'that which is off to the side'.

Once a translator has found the appropriate equivalents for the lexical units of this verse, the problem has in a sense only begun, for an even more complex difficulty is involved in stating accurately the relationships between the parts. The first half of the verse, of course, presents no special problems, but the latter half often involves very special difficulties. The syntactic problems of this verse are caused by two types of factors: (1) the series of process words linked by prepositions (i.e. in English, but by case endings in certain of the Greek forms), and (2) the abrupt shifts in the persons participating in these processes. In the first place, we find that in a high percentage of languages most processes, e.g. walking, running, eating, speaking, and also baptizing, repenting, forgiving, and sinning, are expressed by verb forms. In some cases these verbs may be made into noun-like words, but such noun formations may be quite uncommon in actual usage and especially in the complex kind of arrangement such as occurs in this verse. That is to say, in the series of processes involving baptism, repentance, forgiveness, and sins the predominant pattern in many languages is to treat such words as verbs. However, as verbs such words require the explicit indication of the persons who participate in these processes, and this involves the second major difficulty, the fact that there are such abrupt changes in the participants. For example, after the introductory verb of which *John* is the subject, it is John who does the baptizing and the people who are baptized, but the people are the subject of the repenting, God is the subject of the process of forgiving, and the people do the sinning.

There is a further problem involved in relating the four components baptism, repentance, forgiveness, and sins (these four are, of course, all the object of the preaching). The relationship between the third and fourth units is clear enough, for the sins are the goal (i.e. object, in grammatical terms) of the process of the forgiving: cf. South Toradja 'repentance which treads forgiveness as path'. On the other hand, what is the relationship between the processes of baptism and repentance? The grammar books describe the second unit as a "genitive of characteristic" but that is not much help. However, if the second process is to characterize the first process, just how can this be stated clearly, when the two processes are to be treated as verb expressions, with their own subject constituents? There are probably two most satisfactory means of dealing with this problem: (1) the repenting can be described as simply preceding the baptism (in which case the character or quality is implied by the temporal sequence), e.g. 'preached that the people should repent and be baptized' or 'preached that the people should be sorry on account of their sins and be baptized' (Trique) and (2) the baptism can apply specifically to those who repent, e.g. 'whosoever has changed his mind, he ought to be baptized...' (Balinese). The same meaning is conveyed in Tzotzil, but in a different order 'declares that he gives baptism to whoever receives his heart' (the last expression is the Tzotzil idiom for repentance).

One further complication is involved in the relationship between the preaching and the rest of the clause, namely, that in many languages such a verb of speaking demands direct, rather than indirect discourse (in the Balinese translation, noted above, there is a shift in this direction, but not the use of the second person). That is to say, one must render this passage as, 'John preached, You must repent and be baptized...' If then, we put the entire second clause together, it could be rendered in the indirect form as 'John preached that the people should repent and be baptized so that their sins would be forgiven' (changes into the direct form would be more or less automatic). On the other hand, in languages which have no passive forms of the verbs, the problems are even more complex, for the subjects of the corresponding active verbs must be introduced and the resultant translation may be roughly parallel to, 'preached that the people should repent and he would baptize them so that God would forgive the bad deeds which they had committed'.

5 And there went out to him all the country of Judea, and all the people of Jerusalem; and they were baptized by him in the river Jordan, confessing their sins.

Text: *pantes* 'all' in *Textus Receptus* is placed after *ebaptizonto* 'all were baptized': this reading, based on later mss., is rejected by modern editions of the Greek text.

Exegesis: *exeporeueto* (6:11, 7:15, 19, 20, 21, 23, 10:17, 46, 11:19, 13:1) 'was going out': the imperfect stresses the continuous procession of people as they kept going out to hear John's preaching and receive his baptism. The force of the preposition *ek* is, naturally, to go *out of* the Judean countryside and the city of Jerusalem to the Jordan where John was preaching and baptizing.

pasa hē Ioudaia chōra kai hoi Ierosolumitai pantes 'all the region (of) Judea and all the citizens of Jerusalem'.

chōra (5 : 1, 10, 6 : 55) 'country', 'region', 'land'. The words *pasa* 'all (the region of Judea)' and *pantes* 'all (the citizens of Jerusalem)' are not intended literally (cf. similar expressions in 1 : 32, 33, 37; see also Mt. 2 : 3, 21 : 10; Lk. 7 : 29; Acts 21 : 30). The language describes forcefully and vividly the effect of John's ministry upon many people from both the countryside and the city. Although possible in some contexts, *pasa* and *pantes* 'all' in this passage should not be taken in a qualitative sense (as is done by Weymouth: "people of all classes").

ebaptizonto hup' autou 'were being baptized by him'. The preposition *hupo* 'by' clearly shows that the verb is passive: the rite was not self-administered, as in the case of Jewish proselyte baptism, but was administered by John 'the Baptizer'. Again the imperfect of the verb stresses the continuity of the action: the people came, one by one, and were baptized by John.

baptizō (1 : 8, 9, 7 : 4, 10 : 38, 39, 16 : 16) 'dip', 'bathe', 'immerse', 'baptize' (see Arndt & Gingrich): used only in ritual sense in the N.T.: (1) of Jewish ritual ablution, Lk. 11 : 38 (and Mk. 7 : 4, if the true reading); (2) of John's baptism and Christian baptism (all other occurrences of the verb not listed here); (3) figuratively, as a metaphor of suffering and martyrdom, Mk. 10 : 38-39, Lk. 12 : 50, and of Israel's passage through the Red Sea, 1 Co. 10 : 2.

en tō Iordanē potamō 'in the Jordan river': the construction is parallel to *hē Ioudaia chōra* in which the proper name has the force of an adjective modifying the noun, i.e. 'the Judean region', 'the Jordanian river'. The sense, however, is accurately represented by 'Jordan river' or 'river Jordan'.

exomologoumenoi (only here in Mark) 'as they were confessing'. In the active form the verb means 'promise', 'consent', 'agree' (cf. Lk. 22 : 6); in the middle, 'confess', 'admit', 'acknowledge' (cf. Kennedy *Sources*, 118; Moulton & Milligan give examples from the papyri for 'acknowledge', 'avow openly'—see also Acts 19 : 18, Ph. 2 : 11). In the LXX the verb stands chiefly for *yadhah* 'confess', 'praise' (cf. Field *Notes*, 75). The present tense of the participle in the present passage, in its relation to the principal verb *baptizō* 'baptize', shows clearly what is meant by John's preaching 'a baptism of repentance for remission of sins'. Those who repented and responded to his proclamation came to receive baptism at the hands of John: included in the performance of the rite was their confession of sins, in audible demonstration of their repentance, baptism being its visible representation, the purpose of all of which was the forgiveness granted by God to repentant sinners. Confession here is *open* confession: if an indirect object is to be supplied, it would naturally be God *to whom* confession of sins was made, presumably in a loud voice, and so heard by John (cf. Vincent *Word Studies* I, 24, on Mt. 3 : 6).

Translation: The use of the English expletive *there* in the construction *there went out to him* ...is an attempt to reproduce the effect of the initial verb in the Greek text. However, in most languages it is necessary to use the more direct form, 'all the country of Judea went out to him...'

On the other hand, it is frequently impossible to say 'all the country (i.e. region) went out...', for in many languages 'regions' cannot 'go', only people can go. Hence one must introduce some more acceptable immediate subject, e.g. 'people from all over Judea went' (if 'all' is to be related to Judea) or 'all the people from Judea went' (if 'all' is to be taken with 'people'). The resultant meanings are essentially similar, though the first may reflect more accurately the relative use of 'all' (the Greek *pasa* and *pantes* are certainly not to be taken in their literal sense, any more than the corresponding words thus construed in English or most other languages).

A further syntactic rearrangement may be required in some languages in order that both parts of the subject may be preposed to the verb, e.g. 'people all over Judea and all the people of Jerusalem went out to him'.

Baptize has given rise not only to an immense amount of discussion in terms of its meaning within the Judaeo-Christian historical context, but also continues to introduce serious problems for translators today (see *TBT*, 2.57, 166, 1951; 3.231-32, 1952; 5.76, 1954; and *BT*, p. 232). In many instances the recommendation has been to transliterate, i.e. employing some indigenous equivalent of the sounds of the word in some more prestigeful language spoken in the region, e.g. English, French, Spanish, or Portuguese. Though this solution tends to remove some theological controversies, it does not completely satisfy everyone, for not only does it avoid the problem of the mode of baptism, but it leaves the Scriptures with a zero word. Unfortunately, many of the controversies over the indigenous equivalent of *baptism* arise because of a false evaluation of a word's so-called etymology. For example, in Maya the word for *baptism* means literally 'to enter the water', but this term is used freely by both Presbyterians and Roman Catholics, even though it might appear to be strictly "Baptist nomenclature". Similarly, in Kekchi, an even "stronger" term 'to put under the water' is employed by Nazarenes and Roman Catholics. Obviously the meanings of these Maya and Kekchi words are not derivable from their literal significance but from the fact that they now designate a particular kind of Christian rite. To insist on changing such a well established usage (and one to which immersionists could certainly not object) would seem quite unwarranted. The situation may, on the other hand, be reversed. There are instances in which immersionists are quite happy to use a term which though it means literally 'to put water on the head' has actually lost this etymological value and refers simply to the rite itself, regardless of the way in which it is performed. A translator should not, however, employ an already existing expression or construct a new phrase which will in its evident meaning rule out any major Christian constituency.

There are, of course, a number of instances in which traditional terms for 'baptism' need modification. In some situations the word may mean only 'to give a new name to' (one aspect of christening) or 'to be one who lights' (referring to a custom in some traditions of lighting a candle at the time of baptism). However, in order to reproduce the core of significant meaning of the original Biblical term, it is important to explore the entire range of indigenous usage in order that whatever term is chosen may have at least some measure of cultural relevance. In Navajo, for example, there were four principal possibilities of choice: (1) borrowing some transliterated form of the English word, (2) constructing a phrase meaning 'to touch with water' (an expression which would have been acceptable with some groups in the field, but not with others), (3) using a phrase meaning 'ceremonial washing' (but this expression seemed to be too closely related to indigenous practices in healing ceremonies), and (4) devising an expression meaning 'to dedicate (or consecrate) by water', without specifying the amount of water employed. This last alternative was chosen as the most meaningful and the best basis for metaphorical extension and teaching.

On the other hand, it would be wrong to think that the meaning of 'washing' must be rejected in all languages. For example, it is quite appropriate in Kpelle culture, since it ties in with male puberty rites, and in the San Blas society, since washing is a very important aspect of female puberty ceremonies. In some translations 'water' is introduced into the expression for baptism, but the quantity and means of administering it are left quite ambiguous, e.g. 'to get (take, receive) water' (Tzeltal). South Toradja, Bare'e and Toba Batak render the verb 'to pour water over, give a bath'.

One would assume that an equivalent of *confess* would not be difficult to find, but such is not always the case (see *TBT*, 3.92, 157, 1952; 4.176-78, 1953; and *GWIML*, p. 155). In general the principal problem is to avoid some technical, ritualistic term which will carry over too many non-Christian associations. One of the best translations is simply 'to say openly' (Zacapoastla Aztec, Tzeltal), since this was certainly public confession. There are, however, a number of idiomatic equivalents of confession, e.g. 'to accuse oneself of his own evil' (San Blas), 'telling the truth about their sins' (Kankanae), and 'to take aim at one's sin' (Huastec, an idiom which is derived from the action of a hunter taking aim at a bird or animal).

The principal syntactic difficulty in the second clause involves relating the confession of sins to the process of being baptized. The Greek text implies that confession was an essential element of the process of being baptized, and though the participle meaning 'confessing' follows the main verb and can be rendered with a degree of ambiguity in English, this is usually not possible in other languages. More often than not, one must select the temporal order of the processes, and if this is required by the syntactic structure of the language in question, it is valid to follow the same implied temporal order of verse 4, in which the repentance, if it is to characterize the baptism, is likely to have preceded it. Therefore in this verse, 'confessing' may be described as preceding, e.g. 'after confessing their sins, they were baptized by him in the river Jordan' (Ifugao). In

Shipibo, the necessity of using direct discourse after the verb of speaking results in a modification of order, but temporal sequence is the same: 'Then he washed them, at the Jordan stream, when they said: It is true. We have sinned'. (In Shipibo, a language spoken in the Amazon river basin, one must use a special word designating a mountain stream, so as not to give the impression that the Jordan was in any sense like the vast major tributaries of the Amazon.)

6 Now John was clothed with camel's hair, and had a leather girdle around his waist, and ate locusts and wild honey.

Exegesis: *ēn...endedumenos* 'was clothed'; this verbal phrase, consisting of the auxiliary verb *eimi* 'to be' plus the participle of the main verb *enduō* 'to clothe' does not mean, as it would in classical Greek (cf. Turner, *Journal of Theological Studies* 28.349, 1926-7), 'had been clothed'; it rather denotes the habitual nature of John's dress. 'And John clothed himself', or 'was clothed'.

enduō (6:9, 15:20) 'clothe', 'dress': the forerunner's dress and diet mark him as a man of the wilderness, an ascetic, a Nazirite (Lk. 1:15); his clothing is similar to that worn by Elijah (2 Kings 1:8; cf. Zech. 13:4). Such simple and hardy manner of life was characteristic of one who lived in the wilderness (Lk. 1:80) and was the object of comment by Jesus (Mt. 11:8, Lk. 7:25).

trichas kamēlou 'hairs of a camel' does not mean a camel's *skin*. It stands for a robe, long and loose (cf. Mt. 3:4, *to enduma autou* 'his garment') woven from camel's hair (cf. Moulton & Milligan; cf. Zürich: *Und Johannes war bekleidet mit [einem Gewand aus] Kamelhaaren*).

zōnēn dermatinēn 'leather girdle': a waistband, or girdle, which holds the robe at the waist, enabling it to be tucked up for rapid walking. The *zōnē* is not exactly a belt, such as used by modern Western men, but more in the nature of a waistband wherein money (cf. Mk. 6:8) and other things could be kept (cf. Lagrange; A. C. Bouquet *Everyday Life in N.T. Times*, 60).

osphus (only here in Mark) 'waist': the place where a belt or girdle is fastened (cf. Arndt & Gingrich).

kai (ēn) esthōn 'and was eating': this verbal phrase, consisting of the imperfect of the verb *eimi* 'to be' plus the present participle of the main verb is quite common in Mark (16 instances in all—cf. Taylor, 45). 'He (habitually) ate', 'his food was...'

akris 'locust': to this day the locust is eaten especially by the poorer people in Arabia, Africa, and Syria (cf. Arndt & Gingrich).

meli agrion 'wild honey': there is no need to think of vegetable substances which are found on the leaves of certain trees (cf. Lagrange, 7; Arndt & Gingrich). Natural wild honey is meant.

Translation: The word *now* used to introduce this verse in the RSV (cf. *and* in ASV and KJ), is an attempt to represent the transitional value of Greek *kai*, literally 'and'. It should not, of course, be taken in any temporal sense. In most translations it is probably best to omit any transition, though if some appropriate particle can be found to soften the abrupt transition between verses 5 and 6, such would be justified.

In parts of the world in which camels are not known, one is immediately confronted with the problem of what to do with the name of this strange animal. Some people have thought that Eskimos would want to say 'cloth made of polar bear fur' and people from the South Pacific would understand most satisfactorily if one used 'rough cloth made from palm fibre'. These types of adaptations can be meaningful, but they do not solve the real problems. In the first place, even the most isolated peoples after the introduction of reading, soon become familiar with many areas of the world around them, and very quickly they learn that people in other parts of the world are quite different. Even a very rudimentary education soon teaches them that the life of the Middle East is not similar to their own. Accordingly, they tend to react to such artificially adapted translations as being paternalistic, since they seem to imply that the native people would never learn about the differences in the outside world. On the other hand, it is not very meaningful simply to borrow the word *camel* in transliterated form and give the people no idea what sort of creature this is. One way to solve this problem is to employ certain descriptive classifiers, which may be used in initial translations and then discarded as the level of education in an area rises. For example, one may say 'hair of an animal called camel', which helps to identify the trans iterated form as a name and specifies the class of objects involved. In some of the Quechua dialects of South America translators have used 'hair of a llama-like animal called camel', a somewhat fuller descriptive classifier. In general, however, it is preferable to use the shortest possible expression which will provide the basis for correct, even though partial, understanding.

Since many different peoples in the world eat one or more varieties of locusts or grasshoppers, this verse does not seem to them so strange as it does to us. However, it is important that in obtaining a word for *locusts* one be sure that an edible variety is specified. In some languages, for example, there may be as many as ten different words for such insects, and only certain classes are regarded as edible.

In regions where such insects are not known, one can likewise use a descriptive device, e.g. 'insects called locusts' or simply a generic term 'a kind of insect'.

'Wild honey' is most often translated 'honey from the forest' (cf. Indonesian 'wood-honey'). In Zoque it is actually called 'gentle honey', since it is made by wild bees in the forest, which, however, are stingless.

7 And he preached, saying, "After me comes he who is mightier than I, the thong of whose sandals I am not worthy to stoop down and untie.

Exegesis: *ekērussen* 'he proclaimed' (cf. v. 4): the imperfect continues to describe John's habitual activity, the message which accompanied his baptism.

ekērussen legōn 'he preached saying': this construction, consisting of a verb plus the participle of another verb, which is practically a synonym of the first, is common and reflects Semitic infuence. There is no need, in English translation, to reproduce both verbs (cf. BFBS, Manson, Weymouth, Moffatt, Knox, Zürich).

erchetai 'he comes': the present tense is often used with a future meaning (Moffatt "is to come"); in this verse there is an emphasis on the immediacy of the action, 'is coming' (BFBS), 'is on his way'.

ho ischuroteros mou 'the one stronger than I': *ischus* 'strength' refers primarily to physical strength—by extension it takes on the idea of power, might, greatness (cf. 3:27): 'mightier' (Weymouth, Moffatt, RSV, Manson, Knox), 'greater' (BFBS).

opisō mou 'behind me': the phrase goes with *erchetai* 'is coming behind me'.

opisō (1:17, 20, 8:33, 34, 13:16) 'behind', 'after': as an adverb it refers both to time and to place (not used of time in the N.T.); as a preposition, with the genitive case, as here, it is also used of time and place (Abbott-Smith sees LXX influence). Here the idea is clearly that of time (cf. Acts 13:25 *erchetai met' eme* 'comes after me'), although some commentators see the idea of rank, 'a follower of mine' (see reff. in Arndt & Gingrich).

hou...autou 'whose...of him': this use of the relative *hos* 'who' and the pronoun *autos* 'he', both in the genitive case, is a construction which reflects Semitic influence (Black *Aramaic*, 75: "clear proof of its origin"), although, as Lagrange points out, it is not unknown in Greek itself. In translation, therefore, there is no need to reproduce both the relative *hou* 'whose' and the pronoun *autou* 'of him' since both refer to the same thing, i.e. *ton himanta tōn hupodēmatōn* 'the thong of the sandals' (cf. a similar construction in 7:25, and see Taylor, 60 and literature referred to). The relative *hou* 'whose', it is to be noticed, does not refer to *hikanos* 'worthy' as though it meant 'worthy of *him*': rather, like *autou* 'of him', it refers to 'the thong of the sandals'.

hikanos (10:46, 15:15) "competent, qualified, able, with the connotation worthy...for something" (Arndt & Gingrich).

kupsas lusai 'stooping to loose': such a verbal construction is quite common, in which two different actions are described by the participle of one verb plus the regular form (required by grammar) of the other. The meaning is the same it would be if both verbs were in the infinitive: *kupsai kai lusai* 'to stoop and to loose'.

kuptō (only here in Mark) 'stoop (down)': the participle modifies the subject of *eimi* 'I am', not 'the thong of his sandals'.

luō (7:35, 11:2, 4, 5) 'loose', 'unbind', 'release': to untie the thong of the sandal was the menial task of a slave. On the difference between 'untie' here and 'bear' in Mt. 3:11, see Daube *New Testament and Rabbinic Judaism*, 266 f.

Translation: In most translations the first problem to be encountered in this verse is the existence of the double verbs of speaking, *preached,* *saying*. In many languages one must use one verb or the other, but not both, or people will say, "What did he do, preach or say?" Often these terms are mutually exclusive. On the other hand, there are a number of languages, e.g. several of the Quechua dialects of South America, which use double verbs of speaking, but one is used at the beginning of an utterance, and the other at the end, somewhat parallel to "he said...said he". In a sense they serve in the place of quotation marks and as such are very convenient. In still other instances this Semitic type of expression fits quite naturally, e.g. in Barrow Eskimo.

Having noted (Mark 1:4) that some indirect expressions must be turned into direct ones, we must also indicate the fact that frequently the reverse process is obligatory. For example, in Maninka verses 7 and 8 must be cast into an indirect form: 'he said that after him would come one...'

Comparatives, such as *mightier than I* are seemingly very awkward to translate in some languages, for in such instances comparison is only accomplished by means of a combined positive-negative statement, e.g. 'there is more his power; more there is not my power' (Tzotzil), 'he has great power; I do not have great power' (as in the case of a number of so-called Bantu tongues). These types of positive-negative statements must not be interpreted on the basis of their literal retranslation into English. They are just as much genuine "comparatives" (if we may use the term) as the construction with which we are familiar in Indo-European languages. Another common form of comparative uses a verb meaning 'to surpass', e.g. 'his power surpasses my power'.

What, however, adds to the difficulty of this verse is the fact that the adjective *worthy* is difficult to translate in many languages, for close equivalents are often not adjectives. This should not be surprising, for *worthy* is not an abstraction of easily definable qualities (cf. *red*, *good*, *beautiful*), but of relative social position and capacity. In Amuzgo the phrase *I am not worthy to* is translated 'I can't be used to...' In Huichol *worthy* is 'to have the right to...' In Barrow Eskimo the equivalent is 'to be on the same level so as to...'; in Tzotzil a possible rendering is 'measure up to...'; and in Huave one must say 'reach to'.

The expression *after me comes* must be treated in some languages as a kind of comparative. For example, in the Chontal of Oaxaca this verse reads 'I come first; he comes later'.

Mightier must be interpreted in terms of authority, and not physical strength, e.g. 'will order more people around' (Huichol) or 'will be more a chief' (Huave).

Sandals must often be translated by a type of footgear with parallel functions, even though some details of construction are dissimilar, e.g. 'boots' (Barrow Eskimo) or 'thongless sandals' (Villa Alta Zapotec), which are 'removed' rather than 'untied' ('removing' is the functional equivalent).

In any translation the arrangement of the constituent parts of this verse must be entirely dependent upon requirements of the structure involved, e.g. 'He spoke God's word, saying, Someone is coming after me, his power surpasses mine. I am not worthy to bend over and untie his shoestrings' (Kpelle).

8 *I have baptized you with water; but he will baptize you with the Holy Spirit."*

Text: Before 'water' and 'Holy Spirit' *Textus Receptus* has *en* 'in'. Support for the second *en* is stronger than for the first: Souter, Merk, Kilpatrick, and Soden include *en* in both places, while Tischendorf, Lagrange, and Vogels include it only before 'Holy Spirit'; Nestle, Westcott and Hort, Taylor, and Turner reject *en* in both instances. (It is to be noticed that although in other passages in the N.T. *en* is sometimes used and sometimes not used before 'water' it is *always* used before 'Holy Spirit': Mt. 3:11, Lk. 3:16, Jn. 1:33, Acts 1:5, 11:16).

Exegesis: *egō...autos* 'I...he': the personal pronouns, not being essential in Greek, are emphatic: '*I*, on my part...*he*, on his part'.

ebaptisa 'baptized': the force of the aorist has been the subject of considerable comment. The majority of translations and commentators agree with Lagrange's interpretation: the ministry of the Baptist ends when that of Jesus begins (cf. Howard II, 458 f.: "the aorist of the thing just happened"). In English the perfect 'have baptized' (AV, RSV, Knox, Weymouth, Moffatt, Manson, BFBS; cf. Zürich, Synodale, Brazilian) may convey the meaning 'I have baptized *and am baptizing no more*'. According to such a view the present *baptizō* 'I baptize' of the parallels Mt. 3:11, Lk. 3:16, represents a change of meaning.

There is, however, an alternative way of viewing the aorist tense: without any particular reference to past time it describes or conveys a general truth (called a "gnomic" aorist: cf. Burton *Moods and Tenses*, § 43, Moule *Idiom Book*, 11). When the full force of *ekērussen legōn* 'he was preaching' in the previous verse is noticed, John's message is not represented as having been delivered once, but repeatedly, throughout his ministry. The aorist *ebaptisa* 'I baptized' does not mean, therefore, that the action is past and finished; it is rather the reference to an action in which time is not emphasized, best translated into English by the present, 'I baptize' (see Black *Aramaic*, 93, who argues for this meaning on the basis of the force of the Semitic perfect tense, with examples; cf. Taylor 64, 157; Rawlinson, 8; cf. *Expository Times* 64.286, 1953).

(en) 'in': whether or not the preposition is included before 'water' and/or 'Holy Spirit', the sense adopted by the majority of translations and commentators is 'with', that is, the instrumental. For this very common use of *en* 'in' see Moule *Idiom Book*, 77; Arndt & Gingrich I.4.c, III.1.a. Lagrange, however, prefers the local sense: 'in the water...in the Holy Spirit'.

pneuma hagion (3:29, 12:36, 13:11; cf. *to pneuma* 'the Spirit' 1:10, 12) 'the Holy Spirit'—and so throughout Mark (and the N.T.). The presence or absence of the definite article, in Greek, before 'Holy Spirit' does not establish a difference between the operation, power, or gifts of the Spirit, and the person of the Spirit. With or without the article *pneuma hagion* is always '*the* Holy Spirit'. Whatever may have been the original significance of the phrase in the preaching of John the Baptist (see Taylor and reff.), especially with the addition of *kai puri* 'and with fire' in Matthew and Luke, the meaning intended by the author of the Gospel is fully Christian, i.e. the Holy Spirit of God.

Translation: Undoubtedly no word has given quite so much trouble to the Bible translator as *spirit*, for (1) it includes such a wide range of meaning, from 'evil spirit' to 'poor in spirit' to 'Holy Spirit' and (2) it touches so vitally the crucial comparison and contrast between Christianity and so-called "animism". We cannot go into a detailed examination of all the problems involving in either 'spirit' or 'Holy Spirit', but for some important treatments see *TBT*, 1.3, 131-32, 1950; 2.56,109, 1951; 6.37-39, 62, 72, 1955; *BT*, pp. 210-15; and *GWIML*, pp. 20-21, 37, 44, and 54 (cf. Hooper, *Indian Word List*, pp. 176-77). There are four principal dangers in the choice of a word for Holy Spirit: (1) the term may identify an essentially malevolent spirit, and no mere addition of the word 'holy' or 'good' is likely to change the basic connotation of the word, (2) the word may mean primarily the spirit of a deceased person (hence God must have died—a not infrequent error in Bible translations), (3) the expression used to mean 'spirit' may denote only an impersonal life force, a sort of soul-stuff which may be conceived as indwelling all plant, animal, and human substances (therefore, to say that 'God is spirit' is to deny His essential personality), and (4) a borrowed term may signify next to nothing to the people, and can only be explained by another term or terms, which, if they are adequate to explain the borrowing, should have been used in the first place. It is true that in some instances a borrowed word has seemed to be the only alternative, but it should be chosen only as a last resort.

There is no easy formula to be employed in finding an adequate equivalent for *Holy Spirit*, for what seems to work quite well in one area may not serve in another. One thing, however, is certain: one should not select a term before making a comprehensive study of all kinds of words for spirits and for parts or aspects of personality and thus having as complete a view as possible of all indigenous beliefs about supernatural beings. (The use of the question outline suggested on pp. 212-13 of *Bible Translating* may prove to be very useful for such necessary investigations.)

An almost equally difficult element in the phrase *Holy Spirit* is the unit meaning 'holy', which in the Biblical languages involves a concept of separation (i.e. unto God or for His service). In general, however, it is difficult to employ a term meaning primarily 'separated', for this often leads to the idea of 'cast out'. One must make sure that the concept of 'separated' implies not merely 'separated from' (hence, often culturally ostracized), but 'separated to' (in the idea of consecrated, dedicated, or 'taboo'—in its proper technical sense). Perhaps the most naive mistakes in rendering *Holy* have been to assume that this word can be translated as 'white' or 'clean', for we assume that "Cleanliness is next to godliness," a belief which is quite foreign to most peoples in the world. *Holy* may, however, be rendered in some languages as 'clear', 'pure' (in South Toradja, Bare'e and Javanese 'clean' or 'pure'), 'shining', or 'brilliant' (with the connotation of awesomeness), concepts which are generally much more closely related to 'holiness' than is 'whiteness' or 'cleanness'.

If one encounters any particular difficulties in finding an adequate expression for *Holy Spirit*, it is recommended that the translator get in touch with the Translations Department of the Bible Society for special help and guidance, since a proper solution to this problem is so basic to any and all communication of the Gospel message.

In so far as possible the phrases 'baptize you with water' and 'baptize you with the Holy Spirit' should be parallel. However, if the term for 'baptism' includes the term 'water', then some adjustment must be made. One would not want to say, for example, in Tzeltal 'you take water with the Holy Spirit' in the second clause, even though a combined idiom 'he gives and you take water' describes the total process of baptism. The parallelism is attained, therefore, in Tzeltal by translating, 'I have given you and you have taken water; but he will give and you will take the Holy Spirit'.

9 *In those days Jesus came from Nazareth of Galilee and was baptized by John in the Jordan.*

Exegesis: *kai egeneto* 'and it was' plus the verb in the indicative (*ēlthen* 'came') is one of the three ways in which the LXX and the N.T. translate the Hebraism *wa-yehi...wa* ('and it was...and'); in the Greek, the clause that follows is logically the subject of *egeneto* 'it was' (cf. Burton *Moods and Tenses* §§ 357-59; Arndt & Gingrich *ginomai* I.3.f). This connective phrase has virtually no meaning and is disregarded by RSV.

en ekeinais tais hemerais (8:1, 13:17, 24) 'in those days' is another Hebraism (cf. Ex. 2:11), and relates in a general way that which follows with what precedes.

apo 'from' goes with *ēlthen* 'came' not with *Iēsous* 'Jesus': 'came from Nazareth of Galilee...'

ebaptisthē eis ton Iordanēn 'he was baptized in the Jordan'. There is no difference between 'baptized *en*' (v. 5) and 'baptized *eis*' here (cf. Robertson *Grammar*, 525; Turner *Journal of Theological Studies* 26.15, 1924-5; see further reff. in Taylor).

Translation: If a language has a kind of introductory and transitional particle equivalent to the Greek *kai egeneto* 'and it happened' (translated traditionally as 'it came to pass'), one can and should employ it, but more frequently than not, it is better simply to omit such elements, particularly if instead of contributing to the meaning, they tend to interrupt the sequence, distract the reader or lead to misunderstanding.

In those days may be rendered in some languages as 'at that time' or 'then'. This Semitic idiom is only a general phrase indicating temporal sequence.

In some languages proper names which are entirely unfamiliar may require some type of descriptive classifier. Hence one may translate 'from Nazareth town in the Galilee province... Jordan river' (Otetela). In view of the fact, however, that 'river' is used with 'Jordan' in verse 5, this last classifier may not be necessary.

In languages in which passive constructions must be or are usually shifted to active ones, the second part of this verse may be readily changed to read, 'John baptized Jesus...'

10 And when he came up out of the water, immediately he saw the heavens opened and the Spirit descending upon him like a dove;

Text: Instead of *ek* 'out of' of all modern editions of the Greek text, *Textus Receptus* has *apo* 'from'.

Instead of *eis auton* 'into him' (see *Exegesis*, below) of the majority of modern editions of the Greek text, *Textus Receptus* and Souter have *ep' auton* 'upon him' (for a discussion of the question see Goodspeed *Problems*, 52, who attributes the *epi* to "harmonistic assimilation with Mt. 3 : 16 and Lk. 3 : 22").

Exegesis: *euthus* 'immediately' occurs some 47 times in Mark. Kilpatrick "Notes on Marcan Usage" (*TBT*, 7.3-4, 1956) concludes that "the evidence suggests that we are dealing not with an adverb of time, but with a connecting particle." Howard (II, 446) finds the inferential meaning 'so then' in 1 : 21, 23, 29, 30 (cf. also Moulton & Milligan). RSV rightly connects *euthus* 'immediately' with the main verb *eiden* 'he saw' and not with the participle *anabainōn* 'coming up' (see further Daube *New Testament and Rabbinic Judaism*, 243).

anabainōn (3 : 13, 4 : 7, 8, 32, 6 : 51, 10 : 32, 33, 15 : 8) 'coming up': the participle is temporal 'as he was coming up... he saw' (cf. Moule *Idiom Book*, 102; BFBS 'just as he was coming up...'). The subject is Jesus. As Lagrange points out *anabainōn* 'coming up' presumes a previous *katabainōn* 'going down' (on the full force of this participle see Daube *New Testament and Rabbinic Judaism*, 111f.).

ek 'out of': not precisely the same as *apo* 'from' in Mt. 3 : 16 (cf. Robertson *Grammar*, 561, 597). Turner (*Journal of Theological Studies* 29.281 f., 1927-8) notes that Mark has *ek* half as often again as *apo*, in which he sees reflected a "Semitic atmosphere."

eiden 'he saw': the verb itself cannot indicate whether a vision or an objective phenomenon is meant; the verb means simply 'he saw' and nothing else. The author doubtlessly means to describe actual happenings. There are two direct objects: *tous ouranous... kai to pneuma* 'the heavens ...and the Spirit'.

schizomenous tous ouranous 'the heavens as they were being rent'.

schizō (15 : 38) 'rend', 'divide', 'tear': the verb is used of garments (Isa. 36 : 22, Lk. 5 : 36, Jn. 19 : 24), a veil (Mk. 15 : 38), a net (Jn. 21 : 11), rocks (Isa. 48 : 21, Mt. 27 : 51), a mountain (Zech. 14 : 4), wood (Gen. 22 : 3). The present participle describes the action in progress (cf. Gould).

Grammar does not decide whether the participle is middle ('opening themselves', cf. Synodale, Zürich), or passive ('being opened'): the latter,
however, is probably to be preferred. The idea of violence is present in
the verb; here is a breach in the firmament which separates the abode
of God from earth. Bengel: *"is rent open*, is said of that which had not
previously been open."

tous ouranous 'the heavens': some hold, with Arndt & Gingrich,
that the plural *hoi ouranoi* 'the heavens' refers to the abode of God;
others see reference to the firmament, the sky (cf. Weymouth). At any
rate the Voice comes from heaven, as the abode of God, not just from
the sky (cf. Rawlinson on the plurality of heavens and the Voice).

to pneuma (v. 8) is 'the (Holy) Spirit'.

katabainon (3:22, 9:9, 13:15, 15:30, 32) *eis auton* 'descending upon
him'. The meaning of *eis* here is debated; in the nature of the case
a precise parallel to *katabainon eis auton* 'descending *into* him' is not
to be found (Mt. 3:16 and Lk. 3:22 have *epi* 'upon', as well as some
manuscripts of the Gospel of Mark; cf. *Text*, above). In the LXX the
phrase *katabainein eis* 'descend into' is often used of 'descend into
Egypt' (cf. Gen. 12:10, 26:2, 43:15, 46:3, Num. 20:15); 'descend into
Hades' (Gen. 37:35, Num. 16:30, Job 7:9, 17:16, Ps. 54 (55):15,
113:25 (115:17), 138 (139):8, Isa. 14:11, 15, 19, Ezek. 31:15, 17, 32:27);
'descend into the darkness (of death)' (Tobit 14:10), and of water
which descends into the sea (Joshua 3:16). In all these passages
the meaning 'descend *into*' is the natural one, generally offering no
difficulties.

So far as spirit possession is concerned, the normal way for the LXX
to narrate the coming of the Spirit of God upon someone is by the use
of the phrase *ginesthai epi* 'to come upon' (cf. Num. 23:7, 24:2; Judges
3:10, 11:29; 1 Sam. 19:9, 20, 23; 2 Chr. 15:1, 20:14), or *hallesthai epi*,
ephallesthai epi 'to leap upon', 'to overpower' (cf. Judg. 14:6, 19,
15:14; 1 Sam. 10:6, 10, 11:6, 16:13). Other phrases less frequently
used are *einai epi* 'to be upon' (1 Sam. 16:16, 23), *piptein epi* 'to fall
upon' (1 Sam. 18:10), *anapauein epi* 'to rest upon' (Is. 11:2) and
epelthein epi 'to come upon' (Is. 32:15); cf. also *dounai epi* 'give upon'
(Is. 42:1).

Closer parallels to the Marcan phrase are to be found in Ezek. 37:5,
6, 14 in which God says, 'I will put breath in you' (*dōsō pneuma mou eis
humas*), and 37:10 'the breath went into them' (*eisēlthen eis autous to
pneuma*); in Is. 37:7 the Lord says of the king of Assyria, 'I will put a
spirit in him' (*embalō eis auton pneuma*), while in Eccl. 3:21 the question
is asked, 'Does the spirit of an animal descend into the earth?' (*ei katabai-
nei auto eis tēn gēn*).

Attention has been called to Isa. 63:11ff. as a possible background
of the Marcan language (*Journal of Theological Studies*, NS 7.74 f., 1956).
In this passage God is spoken of as *ho theis en autois to pneuma to hagion*
'he who placed in them the Holy Spirit' (v. 11), and the statement is
further made *katebē pneuma para kuriou kai hōdēgēsen autous* 'the Spirit
descended from the Lord and guided them' (v. 14).

These verbal parallels in the LXX are sufficient to show, (1) that if Mark had meant to say 'the Spirit descended *upon* him' the preposition *epi* would have been used (as Mt. 3:16 and Lk. 3:22 have it), and (2) that *katabainon eis* means 'descending *into*' unless Marcan usage or the context clearly forbids this meaning.

So far as Marcan usage is concerned it is to be noticed that the preposition *eis* follows verbs of motion with 'house' (2:11, 3:20, 5:19), 'mountain' (3:13, 9:2, 13:14, 14:26), 'region' (7:24, 10:1) and 'road' (10:17): wherever the meaning 'into' cannot be literally pressed, the meaning 'to' or 'toward' is to be presumed. More instructive parallels are found in passages in which a person is the object: 'the word which has been sown *in them*' (4:15), 'something that enters *into a man*' (7:15, 18, 19). Passages which deal with spirit possession are particularly pertinent: the spirits of Legion request they be sent *into* the hogs, and they go *into* the hogs (5:12, 13), and Jesus commands the spirit to come out of the lad and never more enter *into* him (9:25). According to Marcan usage, therefore, *to pneuma ...katabainon eis auton* may certainly mean 'the Spirit descending (to enter) into him'.

The majority of translations render *eis* 'upon', and Robertson (*Grammar*, 1393) cites examples of *eis* with the meaning of *epi* 'upon': none of the examples quoted, however, is decisive for this passage. The meaning 'descending into' is supported by Arndt & Gingrich (*katabainō* 1.b) who translate 'come down and enter into him'. Goodspeed discusses the passage at length (*Problems*, 52-54) and concludes that it means 'coming down to enter into him' (cf. also Weymouth, Appendix p. 658: " 'into' i.e. 'to enter into' ").

In the light of all this it seems reasonably clear that Mark does not say that the Spirit came *upon* Jesus at his baptism as the Spirit of God came upon Old Testament leaders: rather he says that the Spirit entered into and possessed Jesus, who henceforth acts with the authority and power of God, as God's Spirit-filled and Spirit-led Son.

hōs peristeran (11:15) 'as a dove'. There are two possible meanings: (1) 'He saw...the Spirit descending like a dove (descends)...' or (2) 'He saw...the Spirit, as (though it were) a dove, descending...' In the first case the figure modifies the mode of descent, and in the second it modifies the Spirit as such, with the meaning 'in the appearance of' i.e. 'in the form of'. Most English translations are ambiguous, even as the Greek is. Matthew (probably) and Luke (certainly) take the narrative to mean that a dove was to be seen. No significant parallels to the phrase are to be found in the Old Testament or early Jewish literature (cf. Taylor). The natural meaning of *eiden...to pneuma hōs peristeran* is 'he saw...the Spirit *in appearance as* a dove' (cf. 8:24), and this certainly seems to be the meaning intended here (cf. Lagrange: "it is the Spirit himself who is like a dove").

Translation: In order to indicate the force of the Greek word *euthus* 'immediately' as a kind of transitional temporal relator, it is possible to translate, 'Just as...then he...' (Balinese) or 'Then just as...he

saw' (Shipibo). On the other hand one may translate 'and when he came ...,
right then he saw ...' In any case the force of *euthus* must be with the
second verb, even though a temporal particle may precede the first.

In some languages (e.g. Ifugao) there are distinct expressions for
'coming out of a stream' and 'coming out from underneath the surface
of the water'. The choice of one or the other expression will be determined
by one's views on the mode of baptism practiced by John. Where,
however, it is possible to use a noncommittal term which will not provoke
unnecessary controversy this should be employed.

A word which will properly designate the rending of the heavens is
not always easy to find, for the Greek term in question does not mean
merely that Jesus saw that the heavens were open, but that he saw them
being rent open. In the Black Bobo language, for example, one must
choose between two words for opening: (1) one which designates the way
a box is opened (whether with care or violently), and (2) one which
characterizes the splitting of a goat skin. The latter term was found to
fit this context more satisfactorily.

Despite the fact that the Voice comes from heaven (cf. verse 11) as
the abode of God, the *heavens* of this verse may refer to the sky. In a
language in which heaven as God's abode is clearly distinguished from
the sky (e.g. 'God's house' in contrast with 'the place of the clouds'), it
would be important to use the latter in this verse, for one would not
wish to give the impression that 'God's house' was being destroyed.

In general there is no difficulty in finding a word for *the sky*. In Loma,
for example, it is simply 'up'. The more complex problem is discovering
some expression which will convey at least some of the meaning of *heaven*
in English. To do this various expresssions have been employed, e.g.
'God's place' (Loma), 'God's town' (Kaka), 'the up above' (Moré *nyingeri*,
in contrast with *saase* 'the sky' which is regarded as lower), and 'the
home above' (San Blas). (See also *BT*, pp. 161, 231).

When an indigenous word for 'Spirit' generally indicates a malevolent
spirit, it is important that the qualifier 'Holy' be added if the context
in question is not very plain. Of course, in this particular verse the
addition of 'Holy' may not be required, because of the connection with
'heaven' and the 'voice' announcing the sonship of Jesus. However, in
verse 12 the addition of 'Holy' is essential in many languages, and even
in this verse it can in some instances eliminate considerable misunderstanding.

Whether one translates 'descended upon him' or 'descended into him'
(see above) is somewhat related to the treatment of 'as a dove', for if
one says that the Spirit had the precise form of a dove (or pigeon) and
then that it entered into him, the resultant impression may be confusing
and disconcerting to the reader. Where, of course, one can preserve the
Greek ambiguity, so that the phrase 'as a dove' may refer to either
mode of descent or form, the problem can be readily resolved, but this
is not a solution to the Matthaean and Lucan expressions. One can,
however, eliminate some of the semantic difficulties by making two
clauses out of one (in fact, this is often necessary) and translate as 'the

Holy Spirit appeared there like a dove and came down into him' (Kpelle). As in this Kpelle rendering the particle 'as' must often be expanded into an expression containing a verb, e.g. 'appeared like'.

11 *and a voice came from heaven, "Thou art my beloved Son; with thee I am well pleased."*

Text: Instead of *soi* 'with thee' of all modern editions of the Greek text, *Textus Receptus* has *hō* 'with whom'.

The construction is quite abrupt. Perhaps *egeneto* 'came' should be omitted, as is done by Turner (cf. *Journal of Theological Studies* 28.151, 1926-7), Tischendorf and Kilpatrick; Nestle and Westcott and Hort include it in brackets; other modern editions of the Greek text include it without any question.

Exegesis: *phōnē ek tōn ouranōn* 'a voice from the heavens': the voice is God's, addressing itself to Jesus. Lagrange: "the voice comes from heaven where God dwells."

su ei ho huios mou ho agapētos 'you are my beloved son': the phrase is a compound of familiar O.T. phrases (Ps. 2:7, Isa. 42:1; cf. also Gen. 22:2, Isa. 44:2, 62:4), full of meaning.

su ei 'you are': a statement of fact, not a promise; it is either a revelation of a truth previously not known or confirmation of a truth already grasped (see Taylor, 162).

ho agapētos (9:7, 12:6) 'the beloved': used in the LXX (and classical Greek as well) of 'favorite', 'only'. In the LXX *agapētos* seven times out of fifteen translates *yaḥidh* 'only one'. Lagrange comments: "in the O.T. there is no great difference between 'beloved' and 'only'." Turner devotes a lengthy study to the phrase (*Journal of Theological Studies* 27.113-29, 1925-6) and concludes: "From Homer to Athanasius the history of the Greek language bears out, I venture to think, the argument of this paper that *agapētos huios* is rightly rendered 'Only Son'." The majority of translations, however, have 'beloved' rather than 'only', which is in the nature of an interpretation (see BFBS).

Grammatically *ho agapētos* may modify *ho huios* 'the son' and be translated 'beloved Son' (ASV, RSV, Lagrange, Knox, Zürich, Synodale, Brazilian), or it may stand independently, as a title, 'my Son, the Beloved (one)' (Manson, Moffatt, Weymouth, Berkeley).

en soi eudokēsa 'in thee I am well pleased'. The force of the aorist *eudokēsa* has been studied, both from the viewpoint of the Greek (Moule *Idiom Book*, 11; Burton *Moods and Tenses*, § 55) and the possible Semitic perfect underlying it (Black *Aramaic*, 93; Howard II, 458). There is agreement that the meaning is best represented in English by the present tense: " 'punctiliar' present" (Moule), "present of general truth" (Black). Cf. Jerome: *in te complacui.*

eudokeō en 'be well pleased', 'take delight' with or in someone (see Arndt & Gingrich): cf. in the LXX Mal. 2:17, Ps. 43:4, 2 Sam. 22:20; in the N.T. see 1 Co. 10:5, 2 Co. 12:10. The translations reflect the

31

meaning in various ways: "be pleased" (AV, ASV, RSV, BFBS); "delight" (Moffatt, Weymouth, Berkeley); "choice" (Manson).

Translation: In some languages one cannot say 'a voice came'. One may, on the other hand, find that the use of some such expression as 'words (or sounds) of a voice were heard coming...' is fully satisfactory (so Indonesian 'a voice was heard'). Though, of course, this is God's voice (i.e. 'God spoke from heaven') it is best, wherever possible, to try to preserve the indefiniteness of the original form, despite its somewhat greater lack of clarity.

For a discussion of "heaven" see under verse 10.

Though there is justification for the translation of 'only' for Greek *agapētos*, generally rendered 'beloved', it is probably more satisfactory to retain the translation used by the vast majority of translators, for undoubtedly even in the Greek expression there is something of the connotation of 'love', despite what may be the more predominant denotation of 'only'.

My beloved Son must in some languages be translated in a paratactic form, '...my Son; I love you', or '...my Son, the one I love' (Zoque).

With thee I am well pleased is a concept which is often translated in other languages by a wide variety of figurative expressions, e.g. 'you are the heart of my eye' (Huastec), 'you arrive at my gall' (Moré, in which the gall is regarded as the seat of the emotions and intelligence), 'I see you very well' (Tzotzil), 'you make me happy' (Popoluca), and 'my bowels are sweet with you' (Shilluk). One must not, however, assume that all languages will have such figurative expressions (in Barrow Eskimo the equivalent of this entire phrase is a single word, with a strictly non-figurative meaning). Nevertheless, there are problems in the choice of an appropriate phrase, for it is entirely too easy to select inadvertently an expression which may refer primarily to satisfaction with food or pleasure in sensual entertainment.

12 *The Spirit immediately drove him out into the wilderness.*

Exegesis: *to pneuma* 'the (Holy) Spirit', 'the Spirit (of God)'.

ekballei 'drives out': the historic present is characteristic of Mark's style. In Mark *ekballō* 'drive out' always denotes strong and, at times, violent action, being used mainly of the expulsion of demons (1 : 34, 39, 3 : 15, 22, 23, 6 : 13, 7 : 26, 9 : 18, 28, 38, 16 : 9, 17); where people are involved force is always indicated (1 : 43, 5 : 40, 11 : 15, 12 : 8), while once it is used of the removal of an eye (9 : 47). In the present passage, the parallels in Matthew (*anagesthai* 'be led') and Luke (*agesthai* 'be led') may argue in favor of force for the Marcan *ekballei* 'drives out'. Cf. Jerome *expellit* and in English "drive" (AV, ASV, RSV, Moffatt, Berkeley); Zürich *treiben*.

Force is certainly involved. There is no need, however, of inferring resistance or unwillingness on the part of Jesus.

tēn erēmon (cf. v. 4) 'uninhabited places', traditionally the haunt of evil powers.

Translation: In this context it is quite important that one make sure that a word used for 'Spirit' carries the proper connotation, for 'driving one out into an uninhabited region' is precisely what demons are usually credited with doing. Hence, in many translations 'Spirit of God' or 'Holy Spirit' should be used here (Balinese, Kpelle, Bolivian Quechua, Shipibo).

There is no doubt about the fact that the Greek word *ekballō* implies a strong action, but it is possible to translate this word in such a way as to give quite a wrong impression. In one language in West Africa the term used meant literally 'to chase him away' and in one Eskimo dialect the word was one generally used of 'driving dogs'. The force of this Greek verb applies primarily to the psychological compulsion, not any physical violence, and hence to use an expression which emphasizes the physical aspects may ultimately result in a distortion of the meaning. Accordingly, many translations simply use a causative form, 'the Holy Spirit made him go' or 'caused him to go'. In Balinese the expression is 'by the might of the Holy Spirit, Jesus went', meaning that the Holy Spirit was the force which caused Jesus to go.

For a discussion of "wilderness" see I : 3.

13 And he was in the wilderness forty days, tempted by Satan; and he was with the wild beasts; and the angels ministered to him.

Text: With the support of later mss. *Textus Receptus* and Kilpatrick include *ekei* 'there' after (the first) *ēn* 'he was'; the majority of modern editions of the Greek text omit it.

Exegesis: *ēn...peirazomenos* 'was...tempted': may be taken as a verbal phrase, 'he was being tempted', or the participle *peirazomenos* 'being tempted' may be independent of the verb *ēn* 'was', and modify 'he': in this case *ēn* would mean 'he was', 'he abode', 'he remained'. Although most translations favor this rendition, separating the participle from the verb *ēn*, Marcan usage is probably decisive in favor of the first meaning. Kilpatrick (*TBT* 7.8-9, 1956): "In Mark *einai* ('to be'), usually in the imperfect, and the present participle may be presumed to form a single tense" (cf. Turner *Journal of Theological Studies* 28.349, 1926-7).

peirazō (8 : 11, 10 : 2, 12 : 15) 'put to the test'; *peirazomai* 'be tried', 'be tempted': here with hostile intent (cf. Kennedy *Sources*, 106-7, Hatch *Essays*, 71-73). The action is portrayed as taking place throughout the whole period of forty days.

Satanas (3 : 23, 26, 4 : 15, 8 : 33) is the transliteration of the Aramaic *saṭana'* (the O.T. *satan* is 'accuser', 'adversary'). In the N.T. the same as *ho diabolos* 'the devil', ruler of the powers of evil, opponent of God, enemy of man.

meta tōn thēriōn 'with the beasts': hyenas, jackals, foxes, gazelles (cf. Swete, Lagrange). The purpose of this clause is to accentuate the wildness of the desert into which the Spirit drove Jesus, the haunt of wild animals, suitable locale for the presence of supernatural forces both

good and evil (for possible theological overtones cf. Isa. 13:21, Ps. 91:
11-13, Job 5 : 22 f.; *Testament Naphtali* viii. 4, 6; *Testament Benjamin* v. 2).

kai hoi aggeloi diēkonoun autō 'and the angels were serving him'.

hoi aggeloi (cf. v. 2) 'the angels': with the single exception of *aggelos*
'messenger' in v. 2, the word, in Mark, always refers to celestial messengers, sent by God.

diēkonoun (1 : 31, 10 : 45, 15 : 41) 'they were serving': the primary
meaning is that of waiting on someone at table, from which it passes
over to the general meaning of service of any kind (cf. Arndt & Gingrich).
The reference here is to physical needs, particularly food (cf. 1 : 31),
recalling the experience of Elijah (1 Kings 19 : 5-8). The imperfect tense
would seem to describe a ministration which continued throughout the
forty days' stay in the wilderness (cf. C. S. Emden, "St. Mark's Use of
the Imperfect Tense," *Expository Times* 55.146-49, 1954).

Translation: *Tempted* is a difficult term, for though it means 'to tempt
to evil' or 'to try' (or 'test'), in this context it obviously must not be
rendered in such a way as to imply that Jesus succumbed to the temptation. In many instances one finds that words for temptation imply
yielding, rather than resisting. They are rarely neutral in connotation.
In such instances, one must attempt to indicate the attempt by Satan,
but not the success, or the entire meaning of the passage will be distorted,
e.g. 'tried to make him sin' (Maninka, Tzotzil, Huave, Kekchi).

In general it is preferable to transliterate, rather than attempt to
translate, the word *Satan*. However, in some languages *Satan* and *devil*
are translated the same way (however, Greek *diabolos* 'devil' does not
occur in Mark).

In order to combine 'tempted by Satan' with the preceding clause it
is often necessary to use a paratactic construction, sometimes with a
shift in grammatical voice, e.g. 'There in the wilderness Jesus remained
forty days; Satan tried Jesus' (Mazatec).

In saying that Jesus was 'with the wild beasts' one should not give
the impression (1) that he 'was sitting right there with them' (as in one
translation in the Philippines) or (2) that he was a kind of animal trainer,
there in company with lions, tigers, and leopards. In Greek there is no
special emphasis on 'wild'; these were simply the animals of the wilderness
(see above). One may translate, 'he was there where the animals of the
deserted places were'.

One must also make certain that it was Jesus and not Satan who was
with the wild beasts, since in many popular beliefs demonic spirits are
associated with wild animals. Hence, one is often justified in introducing
'Jesus' as the subject of this clause, 'Jesus was with the wild beasts'
(Mitla Zapotec, and Huastec).

Finding an appropriate word for *angels* is not easy. In the first place,
one is quite likely to run into false ideas, especially in Latin America,
where in one Indian language angels had been called 'flying saints' and
in another 'dead babies' (since according to popular belief children who
died in infancy became angels). It is, however, difficult to employ the

precise equivalent of Greek 'messenger', since often this term does not bear the proper connotation. For example, in Mixtec a messenger is literally 'hands and feet', but this term must usually be modified if it is to serve in the Scriptures, e.g. '. . . heavenly', or '. . . of God', or '. . . of the Lord', etc. This same problem has occurred in many translations, and as a result a number of possible solutions have been found, 'word-carriers from heaven' (Shipibo), 'heavenly messengers' (Otetela, Kpelle, Balinese), 'spirit messengers' (Shilluk), 'messengers of God' (Piro), 'envoys, messengers' (Toba Batak), and 'holy servants' (Navajo). Some of these terms developed and became somewhat current among believers prior to actual Bible translating, and in other instances the words were accepted through being employed in the Scriptures.

The word *ministered* includes so much that it is often difficult to discover just the right equivalent, without being too specific. In some languages the closest equivalent is 'helped him' and in others 'provided what he needed' or 'took care of him' (South Toradja).

14 Now after John was arrested, Jesus came into Galilee, preaching the gospel of God,

Text: After *euaggelion* 'gospel' *Textus Receptus* has *tēs basileias*, 'gospel *of the kingdom* of God', with considerable mss. support. Although 'of the kingdom' is rejected by Tischendorf, Nestle, Westcott and Hort, Vogels, Kilpatrick, Merk, Souter and Soden, Turner argues for its originality, in which he is followed by F. C. Grant. Considerable weight, notwithstanding mss. evidence, must be given Turner's arguments: "the gospel of God" is far less probable, in Mark, than "the gospel of the kingdom of God."

Exegesis: *meta de to paradothēnai ton Iōannēn* 'after John had been arrested': an introductory temporal clause; *ton Iōannēn* 'John' is the subject of the passive infinitive *to paradothēnai* 'to be arrested'. A free translation could be 'after the arrest of John'.

paradidōmi (20 times in Mark): 'hand over', 'turn over', 'give up a person'; as a technical term of police and courts, 'hand over into (the) custody (of)' (Arndt & Gingrich, 1.b). Moulton & Milligan quote examples from the papyri with the meaning 'deliver up' to prison or judgment.

kērussōn 'proclaiming' (cf. v. 4).

euaggelion 'the gospel' in the technical, Christian sense: the contents of the Christian message (cf. v. 1).

tou theou 'of God' (omitting *tēs basileias* 'of the kingdom'): the meaning is 'the gospel *proceeding from* God' (cf. Gould, Turner). The phrase *to euaggelion tou theou* 'the gospel of God' is called a "Pauline phrase" (cf. Rom. 1:1, 15:16, 2 Cor. 11:7, 1 Thess. 2:8,9; cf. 1 Pet. 4:17). This observation has no bearing, however, on whether or not *tēs basileias* 'of the kingdom' should be read in this passage.

Translation: *Arrested* may be translated in a number of different ways, depending upon the manner in which such an event is described in the language in question, e.g. 'taken prisoner' (Kpelle, Bare'e, Javanese) or 'put in jail' (Balinese).

The verbs for *come* and *go* tend to create all sorts of confusion in translating, since the viewpoint of the writer is so differently interpreted in various languages. There is no help in the Greek at this point for the same verb *erchomai* may be rendered either 'come' or 'go', though 'come' is the more usual meaning. However, Mark does not always preserve the same geographical orientation, for in 10 : 46 he speaks of 'coming to Jericho'. The systems of geographical orientation are, of course, quite different as one goes from one language to another. In some instances one is supposed to preserve the viewpoint of the position of the writer; in others, the position of the eye-witness, i.e. of Jesus' disciples or followers. But whatever may be the type of orientation employed in indigenous narration, it is extremely important that one use this system, for otherwise the reader will be badly confused. In this particular instance, many languages require a verb meaning 'to go', since the viewpoint of the writer is assumed to be that of a companion of Jesus, and hence Jesus would be going to a point away from the writer, rather than coming to a place where the writer was.

If one follows a Greek text omitting 'of the kingdom', the relationship between 'good news' and 'God' is probably subjective. That is to say, this would be 'the good news that comes from God', He being the source of the glad tidings (the possible interpretation 'good news about God', though theoretically possible, is rather unlikely).

If, however, we include 'of the kingdom' the construction becomes distinctly objective (in the grammatical sense), for in this instance the text is certainly speaking about 'the good news about the kingdom of God'. But this expression is very difficult to translate in some languages, for there is simply no ready equivalent of 'kingdom', as this is popularly understood. In the first place, most people do not have kings, but they almost always have rulers, chiefs, headmen, etc. In the second place, in so many societies there is not the emphasis upon geographical extension or territory which the English word *kingdom* seems to imply. However, this should not provide special difficulty, for in Greek the central meaning of *basileia* is not the region, but the rule. In other words, the Greek word applies primarily to the fact of God's rule, rather than the territory over which he governs. Once we understand these two principal limitations, it is not too difficult to construct a functional equivalent. For example, in San Blas the 'kingdom of God' is 'God's government', in Navajo 'what God has charge of', in Kabba-Laka 'God's commanding', in Tzeltal 'the jurisdiction of God' (in the sense of where God has the authority), in Zacapoastla Aztec 'the leadership of God', in Goajira 'where God is chief', in Kekchi 'power (or authority) of God', and in Javanese 'the rule of God'.

15 *and saying, "The time is fulfilled, and the kingdom of God is at hand; repent, and believe in the gospel."*

Exegesis: *hoti* 'that' is recitative, introducing direct ¦speech (cf. 1 : 37,

40, 2:12, etc.). Turner (*Journal of Theological Studies* 28.9-14, 1926-7) catalogues some 45 instances of this use of *hoti* 'that' in Mark.

peplērōtai (14:49) 'is fulfilled'. The verb *plēroō* 'fill up', 'complete' when used of time indicates that a period of time has reached its end (cf. Gen. 29:21). Moulton & Milligan show that this use of the word is not peculiar to Scriptures, quoting a papyrus: "the period of the lease has expired." The verb is used only in the passive in the N.T. and early Christian literature. "The time has run its course and reached its end: the appointed hour has arrived." The implied subject of *plēroō* is God: Jeremias (*Parables*, 12 *et passim*) has abundantly shown that the passive in the N.T. is often a "circumlocution...to indicate the divine activity."

ho kairos (10:30, 11:13, 12:2, 13:33) 'the time': not simply chronological time, but opportune time, appointed time, "season" (Kennedy *Sources*, 153). Cf. 'appointed time' Eze. 7:12, Dan. 12:4,9 (cf. Eph. 1:10). The word (as Arndt & Gingrich 4, point out) is one of the chief eschatological terms in the Bible: *kairos* is supremely God's time.

kai ēggiken hē basileia tou theou: 'and the kingdom of God has drawn near' (or, 'has arrived').

eggizō (11:1, 14:42) 'approach', 'draw near'. The force of the perfect has been the object of much debate. Dodd (*Parables*, 44), Lagrange, Black (*Aramaic*, 260-62) argue that the meaning is 'has come' or 'has arrived' (Manson). Kilpatrick (*TBT* 7.53, 1956) rightly observes that one's conclusion "must be determined in part by other considerations" than purely grammatical ones. Black's argument that the words *ho kairos peplērōtai* 'the time is fulfilled' are decisive for the meaning 'has come' is not lightly to be denied (for a forceful presentation of the meaning 'has drawn nigh' see R. H. Fuller *The Mission and Achievement of Jesus*, 20-49, and W. G. Kümmel *Promise and Fulfilment*, 19-25).

hē basileia tou theou 'the kingdom of God'. Dalman (*Words*, 91-147) has conclusively demonstrated that the meaning of *basileia* is that of exercise of royal power. Arndt & Gingrich: "kingship, royal power, royal rule, especially the royal reign of God."

metanoeite (6:12) 'repent (you, pl.)' (cf. v. 4).

pisteuete en tō euaggeliō 'believe (you, pl.) in the gospel'.

pisteuō (5:36, 9:23,24,42, 11:23,24,31, 13:21, 15:32, 16:13, 14,16,17) 'believe'. Here only in the N.T. is the construction *pisteuō en* 'believe in' to be found (John 3:15 and Eph. 1:13 are not true parallels). Moulton (*Prolegomena*, 67 f.) at one time agreed with Deissmann that *pisteuō* is here used in an absolute sense, being correctly translated "believe in (the sphere of) the Gospel" (cf. Moule *Idiom Book*, 80 f.). Later, however (cf. Howard II, 464), Moulton changed his mind and accepted the construction as translation Greek, meaning simply, "believe the Gospel." Gould comments: "The rendering 'believe *in* the Gospel' is a too literal translation of a Marcan Semitism." Manson translates: "Believe the Good News."

euaggelion (cf. v. 1) 'gospel': some (Taylor, Gould, Lagrange) hold that the meaning here is literally 'the good news' (cf. Weymouth: "this Good News"), while others maintain it has the technical Christian sense

37

of "the Christian message." In the light of v. 1 the latter is to be preferred.

Translation: In rendering *and saying* one must often separate it from the preceding verse and make it an independent verb expression 'he said', with whatever appropriate connective (if any) may be employed.

Since *time* in this instance is a point of time (an opportunity or occasion), its equivalent in many languages is 'day'. One must avoid using a word which implies extent of time (which is an entirely different Greek term, see above).

Is fulfilled is admittedly a difficult expression, unless one translates the idea, rather than the word—this, of course, is fundamentally what one must always do. One can either say 'the day has come' or as in some languages 'this is the day'. In Shipibo there is an interesting idiom 'the when-it-is (referring to any occasion) is already coming-up'—a very appropriate equivalent of the Greek. In some languages, however, one cannot speak of 'days coming' but only of 'people coming to the day', which is equally acceptable, if this is the normal way in which people describe the fulfillment of time.

If in verse 1:14 the *Textus Receptus* is adopted, it is possible to speak of *the kingdom of God* as 'where God rules'; in this verse, however, we must speak of the kingdom in terms of time. Accordingly, in Huastec, even though in 1:14 *kingdom* is translated as 'where God rules' (the more usual form of the expression), in 1:15 it must be rendered as 'now is when God is going to reign'. The idea of immediate future implied in the expression *is at hand* is rendered in Zoque as 'God is soon going to rule'. In Pame the translation is 'God is soon going to make himself the ruler'. Another possibility is 'God the ruler is here'.

For *repent* see 1:4.

A key word in any Scripture translation is *believe*. However, finding suitable equivalents (several are usually necessary depending upon the context) is admittedly very complex, for such expressions as *believe a report, believe a person* and *believe in a person* are frequently treated in other languages as quite different types of expressions. For discussions of some of the problems relating to the translation of *believe* and *faith* (these contain the same basic root in Greek), see *TBT*, 1.139, 161-62, 1950; 2.57, 107-8, 1951; 3.143, 1952; 4.51, 136, 167, 1953; 5.93, 1954; 6.39-41, 1955; *BT*, 230; *GWIML*, 21, 118-22, 125. Cf. Hooper *Indian Word List*, pp. 172-73.

Since belief or faith is so essentially an intimate psychological experience, it is not strange that so many terms denoting faith should be highly figurative and represent an almost unlimited range of emotional 'centers' and descriptions of relationships, e.g. 'steadfast his heart' (Chol), 'to arrive on the inside' (Trique), 'to conform with the heart' (Timorese), 'to join the word to the body' (Uduk), 'to hear in the insides' (Kabba-Laka), 'to make the mind big for something' (Putu), 'to make the heart straight about' (Mitla Zapotec), 'to cause a word to enter the insides' (Lacandon), 'to leave one's heart with' (Kuripako), 'to catch in the mind' (Valiente), 'that which one leans on' (Vai), 'to be strong on' (Shipibo), 'to have no doubts' (San Blas), 'to hear and take into the insides' (Karré), 'to accept' (Bare'e).

Though these are the expressions used in a variety of languages to express faith, one must not conclude that they can be used automatically in all types of contexts. For example, though in Uduk to believe in God is generally translated as 'to join God's word to the body', in this context one must speak of 'joining the joyful word to the body' ('joyful word' is the gospel). In Valiente, however, it is possible to speak of 'catching the word in the mind' (if one is talking about believing a statement), but 'catching God in the mind' (if one is speaking of faith in God). In some instances one must use a kind of paratactic construction to indicate faith in a statement, e.g. 'to declare, It is true'. This type of inserted direct discourse may be rather awkward, but it is an effective equivalent in some languages.

One special problem should be noted, namely, the tendency for some languages to make no distinction between words for 'believe' and 'obey'. At first this may seem to be a clear case of deficiency in the language, but it can be a distinct gain in the task of evangelism, for it prevents people from saying that they believe the gospel when they have no intentions of obeying its implications.

16 And passing along by the Sea of Galilee, he saw Simon and Andrew the brother of Simon casting a net in the sea; for they were fishermen.

Text: Instead of *kai paragōn* 'and passing along' of all modern editions of the Greek text, *Textus Receptus* has *peripatōn de* 'and walking'.

Instead of the unusual compound verb *amphiballontas* 'casting a net' of all modern editions of the Greek text, *Textus Receptus* has the more common *ballontas amphiblēstron* 'casting a net'.

Exegesis: *paragōn* (2 : 14, 15 : 21) 'passing along': the present participle, modifying 'he' (Jesus), indicates manner, and in time is simultaneous with the main verb *eiden* 'he saw': 'as he passed along...he saw'. The phrase *paragō para* 'along—passing along' is rather unusual: Arndt & Gingrich translate 'pass by along' and Lagrange describes it as going by along the lake from the south to the north.

hē thalassa tēs Galilaias (7 : 31) 'the Sea of Galilee'. The use of *thalassa* 'sea' for the more precise *limnē* 'lake' is characterized by Black (*Aramaic*, 96) and Lagrange as a Semitism. *hē thalassa* occurs further in 2 : 13, 3 : 7, 4 : 1, 5 : 1, 13, 21—all referring to the Lake of Galilee.

amphiballō (only here in the N.T.) 'cast a net': it is the word used to describe the throwing out of the circular casting-net (Arndt & Gingrich), called the *amphiblēstron* (cf. Mt. 4 : 18). The net was wound around the arm and thrown out in a rapid circular movement of the arm; this, as Lagrange says, is the meaning of *amphiballō* without a direct object.

en 'in' equals *eis* 'into': cf. Turner, *Journal of Theological Studies* 26.15, 1924-5.

39

Translation: *Passing along* must be rendered in some languages by a more specific 'walking along'.

Sea must be changed in many languages to 'lake', since this was an inland body of fresh water. The use of Greek *thalassa* for both lake and sea is simply a Semitism (see above and compare Luke's use of 'lake').

Along by may be rendered as 'walking along the shore of the lake'.

Sea of Galilee must in some languages be 'lake in the province (or region) of Galilee'.

The phrase *the brother of Simon* tends to cause complications for the translator, for languages reflect such utterly different systems for the classification of family lines relationships. For example, the words for brother may differ depending on such factors as (1) relative age (a younger or an older brother), (2) sex of the person to whom the 'brother' is related (brother of a woman or brother of a man), and (3) father or mother's line (i.e. brothers by the same father or brothers by the same mother). Because of the general practice among Jews of Biblical times to list the name of the older brother first, we may assume that Simon was older than Andrew, and that both had the same father and mother. However, the order of the expressions 'Simon and Andrew' and 'the brother of Simon' must be arranged in accordance with the natural form of expression in any language into which one is translating (the receptor language), e.g. 'Simon and his brother Andrew', 'Simon and Andrew his brother', 'Simon and Simon's brother Andrew', 'the brothers Simon and Andrew', or 'Simon and Andrew; they were brothers'.

It must be noted that both men were casting nets into the lake, but these nets were the circular variety (as much as twenty feet across) which were thrown by a single person in relatively shallow water along the shore. In areas where people are not accustomed to catching fish by nets, one can, however, almost always describe a net (e.g. 'a large fish-trap made of strings').

Fisherman may be translated in languages which do not have an equivalent specialized term as 'men who customarily caught fish' or 'those who lived by catching fish'.

17 *And Jesus said to them, "Follow me and I will make you become fishers of men."*

Exegesis: *deute* (6:31, 12:7) 'come!' 'come here!' is used as the plural of the adverb *deuro* 'here!' 'come!' which is regarded as an imperative. The meaning of the word in this context is not simply that of a physical going after, but of discipleship.

poiēsō...genesthai 'I will make...to become': the full force of the verbal phrase is 'I will make you become *in the future*', after a course of preparation (as Grant says). The verb takes a double accusative: *humas* 'you' and *haleeis anthrōpōn* 'fishers of men'.

haleeis anthrōpōn 'fishers of men': for the figure cf. Jer. 16:16, Ezek. 29:4-5. The genitive *anthrōpōn* 'of men' is not possessive, of course; the meaning is 'fishers *who fish* (or *catch*) *men*'.

40

Translation: *Fishers of men* is such a well-known phrase to us that we seldom suspect that it can provide the basis for considerable misunderstanding in translations. However, it does, for if the expression used for 'catching fish' contains the same verb as is used in speaking of those who round up forced labor (as in parts of Africa) or who arrest people, there will inevitably be misunderstanding. In one language 'I will make you catchers of men' implied that Jesus was going to make his disciples into policemen. In still another language the word for 'getting fish' had the connotation of 'killing fish', and hence the parallel 'getting men' implied that the disciples would become assassins. One of the difficulties is the bold form of the metaphor which does not provide a linguistic clue to the reader that this expression is not to be taken literally. However, by changing the metaphor into a simile most of the trouble is avoided, e.g. 'you will catch men as if you were catching fish' (Barrow Eskimo) and 'just like you catch fish, I will make you catch men' (San Blas). In some instances some of the metaphorical power of the expression is lost but the essential truth can be preserved, e.g. 'give power to bring men' (Black Bobo) or 'make you become ones who are men bringers' (Moré).

18 And immediately they left their nets and followed him.

Text: Instead of *ta diktua* 'the nets' of the majority of modern editions of the Greek text, *Textus Receptus* and Kilpatrick have *ta diktua autōn* 'their nets' (cf. *Exegesis*, below).

Exegesis: *aphentes . . . ēkolouthēsan* 'leaving . . . they followed' is equal to 'they left and followed'. The verb *aphiēmi* is used in the sense of 'abandon' 'leave' some fifteen times in Mark (cf. 2:5; cf. Arndt & Gingrich, 3).

akoloutheō 'follow': used both in the literal sense, and with the meaning 'follow as a disciple'. Kilpatrick (*TBT* 7.6-7, 1956) sees the primary sense of physical following in 5:24, 6:1, 10:32,52, 11:9, 14:13, 54; the derived sense of discipleship in 1:18, 2:14, 8:34, 9:38, 10:21,28, 15:41 (cf. also Arndt & Gingrich, 3; Turner *Journal of Theological Studies*, 26. 238-40, 1924-5).

ta diktua 'the nets': in this context 'their nets' is meant (cf. Turner), without the addition of the possessive *autōn* 'their'. *diktuon* (1:19) is the generic word for "net" of any kind (cf. *amphiblēstron* 'casting net' Mt. 4:18, and *sagēnē* 'drag net' Mt. 13:47).

Translation: In verses 17 and 18 it is essential that an appropriate word for 'follow' be found, since a poor choice at this point may be almost disastrous. There are three principal types of meanings which must be distinguished: (1) to follow a long way off (implying either disinterest or avoidance), (2) to follow in the sense of tracking down (obviously not desirable for disciples), and (3) to follow in the sense of accompaniment, e.g. as a child follows an adult, as a dog its master, or as a friend his companion. One must make certain, however, that such a term does not imply 'failure to work or to participate in an enterprise', in the sense

41

that those who follow along may not take part or do their share.

It is essential that the nets spoken of in this verse be the same as are mentioned or implied in verse 16.

19 *And going on a little farther, he saw James the son of Zebedee and John his brother, who were in their boat mending the nets.*

Text: After *probas* 'going on' *Textus Receptus* adds *ekeithen* 'thence', which is rejected by all modern editions of the Greek text.

Exegesis: *probainō* (only here in Mark) 'advance', 'go forward'.

oligon 'a little' is the accusative of the neuter adjective *oligos* 'little', used adverbially to modify the verb *probainō* 'go forward'.

ton adelphon autou 'his brother' refers, of course, to James, not to Zebedee.

kai autous...katartizontas 'and they (were) mending': this participial clause is a rather clumsy Greek construction reflecting, as Black points out (*Aramaic*, 63, 66), its Semitic character. It is best translated by "while (or, when) they were mending..." (cf. also Howard II, 423). The pronoun *autous* 'they' and the participle *katartizontas* 'mending' are in the accusative case because they stand in apposition to *Iakōbon kai Iōannēn* 'James and John', the direct objects of the verb *eiden* 'he saw'. To translate literally 'they (or, who) *also* were...mending' is inaccurate (Weymouth, Knox, ASV). The best translation will make this clause subordinate to the main one, either in a temporal sense 'while they were mending' or as a relative clause 'who were mending' (RSV).

en tō ploiō 'in the boat'. Grant observes that the definite article need not always be translated (cf. Synodale *dans une barque*), and Lagrange observes that both in Hebrew and in classical Greek the definite article is used to indicate an object naturally to be found in the situation described. On the other hand, 'their boat' (RSV, Moffatt, Weymouth, Berkeley) is a possible translation (cf. Turner, and see v. 18 *ta diktua* 'their nets').

katartizontas ta diktua 'mending the nets'.

katartizō (only here in Mark) "to render *artios*, i.e. 'fit', 'complete'" (Abbott-Smith). The sense is not exclusively that of repairing; the word means 'to adjust', 'to put right'. It may mean here *preparing* the nets for the next fishing (Vincent *Word Studies* I, 31, on Mt. 4:21). Moulton & Milligan also give evidence for this meaning of the word. Arndt & Gingrich: "put in order, restore; put into proper condition."

Translation: The expression *James the son of Zebedee and John his brother* can only rarely be translated literally into another language. In general it must be reorganized to fit the syntactic and lexical requirements of the receptor language, e.g. 'James and John, the sons of Zebedee' (with the relationship of 'brother' left implicit); 'James and his younger brother John, the sons of Zebedee' (Chontal of Oaxaca); 'James and his brother John; their father was Zebedee'; or 'James and John, two brothers, sons of Zebedee' (Mitla Zapotec). The selection of one of these formulae, or some other, will depend entirely upon what type of expression is the closest natural equivalent in the language into which one is translating.

It is not necessary that the nets of verse 19 be the same as those of 16 and 18. The fact that the men were in the boat may suggest that these were long nets let out from boats. The Greek term translated "mending" in the RSV is equivalent to English 'fixing them up'.

While in some parts of the world it may be impossible to find an indigenous term for boat (e.g. along the Sahara the Mossi people have no word for boat, but they call it a 'water-box'), in others one is faced with the problem of selecting out of a number of different terms the name of a craft which would be approximately the size and shape of the fishing boats used on the Lake of Galilee. There were obviously different-sized boats employed for fishing on the lake, but it is probably safest to estimate that the boats which the disciples used would be capable of holding anywhere from six to a dozen persons. They were not, however, huge ships, for they could be drawn up on the shore by hand and they were of relatively shallow draft (so that Jesus could speak to the people on the shore, while being only a little distance off the land).

20 *And immediately he called them; and they left their father Zebedee in the boat with the hired servants, and followed him.*

Exegesis: *ekalesen* (2:17, 3:31, 11:17) 'call': from this basic meaning there develops further the meaning 'to invite', 'to summon' and the word becomes a technical term meaning 'to summon before a court'. From this latter meaning the sense of the verb in this passage is derived 'call to discipleship' (cf. Arndt & Gingrich 1.e; 2).

aphentes...apēlthon 'leaving...they went off' means 'they left and went'.

misthōtōn (only here in Mark) 'hired men': the literal meaning of the noun (from *misthos* 'pay' 'wage') should be observed; these are not *douloi* 'slaves' or *diakonoi* 'servants', but helpers hired for the job (cf. Lagrange).

en tō ploiō 'in the boat' and *meta tōn misthōtōn* 'with the hired men' are connected with Zebedee, not 'they' (i.e. James and John).

apēlthon opisō autou 'went off after him': here is the same idea of discipleship as in *ēkolouthēsan autō* 'followed him' in v. 18 and *deute opisō mou* 'come after me' in v. 17.

Translation: In translating *call* one must make certain that the term chosen in the receptor language conveys something of the meaning of 'call to follow', 'summon to accompany', or 'invite to come', for if not, it may signify only that Jesus shouted at the men. Where necessary, one may use the phrase 'called them to accompany him'.

In some languages it is difficult (and unnecessarily awkward) to distinguish precisely between the two senses in which Zebedee, on the one hand, and the hired servants, on the other, were left by James and John. For

43

example, in Ifugao one would say 'left Zebedee their father and the hired servants in the boat', rather than 'Zebedee with the hired servants'. The important mistake to avoid is linking the hired servants with James and John and hence implying that they went off with Jesus and the disciples, as has been the case in some translations.

In some instances one needs to be very specific about personal reference, but sometimes it is possible to be overly repetitious. In Villa Alta Zapotec, for example, one should not repeat Zebedee in verse 20, for he is already specifically identified in the previous sentence and to repeat the name would be misleading, implying some other Zebedee was meant.

Hired servants are simply 'the workmen' or 'the day laborers'.

21 And they went into Capernaum; and immediately on the sabbath he entered the synagogue and taught.

Text: Instead of *eiselthōn eis tēn sunagōgēn edidasken* 'entering into the synagogue he taught' in *Textus Receptus*, Westcott and Hort, Souter, Vogels, Nestle, Lagrange, and Merk, the reading *edidasken eis tēn sunagōgēn* 'he taught in the synagogue' is adopted by Tischendorf, Soden, Turner, Taylor, and Kilpatrick. The evidence, both external and internal, entitles this reading to consideration.

Exegesis: *eisporeuontai...eiselthōn...edidasken* 'they went into...he entered...and taught': on the change from the third plural of the first verb to the third singular of the next two verbs cf. Turner, *Journal of Theological Studies*, 26.228, 1924-5.

eisporeuomai (4:19, 5:40, 6:56, 7:15,18,19, 11:2) 'enter': here is another use of the Marcan historical present (cf. Moule *Idiom Book*, 7).

euthus tois sabbasin 'immediately on the sabbath': the phrase indicates the following Sabbath (cf. Weymouth, Lagrange).

tois sabbasin 'on the sabbath'. The plural *sabbata* 'sabbaths' is a Greek transliteration of the Aramaic *sabatha'*, taken as a plural form; the singular *sabbaton* 'sabbath' was formed from this (spurious) plural (cf. Abbott-Smith). The LXX uses both *sabbaton* (sg.) and *sabbata* (pl.). The meaning is not that of several sabbaths; when feasts are mentioned the plural form is commonly used (cf. 6:21, 14:1; John 10:22; cf. Arndt & Gingrich 1.b.β). The dative case used to indicate time is, as Lagrange points out, a classical construction.

edidasken (17 times in Mark) 'taught': although some do not agree (e.g. Turner, *Journal of Theological Studies* 28.351, 1926-7), Moule (*Idiom Book*, 9) sees in the imperfect tense of this verb what is called the inceptive force, i.e. an emphasis upon the beginning of the action 'he began to teach' (cf. also C. S. Emden *Expository Times*, 65.146-49, 1954). The Synodale translates *se mit à enseigner*.

sunagōgē (1:23, 29, 39, 3:1, 6:2, 12:39, 13:9) 'synagogue'. The original meaning of the word is that of the act of 'gathering' (from *sunagō* 'gather', 'collect'); the name is then applied to the place, or building, in which this gathering takes place.

Translation: *Went into* must in some languages be changed to 'arrived at' (Zapotec), for though one may 'enter into' a house, a town is regarded as a different type of object, and hence one may 'arrive at' but not 'go in'.

At least at this first occurrence of Capernaum it may be wise to introduce a classifier, e.g. 'they arrived at town Capernaum, its name' (Tzeltal).

Immediately on the sabbath may be rendered as 'as soon as it was...' or 'scarcely was it the sabbath when...'

Sabbath (see *BT*, 239-40) is most generally translated as 'rest day' or 'day for resting' (Tarahumara, Bolivian Quechua, Kituba, Maya, Totonac, Tarascan, Chol, Cashibo, Ifugao, Tagalog, Joloana); cf. 'day of standstill (of work)' in South Toradja. Some persons have used 'God's day', but this tends to be confused with Sunday. One translation employed a phrase 'fear day', a traditional form of expression which was supposed to mean 'day for reverence', but it was quite an inadequate means of expression. One can, of course, transliterate the word *sabbath*, but in some regions this may lead to difficulty, too. For example, the Spanish equivalent is *sabado* 'Saturday' and any transliterated (or borrowed) form will suggest 'Saturday', which is in no sense recognized as a day of rest or one with any special religious significance.

Some translators have transliterated *synagogue*, but on the whole this is not a very satisfactory procedure, despite the fact that there are difficulties in translation since an expression chosen for synagogue tends to be confused with forms used for 'temple' and 'church'. In South Toradja a synagogue is 'meeting-house for discussing matters concerning religious customs'; a church is 'house where one meets on Sunday' and a temple is 'house that is looked upon as holy, that is sacred, that is taboo and where one may not set foot' (lit. 'house where one gets a swollen stomach'). In Bambara a synagogue is 'a worship house' and the temple is 'house of God'; a church is designated by a borrowed term *eglise*. In Navajo a synagogue is a 'house of gathering' and the temple 'a house of worship'. In some languages it has seemed expedient to identify the difference between a church and a synagogue by qualifying a synagogue as being used by Jews, e.g. 'Jews' praise-God house' (Black Bobo). An even closer parallel to church is found in 'church of Jews' for synagogue (Mitla Zapotec, Chontal of Oaxaca). Because of the fact that the ancient synagogues were also used as a place for the instruction of children during the week, some translators have used 'school house', but this is inadequate to convey the religious significance of the structure.

22 And they were astonished at his teaching, for he taught them as one who had authority, and not as the scribes.

Exegesis: *exeplēssonto* (6:2, 7:37, 10:26, 11:18) 'they were astonished': the compound verb is from *plēssō* 'strike', 'smite' (cf. Rev. 8:12), and has a very strong meaning 'they were amazed', 'they were overwhelmed'. Abbott-Smith: 'strike with panic or shock, amaze, astonish'. The third person plural of the verb is appropriately called an "impersonal plural" by Turner: "Mark meant... simply 'people were astonished.'"

45

(*Journal of Theological Studies* 25.378, 1923-4; cf. Black *Aramaic*, 91; Howard II, 447f.).

epi tē didachē autou 'at his teaching'.

epi 'at', 'on the ground of': after verbs which express feelings, opinions, etc. it means 'at', 'because of', 'from', 'with' (cf. Arndt & Gingrich II.1.b.γ).

didachē 'teaching': either in the active sense of the act of teaching itself (cf. 4 : 2, 12 : 38), or in the passive sense of that which is taught, teaching, doctrine (cf. 1 : 27, 11 : 18). There is difference of opinion over the meaning here (cf. Arndt & Gingrich); the context, however, seems to favor the active sense of the word (in v. 27, however, *didachē kainē* 'new teaching' has the passive sense).

ēn...didaskōn 'was teaching': this verbal phrase is better translated into English by 'he was teaching' rather than by 'he taught' (cf. Turner *Journal of Theological Studies*, 28.349, 1926-7; Brazilian *ensinava*).

hōs exousian echōn 'as one having authority': the phrase describes the "manner of an action" (Burton *Moods and Tenses*, §§ 445-46), here, of course, the manner of teaching (cf. the parallel Lk. 4 : 32).

echōn 'having': 'as one who has authority' (cf. Brazilian *como quem tem autoridade*). This participle, however, instead of being independent "*one* having" (as most translations have it), may modify the subject of the main verb 'he was teaching them as though *he had* authority'.

exousian (1 : 27, 2 : 10, 3 : 15, 6 : 7, 11 : 28, 29, 33, 13 : 34) 'authority': the word has several shades of meaning: 'freedom of choice, right to act'; 'ability, capacity, might, power'; 'authority, absolute power' (Arndt & Gingrich).

The whole phrase has been examined by Daube *New Testament and Rabbinic Judaism*, 205-12, who concludes that it here refers to "Rabbinic [i.e. of one ordained] authority, and not like the ordinary teachers." The meaning 'like a king' has been advocated (*Expository Times*, 66.254 1955; 66.350, 1955; 67.17, 1955), receiving some support from Manson: 'with a right to command'.

hoi grammateis (21 times in Mark) 'the scribes'. By the time of the N.T. the word had developed from its original sense of a copyist of the law to that of an authorized interpreter 'a biblical scholar, teacher of the law' (Abbott-Smith), 'experts in the law, scholars versed in the law' (Arndt & Gingrich). Luke uses also *nomikoi* 'lawyers' and *nomodidaskaloi* 'teachers of the law'.

Translation: *To be astonished at*, as might be expected of such a psychologically significant expression, is translated in a variety of ways, some of which are highly figurative, e.g. 'confusing the inside of the head' (Mende), 'shiver in the liver' (Uduk, Kabba-Laka), 'to lose one's heart' (Miskito, Tzotzil), 'to shake' (Black Bobo), 'to be with mouth open' (Huanuco Quechua).

Since the subject of *were astonished* has not been previously identified, one must usually either specify a noun as the object of 'taught' (verse 21) or introduce a subject such as 'the people' as the subject of 'were astonished' in verse 22. More often than not, however, the verb 'to teach' requires an object, and hence an object introduced at the end of 21 provides the appropriate referent for the subject of verse 22. (For a discussion of some of the lexical problems in "teach" see 2:13).

Since *teaching* should probably be taken in the active sense in this context, it is often rendered best as 'astonished at the way he taught'. In Tarahumara this is rendered idiomatically as 'when he taught them they kept quiet'.

Authority is a term with a very wide area of meaning, and in this situation it must usually be qualified in such a way as to make it contextually appropriate. In some languages, of course, one can speak of 'power', 'right', or 'strength to command'; but in other languages one must say 'taught them like a chief not like the writers of the law' or 'taught like a person who had the power to command them'. Cf. Bare'e 'someone who thrones upon (sits on the chair of) authority'.

The *scribes* (see above) were more than mere writers of the law. They were the trained interpreters of the law and expounders of tradition. In Kiyaka, spoken in the Congo, the scribes are designated as 'clerks in God's house' and in Ifugao these are 'men who wrote and taught in the synagogue'. In Navajo a compound expression 'teaching-writers' is used, as an attempt to emphasize their dual function. In Shipibo, however, it seemed enough simply to call such people 'book-wise persons' (knowledge of books and writing would of necessity mean a distinct prestige class to these rather primitive Shipibo people in Upper Amazonia). In San Blas an excellent descriptive phrase has been employed, namely, 'those who knew the Jews' ways'. Among the Loma people of Liberia it has seemed quite enough to call the scribes 'the educated ones', while in Huave the area of learning is more circumscribed, e.g. 'those knowing holy paper', and in Mazahua the equivalent is 'writers of holy words'. In Indonesian they are called 'experts in the Torah' and in Bare'e 'men skilled in the ordinances'.

Some languages require the full form of clauses which in Greek or English may be left elliptical, e.g. *and not as the scribes* becomes 'he did not teach as the scribes taught' (Black Bobo).

23 *And immediately there was in their synagogue a man with an unclean spirit;*

Text: *Textus Receptus* omits *euthus* 'immediately': its inclusion, however, is accepted by all modern editions of the Greek text.

RSV ends the verse at "unclean spirit": all editions of the Greek text, however, include also in this verse *kai anekraxen* 'and he cried out'; the following discussion conforms to the RSV division.

Exegesis: *euthus ēn* 'immediately (there) was': as it stands this phrase is difficult to translate. RSV "immediately there was" is impossible English, unless *was* can mean 'came', 'entered' (which Weymouth's "all at once there was" actually means; cf. BFBS, Berkeley: "just then there was"). The weakened sense 'now' is adopted by some (Manson: "now...there was"); Moffatt connects 'immediately' with 'cried out': "who at once shrieked out." Two alternatives offer themselves: (1) *euthus* may be understood in a general sense 'now', 'then'; (2) *ēn* 'was' may be taken as equivalent to *egeneto* 'came', 'appeared'. The second is probably to be preferred, cf. Gould: "No sooner [was Jesus] in the synagogue than this demoniac appeared." Cf. Brazilian: *Não tardou que aparecesse.* A man with an unclean spirit would not normally be in attendance at the worship service in the synagogue.

anthrōpos 'man' here equals the indefinite pronoun *tis* 'a certain one' (cf. Black *Aramaic*, 251).

en pneumati akathartō 'in an unclean spirit' (1:26, 27, 3:11, 30, 5:2, 8, 13, 6:7, 7:25, 9:25; cf. *pneuma alalon* 'dumb spirit' 9:17, 25; and *to pneuma* 'the spirit' 9:20).

en 'in', 'with' has the force of the Hebrew *be* with the meaning 'having' (cf. 5:2, and Lk. 4:33); Howard (II, 464) calls it a "Semitism of thought." Arndt & Gingrich (I.5.d) translate "under the special influence of a demonic spirit" (cf. Swete "under spiritual influence"), while Lagrange, with particular reference to Rom. 8:9, suggests "a man in whom was an unclean spirit."

pneuma akatharton is best understood as 'a spirit (which makes the man) unclean'. Grant (*Interpreter's Bible*) suggests physical impurity; what is probably meant, however, is ceremonial, moral, or spiritual defilement or pollution. Moulton & Milligan quote a magical papyrus in which the word has the "moral sense of an unclean demon"(cf. Zech. 13:2).

Translation: If *was* is to be interpreted in the sense of 'appeared', which is probably the most likely (demoniacs would not normally be in a synagogue service since the possession of a spirit would make them unclean and hence ceremonially unacceptable), one may translate 'right then a man with an unclean spirit appeared'.

There are a number of different ways in which people speak of demon possession: 'an unclean spirit had hit him' (Mitla Zapotec), 'under the control...' (one Chinese translation), 'someone hit by an evil spirit' (South Toradja), '...standing around inside of' (Navajo), 'a man has an unclean spirit' and 'an unclean spirit has a man'.

In many languages it is impossible to distinguish between the word used for 'spirit' in this context (speaking of 'unclean spirit') and the word for 'demon'. Any attempt to make a distinction, when none actually exists in the language in question, may only lead to misunderstanding. Accordingly, *unclean spirit* may simply be 'unclean demon'.

At the same time, it is not always easy to distinguish between 'unclean spirit' and 'evil spirit'. The latter is not too difficult because such spirits are often regarded as morally bad, hence, evil. However, in many cultures there is no use of 'unclean' in the sense of ceremonially or religiously unacceptable. Some translators have tried to use the equivalent of 'dirty demon', but this has often appeared to be a very strange expression. What is more, the real significance of the term 'unclean' is not primarily the appearance of the spirit itself so much as the fact that the possession of such a spirit made the person in question unclean, i.e. ceremonially and socially unacceptable, e.g. 'spirit which makes foul' (Piro). Similarly, in some languages a word meaning 'unclean' may have no moral significance, but a term such as 'ugly' may. For example, in Chontal of Tabasco the closest equivalent of *unclean spirit* is 'ugly spirit'.

Since in many languages there are a number of different kinds of spirits, it is of extreme importance that one carefully study all the types and be sure that any word chosen for 'spirit' in this context is appropriate. One thing is quite certain, namely, that in most instances it will be different from the word employed in the phrase 'Holy Spirit'.

24 *and he cried out, "What have you to do with us, Jesus of Nazareth? Have you come to destroy us? I know who you are, the Holy One of God."*

Text: The interjection *ea* 'ah!' included by *Textus Receptus* (before *ti* 'what'), is accepted also by Vogels and Soden (who places it in brackets); it is rejected, however, by Tischendorf, Nestle, Westcott and Hort, Kilpatrick, Souter and Turner.

Instead of *oida* 'I know' of most editions of the Greek text, *Textus Receptus*, Tischendorf and Soden have *oidamen* 'we know'.

Exegesis: *anekraxen legōn* 'cried out, saying': modern translations need not adopt Marcan style and translate both the main verb and the participle (cf. the similar construction in v. 7); one verb is sufficient: 'cried out', 'shouted'. It is to be noticed that the subject of the verb is *he* (the man) and not *it* (the spirit); the participle *legōn* is masculine.

ti hēmin kai soi (this same construction is found in 5:7; Mt. 8:29, 27:19; Lk. 4:34, 8:28; Jn. 2:4) literally 'what to us and to you?' In classical Greek the phrase would mean 'What have we in common?' Here, however, it corresponds to the Hebrew 'Why do you meddle with me?' (cf. Taylor; in LXX see Judg. 11:12, 2 Sam. 16:10, 19:23, 1 Kg. 17:18, etc.). BFBS: "Why are You interfering with us?" Goodspeed (*Problems*, 10of.) discusses the phrase at length, and Lagrange succinctly defines its meaning: "It is employed to reject an intervention which is at least premature, not to say inopportune" (cf. H. M. Buck, *TBT* 7.149-50, 1956).

Notice the plurals *hēmin* and *hēmas* 'us': not simply this demonic spirit, but the whole class of unclean spirits is involved. Or else the plural may reflect the feeling of multiple personalities, common in persons suffering from demon possession (cf. 5:1-13).

elthes apolesai hēmas; 'have you come to destroy us?' The phrase is thus understood as a question by Greek editions of the text (Nestle, Westcott and Hort, Kilpatrick, Souter), commentators and translations (Lagrange, AV, ASV, RSV, BFBS, Manson, Knox, Synodale, Zürich,

Brazilian, Weymouth, Berkeley); others have taken it to be an assertion (Tischendorf, Soden, Merk, Vogels, Taylor, Turner, Swete, Rawlinson). There is nothing in grammar or context definitely to decide which should be preferred.

ēlthes 'you came': a few see here the meaning, 'you came *into the world*' (Swete, Taylor); this interpretation, however, has not commended itself to many.

apolesai 'to destroy': the infinitive here expresses purpose. The verb *apollumi* is used in three ways in Mark: (1) in the active 'to destroy', 'to cause to perish', 1:24, 3:6, 9:22, 11:18, 12:9; (2) 'to lose', 8:35 (twice), 9:41; (3) in the middle or passive 'to be destroyed', 'to perish', 'to be lost', 2:22, 4:38.

oida se tis ei literally 'I know you who you are': the personal pronoun *se* 'you' is the object of *oida* 'I know', and the interrogative clause *tis ei* 'who you are' explicitly defines the content of 'I know'. The interrogative pronoun *tis* 'who', though in apposition to *se* 'you' (which is in the accusative case), is in the nominative case because it is the subject of *ei* 'you are' (cf. Robertson *Grammar*, 488).

ho hagios tou theou (also in Lk. 4:34, Jn. 6:69) 'the Holy (One) of God': although the majority of commentators and translations treat this phrase as a Messianic title, Lagrange points out that the phrase is not known in the relevant literature as a Messianic title. The phrase could very well be vocative 'you holy man of God!' (Grant). Whatever may have been the meaning of the words as spoken by the possessed man, it is certain that in Mark the meaning is Christian, i.e. fully Messianic, 'the Holy One of God'. Between the two possible meanings, 'the Holy One *who comes from* God', and 'the Holy One *who belongs to God*', probably the latter is to be preferred.

Translation: *Cried out* means a 'shout' or 'scream' (terms meaning 'weeping' must be carefully avoided).

Note that there are significant shifts in persons in this verse (as in other contexts dealing with demon possession, cf. Mark 5:6-12). The subject of the verb, however, is the man.

The Semitic idiom rendered in the RSV as "What have you to do with us" is variously translated in other languages, e.g. 'why do you bother us', 'what are you going to do to us', 'why do you disturb us', and 'why are we any of your business'.

Jesus of Nazareth must often be rendered as' Jesus from Nazareth town'.

To destroy may be translated in some languages as simply 'to kill', but often people do not use the indigenous expression 'to kill' when speaking of the destruction of demons, since they regard them as a somewhat different type of being. Accordingly, one must in some instances say 'to cause to end' (Tzeltal), 'to put out of sight' (Mitla Zapotec), or 'to blot out completely'.

The Greek verb translated 'know' in this verse implies somewhat more than mere recognition. In some languages the equivalent is 'I know full well'.

The Holy One of God presents a number of problems for the translator. In the first place, some languages do not permit the use of an indefinite 'one' in such a construction. They would require 'person', but this is also a source of difficulty, for 'person' in some languages will not admit of grammatical possession. Hence, in such languages one must use 'Son', if the passage is to make sense (Huichol, Tzeltal, Kekchi). On the other hand, Maninka can quite readily use 'God's Holy Person'. If, however, one adopts the meaning of 'comes from God' some of the grammatical problems are eliminated, e.g. 'the Holy One who comes from God' (Huastec, Ifugao, Kiyaka, South Toradja, Bare'e, Indonesian).

25 But Jesus rebuked him, saying, "Be silent, and come out of him!"

Exegesis: *epetimēsen* (3:12, 4:39, 8:30,32,33, 9:25, 10:13,48) 'he rebuked'. The verb literally means 'to lay a *timē* [price, value] upon' and originally it had a favorable meaning (cf. Abbott-Smith); in the N.T. however, it has the unfavorable meaning of 'censure', 'rebuke' and even 'punish'. Moulton & Milligan: 'censure', 'lay under a penalty'. This idea of censure, however, disappears in many instances; Arndt & Gingrich remark: "*speak seriously, warn* in order to prevent an action or bring one to an end," and Kilpatrick (*TBT*, 7.6, 1956) finds this meaning uniformly in Mark; it is a command, rather than a reproof, and is specifically a prohibition, "desist from an action being performed" (cf. Lagrange: "issue a formal command"). In this verse, therefore, 'prohibit', 'stop', 'command' is to be preferred to 'rebuke'.

autō 'him' or 'it': although, as we saw above, the subject of the verb 'cried out' is the man, not the spirit, the pronoun *autō* in this verse refers to the unclean spirit, as the content of the order which follows shows. A translation should make this clear: "him" (AV, ASV, RSV, BFBS, Manson, Knox) is ambiguous and possibly misleading; "it" (Moffatt) is clear (cf. Weymouth, "the spirit").

phimōthēti (4:39) 'be silent!': the literal meaning of the verb *phimoō* 'bridle', 'muzzle' does not survive in Mark (cf. Arndt & Gingrich, 2); Moulton & Milligan quote Rohde on the use of this word with the sense of *binding* a person by means of a spell so as to make him powerless to harm, and give examples from the papyri. Notice that the only other place it is used in Mark (4:39), it is addressed to the storm.

Translation: The introductory verb in this verse may be translated as 'rebuke' (in the sense of 'scold' or 'censure'), but it is probably more accurately rendered as 'to command sternly'.

The second verb of direct discourse, namely, *saying* is probably better omitted in most languages.

If the language in question distinguishes in pronominal reference between a demon and a man, one should make certain that the object of the command is the demon. In some instances it may even be wise to introduce the noun object, e.g. 'sternly commanded the unclean spirit'.

Be silent is in Greek a firm, but not undignified way of demanding silence, equivalent more to English *keep quiet* than to *shut up*.

Whether onē can translate literally 'come out' depends largely upon the manner in which people speak of demon possession. For example, in Kiyaka demons do not get into people, but are spoken of as 'grabbing people', hence the appropriate term in this case would be 'let go'. In Ifugao the normal way of speaking would be 'get out', not 'come out'. The appropriate term in any language will, as in all such types of problems, depend upon the traditional perspective reflected in normal usage.

26 *And the unclean spirit, convulsing him and crying with a loud voice, came out of him.*

Exegesis: *sparaxan* (9:26) 'convulsing'. The word clearly points to a seizure, a convulsion (cf. 9:20, Lk. 9:39). A man suffering an attack of this sort is described as *anthrōpos sparattomenos* 'a man convulsed' (Arndt & Gingrich).

to pneuma to akatharton 'the unclean spirit' is in the nominative case, and is the subject of all the verbs in the verse.

sparaxan...kai phōnēsan 'convulsing...and shouting' are both aorist participles, whose action is simultaneous with that of the main verb *exēlthen* 'went out'. The RSV "crying" should not be understood in the sense of weeping.

Translation: *Convulsing him* should be translated by a term used to identify such types of seizures as occur in epilepsy. It is not enough to say 'shook him'. Such fits may of course be described in various ways in different languages. In Tzeltal, for example, such an attack is spoken of as 'his wind was stopped'.

Crying with a loud voice is simply 'yelled', but note that the spirit is the one who is credited with the scream, not the man.

In some languages the three actions of 'convulsing', 'yelling', and 'coming out' may have to be placed in a temporal sequence, but generally they can be rendered as 'as the unclean spirit caused the man to have a fit and screamed out, it came out of him'.

27 *And they were all amazed, so that they questioned among themselves, saying, "What is this? A new teaching! With authority he commands even the unclean spirits, and they obey him."*

Text: The reading *pros hautous* (=*heautous*) 'among themselves' of *Textus Receptus* is accepted also by Soden, Souter, Vogels, Merk, Lagrange, Kilpatrick, and (apparently) RSV; the reading *autous* 'they' is preferred by Tischendorf, Nestle, Westcott and Hort, Taylor, Turner.

Instead of *didachē kainē kat' exousian* (disregarding punctuation) 'a new teaching according to authority' of the majority of modern editions of the Greek text, *Textus Receptus* and Kilpatrick have *tis hē didachē hē kainē hautē hoti kat' exousian* 'what (is) this new teaching for according to authority', an obvious expansion of the original for the sake of smoothness.

Punctuation. The clause *kat' exousian* 'according to authority' may be joined either to *didachē kainē* 'new teaching' or to *epitassei* 'he commands'. The first is preferred by Tischendorf, Nestle, Vogels, Soden, Turner, Lagrange, Moffatt, Berkeley, Weymouth, Zürich, Gould, Taylor; the second is favored by AV, ASV, RSV, BFBS, Knox, Synodale, Brazilian, Swete. Field (*Notes*, 24) believes the second is confirmed by the parallel passage Lk. 4:36. Daube's lengthy discussion of the phrase (*New Testament and Rabbinic Judaism*, 212-16) favors the first construction.
    Although there is division of opinion on this passage, it would seem that the prepositional phrase, with adverbial force, rather modifies the verb *epitassei* 'he commands' than the noun *didachē* 'teaching'.

Exegesis: *ethambēthēsan* (10:24, 32) 'were amazed': a strong word, meaning 'be astounded, amazed' (Arndt & Gingrich; cf. Lagrange).
    hōste suzētein 'so as to question': the consecutive particle *hōste* 'so that' plus the infinitive of the verb, to express result, is found also in 1:45, 2:2, 12, 3:10, 20, 4:1, 32, 37, 9:26, 15:5.
    suzētein (8:11, 9:10, 14, 16, 12:28) 'discuss', 'debate' (cf. Moulton & Milligan; Kennedy *Sources*, 155). As Marcan usage demonstrates, a group is always implied (even when the verb is used absolutely, as at 12:28), so that the sense is that of an exchange (if not conflict) of opinions. Even if *autous* 'they' of the Nestle text is read (instead of *pros hautous* 'among themselves' of the RSV), the sense will still be that of debate or discussion.
    didachē 'teaching': here in the passive sense of the content of the teaching, "doctrine" (cf. 1:22).
    kainē (2:21, 22, 14:25, 16:17) 'new': the old distinction between *kainos* 'new' of quality and *neos* 'new' of time (cf. Taylor) is not always observed in the New Testament (cf. R. A. Harrisville "The Concept of Newness in the New Testament", *Journal of Biblical Literature*, 74.69-79, 1955, who concludes that the terms are synonymous in the N.T., implying both qualitative and temporal newness).
    kat' exousian...epitassei 'with authority...he commands', 'authoritatively...he orders'.
    exousia 'authority' (cf. v. 22).
    epitassō (6:27, 39, 9:25) 'order', 'command'.
    kai 'and' has what is called the ascensive force, meaning 'even' (cf. Robertson *Grammar*, 1181).
    hupakoousin (4:41) 'they obey': from the literal idea of 'listen', 'attend' (Abbott-Smith) follows the idea of 'be subject to'. Arndt & Gingrich see here the element of unwillingness, 'they are forced to obey him'.

Translation: It is essential that 'they' refer to the people, not to the immediately preceding referents, namely, Jesus, the man, and the demon. Hence, it is often necessary to introduce a noun subject 'the people'.

It is not easy to distinguish readily between the two Greek terms translated 'amazed' in this verse and 'astonished' in verse 22. In many languages one must use the same expression in both cases. Possibly, however, the expression in verse 27 should be even stronger than in 22, for a miracle had taken place in the meantime and the amazement of the people should have been greatly heightened. (The Tzeltal expression 'felt like dying' is an interesting idiom for extreme amazement.)

Questioned among themselves may be rendered as 'kept saying to one another'. Note, however, that in some languages one must be very precise about words which introduce direct discourse. If, for example, a question follows, one must use a word meaning 'to ask' or 'to question'. If a statement is involved, the introductory verb must be 'to say', 'to declare', etc. If an exclamation follows, some other appropriate term must be chosen. Certain languages require constant attention to such details.

Where it is possible to distinguish neatly between the qualitative and temporal values of 'new', it is entirely legitimate to use a term in this context which implies 'different' (for this type of context this can be the significance of the Greek *kainos*, in contrast with *neos*); hence, 'different teaching' (Ifugao).

If *teaching* is to be taken in the passive sense in this context (and this certainly seems to be the correct interpretation), one may translate 'What different words he teaches!' or 'what different (or new) teachings'.

In some languages *authority* must in this context be made concrete rather than left abstract, e.g. 'as a ruler he commands' or 'as one who has power (or is powerful) he commands'.

Most languages have quite acceptable terms meaning 'to obey', but in this context the specific nature of the obedience may require some descriptive phrase, e.g. 'do what he says', 'take hold of his words' (Black Bobo), or 'accept his orders'.

28 *And at once his fame spread everywhere throughout all the surrounding region of Galilee.*

Text: *Textus Receptus* omits *pantachou* 'everywhere': all modern editions of the Greek text include it. As Turner (*Journal of Theological Studies*, 28.155, 1926-7) says: "A redundant expression quite in Mark's style."

Exegesis: *hē akoē autou* 'the report about (concerning) him'.

akoē (7:35, 13:7) has here the passive sense of something heard, 'fame', 'report', 'rumor'; in the plural in 7:35 it means 'ears' (cf. Lk. 7:1, Acts 17:20).

autou 'of him' means *about* him'.

pantachou (16:20) 'everywhere', 'in all directions', an adverb modifying *exēlthen* 'went out'.

holēn tēn perichōron tēs Galilaias 'all the region of Galilee'.

tēn perichōron 'surrounding territory', 'region round about'. The phrase may be understood in three senses: (1) 'the region which surrounds Galilee' (so AV, BFBS); apparently Matthew understood it thus, in writing *holē hē Suria* 'all Syria' (4:24); (2) 'the whole neighbourhood of Galilee', that is, Galilee itself; the majority take it in this sense (Manson, Knox, Moffatt, RSV; Synodale: *dans toute la contrée environnante, en Galilée*); and (3) 'all the region of Galilee *around Capernaum'*, so Gould and Taylor, who refers to Lk. 4:37 for confirmation. The majority of translations and commentators prefer the second interpretation.

Translation: *His fame spread* is a phrase which must be syntactically reconstructed in many languages, for *his* actually identifies the goal of the process of spreading reputation. For example, in Zacapoastla Aztec one can only say 'they heard about him in all Galilee'. In other languages one may say 'his matter was spoken of much'. In most instances, however, 'fame does not spread' but 'people speak much of a person'—which of course is semantically equivalent to the same thing.

If one adopts the second interpretation of the phrase *throughout all the surrounding region of Galilee* (see above), one may translate 'all the region which was Galilee' or 'in all the area round about there, namely, in Galilee'.

29 *And immediately he left the synagogue, and entered the house of Simon and Andrew, with James and John.*

Text: *exelthōn ēlthen* 'he left and came' of the RSV is the text preferred by Swete, Merk, Taylor; the reading *exelthontes ēlthon* 'they left and came' is preferred by the majority. Turner (*Journal of Theological Studies*, 28.155, 1926-7) is of the opinion that the plural is correct since it would be easier for scribes to change the plural to the singular than vice-versa.

Exegesis: *meta Iakōbou kai Iōannou* 'with James and John' goes with 'they left and came'. Cf. Weymouth: "They came at once, with James and John, to the house..."

Translation: *Immediately* in this kind of context is in many languages equivalent to 'and then' or 'and next'.

Because this verse begins a new section, which is often set off by some sort of section heading or title, it may be advisable to employ 'Jesus' rather than 'he', since the reference tends to be ambiguous, especially when four other persons are specifically named in this verse.

With James and John must be so translated that it does not mean that these two men were also co-owners of the house with Simon and Andrew, a meaning which has been inadvertently implied in a number of translations. In order to avoid the difficulty one may (1) combine James and John with the subject, 'Jesus, accompanied by James and John, ...' (Chol, San Blas) or 'he besides James and John they went into...' (Kpelle), (2) set off James and John as a separate clause or sentence at the end of the verse, '...James and John went along' (Mazahua), 'followed by James and John' (Balinese).

In order to specify that a house belongs to two different people, it is necessary in some languages to be quite specific, e.g. 'house of Simon; he owned it with Andrew' (Popoluca).

30 *Now Simon's mother-in-law lay sick with a fever, and immediately they told him of her.*

Exegesis: *katekeito* (2 : 4, 15, 14 : 3) 'she was lying down', 'she lay sick'. Moulton & Milligan give examples from the papyri with the meaning 'to be ill' and Field (*Notes*, 25) translates "kept her bed, being sick of a fever."

puressousa (only here in Mark) 'feverish', '(with) a fever'. The present participle is in the nominative case modifying *penthera* 'mother-in-law', and has a causative force: "Simon's mother-in-law, *because* she had a fever, was in bed..." Lagrange and Taylor point out that the participle itself does not necessarily mean that a prolonged siege of the fever is implied; all it says is that when Jesus and the others entered the house, she was in bed, sick.

legousin 'they tell': with considerable probability Turner (*Journal of Theological Studies*, 25.378, 1923-4) classifies this as an impersonal plural, meaning simply 'he (Jesus) was told'; Mark does not mean that Simon and Andrew with James and John told him. Taylor, however, is of the opinion that the companions of Simon are meant (cf. Swete and Lagrange).

Translation: The RSV *now* is purely transitional, not temporal.

Simon's mother-in-law may be rendered 'the mother of Simon's wife', unless there are more idiomatic or specific terms for designating such a relationship.

To have a fever seems to us as English speakers to be a perfectly legitimate way of talking about a fever, but in other languages fevers may 'have people'. There are, in fact, a number of different ways in which one may speak of this type of illness, e.g. 'heat was hers' (Black Bobo), 'thrown down by a fever' (Tzeltal), 'making a fever' (Shipibo), or 'taken by God with fever' (Shilluk, in which all illness is spoken of as 'being taken by God', an idiom which cannot be avoided in the Scriptures).

The Greek text implies two elements in 'lay sick', one that the mother-in-law was in bed and the second that she was sick with a fever. Both of these circumstances must be specifically indicated.

If a language distinguishes case, gender, and number (as in most Indo-European languages), it is quite easy to translate the clause *they told him of her* by the use of three pronouns. However, in Mazatec (see *TBT*, 1.136-37, 1950) there are no such distinctions indicated in the verb construction and as a result there can be as many as 32 ambiguities unless nouns are used to distinguish clearly who speaks to whom about what. In fact, if the 'him' and 'her' are ambiguous, this clause is almost inevitably misunderstood, for it would be more natural for the people to tell the woman about Jesus than the reverse. In many languages, therefore, it is necessary to employ nouns rather than pronouns to identify the participants, e.g. 'the people there told Jesus about the woman'.

In some languages, however, a phrase 'about the woman' does not fit the context, because of the specific nature of the information and so the clause must be changed to read 'told Jesus that she was sick' (Tarahumara).

31 *And he came and took her by the hand and lifted her up, and the fever left her; and she served them.*

Text: With considerable mss. support *Textus Receptus*, Vogels, Soden, and Kilpatrick have *eutheōs* 'immediately' after *ho puretos* 'the fever', a reading rejected by the majority of modern editions of the Greek text.

Exegesis: *proselthōn ēgeiren autēn kratēsas tēs cheiros* 'approaching he raised her by (means of) seizing (her by) her hand', i.e. "he came near, grasped her hand and raised her."

proserchomai (6 : 35, 10 : 2, 12 : 28, 14 : 35, 45) 'approach', 'come to', 'draw near': the precise application here is a matter of discussion, the majority taking it to mean 'approaching *the patient*' (cf. Swete); Lagrange, however, takes it to mean 'entering the *room*'.

egeirō 'rise', 'raise' appears in Mark 19 times: (1) without an object, 'rise', 'arise' from a recumbent or sitting position, 3 : 3, 10 : 49; from sleep, 4 : 27 (cf. *diegertheis* in 4 : 39), 14 : 42; from illness, 2 : 9, 11, 12; from death, 5 : 41 (cf. *Exegesis* of 5 : 39), 6 : 14, 16, 12 : 26, 14 : 28, 16 : 6, 14; figuratively 'rise up', 'appear', 13 : 8, 22; (2) with an object, 'raise', 'arouse', 'lift up' from sleep, 4 : 38; from illness, 1 : 31, 9 : 27.

krateō 'grasp', 'seize', 'lay hold (of)': the verb is used in three ways in Mark: (1) 'seize', 'grasp' with the genitive (as here): 1 : 31, 5 : 41, 9 : 27; (2) 'take hold of', 'dominate', 'subdue', 'arrest' with the accusative: 3 : 21, 6 : 17, 12 : 12, 14 : 1, 44, 46, 49, 51; and (3) 'hold on(to)', 'retain', 'observe' with the accusative: 7 : 3, 4, 8, 9 : 10.

diēkonei (cf. v. 13) 'she served': the subject is *penthera* 'mother-in-law'.

Translation: *Came* is probably best taken in the sense of 'came to where she was'.

Lifted her up must be carefully translated, for some languages make quite fine distinctions, e.g. 'raise from a reclining position to a sitting one', 'raise from a sitting position to a standing one', and 'lift entirely off the ground'. (In more than one translation examined this last meaning has been employed, much to the amazement of the readers.) Obviously the first meaning is here most appropriate.

A fever may leave us, but in other languages a patient may 'leave the fever' (Shipibo) or 'become cool' (Huichol), or 'the heat may be driven out' (Black Bobo).

She served them may be rendered as 'she gave them food to eat', 'she took care of their needs', or 'she worked for them' (Kpelle).

32 *That evening, at sundown, they brought to him all who were sick or possessed with demons.*

Exegesis: *hote edusen ho hēlios* 'when the sun set' means '*after* the sun

57

had set' (cf. Manson, Weymouth, Berkeley; Zürich *nach Sonnenuntergang*, Synodale *après le coucher du soleil*).

epheron 'they carried', 'they brought': in his study of the word Turner (*Journal of Theological Studies*, 26.12-14, 1924-5) shows that Mark uses *pherō* in the sense of 'bring' rather than the restricted sense of 'carry'. He finds that meaning in this passage and in 2:3, 7:32, 8:22, 9:17, 19,20, 11:2,7, 15:22. The third person plural 'they brought' is another example of the impersonal plural (cf. 'they told' in v. 30). The imperfect tense of the verb describes a continued process 'they kept bringing'.

tous kakōs echontas (1:34, 2:17, 6:55) literally 'those having (it) badly'. This phrase includes all sorts of sickness and disease, but is always distinguished from demon-possession. Moulton & Milligan cite examples from the papyri of the use of this phrase to describe sick people.

tous daimonizomenous (5:15, 16, 18) 'the demon-possessed (ones)': the verb *daimonizomai* 'to be under the power of a demon' always appears as a participle in Mark describing the condition of a person, or persons, under the power of a demon, or unclean spirit.

Translation: The expression *that evening, at sundown* is not to be interpreted purely as tautological or meaninglessly repetitious. There is a point to this very emphatic statement, for it shows clearly that the people who attended the synagogue and saw the miracle were, however, very pious Jews and would not bring their sick to Jesus until after the Sabbath had passed, namely, until the sun was completely down. The equivalent in some languages is 'late in the day, after the sun had set' (or 'disappeared').

They must often be rendered as 'the people in that place'. Otherwise it will be assumed that the persons mentioned in the immediately preceding section are meant, namely, those of the household of Simon and Andrew.

Sick in this verse should include the most generic term to indicate any and all varieties of ailments.

Possessed with demons (see 1:23) is a phrase which must be carefully studied in the light of the indigenous religious beliefs,—not that the translation should conform to local superstitions, but that the terms employed may not be misleading or meaningless. For example, in Loma one cannot say 'possessed with demons' but 'they had demons behind them'. In Kekchi one must not say that 'demons are in a person' (this may mean simply in the stomach of the victim), but 'with a person'. In Timorese the demon 'mounts the person'.

In a number of languages there is a distinction between two different types of malevolent spirits: (1) those which are disembodied spirits of dead persons and (2) those which inhabit the forest, caves, or forbidden places and which are linked in some cases in an elaborate hierarchy to other even more malicious spirits of the universe, such as the devil. The latter are the spirits which should be identified as demons.

33 *And the whole city was gathered together about the door.*

Exegesis: *holē hē polis* 'the whole city': another instance of a popular and vivid way of describing an event which draws the attention of a large number of people (cf. v. 5).

ēn...episunēgmenē 'was gathered': another example (cf. v. 6) of a verbal phrase consisting of the auxiliary verb *eimi* 'to be' plus the perfect participle of the main verb, whose meaning is *not* past perfect 'had been gathered' but perfect 'was gathered' (cf. Turner *Journal of Theological Studies*, 28.349, 1926-7).

pros tēn thuran 'toward the door'. Swete: "the accusative dwells on the thought of the flocking up to the door...and the surging, moving mass before it" (cf. 2:2, 11:4).

Translation: Obviously in many languages one cannot say 'the whole city gathered together'. This figure of speech, in which one object is used as a name for another, must be adjusted in numerous instances, e.g. 'all the inhabitants of the city came together' (Balinese), 'all those of the city were gathered' (Shipibo), 'and all who belonged to the same town' (Toba Batak), and 'all people of the town came' (Chontal of Tabasco).

Door is the door of the house, not the gate, but many languages have two words for 'door': (1) the object which closes the aperture and (2) the opening through which people pass. Because of the crowd and the likelihood that Jesus was in or near the doorway or that people were passing in and out, it would be better to employ the second, rather than the first meaning.

34 *And he healed many who were sick with various diseases, and cast out many demons; and he would not permit the demons to speak, because they knew him.*

Exegesis: *etherapeusen* (3:2, 10, 6:5, 13) 'he healed', 'he cured', 'he restored': as the context indicates, both in this passage and elsewhere, the meaning is *not* that of caring for, or treating a sick person; it means to effect a cure.

pollous kakōs echontas poikilais nosois 'many who were gravely ill with various diseases'.

kakōs echontas (see v. 32) 'sick', 'ill'.

poikilais nosois (only here in Mark) 'with various diseases': the words are in the dative instrumental case.

kai daimonia polla exebalen 'and he cast out many demons': notice that *hoi daimonizomenoi* 'the demon-possessed ones' in v. 32 are the same as the man *en pneumati akathartō* 'in an unclean spirit' of vv. 23, 26. No distinction is drawn between 'the unclean spirits' and 'the demons'; they are the same.

ekballō (cf. 1:12) 'cast out', 'drive out', i.e. cast out the demon, or spirit, from the person possessed by it.

hoti 'because': here it is causative, not declarative (as Synodale translates it).

59

ēdeisan auton 'they knew him': the demons recognized Jesus himself and knew who he was, not merely what was his mission (Lagrange).

Translation: *Sick with various diseases* is not to be understood that the same people had numerous different diseases. The sense is distributive, many people and different diseases.

Cast out...demons is an expression which must in many instances be adapted to the local psychological viewpoint. For example, in one instance a native speaker asked, "How could Jesus 'throw out' the demons? Was he inside the man in order to do it?" Obviously, the translation in that language had failed to take into consideration the appropriate manner in which one must speak of the process of healing demon-possessed persons. In many languages one must say 'to cause to come out' (Moré), in others 'take out demons' (Mazatec), 'drove many evil spirits from behind them' (Kpelle, Loma).

The same verb for 'know' employed in verse 24 should be used here.

35 And in the morning, a great while before day, he rose and went out to a lonely place, and there he prayed.

Exegesis: *prōi ennucha lian* 'exceedingly early, while still dark': the piling up of three adverbs indicates that it was very early, long before sunrise. The whole adverbial phrase modifies the verb 'to rise'.

prōi (11:20, 13:35, 15:1, 16:2,9) 'early', 'in the morning'.

ennucha (only here in N.T.), an adverb, properly the neuter plural form of *ennuchos* 'in the night', 'at night time'.

lian (6:51, 9:3, 16:2) 'very', 'exceedingly'.

anastas exēlthen kai apēlthen 'rising he went out and (went) away': Turner (*Journal of Theological Studies*, 28.155, 1926-7) notes this use of two almost synonymous verbs as characteristically Marcan.

anastas occurs 17 more times in the sense of 'rise' (it does not appear in Mark with the meaning 'raise'), 'rising up (from bed or from sleep)'.

exēlthen 'he went out (from the house)': some see the additional idea of the town (Capernaum) also (Swete, Turner).

apēlthen 'he went away'. Manson: "went out and away"; Moule (*Idiom Book*, 72) "he left the house and went away".

erēmon topon 'lonely place', 'isolated spot', 'solitary place': there is no desert around Capernaum.

prosēucheto (6:46, 11:24,25, 12:40, 13:18, 14:32,35,38,39) 'he prayed', 'he was praying': the imperfect tense may have the meaning 'he started praying'.

Translation: The equivalent of *in the morning, a great while before day* may be 'it was still very dark' or 'it was a long time before the sun would come up', or 'long before heavens-open-door' (Maninka).

Rose means got up from sleeping.

While in English we must use several words to describe this process of getting up early in the morning before sunup and going out from the town, in Moré this entire idea is expressed by a single verb, this being a very common experience of the people, who set off for their fields very early in the morning hours.

In N.T. Greek *proseuchomai* is one of the most common verbs for praying and as such is the most neutral term. However, in attempting to discover adequate equivalents in other languages the situation is complicated by the fact that Christian prayer is in many respects so different from pagan prayer. In general there are three alternatives: (1) a traditional term which often implies primarily incantation and reciting, e.g. 'to speak doctrine' or 'repeat words', (2) a word which identifies primarily the process of requesting, begging, and seeking, and (3) an expression which implies 'talking with God' (e.g. Pame, Tzeltal, Chol, Ecuadorian Quechua, Shipibo, Cakchiquel, Cuicatec, Zoque, Tarahumara). Though in general the last alternative seems to be the most productive, it does not mean that the first two must never be employed, especially since in certain contexts they fit very well. Moreover, there may be certain connotations of these words which render them quite acceptable. For example, in Tzotzil the word for prayer means primarily 'to beg' or 'to ask', but the full expression is 'to ask with one's heart coming out' (in the sense of 'entreaty'), implying a degree of self-exposure and sincerity, all of which seems to make the expression quite adequate. South Toradja at first used *mangimbo* 'to invoke the gods'; the difficulty was that this 'invocation' was always accompanied by sacrifice, and later it was discovered that the word had the meaning of 'curse' in certain districts. Then the word *masambajang* borrowed from Malay began to be used for 'pray'.

In some instances a word for prayer is not to be interpreted in its literal, etymological sense. For example, in Tarascan prayer is literally 'to say poor', but no Indian would ever think of this meaning. The word is simply a local equivalent of 'to pray'. Huichol uses a verb meaning 'to cause God to know' and Miskito and Lacandon say 'to raise up one's words to God', the latter implying an element of worship, as well as communication.

What one should try to avoid in the selection of a term for prayer is (1) an expression which will mean only the recitation of largely meaningless word formulae and (2) a word which connotes begging insistence, equivalent to teasing God. Neither of these types of expressions can form an adequate basis for the Scriptural teaching about prayer, and they certainly do not fit in this context. For further discussions of terms for prayer, see *BT*, p. 233, and *GWIML*, pp. 42, 158.

36 *And Simon and those who were with him followed him,* 37 *and they found him and said to him, "Every one is searching for you."*

Exegesis: *katediōxen* (only here in N.T.) 'he followed': the verb literally means 'to track down', 'hunt down' and has a hostile sense in such passages as Gen. 31:36; it may also have a good sense as in Ps. 23:6, 1 Kg. 30:22. More is indicated by the verb than the RSV 'followed';

there is an intentness, a determination, not present in the word 'follow'. Cf. Manson "tracked him down"; Swete "tracked him to his retreat"; Brazilian 'searched diligently'.

Simōn kai hoi met' autou 'Simon and those with him', i.e. the other three mentioned in v. 29.

hōti 'that': here recitative, introducing direct speech, and thus correctly omitted in translation.

pantes 'all': notice the same use of this word in 1 : 5, 32, and similar expressions in 1 : 28, 33.

Translation: *Simon and those who were with him* means 'Simon and those who were with Simon', presumably, Andrew, James, and John, but it may have included others. However, the word *him* in this phrase does not refer to Jesus, but to Simon.

Followed is a misleading word, especially when translated literally in some languages, for it might imply that the disciples got up immediately after Jesus did and followed him (keeping him in view all the time) as he went out of the town. This of course is not the case. Evidently, the disciples awoke to find that Jesus had already left, and then they went looking for him. Accordingly, Mezquital Otomí has simply 'went looking' and Shipibo 'went to seek him'. Other languages use expressions which imply that the disciples followed his tracks. The important thing is that the translation realistically reflect what happened.

Many languages have two words corresponding to English *found:* (1) a word which implies that something was discovered which people were not at the time trying to find and (2) a term which indicates that the object found is the result of a planned search. The latter expression is, of course, the one desired here.

The Greek verb *zēteō*, translated in the RSV as "searching", could perhaps be better translated as "looking for you". It may also imply that the people were 'asking about', 'inquiring for', etc.

38 *And he said to them, "Let us go on to the next towns, that I may preach there also; for that is why I came out."*

Text: *allachou* 'elsewhere' is omitted by *Textus Receptus;* all modern editions of the Greek text, however, include it.

Exegesis: *agōmen* (13 : 11, 14 : 42) 'let us go': the subjunctive mode, in this context, has almost the force of an imperative. Here it is not so much a plea, a request, as an exhortation.

allachou (only here in the N.T.) 'elsewhere'. Arndt & Gingrich prefer the meaning 'in another direction' for this passage.

eis tas echomenas kōmopoleis 'to the neighboring towns'.

tas echomenas (cf. Lk. 13 : 33, Acts 20 : 15, 21 : 26) 'neighboring'. The present participle of the verb *echomai* 'have' is used in the specialized sense of 'next', 'adjoining', 'neighboring' either with reference to time or to space.

kōmopolis (only here in the N.T.) 'town', 'village', 'market-town' (cf. Arndt & Gingrich). Swete quotes Lightfoot who defines the word as referring to a small country town.

kai ekei 'and there': *kai* here has the meaning of 'also'.

kēruxō 'I may proclaim', 'I may preach' (see v. 4).

exēlthon 'I came out'. The ordinary meaning of 'I came out (from Capernaum)' is understood by most commentators (Gould, Turner, Rawlinson, Manson, Weymouth); Vincent Taylor takes it to mean 'I came out (on the Galilean mission)'. Swete and Lagrange, however, see a theological meaning 'I came forth *(from the Father)*'; this meaning, however, has not commended itself to many (although it appears that Luke understood the words in this sense; at least that is what Lk. 4:43 means).

Translation: If it is necessary to be more specific in the pronominal reference *he* and *them* may be translated by the appropriate noun expressions. However, all such substitutions, whether of nouns for pronouns or pronouns for nouns must conform to the syntactic requirements of the receptor language in question.

Towns (in Greek a compound word meaning literally 'village-city') in this context refers to places half-way between cities and villages. In some languages this would be 'big villages' and in others 'small cities', depending of course upon the more acceptable way of designating such a place.

For *preach* see 1:4, but note that in this context there is no object of the verb. In many languages, however, one must add a grammatical object to the verb of speaking, e.g. 'to hand down the Way' (Union Version in Chinese), 'declare the word' (Kekchi), or 'speak God's word' (Kpelle).

If it is possible to preserve the ambiguity of 'that is why I came out', well and good, but for the most part one must be more specific about the meaning of *came out*, hence stating specifically either 'I came to this earth' or 'I came out of the city'. The second meaning is recommended, though some translations have followed the first, e.g. Balinese.

39 And he went throughout all Galilee, preaching in their synagogues and casting out demons.

Text: Instead of *ēlthen* 'he went' of the majority of modern editions of the Greek text, *ēn* 'he was' is read by *Textus Receptus*, Turner, Taylor, and Kilpatrick. The evidence of the Greek mss. favors *ēlthen*, but the early versions (Old Latin, Vulgate, Syriac versions) favor *ēn*. Turner's remarks in favor of *ēn* 'he was' have considerable force; besides conforming to Marcan usage, 'he was' is supported by the parallel passage Lk. 4:44, while in Mk. 1:14 we are told that Jesus *came* into Galilee preaching, and here he *continues* preaching in Galilee (cf. *Journal of Theological Studies*, 28.156, 349, 1926-7).

Exegesis: *ēlthen kērussōn...kai...ekballōn* 'came preaching...and...

casting out': with this reading (Nestle and others) *ēlthen* 'he went' goes with *eis holēn tēn Galilaian* 'he went throughout all Galilee', while the two participles *kērussōn* 'preaching' and *ekballōn* 'casting out' function independently and modify 'he' (i.e. Jesus), indicating the manner in which he went into Galilee, 'he went throughout all Galilee, preaching... and casting out'. Should *ēn* 'he was' be preferred, the prepositional phrase *eis holēn tēn Galilaian* 'in all Galilee' will modify *tas sunagōgas autōn*, 'their synagogues throughout all Galilee', while the two verbal phrases *ēn kērussōn...kai...ekballōn* 'was preaching...and...casting out' will stress the continued aspect of the ministry. Cf. Manson "went on making the proclamation", Knox "continued to preach".

autōn 'their' i.e. of the neighboring villages referred to in the previous verse.

Translation: As noted above, the syntactic relationships of the various parts of this verse depend very largely upon the text which is followed, whether, for example, one says, 'he was preaching in their synagogues throughout Galilee' or 'he went throughout Galilee, preaching in their synagogues'.

Galilee may be identified as 'Galilee region' (or 'province'), though by this point in the text the reader should have become somewhat familiar with the significance of Galilee, if classifiers have been used in previous verses.

Their represents a kind of general, impersonal use of the third person plural. In some languages such a pronoun would refer to the immediately preceding third person plural, namely, the disciples addressed by Jesus at the beginning of verse 38. Hence, 'the synagogues of the people' must be employed in some languages (so South Toradja, Bare'e and Javanese).

For *casting out demons* see 1 : 34.

40 *And a leper came to him beseeching him, and kneeling said to him, "If you will, you can make me clean."*

Exegesis: *lepros* (14:3) 'a leper' (cf. the parallel Lk. 5:12 *anēr plērēs lepras* 'a man full of leprosy'). The exact meaning of *lepra* (and of the Hebrew *ṣara'ath*, of which it is the translation) is by no means certain. Arndt & Gingrich point out that in pre-Biblical Greek the term meant psoriasis; there is widespread agreement that, even if the term sometimes denoted leprosy in the Bible, it also included other skin diseases (cf. Arndt & Gingrich, Koehler, Lagrange). Dr. K. P. C. A. Gramberg (*TBT* 11.10-23, 1960) argues that *sara'ath* and *lepra* did not denote leprosy at all. Dr. J. L. Swellengrebel (*TBT* 11.69-80, 1960), in a review of the Biblical evidence, shows that these terms certainly denoted some kind of disease which could be of a serious nature and which carried with it ceremonial uncleanness.

parakalōn...kai gonupetōn legōn 'pleading...and kneeling saying': the three participles describe the manner in which the man *erchetai* 'came' to Jesus.

parakalōn (5:10, 12, 17, 18, 23, 6:56, 7:32, 8:22) 'entreating', 'pleading', 'beseeching'.

gonupetōn (10:17) 'kneeling': literally 'to fall (*piptō*) on the knee' (*gonu*).

hoti 'that': again recitative, introducing direct speech (cf. v. 37).

katharisai (1:41, 42, 7:19) 'to make clean': in the LXX the verb is used of physical and ceremonial cleansing, and means 'to make clean' or 'to declare clean'. Here it is used in the former sense, 'to *make* clean'.

Notice that the request of the leper is conditioned not on Jesus' ability to make him clean ("you can make me clean") but on his desire or willingness ("if you will" or "if you wish").

Translation: A great deal of confusion has existed with respect to the word *leper* (and *leprosy*), for the area of meaning of this word is not the same in the Bible as it is in contemporary medical usage (see above). Moreover, leprosy is not known in certain parts of the world, and in other areas, where it does exist, it may be spoken of in quite idiomatic ways, e.g. 'lazaro sickness' (Shipibo, an expression borrowed into Shipibo from Spanish, which associates leprosy with Lazarus) and 'disease of animals' (Shilluk).

Where leprosy is not known, it is necessary to employ some type of descriptive expression which will indicate something of the seriousness of the disease, but not badly distort its real significance. The following types of expressions are used: 'sickness of skin rotting' (Huichol), 'ulcer sickness' (Tzeltal, in which 'ulcer' refers generally to all types of skin diseases), and 'decaying sores' (Barrow Eskimo).

However, even where leprosy is known, since the meaning of the Biblical term is uncertain, it may be wise to use a more general term or descriptive phrase which none the less conveys the seriousness of the condition, and if possible also carries the connotation of ceremonial uncleanness, e.g. as suggested in Balinese 'ominous disease'. A meaningless loan-word should certainly be avoided.

Beseech may be translated as 'to ask strongly' or 'to ask insistently'. In Huichol the equivalent is 'to give one a desire', an interesting shift of psychological viewpoint.

Kneeling must sometimes be described more specifically as 'kneeling in front of', depending upon local idiomatic requirements.

If you will means 'if you desire to' or 'if you want to'.

Though the "cleansing of lepers" seems to us to be an entirely normal way of speaking, this is quite impossible in many languages. Lepers may 'be healed', but 'not cleansed', for cleansing would imply only washing out of wounds. For example, in several translations it was found that this expression 'to cleanse' or 'to make clean' meant only 'to give a bath to' or 'to wash'. Accordingly in such instances a translator must render the passage as 'if you want to heal me, you can do so'. Moreover, it may be necessary to choose between different words for 'heal', e.g. in Black Bobo *kiri* means to heal external diseases and *kuru* internal ones.

Without a careful distinction at this point the reader could become quite confused.

41 *Moved with pity, he stretched out his hand and touched him, and said to him, "I will; be clean."*

Text: Instead of *splagchnistheis* 'moved with pity' a few manuscripts and versions read *orgistheis* 'moved with anger'. This reading has been adopted as original by Kilpatrick, Turner, Taylor, and Manson. Turner's comments aptly summarize the arguments in favor of *orgistheis* (*Journal of Theological Studies*, 28.157, 1926-7): (1) it is the more difficult reading; (2) Matthew and Luke have nothing corresponding to either 'moved with pity' or 'moved with anger' but there is nothing to explain why they would omit 'moved with pity'; they further omit *embrimēsamenos* 'sternly urged' in v. 43 (as well as *met' orges* 'with anger' in 3:5); and (3) *embrimēsamenos* 'sternly urged' in v. 43 shows that there is indignation on the part of Jesus. There are various explanations for the anger of Jesus, e.g. (1) indignation at the disease or the evil power which caused the disease and (2) anger at the doubt placed on Jesus' willingness to cure the leper (cf. Taylor; Rawlinson 22, 256; Turner; E. Bevan, *Journal of Theological Studies*, 33.186-88, 1931-2; Manson). The observation has been made that no reason is actually given, but there can be no doubt that there was anger and irritation on the part of Jesus toward the man; *embrimēsamenos* 'sternly urged' and *exebalen* 'drove him out' in v. 43 clearly reveal that Jesus was angry with the man. The suggestion is made that perhaps the man approached Jesus as the Messiah.

Exegesis: *splagchnistheis* (6:34, 8:2, 9:22) 'moved with pity': the verb is derived from *splagchnon*, whose plural *splagchna* 'the inward parts' included heart, liver, lungs, etc., as the seat of emotion (the same as *heart* in current English). The verb *splagchnizomai* 'have pity', 'feel sympathy', first appears in Biblical Greek. The participle in this verse is causal, *'because* he was moved with pity he extended his hand...'

ekteinas (3:5) 'stretching out', 'extending', 'reaching out'.

hēpsato (3:10, 5:27, 28, 30, 31, 6:56, 7:33, 8:22, 10:13) 'he touched': the verb *haptomai* literally means 'fasten to', 'cling to', 'take hold of'. Cf. Arndt & Gingrich 2. b.

Translation: Probably either in verse 40 or 41 it will be necessary to substitute 'Jesus' for one of the third person singular pronouns (e.g. in Subanen), since otherwise the reference can become obscure, especially for the slow reader or for one who begins a section at verse 40.

Moved with pity is often paralleled by a figurative expression in other languages, e.g. 'to see someone with sorrow' (Piro) and 'to suffer with someone' (Huastec), and 'one's mind to be as it were out of one' (Balinese). The dependent expression may, of course, be made coordinate in some languages, e.g. 'he pitied the man and stretched out his hand'.

Touched him, perhaps no more than with the fingers, but this was what others would not do, in view of the unclean state of the man.

The translation of *I will* should be as closely related as possible to the corresponding expression in 1:40 'if you will'. In some languages it is simply 'I desire to do so'.

Be clean involves two difficulties: (1) the use of a verb meaning 'to clean' when speaking of a disease such as leprosy (see 1:40), and (2) the passive form of the verb in an imperative mode, a form for which many languages have no close equivalent. In some languages the nearest approximation is 'I make you well', 'I heal you now', or 'now you are well' (Popoluca).

42 And immediately the leprosy left him, and he was made clean.

Text: The words *eipontos autou* 'when he spoke' after the first 'and' are included by *Textus Receptus*, Soden and Vogels, but omitted by the majority of modern editions of the Greek text.

Exegesis: *lepra* (Mt. 8:3, Lk. 5:12,13) 'leprosy': cf. the discussion of *lepros* 'leper' in v. 40.

Translation: *The leprosy left him* seems such a natural type of expression that we almost inevitably assume that it can be translated literally into another language. On the contrary, in some languages one must say simply 'he got well' (Cakchiquel). In Black Bobo the correct phrase is 'the leprosy was driven out'; in Toba Batak 'the leprosy became loose from him'.

He was made clean is in some languages necessarily translated as 'he became well' or 'he was healed'.

43 And he sternly charged him, and sent him away at once,

Exegesis: *embrimēsamenos autō* 'sternly charging him'.

embrimaomai (14:5; cf. also Mt. 9:30, Jn. 11:33,38) 'be indignant', 'scold', 'censure': the verb is rare in classical Greek and in the LXX, and Moulton & Milligan do not have any examples from the papyri to quote. Hatch (*Essays*, 25) is of the opinion that the word is best explained as a translation either of *za'am* 'to be angry' or of *ga'ar* 'to rebuke'. It has also been pointed out that the word means not merely to feel anger, but to show it, while the dative of the personal pronoun *autō* 'with him' indicates the object rather than the cause of the anger. Most translations carry the meaning of 'sternly (or, strictly) charged' (AV, ASV, RSV, Weymouth, Moffatt, Berkeley, Manson); Knox has 'spoke threateningly' while BFBS translates 'was indignant with him'. Some commentators do not agree with the idea of anger. Swete, for example, appeals to the use of the word in Jn. 11:33,38 as indicating "depth and strength of feeling expressed in tone and manner"; Lagrange sees a certain degree of severity, *avec sévérité*; and Taylor quotes with approval Bernard (*International Critical Commentary, Gospel of John*, 392f.):

"inarticulate sounds which escape men when they are physically over-whelmed by a great wave of emotion."

The further use of the verb in Mark (14: 5), however, and the next verb *exebalen* 'he drove out' seem to show that at least some degree of anger is indicated by the verb in this passage.

exebalen (cf. v. 12) 'he drove out': it is not agreed whether 'house' or 'synagogue' should be supplied, while some are of the opinion that neither is implied, the idea being simply that of driving away from his (i.e. Jesus') presence. RSV 'sent away' seems plainly inadequate, for the idea of forcible expulsion appears to be clearly indicated (cf. study of the word in v. 12).

Translation: One of the problems in verses 43 and 44 is the apparent contradiction in temporal sequence. If translated literally (and with certain tense forms), the reader may wonder how it is possible for Jesus to send a man away (verse 43), and still speak to him, apparently later (in verse 44). This may require in some languages the subordination of verse 43 to 44, e.g. 'As he sternly charged...at once, he said to him...' On the other hand, some translations (e.g. Kekchi) reverse the process, and introduce verse 43 as the independent expression and then start verse 44 as 'after he had said to him...'

Sternly charged may be translated as 'commanded him with strong words', 'spoke to him with hard words'.

44 *and said to him, "See that you say nothing to any one; but go, show yourself to the priest, and offer for your cleansing what Moses commanded, for a proof to the people."*

Exegesis: *hora* (8:15,24, 9:4, 13:26, 14:62, 16:7) 'see to it!': the command enforces the prohibition 'say nothing to any one'.

hupage (15 times in Mark) 'depart', 'go', 'away with you'.

seauton deixon tō hierei kai prosenegke 'show yourself to the priest and make (the) offering': cf. Lev. 14:2-32 where the Levitical laws concerning purification rites are set forth.

tō hierei (2:26) 'to the priest': that is, the serving priest, the officiating priest (cf. Taylor; Creed *Commentary* on Luke 5:14). There is division of opinion whether or not this means the priest in Jerusalem or a local priest, but the majority of commentators seem to agree that Jerusalem is implied (cf. Rawlinson).

eis marturion autois (6:11, 13:9) 'for a testimony to them'. There is general agreement that *marturion* here means 'proof', 'evidence' (cf. Manson, Moffatt, Abbott-Smith). There is no agreement, however, concerning *autois* 'to them'. Who is meant? "People" in general is the opinion of some (RSV, Lagrange, Creed, Moffatt). Lagrange conjectures that when the rites had been completed the priest certified in writing that the man had been pronounced clean, and this document would serve as proof to one and all. Others, however, think that "priests" is meant, i.e. those upon whom would devolve the task of officiating at the purification rites (Swete, Turner, Taylor). For translation purposes, if language allows, it is probably better to retain the ambiguity of the Greek and say simply 'to them'.

Translation: *See* must, of course, not be taken in the literal sense, as it has been in some translations. It is equivalent to 'beware lest you' or 'be sure that you do not...'

In contrast with the *prophet*, who spoke to the people on behalf of God, the *priest* represents the people before God. However, in many instances the small, growing Christian community is so strongly opposed to the ways of the religious practices of the paganism around them that they cannot readily accept a word for priest which is even neutral in its connotation. For example, in one area a translator insisted on using a word for priest which carried a very bad connotation whenever the Scriptures spoke of Jewish priests (especially those whom Jesus condemned). In this way the translator thought he could indirectly undermine the influence of the local pagan priests. However, when Jesus is called "our high priest" in Hebrews, this same translator wanted to use an entirely different term. At the same time the problem is complicated by the fact that the priest had many functions: sacrificing of animals, burning of incense, pouring of libations, offering of prayers, and participation in processions. An additional difficulty is that in many areas there are two levels of priesthood. For example, among the Huichol in Mexico there are (1) the local priests (shamans) of the indigenous religion and (2) the Roman Catholic priests, whom the people respect, but of whose ministry they understood very little. In such instances should one use the indigenous term which would imply a shaman-like person or borrow the Spanish term, which would seem to imply that the priests of the Bible were similar to Roman Catholic priests?

However, rather than borrow local names for priests, some of which have unwanted connotations, a number of translations have employed descriptive phrases based on certain functions: (1) those describing a ceremonial activity: Bare'e uses *tadu*, the priestess who recites the litanies in which she describes her journey to the upper or under-world to fetch life-spirit for sick people, animals or plants; Toba Batak uses the Arabic *malim*, 'Muslim religious teacher'; 'one who presents man's sacrifice to God' (Bambara, Maninka), 'one who presents sacrifices' (Baouli, Navajo), 'one who takes the name of the sacrifice' (Kpelle), and 'to make a sacrifice go out' (Habbe); (2) those describing an intermediary function: 'one who speaks to God' (Shipibo) and 'spokesman of the people before God' (Chontal of Tabasco). (See also *BT*, pp. 113, 139, 235.)

Offer for your cleansing may be translated in this context as 'make an offering, seeing that now you have been healed' (or 'cleansed'), or '...because you have been healed'. Because of the temporal sequence involved, the Greek preposition *peri*, which normally would mean 'about', 'concerning', must here imply 'with regard to the fact that...' or 'because of...' (Union Version of Chinese).

What Moses commanded may be expanded, because of its elliptical form, to read 'what Moses commanded you to offer'. In some translations this entire expression reads, 'now that you have been healed, offer what Moses commanded you to offer'.

For a proof to the people may be rendered as 'this will show the people that you are healed' (Black Bobo) or 'to show the people that you have been cleansed' (Subanen). If, of course, one understands the priests as implied in the expression *for a proof to them*, such an interpretation may be suggested by the rendering, 'in order to show the priests that you are healed'.

45 *But he went out and began to talk freely about it, and to spread the news, so that Jesus could no longer openly enter a town, but was out in the country; and people came to him from every quarter.*

Exegesis: *ho de* 'but he': the leper, that is, not Jesus. Some, indeed, in view of *kērussein...ton logon* 'proclaim...the word' (on which, see below), have concluded that Jesus is meant; as Kilpatrick points out, however, (*TBT*, 7.2, 1956), *ho de* in Mark always implies a change of subject.

exelthōn 'went out': probably, of the house (cf. *exebalen* 'drove out' in v. 43).

ērxato kērussein...kai diaphēmizein 'began to proclaim...and spread abroad'.

ērxato 'he began': as an auxiliary this verb occurs some 26 times in Mark. There is general agreement that this use of the verb reflects Semitic speech patterns and, with some exceptions (8:31, 10:47, 14:19, 33, 15:8), is actually redundant, so far as meaning is concerned (cf. the study of the word by Turner, *Journal of Theological Studies*, 28.352-53, 1926-7; Taylor, 48, 63-64; Black *Aramaic*, 91).

kērussein (cf. v. 4) 'proclaim', 'preach'.

diaphēmizein (only here in Mark) 'spread widely', 'disseminate'.

polla 'much': the word is adverbial, modifying *kērussein* 'proclaim', not adjectival 'many things'.

ton logon (21 times in Mark) literally 'the word'. The expression is variously translated: "news" (RSV, Weymouth, Moffatt), "matter" (ASV, Abbott-Smith, Zürich *die Sache*, Lagrange *la chose*), "story" (Manson, Taylor, Knox), "report" (Berkeley); Synodale *le fait*; Brazilian *a notícia*; Swete "the tale". Kilpatrick, in a study of the word in Mark (*TBT*, 7.2-3, 1956), finds that the eleven times the word appears in chapters 1-4 the meaning is "the (Christian) Message," and concludes that in this passage what is meant is that the man proclaimed the cure not simply as an isolated event but as proof of the Messiahship of Jesus. BFBS accordingly translates "the Word." Whether or not this theological meaning is carried by the expression, Mark certainly means to say that the man told to one and all his cure at the hands of Jesus.

dunasthai...eiselthein '(be) able...to enter': Turner's study of the verb *dunamai* in Mark (*Journal of Theological Studies*, 28.354f., 1926-7) concludes that in many cases the meaning of the verb is weakened in Mark and it becomes almost an auxiliary, meaning 'can', 'could', or 'may', 'might'. This passage is an example of this weakened sense, and the verb is properly translated 'could (not)' (most translations).

eis polin eiselthein 'enter a (any) town': the sense is indefinite. In English the word "town" is a better translation than "city" (ASV, Manson, BFBS, Knox).

erēmois topois 'solitary places', 'lonely places' (cf. v. 35) here means, in contrast with *polin* 'town', 'country' (RSV) or 'open country' (Manson).

ērchonto 'they were coming' is another example of the impersonal plural (cf. vv. 30, 32), and the imperfect indicates a continued process 'people kept coming' (cf. v. 32).

Translation: *Went out* whether of the town or a house, is not clear, but in some languages the distinction must be made. Where there is no evidence, as in this case, for or against either choice, either may be selected, though perhaps 'house' fits the context a little more satisfactorily. One must make certain, however, that 'he' refers to the healed man, not to Jesus, which is the subject of the preceding two verses, and is likely to be interpreted as the subject of v. 45, unless clearly indicated to the contrary.

Began to talk freely is 'to tell everyone' (or 'many'). Actually this is the verb translated elsewhere as 'to preach', but its basic meaning is 'to deliver (or proclaim) a message'.

The precise nature of the *news* we do not know (see above), but it would certainly not be wrong to translate this entire phrase as 'he kept telling more people about what had happened'. In Shilluk the idiom for this type of process is 'to visit about it from one to another' and in Puebla Aztec one may say 'to let it drop out of his mouth much'.

So that is in a sense an ambiguous phrase, for though it often refers to purpose, in this instance the meaning is, of course, result. Where necessary a clause introduced by *so that* may be separated from the preceding by a transitional expression, e.g. 'because of this Jesus could not...'

A frequent equivalent of *openly* is 'when people were looking' (Black Bobo, Ifugao).

In the country does not mean the wilderness, as in Judaea, but only out in the country where there were no habitations.

In the last clause an indefinite subject 'people' must very frequently be introduced.

CHAPTER TWO

1 *And when he returned to Capernaum after some days, it was reported that he was at home.*

Exegesis: *di' hēmerōn* 'after some days', literally, 'through (the interval of) days'. These words are rightly connected with *eiselthōn* 'entering' (RSV "returned"), not with *ēkousthē* 'it was heard' (cf. Swete).

ēkousthē 'it was heard' which actually means 'it was said', 'it was reported'. The impersonal use of the verb in the passive voice is quite common.

hoti 'that': some (e.g. Vincent *Word Studies* I, 169) take this to be recitative, introducing direct speech (cf. 1:40); the majority, however, take it to be declarative 'that' introducing indirect speech.

en oikō (cf. *eis oikon* 3:19 [*or* 3:20] 7:17, 9:28) 'in a house': the correct meaning, however, is 'at *home*' (cf. Goodspeed *Problems*, 54; Kilpatrick *TBT* 7.5, 1956). Moulton & Milligan quote examples from the papyri in which the phrase has this meaning. AV and ASV "in the house" are incorrect, as well as Knox "in a house" (cf. Manson, Moffatt, Weymouth, BFBS, Berkeley; Brazilian *em casa*).

Translation: *It was reported* may be rendered as 'the people heard' (Barrow Eskimo), if as in so many languages a passive with indefinite subject cannot be employed.

Because of a possible paragraph break and a section heading introducing this passage, it may be advisable to substitute one of the pronouns (*he*) by 'Jesus'.

At home should be rendered in the appropriate, idiomatic manner, which in some instances requires the addition of a possessive pronoun, e.g. 'in his house'.

2 *And many were gathered together, so that there was no longer room for them, not even about the door; and he was preaching the word to them.*

Text: After the first *kai* 'and' *Textus Receptus*, Soden, Vogels and Kilpatrick add *euthus* 'immediately', omitted by all other editions of the Greek text.

Exegesis: *sunēchthēsan* (4:1, 5:21, 6:30, 7:1) 'they were gathered together', 'brought together', 'collected' (cf. *episunagō* in 1:33).

hōste mēketi chōrein 'so as no longer to be room': for the use of *hōste* with the infinitive of the verb to express result see 1:27.

chōrein (only here in Mark) 'to have space for', 'to hold', 'to contain', 'to be room (for)'.

ta pros tēn thuran (cf. 1 : 33) 'the (places, space) near (toward, about) the door': the meaning is that such a crowd was gathered in the house and overflowing into the street, that not even on the street, near the door, was there room for any more people.

elalei (some 22 times in Mark) 'he was speaking': RSV "preaching," while not incorrect, is not completely consistent. It is better to reserve "preach" for *kērussō* 'proclaim' or *euaggelizomai* 'preach the Gospel'. The imperfect, describing action in progress, tells us what Jesus was doing when the paralytic was brought to him (next verse). Some translations join the last clause of this verse 'and he was speaking the Word to them' directly to the next verse: "And he was speaking to them the Word when..." (Moffatt, Weymouth, Manson, Berkeley).

ton logon 'the word' i.e. the Christian message, the Gospel (cf. Arndt & Gingrich, 1.b.β); Lagrange "the good tidings of salvation." Rather than "the word" it may be preferable to use capitalization—"the Word" or something similar. "The Message" would accurately convey the meaning (cf. 1 : 45 and Kilpatrick's note on *logos* "word" in Mark, there referred to).

Translation: The Greek verb translated *were gathered together*, though a passive in form, is generally best translated as an active, implying not that the people were brought, carried, or forced to come together by the actions of others, but that 'they came together', or 'crowded together'.

In some languages a verb implying the gathering of a crowd may require some statement as to the type of place in which such a gathering may occur. In this instance it is the home of Jesus.

The second clause may be rendered 'so that there was no space for anyone else'.

About the door refers of course to the space outside the house, and the door is in this instance better taken as the opening (where a distinction is made—see 1 : 33), since obviously the door would be open at such a time.

Though *laleō* is a more colloquial term for 'speaking', it is the combination with *logon* 'word' which gives it the strictly theological connotation of 'preaching'. The only equivalent of *the word* in many languages is 'the good news'. In South Toradja and Indonesian 'the word of God' must be used. Certainly this phrase means much more than merely 'he was talking'.

3 *And they came, bringing to him a paralytic carried by four men.*

Exegesis: *erchontai* 'they come' is another example of the impersonal plural (cf. Turner *Journal of Theological Studies* 25.379, 1923-4). Luke (5 : 18) has it 'and behold men were bringing'. Who 'they' are is a matter of conjecture: Lagrange thinks they were the parents of the paralytic, as distinct from the bearers. BFBS "men came". RSV "and they came" is likely to be misleading in light of the immediately preceding "them" of the previous verse.

pherontes 'bringing': here is proof that the verb does not always mean 'carry', since *airomenon* 'being carried' is added to make clear the manner in which the paralytic was brought to Jesus (cf. 1:32).

paralutikon (2:4, 5, 9, 10) 'paralyzed man', 'paralytic', 'lame'.

airomenon (some 20 times in Mark) '(who was) being carried'.

Translation: *They came,* because of its indefinite antecedent, must in many languages be rendered as 'some people came'. If this is not done the impression may be given that the crowd which was gathered together (the last third person plural referent) brought the man.

Because of the two verbs *bringing* and *carried,* it may be that the total number of persons coming with the paralytic were more than four. However, in some languages it is difficult to distinguish between 'bringing' and 'carrying', in view of the fact that the only way to bring this man was to carry him. Many languages distinguish between the processes of (1) leading, (2) accompanying, and (3) carrying, but a verb of such indefinite reference as 'bringing' is often lacking. However, in order to render the two verbs in the passage one may translate 'they had with them a paralytic; four men were carrying him'.

Paralysis is spoken of in a number of different ways in various languages, as one or another feature of the disease is selected as a descriptive base, e.g. 'a sickness which causes one not to be able to move' (Mazahua), 'all dried up' (San Blas), 'one half his body is dead' (Subanen), and 'he could not move' (Zacapoastla Aztec). Since there are paralytics in all societies, there is no difficulty in finding an appropriate term to describe this man's condition.

One problem, however, is posed by the fact that in some languages one must specifically distinguish between maladies which are congenital (occurring at birth) and those which have occurred later in life. In the Scriptures, unless there is a specific statement as to the fact that a person has been suffering from birth, it is to be understood that the disease was not congenital. On the other hand, in languages which distinguish between chronic and acute illnesses, one should probably in this case assume that the paralysis was of some duration.

4 And when they could not get near him because of the crowd, they removed the roof above him; and when they had made an opening, they let down the pallet on which the paralytic lay.

Text: Instead of *prosenegkai* 'bring to' of the majority of editions of the Greek text, *Textus Receptus,* Souter, Kilpatrick and Soden have *proseggisai* 'approach'.

Exegesis: *mē dunamenoi* 'not being able': the participle is causal *'because* (or, *since*) they were unable...'

prosenegkai (10:13) 'bring to' in its literal sense, *not* in the meaning of 'bring (a sacrifice) to (the altar)', as in 1:44.

ton ochlon (some 37 times in Mark; once in the plural *ochloi* 'crowds'

10:1) 'the crowd'. Here not in the sense of a disorganized or an unruly mob, but of the people gathered to hear Jesus speak.

apestegasan tēn stegēn 'they unroofed the roof' (literally).

apostegazō (only here in the N.T.) 'remove the roof'.

stegē (only here in Mark) 'roof': although Mark does not specify it, the roof would be reached, of course, by the outside steps (cf. 13:15). "The roof would be flat, and not made of very thick material, perhaps rough rafters with branches laid across, and the whole plastered with mud, so that 'to take off the roof' and let someone down through it... would be quite easy" (A.C. Bouquet *Every Day Life in New Testament Times*, 28). (Notice that Luke 5:19 speaks of the tiled roof of Roman or Hellenistic construction; cf. Lagrange; Creed, p. 79).

hopou ēn 'where he was', i.e. just above the place where Jesus was: Manson "above the spot where Jesus was"; Weymouth "just over His head"; Moffatt "under which he stood."

exoruxantes (only here in Mark) 'digging out', 'digging through'. This verb further defines the nature of the roof. Arndt & Gingrich: "making an opening by digging through the clay of which the roof was made, and putting the debris to one side, so that it does not fall on the heads of those in the house."

chalōsi ton krabaton 'they let down the pallet'.

chalaō (only here in Mark) 'let down', 'lower' (cf. Acts 9:25). How they lowered the pallet is not made clear. The general presumption is that ropes would be used: Vincent, however, is of the opinion that no ropes would be required (*Word Studies* I, 170). In any case no great distance would be involved since the roof would be quite low.

krabatos (2:9,11,12, 6:55) 'pallet', 'mat': Moulton & Milligan define it: 'the poor man's bed or mattress', a word better suited to the narrative than *klinē* 'bed' in Mt. 9:2 and Lk. 5:18.

katekeito (cf. 1:30) 'he was lying'.

Translation: Because any reference to Jesus is several clauses removed, it is often necessary to translate 'and when they could not get near Jesus'.

Crowd is often just 'many people'.

To remove the roof poses not only problems for the translator but for many readers, especially those who cannot imagine a flat roof such as was common in Palestine in the time of Jesus (and still is). In many instances it is preferable to use rather generalized statements at this point, unless by some picture to be used in the text the fact of flat roofs can be made clear. The first verb may then be translated as 'they took away part of the roof' and the second 'when they had made a hole' (or 'an open place'). Of course, the Greek describes graphically the process of digging out a hole, but this may be difficult, if not impossible, to communicate in another language, especially where people are acquainted only with very steep, thatch-covered dwellings.

Since in most areas of the world people use improvised stretchers to carry people, such a term as is used for these objects can be employed here for *pallet*.

Let down must often be made specific, i.e. 'by hand' or 'with ropes'. Probably the latter is preferable.

5 And when Jesus saw their faith, he said to the paralytic, "My son, your sins are forgiven."

Exegesis: *kai idōn* 'and seeing' is temporal, '*when* he saw'.

tēn pistin autōn 'the faith of them': the phrase refers primarily to the four who were carrying the paralytic, but does not necessarily exclude the paralytic himself (cf. Gould, Lagrange).

pistis (4:40, 5:34, 10:52, 11:22) 'faith', 'belief', 'confidence': in this context, faith in Jesus' ability to cure the man (cf. Arndt & Gingrich 2.b).

teknon (7:27, 10:24,29,30, 12:19, 13:12) 'child', '(my) son': a term of endearment. Nothing may be inferred as to the age of the paralytic from the use of this term; he could have been a lad (Luke 5:18,20 specifically calls him a man). Moulton & Milligan quote examples from the papyri of the word used as it is in this verse, and some English translations stress the meaning of the term by adding *"my* son" (cf. Zürich *Mein Sohn*).

aphientai sou hai hamartiai 'your sins are forgiven': the Gospels record no instance of Jesus' saying "I forgive your sins." In this particular instance it is noteworthy that the Gospel writer has employed the passive 'your sins are forgiven' without defining the subject of the action of the verb 'forgive', even though he goes on to relate that the scribes charge Jesus with blasphemy in assuming the prerogative that belongs to God alone. Again, in v. 10, Jesus says, with reference to himself, "the Son of man has authority on earth to forgive sins": he does not say, "I forgive sins". Both the title 'the Son of man' and the qualifying phrase 'upon the earth' are significant. The present tense *aphientai* 'are forgiven' should not be translated 'are *being* forgiven': this is an example of what is called an aoristic present (Burton *Moods and Tenses*, § 13).

aphiēmi 'send forth', 'go away' (from *apo* 'from' and *hiēmi* 'go'): the verb is used in Mark with three main meanings: (1) 'let', 'allow', 'permit': 1:34, 5:19,37, 7:12,27, 10:14, 11:6,16, 15:36; (2) 'forgive', 'remit', 'pardon': 2:5,7,9,10, 3:28, 4:12, 11:25; (3) 'leave': 12:19,20,22, 13:2 ('leave alone' 14:6); with the sense of 'go away from', 'abandon', 'forsake': 1:18,20,31, 4:36, 7:8, 8:13, 10:28,29, 12:12, 13:34, 14:50; with the sense of 'let loose': 15:37.

Translation: Rather than translate *their* to mean only the faith of the carriers (as is often the case), it would seem better to say 'the faith of these men', so that the paralytic himself might be included in that group, since undoubtedly his confidence that Jesus could help him was an important factor in his having been brought.

For terms for 'faith' and 'believe' see 1:15, but note that in this instance the faith is not in a declaration, as in 1:15, but in what a particular person, namely, Jesus, could do. Hence, the expression used here must imply confidence.

The Greek term *teknon* 'child', which is rendered by the more appropriate "my son" in the RSV, cannot be translated literally into other languages. In the first place, people would immediately question why four men would be required to carry a child and furthermore the statement of Jesus relative to the forgiveness of the paralytic's sins would seem to imply an adult (compare Luke). However, any literal rendering of *my son* is equally subject to trouble, since in many languages one cannot speak in this manner except to one's own offspring. Several different types of expression can be employed: 'young man' (Piro, Zacapoastla Aztec), in which 'young' has been used to represent something of the value of *teknon*; 'friend' (Zoque), 'my friend' (Mazatec).

Are forgiven is a passive expression, which, if it can be reproduced without reference to a logical subject, should be retained. However, in languages where passive expressions simply do not exist or where a passive such as this one cannot occur without the agent of the action, one must make certain modifications by employing the most logical subject 'God', i.e. 'God forgives your sins' or 'May God forgive your sins'.

For *forgive* see 1:4. In this context, however, certain special adaptations of this expression for forgiveness may be required because of the use in some languages of 'I' as the subject and the immediacy of the act. For example, in Black Bobo the rendering is 'I command your sins be cast away from you'. In Tzeltal the appropriate formula is 'your sins are lost'.

6 Now some of the scribes were sitting there, questioning in their hearts,

Exegesis: *ēsan...kathēmenoi kai dialogizomenoi* 'were...sitting and questioning': these verbal phrases, consisting of the imperfect of *eimi* 'to be' plus the present participle of the main verbs, denote continuous action.

tines tōn grammateōn (cf. 1:22) 'some scribes'.

kathēmenoi (2:14, 3:32,34, 4:1, 5:15, 10:46, 12:36, 13:3, 14:62, 16:5) '(were) sitting'.

dialogizomenoi (2:8, 8:16,17, 9:33, 11:31) 'considering', 'pondering', 'reasoning'. Moulton & Milligan note that in the N.T. the word always has the sense of "inward deliberation or questioning."

en tais kardiais autōn 'in their hearts': the meaning is the same as *en heautois* 'in themselves' of v. 8.

kardia (2:8, 3:5, 6:52, 7:6,19,21, 8:17, 11:23, 12:30,33) 'heart': in Hebraic thought the heart is the center of intellectual activity. Lagrange points out that the same concept was true also of the Latins and even of the Greeks. The narrative throughout makes clear that this questioning carried on by the scribes was wholly internal and not outwardly expressed. Cf. Abbott-Smith: "say to oneself, i.e. think, reflect, without saying anything aloud."

Translation: 'Now' is transitional, introducing a new aspect of the situation; it is not temporal.

For *scribes* see 1 : 22.

Questioning can be quite well translated as 'thinking' or even 'speaking to themselves in their hearts'.

Though the *heart* is spoken of in the Bible as the center of intellectual and emotive elements of human experience, in other languages the heart may have no such value. In some languages the corresponding centers are the viscera (Conob), the liver (Kabba-Laka), the stomach (Uduk), the gall (South Toradja) and the head (Anuak), though in the neighboring Shilluk demons may be in one's head, but the liver and heart are the center of most other psychological activities. Whether one is to use 'heart' or some other part or organ of the body depends entirely upon the manner in which in any language such psychological experiences are described.

7 *"Why does this man speak thus? It is blasphemy! Who can forgive sins but God alone?"*

Exegesis: *ti* 'why?': the question is thoroughly rhetorical: 'Can it be that he thus blasphemes?' i.e. 'Why! He thus blasphemes!' (cf. Black *Aramaic*, 88).

houtos 'this one' is probably contemptuous (cf. Taylor)—perhaps something like 'this fellow!'

lalei blasphēmei 'he speaks, he blasphemes' (disregarding punctuation): although most commentators and translations separate the two verbs, translating *blasphēmei* 'he blasphemes', Black (*Aramaic*, 47f.) holds that we have here an example of an Aramaic construction in which the second verb has the force of an adverb, modifying the first one: "What is this man thus blasphemously saying?"

blasphēmei (3 : 28, 29, 15 : 29) 'he blasphemes'; the verb in this passage contemplates God as the object of the blasphemy, 'to speak impiously (of God)', 'to profane (God)'. As such, by O.T. law, it was punishable by death (Lev. 24 : 15, 16, 1 Kings 21 : 13).

tis dunatai...ei mē 'who is able...except...?': the scribes felt Jesus was usurping the right of God and actually forgiving sins, not simply declaring them to be forgiven, as Nathan did (2 Sam. 12 : 13).

heis ho theos 'one, (even) God', 'God alone': it has been suggested (*Expository Times*, 49.363-66, 1938) that the phrase means, in accordance with Hebrew theology, 'the One God' (cf. *TBT*, 2.126, 1951).

Translation: *It is blasphemy* is much more conveniently translated as a verb expression, following the Greek text. In almost all languages there are adequate terms for such behavior, but they are quite diverse in form and cultural content (see *TBT*, 6.44-46, 1955): 'speak evil of God' (Huanuco Quechua), 'to hurt God' (Conob), 'to break God's name' (Black Bobo), 'to spoil the name of God' (Loma), 'to insult God' (Luvale), 'to slande God' (Bare'e, Malay), 'to defame God' (Javanese), 'to bring curses (o 'calamitous words') against God' (Tae), and 'to talk to pieces' (Timorese). In some languages translators have introduced an expression here meaning 'to make oneself equal with God', but this does not seem to be required by the context. It is the insulting of God, rather than the usurping of God's prerogatives, which should be brought out by this second clause. The following sentence specifically indicates the degree to which Jesus was accused of usurping divine authority.

The elliptical expression *but God alone*, in combination with the preceding clause, must in some languages be expanded into a kind of paratactic expression, 'Who can forgive sins? Only God can forgive sins'.

The direct discourse of this entire verse must in some languages be introduced more specifically with a verb of direct address, e.g. 'saying to themselves' or 'asking themselves'. Note that the meaning here is reflexive, not reciprocal, for they did not speak openly to one another but only questioned within their own hearts.

8 *And immediately Jesus, perceiving in his spirit that they thus questioned within themselves, said to them, "Why do you question thus in your hearts?*

Exegesis: *epignous* (5:30, 6:33,54) 'perceiving', 'recognizing'. Some think that the preposition *epi* 'upon' has what is called the perfective force, and that the verb would therefore mean 'to know *thoroughly*', 'to be *fully* aware' (cf. Vincent *Word Studies* I, 170; Lagrange). J. A. Robinson (*Ephesians*, 248ff.), however, has convincingly demonstrated that the verb denotes knowledge reached by directing attention *epi* 'upon', 'toward' a particular person or object. Moulton & Milligan quote examples from the papyri which bear out this sense.

tō pneumati autou 'in his spirit', i.e. 'in himself' (*not* 'in his (Holy) Spirit'). Taylor calls this phrase the 'dative of sphere'; Manson and BFBS translate 'by his spirit'.

pneuma 'spirit': this is the third meaning given the word in Mark (cf. 1:8 and reff. for 'Holy Spirit'; 1:23 and reff. for 'unclean spirit'). The meaning here (and in 8:12 and 14:38) is, as Arndt & Gingrich define it, "the source and seat of insight, feeling, and will, generally as the representative part of the inner life of man." In 14:38 it is opposed to the outer life, the physical.

ti 'why?': Black (*Aramaic*, 88) takes this to be another example of a rhetorical question, expressing dismayed surprise (cf. previous verse).

Translation: It is often difficult to use for *spirit* in this verse the same term which may be employed for *Holy Spirit*, and it is especially important to avoid a word for spirit which will imply a demon or a familiar spirit. That is to say, one must not give the impression that Jesus was using a familiar spirit to ferret out the thoughts of the scribes (the technique ascribed often to mediums) or that he had some magic power to send out his spirit to pry into the thoughts of others (a not infrequent idea of the activity of shaman). On the other hand, this spirit was not

79

the Holy Spirit, but the spirit of Jesus as a focus of intellectual activity and discernment. The equivalent of this aspect of personality is, however, in many other languages spoken of as distinct from any word for spirit. For example, in Bolivian Quechua, Black Bobo, and Chol one must use 'heart' and in Conob one must employ a term which identifies the 'viscera'.

In some languages one cannot 'question within oneself', for the word 'to question' means to ask another. Hence, in this verse, as well as verse 6, one must use a verb such as 'to think' or 'to wonder' (Ifugao).

Because of the shift in subjects, i.e. Jesus as the subject of the perceiving and the scribes as the subject of the questioning, it is often advisable to break the sentence and to begin the latter half as a new sentence, e.g. 'he said to them...' (Shilluk).

9 Which is easier, to say to the paralytic, 'Your sins are forgiven,' or to say, 'Rise, take up your pallet and walk'?

Exegesis: *ti estin eukopōteron* 'what is easier?' The question answers itself: it is easier to *say* "Your sins are forgiven" because this statement is not susceptible of proof, while to say "Rise, take up your pallet and walk" would expose Jesus to ridicule should the paralytic not be able to obey the order. By proving he could do the harder Jesus proved he could do the (apparently) easier (on this type of argumentation cf. Daube *New Testament and Rabbinic Judaism*, 68 : Rabbinic *qal wa-ḥomer* "light and heavy"; cf. Lagrange).

eukopōteron (10:25) 'easier': appears only in the comparative form in the New Testament (*eukopos* 'easy').

egeire (cf. 1:31) 'rise', 'get up'.

peripatei (5:42, 6:48,49, 8:24, 11:27, 12:38, 16:12; used once figuratively of manner of life, 7:5) 'walk', 'go about'.

Translation: Opposites such as 'easy' and 'hard', 'good' and 'bad', and 'smooth' and 'rough', etc., may consist of words having contrastive meanings, or they may occur as positives and negatives. For example, in Tzotzil 'easy' is literally 'not hard' and in Maya 'good' is literally 'not bad'. Accordingly in this verse in Tzotzil one must say, 'what is more not hard'.

Comparatives are expressed in a variety of ways, and hence this sentence must be recast to fit the syntactic and lexical requirements of the language into which one is translating, e.g. 'shall I say to the paralytic, Your sins are forgiven, or shall I say, Rise..., which of the two is not hard' (Black Bobo). The reverse order is used in Tarahumara: 'What manner is not hard? To say...or to say...'

Rise means 'stand up', not as in one translation 'to rise miraculously off the ground'.

Take up your pallet may be rendered in some cases as 'roll up your mat' (Tzeltal) or 'pick up your stretcher'.

Walk does not imply here 'to go home' or 'to leave', but to demonstrate the ability to walk, i.e. 'to walk about'.

10 *But that you may know that the Son of man has authority on earth to forgive sins"—he said to the paralytic—*

Exegesis: *hina de eidēte* 'but in order that you may know': as it stands the sentence is grammatically incomplete. Properly something like the following is to be understood: 'But, in order that you may know...*I will do this*' or, '*I will say this*' (cf. Arndt & Gingrich, *hina* I.6). Instead of saying it, however, Jesus directly addresses himself to the paralytic, thus saying and doing what was necessary in order that the scribes should know.

exousian (cf. 1 : 22) 'authority' rather than 'power' of ASV.

ho huios tou anthrōpou 'the Son of man': much has been written on the origin and meaning of this title in the Gospels. In order that the meaning of the phrase, as used by Jesus in the Gospels, be properly carried over into modern languages, it is necessary either literally to translate the words as a Christian technical term, a title, *"The* Son of man"* or else use some phrase or title that will convey if possible a (messianic) sense of dignity, authority, and responsibility. Strictly to be avoided is any translation which would equate the title merely with 'man', 'a human being'. In Mark the title appears here and in 12 other passages (2:28, 8:31,38, 9:9,12,31, 10:33,45, 13:26, 14:21,41,62).

epi tēs gēs 'upon earth': RSV rightly connects the phrase with 'has authority' (cf. Manson, Weymouth, Synodale, Brazilian).

Translation: There is no easy way to resolve the problem of a grammatical break at the end of the first clause. The expression is simply not completed. However, the sense is relatively clear, and for the most part readers can understand the transition. It is best to leave the expression incomplete, rather than try to edit it, for the translator's task is not to try to improve on the original (which contains the break), but to attempt to discover its closest equivalent. Accordingly, the only thing is to leave the incompleted statement as it is, but to employ some type of mark of punctuation which will reflect this fact.

The phrase *Son of man* is one of the most difficult in the entire N.T., for there are almost innumerable problems, many of which have subtle theological implications. The principal difficulties with this phrase are caused by (1) highly specialized terms for 'son', e.g. 'son of a man', 'son of a woman', 'son of a person' without specification of sex, (2) the absence in some languages of a generic term for 'mankind' (though all languages may speak of mankind in the aggregate as 'people'), and (3) the fact that this expression has a double semantic value in the N.T. In the first place, it is related to the numerous other idioms, having the structure 'son of...', e.g. 'son of peace', 'son of perdition', 'sons of thunder', in which the meaning is 'one who has the essential quality of...'; and in the second place, in the N.T. *Son of man* has become a kind of title with Messianic import, whether derived primarily from the book of Daniel or not. A still further complication exists in this verse by virtue of the fact that in many occurrences of this phrase Jesus speaks of himself

81

in the third person. This is, of course, possible in some languages, but in many translations one must add 'I', e.g. 'I who am the Son of man' or people will insist that Jesus is speaking of someone else, not himself.

In some translations the expression used for *Son of man* has constituted a complete denial of the virgin birth. In some of these languages there are two words for son, one used in speaking of the son of a woman and the other the son of a man. Quite understandably, because of the last part of the phrase 'of man', the latter word for 'son' was chosen, but the resultant meaning was to state emphatically that Jesus was the offspring of a male. Even if a generic term for 'mankind' had been used, the very occurrence of the specialized word for 'son' would have resulted in essentially the same meaning. Accordingly, in these languages, including a number in South America, the phrase which was ultimately chosen meant 'he who was born man' or 'he who was truly man', expressions which would not deny his being the Son of God, but which would be a stereotyped expression to emphasize his humanity. In other languages 'he who became man' or 'he who was born for man' have been employed (cf. South Toradja 'the Son who descended into the the world as man') but in any case a good deal of teaching must be undertaken if people are to understand the appropriate significance of the Biblical title. However, the basic phrase should be such as not to suggest immediately an entirely wrong meaning.

Authority is the 'right' or the 'power'. In some languages this is expressed figuratively or in descriptive phrases, e.g. 'power in his hand' (Loma), 'being able to command' (Chanca Quechua), 'place to show power', 'to hold the handle' (Valiente).

11 *"I say to you, rise, take up your pallet and go home."*

Exegesis: *soi legō* 'to you I say': the order of the Greek makes the personal pronoun *soi* 'to you' emphatic: cf. BFBS 'to you I am speaking'.

eis ton oikon sou 'to your house', i.e. 'go *home*' (presumably in Capernaum itself, where the incident occurred). ASV 'into thy house' is an example of extreme literalism in translation. Cf. *en oikō* 'at home' in 2 : 1.

Translation: In all such verses as this one, in which most of the words are identical with expressions used in previous verses, but where some (the last) are slightly different, one must be sure to maintain parallelism where the wording is the same but not to overlook the minor differences.

12 *And he rose, and immediately took up the pallet and went out before them all; so that they were all amazed and glorified God, saying, "We never saw anything like this!"*

Exegesis: *euthus* 'immediately': Taylor thinks no special emphasis is carried by the word here and BFBS translates 'then' (see the note in 1 : 10).

emprosthen (9:2) 'before', 'in the presence of'.

existasthai (3:21, 5:42, 6:51) 'to be astonished', 'to be amazed': Arndt & Gingrich note that this meaning of the verb *existamai* is peculiar to the Bible and (Greek) works influenced by it. In 3:21 it means 'to be beside himself', 'to be mad'.

doxazein (only here in Mark) 'to glorify', 'to praise', 'to honor': Moulton & Milligan quote examples of this use of the verb in the papyri. Taylor: "ascribing to God the splendour (*doxa*) due to His name."

hoti 'that' is recitative, introducing direct speech.

oudepote (2:25) 'at no time', 'never'.

Translation: *Rose* equals 'stood up'.

Went out before them all may be translated 'walked out while all saw him' (Ifugao). The order of elements may also be changed to read 'all the people saw him walk out'. The reasons for such adaptations are largely determined by the rendering of *before them*. In some languages there are no equivalent prepositional constructions, and hence a verb expression is the only satisfactory parallel.

For *amazed* see 1:22 and 27. In this particular context, however, it may be useful to employ some other more appropriate idiom which may be generally used for indicating amazement, e.g. 'they all opened their eyes' (Mazahua).

Glory and the related word *glorify* occur in such a wide variety of Scriptural contexts and reflect in different languages such a diverse series of cultural settings that it is no wonder that these terms provide a number of complications (see *TBT*, 1.28-29, 1950; 4.72, 169-72, 1953; cf. Hooper *Indian Word List*, 52-53). In general *glorify* (in the sense of glorifying God) is translated by two different types of expressions: (1) those which attribute praise to God, whether (a) directly as 'to praise' (Totonac, Mitla Zapotec, Karre, Black Bobo) or (b) indirectly in the form of direct discourse: 'to say that God is very great' (Tarahumara), 'How good God is, they said' (Tzotzil), and 'they spoke about God as good' (Tzeltal), and (2) those which introduce some special attribute as a significant feature of God's glory, whether of appearance or position, e.g. 'to give God a great name' (Zacapoastla Aztec), 'to give God highness' (Kipsigis), 'to take God out high', in the sense of 'to exalt' (Mazatec), 'to make great, to exalt' (South Toradja, Javanese), 'to lift up God's brightness' (Kpelle), 'to show God to be great' (Pame), 'to make God shine' (Goajira), 'to make God's name big' (Huastec), and 'to make God important' (Isthmus Zapotec). However, in addition to these more usual types of expressions there are some rather strange idioms which are nevertheless entirely acceptable in certain languages; for example, in Amuzgo to glorify God is 'to wake God up'.

The last clause may be slightly adapted to fit indigenous forms of speech, e.g. 'there never was a day when we saw this' (Isthmus Zapotec) and 'this kind of happening has never been seen' (Shilluk, which requires a passive expression in this context).

13 *He went out again beside the sea; and all the crowd gathered about him, and he taught them.*

Exegesis: *exēlthen* 'he went out', i.e. of the house and town (cf. Swete).

palin 'again': probably refers back to 1 : 16, although Lagrange thinks the reference is to 1 : 45.

thalassa 'sea' is the Lake of Galilee (cf. 1 : 16).

pas ho ochlos 'all the crowd': not the same 'crowd', of course, referred to in 2 : 4 (for the same expression *pas ho ochlos* 'the whole crowd', 'all the people' cf. 4 : 1b, 9 : 15).

ērcheto...kai edidasken 'came...and he taught': the imperfect tense of the verbs portrays repeated acts of coming, on the part of groups of people, and of teaching, on the part of Jesus.

ērcheto pros auton 'was coming to him': RSV "gathered about him" is not quite consistent with the translation of the phrase elsewhere (cf. 1 : 45 "came to him" and 2 : 3 "came, bringing to him"), but is not out of keeping in this context.

autous 'them': that is, the people who composed *ho ochlos* 'the crowd'.

Translation: It may be necessary to introduce 'Jesus' as the subject of this verse, since the immediately preceding third person singular reference is the paralytic who was healed.

One must be consistent in the translating of *sea*, which in most instances will be the equivalent of 'lake' (see 1 : 16).

One must make certain that the translation of *all the crowd* does not refer to the *crowd* of 2 : 4, for although undoubtedly some of the same people were in attendance on the two occasions, this is not the same group of people. It is better to translate 'all the people'.

It is most important that a word for *teach* is not such as to imply merely class-room instruction, something which not infrequently happens in translations, since translation helpers assume that the educational processes introduced in mission schools are the only legitimate form of teaching. (We ourselves are often deceived in somewhat the same way, not realizing that the classroom technique, though useful for mass production methods is highly inefficient in essential communication.) One should employ either a descriptive term of common usage, e.g. 'to give to be learned' (Tzeltal), or some well-known figurative phrase which will be fully meaningful, e.g. 'to engrave the mind' (Valiente) and 'to cause others to imitate' (Huichol).

14 *And as he passed on, he saw Levi the son of Alphaeus sitting at the tax office, and he said to him, "Follow me." And he rose and followed him.*

Exegesis: *paragōn* (cf. 1 : 16) 'passing by'.

ton tou Alphaiou 'the (son) of Alphaeus': the regular way of denoting filial relationship.

kathēmenon epi 'sitting at' (*not* 'upon').

to telōnion 'revenue office', 'custom house', 'toll house': BFBS "customs office." This customs office in Capernaum would be in the service of Herod Antipas, tetrarch of Galilee.

akolouthei moi 'follow me (in discipleship)' (cf. 1:18).

Translation: In some languages the transition between 'taught them' and 'passed on' is somewhat too abrupt. This may require the addition of some temporal particle such as 'then', so as to show the proper sequence of events and to avoid the words 'passing on' being confusedly taken as more or less part of the teaching.

The tax office is 'where they received taxes' (or 'customs'). This does not refer to the collection of personal taxes on wealth, but to the collection of customs on produce being transported to or through Capernaum. The equivalent of this type of tax in many communities are the levies imposed on merchants or farmers from surrounding regions who come into a market town to sell their wares or produce.

For an adequate translation of *follow* see 1:17.

15 And as he sat at table in his house, many tax collectors and sinners were sitting with Jesus and his disciples; for there were many who followed him.

Exegesis: *auton...autou* 'he...his': there is some disagreement as to who is referred to in the opening clause. Luke 5:29 expressly says it was Levi's house, and there is general agreement that that is the meaning here: 'his house' is Levi's house. Although some think that 'he sat at table' refers also to Levi, the majority understand this to be a reference to Jesus, an interpretation supported throughout by Marcan usage (cf. BFBS).

katakeisthai (14:3; cf. 1:30) 'recline (on a couch at table)', 'dine' (cf. Arndt & Gingrich). Lagrange says that this manner of eating was universal in the time of Jesus, but others, e.g. Jeremias, insist that such was not the case. With the same meaning of 'recline at meal' or 'dine' Mark uses other verbs as well: *anakeimai* (6:26, 14:18, 16:14), *anaklinō* (6:39), *anapiptō* (6:40, 8:6), *sunanakeimai* (here and 6:22).

telōnai kai hamartōloi (Mt. 9:10,11, 11:19, Lk. 5:30,32, 7:34, 15:1, 18:13) 'tax collectors and sinners'.

telōnai (2:16) 'tax collectors': these are to be thought of as the *portitores*, men who actually collected the dues, rather than the *publicani* to whom the revenues were farmed out (cf. Arndt & Gingrich).

hamartōloi (2:16,17, 8:38, 14:41) 'sinful (men)': the adjective is always used in Mark (with the exception of 8:38) in the plural, as a noun, *hoi hamartōloi* 'the sinners'. There is widespread agreement that 'sinners' were people in general who were not so careful in their observance of the Law, especially with regard to dietary laws, as were the Pharisees. "The *'am ha-'arets* (people of the land) who are sinners, not because they transgress the law, but because they do not hold the Pharisaic interpretation of it" (K. Grayston, Richardson's *Word Book*, article "Sin"). Cf. the discussion in Goodspeed *Problems*, 28f., who translates "irreligious people" (cf. Rawlinson, Turner, Taylor).

kai tois mathētais autou 'and his disciples': this is the first mention of the disciples as such, in Mark. The word *mathētēs* 'disciple' occurs some 43 times in Mark and should always be translated 'disciple', 'follower', 'adherent', while 'apostle' should be kept exclusively for *apostolos*, in Mark only at 6:30 and, perhaps, 3:14.

ēsan gar polloi kai ēkolouthoun autō 'for they were many and they were following him': who is referred to by 'the many' who were following Jesus? Some (Rawlinson, Taylor, and others) understand it to refer to a large company of disciples who were now following Jesus; Turner (*Journal of Theological Studies*, 26.239, 1924-5) observes that this is the first mention of the disciples, and "we are told that they were now many and that they were beginning to 'follow him about'." Others (Swete, Moffatt, Manson, Weymouth, Brazilian) understand that *publicans and sinners* are referred to. Although there is no way by which definitely to prove one or the other interpretation, it would seem that the context favors the second interpretation.

kai ēkolouthoun autō 'and they were following him': this clause has been interpreted in two ways: (1) as suggested by Tischendorf, some connect this clause to the next verse, by making it the beginning of the sentence, as follows: "And there were following him also the scribes of the Pharisees..." (Gould, BFBS; cf. Kilpatrick *TBT*, 7.7, 1956). (2) The majority, however, like RSV, connect the clause with what precedes, and translate it as a relative clause, in accordance with normal Semitic syntax: '*who* also were following him' (Rawlinson, Lagrange, Manson, Weymouth, Synodale, Zürich).

Translation: Because of the confusion of pronominal reference in the first clause of this verse (a confusion which also exists in the Greek, but which needs to be resolved in order for the passage to be intelligible in some languages and which if not made more specific may give an entirely wrong meaning in other languages), it is advisable in many instances to translate, 'and as Jesus was dining in Levi's house...'

The rendering *sat at table* is an obvious adjustment to the requirements of the English cultural setting, since in the Greek the verb means 'to recline'. However, the important thing is that this verb means 'to eat' or 'to dine'. The particular position assumed by the participants surrounding the table, whether reclining or sitting, is not important. What matters is the function.

The tax collectors are the 'ones who take the money' (Cashibo) or as in some instances 'those who take the money for the government', in order to specify their function as being different (at least officially) from those who steal, rob, or cheat.

There is no doubt about the special meaning of *sinners* in this context, for undoubtedly the essential meaning is 'those people who consistently violated religious regulations', in contrast with the Pharisees and others who scrupulously kept all the detailed requirements of the law. However, in most languages it is almost impossible to find a term which accurately describes such persons, without introducing certain alien concepts.

Accordingly, for the most part translators have used one word for sinners throughout the Scriptures, whether the context happens to imply those who were morally reprehensible or those who violated certain religious taboos. For a treatment of the lexical problems in words for *sin*, see 1:4.

Terms for *disciple* are generally of three types: (1) those which employ a verb 'to learn' or 'to be taught', (2) those which involve an additional factor of following, or accompaniment, often in the sense of apprenticeship, and (3) those which imply imitation of the teacher. Expressions which are based on the first class of semantic base include: 'word searchers for' (Valiente), 'those who learned from Jesus' (Kiyaka), 'those who learned' (Navajo, Tarascan, Cuicatec, Lacandon), 'those who studied with Jesus' (Mixteco Alto), 'the ones Jesus taught' (Gbeapo); South Toradja 'child (i.e. follower) of the master'; Indonesian and Javanese 'pupil'. There is, however, always a danger in this first type of expression, namely, that the reader will think that the disciples were simply school boys that Jesus was teaching. Accordingly, in order to convey something of the meaning of continued association and fellowship which was involved in the rabbi-disciple relationship of N.T. times, the Mazahua has 'companions whom Jesus taught'. Kipsigis, Loma, and Zoque use a form which means essentially 'apprentices', implying continued association and learning. In Cashibo the meaning is 'those who followed Jesus' and in Mazatec the expression 'his people' means essentially his followers and is used of the political adherents of a leader.

In Zacapoastla Aztec the word for *disciples* is based on the root 'to imitate', and as such has a good deal to recommend it. For further discussion of *disciple* see *TBT*, 2.109, 1951; 3.168-69, 1952; and 4.180, 1953.

If in the last clause of this verse one follows the second interpretation noted above (one strong support for this interpretation is the occurrence of *many* with *tax collectors and sinners* in the second clause), one must make certain that the reference is clear. In some instances one may have to repeat 'tax collectors and sinners', but in many instances languages possess pronominal elements which refer to the earlier of two such third person plural referents. The confusing element in this last clause, however, is the word *followed*, which is generally used in speaking of disciples, not of tax collectors and sinners.

16 *And the scribes of the Pharisees, when they saw that he was eating with sinners and tax collectors, said to his disciples, "Why does he eat with tax collectors and sinners?"*

Text: Instead of *tōn Pharisaiōn* 'of the Pharisees' of all modern editions of the Greek text, *Textus Receptus* has *kai hoi Pharisaioi* 'and the Pharisees'.

After the second *esthiei* 'he eats' *Textus Receptus*, Tischendorf, Vogels, Merk, Souter, Soden, and Kilpatrick add *kai pinei* 'and drinks'; Nestle, Westcott and Hort, Lagrange, and Taylor omit *kai pinei*.

Exegesis: *hoi grammateis tōn Pharisaiōn* 'the scribes (who belonged to the party) of the Pharisees' (cf. Acts 23 : 9).

hoi grammateis 'the scribes' (cf. 2 : 6).

tōn Pharisaiōn 'of the Pharisees': on the origin and particular beliefs of this religious group, the largest among the Jews in the time of Jesus, cf. the standard dictionaries and commentaries. They are mentioned by name ten more times in Mark (2 : 18, 24, 3 : 6, 7 : 1, 3, 5, 8 : 11, 15, 10 : 2, 12 : 13).

hoti 'why?': although some take *hoti* here as recitative, introducing a direct statement (Souter, ASV, Manson, Weymouth, Synodale), the great majority of commentators and translators take it to be interrogative (cf. Turner *Journal of Theological Studies* 27.58, 1925-6; Moule *Idiom Book,* 159).

Translation: *The scribes of the Pharisees* are 'the scribes who belong to the sect of the Pharisees' or 'the scribes who were Pharisees'. The scribes might be members of one of several different religious sects, of which the three most important were the Pharisees, Sadducees and Essenes.

The word *Pharisees* is derived by most scholars from a verb meaning 'to separate' (T. W. Manson, however, suggests it represents the Aramaic 'Persian'). These persons undertook to separate themselves from the Hellenistic influences which threatened Judaism during the times of the Maccabees. However, by the N.T. period the name had become almost entirely a proper name, and as such should be transliterated, rather than translated. It may, however, be useful in initial contexts to introduce a classifier such as 'sect' or 'religious group', in order to identify something of its significance.

To eat with...must in some languages be restated in terms of a different arrangement of constituents, e.g. 'Jesus and the sinners and the tax collectors were eating in the same place' (Loma).

The verbs for *eating* (and *drinking*) are often troublesome, for they may either require an object, which states what is eaten or drunk, or they may imply in their own form the type of food or drink which is consumed. For example, some languages have several words for 'eat', depending upon whether one eats meat, vegetables, roots, or fruit. Similar contrasts occur with words for 'drink'. When the terms are so specific as to make the context entirely too restricted in meaning, it may be better to use a more generic expression, e.g. 'to sit down at a meal with' or 'to gather with... at a meal' (or 'feast', for this was obviously a special occasion).

17 And when Jesus heard it, he said to them, "Those who are well have no need of a physician, but those who are sick; I came not to call the righteous, but sinners."

Text: After *hamartōlous* 'sinners' *Textus Receptus* adds *eis metanoian* 'to repentance' (assimilated from the parallel passage Lk. 5 : 32): all modern editions of the Greek text reject *eis metanoian.*

Exegesis: *autois* 'to them': that is, to those who asked the question.

chreian (2:25, 11:3, 14:63) 'need', 'necessity': *echein chreian* means 'be in need', 'lack something' (cf. Arndt & Gingrich).

iatrou (5:26) 'of a physician'.

hoi ischuontes 'those who are strong', 'those who are healthy': the verb *ischuō* 'be strong', 'be able' occurs further in 5:4, 9:18, 14:37. In contrast, in this verse, with *hoi kakōs echontes* (cf. 1:32) 'those who are ill', *hoi ischuontes* are 'those who are well', 'those who are in good health'.

ēlthon 'I came': the meaning here is more than merely local and temporal (cf. the same use of the verb in 10:45). There is reference here to the whole mission and purpose of Jesus' ministry (whether or not we understand, with Lagrange, that 'I came' means 'I came *into the world*' with a reference to his preexistence).

kalesai 'call': the word in this passage carries theological content, and does not mean 'invite to eat' (cf. 1:20 see Arndt & Gingrich 2).

dikaious...hamartōlous 'righteous...sinners': the words reflect the attitude of the Pharisees toward themselves (cf. Lk. 16:15) and others (cf. John 7:49). There is, perhaps, a tinge of irony in Jesus' use of these words (cf. Rawlinson).

Translation: *Heard it* may be in some languages best translated as 'heard what they said', in order to make the reference precise.

To them, referring to the scribes, must often be made quite explicit, for there are three other intervening third person plural referents: the sinners, the tax collectors, and the disciples.

Well is often 'strong', 'healthy' or just 'not sick'.

To have no need may be variously rendered: 'do not go looking for' (Subanen), 'do not have to consult' (Barrow Eskimo), 'do not go in search of a physician' (Bare'e).

Physician should be translated by a respectful term applied to the medical profession. This may be either the word used for the foreign mission doctor (if there is a special usage applied to this type of person) or the name of the indigenous medicine man, who may not be highly regarded by foreigners but who may enjoy a great deal more prestige among the local people than a translator may suspect.

The extent of ellipsis which may be employed in translating the clause *but those who are sick* depends upon the syntactic requirements of the receptor language. In some instances the full form must be given, 'but those who are sick need a doctor'.

In order that *came* may mean more than simply 'to come to this banquet', it may be useful to employ the most generic expression possible, which would also be used in phrases referring to 'the coming of the Lord'. This would then permit this phrase to express more of its theological content.

There is a tendency to translate *righteous* merely as 'the good ones'. This may be all that can be done in some languages, but wherever possible it is advantageous to attempt to find some word which will indicate more of the idea of conformity to standard, so that a differentiation may be made between 'good' and 'righteous'. On the other hand, it is not advisable to translate *righteous* as 'to have no sin', for this involves many theological problems which are better not introduced in such a general word as 'righteous'.

The most common expression for *righteous* involves the concept of 'straightness', though this may be expressed in a number of ways: 'to be straight' (Bambara, Black Bobo, Chokwe, Ifugao, Chol, Maninka, South Toradja, Bare'e, Toba Batak), 'to follow the straight way', 'to straight-straight', a reduplicated form (Kabba-Laka), and 'to have a straight heart' (Zacapoastla Aztec, Kekchi). Some languages imply conformity to truth, e.g. 'to do the truth' (Kipsigis), 'to do according to the truth' (Mesquital Otomí), and 'to have truth' (Mazatec). The sense of obligation is highlighted in other instances, e.g. 'to fulfill what one should do' (Piro), 'people who are true' (Indonesian), 'to do just so' (Navajo), and 'to do as it should be' (Anuak). In some languages, of course, certain highly figurative expressions are used, e.g. 'to have a white stomach' (Moré).

In Nuer there is a complex concept of 'right' vs. 'left', in which 'right' indicates that which is masculine, strong, good, and moral, and 'left' denotes what is feminine, weak, and sinful (a strictly masculine viewpoint!) The 'way of right' is therefore *righteousness*, but of course women may also attain this way, for the opposition is more classificatory than descriptive.

But sinners may need expansion into its fuller implied form, i.e. 'but I came to call sinners'.

If the translation in question must follow a text having *to repentance*, see 1:4 for comments on the lexical problems involved in *repentance*. The syntactic problems often require an expansion, e.g. 'call sinners so that they would change their hearts'.

18 *Now John's disciples and the Pharisees were fasting; and people came and said to him, "Why do John's disciples and the disciples of the Pharisees fast, but your disciples do not fast?"*

Text: Instead of *hoi Pharisaioi* 'the Pharisees' of most modern editions of the Greek text, *Textus Receptus* has *hoi tōn Pharisaiōn* 'the (disciples) of the Pharisees' (with slight difference, Soden has this reading also).

Exegesis: *ēsan...nēsteuontes* 'they were...fasting': the meaning is *not*, as AV has it, 'used to fast'; rather it is a historical reference to fasting that was then going on. It is impossible to determine the occasion of this particular fast.

nēsteuō (2:19, 20) 'to fast (as a religious practice)'. The Mosaic Law required only one day of fasting, the Day of Atonement (Lev. 16:29) but the Pharisees, in addition, fasted twice a week (cf. Lk. 18:12), on Mondays and Thursdays (cf. Richardson *Word Book*, article "Fast").

hoi mathētai Iōannou (6:29) 'the disciples of John (the Baptist)'.

erchontai 'they come': here, clearly, an impersonal plural (cf. Turner *Journal of Theological Studies*, 25.379, 1923-4). The meaning is not that 'the disciples of John and the Pharisees' came to Jesus and asked him something, but that 'men came', 'people came' (the parallels Mt. 9:14 and Lk 5:33 understand it differently): cf. BFBS, Manson, Moffatt; Zürich *die Leute*; Brazilian *alguns*.

hoi mathētai tōn Pharisaiōn 'the disciples of the Pharisees': this phrase appears only here in the N.T.

Translation: In order that the temporal setting of the first clause may be properly identified (to the extent that it is equivalent to what is implied in the Greek imperfect), one may translate 'at that time...were fasting'.

For *disciples* see 2:15.

Fasting as an act of religious observance is relatively uncommon in the world. On the other hand, religious feasting is quite common, and hence to speak of going without food as a kind of religious observance often strikes the reader as strange, if not incomprehensible. There is a rather widespread custom of abstaining from food as a symbol that one is angry or distressed about something (e.g. the fasts of Ghandi) or is determined to prove the justice of one's cause (hunger strikes in prisons), but in such situations the hunger is supposed to impress people to such an extent that the provoking circumstances will be altered. On the other hand, the fasting of the Scriptures involves a kind of religious abstention from food designed to stimulate greater piety or gain more merit, concepts which are quite alien to most people's concepts of fasting. It is for this reason that expressions for fasting must in some languages be expanded so that they will be contextually conditioned. For example, to say 'not to eat' would mean little or nothing in Navajo. It might be that there was no food in the house or that the persons in question were so ill that they could not eat. Accordingly, one must say 'to put food away reverently' (that is, with religious intent). Similarly in Cakchiquel one says 'to cause oneself not to eat', that is, to abstain from it purposely.

Frequently *said to him* must be changed to 'questioned him...', for what follows is not a statement, but a question. Close attention to these matters must be given in many languages.

19 And Jesus said to them, "Can the wedding guests fast while the bridegroom is with them? As long as they have the bridegroom with them, they cannot fast.

Exegesis: *mē dunantai...*: 'are they able...?': the implied answer to this form of the question in Greek is negative, 'No!'

hoi huioi tou numphōnos: literally 'the sons of the chamber of the bridegroom': the Greek form of the Semitic idiom *benei ha-ḥepah* (cf. Koehler: *ḥepah* 'chamber of bridegroom'). Commentators are divided over whether the word means, generally, 'wedding guests' (RSV, Weymouth, Berkeley, Torrey, Manson; cf. Vincent *Word Studies* I, 172), or, in a more restricted sense, 'the bridegroom's attendants' (Arndt & Gingrich; cf. Abbott-Smith: "the bridegroom's friends who have charge of the nuptial arrangements"), 'groomsmen' (cf. Turner, BFBS, Knox, Synodale).

For other examples of the Semitic idiom 'sons of...' see 3:17; Mt. 23:15, Lk. 10:6, 16:8, 20:34, 36.

en hō 'in (the time) which', 'during the time', 'while'.

hoson chronon 'so long a time (as)': the accusative case is used to express duration of time.

hosos (12 more times in Mark) 'as long', 'how long' (cf. Arndt & Gingrich).

chronos (9:21) 'time'.

Translation: *Said* must in some languages be 'asked' (e.g. Trique).

There are few languages in which the idiom *sons of the bridechamber* can be reproduced literally. In fact, in some languages it implies the illegitimate children of the couple and in others a crude reference to the consummation of the marriage. One must therefore generally adopt an expression meaning 'wedding guests' or 'friends of the bridegroom', and for either of these terms there are usually very satisfactory equivalents (cf. Bare'e 'those who accompany the bridegroom on the way to the bride's house'). In a number of cultures the second meaning is particularly acceptable since there are customs closely paralleling the wedding practices of N.T. times.

The Greek form of the verse implies a negative reply, hence, 'the wedding guests cannot fast can they...' Many languages clearly distinguish between questions implying positive or negative replies, and accordingly, this subtle, but important, distinction in the Greek should be indicated. (The RSV tends to overlook such distinctions.)

In asking the question as to fasting during the time that the bridegroom is with the wedding guests, the real problem is not whether the guests can, but whether they would want to fast. However, the form of the question occurs with *can*, for this makes the question all the more forceful, and hence the assumed inability to fast should, if possible, be clearly noted.

20 ***The days will come, when the bridegroom is taken away from them, and then they will fast in that day.***

Exegesis: *hotan aparthē* 'when he is taken away': the subjunctive mode of the verb is required by the sentence construction; its meaning, however, is not 'when he *may be* taken away', as though doubt were expressed, but, simply, 'when he *is* taken away', a statement of future fact.

apairō (the word occurs only here and parallel passages Mt. 9:15, Lk. 5:35, in the N.T.) 'take away', 'remove': the verb, as such, does not state whether the removal is natural, or sudden and violent. The context of the whole saying, however, implies a violent removal which will provoke sorrow (cf. the use of the verb in the LXX Isa. 53:8).

nēsteusousin 'they will fast': a declaration of what will happen in the future, not a command.

Translation: In place of *the days* some languages employ 'the day' as an expression of indefinite temporal reference (Ifugao). One may, of course, also translate 'the time will come'.

Is taken away may in some languages be paralleled by 'is caused to go away' or 'is led away', since objects may 'be taken' but people are either 'caused to go' or 'are led'.

21 *No one sews a piece of unshrunk cloth on an old garment; if he does, the patch tears away from it, the new from the old, and a worse tear is made.*

Text: Instead of *ap' autou* 'from it' of most modern editions of the Greek text, *Textus Receptus* has *autou* 'of it' (with considerable change in syntax and meaning; instead of RSV, above, the *Textus Receptus* would be translated 'its new patch takes away from the old'); Kilpatrick changes the word order to *airei ap' autou to plērōma to kainon apo tou palaiou* "the new patch takes away some of the old cloth" (BFBS).

Exegesis: *epiblēma* (only here in Mark) literally 'something placed upon', i.e. 'a cover', 'a patch' (cf. Abbott-Smith).

rakous agnaphou 'of unshrunk cloth'.

rakos (only here and in Mt. 9:16 in the N.T.) 'a rag', 'remnant', 'piece of cloth' (cf. Moulton & Milligan).

agnaphos (only here and in Mt. 9:16 in the N.T.) 'unshrunk', 'uncarded', 'not fulled' (i.e. not treated by the *gnapheus* 'the fuller'): the new, unbleached cloth would shrink considerably with the first washing. Moulton & Milligan quote a papyrus which refers to *kitōna agnaphon leukon* 'a new white shirt'.

epiraptei (only here in N.T.) 'sews on', 'sews upon'.

himation palaion 'old garment'.

himation (5:27,28,30, 6:56, 9:3, 10:50, 11:7,8, 13:16, 15:20, 24) 'cloak', 'garment', 'clothes' (in the plural): as distinguished from the inner garment *chitōn* (6:9, 14:63) 'tunic', the *himation* is 'mantle', 'cloak'; when used generally, as here, it means simply 'garment'.

palaion (2:22) 'old': not simply with reference to time, but to usage, 'worn' by use.

ei de mē 'but if not', 'otherwise': these words (actually a negative clause) negate the (negative) statement 'no one sews' and therefore have an affirmative meaning: 'but should he (*contrary to* the statement) sew...'

airei to plērōma ap' autou to kainon tou palaiou 'the fullness takes (away) from it, the new from the old': most translations give some such meaning as this to these words, the last four words *to kainon tou palaiou* 'the new from the old' standing as an additional explanation of the first clause.

airō 'take away', 'remove': the verb requires a direct object and in this verse it will be something like 'takes away *some* (of the old garment)', removes *part* (of the old)'; cf. BFBS "the new patch takes away some of the old cloth"; RSV "tears away" (meaning 'comes loose', 'tears off'), is not supported by usage of the Greek verb *airō* (cf. Arndt & Gingrich 4).

to plērōma (6:43, 8:20) 'that which fills' in the sense of a supplement, a complement (here obviously equivalent to *epiblēma* 'a patch' of the previous clause). As the subject of *airei* 'removes' the word is in the nominative case, being translated 'the patch removes (part)...'

ap' autou 'from it', i.e. from the old garment.

to kainon tou palaiou 'the new (patch) from the old (garment)': an additional clause which explains the previous one.

kai cheiron schisma ginetai 'and a worse tear results'.

cheiron 'worse': the comparative form of *kakos* 'bad'; here 'worse' than the original tear the patch was supposed to mend.

schisma (only here in Mark) 'tear', 'crack', 'rent' (cf. the verb *schizō* 'to tear' in 1:10).

ginetai 'takes place', 'happens', 'results': for this use of the verb see Arndt & Gingrich I.1.b.β.

For another possible translation of the text cf. *Expository Times*, 60.26f., 1944. The meaning of the text as it stands is accurately conveyed by RSV (with exception of *airei* 'removes' as seen above); cf. BFBS: "No one sews a piece of unshrunken cloth on to an old garment, otherwise the new patch takes away some of the old cloth, and the rent becomes worse."

Translation: The basic difficulty of this verse in many languages is that it poses a seemingly insurmountable problem in intelligibility for the reader, not by virtue of any words used but because of the idea expressed, something which is so entirely contrary to what happens in so many parts of the world. The idea that one would even hesitate to sew a new, unshrunk piece of cloth on an old garment seems almost incredible to many people, for as one may observe in many regions of the world there are garments so patched that it is not always easy (in fact, at times very difficult) to determine what was the cloth of the original garment. Nevertheless, despite the problems of understanding, as posed by the cultural diversities, the only thing which we may do is to translate, leaving the matter of cultural discrepancies to explanation, whether oral or written.

The use of *no one* is a means of introducing a generic negative. However, in some languages, the equivalent is 'we (incl.) do not...' (Trique), 'you do not...' (Tzeltal), 'people do not...', or 'they do not...'

Unshrunk may be translated as 'unwashed' (Ifugao, Subanen) or 'entirely new' (Barrow Eskimo, Indonesian, Javanese). Most people are well aware of the effects of cloth which has not been shrunk by the process of washing, and hence there is generally little difficulty at this point. The best way to find the appropriate vocabulary is to spend time observing proficient seamstresses, and finding out how they would describe such processes as sewing, ripping, shrinking, etc.

If he does may in some instances require expansion, e.g. 'if one does sew on such a patch'. (Note the generic English pronoun *he*, a purely grammatical relationship.)

The *patch* may be variously rendered, depending upon the degree of description required or the usage of the receptor language, e.g. 'the cloth that was sewn on', 'the small piece of cloth', or 'the cloth that was added'. It is 'this new cloth which tears away some of the cloth of the old garment, thus making the hole bigger' (Barrow Eskimo).

22 And no one puts new wine into old wineskins; if he does, the wine will burst the skins, and the wine is lost, and so are the skins; but new wine is for fresh skins."

Text: After (second) *ho oinos* 'the wine' *Textus Receptus* adds *ho neos* 'new': all modern editions of the Greek text reject this addition.

Instead of *kai ho oinos apollutai kai hoi askoi* 'and the wine is lost and the skins also' of all modern editions of the Greek text, *Textus Receptus* (from the parallels Mt. 9:17, Lk. 5:37) has *kai ho oinos ekcheitai kai hoi askoi apolountai* 'and the wine is poured out and the wineskins are ruined'.

After the last words *askous kainous* 'fresh skins' *Textus Receptus* adds *blēteon* (from the parallel Lk. 5:38) 'must be put': all modern editions of the Greek text reject this addition.

Exegesis: *ballei* (some 17 times in Mark) here in the sense of 'place', 'put', 'pour' (cf. Arndt & Gingrich 2.b): Moulton & Milligan illustrate from the papyri this unemphatic use of the verb.

oinon neon 'new wine', i.e. still fermenting. On *neos* 'new' as distinguished from *kainos* 'new' see 1:27 and reff.

askous palaious 'old wineskins' (AV 'bottles' is quite misleading today).

askos 'a leather bag', particularly a wineskin (cf. Arndt & Gingrich).

palaios 'old' has here the same meaning as in the previous verse; an "old wineskin" is one which has long been used and lost its elasticity, being unable to expand with the fermenting wine.

rēxei (cf. 9:18) 'will burst', 'will tear', 'will break'.

kai ho oinos...kai hoi askoi 'and the wine...and the skins': this construction in Greek is translated '*both* the wine...*and* the skins'.

apollutai (cf. 1:24) 'is lost', 'is destroyed', 'is ruined'.

eis 'into': instead of RSV "new wine *is for* fresh skins", it is probably better to translate 'new wine (*is to be poured*) into fresh skins'.

Translation: The generic negative expression used to introduce verse 21 should also be used in the parallel construction in verse 22.

In the selection of a term for *wine* in this passage it is essential that in so far as possible the concept of fermentation be present or at least understandable in the context. For that reason, for example, most translations in central Africa have used the local equivalent of palm wine, in which the processes of fermentation are well-known. Some missionaries have, however, insisted on the use of a borrowed word which would be more likely to relate the meaning to the foreign product, which may be known but rarely consumed by the local population, e.g. 'drink called vin' (or 'wain' or 'vino', depending upon the source of the borrowing). There may be special reasons for the choice of a nonindigenous term for wine in other contexts, but for this particular passage it would seem that a well-known local product would be considerably more meaningful than any foreign one. *New wine* may be rendered as 'wine beginning to ferment'.

Wineskins are variously described as 'leather containers for wine' (Subanen), 'bottle-like objects made of leather for wine', 'animal skins used as containers for wine', and 'animal skins into which wine is poured, to be kept'. South Toradja uses a loan word; Bare'e has 'goat-skin', and Javanese 'bladder (of an ox)'.

Old in this context should refer to 'used' or 'worn out'.

As may be required, the ellipsis in *if he does* may be expanded (see verse 2 : 21).

In some languages different verbs must be used to describe what happens to the wine and the skins. For example, 'the wine runs out and the skins are ruined' or 'the wine is lost and the skins are made useless'.

The last clause may be translated as 'fermenting wine should be put into new skin containers'.

23 *One sabbath he was going through the grainfields; and as they made their way his disciples began to pluck ears of grain.*

Text: Instead of *paraporeuesthai* 'go along' of most modern editions of the Greek text, *Textus Receptus*, Souter, and Westcott and Hort prefer *diaporeuesthai* 'go through'.

Exegesis: *kai egeneto...paraporeuesthai* 'and it happened...(that he) went along': for this Semitic construction see 1 : 9.

en tois sabbasin 'on the sabbath day' (on the use of the plural cf. 1 : 21).

paraporeuesthai dia tōn sporimōn 'to go along through the grain fields': the subject, of course, is *auton* 'he' (it is understood that the disciples were accompanying him).

paraporeuomai (9 : 30, 11 : 20, 15 : 29) 'go by', 'pass by'; plus *dia* 'through', it means 'go through'.

sporimos (only here in Mark) is an adjective 'sown', 'fit for sowing'; as a plural substantive *ta sporima* means here 'grain fields', 'standing grain' (cf. Arndt & Gingrich). It is to be noticed that 'cornfield' of AV, ERV and BFBS is not what American 'corn' (i.e. maize) is: the grain referred to is wheat or barley; see Goodspeed *Problems*, 55f.

ērxanto hodon poiein tillontes 'they began to make way plucking': it is agreed that *hodon poiein* means what in classical Greek would be *hodon poieisthai* 'journey', 'go along' (cf. Latin *iter facere*), and does *not* mean 'make a road' (for the same use of this idiom see LXX Judges 17 : 8). The words *hodon poiein*, therefore, are to be translated 'as they went' (ASV, BFBS, Manson, Weymouth): cf. Field *Notes*, 25; Vincent *Word Studies* I, 172f. The disciples were going along a regular path through the wheat fields (cf. Rawlinson).

ērxanto...tillontes 'they began...plucking': according to rules of grammar *ērxanto* 'they began' should go with *hodon poiein* 'to make (their) way'; it is generally agreed, however, that here the meaning is rather 'they began plucking' (cf. Lagrange, Taylor). As Gould says, there is not actually much difference between 'they began to go along, plucking the ears' and 'they began, going along, to pluck'. *tillō* 'pluck', 'pull off' is found only here in Mark.

tous stachuas (4:28) 'the ears (or, heads) of grain' (i.e. wheat).

Translation: Since the last specific previous reference to Jesus is in verse 19, and there are several intervening third person singular referents, it is often necessary to employ 'Jesus' as the subject of the first clause.

For *sabbath* see 1:21.

It is quite evident that Jesus was going along with his disciples, and that they were not walking out through a grainfield, but along a path. However, in order that the reader may properly understand the obvious intent of the Greek text, it is sometimes necessary to regroup the subject constituents, e.g. 'Jesus and his disciples were going along a path through the grainfields' (Ifugao).

The grainfields refer to fields of wheat. In some parts of the world there is practically no equivalent, and hence 'corn' (in the meaning of 'Indian corn' or 'maize') is used, even though the particular activities are in such instances not accurately represented. In some languages the wheat is described as 'ricelike grain' (Kiyaka) or 'millet-like grain' (Gurunse), and in other languages it may have some special designation, e.g. 'Mexican grain' vs. 'Indian grain', that is to say, wheat vs. maize (Tzeltal), and 'field for grain for flour' (Barrow Eskimo, in which there is a perfectly good word for wheat 'flour', but no knowledge of wheat as a grain).

Ears of grain must in some languages be variously rendered as 'stalks of seeds', 'heads of grain', 'clusters of seeds', or 'fruit of seeds'.

Note that though Jesus and the disciples were walking together, only the disciples are described as plucking off the heads of grain. The question of the Pharisees, however, is directed only to Jesus.

24 And the Pharisees said to him, "Look, why are they doing what is not lawful on the sabbath?"

Exegesis: *hoi Pharisaioi* 'the Pharisees': cf. 2:16.

ide (3:34, 11:21, 13:1,21, 15:4,35, 16:6) 'look!', 'see!': no longer strictly an imperative of the verb but an interjection (cf. *hora* 'see' in 1:44).

ti...; 'why...?': again a rhetorical question (cf. 2:7): this is not a request for information, but is an accusation of wrong doing (cf. Black *Aramaic*, 88). Cf. Moffatt: "Look at what...! That is not allowed."

ho ouk exestin 'that which is not lawful': i.e. reaping, which the Mosaic law prohibited on the sabbath (cf. Ex. 34:21). It is to be noticed that the disciples are not accused of stealing or plundering someone

97

else's field; the charge has to do with work prohibited on the sabbath.

exestin (2:26, 3:4, 6:18, 10:2, 12:14) 'it is lawful', 'it is permitted', 'it is proper' (an impersonal verb).

Translation: *Said* may need to be translated as 'asked', because of the interrogative fórm of the following.

They must be rendered in some languages more specifically as 'your disciples'.

Not lawful is a somewhat complex idea, which in a number of languages must be translated in a more descriptive manner, e.g. 'what the law does not allow' (Mitla Zapotec), 'what the law says should not be done', 'what the law prohibits people from doing', or 'what the law says is bad', if specific reference is to be made to the 'law' as codified rules of behavior. Rather, however, than the 'law speaking' (which it cannot do in some languages), one can translate 'what people read in the law should not be done'. On the other hand, it is more satisfactory in some instances to translate 'what people should not do'(South Toradja has simply 'that which is not done'), without attempting to identify the codified form of the commandment, though the Greek text clearly implies a challenge to the authority of the Law.

25 And he said to them, "Have you never read what David did, when he was in need and was hungry, he and those who were with him: 26 how he entered the house of God, when Abiathar was high priest, and ate the bread of the Presence, which it is not lawful for any but the priests to eat, and also gave it to those who were with him?"

Text: *pōs* 'how' in v. 26 is omitted by Kilpatrick, but included by all other modern editions of the Greek text (Nestle and Westcott and Hort have it in brackets).

Exegesis: *oudepote anegnōte...*; 'have you never read...?': another rhetorical question. There is no doubt that they had read; the point is they are being accused of not having understood what they read (cf. Daube *New Testament and Rabbinic Judaism*, 433).

anaginōskō (12:10,26, 13:14) 'read', 'read aloud': the incident referred to is related in 1 Sam. 21:1-6.

chreian eschen (cf. 2:17) 'he had need', 'he had necessity'.

epeinasen (11:12) 'he got hungry' (to be distinguished from *nēsteuō* 'fast'; cf. 2:18).

hoi met' autou 'those with him', 'his companions' (cf. 1:36).

pōs 'how?': in omitting this interrogative, BFBS places the question mark at the end of v. 25 and makes of v. 26 a statement; in including *pōs* 'how?' the other editions of the Greek text extend the question to the end of v. 26 (as does RSV).

ton oikon tou theou 'the house of God': in the time of David, of course, it was the Tabernacle (not the Temple).

epi Abiathar archiereōs 'when Abiathar was high priest'.

epi 'upon' with the genitive here indicates time: 'in the time of', 'under' (cf. Lk. 3:2, Acts 11:28); see Arndt & Gingrich I.2.

Abiathar 'Abiathar': for the problem involved in the fact that the high priest was actually Ahimelech, the father of Abiathar (cf. 1 Sam. 21:1, 22:20), see the commentaries. It has been suggested (*Journal of Theological Studies* NS 1.156, 1950) that the phrase here employed, like *epi tou batou* 'in the passage about the bush' in 12:26 (which see), means 'at the passage of Scripture concerning (or, entitled) Abiathar the High Priest'. The suggestion, however, is none too convincing (cf. *Journal of Theological Studies* NS 2.44-45, 1951, and see also Lagrange).

archiereus 'high priest' (the singular is found further in 14:47,53, 54,60,61,63,66; the plural *hoi archiereis* 'the chief priests' occurs 14 times in Mark: see 8:31).

tous artous tēs protheseōs literally 'the loaves of the presentation': a translation of *lehem ha-panim* 'bread of the face (of God)' (see Lev. 24:5-9 for instructions concerning the twelve loaves laid on tables before God every week by the priests). For the Greek phrase see LXX Lev. 24:8. In keeping with the meaning and purpose of these loaves, the accurate translation is 'bread of the Presence (of God)' (RSV, BFBS).

hous ouk exestin phagein ei mē tous hiereis 'which (bread) it is not lawful (for anyone) to eat except the priests': though a rather awkward construction, the meaning is clear.

kai edōken kai tois sun autō ousin 'and he gave it also to those who were with him'.

kai (the second one) means here 'also', 'furthermore', 'in addition'.

tois sun autō ousin 'to his companions' (the meaning is the same as that of *hoi met' autou* of v. 25).

Translation: *Said* is in this verse more specifically 'answered' or 'asked', depending upon the requirements of the context as specified in a receptor language.

In some languages there are special forms of questions which are essentially rhetorical, i.e. asking not for the sake of the information communicated but asked to make a point in the very asking. Since this question directed to the Pharisees by Jesus is so obviously rhetorical—the Pharisees had read the Scriptures many times but had not taken them to heart—it may be essential to give the sentence a special form characteristic of such questions.

Because of the unusual placement of the appositional double subject *he and those who were with him* after the principal subject *David* (and separated from the latter by an intervening clause), it is often necessary to regroup the constituents as follows: 'what David did when he and those who were with him were in need and were hungry' (Ifugao).

To be in need may be translated as 'had nothing', or in some instances as 'were in difficulty'.

Because of the syntactic awkwardness of continuing the question with the beginning of verse 26, thus making two clauses dependent upon *read*:

namely, 'What David did...' and 'how he entered...', it is sometimes preferable to begin verse 26 as a statement, 'he entered...'

One should use 'house of God', despite the fact that this may have been selected as a term for the temple rather than for the tabernacle. In some languages, however, it is 'the house for God' rather than 'God's house', which could refer only to heaven.

High in the phrase *high priest* is generally translatable as 'the biggest', 'the strongest', 'the most important', or 'the chief'. Rarely does elevation, i.e. literally 'high', come into the figure.

Bread of the Presence involves two principal problems: (1) the traditional translation as 'showbread', which would give rise to translations meaning 'bread which was displayed', 'bread put out to be seen', or 'bread laid out' (Tzeltal) and (2) the problems of rendering *presence*, without specifying whose presence is involved. The meaning in this latter type of phrase is that the bread was displayed before the presence of God, in which case the word 'Presence' would signify God Himself. In so many languages, however, it is quite impossible to talk about 'presence' without stipulating whose presence one is referring to, a problem not only presented by the semantic character of the phrase but by the very syntactic relationships of words, e.g. 'presence' is often either a verb which must have a subject or a noun which demands an actor possessor. In either case, therefore, 'God' would have to be specified. In some languages, accordingly, the closest equivalent of *bread of the Presence* would be 'bread set before God' or 'bread set before the face of God' (Luvale); 'loaves which are laid before the face (of God)' (South Toradja).

It is not lawful for any but involves a double negative, reproduced in some languages as 'only the priests could eat'.

It is essential that the last clause be fully reproduced in any translation, for so much of the meaning is attached to the fact that David gave to those with him, a specific parallel to what Jesus was doing in permitting his disciples to do what was forbidden on the Sabbath.

27 And he said to them, "The sabbath was made for man, not man for the sabbath; 28 so the Son of man is lord even of the sabbath."

Exegesis: *dia ton anthrōpon* 'on account of man', 'for the sake of man': the preposition *dia* indicates here the reason for the institution of the sabbath (cf. Arndt & Gingrich B.II.1; Moule *Idiom Book*, 55).

egeneto 'became', i.e. 'was made', 'was established' (for this use of *ginomai* 'become' see Arndt & Gingrich I.2.a).

hōste (with the indicative, 10:8) 'therefore', 'consequently', 'so', 'accordingly' (cf. Moule *Idiom Book*, 144; for *hōste* with the infinitive see 1:27).

kurios 'lord', 'owner', 'ruler', 'master' (cf. Arndt & Gingrich II.1. a.α).

ho huios tou anthrōpou 'the Son of man' (cf. 2:10).

kai tou sabbatou 'even of the sabbath' (for this use of *kai* 'and' see

1 : 27); the meaning could possibly be *'also* (i.e. in addition to being lord of other things) of the sabbath': most translations and commentators, however, prefer the first meaning.

Translation: Since Jesus is not only the one who asked the question beginning in verse 25, but who also made the statement in this and the succeeding verse, it is sometimes necessary to make this relationship explicit, frequently by repeating the noun subject, i.e. 'Jesus'. *Them* refers to the Pharisees and may be translated as such if there is danger of any other intervening third person plural referent being understood.

Such aphoristic expressions as occur in this verse are almost always difficult to translate because of (1) their shortness (much is left implicit), (2) the double meanings of words involved (it is one thing to speak of man being 'made', but for 'a sabbath to be made' is often quite a different matter), and (3) the somewhat tenuous relationship to the context. In this instance the context assists materially in the understanding of the passage, but this is not always true, and even in this instance what is evident to the translator may not be equally clear to the reader.

For *sabbath* see 1 : 21.

In many languages one must use different verbs in speaking of instituting the sabbath and of creating man (in Greek and in English the verb 'to make' serves quite well). For example, in some instances one must say 'the sabbath was set aside' (or 'ordained', 'commanded'), or if an active rather than passive expression is required 'God ordered the day of rest for the sake of people; he created people, but not just in order that they could keep the laws of the rest day'. This expansion involves several matters: (1) the need of employing a fully generic term for *man* (in English and Greek we may use a singular for a generic, but in many languages a plural is necessary for the same meaning), (2) the necessity of placing a negative with the element negativized (e.g. one cannot say in some languages 'he did not create men for the sabbath', for by placing the negative particle with the verb one would imply a negation of creation; the negative must go properly with the negativized element, namely, the purpose), and (3) the lack of parallelism in (a) the principal verbs ('ordered' and 'created') and (b) the expressions of 'for', since something done for a person often requires quite a different type of expression than the fact of a person existing for the sake of a particular institution. This means that one must employ quite different descriptions of the relationships between the individuals and the institutions, depending upon the so-called actor-goal relationship. The complex relationships are expressed in a temporal context in Trique 'God first made people, then the day of rest for the sake of people; he did not first make the day of rest and then make people for the day of rest'. The relationship between the sabbath and man is defined somewhat more explicitly in Mazahua as 'the day of rest was made to help people; people were not created to help the day of rest'; Toba Batak 'the sabbath was instituted for man; man has not been formed for the sabbath'.

For *Son of man* see 2 : 10.

Because of the third person reference to himself in this passage, it may be necessary to specify the relationship between the speaker and the subject by saying 'I, the Son of man' (cf. 2 : 10).

Lord of ... is equivalent to 'has the right to command' (Huave) or 'has control over' (Tarahumara), or 'says what should be done on the rest day' (Huastec).

CHAPTER THREE

1 *Again he entered the synagogue, and a man was there who had a withered hand.*

Exegesis: *palin* 'again': refers back to 1:21.

eis sunagōgēn 'into a synagogue': the exact shade of meaning would be akin to the idiom in English "he went to church" (cf. Taylor); Lagrange translates *en synagogue*.

anthrōpos...echōn 'a man...having' i.e. 'a man who had'.

exērammenēn...tēn cheira 'withered...the hand': the definite article *tēn* 'the' is customary with parts of the body, and means 'his hand' (cf. 1:41).

xēraino (4:6, 5:29, 9:18, 11:20,21) 'dry up', 'wither': what is indicated is a stiffness, an inability to use the hand (cf. Arndt & Gingrich). It is an overrefinement to see in the use of the perfect passive participle an indication that the paralysis of the hand was due to an accident, rather than being congenital (as do Swete, Vincent).

Translation: For *synagogue* see 1:21.

Withered, which is in itself a figurative expression, corresponds to different types of figurative and descriptive terms, e.g. 'dead hand' (Ifugao, Subanen, Gurunse), 'a weak hanging-down hand' (South Toradja), 'a crooked-grown hand' (Javanese), 'dried up hand' (Black Bobo), 'stiff hand', 'a hand which could not be moved', and 'a hand without flesh' (Shipibo).

Languages differ considerably in the divisions of human anatomy. For example, one term may include only the hand, and not the wrist, but in another language a word for the hand may include the entire forearm, or even the arm as a whole. In other instances the palm of the hand is distinguished from the fingers. The Greek term may itself even include the entire arm, but probably in this context the best correspondence is what we would understand by hand, wrist, and possibly forearm, since the 'withering' often includes the entire portion.

2 *And they watched him, to see whether he would heal him on the sabbath, so that they might accuse him.*

Exegesis: *paretēroun* (only here in Mark) 'they were watching': it is not necessary to suppose with Turner (*Journal of Theological Studies*, 25.379, 1923-4) that this is an impersonal plural 'people were watching'. The context indicates that it was the adversaries of Jesus who were watching, identified as the Pharisees in v. 6.

paratēreō 'watch closely', 'observe with care': when used in a hostile sense, as here, it means 'lie in wait for' (cf. Arndt & Gingrich). Moulton

& Milligan quote an example of the word in the papyri in the sense of keeping a careful watch over criminals.

ei...therapeusei 'if...he shall heal': the future tense is used from the point of view of the spectators. Though the use of the future tense of the verb in such a construction as this is rare, it is perfectly correct (cf. Lagrange).

ei 'if': here it is used as an interrogative particle, in an indirect question, 'whether'. In direct form, it would be: 'Will he heal?' For this use of *ei* cf. Arndt & Gingrich V.2.a.

hina katēgorēsōsin autou 'in order that they might accuse him'.

hina 'in order that' goes back to *pareteroun*: 'They were watching him...in order that...'

katēgoreō (15: 3, 4) 'accuse', 'bring charge against': a technical term meaning to bring charge in court against someone.

Translation: *They* (identified specifically as Pharisees in verse 6) may probably be best rendered as 'the people there', for no doubt more than just the Pharisees were intent to see what Jesus would do, since they would be acquainted with his fame as a healer and his reputed defiance of certain Sabbath traditions.

The succession of pronouns *him, he, him,* may require some clarification in languages which do not have the same system of pronominal reference as Greek, e.g. 'the people watched Jesus in order to see whether he would heal the man on the sabbath'.

Verbs for *healing* are not infrequently quite specific in their area of reference, e.g. internal disorders vs. external ones, sores vs. dislocations, organs of movement vs. those of sense, etc.

Accuse may be translated simply as 'to say that he had done wrong'.

3 And he said to the man who had the withered hand, "Come here."

Exegesis: *xēran* (only here in Mark) 'dried up', 'withered', 'immobile' (the same meaning as *exērammenēn* in v. 1).

egeire eis to meson 'rise (and stand) in the middle' (cf. Lk. 6:8).

to meson as a noun means 'the middle', 'the center', meaning 'in the sight of all': cf. Manson "stand up where everybody can see you"; Synodale *Lève-toi et tiens-toi au milieu de nous.* RSV "come here" is not completely accurate, while BFBS "stand in the middle" may be misleading. Better, "Rise and come forward" (Moffatt; cf. Goodspeed, Weymouth). Cf. *eis meson* 'in the midst', 14:60.

egeire (cf. 1:31) 'rise', 'get up'.

4 And he said to them, "Is it lawful on the sabbath to do good or to do harm, to save life or to kill?" But they were silent.

Exegesis: *exestin* (cf. 2:24) 'it is lawful'. As in 2:24 the standard of reference is the Mosaic Law.

agathon poiēsai ē kakopoiēsai 'to do good or to do bad': it is debated whether the verbs are to be understood in a moral sense 'do right...do wrong' or in the sense of assistance 'to help...to harm'. Hatch (*Essays*, 7) contends that Biblical usage favors the second meaning. AV, BFBS, Weymouth, Manson, have 'to do evil'; ASV, RSV, Knox, Moffatt, Torrey, translate 'to do harm'. The context, especially the words that follow, would seem to support the second meaning.

psuchēn sōsai ē apokteinai 'to save life or to kill'; these words further define what is meant by 'do good...do harm'.

psuchē (8:35,36,37, 10:45, 12:30, 14:34) 'life', 'soul', 'self': the various meanings of the word can be traced back to its use in the LXX (cf. Hatch *Essays*, 101-2). In Mark three general uses may be distinguished: (1) of earthly life itself, including the reflexive sense of 'oneself', 8:35a,b, 10:45, 14:34; (2) of the inner life of man, his feelings and emotions, 12:30 (possibly 14:34 should be included here); (3) of the life which transcends earthly existence, 8:36,37. The precise meaning of the word here is probably to be included in the first category in the sense of a living creature, person: 'to save a person's life or to destroy it?' (cf. Arndt & Gingrich; for *psuchē* as "person", "man" cf. Acts 27:37).

sōzō 'save': this word in Mark is used in the following senses: (1) 'rescue' (from death) 15:30,31, 'preserve' (life) 3:4, 8:35a, and in the passive, 'survive' 13:20; (2) 'heal', 'cure' 5:23, 28,34, 6:56, 10:52; (3) of 'salvation' in the theological sense, 8:35b (probably: cf. Arndt & Gingrich 3), 10:26, 13:13 (cf. Arndt & Gingrich 2.b), 16:16. In the present passage the word falls into the first category: "Is it better to preserve a man's life or destroy it?"

apokteinō (6:19, 8:31, 10:34, 12:5,7,8, 14:1) 'kill'.

hoi de esiōpōn 'but they were silent'.

siōpaō (4:39, 9:34, 10:48, 14:61) 'keep silence', 'be silent': the meaning here is best expressed by 'they remained silent'.

Translation: *Said* may be changed to 'asked' if the following question requires such an introductory verb.

Lawful in this context (as in verse 2:24) refers to 'what one should do' or 'what one is allowed to do' (hence, lawful). That is to say, 'On the Sabbath ought one to do good...', 'is it proper to do good...', 'is it allowable to do good...', or as in Tzeltal, 'on the rest day is it good for one...'

Some languages require objects of expressions such as 'to do good' and 'to do harm'. The logical grammatical objects would be persons, e.g. 'to do good for people or to do them harm'. The following clause is a further elaboration, and may need to be introduced by another main verb, 'is it proper to save a man's life or to kill him'.

5 *And he looked around at them with anger, grieved at their hardness of heart, and said to the man, "Stretch out your hand." He stretched it out, and his hand was restored.*

Text: At the end of the verse *Textus Receptus* adds *hugiēs hōs hē allē* 'sound as the other (hand)' (from the parallel passage Mt. 12:13): all modern editions of the Greek text omit this phrase.

Exegesis: *periblepsamenos* (3:34, 5:32, 9:8, 10:23, 11:11) 'looking around': the aorist participle indicates manner, and this verb is used in Mark (with the exception of 9:8 and 11:11) of Jesus' looking upon friends or enemies.

met' orgēs (only here in Mark) 'with anger', 'wrathfully'.

sullupoumenos (only here in the N.T.) 'grieved': in ordinary usage this compound verb means 'to grieve with (somebody)', 'to sympathize', and Lagrange and Swete suggest that here it indicates a mixture of grief with anger; most commentators, however, see here only a strengthened form of the simple verb 'deeply grieved' (cf. Arndt & Gingrich), or else the Greek equivalent of the Latin *contristare* 'grieve', 'mourn' (Moule *Idiom Book*, 192).

epi tē pōrōsei tēs kardias autōn 'at the hardness of their heart'.

epi 'at', 'because': for this use of *epi* see 1:22.

pōrōsis (only here in Mark) 'hardness': it is generally agreed that the word in the N.T. (also Rom. 11:25, Eph. 4:18) has the meaning of 'dullness', 'insensibility', 'insensitiveness', 'obstinacy' (J. A. Robinson *Ephesians*, 264-74: "obtuseness or intellectual blindness"), BFBS *Glossary*, Manson "stupidity", Moffatt "obstinacy".

kardia 'heart' (see 2:6 for the meaning of 'heart').

ekteinon 'you stretch out' (cf. 1:41).

apekatestathē (8:25, 9:12) 'it was restored', i.e. returned to its original soundness.

Translation: Since the clause *grieved at their hardness of heart* describes the reason for the anger, it must in some languages precede (Navajo). In all such instances, however, the proper antecedent of 'their' must be clearly evident.

Since *anger* has so many manifestations and seems to affect so many aspects of personality, it is not strange that expressions used to describe this emotional response are so varied: 'to be warm inside' (Trique), 'to have a cut heart' (Mende), 'to have a split heart' (Miskito), 'to have a hot heart' (Tzotzil), 'a swollen heart' (Moré), 'fire of the viscera' (Conob), 'pain in the heart' (San Blas), 'not with good eye' (Ecuadorean Quechua).

There are, of course, differing degrees of anger which may be indicated in various languages, but there is no reason to think that some relatively weak form of anger should be referred to here, just because Jesus is the subject of the sentence. This was genuine indignation and anger because of the callous disregard of the people for human welfare.

Since 'anger' is so often expressed as a process, it must be combined with the main verb of its clause as another related event, e.g. 'Jesus' heart was hot as he looked around' or 'as he looked around..., his heart was swollen'.

In this verse *grieve* is not to be associated with weeping or mourning for the dead (a common meaning of the term), but with the concept of deep emotional upheaval and disturbance, often described in very figurative language, e.g. 'his liver was ruined because of...' (Shilluk).

Hardness of heart is one idiom which in a great many languages must be replaced by quite different types of expressions. For one thing, 'hard heart' may have quite different meanings in other languages: 'brave' (Tzotzil, Tzeltal, Shilluk), 'bad character' (Trique), 'endurance' (Popoluca), and 'to be in doubt' (Piro). In still other languages a phrase such as 'hard heart' would not mean any more than a 'stony lung' would mean to English-speaking persons. If, then, we are to make sense in such languages, we must adopt an expression which is the natural equivalent in this type of context as e.g. 'large heart' (Huave), 'tightness of heart' (Shilluk), 'blind in their thoughts' (Zoque), 'hard heads' (Trique), 'ears without holes' (Shipibo), 'do not have pain in their heart' (Tzotzil, Tzeltal).

Restored may be rendered as 'was made like it was before' or 'became good again'.

6 The Pharisees went out, and immediately held counsel with the Herodians against him, how to destroy him.

Text: Instead of *edidoun* 'they were giving' of the majority of modern editions of the Greek text, *Textus Receptus* and Souter have *epoioun* 'they were making', and Tischendorf has *epoiēsan* 'they made'.

Exegesis: *exelthontes* 'going out (of the synagogue)'.
Hērōdianōn (12 : 13) 'Herodians': partisans and friends of Herod Antipas, tetrarch of Galilee.
sumboulion edidoun 'they held counsel', 'they plotted', 'they planned': not simply the idea of consultation, but that of deliberation, resolution (cf. Lagrange). Arndt & Gingrich (*sumboulion* 1) take this phrase to be the equivalent of the Latin *consilium capere* 'to plan', 'to purpose'. The imperfect tense of the verb here may have the meaning 'they *began* to counsel'.
hopōs 'in order that', 'so that': as an adverb *hopōs* expresses manner 'how' (so RSV); if used as a conjunction, it indicates purpose, '*so that* they might destroy him' (Burton *Moods and Tenses*, §§ 205, 207); or, following a verb meaning 'to plan', *hopōs* may mean 'with a view to' (Arndt & Gingrich 2.b).
apolesōsin (cf. 1 : 24) 'they might destroy him', i.e. put him to death.

Translation: *Went out*, i.e. of the synagogue.
Herodians, the political followers and friends of Herod, may be identified as 'those who walked with Herod' (Mitla Zapotec).
The Shilluk idiom for *taking counsel* is an interesting and typical one, 'gathered mouths together'.
Against him, how to destroy him may give rise to serious difficulties if one attempts to translate literally. However, the expression can be efficiently related to the preceding by translating as 'got together with

the followers of Herod in order to plan how they could destroy Jesus' (or 'kill him'). This was no plot merely against his influence, but against his life.

7 Jesus withdrew with his disciples to the sea, and a great multitude from Galilee followed; also from Judea 8 and Jerusalem and Idumea and from beyond the Jordan and from about Tyre and Sidon a great multitude, hearing all that he did, came to him.

Text: Verse 8. Before *peri* 'about' *Textus Receptus* and Soden (in brackets) add *hoi* 'the (people)'; it is omitted by all other modern editions of the Greek text.

Exegesis: *anechōrēsen* (only here in Mark) 'he withdrew', 'he retired': whether flight is implied is a debated question; Moulton & Milligan cite examples from the papyri with the meaning 'take refuge'.

tēn thalassan 'the sea' is the Lake of Galilee (see 1:16).

plēthos (in these two verses only) 'quantity', 'large number': used generally of a crowd.

The 'great multitude' comes from Galilee and all points of the compass: Judea, Jerusalem and Idumea, in the south; beyond the Jordan, to the east; and the regions of Tyre and Sidon, to the northwest.

peran tou Iordanou (10:1) 'beyond the Jordan': a set phrase in the New Testament to designate the country east of the river Jordan called by Josephus and others *Peraia* 'Perea'. *peran* is an adverb of place and means 'on the other side'.

peri Turon kai Sidōna 'the neighborhood of Tyre and Sidon' (cf. Arndt & Gingrich *peri* 2.a.γ; Moule *Idiom Book*, 62).

akouontes 'hearing': either temporal *'when* they heard' (BFBS), or possibly causal *'because* they heard'.

hosa 'how many things', 'everything that': indicates quantity.

Translation: *Withdrew* may be rendered as 'went away with'.

A *multitude* is simply a 'very large crowd' or 'many, many people'.

Followed should be translated in the sense of 'went along with' (or 'behind'), but not in the meaning of 'tracked down' (see verse 1:17) or in the sense of 'to be his disciples'. The crowd is composed of interested listeners, but not committed adherents.

The order of elements in the clause *also from Judea...came to him* must frequently be changed, because of the awkward relationship of constituent parts, e.g. 'Also those which were of the land Judea and the city Jerusalem and the land Idumea and from the land on the other side of the Jordan river and from the country around the cities Tyre and Sidon they heard all that Jesus did; therefore very many of them came to him'. This type of recasting may be necessitated by several syntactic requirements: (1) the use of classifiers with unfamiliar place names, e.g. Tyre, Idumea, Sidon, etc., (2) the shift from subordinate (hypotactic) to paratactic structure (rather than, '...when those which ...heard...that

Jesus did... they came', a structure containing three dependent clauses which telescope one within another and are all dependent upon the last clause), and (3) the parallelism of subject-predicate structure (what is important is not the relative order of constituents but the tendency toward parallelism, which tends to reenforce correct interpretation, rather than produce confusion).

9 *And he told his disciples to have a boat ready for him because of the crowd, lest they should crush him;* 10 *for he had healed many, so that all who had diseases pressed upon him to touch him.*

Exegesis: *hina ploiarion proskarterē autō* 'that a boat be ready for him': in this clause *hina* does not denote purpose 'in order that' but simply indicates the content of the order given the disciples (cf. Moulton *Prolegomena*, 206-9).

ploiarion (only here in Mark) 'a boat': the diminutive of *ploion* (cf. 1 : 19) 'boat'. It is not necessary to suppose, however, that a very exact distinction between the two is made by the evangelist.

proskartereō (only here in Mark) 'attend constantly', 'wait on': used here of a boat it means 'stand ready, be in constant attendance' (cf. Gould).

hina mē thlibōsin auton 'in order that they not crush him': here is the purpose (*hina* 'in order that') of the command that a boat be at hand.

thlibō (7 : 14) 'press upon', 'crowd', 'crush': 'they' refers to *ho ochlos* 'the crowd' of the preceding clause.

etherapeusen (cf. 1 : 34) 'he healed': ASV and RSV "had healed" is not to be understood in the sense that the healing ministry was finished; cf. "healed" of Moffatt, BFBS (cf. Manson "made many cures").

hōste epipiptein (cf. 1 : 27 for this construction) 'so as to press upon': the verb *epipiptō* (only here in Mark) means literally 'to fall upon' and is here used in the sense 'to crowd upon', 'to approach impetuously' (cf. Arndt & Gingrich).

autou hapsōntai (cf. 1 : 41) 'that they might touch him'.

hosoi eichon mastigas 'as many as had diseases', 'all who had diseases'.

mastix (5 : 29, 34) 'whip', 'scourge', 'torment': used of disease and suffering as divine chastisement. It is probable, however, that the word had lost its original sense of 'scourge' inflicted by the gods and meant simply 'disease' (cf. Lagrange). Cf. the similar use, in English, of the word 'plague'.

Translation: After the verb *told* it is quite frequent that the following order of Jesus must be stated in a direct form, e.g. 'told his disciples: Have a boat ready for me because...'

To have a boat ready is not always an easy idea to translate literally. Some languages may speak of people being 'ready' (i.e. 'prepared for action') but inanimate objects such as boats cannot be spoken of as 'ready'. The closest equivalent in Huave, for example, is to say 'to have a boat tied (anchored) near by', Bare'e and Javanese, 'a little ship had to be close-by'. On the other hand, one can usually speak of 'preparing a boat for a person' and this may be the best equivalent in some languages.

The two expressions (1) *because of the crowd* and (2) *lest they should crush him* are better coalesced into one clause in some languages since the logical subject is identical for each, e.g. 'in order that the crowd would not push hard against him'.

The conjunction *for* introducing verse 10 may pose certain difficulties, since, if it is understood to suggest a reason for the immediately preceding action, there is a non sequitur, that is to say, people will not be able to understand why the people would crush him because he had healed so many. Actually, this conjunction introduces a reason, not for the immediately preceding action, but for the previous statement by Jesus, namely, that the disciples should keep a boat ready for him. In order to make the relationship quite clear one may render the passage as 'Jesus did this because he had healed many and as a result all who...'

Pressed upon him to touch him must be translated with care, for 'to press upon' may imply by its very form physical contact. Accordingly, readers may wonder why the phrase 'to touch him' should be added. However, the description of what was happening in this crowd can be readily described as 'they kept pushing one another in order to touch him' (Ifugao) or 'kept shoving toward him in order to touch him' (Chontal of Tabasco).

11 And whenever the unclean spirits beheld him, they fell down before him and cried out, "You are the Son of God." 12 And he strictly ordered them not to make him known.

Exegesis: *hotan auton etheōroun, prosepipton autō kai ekrazon* 'whenever they saw him, they fell before him and shouted'.

hotan 'whenever', 'at the time', 'when': with the three verbs in the imperfect tense, the action is portrayed as being repeated (cf. 11:19). Cf. Arndt & Gingrich on *hotan* 'whenever': "of an action that is conditional, possible, and repeated."

theōreō (5:15, 38, 12:41, 15:40, 47, 16:4) 'look (upon)', 'gaze', 'behold'.

prospiptō (5:33, 7:25) 'fall before', 'fall at the feet of'.

krazō (11 times in Mark) 'call', 'call out': of evil spirits, 'shriek', 'scream'.

polla (cf. 1:45) used adverbially 'strongly', 'insistently': it does *not* mean here 'many times', 'often'; cf. Vulgate *vehementer*, Lagrange *enjoignant fortement*, BFBS 'warned strongly'.

epetima (cf. 1:25) 'he commanded', 'he warned'.

hina 'that': as in v. 9 *hina* denotes here the content of the order, *not* purpose 'in order that'.

phaneron poiēsōsin 'they should make known', 'they should reveal' (cf. Mt. 12:16) : the meaning is 'reveal the identity of (someone)', cf. 1:34.

Translation: There is a tendency for translators to render this passage as 'whenever people who had unclean spirits looked at Jesus, they fell...' Despite the fact that this may seem to make better sense, it is advisable not to depart from the original in this regard. Even though passages which speak of evil spirits seem to involve certain confusion between the action of the demonic spirits and the men in whom they dwelt, this very confusion is a highly significant factor (see 1:24).

For *unclean spirits* see 1:26,32.

Not to make him known may be translated in some languages as 'not to say who he was'. If this must be adapted to the requirements of direct discourse the form would be 'he strictly ordered them: You must not say: He is the Son of God' (or as may be necessary in some instances, 'You are the Son of God', using the expression of verse 11). Such a series of included direct discourse is not uncommon.

13 And he went up into the hills, and called to him those whom he desired; and they came to him.

Exegesis: *anabainei* (cf. 1:10) 'he goes up'.

eis to oros (cf. 6:46, 13:14) literally 'into the hill': what is meant is the hill district as distinct from the lowlands, especially above the Lake of Galilee, (cf. Arndt & Gingrich, Turner, Swete).

proskaleitai hous ēthelen autos 'he calls to himself those whom he himself wished'.

proskaloumai 'summon', 'call to oneself', 'invite': with one exception (15:44, Pilate to the centurion) this verb in Mark is used always of Jesus' calling the disciples (3:13, 6:7, 8:1, 10:42, 12:43) or the crowd (3:23, 7:14, 8:34).

thelō (some 24 times in Mark) 'desire', 'will', 'wish': Arndt & Gingrich hold that the verb here indicates purpose and will, rather than desire; and Turner (*Journal of Theological Studies*, 28.356, 1926-7) concludes that *thelō* in Mark must not be translated 'wish' or 'desire', and that in the present passage the sense of the verb is that of choice: 'whom he willed'.

autos 'he': since the personal pronoun is unnecessary with the verb, in Greek, it is normally emphatic when used: 'he himself'. Turner, however, takes it to be unemphatic in Mark, meaning, simply 'he'.

kai apēlthon pros auton 'and they went off (from the crowd) to him'.

Translation: *Into* the hills, if translated literally, can be badly misunderstood. In Kekchi, for example, one must translate 'on the face of the hill'. In other languages it must be 'in the region of the hills' or 'among the hills'.

For *call* see 1:20.

Desired in this context should not be understood in the sense of 'personal pleasure in' (a not uncommon mistake, and one which can lead to gross misinterpretation). The appropriate area of meaning in some languages seems to lie about half-way between 'want' and 'choose'.

14 *And he appointed twelve, to be with him, and to be sent out to preach* 15 *and have authority to cast out demons:*

Text: After *dōdeka* 'twelve' Westcott and Hort add *hous kai apostolous ōnomasen* 'whom he also called apostles': the great majority of the modern editions of the Greek text reject this clause (cf. Swete's arguments, however, for its inclusion).

Verse 15. After *exousian* 'authority' *Textus Receptus* adds *therapeuein tas nosous kai* 'to heal the sicknesses and': this reading is rejected by all modern editions of the Greek text.

Exegesis: *epoiēsen dōdeka* 'he appointed twelve': for this use of *poieō* 'do', 'make' cf. (in the LXX) Ex. 18:25, 36:1, and in the N.T. Heb. 3:2. The influence of the LXX is seen in this use of the verb (cf. Rawlinson, Lagrange).

The two *hina* 'in order that' clauses indicate purpose and are coordinate: 'that they be with him and that he send them' are the two purposes for which Jesus appointed the twelve men.

hina apostellē autous 'that he should send them out': it is better to translate the verb as an active form, with Jesus as subject, than to translate it by a passive (as does RSV) 'to be sent out'.

apostellō (cf. 1:2) 'send out': from this verb the noun *apostolos* (6:30) 'apostle' is formed (cf. 6:7 for the 'sending out').

kērussein kai echein exousian 'to preach and to have authority': the two infinitives 'to preach' and 'to have authority' are coordinate, and are both the object of *apostellō* 'send out'. A translation should preserve this construction if possible rather than make the second infinitive a subordinate clause (as does BFBS).

kērussō (cf. 1:4) 'proclaim', 'announce', 'preach'.

echein exousian (cf. 1:22) 'to have authority'.

ekballein ta daimonia (cf. 1:34) 'to cast out the demons': this infinitive clause is the object of *echein exousian* 'to have authority'.

Translation: *Appointed* is not always an easy term to translate. In general the cultural background which may provide an adequate equivalent is to be found in many societies in the practice of (1) medicine men who appoint associates or (2) chiefs or kings who designate certain men to offices of responsibility. When this is done the process is often described in more concrete terms, e.g. 'gave them jobs to do', 'gave them important names', or 'chose them for tasks'. Such expressions can generally be adapted to this type of context. Cf. South Toradja 'he exalted (the status of) twelve people'; Bare'e and Indonesian 'he appointed twelve people for good'.

Twelve must usually have some added noun, e.g. 'twelve men', 'twelve persons', or even 'twelve followers'. Most languages require some type of classifier with a numeral such as 'twelve'.

If the full meaning of *to be with him* is to be understood it must often be elaborated in one of two directions: (1) by some verbal mode or aspect which would indicate that the apostles were to remain with him in some more permanent relationship than the crowds which followed, or (2) by related lexical elements, e.g. 'to remain with him', 'to be associated with him', or 'to be with him more constantly'. Note, however, that their appointment was for a double purpose—not only association, but commission to go out. The words used at this point should not be contradictory. On the other hand, their close association with the Master was to precede their being sent out on their own.

For *preach* see 1 : 4.

For *authority* see 2 : 10, but note that the important aspect of the word *exousia* 'authority' is that of delegated power. Accordingly, in this passage 'to receive power (or strength) to cast out' would be quite satisfactory.

For *cast out*, in speaking of demons, see 1 : 34.

16 *Simon whom he surnamed Peter;*

Text: At the beginning of the verse Tischendorf, Nestle, Westcott and Hort, Soden, Vogels, Kilpatrick, Lagrange, and Merk add *kai epoiēsen tous dōdeka* "and he appointed the twelve": this clause is omitted by *Textus Receptus*, Souter, ASV, RSV, Taylor (cf. Taylor for arguments for omitting it). Although not decisive, the evidence for retaining the clause, with Nestle and others, seems to outweigh the evidence for omitting it.

Exegesis: *kai* 'and': here with the meaning 'so' (BFBS, Manson).

tous dōdeka (4 : 10, 6 : 7, 9 : 35, 10 : 32, 11 : 11, 14 : 10, 17, 20, 43) 'the Twelve': not simply a number, as in v. 14, but a title: 'the Twelve' (BFBS); Lagrange *les Douze*.

kai epethēken onoma tō Simōni Petron 'and he added to Simon the name Peter'.

epitithēmi (3 : 17, 5 : 33, 6 : 5, 7 : 32, 8 : 23, 25, 16 : 18) 'lay', 'set', 'place upon': the phrase *epitithenai onoma* means 'give a surname' (cf. Arndt & Gingrich 1.a.β).

Translation: Verses 16 through 19 consist of a list of the names of the apostles, but this list is grammatically in apposition with the *twelve*, spoken of in verse 14. In most languages this type of apposition is so distant that without some clarification or more explicit reference, misunderstanding is likely to arise. For example, in one translation the list of names (all strange ones) was taken to be a list of the demons that were to be cast out, for the list immediately followed reference to the demons. Accordingly, verse 16 must often begin as 'these men were...' (Chontal of Oaxaca) or 'the ones he appointed were...' (Trique).

Surnamed is 'to give an additional name to' or 'to give a second name to'. This practice is a good deal more common in many cultures than in our own, and hence is not likely to be misunderstood.

For problems of transliteration of proper names and the adjustments

113

which must be made in the case of certain familiar names see *Bible Translating*, 243-46. Note, however, that in many instances there are strong pressures for the adoption of arbitrary orthographic conventions in the case of well-known proper names (e.g. taking over the spelling of French, Spanish, or Portuguese, despite the fact that the people do not pronounce the names according to such consonant-vowel representations). In most instances one must accede to these pressures and use the orthographically approved form of the prestige language of the area. This principle often applies to such names as Peter, James, John, Philip, and Thomas, but would not be likely to apply to Bartholomew, Alphaeus, or Thaddaeus.

17 James the son of Zebedee and John the brother of James, whom he surnamed Boanerges, that is, sons of thunder;

Text: Instead of *onoma* 'name', *Textus Receptus*, Tischendorf, Soden, Souter, Vogels, Lagrange, and Merk have *onomata* 'names'; the singular is preferred by Nestle, Westcott and Hort, Taylor, Kilpatrick.

Exegesis: *Iakōbon ton tou Zebedaiou* 'James *the son of* Zebedee' (cf. the same construction in 2:14).

Boanērges 'Boanerges': cf. Dalman *Words*, 49, and Arndt & Gingrich for problems connected with the correct understanding of this proper name, and possible solutions.

huioi brontēs 'sons of thunder': the Semitic idiom means that the men thus named are characterized by a wrathful disposition, and so are like thunder (cf. same idiom 2:19 *huioi numphōnos* 'sons of the bridegroom's chamber').

Translation: For a discussion of the order of names and attributive expressions in *James the son...of James*, see 1:19. In this passage a frequently acceptable equivalent is 'James and his younger brother John, both the sons of Zebedee'.

Whom he surnamed Boanerges may be translated as 'he also called them a second name Boanerges'. This last term should be transliterated, following the principles of sound equivalence established for the handling of such infrequent proper names.

That is (reflecting Greek *ho estin*) is a kind of formula for 'which means'. The interpretation of such strange names in a language may need to be introduced as 'which means in our language' or 'which tries to say'.

Sons of thunder, translated literally, has been misunderstood in a number of translations in which readers have assumed that Jesus was actually describing these men as the supernatural offspring of the local deity "Thunder" (the fact that the men had a stated human father seemed either noncontradictory, or as in one instance, Zebedee was taken to be the name of Thunder). In order that the reader may understand precisely what is the meaning of this Semitic idiom, many translations have used certain equivalent phrases, e.g. 'men like thunder'

(Huave, Navajo, Pame), 'sons like thunder' (Ifugao), and 'men who are strong like thunder' (Sierra Aztec, Chontal of Oaxaca). In some languages one may find that the phrase 'sons of thunder' is already in use in a very specialized meaning. For example, in Trique the expression is the name of a small toad, so named after an ancient pagan rain god. However, by changing the phrase somewhat by the introduction of 'noise', the proper referent was understood, e.g. 'sons of the noise of thunder'.

18 *Andrew, and Philip, and Bartholomew, and Matthew, and Thomas, and James the son of Alphaeus, and Thaddaeus, and Simon the Cananaean,* 19 *and Judas Iscariot, who betrayed him. Then he went home;*

Text: In verse 19 instead of *erchetai* 'he goes' of Tischendorf, Merk, Souter, Westcott and Hort, Taylor, and Nestle, the plural *erchontai* 'they go' is preferred by *Textus Receptus*, Soden, Vogels, Lagrange, and Kilpatrick.

Exegesis: *Iakōbon ton tou Alphaiou* 'James the son of Alphaeus' (cf. 2:14).

Simōna ton Kananaion 'Simon the Cananaean': this is *not* 'Simon from Cana' (which would be *Kanaios*) or 'Simon the Canaanite' (which would be *Chananaios,* cf. Mt. 15:22); rather as a transliteration of the Aramaic *qan'an* 'enthusiast', 'zealous', it means 'Simon the Zealot' (cf. Lk. 6:15 and Acts 1:13). Instead of "Cananaean" (RSV, BFBS), therefore, it would be better, in order to avoid misunderstanding, to translate "Zealot" (Goodspeed, Moffatt, Brazilian, Lagrange); some (Swete, Lagrange) see the name as an indication of religious fervor, rather than adherence to the extremist party of Zealots (cf. Manson, "the Zealous").

kai Ioudan Iskariōth, hos kai paredōken auton 'and Judas Iscariot, who also delivered him up'.

Iskariōth 'Iscariot': generally taken to be a transliteration of *'ish qerioth* 'man from Kerioth' (for other suggestions cf. Taylor).

kai 'also': should not be omitted, as does RSV (cf. Swete): it means 'in addition to being one of the Twelve'; it does not mean 'who also (besides other men) delivered him up'.

paradidōmi (cf. 1:14) 'hand over', 'deliver up (to judgment or prison)': in certain contexts it is better to preserve the literal sense of the word in a translation rather than use the common 'betray' (cf. 1:14 and Mt. 26:15 as striking examples of the use of the verb where 'betray' would be grossly inaccurate). The 'delivering up' of Jesus was in fact a betrayal on the part of Judas; that does not mean, however, that *paradidōmi* means 'betray' (cf. *prodidōmi* 'betray', Liddell and Scott).

eis oikon 'home' (RSV), 'His home' (BFBS): cf. *en oikō* 'at home' in 2:1 (see Goodspeed *Problems,* 56f.).

Translation: *Cananaean* should be translated in the same manner as *Zealot.* In general this term, which comes out of a complex religious, social and political context, is perhaps most appropriately related to what

115

might be primarily a political entity in another culture (though politics are rarely separable from social and religious considerations). Some translators have used designations which would imply that Simon was one of the 'nationalist party'. Others have characterized him as 'always campaigning' (i.e. politically zealous, without specifying his cause). The Subanen describe this type of zealous, politically-minded person as 'brave to speak'. Within this general area of significance it is usually possible to find some relatively adequate equivalent.

Judas Iscariot should in general be transliterated, rather than translated, in the sense of 'the man from Kerioth'.

Betrayed in this context may be rendered as 'handed him over to enemies' (Conob) or 'cause his enemies to apprehend him' (or 'to arrest him').

20 *and the crowd came together again, so that they could not even eat.*

Exegesis: *kai sunerchetai palin ho ochlos* 'and the crowd gathers again'.

sunerchomai (14:53) 'assemble', 'gather', 'come together'.

palin 'again': looks back at 3:7. It would not be correct to say 'the *same* crowd': it is simply the gathering together again of a crowd about Jesus.

hōste mē dunasthai autous (cf. 1:27 for this construction) 'so that they were unable', 'so that they could not'.

autous 'they': the reference is most likely to Jesus and his disciples (cf. Bruce *Expositor's Greek Testament* I, 360).

mēde arton phagein 'not even to eat bread', i.e. eat, "take food" (BFBS).

Translation: In order to avoid the impression that this was identically the same crowd following Jesus (though admittedly made up of many of the same people), one may say, 'And again a crowd gathered together there...' The occurrence of the article in Greek does not require one to translate as 'the crowd', identifying these people with the group in 3:9.

They is likely to be badly misunderstood unless the reference is made more specific, for in many languages the only antecedent would be the 'crowd'. Accordingly in some languages the subject is made explicit as 'Jesus and his disciples' (Huave, Ifugao).

21 *And when his friends heard it, they went out to seize him, for they said, "He is beside himself."*

Exegesis: *hoi par' autou* literally 'those along with him': this idiom may mean 'his followers', 'his friends', or 'his family'. AV, ASV, RSV prefer 'his friends'; it would seem, however, that 'his family', 'his relatives' is what is indicated, in light of vv. 31ff. (cf. Arndt & Gingrich *para* I.4.b.β; Moulton & Milligan; Moule *Idiom Book*, 52; Field *Notes*, 25f.): this rendering is adopted by Manson, Moffatt, Goodspeed, Weymouth, BFBS, Brazilian, Synodale.

kratēsai (cf. 1 : 31) 'to seize', 'to take control of' (BFBS), 'to seize by force' (Weymouth).

elegon gar 'for they were saying': there is division of opinion over who is referred to by '*they* were saying'. Most translations assume that the subject is 'his relatives' ('his friends') of the previous clauses; following Turner (*Journal of Theological Studies*, 25.383f., 1923-4), however, some see here another example of the impersonal plural (cf. 2 : 18) whose meaning would be 'people were saying', 'it was being said': so Moffatt, BFBS; Lagrange *on disait*. There is no way finally to determine which interpretation is correct.

hoti 'that': recitative, introducing direct speech.

exestē (cf. 2 : 12) 'he is beside himself', 'he has lost his senses' (Arndt & Gingrich). As Burton (*Moods and Tenses*, § 47) points out, this aorist describes a present state, the result of a past action, and is best translated by the present tense.

Translation: It would seem from the context that a somewhat more intimate group than 'friends' were those so concerned about Jesus' health as the result of his being constantly with the thronging crowd. Accordingly, one may use 'those of his household' (a common equivalent of family and relatives) or 'those who were close to him' (a close rendering of the Greek phrase). Indonesian and Javanese render 'his blood-relations'.

Seize must be carefully translated or the wrong connotation may be given. After all, his family wanted to rescue him from the importuning crowd, not to manhandle him, a not uncommon connotation of words meaning 'to seize'.

Two types of mistakes tend to occur in translating *He is beside himself*: (1) that Jesus was demented and (2) that he was demon possessed (particularly in view of the following charge by the scribes). There is no doubt that the Greek term is a strong one, and often does signify complete mental derangement, but in this context it means that Jesus' family thought he was demented. It was this fear which prompted his solicitous associates to try to rescue him. In Tzeltal the appropriate equivalent is 'his head had been touched', which is an expression to identify what might be called the half-way stage to insanity. In Ifugao one may say 'he acts as though he were crazy'. In Shilluk the equivalent is 'he is acting like an imbecile', and in Shipibo one may say 'his thoughts have gone out of him'. In Bare'e the translation is 'he is outside his senses', in Indonesian 'he is not by his reason'.

22 *And the scribes who came down from Jerusalem said, "He is possessed by Beelzebul, and by the prince of demons he casts out the demons."*

Exegesis: *hoi apo Ierosolumōn katabantes* 'who came down from Jerusalem': one *went up* to the capital (cf. 10 : 32) and *came down* from it (cf. similar usage with regard to London) (cf. Lk. 2 : 51, 10 : 30f., Acts 8 : 26).

For *hoi grammateis* 'the scribes' cf. 1 : 22.

elegon hoti...kai hoti 'they were saying that...and that': both times *hoti* is recitative, introducing direct speech. This being so, it would be more accurate to punctuate the translation in such a way as to indicate *two* direct statements: The scribes...were saying, "He is possessed by Beelzebul," and, "By the prince of demons he casts out demons."

elegon 'they were saying': the statement was repeated (cf. C. S. Emden, *Expository Times*, 65.147, 1954; cf. Taylor).

Beezeboul echei 'he has Beelzebul', i.e. 'he is possessed by Beelzebul'. On the variant forms of the name and possible etymologies cf. Arndt & Gingrich, Rawlinson. Commentators are divided over whether or not 'Beelzebul' and 'the prince of the demons' are the same one, or refer to two different evil spirits.

en tō archonti tōn daimoniōn 'in the ruler of the demons'.

en 'in', 'by', i.e. 'in the name of', 'by the power of' (cf. Arndt & Gingrich *en* III.1.b: "with the help of").

ho archōn (only here in Mark) 'ruler', 'chief': in form it is the present participle of the verb *archō* 'to rule'.

ekballei ta daimonia 'he drives out the demons' (cf. 1 : 34).

Translation: For *scribes* see 1 : 22.

In many languages expressions of coming and going, whether up to or down from, are used with great precision and care, something which is not typical of the Gospels. Accordingly, if one is to use such expressions in a translation in a language which maintains a scrupulous consistency in such details of movement, it is obligatory that one maintain the same expressions throughout. Otherwise the reader is likely to be utterly confused.

For expressions dealing with *possession* see 1 : 23. A literal translation of this type of expression 'has Beelzebul' or 'is possessed by Beelzebul' can give rise to entirely wrong meanings. For example in Izthmus Zapotec to say only 'is possessed by' would mean 'to speak filthy words'. On the other hand, if one wants to designate demon possession, one must say 'he talks with Beelzebul'. Despite the fact that the literal expressions in this language do not seem to carry this proportionate scale of intensity in meaning, nevertheless, they do, and what counts is not the literal words but the meaning.

If one wishes to identify Beelzebul with the prince of the demons, one may translate 'and by this prince of demons' (Huave).

The last clause of this verse introduces a difficult problem of secondary agency. That is to say, the primary agent is 'he (i.e. Jesus), but the secondary agent (secondary in terms of the grammatical structure, but primary in importance as far as the scribes were concerned) is the prince of demons. In languages in which such secondary agency can be expressed by a prepositional phrase, as in Greek or English, the problem is simple enough, but in many languages this is not possible. The alternatives are of two types: (1) the secondary agent becomes the primary agent of a causative expression, e.g. 'the prince of demons causes him to cast out demons' or '...gives him power to cast out...' (Zoque) and (2) the secondary agent becomes the source of power for the accomplishment of an activity, e.g. 'Jesus receives power from the prince of demons so that he can cast out demons'.

Prince is 'the chief' (Zoque, Black Bobo) or 'the ruler'. In Shipibo one may say 'the strong one among the demons'.

For *demons* see 1 : 26, 32.

23 And he called them to him, and said to them in parables, "How can Satan cast out Satan?

Exegesis: *proskalesamenos* (cf. 3 : 13) 'calling', 'summoning', 'calling to oneself'.

en parabolais 'in parables', 'by means of parables', 'in figurative language': the phrase indicates the manner in which he spoke to them.

parabolē 'parable', 'figure', 'comparison', 'analogy', 'illustration': in the LXX *parabolē* translates *mashal* which covers a whole range of figurative language: 'parables', 'proverbs', 'figures' and even 'riddles' (cf. Hatch *Essays*, 64-71). The word appears 13 times in Mark: 3:23, 4:2, 10, 11, 13 (twice), 30, 33, 34, 7:17, 12:1, 12, 13:28. As a technical Christian term designating (in the Synoptics) Jesus' customary form of teaching, *parable* serves as a translation in all these passages with the exception of two: 7:17, where "figure" (Goodspeed) or even "lesson" (Berkeley) better fits the context, and 13:28 where "illustration" or "lesson" (RSV, Weymouth, Goodspeed) is meant.

satanas (cf. 1:13) 'Satan', the ruler of the demons. The meaning is not that of one satan driving out another, but of Satan driving out himself. That is what Satan would be doing were he to drive out the demons who compose his empire (cf. Lagrange).

Translation: *Them* is of uncertain reference in this passage, but taken literally in many languages it would mean only the scribes, the closest third person plural referent, other than the demons. Probably, however, one should make the reference more explicit by substituting 'the people'.

In some languages there are quite good equivalents of *parable*, since such forms of expression are common. However, in other cases one must develop some type of expression which conveys the meaning implied by *parable*, without being too elaborate and detailed a definition. Such descriptive terms are of two types: (1) those which emphasize the nature of the parable as a comparison or illustration and (2) those which specify its use in teaching and instruction. The first type may be illustrated by 'picture with words' (Piro), 'message in the manner of a comparison' (Bare'e), 'comparison word' (Totonac, Bolivian Quechua), 'picture story' (Tzeltal), 'likeness word' (Maya, Tarahumara), and 'story which says like that' (Cashibo). The second type may be found in 'story told for teaching' (Trique, Goajiro), 'story from which understanding comes' (Navajo), 'notice from which comes teaching' (Conob).

In a number of languages a literal translation of *Satan cast out Satan* will imply that there are at least two Satans. In such a language one should translate 'How can Satan cast himself out' (Tzeltal, Huastec).

24 *If a kingdom is divided against itself, that kingdom cannot stand. 25 And if a house is divided against itself, that house will not be able to stand.*

Exegesis: *basileia* (cf. 1:15) 'kingdom': here a political entity, in the sense of a country ruled by a king (cf. Arndt & Gingrich 2).

eph' heautēn 'upon itself', i.e. 'against itself' (Arndt & Gingrich *epi* III. 1.a.ε).

meristhē (3:24,25,26, 6:41) 'be divided', 'be split', 'be disunited'.

dunatai...dunēsetai 'it cannot...it will not': simply a stylistic change from the present to the future tense.

stathēnai...stēnai 'stand...stand': the meaning of both infinitives is the same, though one is passive and the other active: 'stand', 'maintain itself', 'endure' (the verb *histēmi* used absolutely, without an object, may mean 'stand firm').

oikia 'house': not simply a building, but the people who live in it: 'household', 'family' (cf. Arndt & Gingrich 2). Rawlinson points out that in Aramaic usage the word may be used in a broad sense for a political domain.

Translation: In some languages one cannot speak of a 'kingdom' as 'being divided against itself'. This type of passive is especially complex because there is no agent, other than the kingdom itself. Therefore, one must often render this passage in terms of 'the people of a kingdom' causing this type of division.

The division spoken of in this verse is essentially a state of enmity and war among the people of a region, not an actual division of a territory. Accordingly, this clause must often be translated as 'if the people of a kingdom fight against each other' (Mitla Zapotec, Tarahumara). However, this division may also be spoken of in terms of antipathy, e.g. 'hate one another' (Zoque).

Cannot stand is rendered in some languages as 'cannot continue to exist', 'cannot remain', or 'cannot be any longer'.

A literal rendering of verse 25 can also be interpreted in a completely materialistic manner, thus missing the significance of the passage. As in the case of verse 24, one may translate 'the people of a family fight among themselves' (Zoque). Since clan squabbles are not at all uncommon in many societies, this reference to the family, especially in its extended clan form, can be very meaningful (cf. South Toradja 'the members of a family', Indonesian 'the inmates of the house').

26 *And if Satan has risen up against himself and is divided, he cannot stand, but is coming to an end.*

Text: Instead of *kai emeristhē* 'and is divided' read by the majority of the modern editions of the Greek text, *Textus Receptus* and Soden read *kai memeristai* 'and has been divided'; Tischendorf and Kilpatrick read *emeristhē kai* 'is divided and'.

Exegesis: *anestē eph' heauton kai emeristhē* 'he rose against himself and is divided': i.e. if Satan is at war against himself, if there is faction or division in his kingdom, among his subordinates.

telos echei (cf. Heb. 7 : 3) 'he has an end', i.e. "he is done for" (Manson), "he is finished", "that is the end of him" (BFBS). What is meant is the end of his power, or his kingdom (cf. Lagrange), rather than the end of his existence (as Brazilian *perece* has it).

Translation: *Risen up against himself* may be rendered as 'Satan fighting against himself' (Ifugao, Shilluk). On the other hand, one may employ a less violent, but equally meaningful type of equivalent, as in Kekchi e.g. 'if Satan hates himself' (literally, 'looks mean at himself').

To speak of Satan as being 'divided' may mean that he is literally cut into two pieces, obviously not the meaning of the passage. On the other hand, it is quite possible to speak of 'his power is divided', and by this means employ a very close equivalent.

Cannot stand may be treated as in the preceding two verses.

In some languages a person cannot 'come to an end', but 'his power will end' (Loma). In others, one may translate 'he will disappear' or 'he will no longer exist'.

It should be noted, that though these conditional sentences (verses 24-26) are given as simple conditionals: 'if...is..., is (or, will)'; nevertheless, they are essentially conditions contrary to fact: 'if...should be ..., then...would be...' One must often be quite careful to distinguish between simple conditions, which in this case would imply that Satan cannot stand, as of now, and conditions contrary to fact, implying that Satan was not divided against himself, for certainly Jesus was not acting on the authority of Beelzebul.

27 *But no one can enter a strong man's house and plunder his goods, unless he first binds the strong man; then indeed he may plunder his house.*

Exegesis: *all'* 'but': does not contradict the statement of the previous verse, but the charge that Jesus is acting in the name of the ruler of the demons. *On the contrary*, the household of the strong man can be plundered only if he is bound by a stronger man.

dunatai...eiselthōn...diarpasai 'able...entering...to plunder', 'able to enter and plunder'.

tou ischurou 'of the strong man': RSV, BFBS and others translate "of *a* strong man" in a general sense; since figurative language is being employed, however, it is perhaps better to translate literally '*the* strong man' (which may mean Satan himself: cf. Taylor, and footnote in BFBS).

ta skeuē autou (11 : 16) 'his goods', 'his belongings'; rather than the restricted sense of 'implement', 'instrument' (cf. Gould) the meaning here is broader, including all goods or possessions. To 'plunder his goods' in this clause is the same as to 'plunder his house' in the next.

diarpasai (here only in Mark) 'to plunder', 'ransack', 'rob'.

dēsē (5 : 3, 4, 6 : 17, 11 : 2, 4, 15 : 1, 7) 'he should restrict', 'he should bind', 'he should tie'.

Translation: Despite the more or less concrete form of this statement, it is essentially generic (unless there is a subtle reference to Satan, an allusion which would be difficult to render, even at best). Hence, though the Greek form speaks of 'no one', in many languages generic forms must be either plural, e.g. 'people cannot enter the houses of strong men...' or second person, e.g. 'you cannot enter a strong man's house...' (Tzeltal).

Enter here is 'force an entrance', 'go in by force', or 'push your way in'. This distinction must be maintained in some languages.

Strong refers primarily to physical strength, but having great socio-political power or reputation is in some cultures the closest equivalent. This is suggested in the Chontal of Tabasco as 'one who is not afraid of anything'.

Plunder his goods is equivalent to 'take away what a person has'.

The order of temporal sequence may be of such importance in a language that one must reorder the clauses of this verse, e.g. 'First, you must bind a strong man, then and only then can you enter his house and take away all he has in his house'.

28 ***Truly, I say to you, all sins will be forgiven the sons of men, and whatever blasphemies they utter;***

Punctuation of the Text: As Nestle, *Textus Receptus*, Tischendorf, Kilpatrick, Merk, and Souter are punctuated, with no comma after *anthrōpōn* 'men', the word *panta* 'all' modifies *ta hamartēmata* 'sins', i.e. 'all sins' (so AV, ASV, RSV, BFBS, Moffatt, Weymouth); if, however, a comma be placed after *anthrōpōn* 'men' as is done by Westcott and Hort, Lagrange, Taylor, *panta* 'all' is used absolutely as the subject of *aphethēsetai* 'will be forgiven', i.e. 'all (things) will be forgiven', while *ta hamartēmata kai hai blasphēmiai* 'the sins and the blasphemies' stand in apposition to 'all', further explaining it (so Manson, Goodspeed, Brazilian).

Exegesis: *amēn* (13 times in Mark) 'truly', 'verily', 'solemnly': the Greek equivalent of the Hebrew *'amen* from the verb *'aman* 'to be firm'. This Hebrew adverb is used to emphasize the importance of the statement that follows.

aphethēsetai (cf. 2 : 5) 'will be forgiven': the statement is not to be understood absolutely as if Jesus were saying that all sins will assuredly be forgiven by God, whether or not men change or repent. As the context makes clear, he is saying that there is forgiveness for all sins, all sins are capable of being forgiven, except blasphemy against the Holy Spirit, which cannot be forgiven.

tois huiois tōn anthrōpōn 'to the sons of men': the Semitic way of saying 'men' in a general way.

ta hamartēmata (here and next verse) 'sins': in Mark the distinction between *hamartēma* as 'specific act of sin' and *hamartia* as 'sin in general', 'the sinful principle', is not observed (cf. 1 : 5).

hai blasphēmiai hosa ean blasphēmēsōsin 'and whatever blasphemies they may utter'.

hai blasphēmiai (7 : 22, 14 : 64) 'blasphemies', i.e. impious or irreverent speech against God.

hosa (cf. 3 : 8) 'as many...as': though the neuter form of the word does not agree with the feminine *hai blasphēmiai* 'the blasphemies' the sense is quite clear: 'as many times as they may blaspheme', 'however often they utter blasphemies'.

blasphēmeō (cf. 2 : 7) 'blaspheme': "defiant hostility to God...in speech which defies His power and majesty" (Vincent Taylor).

Translation: *Truly* qualifies the certainty of the statement *all sins will be...* In many languages this type of qualifier must be more closely associated with the verb expression which it modifies, e.g. 'I tell you, All sins will certainly be forgiven...'

For *sins* see 1 : 4; for *forgiveness* see 1 : 4; and for *blasphemies* see 2 : 7. In this context, however, an expression such as 'bad words' or 'harmful sayings' (often used as an equivalent of blasphemy, at least in certain contexts) is often inadequate. At the same time, one cannot use 'to make oneself equal with God' (as a rendering of blaspheme), for this is too specific. The better rendering would be more or less equivalent to 'speaking against God' or 'talking God down'.

Sons of men, if translated literally into some languages, would mean nothing more than 'children' (Huave, Shilluk). Of course, God is usually regarded as being quite forgiving toward children, and hence the reader is likely to miss completely the significance of this passage, in which the real meaning is simply 'will be forgiven people'. South Toradja uses the expression 'the offspring of Adam'.

Since there are two subjects of *will be forgiven*, namely, *all sins* and *whatever blasphemies...* (see above, under *Punctuation of the Text* for the alternative), it is necessary in many languages to change the order so that both of the subject expressions are in a parallel relationship to the verb, whether preceding or following, e.g. 'all sins and whatever blasphemies...will be forgiven'.

29 but whoever blasphemes against the Holy Spirit never has forgiveness, but is guilty of an eternal sin"— 30 for they had said, "He has an unclean spirit."

Text: Instead of *hamartēmatos* 'sin' *Textus Receptus* has *kriseōs* 'judgment', 'condemnation': this clearly inferior reading is rejected by all modern editions of the Greek text.

Exegesis: *eis to pneuma to hagion* 'into the Holy Spirit': *eis* here has a hostile meaning 'against' (cf. Arndt & Gingrich 4.c.α).

aphesin (cf. 1:4) 'forgiveness' (for the verb *aphiēmi* 'forgive' see 2:5).
eis ton aiōna 'into the age', i.e. the 'future age'.

eis 'into' indicates duration of time (Arndt & Gingrich 2.b).

aiōn (4:19, 10:30, 11:14) 'age': the word reflects the Hebrew concept of time as divided into ages, generally the present age (cf. 4:19) and the future age, the age to come (cf. 10:30). In this passage the phrase means 'eternally', 'forever' as the parallel in Mt. 12:32 makes explicit: 'either in this age or in the coming age'. Cf. Vulgate *in aeternum*; Lagrange *à jamais*.

enochos (14:64) 'guilty of', 'charged with', here indicates the crime of which the man is guilty, *not* the punishment to which he is liable.

aiōniou 'of the age', 'age-long': that is, 'eternal', 'endless'.

hoti elegon 'because they were saying': these are words of explanation which the evangelist adds. *hoti* is causative 'because', giving the reason why Jesus said what he did concerning the unforgivable sin.

elegon 'they were saying' is better than 'they had said' of RSV (cf. *Expository Times*, 65.147, 1954; Vincent *Word Studies* I, 180). 'They' are the scribes referred to in v. 22.

pneuma akatharton 'unclean spirit', the same as saying 'he has Beelzebul' (v. 22) or 'he has a demon' (cf. 1:34).

Translation: *Blasphemes against the Holy Spirit* may be rendered as 'to speak against the Holy Spirit' or 'to say evil words about the Holy Spirit' (for "Holy Spirit" see 1:7).

Has forgiveness is a difficult expression to translate literally, for in general one must speak of 'to be forgiven' or 'to receive forgiveness' (but for numerous idioms for *forgiveness* see 1:4). In languages in which an active form of the verb is required, the subject 'God' must be introduced, 'God will never forgive a man who speaks evil of the Holy Spirit'.

To be guilty of an eternal sin can only rarely be translated literally. Rather, this phrase must be rendered by various types of idiomatic expressions, e.g. 'his sin stays on his head for the time that never ends' (Gurunse), 'he carries the weight of his sin that lasts forever' (Kiyaka), 'his sins will be continually taken into account' (Bare'e),' he will always have his sin' (Chontal of Oaxaca), and 'he has a sin that will never be taken away' (Huichol).

In some way, the abrupt transition before the clause *for they had said...* must be marked, either by some kind of a dash, or by a complete new sentence, or by some transitional expression, e.g. 'Jesus said this because they had said...' (Bolivian Quechua). The reason for making this break evident is that one must not translate as 'he is guilty of an eternal sin because of what they had said' (though indirectly this is true). Nevertheless, the last sentence must be construed with all that precedes, not merely with the last clause.

31 *And his mother and his brothers came; and standing outside they sent to him and called him.*

Exegesis: *exō stēkontes* 'standing outside (the house)': Jesus is inside (see vv. 32, 34).

stēkō (11 : 25) 'stand': in the LXX and N.T. this verb is equal in meaning to the intransitive use of *histēmi* 'stand' (cf. Kennedy *Sources*, 158).

apesteilan pros auton 'they sent (a message) to him' (or, 'they sent for him').

kalountes auton 'calling him': this is the message they sent.

Translation: *Brothers* should be understood as 'younger brothers' by the same mother, where as in so many languages special words are employed for brothers, whether younger or older (Zoque, Tzeltal), or of the same mother or father (Navajo, Gurunse).

Because of the distance of this verse from any previous reference to Jesus it would probably be necessary in some languages to introduce 'Jesus' (Huave).

32 And a crowd was sitting about him; and they said to him, "Your mother and your brothers are outside, asking for you."

Text: After *hē mētēr sou* 'your mother' Tischendorf, Nestle, Soden, Vogels, and Kilpatrick add *kai hai adelphai sou* 'and your sisters': this clause is omitted by *Textus Receptus*, Westcott and Hort, Taylor, Lagrange, Merk, RSV. Since the manuscript evidence is not decisive one way or the other, internal evidence will determine whether or not the words should be included (cf. Westcott and Hort *Notes on Selected Readings*, 24, for arguments for omitting them).

Exegesis: *idou* (cf. 1 : 2) 'look', 'see': should not be omitted (as is done by RSV).

exō zētousin se 'outside they are asking for you'.

exō 'outside': ordinarily taken with 'mother and brothers': 'your mother and brothers *are outside*'. Moffatt, however, joins it to the verb, 'wanting you outside'.

zēteō 'search for', 'ask', 'request': here in the latter sense of 'asking', 'wanting': they were not *looking* for him since they knew him to be there. In Mark *zēteō* is used in both ways: (1) 'search for', 'seek' (1 : 37, 14 : 55, 16 : 6); with the idea of 'examine', 'consider' (11 : 18, 14 : 1, 11); (2) 'want', 'request', 'ask' (3 : 32, 8 : 11, 12); with the idea of 'attempt', 'try' (12 : 12).

Translation: Though the equivalent of Greek *idou* 'behold', 'look', 'pay attention' should be rendered in some manner, it is not always easy to find just the right introductory particle. Probably, the meaning here is really not 'look!', but rather a kind of polite way in which the crowd could interrupt Jesus, in order to call his attention to the request of mother and brothers. One must choose a form which would be appropriate for the context, e.g. 'listen' (Tzeltal), 'but listen' (Shilluk).

33 *And he replied, "Who are my mother and my brothers?"* 34 *And looking around on those who sat about him, he said, "Here are my mother and my brothers!* 35 *Whoever does the will of God is my brother, and sister, and mother."*

Text: In v. 33 instead of *kai* 'and' of all other modern editions of the Greek text, *Textus Receptus* and Soden have *ē* 'or'.

In v. 34 the order of words in *Textus Receptus* is changed so as to make *kuklō* 'in a circle' modify *periblepsamenos* 'looking', i.e. 'looking around'; all modern editions of the Greek text follow the same word order as Nestle's, whereby *kuklō* modifies *tous kathēmenous*, i.e. 'those seated in a circle'.

Exegesis: *apokritheis...legei* 'answering...he says': there are some 15 instances of this construction throughout the gospel of Mark. A translation in English need only give the sense 'he answered' without reproducing both verbs in a literal form (cf. 1:7 and 1:24 for similar constructions).

periblepsamenos (cf. 3:5) 'looking around (him)'.

tous peri auton kuklō kathēmenous 'those seated in a circle about him'.

kuklō (6:6, 36) is adverbial 'round about', 'around'.

ide (cf. 1:2) 'see!' 'here'.

hos an poiēsē 'he who does': the subjunctive mode of the verb is required by the construction of the sentence; there is no idea, however, of doubt or futurity. The meaning is 'whoever does', 'he who does'.

thelēma (only here in Mark) 'will'.

Translation: The form of the question *Who are my mother...* is ambiguous from the standpoint of some languages which must distinguish between identificational questions and qualificational ones, i.e. 'who are these...' and 'what sort of persons are...' Note, however, in languages which must translate this sentence as qualificational, one does not question the characteristics of Jesus' mother and brothers, but asks what sort of characteristics of people make it possible for them to be recognized as 'mother and brothers'. The equivalent would be 'Who are the sort of people who are my mother and my brothers?'

The adverb *here* may be translated by a gesture-like word or phrase 'these here' or 'right here'.

Does the will of God is often translated as 'does what God wants him to do'. In Huichol this is 'follow God's heart'.

In a number of languages brothers and sisters of the same mother are grouped under a single term, meaning siblings of the same maternal line. In such languages, e.g. Totonac, Barrow Eskimo, Navajo, and Sierra Aztec, it would be quite wrong to try to use two words just because Greek has two words, when a single word is the more accurate and satisfactory term. This same word can be employed for 'brothers' throughout this passage, beginning with verse 31.

CHAPTER FOUR

1 *Again he began to teach beside the sea. And a very large crowd gathered about him, so that he got into a boat and sat in it on the sea; and the whole crowd was beside the sea on the land.*

Exegesis: *ochlos pleistos* 'a very large crowd', 'a huge crowd': *pleistos* is the superlative of *polus* 'many', 'much'.

sunagetai (cf. 2:2) 'gathers together', 'collects' (cf. 3:20).

hōste auton...kathēsthai (cf. 1:27 for this construction) 'so that he... sat'.

eis ploion embanta 'having entered a boat': the two clauses together may be translated as coordinate: 'so that he entered a boat and sat (in it)'.

embainō (5:18, 6:45, 8:10,13) 'enter': in Mark used only in connection with a boat: 'embark'.

en tē thalassē 'in the sea' (i.e. the Lake of Galilee: cf. 1:16): the words are connected with *kathēsthai* 'he sat in the Lake', but the meaning is clear enough. Jesus was in (or, on) the Lake, seated in a boat, while the crowd was *pros tēn thalassan* 'on the beach', 'near the water', *epi tēs gēs* 'on land'.

en 'on' (cf. Arndt & Gingrich I.1.b).

(Note: care should be taken to avoid the error into which several translations have fallen, namely, that of having Jesus sitting in the water! Cf. *The Bible Translator*, 2.143, 1951. Most English translations say simply 'on the water', no misunderstanding resulting. Some, however, use a descriptive phrase: Weymouth 'a little way from the land'; Manson 'lie off-shore'; cf. Brazilian 'pulling away from the beach'.)

pros tēn thalassan 'by the sea-side' (cf. Arndt & Gingrich *pros* III.7) i.e. on the shore.

Translation: *Beside the sea* must be specific in some languages, i.e. 'on the shore, along the lake', or 'at the mouth of the sea' (Conob).

It is essential that one be consistent in the size and shape of boats depicted as being used on the Lake of Galilee (cf. 1 : 19).

In order to avoid the common mistake of having Jesus sit down in the water, it is necessary in some languages to specify that 'he got into a boat which was floating in the water and he sat down'. After all, it is possible to get into a boat which has been drawn up onto the shore, hence this detailed rearranging of the semantic components is required in some languages (e.g. Trique, Barrow Eskimo, Mazahua, and Kekchi).

In a number of languages there is no ambiguous way of speaking about the crowd as 'being beside the sea on the land'. One must specify whether the people were seated, standing, moving about, etc. In general it is preferable to employ a word meaning 'to be seated', since this is often also the most generic term indicating 'to be in a place'.

2 *And he taught them many things in parables, and in his teaching he said to them:* 3 *"Listen! A sower went out to sow.*

Exegesis: *en parabolais* (cf. 3:32) 'in parables', 'by means of parables'.
polla 'many things' (adjectival), *not* adverbial 'much' (cf. 1:45, 3:12).
en tē didachē autou (cf. 1:22) 'in his teaching', i.e. 'as he taught': the sense of *didachē* here is active 'the act of teaching' and not passive 'the thing taught', 'doctrine'.
akouete. idou 'listen!' (impv.) look!' (cf. 1:2). The second word simply strengthens the note of urgency and demand in the first, and need not be translated literally (cf. RSV, BFBS, and the majority of English translations which omit it).
ho speirōn 'the sower', 'the man who sows' (4:14): the present participle of the verb is to be taken as an active noun.
speirō (4:4, 14, 15, 16, 18, 20, 31, 32) 'sow'—only in this chapter, in Mark. The infinitive *speirai* 'to sow' indicates purpose: 'the sower went out *in order to* sow'. It should be noticed that the method employed in sowing was that of scattering the seed over the soil, as the sower walked through the field, and *not* that of dropping each seed individually into a hole previously dug in the ground for that purpose.

Translation: For *parables* see 3:23.
In his teaching may be rendered 'as he was teaching them', in order to emphasize the active process, not the passive content of the teaching.
In many regions of the world this parable causes almost unbelievable difficulty because the method of sowing is not understood. For example, in a great many parts of the world the common process of sowing involves the use of a dibble stick by which a hole is made in prepared soil and in this hole a number of grains are dropped, after which the hole is carefully covered up and the soil sometimes tamped. The idea that a sower would be so utterly profligate as to throw seed broadcast is sometimes interpreted as a sure sign of incurable laziness or even of insanity. The reader then judges that for some of the seed to be lost to the birds, choked by weeds, or ruined by sprouting too soon in shallow soil is only to be expected in view of such an incredibly stupid method of sowing. On the other hand, it is impossible to change the method of sowing as spoken of in this parable, for the parable itself is not understandable except in terms of such a procedure. The only thing that one can do is to make certain that one does indicate that this was broadcast sowing 'scattering the seed on plowed ground' (or 'prepared ground'), 'to sow-scatter', used of upland rice (Ifugao), and 'to plant by throwing' (Chontal of Oaxaca). This is much better than implying that the sower was so utterly lacking in judgment that he would have used a dibble stick on stony ground or in a path.
Fundamentally, the translator is confronted by three types of meaning:

syntactic (the meanings of grammatical constructions), lexical (the meanings of individual words and phrases), and cultural. The first two he must deal with in terms of the closest natural equivalent (the meanings of concepts within a cultural framework). The latter can only be treated in commentaries, or at best through necessary marginal notes. What he must avoid, however, is deciding upon syntactic and lexical solutions which will make cultural meanings more difficult.

It is not necessary to repeat the lexical items 'sower' and 'sow'. If this would be stylistically awkward in a receptor language, one may say only 'a man went out to sow'.

4 *And as he sowed, some seed fell along the path, and the birds came and devoured it.*

Text: After *ta peteina* 'the birds' Textus Receptus adds *tou ouranou* 'of the heaven': all modern editions of the Greek text omit this addition.

Exegesis: *kai egeneto* 'and it was' plus the indicative *epesen* 'it fell': for this Semitic construction see 1 : 9, 2 : 23.

en tō speirein (cf. 6 : 48 for identical construction) 'in the sowing', 'as he sowed': a Semitic construction (Taylor, 62), but found also in Greek (Moulton *Prolegomena*, 249; Moule *Idiom Book*, 76f.).

ho men epesen 'some (seed) fell': throughout the whole parable (vv. 5, 7, 8) *sperma* 'seed' is to be understood.

ho ('some') is the neuter of the relative *hos* 'who', 'which': it is here used as a demonstrative 'this (seed)', 'this portion (of the seed)': cf. Arndt & Gingrich *hos* II.2. In connection with *allo* (v. 5) *allo* (v. 7) and *alla* (v. 8) the whole series may be translated: 'some...and other...and other...and others'. Notice that *ho* 'some' and *auto* 'it' are collective, meaning '*some* seed' (not singular, '*a* seed').

piptō (4 : 5,7,8, 5 : 22, 9 : 20, 13 : 25, 14 : 35) 'fall'.

para tēn hodon literally 'by (alongside) the path': some (Black *Aramaic*, 120) see in the Greek phrase a mistranslation of the underlying Aramaic, since the meaning, clearly, is '*on*' the beaten path that ran through the field, on which the sower walked as he scattered his seed (cf. Lk. 8 : 5 'and it was trodden upon'). "Along" (RSV) is ambiguous enough; some (Manson, Moffatt, Berkeley) have "on".

ta peteina (4 : 32) 'the birds'.

katephagen (12 : 40) 'they ate', 'they ate up', 'they devoured'.

Translation: Probably 'on the path' is a more justified translation, if one cannot use an ambiguous expression for the Greek phrase (see above).

The birds (as indicated in the added phrase *of heaven*) refer to the undomesticated song birds or wild birds, to be distinguished in a number of languages from domesticated fowl. In Tzeltal these former are the 'field birds'.

Many languages distinguish carefully the way in which a bird eats from the manner in which people or animals eat. One must make certain to employ the right term.

5 *Other seed fell on rocky ground, where it had not much soil, and immediately it sprang up, since it had no depth of soil; 6 and when the sun rose it was scorched, and since it had no root it withered away.*

Exegesis: *epi to petrōdes hopou ouk eichen gēn pollēn* 'on rocky (stony) ground where it did not have much soil': what is meant is a shallow layer of soil covering the outcropping of an underlying bedrock (cf. Vincent *Word Studies* I, 77 on Mt. 13:5).

Grammatically *allo* 'other (seed)' is the subject of *ouk eichen* 'it had not' and *to mē echein* 'not to have': this other portion of seed *did not have* much soil, and it sprang up immediately because *it did not have* any depth of soil. The same meaning, however, may be achieved in another way: 'where *there was not* much soil...because *there was no* depth of soil' (cf. Goodspeed, Brazilian).

euthus exaneteilen 'immediately it sprang up', 'quickly it sprouted'.

hote aneteilen ho hēlios (16:2) 'when the sun rose', 'after the sun had risen' (cf. 1:32 'when the sun set'). This does not mean 'at sunrise': what is meant is that the sun, high in the sky, was sufficiently hot to scorch the newly sprouted plant.

ekaumatisthē (only here in Mark) 'it was burned', 'it was scorched'.

dia to mē echein rizan 'because it had no root': *dia* 'on account of' with the infinitive indicates cause.

riza (4:17, 11:20) 'root': due to lack of soil the roots barely developed.

exēranthē (cf. 3:1) 'it was withered', 'it was shrivelled up'.

Translation: *Rocky ground* in this passage must be translated in such a way that people understand it not as soil having many stones, but as soil consisting of a thin overlayer on bedrock. This is done in some languages by saying 'fell into thin soil which was lying on huge rocks' (as a way of combining the first two clauses into one).

Some translators have failed to translate the second part of verse 5 correctly because they themselves did not understand it. This passage refers to the fact that in the spring of the year thin soil over bedrock or near outcroppings becomes warm faster than deep soil. This contributes to the more rapid germination of the seed. Hence, the seeds do actually spring up quickly, precisely because the soil is thin.

In the English text the seed is referred to collectively, and the pronominal reference in the singular *it* identifies the portion of seeds which fell in one place or another. In many languages, however, plurals are required, e.g. 'other seeds fell...and immediately they sprang up...'

When the sun rose should not be restricted merely to the position of the sun in the eastern sky (a typical mistake), but to the sun high in the heavens, scorching the vegetation (the early morning sun is not likely to scorch any vegetation).

In verse 6 *it* refers to the germinated seeds, hence, 'the plants'. Accordingly, in some languages one must speak of 'the seeds' in verse 5 and 'the small plants' in verse 6.

Since it had no root must not be taken in the absolute sense, or these plants would be quite miraculous. The meaning therefore is 'because they did not have much root' or 'because they did not have deep roots'.

It might seem that in indicating the extent to which a translator is required in some languages to be more specific than the text we are being unnecessarily pedantic or quibbling. This is not the case. We are only calling to the attention of the translator the fact that in many languages, especially of predominantly horticultural peoples, lexical distinctions between words require the selection of forms which are more specific than the corresponding Greek text.

7 *Other seed fell among thorns and the thorns grew up and choked it, and it yielded no grain.*

Exegesis: *eis tas akanthas* 'among the thorns': in clearing the ground for planting, the roots of these thorns and weeds had not been removed, and in time they sprang up and choked the tender plants (cf. Rawlinson).

akanthai (4:8) 'thorns', 'thistles', 'weeds': cf. Arndt & Gingrich for identification; Dalman *Sacred Sites and Ways*, 247f.

eis 'among' (cf. Arndt & Gingrich 1.a.β).

anebēsan (cf. 1:10) 'came up': here as a synonym of *exanatellō* (v. 5) 'spring up', 'sprout'.

kai sunepnixan auto 'and they choked it', i.e. the plant sprouting from the seed which had been sown, not (clearly) the seed itself in the ground.

sumpnigō (4:19) 'crowd together', 'choke off'.

karpon ouk edōken 'it yielded no fruit': referring to grain, "yielded no grain" (Goodspeed, RSV), "bore no crop" (cf. BFBS).

karpos (4:8, 29, 11:14, 12:2) 'fruit'.

Translation: *Other seed* (which is collective) may be rendered as 'other seeds' or 'other grains'. In Chontal of Oaxaca one may say 'two and three seeds', for this is the idiomatic way of saying 'some'. In Tzeltal the equivalent expression is 'another hand-full of seeds'.

These seeds did not actually fall among thorns, in the sense of growing plants, but where thorns had been growing or where there were roots of thorn plants, for note that the effect upon the seed is not seen until the "thorns grew up". In some languages, therefore, one may translate 'where thorn plants had been' or 'where thorn-plant roots were'.

Choked is a good idiom in English and Greek, but not acceptable in many languages. In Kekchi one must say, 'the thorns grew up and made a shadow' (thus preventing the growth of the grain). In Tzeltal one may say 'the plants made it to stop growing'; in Tarahumara and Subanen 'made them unable to grow'; in Huave 'shaded them under'; in Chontal of Tabasco 'took them under'; in South Toradja and Javanese 'they held it under' and in Bare'e 'they overshadowed it'.

131

8 *And other seeds fell into good soil and brought forth grain, growing up and increasing and yielding thirtyfold and sixtyfold and a hundredfold."*

Text: The reading *eis...en...en* 'in...in...in' of the Nestle text is also adopted by Westcott and Hort, Merk, and Vogels; *Textus Receptus*, Lagrange, Kilpatrick, and Taylor have *hen...hen...hen* 'one...one... one' (cf. Vulgate *unum...unum...unum*); Soden has *heis...heis...heis* 'one...one...one'; Swete, Souter and Tischendorf have *eis...eis...eis* 'in...in...in'. Although there is considerable division of opinion over the exact form of the expression, there is no doubt as to the meaning (cf. *Exegesis*, below). Lagrange and Taylor consider the Nestle reading intolerable and bizarre; in light of probable Semitic correspondence, it is probable that their reading *hen...hen...hen* is to be preferred.

Exegesis: *alla* 'other seeds' (in contrast with *ho...allo...allo* (vv. 4, 5, 7) 'some...other...other', which speak of portions in general): the plural is here used since different individual returns are to be listed.

tēn gēn tēn kalēn 'the good soil'.

kalos "primarily of outward form, *fair, beautiful*" (Abbott-Smith): from this primary meaning there developed the sense of 'good', 'useful'. In Mark the word is used in three different ways: (1) 'good', 'useful', 'fine' 4:8, 20, 9:50, 14:6; (2) 'advantageous', 'fitting', 'right' 7:27, 9:5; and (3) the comparative sense 'better' 9:42, 43, 45, 47, 14:21.

kai edidou karpon...kai epheren 'and it yielded grain...and bore': the two imperfects are coordinate, the second explaining the first.

pherō (cf. 1:32) 'bear (fruit)': cf. Arndt & Gingrich 2.

anabainonta kai auxanomena 'springing up and growing': the two participles modify *alla* 'other seeds'; as to time, they are properly simultaneous with *edidou karpon* 'yielded grain, as they sprang up and grew, (and bore)'. BFBS "and coming up and growing produced a crop and bore..." admirably ties together the two verbs and the two participles.

anabainō (cf. v. 7) 'come up', 'spring up', 'sprout'.

auxanō (only here in Mark) 'grow', 'increase', 'develop'.

eis...en...en (Nestle) 'in...in...in' (or, better, *hen...hen...hen* 'one...one...one'—see *Text*). The use of *heis* 'one' as a distributive (cf. Arndt & Gingrich *heis* 4) is patterned after the Semitic fashion (cf. Black *Aramaic*, 90): *hen triakonta kai hen exēkonta kai hen hekaton* means 'one, thirty, and one, sixty, and one, a hundred', i.e. 'thirtyfold, sixtyfold, and a hundredfold'.

Translation: Because of the complications of temporal order involved in the sequence as translated in the RSV, it is preferable to shift to an approximation of the BFBS order, which however must be rendered in some languages as four coordinate expressions, 'sprang up, grew, bore mature seeds, and gave thirtyfold...' (Tarahumara).

The statements of ratio (*thirtyfold, sixtyfold, and a hundredfold*) almost always cause certain complications in translating, unless one is fortunate enough to discover some ready-made formula for this type of expression.

However, the ideas expressed in this verse can always be stated, even if they seem somewhat paraphrastic: 'some plants produced thirty grains, other plants produced sixty grains, and still other plants produced one hundred grains' (Tzotzil, Tetelcingo Aztec, Gurunse, Ifugao, and Barrow Eskimo). In Loma, however, one must refer to the head of wheat, e.g. 'one head of seed had thirty seeds, another had sixty seeds...' A different perspective is used in Totonac, 'people got thirty grains from some plants, sixty from other plants...' Statements which describe the increase in terms of the number of seeds produced by various plants are quite justified, since each plant results from a single seed and hence a plant producing thirty, sixty, or a hundred seeds would represent this extent of increase.

9 *And he said, "He who has ears to hear, let him hear."*

Exegesis: For the whole expression cf. 4:23, 7:16, and in the O.T. Deut. 29:4, Psalm 115:6. The meaning is "If any one is able (and willing) to learn, let him pay attention!"

ōta (4:23, 7:33, 8:18) 'ears'.

akouein 'to hear': the infinitive indicates purpose (cf. 4:3).

Translation: This aphoristic expression is a very effective one, but in some languages it must be slightly modified in order to be intelligible. In the first place, its generic quality sometimes must be altered from singular to plural 'all those who have...' In the second place, in a number of languages the *ears* must be the inner ears, by which one hears, not the outer projections from the head (cf. Spanish, Totonac). In the third place *let him hear* is not an expression of permission, but an exhortation, therefore, equivalent to 'he ought to listen' or 'they should pay attention' (Shilluk). *Ears to hear* may be rendered as 'ears with which he (or 'they') can hear'.

10 *And when he was alone, those who were about him with the twelve asked him concerning the parables.*

Exegesis: *kata monas* (only here and Lk. 9:18 in N.T.) 'alone': no place is specified in the text; it is simply indicated that Jesus withdrew from the crowd.

ērōtōn (7:26, 8:5) 'they asked', 'they asked a question' (in this passage and in 8:5); in late Greek it came to mean 'request', 'ask for' (as in 7:26): see Field *Notes*, 101-2.

hoi peri auton 'those about him', i.e. 'his followers' (cf. Lk. 22:49, Acts 13:13): see Arndt & Gingrich *peri* 2.a.δ. Compare *par' autou*, 3:21.

sun tois dōdeka 'with the Twelve': a title, not simply a number (cf. 3:16).

Translation: The clause *when he was alone* can, in a literal rendering, introduce a very confusing contradiction. People often ask, "How could he be alone, and still be in the presence of those who could ask him questions?" Obviously, the expression *was alone* must not be taken in the absolute sense, or it cannot be harmonized with the following clause. In some languages the only way to treat this expression satisfactorily is to render it 'when he was no longer with the crowd' or 'when the crowd was no longer there', for this is the meaning of the expression in the Greek text.

Those who were about him with the twelve poses a problem in some languages: "Who asked the question? Those who were about him, not including the twelve apostles, or should the twelve be included in the group of interrogators?" The English form of this expression might lead one to think that those who asked the question were the ones around Jesus and the twelve. The Greek text, however, makes it clear that Jesus was questioned by the twelve and those who clustered around, namely, his somewhat larger band of followers. In many languages this relationship must be made more explicit, e.g. 'when the twelve and those who were also around Jesus...' (Kiyaka), 'those who were around Jesus and also the twelve...' in which it is quite clear that the preposition 'around' goes only with Jesus and not with the twelve (Chontal of Oaxaca).

As noted in 3:14, it is often necessary to add some classifier to the expression 'the twelve'.

For *parables* see 3:23.

11 And he said to them, "To you has been given the secret of the kingdom of God, but for those outside everything is in parables;

Text: Before *to mustērion* 'the secret' *Textus Receptus* and Kilpatrick add *gnōnai* 'to know', which is omitted by all other editions of the Greek text.

Exegesis: *to mustērion...tēs basileias tou theou* 'the mystery of the kingdom of God': the probable meaning is 'the mystery *concerning* the kingdom of God' (although another meaning is possible: 'the mystery *which is* the kingdom of God').

mustērion (only here in Mark) 'mystery', 'secret' (cf. Hatch *Essays*, 57-62).

hē basileia tou theou 'the kingdom of God': cf. 1:14.

humin...dedotai 'to you...has been given', i.e. by *God* (cf. Jeremias *Parables*, 13; cf. *peplērotai* 'has been fulfilled' in 1:15).

ekeinois de tois exō 'but to those who are outside', i.e. those who, in contrast with *humin* 'you', do not belong to the immediate group of disciples to whom God has given the secret (cf. Swete); some (cf. Gould) refer the 'outsiders' to those who are outside the Kingdom.

en parabolais 'in parables', 'by means of parables' (Moule *Idiom Book*, 77). The sense of 'parables' here is clearly that of something hard to understand, i.e. 'riddles' (cf. Jeremias *Parables*, 14), after the Hebrew *mashal* 'parable' (cf. 3:23). In the Marcan context, however, *parabolē* 'parable' is a Christian technical term and means the stories Jesus used as illustrations in his teaching about the kingdom of God.

ta panta ginetai 'all things are', 'all things come': Arndt & Gingrich *ginomai* I.3.b.γ, 'those outside receive everything in parables'; Lagrange *tout arrive en paraboles*. *ta panta* 'all things' in this context refer to the teachings, the truths, the explanations concerning the kingdom of God.

Translation: In the expression *to you has been given the secret...* there is a passive construction which cannot be translated into a number of languages. However, two adaptations are possible: (1) the introduction of the agent, e.g. 'God has given (or 'is giving') to you the secret...' (Mezquital Otomí) or (2) the substitution of the active correspondent of give, namely, 'receive', e.g. 'you have received the secret...'

A *mystery* in the Biblical sense is essentially knowledge which has not been known to people in general, but revealed to the initiated, i.e. to the believers. Some translators have employed a phrase meaning 'that which is not known' (as the closest equivalent of *secret*), but this obviously will not do, for a mystery is not an unknown fact, but a specially revealed one. This particular value of the Greek expression can be expressed in various ways, e.g. 'that which was hidden' with the connotation that it is no longer so (Huave), 'that which has not been known' with the implication that it is now known (Mazahua), 'what is hard to understand', in which the meaning of 'riddle', 'difficult saying' is approximated (Barrow Eskimo).

If, as is most generally the case, one assumes the relationship between 'secret' and 'Kingdom' to be an objective one, the translation may be 'what was previously hidden about God's rule' (Huave), 'you have learned what was not formerly known about God's government' (Putu), and 'secret about how God rules' (Zoque).

If the appositional interpretation is followed, the problems of rendering are much greater, e.g. 'learned about the secret, and the secret is how God rules'.

Those outside if translated literally may mean nothing more than 'those outside the house' or 'those outside the village'. In many languages the contrasting expression with 'you' is simply 'the others' (Kiyaka) or 'other people'.

Everything may be rendered as 'all knowledge' or 'all the truth', e.g. 'other people receive all the knowledge in likeness-stories'.

12 *so that they may indeed see but not perceive, and may indeed hear but not understand; lest they should turn again, and be forgiven."*

Text: After *aphethē autois* 'it be forgiven them' *Textus Receptus* adds *ta hamartēmata* 'the sins', which is omitted by all modern editions of the Greek text.

Exegesis: This verse poses great difficulties to the interpreter; to the translator, however, there are somewhat fewer complications, for despite the difficulties in understanding, it should be rendered in a simple, straightforward manner.

hina 'in order that' expresses purpose. As the commentators note, with special reference to the divine will, purpose and result in Jewish thought are united into one. Cf. Arndt & Gingrich *hina* II. 2: "purpose and result are identical in declarations of the divine will." The words which follow are a free paraphrase of Isa. 6 : 9-10. (On the whole verse see commentaries *in loc.*; Jeremias *Parables*, 14-15; Black *Aramaic*, 153-58).

blepontes blepōsin...*akouontes akouōsin* 'seeing they may see...hearing they may hear': a Semitic way of intensive statement: 'that they may look and look...that they may listen and listen'.

kai mē idōsin...*kai mē suniōsin* 'and not see...and not understand', i.e. '*yet* not really see...*yet* not understand at all'.

suniēmi (or, *suniō*) (6:52, 7:14, 8:17, 21) 'understand', 'comprehend', 'gain insight'.

mēpote epistrepsōsin 'lest they should turn', 'so that they should not turn'.

mēpote 'lest': denotes purpose 'in order that...not' (cf. Arndt & Gingrich 2.b.α): cf. Brazilian *para que não*; Zürich *damit...nicht etwa*.

epistrephō (5:30, 8:33, 13:16) 'turn', 'return': in the spiritual sense of repent (cf. Act. 3:19, 26:20). The equivalent of the O.T. *shubh* 'turn': cf. 1 : 4 on *metanoia* 'repentance'.

kai aphethē autois 'and it be forgiven them': that is, 'and *God* should forgive them'. Cf. *aphiēmi* 'forgive' in 2:5, and *aphesis* 'forgiveness' 1:4.

Translation: It is not always easy to relate the purpose clause of verse 12 to the preceding expression in verse 11. In some languages one may insert a transitional element 'this happens in order that...'

Despite those who would assume some sort of result clause at this point, rather than purpose, it seems quite certain that Mark meant to express the purpose of God's way of revealing the mystery, an aspect of the providence of God which is almost incomprehensible to man, but which is as much a part of the Biblical perspective as any other (cf. God's hardening of Pharaoh's heart). To try to "water down" or alter this essential meaning which Mark evidently intended at this point is to do violence to one's commission as a translator.

These clauses pose a problem in some languages because of the positive-negative sequence within the purpose clause itself. In other words there are two purposes, one that people may see, but at the same time not perceive (the parallel is that they may hear, but at the same time do not understand). The first of these must be considered as a kind of concessive clause in some languages, and placed after the primary purpose (in this case the negative purpose), e.g. 'in order that it may not reach the heart (i.e. perceive), even though the people look and look at; and in order that they may not understand it, even though they listen and listen' (Tzeltal). In other languages the order of the Greek may be retained, and the concessive clause preposed, e.g. 'it is for this reason that though they look and look they do not see...' (Kiyaka).

To turn again is the translation of the Greek word traditionally rendered as 'to be converted'. This type of expression is translated in a number of ways in different languages, e.g. 'to change completely' (Barrow Eskimo), 'to turn around' (Tarascan), 'to have one's life changed' (Totonac), 'to make pass over bounds within' (Mazatec), 'turn the heart toward God' (San Blas), 'the heart turns itself back' (Chol), 'self-heart change' (Zacapoastla Aztec), 'to turn away from, unlearn something' (Bare'e), 'to turn around from the breast' (Cuicatec), and 'to return' (Luvale). One of the difficult distinctions to be made in translating is the difference between repentance and conversion, words which in some contexts are not perceptively different in areas of meaning. Both are closely related spiritual experiences, but the one is generally described as preceding the other and the second as being a more complete transformation than the former. The following contrasting sets are illustrative:

Language	'repentance'	'conversion'
Ngok Dinka	'to turn the heart'	'to turn oneself'
Balinese	'to put on a new mind'	'to put on a new behavior'
Tzeltal	'to cause one's heart to return because of one's sin'	'to cause one's heart to return to God's presence'
Northern Sotho	'to become untwisted'	'to retrace one's steps'
Timorese	'to turn the heart upside down'	'to return'

The final clause introduced by *lest* in English is an expression of negative purpose, which is dependent, not upon the immediately preceding clause, but upon the final clause of verse 11. Because of the grammatical distance involved in this relationship, one must introduce in some languages a further transitional element, 'this has happened in order that...'

For *forgiveness* see 1·4.

13 *And he said to them, "Do you not understand this parable? How then will you understand all the parables?*

Exegesis: *ouk oidate tēn parabolēn tautēn*; 'do you not understand this parable?': as a question, this is purely rhetorical, since it is not a request for information, but stands as an accusation. It may be taken as a statement, however: 'You don't understand this parable! How then...?' Or it may be taken as a condition: 'If you don't understand this parable... how will you...?' (cf. Goodspeed, Berkeley, Williams).

oidate...gnōsesthe 'you know...you will know': it is precarious to try to maintain a strict distinction between *oida* 'know by intuition or insight' and *ginōskō* 'know by experience or observation' as do Swete, Taylor. *oida* occurs some 23 times in Mark and *ginōskō* 12.

Translation: Note that the direct discourse may consist of questions, in which case the introductory verb must often be 'questioned' rather than 'said'. On the other hand, the first expression may be a statement (see above), followed by a question. In any event the questions are strictly rhetorical, and if such questions are treated in any particular manner in the receptor language this fact should be consistently indicated.

14 *The sower sows the word.* **15** *And these are the ones along the path, where the word is sown; when they hear, Satan immediately comes and takes away the word which is sown in them.*

Text: Instead of *eis autous* 'in them' in v. 15 read by Nestle, Westcott and Hort, Souter, Taylor, and Kilpatrick, *Textus Receptus* has *en tais kardiais autōn* 'in their hearts'; Tischendorf, Soden, Vogels, Merk, and Lagrange have *en autois* 'in them'.

Exegesis: *houtoi...hoi para tēn hodon* 'these...(are) the ones along the path': it is to be noticed that in the explanation of the parable (vv. 15-20) the demonstratives, prepositional phrases and participles are all masculine, not neuter. The explanation of the parable has in view men (not seeds), i.e. the listeners, those who in one way or another receive the word (proclaimed to them).

hoi para tēn hodon 'the ones along the path': it is not said of these (as it is of the others, vv. 16, 18, 20) '*sown* on the path' since they were not properly sown at all—they *fell* on the path without penetrating the soil.

In the explanation, by a change of figure, the various kinds of soil become various kinds of men who (literally) are *sown therein*. Properly what is sown is the (same) Word, and the soils represent the different classes of hearers: in the explanation, however, the various classes of hearers are *sown*. Though there is inconsistency in figures between the parable and its explanation, the meaning is clear throughout, and a straightforward translation will reproduce the meaning accurately.

ho logos 'the Word', 'the (Christian) Message' (cf. 2:2).

eis autous 'in them' (*not*, 'among').

airei (some 20 times in Mark) 'carry away', 'take off'.

Translation: In some languages a metaphor such as 'the sower sows the word' is meaningless, but a simile is completely understandable, and in fact is the closest natural equivalent, e.g. 'the sower, as it were, sows the word'. This little element 'as it were' (whether a complete phrase, a particle, or even a suffix on the verb) gives the clue to the reader that this is not to be understood literally, but in a figurative sense. Such shifts from strict metaphors to similes are frequently required for proper sense.

The word is in this context 'the message', 'the pronouncement', or even 'the good news', for this is the technical use of Greek *logos* to represent the Christian message.

There is a certain difficulty in the words used to introduce the series of four types of persons. In the RSV the words used are *these* (verse 15), *these* (verse 16), *others* (verse 18) and *those* (verse 20). In other languages one may need to adapt this series somewhat in order to produce an intelligible sequence, e.g. 'some...others...still others...finally those'.

These are the ones along the path...is a metaphorical expression which may be shifted into the form of a simile by some verb such as 'represent', 'stand for', or 'mean', e.g. 'some represent the people along the path...'

Sown in them must in many languages be 'sown in their hearts'.

16 And these in like manner are the ones sown upon rocky ground, who, when they hear the word, immediately receive it with joy; 17 and they have no root in themselves, but endure for a while; then, when tribulation or persecution arises on account of the word, immediately they fall away.

Exegesis: *homoiōs* (15:31) 'likewise', 'in like manner': that is, *these* are (like *those*, in v. 15, who are along the path) those who are sown upon rocky places.

hoi epi ta petrōdē speiromenoi 'they who are sown upon rocky places': notice plural *petrōdē* 'rocky places' instead of the sing. *petrōdes* in v. 5.

meta charas lambanousin auton 'with joy receive it'.

chara (only here in Mark) 'joy', 'happiness'.

lambanō (some 20 times in Mark) 'receive', 'accept'.

ouk echousin rizan en heautois 'they have no root in themselves', that is, have no depth of conviction or belief: due to the sparsity of soil the roots do not develop and sink as deeply as they should. The figure is that of lack of firmness, stability, endurance: they are *proskairoi* 'lasting only for a time', 'temporary'.

eita genomenēs thlipseōs ē diōgmou 'then when affliction or persecution comes'.

thlipsis (13:19,24) 'tribulation', 'affliction', 'distress' (BFBS "trouble" is not quite adequate): cf. Lagrange.

diōgmos (10:30) 'persecution'.

euthus skandalizontai 'immediately they are scandalized': this clause parallels that of v. 16 'immediately they receive it with joy'.

skandalizomai literally 'to be ensnared', 'be trapped' (cf. Moulton & Milligan, Lagrange). The word appears in Mark in the active and in the passive: (1) in the active it is causative, 'cause to be ensnared', 'cause to stumble', 9:42,43,45,47; (2) in the passive 'to be ensnared', 'be offended', 4:17, 14:27,29; in 6:3 'to be offended *by* (someone)'.

The English "scandalize" does not adequately *translate* the Greek verb, and other verbs are used to convey the meaning: "fall away" (RSV, BFBS, Montgomery), with its note of finality, is perhaps too strong; "are repelled" (Moffatt), "stumble" (ASV), "stumble and fall" (Berkeley, Weymouth), Zürich *nehmen sie Anstoss* 'they take offence', are other possibilities. The idea conveyed by the Greek verb is that of being offended and repelled to the point of abandoning (whether temporarily or perma-

139

nently, the word itself does not specify) belief in the Word (cf. Lk. 8:13), or one's relation with Jesus (14:27, 29).

Translation: The phrase *in like manner* helps to indicate the symbolic character of the passage, and may serve to make the figurative expression more like a simile, e.g. 'in a similar way others are the people who are sown...' At this point, however, one must be careful that the resulting phrase 'sown on the rocky ground' does not mean 'thrown down on the rocks' (as in some translations). It is all right to speak of 'seed being thrown into the rocky ground' but to speak of 'people being thrown into rocky ground' may completely destroy the value of the figure. This difficulty may be solved by translating 'others are the people who are there where the rocky ground is...'

The syntax of the constructions 'these...the ones...who, when...; then when...' is very complex, and usually some drastic alterations must be made to adapt this to the grammatical requirements of the receptor language, e.g. 'these are the people in the rocky ground; just as soon as they hear the word they hold it in their heart (Shilluk) accept it and are happy. But they do not have a sort of root in themselves, and they only last for a little while. When difficulties come and people hate them because of the good news, they immediately give up'.

Since the phrase *receive with joy* involves two processes, it is often translated as two related events, e.g. 'agree quickly and are happy' (Loma), 'they hear it and are glad' (Popoluca), 'they receive it while their heart is glad' (Toba Batak). In other cases the expression may be combined as a single phrase 'hold it in their heart' (Shilluk), which involves the meaning of not only accepting the truth but receiving it with gladness.

They have no root in themselves must be treated as a simile in many languages, e.g. 'they do not have as it were any root' or 'their hearts do not have any root-like thing'.

Endure for a while is idiomatically translated in Kekchi as 'they are like passers by', an apt description of the transient enthusiast for Christianity. Cf. South Toradja 'their heart is shallow', Javanese 'they are not steadfast', Bare'e 'only a moment is their heart quiet'.

Tribulation may be rendered as 'difficulties', 'hardships', 'troubles'. These are events which may or may not have human instigation. The *persecution*, however, is the result of hatred, enmity, or malintent of others, e.g. 'being hated' (Zoque), 'caused to see trouble', or 'being stoned'—an expression used in Pame to include all types of persecution.

There are a number of senses in which the Greek verb *skandalizō* may be taken in this context and only rarely can one use the meaning of 'to stumble'. In various languages the resulting equivalent expressions vary widely, e.g. 'to give up' (Tzeltal, Tarascan), 'no longer like it' (Navajo, Zoque), 'get rid of it right away' (Kituba,—reminding one of our game of "hot potato"), 'to turn back' (Huichol), and 'to go by another road' (Piro). This last expression is particularly suggestive of the moral and spiritual issues involved.

18 *And others are the ones sown among thorns; they are those who hear the word,* 19 *but the cares of the world, and the delight in riches, and the desire for other things, enter in and choke the word, and it proves unfruitful.*

Exegesis: *kai* (at the beginning of v. 19) is adversative 'but': so the great majority of modern translations have it.

hai merimnai tou aiōnos 'the anxieties of (this) age', that is, of the present life.

merimna (only here in Mark) 'anxiety', 'worry', 'care'.

aiōn (cf. 3:29) 'age': here it means the present age; by an extension of meaning the word denotes the *scene* of this age, the *place* where this age is effective, i.e. "this *world*" (RSV, BFBS).

hē apatē tou ploutou 'the deceit of riches'.

apatē (only here in Mark) may mean 'deceitfulness' (ASV, Weymouth, BFBS) or 'pleasure' (in a bad sense) (Goodspeed, Montgomery, RSV; cf. Lagrange *les délices de la richesse*). Williams combines the two ideas 'deceiving pleasures'; Manson has 'glamour'; Brazilian 'fascination'.

ploutos (only here in Mark) 'wealth', 'riches'.

hai peri ta loipa epithumiai 'and the desires for other things'.

epithumia (only here in Mark) 'desire', 'longing', 'craving': usually in a bad sense; Arndt & Gingrich classify its use here as neutral.

to loipon (14:41, 16:13) 'the remaining', 'the rest'; *ta loipa* means 'the other things' (i.e. besides *riches* of the previous clause). *peri ta loipa* 'for other things'.

eisporeuomenai (cf. 1:21) 'entering', 'coming in': all these things come into the individual's heart, or life, where the seed has been planted.

sumpnigousin ton logon 'they choke the (Christian) message' (cf. v. 7) which has been sown.

kai akarpos ginetai 'and it (the Word) becomes fruitless': this is not to be taken in the sense of becoming fruitless after having been fruitful; rather, the Word bears no fruit at all.

Translation: Even though it may be necessary to introduce the other classes of persons (or soil) (verses 15 and 16) by some sort of simile (or equivalent expression), it may be that by this verse the metaphor may be preserved without any clue phrase. But if not, or if the parallel construction would make the passage more intelligible, then all four elements in the series may be introduced in a similar manner.

The word must be translated the same in each instance, cf. verses 14, 15, 16, 17, and 18. There should be no confusion at this point that *the word* refers to the Christian message.

The basic problem encountered by many translators in rendering verse 19 is the fact that those factors which make the persons unfruitful are given in Greek as nouns, but they really refer to processes, i.e. events, and as such, must be translated in many languages as verbal expressions, often with a full complement of subjects and objects. *The cares of the world* is in some languages rendered as follows: 'they think very much about these days now', in which for Greek *aiōn* a time equivalent of

141

'days' is better than a spatial one of 'world' (Kekchi); 'they begin to worry about this world-things' (Gurunse); 'their hearts are gone doing what they do when they pass through world', in which the last phrase is an idiomatic equivalent for 'this life' (Tzeltal); 'they think intensely about things in this world' (Mitla Zapotec, Huave); 'all the time they think about things in the world' (Eastern Otomí); 'the longing for this world' (Bare'e); 'they are very occupied about things in the world' (Tzotzil); 'they are very much afraid about what will happen in the world' (Tarahumara); and 'the heavy talk about things in the world' (Shilluk).

The traditional interpretation of *deceitfulness of riches* generally causes more complications than the exegetically preferable *delight in riches* since the former phrase breaks the sequence of objective relationships (i.e. 'cares about the world' and 'desire for other things', in which the second element is the object of the process implied in the first) with a subjective relationship, i.e. 'riches deceive'. However, this idea may be translated, but it must in many languages be somewhat expanded in form, e.g. 'because they have much in their pockets they are deceived' (Huichol), 'fooled themselves in wishing to get rich' (Tarascan), 'they wanted to get rich; but they deceived themselves' (Mixtec), and 'their money deceives them' (Zacapoastla Aztec). The objective relationship, in which the riches are the object of the delight, may be translated as follows: 'they are happy with riches' (Gurunse), 'they are so delighted to be rich', and 'they take much pleasure in all the things they have'.

The desire for other things must frequently be translated as a verb expression, and with some type of contrastive generic value added to 'other things', i.e. 'all sorts of other things', since the equivalent of *riches* is often a word meaning abundance of 'things', 'possessions', and 'objects', e.g. 'they get all tied up for other sorts of things' (Shilluk), 'they crave many things' (Zacapoastla Aztec), 'they intensely desire other things' (Gurunse), and 'they covet all sorts of things' (Navajo).

If one has translated the processes 'cares...delight...and...desire' by verbs, it is usually impossible to talk of these experiences as 'entering in'. The equivalent is simply that 'people care...delight in...and desire...; therefore the word cannot grow' (or 'gets shut off', 'gets shaded over', or 'is closed off'). *Proves unfruitful* means 'does not produce anything', 'did not grow anything' (Barrow Eskimo), and 'was killed'.

20 **But those that were sown upon the good soil are the ones who hear the word and accept it and bear fruit, thirtyfold and sixtyfold and a hundredfold."**

Text: Instead of *en...en...en* 'in...in...in' read by Tischendorf, Nestle, Westcott and Hort, Soden, Vogels, Merk, and Souter, *hen...hen...hen* 'one...one...one' is read by *Textus Receptus*, Lagrange, Kilpatrick, and Taylor (cf. v. 8).

Exegesis: *ekeinoi...hoi...sparentes* 'those...who...(were) sown': prob-

142

ably some distinction should be made between *ekeinoi* 'those' and *houtoi* 'these' of vv. 15, 16 (*alloi* 'others' v. 18); some difference, likewise, is probably intended by the use of the aorist participle *sparentes* 'sown' in the present verse, instead of the present participle *speiromenoi* 'sown' of vv. 16, 18.

hoitines (9:1, 12:18, 15:7) 'those who', i.e. 'the *very ones who*' (referred to in the previous clause).

paradechontai (only here in Mark) 'they receive', 'they accept': here used as a synonym for *lambanousin* 'they receive' of v. 16.

karpophorousin (4:28) 'they bear fruit', 'they produce a crop'.

Translation: *Accept it* must mean more than simply 'receive it' or 'hear it'. The implication here is that people believe the word, e.g. 'put it in their hearts' (Tzeltal), 'take the word with truth' (Loma), or 'to hear and understand' (Tumbuka).

Bear fruit is all right when speaking of plants, but the figure may not be acceptable when speaking of persons. Hence, one must often substitute a phrase meaning 'to produce results' or 'to cause blessing'.

For an analysis of *thirtyfold, and sixtyfold and a hundredfold* see 4:8.

21 **And he said to them, "Is a lamp brought in to be put under a bushel, or under a bed, and not on a stand?**

Text: Instead of *tethē* 'put' (after *luchnian* 'lampstand') of all modern editions of the Greek text, *Textus Receptus* has *epitethē* 'put upon'.

Exegesis: The verse contains three questions, the first two of which expect a negative answer, and the last a positive answer. A translation should make this clear.

mēti erchetai 'does it come (to be put under a bushel)? (No!)': the verb *erchetai* 'come' is here used with the meaning 'is brought' (Arndt & Gingrich I.1.c.β).

luchnos (only here in Mark) 'lamp': this is an oil-burning wick lamp, the wick lying in a shallow bowl filled with oil.

hina hupo ton modion tethē 'in order that it be placed under the bushel'.

modios (only here in Mark) 'bushel': a dry measure of about two gallons; in this passage, as Lagrange points out, the reference is probably to a large bowl used to hold (and measure) the grain, under which the lamp would be placed at bedtime. Cf. BFBS "measuring-vessel".

tithēmi 'place', 'put': in Mark used in the passive here and 15:47; in the active, 4:30, 6:29,56, 8:25, 10:16, 12:36, 15:19,46, 16:6.

klinēn (7:30) 'bed' 'couch': perhaps the couch that went with the table at which they reclined for meals. Not to be confused with the *krabatos* 'pallet' of 2:4.

luchnian (only here in Mark) 'lampstand': "candle" and "candlestick" (AV) are not, of course, an accurate translation of the Greek words.

Translation: *Said* must be translated as 'asked' in some languages because of the questions which follow.

143

Since two of the questions imply negative answers and one a positive one, some languages require that these be split, e.g. 'People do not bring a lamp in and put it under a bushel or under a bed, do they? Don't they bring it in and put it on a stand?'

As noted above, the *lamp* in this context is a kind of oil lamp, not a candle or a torch.

The equivalent of 'measuring vessel' may be in some languages 'bucket', 'pail', or 'vessel'. In some instances there are a number of terms, each denoting a special shape and size of container. In so far as possible the most general object of the approximate equivalent size should be chosen, provided that it is not of material which would immediately ignite (as was done in one language in which the name of a small loosely woven basket was used).

In some instances people do not have an indigenous word for bed, since they sleep either on skins or mats on the floor or in hammocks. In such instances one may use 'benches for sleeping' or 'wide shelf for sleeping' (Tarahumara). Since most South Toradjas still sleep on a mat on the floor the expression is here translated 'in the space under the house' (the house being built on piles).

The *stand* may be described as 'the elevated (or high) place for the lamp'.

22 *For there is nothing hid, except to be made manifest; nor is anything secret, except to come to light.* 23 *If any man has ears to hear, let him hear."*

Text: *ti* 'anything' in v. 22 is omitted by Westcott and Hort, Lagrange, and Taylor, but retained by *Textus Receptus* and the great majority of modern editions of the Greek text.

Exegesis: The two parallel clauses, in Semitic style, both state the same truth: 'if something is hidden, it is in order that it (eventually) be manifested; if something is covered up, it is in order that it (eventually) be brought out into the open'.

krupton (only here in Mark) 'hidden'.

phanerōthē (16: 12, 14) 'that it be revealed', 'that it be manifested'.

apokruphon (only here in Mark) 'covered up', 'secret'.

elthē eis phaneron (cf. 3 : 12) 'that it come into the open', 'that it become known'.

For v. 23 see 4 : 9.

Translation: It is often quite difficult to treat the double negatives in verse 22, literally 'nothing...if not'. In some languages such a construction must be rendered by positives (e.g. Cashibo and Amuzgo) 'everything that is hidden is that way in order that it may be made to be seen'.

In the words 'hid' there is no implication that such objects were purposely hidden. The Greek does not imply in this first instance any process, only a state of being. On the other hand, in the second form of essentially this same concept (typical of Hebrew parallelism) the Greek verb *egeneto* may imply that something 'has become hidden', e.g. 'if there is anything that has become hidden, it is that way in order that it will be put out in the light' or 'everything that has become hidden...' On the other hand, *egeneto* may be only a stylistic variant of the previous *estin*.

For verse 23, see 4 : 9.

24 *And he said to them, "Take heed what you hear; the measure you give will be the measure you get, and still more will be given you. 25 For to him who has will more be given; and from him who has not, even what he has will be taken away."*

Exegesis: *blepete ti akouete* 'see what you hear', i.e. 'pay attention to what you are listening to!'

en hō metrō metreite metrēthēsetai 'in the (same) measure you measure (for others) it will be measured out (to you)'.

metron (only here in Mark) 'measure': a measure of capacity.

metreō (only here in Mark) 'measure out': Arndt & Gingrich 2, 'give out', 'apportion', 'deal out' something to someone.

prostethēsetai (only here in Mark) 'more shall be given', 'shall be added', 'shall be given in addition'. The two passives *metrēthēsetai humin kai prostethēsetai humin* 'shall be measured out to you and more shall be added to you' are to be referred to God, as the subject (cf. v. 11; cf. Dalman *Words*, 224).

dothēsetai...arthēsetai 'shall (more) be given...shall be taken away': these two passives also, as in the previous verse, are to be referred to God as the subject.

hos ouk echei, kai ho echei 'he who has not, even what he has': the meaning, naturally, is 'he who has very little, even the little that he has will be taken away'—it would, of course, be impossible to take away from someone something he actually does not have.

Translation: *Take heed what you hear* is translated in two different ways: (1) 'pay attention to what you hear' (the preferred rendering) and (2) 'discriminate carefully between the things which you might hear', e.g. 'select the right things to listen to'. This latter rendering does not seem to fit this type of context, especially after verse 23.

Take heed is translated in Conob as 'to hear dying'. The word 'dying' added to the admonition 'to hear' indicates the importance of listening, a kind of "life or death matter".

In some languages the order of constituents in the expression *the measure...you get* must be changed so that the persons participating are the active subject, rather than the measure, e.g. 'you will receive the same kind of measure that you measure out to others'. In other languages the *measure* is treated in somewhat more generic terms, 'what you have given to others will be what you get' in which the meanings

145

'to give' and 'to measure out to' are rendered by the same word (Subanen).

The last clause in verse 24 must in some instances be shifted so that the grammatical subject is the personal participant, even as in the previous clauses, e.g. 'and you will receive even more' (Shipibo). If *Textus Receptus* is followed, there may be even greater need of a shift in subject expression, e.g. 'you who hear will receive more' (Zoque, Eastern Otomí).

The passive expression in the first clause of verse 25 may be shifted to active, e.g. 'the one who has some will receive even more' (or in the passive form, 'will be given even more'). Where, however, the logical subject of the process of giving must be introduced, one may translate as 'God will give even more to the one who has some'.

The hyperbole about taking away from a man what he does not have can often be rendered as 'even if a man does not have anything, even the little that he does have will be taken away', thus preserving some measure of the extreme statement.

26 And he said, "The kingdom of God is as if a man should scatter seed upon the ground, 27 and should sleep and rise night and day, and the seed should sprout and grow, he knows not how.

Exegesis: *hōs ... balē* 'as though he might throw' (cf. Moule *Idiom Book*, 23).

ballō (cf. 2:22) 'throw': here used of scattering seed upon the ground in the process of sowing (cf. 4:3).

sporon (4:26, 27) 'seed': used as a synonym for *sperma* 'seed' (4:31).

kai katheudē kai egeirētai 'and he should sleep and rise': notice the two present tenses here in contrast with the aorist *balē* 'throw'. 'Sleep and rise night and day' means 'sleep at night and rise by day' (cf. Moffatt) i.e. the normal routine of daily activities: cf. Lagrange *sa vie tranquille*.

katheudō (4:38, 5:39, 13:36, 14:37,40,41) 'sleep'.

egeirō 'rise': here, rise from sleep (cf. 1:31).

blasta (only here in Mark) 'it sprouts', 'it buds'.

mēkunētai (only here in Mark) 'it becomes long' (from *mēkos* 'length'), 'it grows'.

hōs ouk oiden autos 'he doesn't know how': i.e. the man does not know how this process of germination and growth of the seed he planted takes place.

Translation: For *kingdom of God* see 1:15 and 4:11.

Is as if introduces a difficult grammatical construction, which requires some expansion in some languages, e.g. 'This is how God rules; it is as a man who...' (Zoque).

For *scatter seed* in the sense of 'sowing' see 4:3.

Ground should be 'prepared soil' or some other expression denoting the ground for planting, not just thrown on the ground indiscriminately.

The generic *seed* must often be translated as plural 'seeds' or 'grains' (Chontal of Tabasco).

If one translates literally *sleep and rise night and day* it may mean as in one language that the person is constantly disturbed night and day while he is sleeping. Many languages require that the sleeping and rising be properly paired with the night and day, e.g. 'sleep in the night and rise in the day' (Mazahua, Zacapoastla Aztec, Trique, Subanen, Black Bobo). However, in some languages one must shift the order of 'night and day' to 'day and night', since the ordinary way of speaking of such succession is first to mention the day and then the night (Tetelcingo Aztec).

He does not know how must in some instances be expanded because of the implied ellipsis following *how*, e.g. 'he does not know how this happens' (or '...how they grow'), referring to the germination and growing process (Barrow Eskimo; cf. South Toradja and Indonesian 'but he does not know how the growth goes').

28 The earth produces of itself, first the blade, then [the ear, then the full grain in the ear.

Exegesis: *automatē* (only here and in Acts 12:10 in the N.T.) 'of itself': of something which happens without visible cause (Arndt & Gingrich).

karpophorei (cf. 4:20) 'it bears fruit', 'it produces', 'it yields a crop'.

chorton (6:39) 'grass', 'hay'; also refers to stalks of grain in their early grass-like stages (cf. BFBS "green shoot").

stachun (cf. 2:23) 'head' or 'ear' (of grain).

plērēs (8:19) 'full': here in the sense of 'full grown', 'mature', 'ripe'.

sitos (only here in Mark) 'wheat' or 'grain'.

Translation: In some languages the relationship of the earth to the production of vegetation is quite easily expressed, e.g. 'the earth is the mother of the seed' (Tzeltal), but in others one cannot say that the 'earth' (which may mean only 'the dirt') produces plants of itself. In such instances one can say 'plants come from the ground' or 'plants grow out of the earth' (Kekchi).

The three stages of growth are variously described in different languages, e.g. 'first the leaf, then the seed-container and then the grain' (Subanen), and 'first the grass, then the green wheat, and then the ripe wheat' (Mitla Zapotec).

Ear must be altered in many languages, e.g. 'eyes of the grain' (Shilluk), referring to the tender grain in formation, and 'heads of the grain', denoting the ripened grain.

In this context it is not necessary to try to specify the details of the growth of wheat, especially in areas where such plants are not known. One can just as appropriately use Indian corn (Kekchi, Totonac, Zoque).

29 But when the grain is ripe, at once he puts in the sickle, because the harvest has come."

Exegesis: *hotan de paradoi ho karpos* 'when the fruit allows', i.e. 'when the crop permits': so, in a general sense, "when the grain is ripe" (RSV).

paradidōmi here has the sense of 'permit', 'allow' (Arndt & Gingrich, 4; cf. Turner; cf. Taylor, who quotes examples from classical Greek; Black *Aramaic*, 121f., agrees that this is the sense of the Greek text, but thinks that the underlying spoken Aramaic probably meant 'when the fruit has been produced'). For the use of *paradidōmi* 'hand over' see 1:14, 3:19.

apostellei to drepanon, hoti parestēken ho therismos 'he sends forth the sickle, because the harvest has come': the words reflect an O.T. passage, Joel 3:13 (LXX, 4:13).

apostellō 'send': Field (*Notes*, 26) argues for the meaning 'put forth' on the basis of the Hebrew verb *shalah* 'send', 'send forth', 'stretch out' which in Joel 3:13 the LXX translates *exapostellō* 'send forth'.

to drepanon (only here in Mark) 'sickle': by a change of figure "sends forth the sickle' stands for 'sends out *the reapers*' (Gould; cf. Weymouth).

hoti here is causative 'because'.

paristēmi (14:47,69,70, 15:35,39) 'is present' 'stands by'; 'is ready' (Arndt & Gingrich 2.b.β).

ho therismos (only here in Mark) 'harvest', 'time of harvest', 'harvesting'.

Translation: *Ripe* is rendered variously as 'hard', 'complete', 'ready', and 'fully grown'.

Puts in the sickle may refer to either (1) the immediate process of cutting the grain (by the grammatical subject of the expression), e.g. 'he cuts it down' (Zoque, Subanen) or 'cuts with a rounded machete' in which 'rounded machete' is the name of the harvesting sickle (Chontal of Tabasco), or (2) the sending of workmen into the harvest fields to do the work (seemingly the preferable rendering), e.g. 'sends those who bear the knives', in which 'knives' is the cultural equivalent of *sickle* (Shipibo); 'gives the order to those who cut with the sickle' (Toba Batak).

Harvest is 'the time of cutting' (Barrow Eskimo) or 'harvesting-time' (Shipibo).

30 *And he said, "With what can we compare the kingdom of God, or what parable shall we use for it?*

Text: Instead of *pōs* 'how' of all modern editions of the Greek text, *Textus Receptus* has *tini* 'with what'.

Instead of *tini* 'with what' (in the second clause) of all modern editions of the Greek text, *Textus Receptus* has *poia* 'what kind'.

Instead of *thōmen* 'may we put' of most modern editions of the Greek text, *Textus Receptus* and Kilpatrick have *parabalōmen* 'may we compare'.

Exegesis: *homoiōsōmen* (only here in Mark) 'shall we compare', 'shall we liken'.

parabolē (cf. 3:23) 'parable': here the sense 'figure' (Goodspeed), 'similitude' (Taylor), 'comparison' is indicated, as the parallelism of the two clauses shows. In light of the whole Marcan context, however, *parable* as a technical Christian term is probably meant (cf. 4:11).

thōmen (cf. 4:21) 'shall we place (it)': the meaning is 'present' (Brazilian; cf. Arndt & Gingrich I.1.b.ε); Cf. ASV 'set forth'; Weymouth, Synodale 'represent'; Lagrange *le mettre en*.

Translation: For *kingdom of God* see 1:15 and 4:11, and for *parable* see 3:23.

Compare must be rendered in some languages by a somewhat expanded descriptive expression, e.g. 'saying what shall we say they are like' (Tarahumara) and 'with what things can we make it equal' (Shipibo).

Use for it is equivalent in some languages to 'use in speaking about it'.

31 *It is like a grain of mustard seed, which, when sown upon the ground, is the smallest of all the seeds on earth;*

Exegesis: *kokkō sinapeōs* (only here in Mark) 'grain (seed) of mustard': the plant is identified as the *sinapsis nigra* (cf. Lagrange). The mustard grows wild in Palestine: it is an annual plant, growing from seed, and, especially when cultivated, may reach a height of 10 to 12 feet. A garden herb (cf. *lachanon* 'herb' next verse), it is, not quite accurately, called a 'tree' (Lk. 13:19), due to its large size.

mikroteron on 'being smaller (than)': as is common, the comparative 'smaller than' is used for the superlative 'smallest of'. The neuter tense of the adjective and participle is probably due to the neuter *spermatōn* 'seeds' which follows.

on 'being': the participle is concessive '*though* it is' (Burton *Moods and Tenses*, § 437).

spermatōn (12:19, 20, 21, 22) 'seeds' (notice *sporos* 'seed' in v. 27, and *kokkos* 'grain', 'seed' in this verse).

Translation: *It* must be translated so as to refer to 'the kingdom of God'.

Grain of mustard seed may be rendered as 'a seed of a plant called *mustard*', employing a word borrowed from the dominant prestige language of the area (Tarahumara, Eastern Otomí). Frequently, one can find a type of local mustard plant, which, though somewhat different, can still be used as a basis for the translation, e.g. 'a seed of a kind of... plant' (in which the appropriate close equivalent can be used; cf. Taungthu). South Toradja, Indonesian and Javanese use *sawi*, a sort of mustard plant (*Brassica rubosa*), the leaves of which are eaten as vegetables.

The constructions introduced by *which, when* are such that they frequently require some rather radical readjustments, e.g. 'it is like the grains of a plant called mustard; when these seeds are sown in the earth, they are the smallest...' In this rendering we have suggested the plural for singular, since in a number of languages such generic statements must be regularly in the plural form. However, for the sake of the follow-

149

ing verse, it is preferable, if at all possible, to employ the singular through-out. Note also the change of *sown upon* to 'sown in', as in a number of languages.

Despite the fact that the statement *smallest of all the seeds on earth* cannot be taken in any absolute sense, one should nevertheless translate the text as it is.

32 *yet when it is sown it grows up and becomes the greatest of all shrubs, and puts forth large branches, so that the birds of the air can make nests in its shade."*

Exegesis: *kai* 'and' (the first word): here with the meaning 'but', 'yet'.

anabainei (cf. 4:7) 'it grows'.

meizon pantōn tōn lachanōn 'bigger than all the shrubs': as in the previous verse the comparative 'bigger than' is used with the meaning 'biggest of'. The neuter *meizon* 'bigger' is due either to *sperma* 'the seed is bigger' implied in the statement, or to *tōn lachanōn* 'of the shrubs' which follows.

lachanōn (only here in Mark) 'vegetable', 'edible garden herb' (cf. Arndt & Gingrich).

poiei kladous megalous 'it makes large branches'.

poieō here means 'produce', 'send out' (cf. Arndt & Gingrich I.1.b.η).

klados (13:28) 'branch', 'limb'.

hōste dunasthai...kataskēnoun (for the construction see 1:27) 'so that they (the birds) are able to live'.

kataskēnoō (only here in Mark) 'live', 'dwell', 'settle': of birds, 'nest'. The saying about the birds nesting in the shade reflects O.T. passages such as Dan. 4:12 (cf. Ezek. 17:23, 31:6; Ps. 104:12).

tēn skian autou 'its shade', i.e. of the grown mustard plant.

skia (only here in Mark) 'shadow', 'shade'.

Translation: The Greek term translated here as *shrubs* refers primarily to large annuals. One should not render this as 'trees of the forest' (as in some translations, merely in order to emphasize the extent of growth of the plant). Where a language possesses a generic term for annuals (a not infrequent classification), one can make ready use of this word. In some instances, however, in order to use some relatively satisfactory equivalent, translators have used 'plants that grow for a year' (Totonac).

For *birds of the air* see 4:4. A literal translation of this expression can be quite misleading. In one language in Latin America this phrase was taken to refer to the Holy Spirit, for it was understood to mean 'doves from heaven', and since the dove is employed in Roman Catholic ritual as a symbol for the Holy Spirit, the meaning of the passage was entirely misconstrued. The meaning here is simply 'field birds', 'birds of the forest', or 'undomesticated fowl'.

Nests in its shade must in some instances be more precise, i.e. 'nests in its branches under its shade', or the use of 'shade' would imply nests on the ground beneath the plant.

33 *With many such parables he spoke the word to them, as they were able to hear it;* **34** *he did not speak to them without a parable, but privately to his own disciples he explained everything.*

Exegesis: *toiautais parabolais pollais* 'with many parables such as these'.

toioutos (6:2, 7:13, 9:37, 10:14, 13:19) 'such', 'of this kind', 'of this sort'.

elalei autois 'he was speaking to them (all)': *autois* 'them' includes the crowd (4:1) and the disciples; only to the disciples was the explanation given (cf. parallel Mt. 13:34).

kathōs ēdunanto akouein 'as they were able to hear', 'in proportion to their ability to hear' (cf. Jn. 16:12, 1 Cor. 3:2).

chōris (only here in Mark) 'apart from', 'without'.

kat' idian (6:31,32, 7:33, 9:2,28, 13:3) 'privately', 'alone'.

tois idiois mathētais 'to his disciples': although *idios* is properly 'one's own' (as distinct from 'another's own') it is often used simply as a synonym of the possessive pronoun 'his'—and that would appear to be its meaning in this passage.

epeluen (only here in Mark) 'he interpreted', 'he explained'.

Translation: For *parables* see 3:23.

Spoke the word is the equivalent of 'to preach', 'to announce', or 'to tell them the message'. For *preach* see 1:4.

Because of the double reference in this verse, first to the people in general, identified as *them*, and later to the disciples, it may be necessary in some languages to translate as 'Jesus told the good news to the people by means of many likeness-stories such as these'. In Tarahumara this passage is rendered as 'when he spoke...he only told them stories'.

As they were able to hear involves a rather complex type of proportion, rendered in Tzeltal as 'as much as they could put in their hearts', in Barrow Eskimo as 'just as long as they could understand', and in Indonesian 'according as they could understand'.

The double negative *not...without* must in some languages be rendered in a positive form: 'he cnly spoke to them with parables'.

Privately is translatable as 'when he was alone with his disciples'.

Explained everything may be translated as 'he told them what the stories meant'.

35 *On that day, when evening had come, he said to them, "Let us go across to the other side."* **36** *And leaving the crowd, they took him with them, just as he was, in the boat. And other boats were with him.*

Exegesis: *opsias genomenēs* (1:32, 6:47, 14:17, 15:42) 'when evening had come': presumably at, or after, sunset.

dielthōmen eis to peran 'let us go to the other side'.

dierchomai (10:25) 'go *through*' literally; here 'go', 'go across',

eis to peran 'to the other side': normally, as here, meaning Perea.

the country east of the Lake of Galilee (cf. 5:1), or of the Jordan river (cf. 3:8, 10:1). In the literal sense 'to the other side' it is used in 5:21, 6:45, 8:13.

kai aphentes...paralambanousin 'and leaving...they take': the subject is 'the disciples'.

aphiēmi (cf. 1:18, 2:5) 'leave', 'abandon'; some translate "dismiss", which is not supported by Marcan usage (*apoluō* is 'dismiss', 'send away': cf. 6:36,45, 8:3,9).

paralambanō (5:40, 7:4, 9:2, 10:32, 14:33) 'take', 'take with' (or 'along'): there is no idea of force implied (cf. Lagrange).

hōs ēn en tō ploiō 'as he was in the boat': *hōs* 'as', denoting comparison, means that Jesus still was in the boat in which he had pushed off from shore to teach the crowd (4:1), without having gone ashore. BFBS takes *hōs* as temporal 'while': the great majority of translations, however, assume the meaning 'as'.

alla ploia ēn met' autou 'other boats were with *him*': so the great majority of translations; BFBS, however, has "it" (the boat).

Translation: Because of possible confusion in rendering *them*, in view of the fact that for the most part the crowd has been referred to by such a third person plural pronoun, it may be advisable to translate 'said to the disciples'.

Go across must be made quite specific in some languages. For example, in Aymara, a language spoken by about one million Indians around Lake Titicaca in the Andes between Bolivia and Peru, one must specify whether 'going across' denotes from one side of the lake to another or from one projection of land (into the lake) to another such projection. In this context, one would seem to be dealing with a passage across the main body of the lake to Perea.

To the other side must often be elaborated to mean 'to the land on the other side of the lake' (Kekchi).

One must be quite careful in translating *took him*, for in some languages the connotation is one of 'forceable arrest' or 'manhandling'. One may, however, say 'go with him' or 'have him go with them'.

Just as he was does not refer to Jesus' appearance, but his place, already in the boat. This meaning may be indicated by some paratactic constructions, e.g. 'the disciples had him go with them in the boat; he was already there in the boat'.

For problems involving the size of the boat, see 1:19.

Were with him is equivalent in some languages to 'went along at the same time'. Note, however, that verbs used in speaking of boats 'going' may be entirely different from those used of motion by birds, animals, or persons.

37 *And a great storm of wind arose, and the waves beat into the boat, so that the boat was already filling.*

Exegesis: *lailaps megalē anemou* 'a great storm of wind'; Arndt & Gingrich: 'a fierce gust of wind'.

lailaps (only here in Mark) 'whirlwind', 'hurricane', 'squall'.

anemos (4:39, 41, 6:48, 51, 13:27) 'wind'.

ta kumata epeballen 'the waves were spilling on (into the boat)'.

kuma (only here in Mark) 'wave'.

epiballō (11:7, 14:46,72) 'throw upon': without an object, in the active voice, as here, the verb means 'to throw oneself' or 'to beat upon' (cf. Arndt & Gingrich 2.a).

hōste ēdē gemizesthai (see 1:27 for this construction) 'so that it was already getting full (of water)'.

gemizomai (15:36) 'be filled', 'become full'.

Translation: In some languages one cannot say 'a great storm of wind arose'. The only equivalent may be 'suddenly the wind blew very fiercely' or 'the wind ran with strength'.

The waves may be spoken of as 'falling into the boat', rather than *beating into the boat*.

Rather than *the boat...was filling* one may need to say in some languages 'water was filling the boat' or 'the boat was already getting full of water'.

38 *But he was in the stern, asleep on the cushion; and they woke him and said to him, "Teacher, do you not care if we perish?"*

Text: Instead of *en* 'in' of all modern editions of the Greek text *Textus Receptus* has *epi* 'upon'.

Exegesis: *kai autos ēn...katheudōn* 'and he was...sleeping': a verbal phrase, in accordance with Marcan usage (cf. 1:6 *ēn esthōn* 'he was eating').

prumnē (only here in Mark) 'stern'.

proskephalaion (only here in Mark) 'pillow', 'cushion': probably the sailor's cushion used in rowing. The phrase 'on the cushion' means, of course, that Jesus was sleeping with *his head* on the cushion.

egeirousin auton (cf. v. 27) 'they rouse him (from sleep)' (cf. 1:31).

didaskale (5:35, 9:17,38, 10:17,20,35, 12:14,19,32, 13:1, 14:14) 'Teacher', 'Master'—the equivalent to the Aramaic 'Rabbi' (which Mark uses only 4 times—see 9:5). Cf. Dalman *Words*, 336-40.

ou melei soi 'is it no concern to you?', 'do you not care?': the implied rebuke is unmistakable.

melei (12:14) 'it is a care', 'it is a concern': an impersonal verb.

apollumetha (cf. 1:24) 'we are perishing', 'we are dying' (the middle voice of *apollumi* 'kill', 'destroy'). As the context makes clear, 'do *you* not care that *we* are perishing?', the 'we' refers to the disciples. The present tense 'we are perishing' here means, probably, 'we are about to perish'.

Translation: *He* may be rendered as 'Jesus' if the pronominal reference is not clear.

In a number of rough-draft translations people have discovered that Jesus was described as being asleep in the water, out behind the boat. The trouble is that we too often describe boats in terms of our own ideas, e.g. the front, the back, etc. In Shilluk, for example, boats may be described as having 'a throat' (the prow), 'a foot' (the stern), and 'a back' (the bottom). Words for position within a boat must be carefully chosen, e.g. 'he was sleeping in the boat's tail' (Zoque).

On a cushion does not mean that he was curled up on a pillow (in the position of a dog—as discovered in one translation), but asleep in the stern of the boat, with his head on a pillow, literally, 'rest for the head' in Kekchi.

For *teacher* see 2 : 13.

Because of the specialized nature of this context *do you not care* may be rendered in a number of ways, e.g. 'don't you have a heart' (Tzeltal), 'aren't you going to do anything' (Piro), 'we are drowning; do you think: What is that to me?' (Navajo), 'does it not burden you, that we are perishing?' (Bare'e).

For languages in which there is a contrast between inclusive and exclusive first person plural, i.e. between forms which include those spoken to and those which exclude them, this verse presents somewhat of a problem. Should one translate "we" by an exclusive form, implying that the disciples thought that they would drown, but that Jesus would not, or are they to be understood as using an inclusive form, with the implication that all would perish together? Of course, there is no hint in the Greek grammatical forms as to which rendering to employ, for Greek does not make such a distinction. On the other hand, in a language with such an inclusive-exclusive contrast (and this includes hundreds of languages throughout the world) there is no way to avoid a decision. One can decide such a problem, however, only on the basis of the context: Are the disciples so concerned about their own safety that they would use an exclusive form, quite without regard to a concern for Jesus' own welfare, or are they more likely to think of Jesus as so preoccupied with his spiritual ministry as to be utterly unaware of material dangers to himself as well as to the disciples? If one chooses the exclusive form, it is possible to interpret this passage as meaning that the disciples thought that Jesus would in some way make a miraculous escape, leaving them to their doom, while if the inclusive form is employed, there is some lessening of the intense concern of the disciples for their own welfare. In general, translators have seemed to prefer the inclusive form, but many are equally sure that the exclusive is better. This is an instance in which the more precise limitations of meaning imposed by more subtle categories do not materially improve understanding or appreciation of a passage.

39 *And he awoke and rebuked the wind, and said to the sea, "Peace! Be still!" And the wind ceased, and there was a great calm.*

Exegesis: *diegertheis* (only here in Mark) 'awakening', 'arousing'.

154

epetimēsen (cf. 1:25) 'he stopped', 'he checked'.
siōpa (cf. 3:4) *pephimōso* (cf. 1:25) 'Be silent!', 'Be quiet!' (used with the unclean spirit in 1:25).
ekopasen (6:51) 'it abated', 'it ceased', 'it stopped'.
galēnē (only here in Mark) 'calm', 'stillness'.

Translation: *Rebuked* is equivalent in some instances to 'scold', but in many instances must be translated as 'commanded the wind strongly'.
The sea is 'the lake' or 'the water in the lake'.
Peace is often translated by two different types of expressions: (1) a term indicating cessation of war and (2) one denoting quietness, inactivity, or calm. It is the latter meaning which is important here, e.g. 'be quiet', 'be calm'. In Subanen one may say 'calm; that's enough'.
In Greek the word translated in the RSV as *be still* refers primarily to quietness, in contrast with noise. However, in some languages the figure of cessation of violent movement (speaking of the waves) would be more meaningful, especially as the second part of the command to the waters of the lake.
The wind ceased is expressed in a number of ways 'the wind stopped', 'the wind went down', 'the wind stood still', 'the wind passed over' (Chontal of Tabasco), and 'the wind healed' (Bolivian Quechua).
There was a great calm is in Piro 'the water was doing nothing at all'. 'There were no waves' can also be used.

40 **He said to them, "Why are you afraid? Have you no faith?"**
41 **And they were filled with awe, and said to one another, "Who then is this, that even wind and sea obey him?"**

Text: In v. 40 after *este* 'you are' *Textus Receptus*, Nestle, Tischendorf, Soden, Vogels, Taylor and Kilpatrick add *houtōs* 'thus' which is omitted by Westcott and Hort, Lagrange, Souter, Merk and RSV.
In v. 40 instead of *pōs ouch echete* 'how (is it that) you do not have' read by *Textus Receptus*, Tischendorf, Merk and Nestle; *oupō echete* 'do you not (yet) have' is preferred by Westcott and Hort, Souter, Soden, Vogels, Taylor, Lagrange, RSV, Kilpatrick.

Exegesis: *deiloi* (only here in Mark) 'timid', 'fearful', 'cowardly'.
pōs 'how?', 'how is it possible that...?'
pistin (cf. 2:5) 'faith', 'belief', 'trust': whether in God, or in Jesus himself, the text does not specify.
ephobēthēsan phobon megan 'they feared a great fear': a Semitic manner of intensive statement 'they feared greatly', 'they were very much afraid'.
phobeomai (5:15,33,36, 6:20,50, 9:32, 10:32, 11:18,32, 12:12, 16:8) 'to be afraid', 'to be awed'.
pros allēlous (8:16, 9:34, 15:31; *en allēlois* 9:50) 'to themselves', i.e. 'to one another' (*not* privately, each one to himself, but in the group, one to the other).

ara (11:13) 'then', 'therefore': as an inference from all that has preceded; 'In light of this, who, then, is this man?'

kai ho anemos 'even the wind': so the great majority of modern translations (ASV, RSV, Goodspeed, Berkeley, Manson, Weymouth, Williams, Montgomery, Zürich, Brazilian); BFBS, however, "*both* wind and..."

hupakouei (cf. 1:27) 'they obey'.

Translation: *Them* must in some languages be clearly indicated as 'disciples' because of the immediately preceding reference to the 'wind and sea'.

The description of fear leads to a number of idioms, e.g. 'your heart trembles' (Tzeltal), 'shiver in your liver' (Uduk), and 'to have such little hearts' (Tzotzil). This fear must be carefully distinguished from the meaning of fear as reverence or respect.

For *faith* see 1:15. In some languages, however, one cannot speak of faith without indicating the object of the faith. Despite the fact that the Greek does not specify whether this is faith in Jesus or God, it is probably more acceptable to translate as 'faith in God', since it would seem that faith is here spoken of in terms of its widest application to experiences of confidence and trust, rather than with regard to specific reliance on Jesus' own leadership and provision for their needs.

Filled with awe is equivalent in some instances to 'completely amazed', 'their thoughts left them', 'their hearts fell'.

Who, introducing the last question, is not a simple interrogative pronoun relating to identity. It rather asks 'what sort of person is this that...' Or, as in some languages, 'who is this sort of person that...' At any rate, there must usually be some type of qualifier to supplement the words as they stand in the English text.

Obey him may be rendered as 'do what he says' (or 'commands').

CHAPTER FIVE

1 *They came to the other side of the sea, to the country of the Gerasenes.* **2** *And when he had come out of the boat, there met him out of the tombs a man with an unclean spirit,*

Text: Instead of *Gerasēnōn* 'Gerasenes' of the great majority of the modern editions of the Greek text, *Textus Receptus* and Vogels have *Gadarenōn* 'Gadarenes' (the correct reading in Mt. 8:28).

Exegesis: *tēn chōran tōn Gerasēnōn* 'the region of the Gerasenes' (cf. 1:5 for *chōra* 'region'): for the exact identification of this region, which is disputed, see the commentaries *in loc.*; Dalman *Sacred Sites and Ways*, 177-79.
 hupēntēsen (only here in Mark) 'he met', 'he encountered': sometimes in a hostile sense (cf. Lk. 14:31).
 ek tōn mnēmeiōn 'out of the tombs', i.e. *'coming out* of the tombs' (cf. Goodspeed, Manson, Weymouth).
 mnēmeion (6:29, 15:46, 16:3,5,8) 'grave', 'tomb' (synonym of *mnēma* 'tomb' vv. 3, 5).

Translation: For difficulties involved in expressions of 'going to the other side', see 4:35.
 The country of the Gerasenes may be variously translated, depending upon the usage of the receptor language in question, e.g. 'land where the Gerasenes lived', 'land which belonged to the Gerasene people', 'region inhabited by the Gerasene tribe'.
 The apposition involved in the expressions *to the other side...to the country...* may be treated in some instances as two paratactically combined clauses: 'they went to the other side of the lake; this was the land of the Gerasene people'.
 For problems involved in verbs for 'coming' and 'going' see 1:14. In many languages one must translate *came to the other side* as 'arrived at the other side' and *come out of the boat* as 'went out of...' or 'climbed out of...'
 The word *tombs* refers either to cave-like rooms cut into the rock or small mausoleum-like structures, which might provide some shelter for the demoniac. If people have a custom of burying the dead in such places, there is generally no problem, except where, as in one language, the informants insisted that the demoniac could not come out of more than one tomb at a time, hence, 'met him, coming out of a tomb' or 'met him, coming from where the tombs were'. On the other hand, if people bury only in holes in the ground, it would be quite misleading to imply that the demoniac came out of the graves in the ground. In

such instances, the closest equivalent is usually 'came from where the dead were buried', i.e. from the cemetery.

For *unclean spirit* see 1 : 26.

3 who lived among the tombs; and no one could bind him any more, even with a chain; 4 for he had often been bound with fetters and chains, but the chains he wrenched apart, and the fetters he broke in pieces; and no one had the strength to subdue him.

Exegesis: *katoikēsin* (only here in the N.T.) 'dwelling', 'residence', 'home': 'who made his home...', 'who lived...'

en tois mnēmasin 'among the tombs': these would probably be caverns, natural and artificial, in the rocks (cf. Rawlinson; Vincent *Word Studies* I, 186).

mnēma (5:5, 15:46, 16:2) 'tomb', 'grave'.

halusei (only in these two verses in Mark) 'with a chain', 'with a bond'.

kai oude halusei ouketi oudeis (notice the repetition of negatives) 'and not even with a chain (could) any one any longer (bind him)'.

dēsai (cf. 3:27) 'bind', 'restrict', 'confine', 'keep prisoner'.

dia to auton...dedesthai kai diespasthai...kai...suntetriphthai 'because he...had been bound, and (the chains) had been shattered...and (the fetters)...had been smashed': the three verbal infinitives, all perfect passives, are governed by the preposition *dia* 'on account of', 'because'. As Burton (*Moods and Tenses*, § 408) points out, this clause presents the *evidence* for the preceding statement (that the man no longer could be bound) rather than the cause.

diaspaō (only here in Mark) 'tear apart', 'shatter'.

suntribō (14:3) 'crush', 'smash', 'break'.

It is to be noticed that the perfect infinitive *dedesthai* describes an action in the past whose result no longer existed at the time of speaking, but had ceased at an undefined point in the past: 'he *had been* bound' (cf. Burton *Moods and Tenses*, § 108).

pedais (only here in Mark) 'with fetters', 'with shackles'.

kai oudeis ischuen auton damasai 'and no one was strong enough to subdue him': a summary statement of the whole detailed description of the demoniac's superhuman strength.

ischuō (cf. 2:17) 'to be strong', 'to be able': Field *Notes*, 26 (against RSV) contends for the weakened sense 'was able', 'could'. The use of *edunato* 'could' in the previous verse, however, would seem to require for *ischuen* the meaning RSV gives it.

damazō (only here in Mark) 'subdue'; of animals, 'tame'.

Translation: *Lived among the tombs* is equivalent to 'had his home among the tombs' or 'continually stayed among the tombs'.

It should be noted that in the RSV text verses 2-4 are punctuated as one sentence. Because of the complex nature of the clauses, involving as they do several shifts in subject expressions, it is necessary in many languages to break these up into several complete sentences, depending upon the syntactic requirements of the receptor language into which one is translating.

Chains are known as 'iron ropes' in some areas (Tarahumara, Bolivian Quechua), and in the second part of verse 3 may be incorporated as follows: 'no one could tie him up any more, not even when they used iron ropes'. In some instances *no one could* is more naturally rendered as 'people could not'.

Fetters were used to bind the legs and feet and the *chains* were used to bind the hands and arms. Where a specific word for fetters is not known, it is possible to translate this passage as 'put chains on his hands and feet' (Tetelcingo Aztec, Tarahumara); South Toradja has 'block in which the feet are put'.

The chains he wrenched apart refers to the violent action of his arms in breaking the chains and *the fetters he broke* may refer to his smashing of the fetters by stones or slamming them against rocks or on the ground, translated in some instances as 'he pulled in two the chains around his arms and he smashed into pieces the iron that was fastened on his legs'.

Had the strength to is in some languages equivalent to 'was strong enough to' or 'was able to'.

Subdue may be translated either as a reference to taming wild animals, e.g. 'to teach him to drink' (Shilluk), or to controlling possessed persons, e.g. 'to keep him quiet' (Tzotzil).

5 Night and day among the tombs and on the mountains he was always crying out, and bruising himself with stones.

Exegesis: *dia pantos nuktos kai hēmeras* 'continually, night and day' (cf. Moule *Idiom Book*, 39).

ēn krazōn kai katakoptōn 'he was shrieking and cutting'.

krazō (cf. 3:11) 'shriek', 'cry out', 'shout'.

katakoptō (only here in N.T.) 'cut', 'gash': Field (*Notes*, 27) contends for the meaning 'beating himself', which the verb sometimes has. The great majority of commentators and translations, however, prefer the usual meaning.

lithois (12:10, 13:1,2, 15:46, 16:3,4) 'with stones', 'with rocks'.

Translation: *Night and day*, as an expression of 'all the time' or 'continually', may in some instances need to be altered in order, e.g. 'day and night', depending on the more usual order of speaking. On the other hand, it may be necessary to expand the phrase somewhat, e.g. 'all the time, both night and day', in order that the reader may understand this action as continuous.

Crying out is here 'shrieking', 'howling', and 'screaming'.

6 And when he saw Jesus from afar, he ran and worshiped him; 7 and crying out with a loud voice, he said, "What have you to do with me, Jesus, Son of the Most High God? I adjure you by God, do not torment me."

Exegesis: *apo makrothen* (8:3, 11:13, 14:54, 15:40) 'from afar', 'from a distance'.

ed ramen kai prosekunēsen auton 'he ran and prostrated himself before him'.

trechō (15:36) 'run'.

proskuneō (15:19) 'do reverence', 'make obeisance', 'bow down to', 'worship': not in the technical Christian sense of worshiping Jesus, but in the general sense of paying him reverence (cf. 3:11 *prosepipton autō* 'they fell down before him'; cf. the parallel Lk. 8:28 *prosepesen autō* 'he fell down before him'). Most English translations have "knelt before him".

ti emoi kai soi (cf. 1:24) 'why do you bother me?'

huie tou theou tou hupsistou 'son of the Most High God'.

hupsistos (11:10) '(the) Most High': title of the God of the Jews. The word is the superlative form of the adverb *hupsi* 'on high'.

horkizō se ton theon 'I implore you by God': the accusative *ton theon* 'God' denotes the thing (or, name) by which one swears (cf. Acts 19:13 *ton Iēsoun* 'by Jesus').

horkizō (only here in Mark) 'put on oath' (*horkos* 'oath'), 'cause to swear', 'adjure', 'entreat earnestly', 'implore'.

basanisēs (6:48) 'torment', 'torture': here probably with the idea of temporal punishment (Mt. 8:29 and Lk. 8:28,31 interpret it of eschatological punishment).

Translation: *Worshiped* is most generally rendered as 'knelt down before' or 'fell down before in reverence'.

Crying with a loud voice is equivalent to 'shouted out strong' or 'yelled'.

For a discussion of some of the problems in the idiom "What have you to do with me", see 1:24. In this context Tzotzil has 'what does it serve you to me' and Loma has 'what is your palaver on me'.

The superlative *Most High* cannot always be translated literally. In some instances, even though a superlative form does not exist, some relatively satisfactory equivalent may be used, e.g. 'extremely high above' (Kekchi). In other cases, one must substitute location, e.g. 'high in heaven' (Huichol), for an expression meaning 'highest' would refer only to physical size. In still other languages, one must substitute general size for height, as an expression of distinction, e.g. 'really great' (Conob).

Adjure is variously translated, e.g. 'tell you before God' (Zoque), 'ask in front of God' (Mazatec), 'ask you by God' (Eastern Otomí), 'ask you in God's presence' (Subanen), 'I swear, calling on the name of God, requesting you' (South Toradja), 'I want your oath by God' (Indonesian), 'will assure me by using a curse on yourself calling on the name of God' (Bare'e), and 'ask you; God has seen it' (Tzotzil). The concept of *adjure* involves two relationships: (1) the asking of the person and (2) the witness or participation of the deity called to witness or validate the request. Such actions, though rather unfamiliar to people in our Western culture, are common enough in most societies.

Torment may be rendered as 'cause to suffer'.

8 *For he had said to him, "Come out of the man, you unclean spirit!"* 9 *And Jesus asked him, "What is your name?" He replied, "My name is Legion; for we are many."*

Exegesis: *elegen gar autō* 'for he was saying to him' (so Goodspeed, Montgomery, Williams); 'for he said' (ASV, BFBS); 'for he had said' (RSV, Moffatt, Berkeley); 'for he had been saying' (Taylor). The imperfect indicates either (1) that Jesus was in the act of exorcising the unclean spirit when interrupted by the demoniac; or (2) Jesus was repeating his command (cf. Goodspeed and others). Manson's "Jesus was already saying to him", favors the first interpretation. The meaning of the verb *legō* 'say' here is 'command', 'order' (cf. Black *Aramaic*, 236; Arndt & Gingrich II.1.c).

autō 'to him': refers to the unclean spirit, to whom the command to come out is addressed. The confusion between the man and the unclean spirit (or spirits) who possessed him is seen throughout.

to pneuma to akatharton 'you unclean spirit': though the form is nominative, this is the vocative use, the case of address.

kai epērōta auton 'and he (Jesus) asked him (the man)': the masculine pronoun *auton* 'him' shows that the man is being addressed. Again, in such cases, it is impossible to separate the man from the spirit.

eperōtaō (some 25 times in Mark; cf. *erōtaō* in 4: 10) 'ask a question'.

legiōn (5: 15) 'Legion': a Latin loanword. In the time of Augustus a legion of soldiers comprised about 6000 men.

hoti polloi esmen 'because we are many': the masculine *polloi* 'many' does not agree in gender with *ta pneumata ta akatharta* 'the unclean spirits' (v. 13). It must be understood in a general sense (cf. the masculine participle *legontes* 'saying' in v. 12; cf. 9:26 where masculine participles modify the neuter 'spirit'), as applying to the spirits themselves (although it is possible that the masculine is influenced by *legiōn* which is masculine—cf. v. 15).

Translation: In order that the sequence of actual events between verses 7 and 8 may be made clear, it is necessary to indicate explicitly that the statement made by the demon-possessed man is in response to what Jesus had already said, e.g. 'For Jesus had already said to the man,...' (or 'was already saying').

Despite the apparent confusion between words addressed to the man and the responses of the demon (or demons), it is important in so far as possible to preserve this confusion, as being an essential element in the psychological situation. In the beginning of verse 8, it is vital that one have as the object of the verb 'said' a pronominal element (or noun) which will identify the demon, since the following words are specifically addressed to the unclean spirit. However, in the beginning of verse 9, *asked him* is probably better interpreted as being addressed to the man, even though the demon seems to reply.

What is your name is rendered in a number of different ways in various languages, e.g. 'how do you call yourself', 'what name has been given to you', 'what do people speak in calling you', and 'what are you named'.

Legion has been treated in several different ways: (1) by transliteration, but this is usually quite meaningless, (2) by some reference to a number of soldiers, e.g. 'many soldiers' (Mazahua), 'an army' (Trique), 'thousands of soldiers' (Kekchi), and (3) by some word or phrase indicating a large crowd or group, e.g. 'a multitude' (Black Bobo), 'ten thousand' (Toba Batak), 'a crowd' (Ifugao, Subanen, Bolivian Quechua), and 'many' (Amuzgo). Either of these latter types of alternatives seems to be quite adequate.

For we are many may be 'for there are many of us' or 'for our number is very great'.

10 And he begged him eagerly not to send them out of the country.

Exegesis: *kai parekalei auton polla* 'and he entreated him strongly': the subject could be 'the unclean spirits' (with which *auta* 'them' would be in agreement) as Moffatt, Taylor, Manson, and Goodspeed interpret it (cf. the parallel Lk. 8:31 'and they begged him'); it is probable, however (with ASV, RSV, BFBS, Weymouth, Brazilian, Lagrange and others), that the subject is 'he' (the man himself), as it is in the identical form *parekalei* 'he begged' in v. 18 (and notice the plural of the verb *parekalesan* 'they (the spirits) begged' in v. 12).

polla (cf. 1:45, 3:12) is adverbial 'insistently', 'strongly', 'urgently'.

hina mē auta aposteilē 'that he not send them off': the clause begun with *hina* 'that' denotes the content of the request—it is not a purpose clause (cf. 3:9, 12).

apostellō (cf. 1:2) 'send away', 'send'.

exō tēs chōras 'outside the region' (i.e. of the Gerasenes, v. 1): for *chōra* 'region' see 1:5.

Translation: *Begged him eagerly* indicates the heart-felt nature of the entreaty, expressed in Tzotzil as 'he asked with his heart coming out'.

In many languages the object of the entreaty must be in the form of direct discourse, e.g. 'the man asked Jesus strongly, Do not send the unclean spirits away from this place'. This type of expression need not imply any fond attachment which the man had for the demons which possessed him, but he uttered this request as the spokesman for the demons.

11 Now a great herd of swine was feeding there on the hillside; 12 and they begged him, "Send us to the swine, let us enter them."

Text: Verse 12. After *auton* 'him' *Textus Receptus* adds *pantes hoi daimones* 'all the demons' which is omitted by all modern editions of the Greek text.

Exegesis: *ēn...boskomenē* 'it was...feeding': according to Marcan usage, the two are to be taken together as a single verbal phrase (cf. *ēn esthōn* 'he was eating' in 1:6).

boskō (5:14) 'graze', 'feed' (in the passive, of livestock); 'tend', 'feed' (in the active, of herdsmen—v. 14).

agelē (5:13) *choirōn* (5:13,16) 'a herd of pigs' (this would be in Gentile territory, on the east side of the Lake of Galilee—cf. Lagrange).

kai parekalesan auton legontes 'and they begged him saying': the subject is neuter 'the unclean spirits' and the nominative masculine participle *legontes* 'saying' must be taken in a general way, the concordance not being precise.

parakaleō (cf. 1:40) 'beg', 'entreat', 'implore'.

pempson hēmas eis tous choirous 'send us to the hogs'.

pempō (only here in Mark) 'send'.

eis 'into' (ASV, BFBS, Moffatt), 'among' (Manson), or 'to' (RSV, Weymouth, Berkeley, Brazilian, Synodale). The translation of this *eis* will depend on the translation of the next clause; 'to', however, seems preferable here.

hina eis autous eiselthōmen 'so that we might enter (into) them': if *hina* here be taken to denote purpose 'in order that', 'so that', it would seem that *eis* in the former clause (see above) means 'to', since *eis* here is manifestly 'into'. It is possible, however, to take *hina* in the imperative sense (as it is often used in the N.T.) and understand this second clause simply as a repetition of the first clause, which is imperatival (*pempson* 'send'): 'Send us to (into, among) the hogs, let us enter them' (so Goodspeed, BFBS, RSV).

Translation: In some languages careful distinctions are made in words designating a 'herd', depending upon what types of animals are involved. (Compare the English use of *herd of cattle, flock of geese, swarm of bees,* and *covey of quails*.)

Swine must be a domesticated variety, or the following portion of the story will be incomprehensible. Where pigs are not known, a borrowed word may be used with a classifier, e.g. 'animals called pigs', or some descriptive expression, if possible one already employed by the people, e.g. 'queer deer', a phrase in use among the Barrow Eskimo.

Note that though the man is the subject of the entreaty in verse 10, the unclean spirits are specifically identified as the subject of the begging in verse 12.

Let us is equivalent to 'permit us' or 'allow us'.

Was feeding may be rendered in terms of 'being pastured' or 'hunting for something to eat' (Chontal of Tabasco).

13 *So he gave them leave. And the unclean spirits came out, and entered the swine; and the herd, numbering about two thousand, rushed down the steep bank into the sea, and were drowned in the sea.*

Text: After *autois* 'them' *Textus Receptus*, Soden, and Kilpatrick add *eutheōs ho Iēsous* 'immediately Jesus', which is omitted by the rest of the modern editions of the Greek text.

163

Exegesis: *epetrepsen* (10 : 4) 'he permitted', 'he allowed', 'he consented'.
hōrmēsen (only here in Mark) 'it rushed', 'it swarmed'.
kata tou krēmnou eis tēn thalassan 'down (from) the cliff into the lake'.
kata 'down', 'down from' (cf. Arndt & Gingrich I.1.a).
krēmnos (only here in Mark) 'steep slope (or, bank)', 'cliff'.
thalassa (cf. 1 : 16) 'lake (of Galilee)'.
epnigonto (only here in Mark; cf. *sunpnigō* in 4 : 7) 'they choked', 'they strangled', i.e. 'they drowned'.

Translation: *Gave them leave* is an obsolescent expression in English, meaning 'he permitted them to go' or, as in some languages, 'he said, You may go'.

Came out must be more explicitly defined in some instances as 'came out of the man'.

In speaking of the demons entering the swine it is probably necessary to adopt the same type of expression as in the case of demons entering into people, e.g. 'went into the hearts of the pigs' (Trique).

In many languages numbers of large magnitudes, such as this figure of 2,000, are very difficult to express in the indigenous system of numeration. For example, in Maya, which has a system based on 20's, such a figure though apparently easy, is actually much more complicated than the Spanish terms, which are used almost exclusively for such higher numbers. In some cases, however, one can use the receptor language system, e.g. 'two hundred ten times' (Shilluk) and 'twenty one-hundreds' (Barrow Eskimo). However, in the choice of such a number the important consideration is not the apparent relative ease or difficulty of the expression, but which type of term would be more readily understandable.

There are usually no difficulties in finding adequate terms for 'drowning', but some are quite specialized and descriptive, e.g. 'choked on water' (Tzeltal) and 'went under up to the nose' (Maya).

14 *The herdsmen fled, and told it in the city and in the country. And people came to see what it was that had happened.*

Exegesis: *kai hoi boskountes autous* 'and the men tending them (the pigs)', i.e. 'the (their) herdsmen'.
ephugon (13 : 14, 14 : 50, 52, 16 : 8) 'they fled', 'they ran away'.
apēggeilan (5 : 19, 6 : 30, 16 : 10, 13) 'they announced', 'they told', 'they related'.
eis tēn polin kai eis tous agrous 'in the city and in the country towns'.
hē polis 'the city' would be here the important city of that region.
agros 'field', 'country': the word is used in three ways in Mark: (1) meaning literally 'field' (i.e. a plot of ground) in singular and plural, 10 : 29, 30, 11 : 8, 13 : 16; (2) meaning 'country towns', 'hamlets', in the plural only, 5 : 14, 6 : 36, 56; (3) meaning 'rural region', 'country district' (as opposed to the urban region), in the singular and without the definite article, 15 : 21, 16 : 12.
ti estin to gegonos 'what is it that has happened': the neuter perfect participle of *ginomai* 'happen', 'take place'.

ēlthon 'they came': another impersonal plural, i.e. 'people' in general (RSV), 'men' (BFBS). Cf. Turner *Journal of Theological Studies* 25. 380, 1923-4.

Translation: The *herdsmen* are 'those who watched the pigs', or 'those who took care of the pigs', or 'those who guarded the pigs while they ate'.

Told it must in some instances be expanded to 'told the people what had happened'.

In the city and in the country must usually modify 'people', i.e. 'told the news to the people in the city and to the people in the country'. The repetition of 'people' may be required because the same people could not be both in the city and in the country at the same time.

15 And they came to Jesus, and saw the demoniac sitting there, clothed and in his right mind, the man who had had the legion; and they were afraid.

Exegesis: *erchontai* 'they come': the same people referred to in the previous verse *ēlthon* 'they came'.

kai theōrousin ton daimonizomenon 'and they see the demon-possessed man'.

theōreō (cf. 3 : 11) 'look upon', 'gaze', 'behold'.

ho daimonizomenos (cf. 1 : 33) 'the demon-possessed man': simply identifying the man, not stating that he was still possessed.

kathēmenon himatismenon kai sōphronounta 'seated, clothed and sane': the three participles describe the man.

kathēmai (cf. 2 : 6) 'seated', i.e. as a disciple (at the feet of Jesus, Lk. 8 : 35).

himatizomai (only here in Mark) 'be dressed', 'be clothed' (he had gone about naked, Lk. 8 : 27): from *himation* 'clothes' (cf. 2 : 21).

sōphroneō (only here in Mark) 'to be of sound mind', 'be sane'.

ton eschēkota ton legiōna 'he who had the Legion': the perfect participle here is to be translated 'he who had had'—since he had it no longer (cf. Burton *Moods and Tenses*, § 156).

ton legiōna 'the Legion': it seems better to take it as a proper name (BFBS) than as a common noun (RSV).

kai ephobēthēsan (cf. 4 : 41) 'and they were afraid'.

Translation: *Demoniac* must be translated with care, so as not to imply that he was still possessed by demons. Therefore, it is often advisable to employ a phrase, e.g. 'the man who had had the unclean spirits' or 'the man in whom unclean spirits had lived' (see 1 : 26).

Sitting there, clothed and in his right mind are three rather diverse expressions, which must in some instances be divided into separate clauses, e.g. 'he was sitting there; he had clothes on and his thoughts were straight'.

In his right mind is rendered in a variety of ways, e.g. 'his mind had returned' (Ifugao), 'his heart was sitting down' (Tojolabal), 'his head was healed' (Trique), 'his mind was straightened' (Tzotzil), 'with a clear mind again' (Javanese), and 'come to his senses' (Indonesian).

The appositive phrase *the man who had had the legion* is in some instances better handled as a separate clause, e.g. 'this was the man who had had the legion', or as interpreted by some 'this was the man who had had the name Legion'.

For *afraid* see 4:40.

16 And those who had seen it told what had happened to the demoniac and to the swine. 17 And they began to beg Jesus to depart from their neighborhood.

Exegesis: *kai diēgēsanto autois hoi idontes* 'and the eye-witnesses described to them'.

diēgeomai (9:8) 'relate', 'describe', 'narrate', 'explain'.

pōs egeneto tō daimonizomenō 'what had happened to the demon-possessed man': *pōs* usually means 'how' (cf. 2:26) and could be so translated here '*how* it happened to the demon-possessed man'; it may mean, as it probably does here, 'what' (RSV, BFBS; cf. Arndt & Gingrich *ginomai* I.3.b.β).

kai peri tōn choirōn 'and (also) about the pigs': additional explanation supplied by the eye-witnesses.

tōn horiōn autōn 'their regions': the word *horion* (7:24, 31) 'boundary', 'limit' in the N.T. is always used in the plural 'boundaries', with the resultant meaning of the region encompassed by the boundaries—'region', 'district', 'province' (cf. Arndt & Gingrich).

Translation: The syntax of verse 16 is complicated by the double grammatical reference to the same event through the use of *it* and *what had happened to the demoniac and to the swine*. These eyewitnesses simply reported what they had seen. This means that in some languages the descriptive statement 'what happened to the demoniac and the swine' must be attached to the verb of 'seeing', e.g. 'those who had seen what happened to the demoniac and to the swine told this to the people'.

As in verse 15, the translation of *demoniac* must not indicate his continued possession.

They of verse 17 refers to the people in general, not just to the eye-witnesses specified in verse 16. That is to say, after the people heard what had happened, they asked Jesus to depart out of their country or territory.

18 And as he was getting into the boat, the man who had been possessed with demons begged him that he might be with him.

Exegesis: *embainontos autou eis to ploion* 'as he was embarking': the present participle is to be thus translated.

embainō (cf. 4:1) 'enter', 'go into'.

parekalei auton ho daimonistheis 'he who had been demon-possessed begged him': the aorist participle describes the past condition of the man.

hina met' autou ē 'that he might stay with him': i.e. accompany Jesus about as a disciple (cf. 3:14).

hina 'that': describes the content of the request, not the purpose of it (cf. Arndt & Gingrich II.1.a.γ).

Translation: *Getting into the boat* may be described in various ways: 'climbing into...', 'going down into...', 'jumping into...' One should employ the typical manner of describing the boarding of this type of small craft.

Begged him that he might be with him may result in obscurity unless some of the pronouns are made more specific, e.g. 'Begged Jesus that he could remain with him'. For languages in which this type of expression must be in direct discourse, the following pattern may be followed: 'begged Jesus, I want to stay with you'.

In a number of translations it has been found that the last clause of verse 18 was understood as a request by the former demoniac that Jesus would remain there in the land of the Gerasenes, a not unusual type of interpretation, but one which should be carefully avoided.

19 **But he refused, and said to him, "Go home to your friends, and tell them how much the Lord has done for you, and how he has had mercy on you." 20 And he went away and began to proclaim in the Decapolis how much Jesus had done for him; and all men marveled.**

Text: Instead of *kai* 'and' (at the beginning of v. 19) of all modern editions of the Greek text, *Textus Receptus* has *ho de Iēsous* 'and Jesus'.

Exegesis: *ouk aphēken* (cf. 2:5) 'he did not allow', 'he did not permit'.

hupage eis ton oikon sou (cf. 2:11) 'go home'.

pros tous sous 'to your own family (or, people)' (cf. BFBS), rather than 'friends' (RSV).

hosa ho kurios soi pepoiēken kai eleēsen se 'how much the Lord has done for you and (how) he had pity on you'.

hosa (cf. 3:8) is here adverbial 'how much', 'how greatly' (modifying both 'has done' and 'had pity'), rather than adjectival 'how many things' (cf. Lagrange).

pepoiēken kai eleēsen 'he has done and he showed mercy': the proper distinction should be observed, where language allows, in translating the two tenses, the perfect of the first verb and the aorist of the second verb (cf. Taylor). RSV 'he has had mercy' is not a fully satisfactory translation of *eleēsen*.

kērussein (cf. 1:4) 'proclaim'.

en tē Dekapolei (7:31) 'in the Decapolis': a league originally consisting of 10 cities, east of the Jordan. It is not necessary to suppose that the man proclaimed his cure in all the cities, but simply that he announced it in the region of the Decapolis.

kai pantes ethaumazon 'and all men (who heard of it) marveled'.
thaumazō (6:6, 15:5,44) 'marvel', 'wonder'.

Translation: Probably the use of 'Jesus' as subject of 'refused' is justified, in order to avoid ambiguity.

Your friends, as a rendering of the Greek *tous sous*, is equivalent in many languages to 'your clan', implying the man's family, both immediate and extended.

Lord is here undoubtedly a reference to God, but probably employed purposely by Mark with a kind of double reference, to God and to Christ. For a discussion of problems relative to *Lord* see 1:3, but note also the fact that in some languages 'Lord' must always be possessed. A man cannot be 'lord' without being 'lord of someone'. This means that in a verse such as this one must translate 'how much your Lord has done'.

Mercy is not a process which is easy to describe, for it involves a psychological state and an overt response in the form of behavior. As in the case of so many related words, e.g. *love, kindness, grace,* and *goodness,* this term likewise has a number of different types of equivalents, of which the most common are: (1) those based on the quality of heart, or other psychological center, e.g. 'tender heart' (Valiente), 'white heart' (Miskito), 'what arises from a kind heart' (Ifugao), and 'purity of heart' (Vai); (2) those which introduce the concept of weeping or extreme sorrow, e.g. 'his abdomen weeps' (Conob), 'to cry inside' (Kipsigis), 'to cry continually within' (Shilluk), and 'to feel great sorrow', with the connotation of being about to cry (Navajo); (3) those which involve willingness to look upon or to recognize the condition of others, e.g. 'to see misery' (Kpelle) and 'to know misery' (Habbe); and (4) those which involve a variety of intense feelings, e.g. 'to be in pain for' (Tarascan), 'to be very sorry for' (Mixteco Alto), and 'to have increasing love for' (Mezquital Otomí). In one language, Cuicatec, *mercy* is closely identified with grace as 'showing undeserved goodness'.

Decapolis may be rendered 'in the country of the ten cities' or 'in the region called Ten Cities'.

The type of marveling referred to in this verse may be described in different ways, e.g. 'listened quietly' (Tarahumara), 'they forgot listening'— in which the meaning is that they were so absorbed in what they heard that they forgot everything else (Mixtec), and 'it was considered very strange by them' (Tzeltal).

21 *And when Jesus had crossed again in the boat to the other side, a great crowd gathered about him; and he was beside the sea.*

Text: Instead of placing *palin* 'again' before *eis to peran* 'to the other side', as do the majority of the modern editions of the Greek text, Lagrange, Taylor, and Kilpatrick place it after *eis to peran* 'to the other side' (so that it thus modifies *sunēchthē* 'gathered'); although Tischendorf also places *palin* after *eis to peran*, by putting a comma after it he joins it to *eis to peran* 'again to the other side'.

Exegesis: *diaperasantos...palin eis to peran* 'going across...again to the other side', this time to the west side of the Lake.

diaperaō (6:53) 'go across', 'go over'.

eis to peran (cf. 4:35) 'to the other side'.

sunēchthē ochlos polus ep' auton 'a great crowd gathered around him'.

sunagō (cf. 2:2) 'gather together': cf. 3:20 and 4:1 for other instances.

epi 'upon': here, 'around' or 'to' (Arndt & Gingrich III.1.a.γ).

kai ēn para tēn thalassan 'and he was by the sea' (cf. 2:13, 4:1).

thalassa (cf. 1:16) 'sea': the Lake of Galilee.

Translation: For a discussion of *crossed...to the other side* see 4:35.

A great crowd may be equivalent to 'very many people', though in general it is not difficult to find words which designate a throng.

In some languages one must specify more exactly what is meant by *beside the sea*. Was he, for example, 'on the very shore of the lake', within a distance of a hundred yards or so, or with the lake at a distance of a mile or so on the horizon? All of these are different ways of being 'beside the lake'. Where a choice is required in designating distance, probably the first alternative is preferable (though the second is not incorrect), for it would indicate the immediacy with which the crowd thronged around him as he returned with his disciples. Cf. Indonesian 'he was close by the sea', South Toradja 'He was there, where the beach of the sea is'.

22 *Then came one of the rulers of the synagogue, Jairus by name; and seeing him, he fell at his feet,* **23** *and besought him, saying, "My little daughter is at the point of death. Come and lay your hands on her, so that she may be made well, and live."*

Exegesis: *heis tōn archisunagōgōn* 'one of the rulers of the synagogue'.

heis 'one' may be the equivalent of *tis* 'a certain one': 'a certain ruler of the synagogue' (cf. Black *Aramaic*, 249).

archisunagōgos (5:25, 36, 39) 'leader of the synagogue' charged with administrative duties, not spiritual (cf. Swete). The plural here 'rulers of the synagogue' is not to indicate that there were necessarily several in that particular place: it indicates simply the class to which Jairus belonged.

piptei pros tous podas autou 'he falls at his feet', 'he prostrates himself'.

piptō (cf. 4:4) 'fall'.

pous (6:11, 7:25, 9:45, 12:36) 'foot'.

parakalei auton polla 'he begged him urgently', 'he entreated him insistently'.

parakaleō (cf. 1:40) 'request', 'beg', 'entreat'.

polla (cf. 5:10) is adverbial 'much', 'strongly', 'urgently'.

eschatōs echei (only here in Mark) 'is in a critical stage', 'is at the point of death': for a similar construction cf. *kakōs echei* 'is in a bad way' in 1:32. Notice that Matthew (9:18) has *arti eteleutēsen* 'just now died' and Luke (8:42) says *apethnēsken* 'is dying'.

hina elthōn epithēs 'so that you may come and place': it is generally agreed that this construction represents the use of *hina* to express an imperative (here a request, rather than a command): 'Come and place...' (cf. RSV, BFBS, Manson, Goodspeed, Moffatt; Arndt & Gingrich *hina* III.2; Moule *Idiom Book*, 144; Moulton *Prolegomena*, 178-79).

epitithēmi (cf. 3:16) 'place upon', 'lay', 'set': for the phrase 'place the hand (hands) upon' in Mark see 6:5, 7:32, 8:23,25, 16:18.

hina sōthē kai zēsē 'that she may be healed and live': the two verbs represent two ideas, both of which should be expressed.

sōzō (cf. 3:4) 'save'; here, in the passive, 'be healed', 'be made well'.

zaō (12:27, 16:11) 'live'.

Translation: Since the phrase *one of the rulers of the synagogue* does not refer to Jairus as being one of several rulers of the particular synagogue in question, but simply to him as being a person with a particular function, one must in some languages recast this phrase as 'a man, named Jairus, who was a ruler in a synagogue' or 'a man, he was called Jairus, was one who had command over the affairs of the synagogue'.

Jairus by name is an awkward construction even in English. The equivalent is more likely to be 'he was called Jairus', 'people called him Jairus', or 'he had the name Jairus', often expressed as a paratactically combined clause.

The order of the constituents in the first part of verse 22 must often be rearranged, for the order is unusual in that Jairus is separated from the pronominal referent 'one'.

The pronouns *him, he...his* may need more specific identification, e.g. 'when Jairus saw Jesus, he fell at his feet'.

In translating the expression *fell at his feet* one must make certain that the phrase in the receptor languages does not mean—as it often has—stumbled and collapsed at Jesus' feet. The equivalent in many languages is 'bowed himself to the ground at Jesus' feet' or 'lay face down at the feet of Jesus'.

As in so many instances *besought...saying* may be better translated by a single verb.

At the point of death may be rendered as 'about to die'.

Live must be translated with care in some languages which clearly indicate aspectual differences. For example, in Kekchi one cannot use the verb 'to live' in the future. One may 'continue to live', but 'will live' means 'will be born'. A better rendering at this point, however, is 'so that she may...not die'.

24 And he went with him. And a great| crowd followed him and thronged about him.

Exegesis: *ēkolouthei* (cf. 1:18) 'it was following': here simply in a physical sense, and not as disciples.

ochlos polus (cf. v. 21) 'a large crowd'.

sunethlibon (5:31; cf. *thlibō* 3:9) 'pressed upon', 'crowded about'.

Translation: Note the importance of a paragraph break in the middle of this verse (cf. RSV).

Followed is better translated in some languages as 'went along with him', for 'followed' might give the idea of stringing out behind him.

Thronged may be translated as 'kept pushing around him' or 'pushed in against him'.

25 *And there was a woman who had had a flow of blood for twelve years,* **26** *and who had suffered much under many physicians, and had spent all that she had, and was no better but rather grew worse.*

Exegesis: *ousa en rusei haimatos* 'being in a flow of blood', 'had a hemorrhage'.

ousa 'being': the present participle describes a state begun in the past and still in effect at the present (cf. Burton *Moods and Tenses*, § 131).

en 'in': describes the condition, or state, the woman was in (cf. Arndt & Gingrich *eimi* III. 4; cf. *en pneumati akathartō* 'in an unclean spirit' 1:23).

rusis (only here in Mark) *haimatos* (5:29, 14:24) 'flow of blood', 'hemorrhage'.

dōdeka etē 'during twelve years': the accusative case describes duration of time (cf. 2:19 *hoson chronon* 'so [long] a time [as]'). It is not to be inferred that the woman had had an unchecked hemorrhage lasting twelve years: what is said is that she suffered from hemorrhages during these twelve years without being cured. In such a condition she was ceremonially unclean (Lev. 15:25) as well as physically ill.

kai...pathousa...kai dapanēsasa...kai mēden ōphelētheisa alla... elthousa 'and suffering...and spending...and not improving a bit but...getting (worse)': all four aorist participles describe the condition of the woman during the twelve years.

polla (cf. 1:45) *pathousa* (8:31, 9:12) 'suffering much'.

hupo pollōn iatrōn 'under (the care of) many physicians', 'at the hands of many physicians' (*iatros* 'physician' cf. 2:17).

dapanēsasa ta par' autēs panta 'having spent all she had', 'spent all her property' (cf. Arndt & Gingrich *para* I.4.b.α; Moule *Idiom Book*, 51f.).

kai mēden ōphelētheisa 'yet profiting nothing', 'yet benefiting nothing'.

ōpheleō (7:11, 8:36) 'profit', 'benefit', 'help'; in the passive, as here, 'receive help', 'be benefited': the meaning here is 'she didn't improve...'

alla mallon (7:36, 9:42, 10:48, 15:11) 'rather, on the contrary'.

eis to cheiron elthousa 'she got worse', 'her condition grew worse'.

eis 'into' expresses degree (cf. Arndt & Gingrich 3).

cheiron (cf. 2:21) 'worse': the comparative of *kakos* 'bad'.

elthousa 'coming (into a worse condition)': for this use of *erchomai* 'come' cf. Arndt & Gingrich I.2.c.

Translation: The Greek of verses 25 and 26 consists of a series of connected participial constructions which must usually be broken into several complete sentences. However, in order to introduce this woman it is often necessary to "locate" her with respect to the actual context, i.e. 'a woman was there who...'

Flow of blood (or as in the AV "fountain of blood") has frequently been badly translated. In one language the translator had employed a literal 'fountain of blood', which people assumed was a miraculous source of blood which the woman had, apparently in her courtyard or somewhere on her property. However, the people could not understand why the woman would be so poor, since blood in that region was sold at a good price for use in preparing food. In another language the translation referred not to menstrual flow, but to blood coming from a wound, and to have had an open wound for twelve years seemed entirely incredible to the people. Accordingly, it must be made quite clear—though not vulgarly so—that this flow of blood refers to a menstrual disorder. Ways of speaking of this are varied: 'for twelve years her water was running out', in which menstrual flow is always called 'water' in contrast to blood from a wound (Mazahua), 'her month did not pass for twelve years' (Tojolobal), 'suffered month for twelve years' (Trique), and 'sickness of blood lasted twelve years' (Eskimo). In Shilluk menstrual flow is always called 'blood of the moon'.

Suffered much under many physicians is translatable in two different ways: (1) 'suffered much while she was being treated by many doctors' or (2) 'many doctors who treated her caused her to suffer much'.

Spent may be equivalent to 'had paid out' or in some instances to 'this cost her all that she had'.

The last clause may be rendered as 'she did not get better; she got worse', or 'rather than getting better, she got worse'.

27 She had heard the reports about Jesus, and came up behind him in the crowd and touched his garment.

Exegesis: *akousasa* 'hearing': the participle may express time '*when* she heard' or cause '*because* she heard'. Notice that in Greek the whole sentence runs from v. 25 through v. 27, without a break: the subject *gunē* 'woman' at the beginning of v. 25 is followed by seven participial clauses, with the principal verb *hēpsato* 'she touched' coming at the end of v. 27.

ta peri tou Iēsou 'the things concerning Jesus', 'reports about Jesus', i.e. specifically his miracles of healing.

elthousa...opisthen 'coming from behind': as the crowd accompanied Jesus down the road toward the house of Jairus, the woman came from behind, working her way through the crowd toward Jesus.

hēpsato (cf. 1:41) 'she touched': not accidentally but on purpose.
himatiou (cf. 2:21) 'clothes', 'garment'.

Translation: *Reports about Jesus* are often 'what people were saying about Jesus'.

One must be careful about the word for 'garment', since more may be communicated than one may think. For example, in some languages there is no general word for 'garment', only the specific names for various articles of clothing: pants, shirt, loin cloth, sheet, blanket, etc. If one selects one or another of these garments, Jesus may be immediately identified as a foreigner, a proud person, a non-conformist, etc. This difficulty may be avoided in some languages by using a clause 'what he was wearing'.

Garments, both here and in verse 30, must usually be rendered by a singular 'garment' (or the equivalent), since it is not likely that the woman touched more than one article of clothing.

28 *For she said, "If I touch even his garments, I shall be made well."* 29 *And immediately the hemorrhage ceased; and she felt in her body that she was healed of her disease.*

Exegesis: *elegen gar* 'for she said': not aloud, but to herself (cf. Mt. 9:21). Verse 28 is parenthetical, being added to show why the woman did what she did.

ean apsōmai kan tōn himatiōn autou 'if I get to touch at least his clothes'.

kan (the contraction of *kai ean* 'and if') (6:56, 16:18) 'if only', 'at least', 'just' (cf. Arndt & Gingrich 3): modifies 'his clothes', not 'if I touch'.

sōthēsomai (cf. v. 23) 'I shall be made well', 'I shall be healed'.

exēranthē (cf. 3:1) 'it became dry', i.e. 'ceased', 'stopped'.

pēgē (only here in Mark) 'spring', 'fountain'.

kai egnō tō sōmati hoti iatai 'and she knew in her body that she has been healed': notice the distinction between the aorist *egnō* 'she knew' and the perfect *iatai* 'she has been healed'.

iaomai (only here in Mark) 'heal': in the passive 'to be healed'.

mastigos (cf. 3:10) 'of (her) affliction', 'suffering'.

Translation: It may be necessary to specify the manner in which the woman spoke about her intention expressed in verse 27, for languages may distinguish between 'speaking to people' and 'speaking to oneself'. Obviously, the woman speaks to herself (see above), for she was trying to remain unnoticed by the crowd.

The same Greek verb (here *sōthēsomai*) may mean 'to be saved' and 'to be healed'. It is rarely possible to combine these two ideas in any single word in a receptor language (though this does happen to be the case in Tzeltal). In this context the meaning must obviously be related to the healing process.

Some languages have a number of verbs meaning 'touch', depending upon the degree of contact and the manner in which it is done. Here the contact was no doubt with the fingers and as slight as possible, for fear of detection.

The hemorrhage ceased is expressed in various ways, e.g. 'her disease sat down' (Chontal of Tabasco), 'she became well', and 'she no longer suffered'.

Was healed is a passive construction, which may be changed to an active one 'that Jesus had healed her' (where active expressions containing agents are required) or which may be shifted to one expressing state of being 'was well', 'no longer had the disease', or 'the sickness had left her'.

30 *And Jesus, perceiving in himself that power had gone forth from him, immediately turned about in the crowd, and said, "Who touched my garments?" 31 And his disciples said to him, "You see the crowd pressing around you, and yet you say, 'Who touched me?'"*

Exegesis: *epignous en heautō* (cf. 2 : 8 *epignous...tō pneumati autou*) 'perceiving in himself', 'sensing in himself' (cf. Arndt & Gingrich *epiginōskō* 2.c).

tēn ex autou dunamin exelthousan 'the power from him which had gone out': the meaning here, clearly, is 'sensing that (the) power had gone out from him'. Taylor, however, following Swete, argues that *ex autou* 'from him' is an additional statement concerning the power that resided in Jesus, and defends the ASV rendition 'the power *proceeding* from him had gone forth'. As Field (*Notes*, 27) points out, however, what is said is not that Jesus was conscious of his power: he was conscious that it had gone forth. This is the meaning that practically all modern translations give to the phrase.

dunamis 'power', 'strength' is used in Mark in three ways: (1) in the sense of 'power' as such, 5 : 30, 9 : 1, 12 : 24, 13 : 26; (2) with the meaning 'miracle': in the sg. 6 : 5, 9 : 39, in the pl. 6 : 2, 14; (3) personalized, 13 : 25 ('the powers in the heavens') and 14 : 62 ('the Power', i.e. God).

epistrapheis (cf. 4 : 12) 'turning', 'turning around'—here in a physical sense.

sunthlibonta (v. 24) 'pressing', 'crowding', 'jostling'.

Translation: *Power* must be translated with care, since a literal rendering may result in bad distortion of the meaning of the passage. For example, in Loma a literal rendering would denote that Jesus had lost his strength, i.e. had become helpless. In another language, this expression about 'power going out of a person' is a euphemistic, but common, way of speaking about the male function in sexual intercourse. In some languages, therefore, certain adaptations must be made, e.g. 'person-heal-power' (Loma) and 'medicinal power', in which 'medicinal' means essentially 'healing' (Chontal of Tabasco), and 'know-how' (Chontal of Oaxaca), in which one must use 'know-how' rather than literally 'power' or 'strength', for the latter would be equivalent to saying that having lost his strength, he could do nothing in the future, until this was magically recovered— a parallel to common practices in witchcraft. Bare'e renders 'a miracle-power had gone out from Him', a precise and accurate expression.

It is not easy to render the obvious irony in the voices of the disciples who exclaim *and yet you say*... This may be approximated in some languages by employing a double question, e.g. 'You see the crowd pressing around you; then how can you say, Who touched me?' Cf. South Toradja 'But you see that the crowd is pressing round you, and then you say...'

32 *And he looked around to see who had done it.* 33 *But the woman, knowing what had been done to her, came in fear and trembling and fell down before him, and told him the whole truth.*

Exegesis: *perieblepeto* (cf. 3:5) 'he looked around him'.

idein 'to see': the infinitive indicates purpose; here the verb is practically equivalent to 'to discover', 'to find'.

tēn touto poiēsasan 'the one who had done this': literally, 'the (*woman*) who did this'. This, of course, is from the author's viewpoint, not from the point of view of Jesus, who did not know whether man or woman had touched him. It is fanciful to suppose that from the touch Jesus sensed it was a woman (as does Bruce *Expositor's Greek Testament* I, 375).

phobētheisa (cf. 4:41) 'afraid', 'fearful'.

tremousa (only here in Mark) 'trembling'.

eiduia 'knowing': probably causal, 'because she knew' (cf. BFBS).

prosepesen autō (cf. 3:11) 'she prostrated herself before him'.

pasan tēn alētheian 'the whole truth': not only about her cure, but all the facts concerning her illness (narrated in vv. 25-28).

alētheia (12·14, 32) 'truth'.

Translation: *Fear and trembling* must in some languages be related subordinately, rather than coordinately, as in Greek (and English). For example, in Zoque the equivalent expression is 'for fear she was trembling'. This type of arrangement with *and* makes possible an implication which is readily understood by English speakers, but not by certain others, namely, the specific connection between 'fear' and 'trembling' or the fact that 'trembling' designates a psychologically significant experience.

For problems in translating *fall down*, see 5:22.

Where languages may lack an abstract term *truth*, which can be used in this type of context, it may be possible to employ a phrase 'she told him exactly what had happened'.

34 *And he said to her, "Daughter, your faith has made you well; go in peace, and be healed of your disease."*

Exegesis: *thugatēr* (5:35, 6:22, 7:26,29) 'daughter'—a term of endearment (cf. *teknon* 'child' 2:5) the nominative form used for the vocative case (cf. 5:8 for similar instance).

hē pistis sou sesōken se 'your faith has made you well': for this use of the verb *sōzō* 'save' see v. 28 (cf. also 3:4).

hupage eis eirēnēn 'go in peace': a Jewish mode of saying farewell (cf. 1 Sam. 1 : 17). It should not, however, be translated simply 'goodbye', as a mere dismissal.

eirēnē (only here in Mark) 'peace': the Hebrew word it represents has more the idea of soundness, wholeness, well-being, than that of lack of conflict or strife (cf. Kennedy *Sources*, 98f.).

isthi hugiēs apo tēs mastigos sou 'and you be (or, continue) sound (freed) from your affliction' (cf. Arndt & Gingrich *hugiēs* 1.a): this is an additional statement, not simply to be equated with the previous one.

hugiēs (only here in Mark) 'sound', 'healthy', 'whole'.

mastix (cf. 3 : 10) 'affliction', 'suffering'.

Translation: There are relatively few languages in which one can translate literally 'daughter', without resultant misunderstanding, for people would assume that in some quite inconceivable way Jesus was addressing his own daughter. Accordingly, one must adopt an expression which conveys something of the tenderness of the Greek form of address, while at the same time being culturally explicable, e.g. 'woman' (Kiyaka), 'my little woman', in which this phrase reflects some degree of sympathy and endearment (Mazatec), and 'old lady', a phrase which, though denoting a person of quite different relative age, is, nevertheless, the exact cultural equivalent in this context (Shipibo).

Your faith has made you well involves a problem for many translators since *faith* must be rendered in many instances by a verb, and this may make it impossible to say literally that 'believing has made'. However, in order to show the causal relationship between the faith and the healing, one may translate as 'because you believe in your heart, you have been made well' (Tzeltal), and 'you are well because you have believed' (Huave).

Go in peace is an idiomatic expression of farewell which is translatable in different ways in other languages: 'go with sweet insides' (Shilluk), 'rejoice as you go' (Mazahua), 'go in quietness of heart' (Chol), 'go happy' (Zacapoastla Aztec), 'being happy, go' (Tarahumara), and 'go and sit down in your heart' (Tzeltal).

Be healed of your disease is a passive command, a relatively rare type of construction which has no close counterpart in many languages. The closest equivalent may be a strong type of future 'you will remain healed' (Kekchi), an intensive expression of assurance 'once for all your sickness has gotten well' (Tzeltal), or an active assertion 'your disease will never come back to you'.

35 *While he was still speaking, there came from the ruler's house some who said, "Your daughter is dead. Why trouble the Teacher any further?"*

Exegesis: *eti autou lalountos* 'while he was speaking': the present participle portrays the action still in progress.

erchontai apo tou archisunagōgou 'they come from the (house of the) ruler of the synagogue': so the majority of modern translations. Another translation is possible by understanding *apo* 'from' to mean *'some* from' (cf. Black *Aramaic*, 251): the phrase would then mean 'some men of the household of the ruler of the synagogue' (cf. BFBS 'some of the men of the officer of the synagogue').

erchontai 'they come' is another example of the impersonal plural: 'men come' (cf. Turner *Journal of Theological Studies*, 25.380, 1923-4).

apethanen (5:39, 9:26, 12:19,20,21,22, 15:44) 'she died', 'she is dead'.

ti eti skulleis ton didaskalon 'why are you still bothering the Teacher?' *skullō* (only here in Mark) literally 'flay'; 'bother', 'annoy', 'trouble'. *ho didaskalos* (cf. 4:38) 'the Teacher', 'the Rabbi'.

Translation: The impersonal indirect type of expression *there came... some* must frequently be shifted to a more direct form, e.g. 'some men from the ruler's house came...' or 'some men came from the ruler's house'.

Though the Greek has only 'ruler of the synagogue', a type of compound, it is often necessary to add 'the house' (as in English). One may, of course, also use 'synagogue' in this phrase if this is required by the context, but generally the complete expression, as given in 5:22, is sufficiently full that in verse 5:35 one need only speak of the 'ruler' or the 'leader'.

Said must in some languages be expanded to include the object of the saying, namely, the ruler of the synagogue.

The sequence of events may require *is dead* to be rendered as 'is now dead' or 'has now died'.

For the translation of *teacher*, see 2:13.

36 *But ignoring what they said, Jesus said to the ruler of the syna-gogue, "Do not fear, only believe."*

Text: Instead of *parakousas* 'ignoring' of all modern editions of the Greek text, *Textus Receptus* has *eutheōs akousas* 'immediately hearing'; Kilpatrick has *euthus parakousas* 'then ignoring'.

Exegesis: *parakousas* (only here in Mark) 'ignoring', 'disregarding', or, 'overhearing': the meaning of the verb here is disputed, with the majority of translations favoring the sense 'ignoring', 'disregarding' (ASV, RSV, BFBS, Goodspeed, Moffatt, Weymouth, Montgomery, Williams, Zürich, Synodale, Brazilian; among the lexicons and commentators, Abbott-Smith, Thayer, Swete, Taylor); others, however, favor the meaning 'overhearing' (Berkeley, Manson, Turner, Arndt & Gingrich, Liddell and Scott, Kittel); the meaning 'pretending not to hear' is favored by Field (*Notes*, 28) and Souter. Cf. the discussion in Taylor, *in loc.*, and other commentaries.

ton logon laloumenon 'the message being delivered': i.e. while they were still talking, Jesus interrupted and spoke to Jairus.

mē phobou (cf. 4 : 11) 'do not be afraid', 'quit being afraid': the further injunction 'only believe' shows that 'do not be afraid' in this particular context has the meaning 'do not be unbelieving', 'do not doubt'.

monon pisteue 'only believe': a command.

monon (6:8) 'only': an adverb, modifying the verb 'believe' (for *monos* 'only' as an adjective cf. 6 : 47).

Translation: The meaning of *ignoring* may be translated as 'he paid no attention'. *Overhearing* may be rendered as 'he heard what the men had just said to the ruler'.

For *ruler of the synagogue*, see 5 : 22, though note that since this is a title, more than a specific designation of his role in a particular synagogue, it may be more correct to translate 'the ruler of a synagogue'.

Fear must refer in this context to 'fearful of the outcome' or 'doubtful'.

For *believe*, see 1 : 15, but in this context difficulties may arise if the verb 'to believe' requires an object. In such instances it may be better to adopt an alternative expression such as 'have confidence' or 'keep your heart firm'.

37 And he allowed no one to follow him except Peter and James and John the brother of James.

Exegesis: *aphēken* (cf. 2 : 5) 'he allowed', 'he permitted'.

sunakolouthēsai (14 : 51) 'to go along with', 'to accompany': cf. *akoloutheō* 'follow' in 1 :18.

ei mē (cf. 2 : 7) 'except', 'but', 'with the exception of' (occurs some 16 times in Mark).

Translation: *Follow* here has the sense of 'to go with'. (cf. 1 : 17).

For a discussion of problems relating to expressions of lineage and relationships such as *James and John the brother of James*, see 1 : 19 and 3 : 17. Here the equivalent of such an expression may be 'James and his brother John', 'the brothers James and John', or 'James and John, they were brothers'.

38 When they came to the house of the ruler of the synagogue, he saw a tumult, and people weeping and wailing loudly.

Exegesis: *eis ton oikon* 'into the house (home)', 'to the house (home)': *eis* here probably means 'to', since in v. 39 it is said 'and he went in' (*into the house*), while in v. 40 we read 'and he entered (the room) where the child was'. *eis ton oikon* may mean literally 'into the house' or, 'into (the courtyard of) the house': the meaning accepted by RSV, BFBS and others, however, seems to be the preferred one.

oikos 'house' or 'home' (cf. 2 : 1, 3 : 19; cf. Kilpatrick *The Bible Translator*, 7.5-6, 1956).

theōrei (cf. 3 : 11) *thorubon* (14 : 2) 'he sees a tumult': the word *thorubos* means 'turmoil', 'excitement', 'uproar' (cf. Arndt & Gingrich 3).

kai klaiontas kai alalazontas polla 'and (people) crying and lamenting much': this phrase describes in detail the *thorubon* 'turmoil' Jesus saw. The two masculine participles are in the accusative case, as the object of the verb *theōrei* 'he sees', and both refer to *people* crying and *people* wailing.

klaiō (5:39, 14:72, 16:10) 'weep', 'cry'.

alalazō (only here in Mark) 'wail', 'cry out', 'lament'.

polla (cf. 1:45) adverbial 'much': here, 'loudly', 'grievously', 'bitterly'.

Translation: It may be well at this point to specify *he* more exactly as 'Jesus' because of the other intervening third person referents.

Tumult is 'many people making a lot of noise'.

Weeping and wailing is equivalent to 'crying and yelling out' (Maya) or 'crying and making a noise' (Tarahumara). Wailing appears to most peoples as quite appropriate at the time of death, but in some tribes wailing is carefully avoided so as not to prevent unduly the passage of the spirit from this world to the next.

39 *And when he had entered, he said to them, "Why do you make a tumult and weep? The child is not dead but sleeping."*

Exegesis: *eiselthōn* (cf. previous verse) 'entering (the house)': in the next verse *ekbalōn* 'driving out (of the house)'.

ti thorubeisthe (only here in Mark) 'why do you make a tumult?' (cf. the noun *thorubos* in the previous verse).

to paidion (5:40,41, 7:28,30, 9:24,36,37, 10:13,14,15) 'the child', 'the infant': here, a twelve year old girl (v. 42).

ouk apethanen alla katheudei 'she did not die but is sleeping', 'is not dead but sleeps'.

apothnēskō (cf. v. 35) 'die'.

katheudō (cf. 4:27) 'sleep': this word offers no problem to the translator since its meaning is 'to sleep' whatever may have been the sense in which it was used by Jesus (whether literal or metaphorical: cf. R. E. Ker, *Expository Times* 65.315 f., 1954; 66.125, 1955; and, in reply, W. Powell, *Expository Times* 66.61, 1954; and 66.215, 1955).

Translation: *Entered* must in some languages specify 'entered the house'.

Child offers certain problems to the translator since languages frequently have a number of terms, depending upon the age and stage of maturity. Note that the age is specifically given in verse 42, and it may be assumed that she had not experienced puberty (this latter event is the decisive distinction in many indigenous terms for 'child' or 'girl').

40 *And they laughed at him. But he put them all outside, and took the child's father and mother and those who were with him, and went in where the child was.*

Text: At the end of the verse, after *paidion* 'child' *Textus Receptus*,

Soden, Vogels, Merk, and Kilpatrick add *anakeimenon* 'lying', which is omitted by Tischendorf, Nestle, Souter, Westcott and Hort, Lagrange, and Taylor.

Exegesis: *kategelōn* (only here in Mark) 'they were laughing at', 'they were jeering', 'they were ridiculing'.
ekbalōn (cf. 1:12) 'expelling', 'driving out', i.e. forcibly.
paralambanei (cf. 4:36) 'he takes along', 'he takes with (him)'.
tous met' autou 'those who were with him', i.e. the three disciples he allowed to accompany him (v. 37).
eisporeuetai hopou ēn to paidion 'he entered (the room) where the child was'.
  eisporeuomai (cf. 1:21) 'go in', 'enter'.

Translation: There is generally no problem in finding an equivalent of *laughed at*, but this type of expression of scorn is in some languages translated quite idiomatically, e.g. 'burped at him' (Shilluk).
Outside may be rendered as 'outside the house'.
Went in no doubt refers to a separate room in which the child lay.

41 *Taking her by the hand he said to her, "Talitha cumi"; which means, "Little girl, I say to you, arise."*

Text: Instead of the masculine form *koum* of the great majority of modern editions of the Greek text, *Textus Receptus*, Souter (and RSV) have the feminine form *koumi* (cf. the discussion in Lagrange).

Exegesis: *kratēsas tēs cheiros* (cf. 1:31) 'seizing her hand'.
legei autē 'he says to her': the concordance of genders is logical 'her', i.e. 'the girl' and not grammatical (since the antecedent *tou paidiou* 'the child' is neuter).
tulitha koum: a Greek transliteration of the Aramaic *ṭelitha' qum* 'damsel arise'.
ho estin methermēneuomenon 'which is, translated', i.e. 'which, translated, means' (cf. Moule *Idiom Book*, 17).
  methermēneuomai (15:22, 34) 'be translated', 'be interpreted'.
to korasion (5:42, 6:22,28), 'maiden', 'girl': another use of the nominative form for the vocative case (cf. 5:8, 34).
egeire (cf. 1:31) 'rise', 'get up'. Whether this means simply 'rise from the bed', or 'rise from the dead' will be determined by the meaning given the statement of Jesus concerning the girl in v. 39.

Translation: *Taking her...he said* may be rendered by two coordinate expressions 'he took hold of her hand and he said'.
Talitha cumi should be transliterated in such a way as to represent the closest sound equivalents in the receptor language. For a discussion of problems of transliteration, see *Bible Translating*, 243-46.
For the treatment of a phrase such as *which means*, see 3:17.
Little girl is very frequently translated by the same term as is used for child in verses 39 and 40. It is most important that one not employ

a word which would imply a person of different age or maturity status.

Arise should be interpreted in this context as 'stand up' (see the following verse). It is quite unnecessary, and misleading to translate 'arise from the dead', for note that Jesus was sincerely trying to understate the extent of the miracle (see verse 39).

42 *And immediately the girl got up and walked; for she was twelve years old. And immediately they were overcome with amazement.*

Exegesis: *anestē kai periepatei* 'got up and walked': perhaps, 'rose and started walking about' (cf. *Expository Times* 65.147, 1954).

anistēmi (cf. 1:35) 'rise', 'get up'.

peripateō (cf. 2:9) 'walk', 'walk about'.

exestēsan...ekstasei megalē 'they were amazed with a great amazement' (cf. 4:41 'they feared a great fear' for another example of this form of intensive statement).

existēmi (cf. 2:12) 'to astonish', 'to amaze', 'to confound': in the active aorist (as here) the verb has a passive sense, 'to be astonished', 'to be amazed'.

ekstasis (16:8) has the weakened sense of 'bewilderment', 'astonishment' (cf. Kennedy *Sources*, 121f.).

Translation: The Greek imperfect in the verb translated 'walked' has suggested to some translators the value of translating 'was walking', but this may not always be done. For example, in one translation the imperfect tense suggested that she was walking before she got up. Hence, 'stood up and started to walk' is preferable.

Twelve years is translated quite idiomatically in some languages, e.g. 'her winters are twelve' (Navajo) or 'her seasons were ten on the head of which two' (Shilluk).

43 *And he strictly charged them that no one should know this, and told them to give her something to eat.*

Exegesis: *diesteilato...polla* 'commanded...much', i.e. 'gave strict orders'.

diastellomai (7:36, 8:15, 9:9) 'command', 'order'.

polla (cf. 3:12, 5:10,23) is adverbial 'much', 'strictly'.

hina 'that' denotes content (cf. 5:18), not purpose.

eipen dothēnai autē phagein 'he said to be given to her to eat', i.e. 'he said that she be fed'.

Translation: *Strictly charged* may be rendered as 'strongly commanded' or 'spoke to them in hard words'.

In some languages the rendering seems to imply a complete inconsistency between Jesus' order to the parents of the child and the fact that others should not know. What was really meant in the command of Jesus was that they should not tell others what had happened. Hence, one may translate as 'that no one else should come to know about', or 'that no other people should hear about', or 'that they should not tell others about'.

CHAPTER SIX

1 *He went away from there and came to his own country; and his disciples followed him.*

Exegesis: *eis tēn patrida autou* 'to his own native place': rather than the generalized sense of 'fatherland', 'country' (RSV), the word *patris* (6:4) has here the more specialized meaning of 'home town' (Cf. Moulton & Milligan; Field *Notes*, 10; Manson). The town of Nazareth is meant (cf. 1:9, 24).

akolouthousin (cf. 1:18) 'they follow', 'they accompany': in the physical sense of going along with, not the specialized sense of 'follow as a disciple'.

Translation: *His own country* must be translated in the sense of 'region (or 'place') in which he lived', not 'the land which he owned', as is sometimes the case in poor translations. Cf. 'the town where he grew up' (South Toradja), 'the town from which he came' (Javanese).

For *disciples*, see 2:15, and for *follow* see 1:17.

2 *And on the sabbath he began to teach in the synagogue; and many who heard him were astonished, saying, "Where did this man get all this? What is the wisdom given to him? What mighty works are wrought by his hands!*

Text: Before *polloi* 'many' *Textus Receptus*, Souter, Kilpatrick (and, apparently, RSV) omit *hoi* 'the', which is included by all other modern editions of the Greek text.

Instead of *kai hai dunameis* 'and the mighty works' of most editions of the Greek text, *Textus Receptus*, Soden, and Kilpatrick have *hoti kai dunameis* 'for even mighty works'; Tischendorf has *kai dunameis* 'and mighty works'.

Exegesis: *genomenou sabbatou* (cf. 1:21) 'when the sabbath came', 'when it was the sabbath'.

ērxato didaskein en tē sunagōgē (cf. 1:21, 3:1) 'he began to teach in the synagogue'.

hoi polloi akouontes exeplēssonto 'the many who were listening to him were astonished'.

hoi polloi 'the many': with the article (cf. *Text*, above) the phrase here means 'the many (*who were there*) as they heard him', *not*, as RSV has it, 'many (of those there)...', i.e. 'many, but not all'. Cf. Arndt & Gingrich *polus* I.2.a.β (cf. 9:26).

ekplēssomai (cf. 1:22) 'be astonished', 'be overwhelmed'.

The three clauses that follow, understood either as questions or as exclamations, lack finite verbs, being thus grammatically incomplete: they express quite vividly the surprise and astonishment that gripped the large crowd.

toutō (cf. 2:7) 'to this one': expresses contempt. By underscoring the personal pronouns Manson graphically portrays the astonishment and resentment of Jesus' townspeople.

tis hē sophia hē dotheisa toutō; Manson: 'What sort of wisdom is it that has been conferred on *him*?'

sophia (only here in Mark) 'wisdom'.

hai dunameis toiautai 'miracles such as these!'

dunamis (cf. 5:30) 'mighty work', 'miracle'.

dia tōn cheirōn autou ginomenai 'which are being done through his hands': or, simply, 'which are being wrought by him'.

Translation: A number of key words in this verse have already been treated: *sabbath* (1:21), *teach* (2:13), *synagogue* (1:21), and *astonish* (1:21,27).

Teach often requires an object: 'teach the people'.

Astonished, saying is frequently rendered as 'were astonished; they said'.

It is important that *get all this* does not refer exclusively to 'wealth' or 'material possessions'. To avoid such a denotation one may translate as in Popoluca, 'from where did he bring these thoughts'.

It should be noted that these questions are not requests for information, but are types of exclamatory expressions. They should be so treated in languages which have special forms for such questions or utterances.

Wisdom is not always translatable by a noun, for it involves the result of a process of learning and the application of special mental faculties. Hence in some instances wisdom is 'what he has learned'. In other languages, however, *wisdom* is equivalent to 'mind', e.g. 'what mind has been given to him' (Chontal of Tabasco) and 'how was this man made a person of big mind' (Ifugao).

The passive concept expressed in *is given* is not always easily rendered, for where the agent is required, one must completely alter the form, either making Jesus the subject of the process of acquiring the wisdom, e.g. 'how has he learned so much', or indicating that God is the source of the special gift of wisdom, e.g. 'how is it that God has given such wisdom to him'. However, this last question does not seem to fit the context, for these people were not inclined to recognize Jesus' God-given ministry or abilities. Hence, the former question is probably closer to the original meaning, though not closer to the formal sentence structure.

Mighty works translates the Greek *dunameis*, a regular term for 'miracles', though meaning literally 'powers'. (For a discussion of certain problems in translating this term see *The Bible Translator* 7.42-47, 1956; and *Bible Translating* 217-18). One of the most common ways of talking about miracles is to call them 'things that no one has ever seen before' (San Blas). A second semantic perspective involves the process of amazement, wonder, and awe, e.g. 'thing marveled at' (Cuicatec), 'breathtaking thing' (Valiente), and 'long-necked thing' referring to the onlookers who stretch their necks to see (Mazatec). A third means of talking about miracles makes use of expressions of power and strength (similar to the Greek), e.g. 'sign done by God's power' (Moré), 'supernatural power' (Javanese), and 'things that have heaven-strength' (Totonac). It is usually necessary in employing these terms for strength or power to specify the source or the nature of the manifestation of power. Otherwise ambiguity or obscurity is likely to occur.

By his hands, if translated literally, may give rise to misinterpretation, for in a receptor language this may be used to refer only to artefacts. Hence, 'by him' may be used in a passive construction or 'he does' in an active one.

3 *Is not this the carpenter, the son of Mary and brother of James and Joses and Judas and Simon, and are not his sisters here with us?" And they took offense at him.*

Exegesis: *ho tektōn* (only here in Mark) 'the carpenter': cf. Mt. 13:55 'the son of the carpenter'.

ho huios tēs Marias 'the son of Mary': very probably stated as an insult (cf. Rawlinson; J. K. Russell *Expository Times* 60.195, 1949).

kai eskandalizonto en autō (cf. 4:17) 'and they took offense at him' (RSV, BFBS, Goodspeed, Weymouth: cf. Arndt & Gingrich *skandalizō* 1.b).

en 'in': denotes that toward which the feeling is directed (cf. Arndt & Gingrich III.3.b).

Translation: *Carpenter* is best rendered as 'house-builder' or 'builder', for the Greek term may refer to one who uses either wood or stone.

Brother must be in many languages 'older brother'.

Sisters would be 'younger sisters' in languages which make a distinction as to relative age.

In some languages there are precise distinctions made between full brothers and half-brothers. Some translators have felt that because Jesus was conceived by the Holy Spirit, they should use a term for half-brother, but generally this is not a wise procedure, for it introduces all sorts of other problems, implying as it does that Mary had two husbands.

Offense in this verse cannot usually be translated in the same way as the corresponding word (in the Greek text) of 4:17. There the reference is more to loss of faith, but in this verse the reaction is one of jealousy and personal animosity: 'they were jealous and angry against him' (Sierra Popoloca), 'they had no more respect for' (Sierra Aztec), 'they were distrustful' (Indonesian), 'they felt offended because of His dignity' (Javanese), 'they despised' (San Blas), 'a grudge arose in their hearts' (Tzeltal), 'they were angry to see him' (Huave), and 'they hated him' (Zoque).

4 *And Jesus said to them, "A prophet is not without honor, except in his own country, and among his own kin, and in his own house."*

Exegesis: *prophētēs* (cf. 1:2) 'prophet': not to be thought of simply as a soothsayer or diviner, but as 'proclaimer and interpreter of the divine revelation' (Arndt & Gingrich).

atimos (only here in Mark) 'unhonored', 'dishonored'; to be dishonored is not to receive one's due honor and respect.

en tē patridi autou (cf. v. 1) 'in his native place', 'in his own hometown'.

en tois suggeneusin autou 'among his own kinsmen', 'among his own relatives'.

suggenēs (only here in Mark) 'related', 'akin to': here in the sense of 'relative', 'kinsman' (cf. Moulton & Milligan).

Translation: For *prophet*, see 1:2.

The expression *a prophet is not without honor* may be difficult for two reasons: (1) *honor* must often be translated as a verb, not as a noun, and (2) the double negative involved in *not without* may require two entirely different sentences, in order to produce the required contrast. Furthermore, in some instances the contrast must be precisely stated by a somewhat redundant, but necessary, repetition (see the Mitla Zapotec rendering below). The following renderings are typical: 'a messenger of God is surely respected; only in his own land...he is not respected' (Tzeltal), 'a prophet has respect everywhere, but not with his towns-people,...they don't have respect' (Mitla Zapotec), 'prophets are every-where praised, but not in their own towns...' (Rinón Zapotec), 'in his own country,...he is not honored, but everywhere else he is honored' (Chontal of Oaxaca), 'one who speaks the word of God is wanted, but he is not wanted in his own town...' (Huave).

Own country may be well translated as 'birth town' (Loma). *Kin* refers to the 'clan', and *his own house* means 'his family'.

5 *And he could do no mighty work there, except that he laid his hands upon a few sick people and healed them.* 6 *And he marveled because of their unbelief. And he went about among the villages teaching.*

Exegesis: *dunamin* (cf. 5:30, 6:2) 'mighty work', 'miracle'.

oligois arrōstois epitheis tas cheiras etherapeusen '(by) laying his hands on a few sick ones he healed (them)'.

arrōstos (6:13, 16:18) 'powerless', i.e. 'sick', 'ill'.

epitithenai tas cheiras (cf. 5:23) 'to lay hands upon'.

therapeuō (cf. 1:34) 'heal', 'cure'.

ethaumasen (cf. 5:20) 'he marveled', 'he was surprised'.

dia tēn apistian autōn 'on account of their unbelief': most English translations (cf. also Synodale, Lagrange, Brazilian) have it '*at* their unbelief' translating *dia* not as cause but as the object of the surprise of Jesus (cf. Arndt & Gingrich *thaumazō* 1.a.β).

apistia (9:24, 16:14) 'lack of belief', 'lack of trust' in Jesus (cf.

faith, confidence, in Jesus, 2:5, 5:34). In this context the word describes the unwillingness of the people of Nazareth to believe that Jesus could work miracles.

kai periēgen tas kōmas kuklō didaskōn 'and he went around among the adjacent villages teaching'.

periagō (only here in Mark) 'go about', 'make a tour'.

kōmē (6:36, 56, 8:23, 26, 27, 11:2; cf. *agros* 5:14) 'village', 'small town'; in general smaller than *polis* 'city' but larger than *agros* 'hamlet'—cf. especially 6:36, 56.

kuklō (cf. 3:34) 'round about', 'around': here modifies *tas kōmas* (cf. Moule *Idiom Book*, 108f.) 'surrounding villages' (cf. Arndt & Gingrich *periagō* 2, 'the nearby villages').

Translation: *Could* evidently means that though Jesus had the power to perform miracles, in Nazareth he was unable to use his power because of the lack of faith on the part of the people.

For *mighty work*, see 6:2.

Few is a relative word, which receives its meaning from the context. In other languages there are often equally arbitrary delimitations. For example, in Tzeltal the equivalent of *few* is 'two or three', but this does not mean literally two or three, but as in the case of English *few* acquires its meaning from the context; compare 'a few people in town' and 'a few people in our living room', obviously capable of quite different meanings.

Unbelief may be rendered as a phrase 'they did not believe' or 'they did not have confidence in him'.

Villages would imply the hamlets surrounding Nazareth, e.g. 'he went around from hamlet to hamlet, teaching the people'.

7 And he called to him the twelve, and began to send them out two by two, and gave them authority over the unclean spirits.

Exegesis: *proskaleitai* (cf. 3:13) 'he summons', 'he calls to himself'.

hoi dōdeka (cf. 3:14, 16) 'the Twelve' as a title, not simply as a number of men (RSV 'the twelve').

apostellein (cf. 1:2, 3:14) 'to send off': a commission and authority to carry out the ministry of Jesus, in accordance with their call as disciples (cf. 3:14-15).

duo duo 'by the twos', 'two by two': the use of the cardinal numbers in a distributive sense is not only Semitic but thoroughly Greek as well (cf. Arndt & Gingrich 5).

exousian tōn pneumatōn tōn akathartōn 'authority over the unclean spirits', i.e. authority or power to cast them out.

exousia (cf. 1:23, 3:15) 'authority', 'capacity', 'power'.

ta pneumata ta akatharta (cf. 1:23) 'the unclean spirits'.

Translation: For problems in translating *the twelve*, see 3:14. For *authority* see 2:10, and for *unclean spirits* see 1:26.

Called must not be interpreted in the sense of 'call out to' or 'to summon' (in the legal sense). Moreover, in this context, we are not dealing with the 'commissioning' of 3:13. In some languages the equivalent is 'he spoke especially to the twelve followers' or 'he addressed himself to the twelve learners'.

Send them out may be rendered as 'told them to go out', for their going out was in response to a verbal command.

Two by two must be distributive, not collective, i.e. two men went in one direction and two others in another.

Authority over may be rendered simply as 'power (or 'strength') to cast out' (or 'to command'). It should be noted, however, that this was a delegated power, not an inherent capacity.

8 *He charged them to take nothing for their journey except a staff; no bread, no bag, no money in their belts;* 9 *but to wear sandals and not put on two tunics.*

Exegesis: *kai parēggeilen autois hina* 'and he commanded them that...': as in previous cases (cf. 5:18) *hina* 'that' does not indicate purpose, but the content of the command.

paraggellō (8:6) 'give orders', 'command'.

eis hodon 'in the road', i.e. 'for the journey' (cf. Arndt & Gingrich *hodos* 1.b).

ei mē rabdon monon 'except a staff only', *not* 'except (for) one staff': *monon* 'only' is an adverb (cf. 5:36), not an adjective, and modifies *ei mē* 'except', 'but'.

rabdos (only here in Mark) 'staff', 'rod' used in travelling.

pēran (only here in Mark) 'knapsack', 'traveler's bag': here, more explicitly, a *beggar's bag* (cf. Deissmann *Light*, 108-10). Lagrange points out it would be pointless to prohibit taking a bag for provisions when the taking of bread had already been forbidden.

mē eis tēn zōnēn chalkon 'no money in their belts'.

zōnē (cf. 1:6) 'girdle', 'belt'.

chalkos (12:41) 'copper', 'brass'; 'copper coin'; 'money'.

In verse 9 the construction changes: instead of clauses governed by *hina* 'that' as in v. 8, there is one participial clause which is the direct object of the verb 'he commanded', and one clause which is in the form of direct speech. For purposes of translation, however, there is no need literally to reproduce the Greek grammatical constructions; the content, not the form, is what matters.

alla hupodedemenous sandalia 'but to wear sandals' (i.e. rather than go barefooted).

hupodeomai (only here in Mark; cf. *hupodēma* 1:7) 'bind under': of sandals, 'to put on', 'to wear'.

sandalion (only here in Mark) 'sandal' (a synonym of *hupodēma* in 1:7).

kai mē endusēsthe duo chitōnas 'and do not wear two tunics'.

enduō (cf. 1:6) 'put on', 'wear'.

chitōn (14:63; cf. *himation* 2:21) 'tunic', 'shirt', worn next to the skin (cf. Arndt & Gingrich for references concerning the wearing of two

187

tunics): the command not to wear two tunics meant that one only was sufficient.

Translation: Verses 8 and 9 present serious problems for translators because (1) the grammatical form shifts in the middle of the passage, from an indirect to a direct form, and (2) there are two awkward exceptions: the staff is an exception in what should be carried, and the extra tunic is forbidden in an otherwise positive command, i.e. to wear sandals and one tunic. This means that in a number of translations this passage must be recast to fit the requirements of the receptor language.

Charged them to take...may be altered in many languages into a form of direct command, for this greatly simplifies the syntactic problems in the rest of the passage, e.g. 'he commanded them, Do not take...'

In verse eight there is a shift from negative to positive and again to negative in the RSV order: *nothing...except a staff; no...* In many languages this would be clearer if the exception to the negation were placed at the end, e.g. 'do not take anything for your journey: do not take bread, a bag, or money in your girdles, take only a walking stick'. In some languages (Black Bobo), however, the positive would normally precede the negative, e.g. 'take a stick in your hand, do not take anything else...'

Put on two tunics is equivalent in many instances to 'wear two shirts'. As Arndt and Gingrich point out the wearing of two tunics was a sign of effeminacy.

10 And he said to them, "Where you enter a house, stay there until you leave the place.

Exegesis: The sense of the order is: 'whenever you enter a town stay in the same house until you leave that town' (cf. Mt. 10:11).

menete (14:34) 'stay', 'remain', 'abide'.

heōs an (9:1, 12:36) 'until': the verb which follows is in the subjunctive mode.

Translation: If this verse is translated literally, it may result in non-sense, e.g. 'when you enter a house, stay in the house, till you leave the house'. This is precisely what a number of translations mean, and it is not without reason that readers are puzzled. The meaning (see the Matthaean parallel, Mt. 10:11) is 'when you enter a house as a guest, do not change residence till you leave the town'. This was designed to prevent the practice employed by some religious teachers who went from house to house, imposing on the hospitality of as many people as possible.

11 And if any place will not receive you and they refuse to hear you, when you leave, shake off the dust that is on your feet for a testimony against them."

Text: Instead of *hos an topos mē dexētai* 'whatever place may not receive'

188

of all the modern editions of the Greek text, *Textus Receptus* has *hosoi an mē dexōntai* 'whoever (pl.) may not receive'.

At the end of the verse *Textus Receptus* adds *amēn legō humin, anek-toteron estai Sodomois ē Gomorrois en hēmera kriseōs, ē tē polei ekeinē* 'Truly I tell you, it shall be more tolerable for Sodom or Gomorrha in the day of judgment, than for that city'. All modern editions of the Greek text reject this addition which, for the sake of harmony, was introduced here from Mt. 10:15.

Exegesis: *os an topos mē dexētai humas* 'whatever place may not receive you': the presumed meaning would be, 'whatever town', or 'whatever city'. Manson, however, suggests that 'place' here probably refers to the synagogue as the place of worship where the disciples would naturally go to deliver their message. In light of the following clause 'nor should they hear you' this conjecture is reasonable.

dechomai (9:37, 10:15) 'receive', 'accept', 'welcome'; 'receive as guest'.

ekporeuomenoi (cf. 1:5) 'going out', 'leaving': this participle probably should not be understood as temporal 'when you go out' (RSV) but in light of the imperative mode of the principal verb 'shake off', should be translated as an imperative 'go out!' 'leave!' (on the use of the participle in the imperative sense cf. Moule *Idiom Book*, 179f. and references).

ektinaxate ton choun ton hupokatō tōn podōn humōn eis marturion autois 'shake off the dust which is under your feet as a testimony to them': cf. Acts 13:51, 18:6, for examples of this practice, and see Lagrange, and Manson *Mission and Message*, 368, for the significance of this act.

ektinassō (only here in Mark) 'shake off'.

chous (only here in Mark) 'dust', 'dirt'.

eis marturion autois (cf. 1:44) 'as a testimony to them' probably in a hostile sense 'against them' (RSV), though Taylor objects (cf. BFBS 'to them'); *autois* 'them' refers to the citizens of the town.

Translation: *Any place* must in many instances be 'the people of any place' ('town' or 'synagogue').

Receive is in some languages 'to welcome' or 'to let you enter their town' or 'to say, Welcome' (Cashibo), or 'to respect', literally, 'to consider big' (Tzeltal).

Refuse to hear is translatable as 'will not listen to'.

Testimony against them (or possibly 'to', see above) is rendered in a number of ways, for this context does not employ the Greek term *marturion* 'witness' in the more usual sense. Some of the ways in which this expression may be translated are 'in order to show them what they have done' (Navajo), 'that shall become a testimony in their eyes' (Tzeltal), 'a sign, that witnesses to their guilt' (South Toradja), 'to show that they are responsible' (Barrow Eskimo), and 'so that it will be known about them' (Mazahua).

For translators who follow *Textus Receptus*, there are added complications in the comparative expression *more tolerable for*, which is rendered variously in different languages (for a discussion of some comparative expressions see 1:7). *More tolerable for* is often translated as 'the people of Sodom and Gomorrha will suffer less than the people of that city'. In some instances one must use a double expression, e.g. 'that city will suffer much, Sodom and Gomorrha will suffer little' (Chol). Some languages employ an idiom meaning 'to surpass', e.g. 'the people of that city will surpass in suffering what the people of Sodom and Gomorrha suffer'.

Day of judgment may be rendered as 'day when God judges' or 'day when God will say people have sin' (Tzotzil), or 'day when people will be judged'.

Note that in many instances one cannot speak of 'a city suffering', but only of 'the people of a city suffering'.

12 *So they went out and preached that men should repent.* 13 *And they cast out many demons, and anointed with oil many that were sick and healed them.*

Exegesis: *ekēruxan hina metanoōsin* 'they (the Twelve) preached that they (the hearers) should repent': *hina* 'that' indicates the content of the preaching, not its purpose (cf. 5:18).

kērussō (cf. 1:4; cf. 3:15) 'preach', 'proclaim'.

metanoeō (cf. 1:15) 'repent'.

daimonia polla exeballon (cf. 3:15, 1:34) 'they cast out many demons'.

ēleiphon elaiō pollous arrōstous 'they anointed with oil many sick people'.

aleiphō (16:1) 'anoint': here for the purpose of healing (cf. Lagrange on this practice both in the past and in the present). It is generally assumed that the oil would be rubbed on, but Lk. 10:34 speaks of oil being poured on.

elaion (only here in Mark) 'oil', i.e. 'olive-oil'.

kai etherapeuon 'and they healed (them)' (cf. 1:34).

Translation: *They* should in many languages be 'the twelve disciples', for between this pronoun and the proper referent there are several confusing third person plural referents in the intervening verses.

Went out refers to their journey, not to the process of going out of a house—as is implied in some translations. One may simply say 'they left'.

Preached that...may be shifted to a direct form, 'announced to people, You should repent'. (For *preach* and *repent*, see 1:4).

For expressions relating to *casting out of demons*, see 1:34, and for words for *demons* see 1:26 and 32.

Anointed introduces a process which is quite foreign to many people. Accordingly, one needs to be careful as to how this act is described. In one language the translator had used a word meaning 'to give a massage to'; and in another, 'to touch with oil'. As suggested above, the meaning is probably 'to rub on', but not implying over the entire body or even any major part of it. The act was essentially symbolic, rather than therapeutic. If, as in some languages, the place of anointing must be specified, the 'head' is as likely to be correct as any other supplied term.

The *oil* should be some type of vegetable oil, not kerosene or motor oil. ('Daubed with crankcase oil' is too frequent a rendering of this term).

Healed is 'made them well' or 'caused them to be well'.

14 King Herod heard of it; for Jesus' name had become known. Some said, "John the baptizer has been raised from the dead; that is why these powers are at work in him."

Text: Instead of *elegon* 'they said' read by Nestle, Westcott and Hort, Soden, Vogels, Lagrange, Taylor, Kilpatrick, and RSV, *elegen* 'he said' is read by *Textus Receptus*, Tischendorf, Merk, and Souter.

Exegesis: *ho basileus Hērōdēs* (6:22, 25, 26, 27) 'King Herod': this was Herod Antipas, tetrarch of Galilee and Perea, son of King Herod the Great.

basileus 'king': besides the above references to Herod, the word is used in a general sense in 13:9, and with reference to Jesus in 15:2, 9, 12, 18, 26, 32.

phaneron (cf. 3:12, 4:23) 'manifest', 'known'.

kai elegon 'and they were saying': *kai* may here be the equivalent of *hoti* 'that', i.e. 'King Herod heard...that they were saying' (cf. Arndt & Gingrich *kai* I.2.b; cf. Taylor).

elegon 'they were saying' is clearly an impersonal plural '*some* were saying' followed up in v. 15 by *alloi de...alloi de* 'and others...and others'.

ho baptizōn (cf. 1:4) 'the Baptizer': a title.

egēgertai ek nekrōn 'he has been raised from the dead'.

egeirō (cf. 1:31) 'rise'; in the passive 'be raised'.

ek nekrōn (9:9,10, 12:25, 16:14) 'from (out of) the dead': besides its use in this phrase, *nekros* 'dead one' is used also in 9:26, 12:26,27.

energousin hai dunameis en autō 'the (miraculous) powers are working in him'—so most translations. Dalman (*Words*, 201) suggests that the corresponding Aramaic may have meant, 'mighty deeds are done by him'.

energeō (only here in Mark) without an object means 'to be at work', 'to operate' (cf. Robinson *Ephesians*, 241-47).

hai dunameis (cf. 5:30) 'the powers', 'the mighty deeds'.

Translation: *King* is not easily translated in some languages, for there is no exact equivalent. Moreover, one cannot say 'greatest chief' (as might be thought), for such a superlative expression must usually be reserved for the Roman emperor, who had authority even over Herod, the king. One can, however, use such expressions as 'a great one' (Piro), 'the ruler', 'the *Inca*', a borrowing from Quechua (Shipibo), 'the big boss' (Totonac), and 'the one who commanded' (Huichol).

Jesus' name had become known is quite intelligible in English, but not in other languages. For example, in Sierra Popoluca one must say 'the people spoke-spoke-spoke about him' (the reduplicated form indicates the extent of the process). In Huave one says 'his name had reached all the people', and in Subanen 'the people heard his name'.

Some is 'some of the people'.

The shift from *Jesus' name* to *John the Baptist* may not be evident in some languages. Accordingly, in order that the proper identification may be made, one must say in Trique 'this man is John the baptizer, who...'

For *John the baptizer*, see 1:4.

Raised from the dead presents a number of difficulties. In the first place, the expression is passive, without the agent identified. In the second place, *from the dead* appears to refer to persons (as it does in Greek), but in many languages the idea of resurrection is normally spoken of as 'living again', without reference to other dead. In some instances one can only speak of 'died and is alive again' or 'died and has been caused to live again'. To say 'God has made him live again' would seem to be too specific about the implied agent, and hence a shift from passive to active, without the agent, is probably preferable. The Greek specifies 'from among the dead', translated in some instances as 'got up and left the dead' (this is necessary in languages which have no such preposition as *from*).

For *powers*, see 6:2, but note that in many instances the passive expression *are at work in him* must be changed to 'he does these...' This is particularly necessary if *in him* would refer only to an activity going on within his body.

15 But others said, "It is Elijah." And others said, "It is a prophet, like one of the prophets of old." 16 But when Herod heard of it he said, "John, whom I beheaded, has been raised."

Text: At the end of verse 16, after *ēgerthē* 'was raised' *Textus Receptus* adds *ek nekrōn* 'from the dead', which is omitted by all modern editions of the Greek text.

Exegesis: *Ēlias* (8:28, 9:4, 5, 11, 12, 13, 15:35, 36) 'Elijah': cf. Mal. 3:1, 4:5, for O.T. references to the coming of Elijah as predecessor of the Messiah, and see Mk. 9:9-13 for the application of this prophecy to the Baptist.

prophētēs (cf. 1:2) 'prophet'.

hōs heis tōn prophētōn 'as one of the prophets': generally taken to mean 'as one of the Prophets of old' as Lk. 9:8 has it (cf. Weymouth 'like one of the great Prophets'). Black (*Aramaic*, 249 n. 4), however, suggests 'a prophet, like any (true) prophet'.

hon egō apekephalisa Iōannēn houtos ēgerthē 'John, whom I beheaded, he was raised': in a construction not at all unusual in Greek, the relative pronoun, which is the object of the verb and thus in the accusative case, is placed *before* its antecedent; the antecedent, being incorporated into the relative clause, is, by what is called "inverse attraction," also in the accusative case (cf. Robertson *Grammar*, 717-19). This construction is equivalent to *Iōannēs, hon egō apekephalisa, houtos ēgerthē*: 'John' in the nominative case, as the subject of the sentence; 'whom' the relative is in the accusative case as the object of 'I beheaded'; *houtos* 'this one' the demonstrative pronoun is in the nominative case agreeing with 'John' to which it refers.

apokephalizō (6:28) 'behead'.

egeirō (cf. 1:31) 'rise'.

Translation: The contrast between *some* (verse 14)...*but others*...*and others* must be quite explicit in some languages, e.g. 'some people...other people...and still other people'.

Elijah should be transliterated in the form which will be employed in the Old Testament. Some translators have endeavored to use one system of transliteration when reproducing the Greek forms of names and another when transcribing the Hebrew equivalents. However, it is a mistake to spell the name of an Old Testament person in one way in the Old Testament and in another way in the New Testament. On the other hand, one should not take a name such as *Jesus* and make it identical with *Joshua*, even though they are etymologically related.

For *prophet*, see 1:2.

Prophets of old must not be rendered as 'old prophets' referring to the age of the men in question. The meaning is 'one of the prophets who lived long ago' or 'one of the prophets who lived in the days of our ancestors'.

Heard of it is in some languages 'heard what Jesus was doing', since *it* may be entirely too vague a reference to be intelligible.

Beheaded poses a subtle problem in some languages which distinguish carefully between primary and secondary agency, i.e. whether the grammatical subject actually performed an action or whether he caused it to be done through another. Obviously, Herod himself did not do the beheading, and hence, one may translate 'caused to be beheaded' or 'ordered men to cut off his head'.

Has been raised is 'has come back to life' or 'is living again' (see 6:14).

17 For Herod had sent and seized John, and bound him in prison for the sake of Herodias, his brother Philip's wife; because he had married her.

Exegesis: *autos gar ho Hērōdēs* 'for Herod himself': most translations disregard the personal pronoun *autos* 'he' as being redundant (cf., however, Manson 'for this same Herod...').

This whole narrative (6:17-29) of the imprisonment and death of John the Baptist is parenthetical, being here inserted to explain the statement (v. 14) that Jesus was John risen from the dead. The order of events here is not chronological: the arrest of John had taken place before Jesus began his ministry in Galilee (1:14), but we are not given the precise time of his subsequent death at the hands of Herod Antipas.

aposteilas ekratēsen 'sending he arrested': 'he sent and arrested'. Arndt & Gingrich (*apostellō* 1.d) classify this use of the verb 'send' as an auxiliary meaning that 'the action has been performed by someone else': here it would mean 'he had John arrested'.

krateō (cf. 1:31) 'seize', 'arrest'.

kai edēsen auton en phulakē 'and he bound him in prison' not in the sense that he was in prison, tied up, but 'bound him (and put him) in prison' (cf. Arndt & Gingrich *deō* 1.b).

deō (cf. 3:27) 'bind', 'restrict'.

phulakē (6:28, 48) 'prison'; in 6:48 it means 'watch' (i.e. an interval of time).

dia Herōdiada 'on account of Herodias': RSV 'for the sake of' may be misunderstood.

On the identity of the Philip here referred to, see the commentaries.

hoti autēn egamēsen 'because he (Herod) married her': this clause explains the statement that John had been placed in prison on account of Herodias.

gameō (10:11, 12, 12:25) 'to marry': generally used of *men* (cf. Arndt & Gingrich for exceptions to the rule; cf. Moulton & Milligan).

Translation: *Sent and seized* is either 'sent men to seize' or 'caused John to be seized'. *Seized* should here be translated as 'arrested'.

Bound him in prison is 'had him put in prison' or, where the idiom may require, 'tied him up in jail', but not necessarily with the literal meaning of 'to bind'.

For the sake of Herodias may be variously translated, depending upon the perspective in question: 'because of Herodias' (meaning, because of what she had done, asked, or wanted), 'in order to please Herodias', or 'he did this for Herodias'.

Contemporary historical sources indicate that there are some difficulties involved in this statement of the relationship of Herodias to Philip, but the translator is not called upon to re-edit, but to translate. Hence, one may say 'Herodias had been the wife of Philip, Herod's brother' ('younger brother', if such a distinction is required).

Because he had married her is very loosely connected with the preceding. If translated without some more precise transition, it may mean in some languages that 'Herodias was Philip's wife because he (i.e. Philip) had married her'. As a result, one must recast the sentence somewhat to read, 'this happened because Herod had married Herodias'. The pronominal element should refer to all the preceding sequence, including if possible the concern of Herod, the imprisonment of John, and Herod's actions in order to please Herodias.

Note that the sequence of events as described: (1) the worry of Herod, (2) the beheading of John, (3) the imprisonment of John, and (4) Herod's marriage to Herodias are told in reverse order of their temporal sequence. In some languages this requires very careful handling of conjunctions or tense forms of the verbs.

18 *For John said to Herod, "It is not lawful for you to have your brother's wife."* 19 *And Herodias had a grudge against him, and wanted to kill him. But she could not,*

Exegesis: *elegen gar ho Iōannēs tō Herōdē* 'for John said to Herod': this clause gives the reason why Herod had imprisoned John.

elegen may be the equivalent of the pluperfect 'had been saying' in this context (Moule *Idiom Book*, 10).

exestin (cf. 2 : 24) 'it is right', 'it is lawful'.

echein 'to have', 'to possess' as wife (cf. Arndt & Gingrich I.2.b.α).

eneichen (only here in Mark) 'she was hostile to', 'she bore a grudge against': the American colloquialism 'to *have it in for* someone' corresponds to this use of the Greek verb *enechō* (cf. Field *Notes*, 28f.).

kai ēthelen...kai ouk ēdunato 'and she wanted...but could not'.

Translation: *John said to Herod* poses certain problems of sequence, for this is no longer in the reverse order, noted in the preceding verse, but fits between events 3 and 4. Only careful use of conjunctions and tense forms is likely to avoid confusion.

Not lawful is not always an easy expression, especially in the languages of people who have no formal written legal codes. In Trique the best equivalent seemed to be 'God does not permit' (a common way of referring to the highest sanctions for behavior). In Huastec one may say 'you are not allowed', without reference to the one doing the allowing. In Tzeltal the proper expression is 'this is against the command' and in Popoluca one says 'the law [a borrowing from Spanish] does not help you'.

Have your brother's wife is better rendered as 'to live with your brother's wife' than to say 'to marry your brother's wife', for the latter might be interpreted as meaning that Herod had married her after the death of Philip, his brother.

Had a grudge is often 'was very angry with' or 'was mad at'.

In languages in which careful distinctions are made between primary and secondary agency, *wanted to kill him* may be translated as 'wanted to cause him to be killed'.

She could not does not refer to her lack of strength (as some translators have rendered the passage), but her inability to get Herod to do what she wanted.

20 *for Herod feared John, knowing that he was a righteous and holy man, and kept him safe. When he heard him, he was much perplexed; and yet he heard him gladly.*

Text: Instead of *ēporei* 'he was puzzled' of all modern editions of the Greek text, *Textus Receptus* has *epoiei* 'he was doing'.

Exegesis: *ephobeito* (cf. 4 : 40) 'he held (John) in awe', 'he feared', 'he respected'.

eidōs auton andra dikaion kai hagion 'knowing him (to be) a righteous

195

and holy man': the participle *eidōs* 'knowing' is causal: *'because* he knew'.

dikaios (cf. 2 : 17) 'righteous', 'just', 'upright'.

hagios (only place in Mark used of a man) 'holy'.

sunetērei (only here in Mark) 'he kept safe', 'he protected': i.e. from Herodias.

kai akousas autou polla ēporei 'and when he heard him he was much perplexed': the majority of translations take *polla* 'much', 'often' with the principal verb *ēporei* 'he was puzzled': BFBS, however, takes it with the participle *akousas* 'he often heard him' (cf. Kilpatrick, *The Bible Translator* 7.8, 1956).

aporeō (only here in Mark) 'be undecided', 'be puzzled' (from *a* privative 'not' and *poros* 'passage': literally, 'without a way'). The verb may mean 'raise questions' (cf. Liddell & Scott I.2), which is suggested for this passage by Field (*Notes*, 29f.); cf. Arndt & Gingrich.

kai hēdeōs autou ēkouen 'yet he heard him gladly', 'yet he liked to hear him'.

hēdeōs (only here in Mark) 'gladly', 'with pleasure'.

Translation: *Feared* in this context means 'had a great deal of respect for', 'had honor for him', or 'saw him big' (as in some languages).

For *righteous* see 2 : 17. In this context some languages have rather interesting expressions: 'did what he should' (Eastern Otomí), 'walked straight' (Popoluca), 'was a man with a good heart' (Huichol), 'his life was straight' (Black Bobo), and 'was completely good' (Huave). (This last expression does not imply sinless perfection.)

Holy has been discussed (see 1 : 7) in connection with the word *Spirit*. When applied to persons there may need to be certain adaptations, e.g. 'good' (Black Bobo), 'without sin' (Huichol), and 'uncontaminated' (Vai).

Kept him safe may be translated as 'kept him from being harmed'.

Perplexed is equivalent to 'worried', e.g. 'his heart was gone' (Tzeltal), 'hard chased' (Piro), 'his mind was killing him' (Navajo), 'his stomach rose up' (Gurunse), 'he was very irresolute' (lit., 'it was all wrong with him') (Indonesian), and 'his heart was very divided' (Javanese).

21 **But an opportunity came when Herod on his birthday gave a banquet for his courtiers and officers and the leading men of Galilee.**

Exegesis: *genomenēs hēmeras eukairou* 'an opportune day arriving': for the use of the participial genitive clause to express time, cf. 6 : 2, *genomenou sabbatou* 'when the Sabbath came'.

eukairos (only here in Mark) 'timely', 'opportune', 'suitable': so most translations; some, however, hold that the meaning here is 'a festal (day)' (cf. Moulton & Milligan)—Moffatt and Goodspeed give it this meaning.

tois genesiois autou (only here in Mark) 'on his birthday': properly the dative of the neuter plural of the adjective *genesios* 'relating to (one's) birth', with the meaning 'birthday celebration' (for the use of the plural cf. *ta sabbata* 'Sabbath' in 1 : 21).

deipnon epoiēsen 'he gave a banquet'.

deipnon (12:39) 'a formal meal', 'a banquet', 'a dinner'.

poieō 'do', 'make': for its use in the sense of *giving* a banquet, cf. Arndt & Gingrich I.1.b.ζ.

tois megistasin (only here in Mark) 'chief men', 'nobles'.

tois chiliarchois (only here in Mark) 'high-ranking military officers': the *chiliarchos*, leader of 1000 soldiers, was the equivalent of the Roman *tribunus militum*, commander of a cohort (about 600 men). The word is used here in the general sense of high-ranking officers.

kai tois prōtois 'and the most prominent men (of Galilee)': cf. Lagrange, 'the aristocracy of the country' (cf. Arndt & Gingrich *prōtos* 1.c.β).

prōtos (9:35, 10:31,44, 12:20,28,29, 14:12, 16:9) 'first'.

Translation: *Opportunity* is 'the right time' or 'a special time', but to make sense one must sometimes specify for whom such an occasion was opportune. Obviously, the proper person would be Herodias, *viz*, 'a day for Herodias' (Subanen).

Birthday must usually not be translated literally, as has been done in some languages. For this was not the day of Herod's birth, but the day on which he celebrated his birth. (As the result of one translation the people were very much amazed at the precocious nature of the baby Herod, for according to the Scriptures he apparently put on a banquet on the very day of his birth and was much impressed by the dancing of Herodias' daughter.) Equivalents of *birthday* are quite varied: 'day he was remembering his birth' (Kiyaka), 'when day of his birth comes up again' (Trique), 'day when he completed another year' (Eastern Otomí), and 'day of his year' (Chol).

Gave a banquet may be rendered as 'provided much food' or 'caused to get together to eat' (Zoque). The giving of a feast is such a widespread custom in so many societies that there are usually no special problems involved in finding a satisfactory equivalent.

Courtiers and officers and the leading men of Galilee represent three classes of people: (1) the civil government, officials, (2) the military officers, and (3) the leading citizens of the realm, i.e. members of influential, rich families. This phrase can be rendered as 'his under-rulers (i.e. those beneath him), and the rulers of his soldiers, and the wealthy people in Galilee'. (Wealth and social prestige were as much equated in Biblical times as they are today.) In some languages leading men are 'the chiefs' or 'the headmen' (Navajo).

22 *For when Herodias' daughter came in and danced, she pleased Herod and his guests; and the king said to the girl, "Ask me for whatever you wish, and I will grant it."*

Text: With the support of many early mss. Westcott and Hort have *tēs thugatros autou Hērōdiados* 'his (i.e. Herod's) daughter Herodias', instead of *tēs thugatros autēs tēs Hērōdiados* 'the daughter of Herodias' of all other editions of the Greek text. The textual problem is discussed in the commentaries; Lagrange admits the weight of the external evidence in favor of the Westcott and Hort text, but concludes: "It is a case where one is compelled to reject the best manuscripts."

Exegesis: *autēs tēs Hērōdiados* literally 'of Herodias herself': here, however, is probably another example of the same Semitic idiom observed in 1:7 *hou...autou* 'whose...his' in which the pronoun is redundant, expressing the same idea as the genitive case of the noun (cf. Black *Aramaic*, 72). It simply means 'of Herodias'.

orchēsamenēs (only here in Mark) 'dancing'.

ēresen (only here in Mark) 'she pleased', 'she delighted'.

tois sunanakeimenois (cf. 2:15) 'those reclining (at meal) with him', i.e. 'his guests'.

korasiō (cf. 5:41) 'maiden', 'girl'.

aitēson (6:23, 24, 25, 10:35, 38, 11:24, 15:8, 43) 'ask (for something)', 'request'.

Translation: *Came in* refers to her entry into the banquet room, i.e. 'came into the room'.

Danced does not specify the type of dance, but in languages in which there are different words depending upon the type of movements involved, one should choose a word which is most likely to fit this type of context— a stag party given by a notoriously sensuous ruler.

She pleased Herod... must be recast in some languages, 'Herod and his guests were pleased with her'.

Girl is variously translated in different receptor languages, depending upon the presumed age of Herodias' daughter. The pleasure shown by Herod and his guests would seem to indicate that Salome was probably beyond puberty.

Ask is not the asking of questioning, but the asking of requesting. In Tzeltal the idiom is 'ask me what you ask me', meaning 'ask me for anything'.

Grant it may be rendered as 'give it to you' or 'let you have it'.

23 And he vowed to her, "Whatever you ask me, I will give you, even half of my kingdom."

Text: After *ōmosen* 'he swore' Taylor and Kilpatrick add *polla* 'much', which is omitted by all other editions of the Greek text.

Exegesis: *ōmosen* (14:71) 'swore', 'vowed', 'took an oath'.

heōs hēmisous 'up to one-half', 'as much as one-half'.

Translation: *Vowed* means 'swore an oath', a practice which in its so-called proper sense is more common in other cultures than in ours. In English *to swear* usually implies cursing and indiscriminate use of names of Deity. But in this passage one has an instance of a culturally common practice of making a promise while calling on God to witness and implying that failure to perform an oath would invoke divine sanctions. Such an action is describable in quite different ways, e.g. 'God sees me, I tell the truth to you' (Tzeltal), 'he loaded himself down' (Huichol), 'to speak-stay', implying the permanence of the utterance (Popoluca), and 'to say what he could not take away' (San Blas).

Half of my kingdom may be 'half of the land I rule over' (Popoluca) or 'half of my land' (Shipibo).

24 And she went out, and said to her mother, "What shall I ask?" And she said, "The head of John the baptizer."

Exegesis: *ti aitēsōmai* 'what should I ask for?': not simply futuristic, but with the element of deliberation.

kephalēn (6:25,27,28, 12:10, 14:3, 15:19,29) 'head'.

Iōannou tou baptizontos (cf. 1:4, 6:14) 'of John the Baptizer': as in both other cases a title.

Translation: *Went out* means 'went out of the room'.

Said to her mother must in many instances be changed to 'asked her mother'.

What shall I ask may be more precisely translated as 'what do you want me to ask' (Subanen).

She said is translated in some languages as 'she replied'.

Though the phrase *the head of John the baptizer* is the grammatical object of the preceding verb 'said' or 'replied', it is actually the object of an elliptical verb 'ask for'. This ellipsis must be filled in some languages, e.g. 'and she replied, Ask for the head of John the baptizer'.

For *John the baptizer* see 1:4.

25 And she came in immediately with haste to the king, and asked, saying, "I want you to give me at once the head of John the Baptist on a platter."

Exegesis: *meta spoudēs* (only here in Mark) 'with haste', 'in a hurry'; perhaps 'eagerly' (Lagrange).

ētēsato legousa 'she requested, saying': it is not necessary, however, in English, to translate both verbs (as does RSV); simply 'she requested'.

thelō hina 'I want that': as in 5:23 the force of the phrase here is probably imperatival; *thelō hina...dos moi* 'Give me' (it may be that *thelō hina* is equivalent, as in later Greek, to 'please').

exautēs (only here in Mark) 'at once', 'immediately' (the whole phrase is *ex autēs tēs hōras* 'this very hour').

pinaki (6:28) 'platter', 'dish'.

Iōannou tou baptistou (8:28) 'of John the Baptist' (cf. *ho baptizōn* 'the Baptizer' in 1:4).

Translation: *Immediately with haste* reflects a double expression in the Greek text. The idea is that the girl not only returned very soon, but she was obviously hurrying to deliver her request.

The closest equivalent of *platter* is often 'serving tray', whether consisting of earthenware, wood, or basketry. It must be a sufficiently large object, so as to hold a human head, but not one in which the head would be hidden from view, as in the case of a basket. Evidently, Herodias was eager that her triumph might be clearly witnessed by all who were present.

26 *And the king was exceedingly sorry; but because of his oaths and his guests he did not want to break his word to her.*

Exegesis: *perilupos* (14:34) 'very sad', 'deeply grieved'; possibly 'greatly annoyed' (Manson), 'very vexed' (Moffatt).

orkous (only here in Mark) 'oaths', 'vows'.

anakeimenous (14:18, 16:14) '(the men) reclining at (the table)', i.e. 'the guests'. Most translations take 'because of his oaths and his guests' with what follows (as does RSV); BFBS, however, takes it with what precedes: 'The king was deeply distressed on account of his oaths and those dining with him'.

ouk ēthelēsen athetēsai autēn 'he did not want to refuse her'.

atheteō (7:9) 'reject'; the meaning here could be 'disappoint her' (by breaking his word to her): cf. Field *Notes*, 30; Arndt & Gingrich 1.b translate 'did not want to refuse her'.

Translation: It is usually necessary to distinguish carefully between *sorry* and *sorrow*, (though the Greek *perilupos* may be used for both concepts), especially if the receptor language distinguishes between emotional feelings which are caused by what one has done himself and those which arise because of sympathy for the plight of others. Expressions for *sorry* are often quite figurative, e.g. 'to be heavy in the stomach' (Uduk) and 'to have a painful heart' (Kpelle).

For *oath*, see *vowed*, 6:23. Amuzgo renders this expression as 'because of the tight (i.e. 'binding') word which he had said to her face' (a verb, rather than noun, is required). In some languages for *oath* one can use 'a strong promise' (Barrow Eskimo).

Guests may be described as 'people who had been invited to the feast', but there is generally some more direct and specific way of designating such persons.

Break his word to her is strictly figurative language, and in many languages one cannot 'break a word', but it may be possible 'to kill a word' or 'to forget a word'. In Cashibo one must say 'did not want to say, I will not do it', a full description in the form of direct discourse. Amuzgo renders this expression as 'he did not want to have his heart change his word to that woman's face', in which the term 'face' is a means of identifying the direction of speaking.

27 *And immediately the king sent a soldier of the guard and gave orders to bring his head. He went and beheaded him in the prison, 28 and brought his head on a platter, and gave it to the girl; and the girl gave it to her mother.*

Exegesis: *aposteilas...epetaxen* 'sending...ordered', 'sent and ordered': the sense is 'sent with orders' (Goodspeed, Moffatt, BFBS).

epitassō (cf. 1 : 27) 'give orders', 'command'.
spekoulatora (only here in the N. T.) 'courier', 'scout', and, by extension of the meaning, 'executioner' (a loan-word from the Latin *speculator*).

Translation: It is important that the sequence of events in the first clause not be confused, for a literal translation into some languages would make the text mean that Herod first sent off a soldier and then gave the orders. This may be recast in such instances to read 'the king sent off a soldier of the guard with orders to bring John's head', or 'the king gave orders to a soldier of the guard and sent him off to bring John's head'.

His must in several languages be made more specific, since the reference is back in verse 25.

Beheaded is simply 'cut off his head', and if the receptor language requires an indication of instrument, a 'sword' is most likely.

Brought is 'carried', but in some languages there are a number of words for 'carrying' depending upon the type of object and how it is carried. The term chosen must fit this type of context.

29 When his disciples heard of it, they came and took his body, and laid it in a tomb.

Exegesis: *hoi mathētai autou* 'his (i.e. John's) disciples' (cf. 2 : 18).
ptōma (15 : 45) '(fallen) body', 'corpse' (from *piptō* 'fall').
ethēkan (cf. 4 : 21) 'they placed', 'they put'.
en mnēmeiō (cf. 5 : 2) 'in a tomb', 'in a grave'.

Translation: *His* must be rendered as 'John's' in many languages, since the usual referent of *his* in a phrase speaking of disciples would be Jesus, and in a number of instances people have wrongly thought that this was an act of kindness on the part of Jesus' disciples toward John.

Came is probably better rendered as 'went', unless one wishes to portray the writer Mark as narrating from Herod's court. (For a discussion of problems involving 'come' and 'go', see 1 : 14.)

30 The apostles returned to Jesus, and told him all that they had done and taught.

Exegesis: *kai sunagontai hoi apostoloi* 'and the apostles come together'.
sunagō (cf. 2 : 2) 'gather', 'come together'.
hoi apostoloi (unless in 3 : 14 also, only here in Mark) 'the apostles', i.e. the Twelve whom Jesus sent out (*apostellein* 6 : 7) in pairs on a preaching and healing ministry.
apēggeilan (cf. 5 : 14) 'they announced', 'they related', 'they told'.

Translation: The use of section headings helps to bridge the abrupt transition from verses 29 to 30 (see list of section headings in the Appendix).

Apostles is rendered primarily in two ways: (1) a word or phrase meaning 'the sent ones' (Eastern Otomí, Tzeltal, Conob, Tarascan, Navajo, Zoque, Chol) and 'messengers' (Kituba, Bare'e, Mezquital Otomí, Pame). In some languages there are certain special adaptations: 'word carriers', practically equivalent to 'messengers' (Valiente), 'those commanded to carry the message' (Subanen), 'witnesses to God', meaning 'those who speak up and out for God' (San Blas). A still further method of dealing with the word *apostles* is to borrow the term used in the prestige language of the area. Unless, however, there is a rather extensive Christian tradition, transliteration of a borrowed word is not recommended.

31 *And he said to them, "Come away by yourselves to a lonely place, and rest a while." For many were coming and going, and they had no leisure even to eat.*

Exegesis: *deute humeis autoi kat' idian eis erēmon topon* 'you yourselves come in private to an isolated spot'.

deute (cf. 1 : 17) 'come'.

kat' idian (cf. 4 : 34) 'privately', 'alone'.

eis erēmon topon (cf. 1 : 35, 45) 'to a lonely place', 'to an isolated spot'.

anapausasthe (14 : 41) 'rest ye'.

oligon is adverbial 'a little (while)' expressing time (cf. 1 : 19 where it expresses distance).

hoi erchomenoi kai hoi hupagontes 'those (who were) coming and those (who were) going'.

hupagō (cf. 1 : 44) 'go', 'depart'.

kai oude phagein eukairoun 'and they [i.e. Jesus and his disciples] did not have time even to eat'.

eukaireō (only here in Mark; cf. *eukairos* 6 : 21) 'have a favorable time', 'have opportunity': here used of time (cf. Moulton & Milligan). For a similar situation cf. also 3 : 20.

Translation: *Said* must in some languages be translated as 'commanded' or 'urged', since the following expression is not a declarative sentence, but in the form of a command.

Come away by yourselves may be very misleading if translated literally, for it might mean that the disciples were to gather as a group without Jesus. The meaning is that they were to go together with Jesus to an isolated place. This may be rendered in some languages as 'come away with me so that we may be alone together'. Cf. Javanese 'You come here and go alone with me'.

Many must refer to the people in general, the crowds. One may translate, 'for many people were coming and going' (literally, in some languages, 'coming to where the disciples were and later leaving', or 'joining with the disciples and then departing'.) *Coming and going* must not be translated in such a way as to refer to the passing of people on the thoroughfare, but the coming of people to talk with Jesus and the disciples.

Leisure to eat is really 'an opportunity (or 'a chance') to eat'.

32 *And they went away in the boat to a lonely place by themselves.*
33 *Now many saw them going, and knew them, and they ran there on foot from all the towns, and got there ahead of them.*

Text: In v. 33 after *hupagontas* 'going' *Textus Receptus* adds *hoi ochloi* 'the crowds', omitted by all modern editions of the Greek text.

After *epegnōsan* 'recognized' *Textus Receptus* adds *auton* 'him'; Tischendorf, Merk, Soden, and Kilpatrick add *autous* 'them'; no addition is made by Nestle, Westcott and Hort, Vogels, Souter, Lagrange, and Taylor.

At the end of the verse after *autous* 'them' *Textus Receptus* adds *kai sunēlthon pros auton* 'and they gathered to him', which is omitted by all modern editions of the Greek text.

Exegesis: *kai eidon* 'and they saw': most translations take *polloi* 'many' to be the subject of *eidon* 'saw'; some, however, understand *eidon* in an impersonal sense, 'people saw', with *polloi* 'many' the subject of *epegnōsan* 'recognized' alone—so Weymouth 'but the people saw them going, and many recognized them' (cf. Lagrange, Taylor).

epegnōsan (cf. 2 : 8) 'they perceived', 'they recognized': this rendering better expresses the meaning of the verb here than 'knew' (RSV).

pezē (only here in Mark) 'by land' (opposed to *en ploiō* 'by boat'), 'on foot' (cf. Arndt & Gingrich).

apo pasōn tōn poleōn 'from all the cities': cf. 1 : 5 for another example of this vivid manner in portraying an action involving many people.

sunedramon ekei kai proēlthon autous 'they ran there and arrived before them': the adverb 'there' refers to the lonely spot to which Jesus and his disciples were going.

suntrechō (only here in Mark) 'run together': used of a number of persons who run to a place and gather there (Arndt & Gingrich).

proerchomai (14 : 35) 'come ahead', 'arrive before (someone)' (cf. Arndt & Gingrich 3).

Translation: *They went away* must refer to Jesus as well as the disciples.

Lonely place is 'an uninhabited place' or 'a place where there were no people living'.

Many is often rendered as 'many people'.

Knew them is often better translated as 'recognized them' or 'knew who they were'.

There is a very ambiguous adverb, which must be made more precise in some languages, e.g. 'to where the boat was headed' or 'to where the disciples and Jesus were going'. A number of languages require very well defined distinctions of place and direction, as determined by the position of the participants in an action. Care must be exercised to be sure that the proper adverb, or adverbial phrase, is employed.

Ahead of them means, of course, 'before Jesus and his disciples arrived', though it is rarely necessary to employ such an extensive paraphrase.

34 *As he landed he saw a great throng, and he had compassion on them, because they were like sheep without a shepherd; and he began to teach them many things.*

Exegesis: *exelthōn* 'coming out (of the boat)', 'when he landed'.

polun ochlon (cf. 5:21,24) 'a large crowd'.

esplagchnisthē (cf. 1:41) 'he was moved with compassion', 'he was touched with pity', 'he felt sorry'.

hōs probata mē echonta poimena 'as sheep not having a shepherd': the words reflect O.T. passages such as Num. 27:17, I Chron. 22:17, Ezek. 34:5.

probaton (14:27) 'sheep'.

poimēn (14:27) 'shepherd'.

polla either adverbial 'much' (Taylor, Moffatt, Lagrange) or adjectival 'many things' (ASV, RSV, Weymouth, Goodspeed, Manson, Brazilian).

Translation: Depending upon the extent to which Jesus may have been introduced into the preceding verses, it may be necessary to employ 'Jesus' in place of the first *he*.

Landed is in some languages 'climbed out of the boat onto the land'.

Compassion is an emotion frequently described in terms closely related to words for 'pain' and 'crying', e.g. 'he cried in his insides' (Shilluk), 'pain came to his heart' (Tojolabal), 'his heart was full of mercy' (Bare'e), and 'he died of pity' (Kiyaka). This is the highest type of sympathy.

Sheep without a shepherd are 'sheep which had no one to care for them' or 'sheep which no one helped' (or 'guarded', 'protected').

Sheep are known throughout most of the world, even though, as in Central Africa, they are a far cry from the fleecy wool-producing animals of colder climates. Where such animals are known, even by seemingly strange names, e.g. 'cotton deer' (Maya) or 'woolly goat' (Barrow Eskimo), such names should be used. In some instances, one may wish to borrow a name and use a classifier, e.g. 'an animal called *sheep*'. In still other instances translators have used 'animal which produces wool', for though people are not acquainted with the animals they are familiar with wool.

We may say *teach many things*, but in other languages one can only 'teach many words', 'teach much', or 'explain long' (referring to the time occupied in speaking).

35 *And when it grew late, his disciples came to him and said, "This is a lonely place, and the hour is now late;* **36** *send them away, to go into the country and villages round about and buy themselves something to eat."*

Text: Verse 36. Instead of *ti phagōsin* 'what they may eat' of all modern editions of the Greek text, *Textus Receptus* has *artous· ti gar phagōsin ouk echousin* 'bread: for they have nothing to eat'.

Exegesis: *ēdē hōras pollēs genomenēs* 'it was already a late hour': for the participial genitive clause used to express time cf. 6:21.

ēdē (4:37, 8:2, 11:11, 13·28, 15:42,44) 'already', 'by now'.

hōra (11:11, 13:11,32, 14:35, 37,41, 15:25,33,34) 'hour': the expression *hōra pollē* means 'late hour'.

proselthontes (cf. 1:31) 'coming to', 'approaching', 'drawing near'.

apoluson autous 'dismiss them', 'send them away'. The verb *apoluō* appears in Mark with three meanings: (1) 'send away', 'dismiss' 6:36, 45, 8:3,9; (2) 'divorce' 10:2,4,11,12; (3) 'release', 'set free' 15:6, 9,11,15.

eis tous kuklō agrous kai kōmas 'to the nearby villages and towns'.

kuklō (cf. 3:34) 'around'; 'surrounding', 'nearby'.

agros (cf. 5:14) 'hamlet', 'small country town'.

kōmē (cf. 6:6) 'village', 'town'.

hina...agorasōsin heautois ti phagōsin 'in order that...they may buy for themselves something they may eat'.

agorazō (6:37, 11:15, 15:46, 16:1) 'buy', 'purchase'.

ti phagōsin 'what they may eat': the interrogative pronoun *ti* is used here as a relative 'something' (cf. Arndt & Gingrich *tis* 1.b.ζ): cf. 8:1, 2 for further examples.

Translation: *Grew late* probably refers to late in the afternoon, perhaps toward sundown, but not late at night, for it is presumed that the village market places would still be open.

Send them away must not be understood in the sense of 'getting rid of the people', but simply urging them to go and provide for themselves.

37 *But he answered them, "You give them something to eat." And they said to him, "Shall we go and buy two hundred denarii worth of bread, and give it to them to eat?"* 38 *And he said to them, "How many loaves have you? Go and see." And when they had found out, they said, "Five, and two fish."*

Exegesis: *apokritheis eipen* (cf. 3:33 for this construction) 'he answered'.

dote...humeis 'you...give': the personal pronoun here is emphatic— '*you yourselves* give (them something to eat)' (cf. Weymouth, Moffatt, Goodspeed, BFBS).

dēnariōn diakosiōn artous 'loaves of two hundred denarii': the genitive expresses the price, 'two hundred denarii worth of loaves'.

dēnarion (12:15, 14:5) 'denarius': at the time of Jesus the coin is generally supposed to have been the equivalent of a rural worker's daily wage, as in Mt. 20:2 (cf. Manson (ed.) *A Companion to the Bible*, 498).

artos 'bread', 'loaf': in this incident probably barley loaves are indicated (cf. Jn. 6:8).

posous echete artous; 'how many loaves have you?'

posos (8:5, 19,20, 9:21, 15:4) 'how much', 'how many'.

ichthuas (6:41, 43) 'fish': here, of course, not fresh fish but prepared fish, either cooked or pickled (cf. Jn. 6:19).

Translation: *Answered* is not used in the sense of 'answer a question', but 'reply to their statement' or 'speak in return'.

The question of the disciples is probably best interpreted as a rhetorical question, not a request for permission or authorization to go and buy; a kind of exclamatory question, implying the utter foolishness of such an idea (compare the parallel passages: Mt. 14:13-21, Luke 9:11-17, and John 6 : 5-13).

Denarii poses a problem in translation, for though it was a coin for which the silver content would be equivalent to about 20 cents in American money, its buying power was much greater, as a result of the relatively low standard of living prevailing in Palestine in those days among the lower classes. It would not be reasonable to translate it by some equivalent coin equal to 20 cents U.S. Moreover, if one chooses any local currency the translation may be badly out of line within a short time, due to extreme inflation, as has occurred in so many parts of the world. (Some countries have seen inflationary pressures within the last two or three years change currency rates from as much as 100 to 1—in terms of the dollar—to as much as 10,000 to 1.) In areas where there is a relatively stable currency and there is a unit of currency roughly equivalent to a day's wage of a common laborer, such a coin may be used. In most instances, however, it has seemed best to borrow the Greek word *denarius*, and speak of 'bread worth 200 denarius coins' (or 'pieces of money'). One can then use a footnote and explain that a denarius (or whatever the appropriate transliterated form might be) was equivalent to a day's wage. It is recommended that one employ a short table of Weights and Measures (see appendix) in publications of New Testaments or Bibles, and that in such a table the various units of currency be related to the basic unit of the denarius.

Five, and two fish must be reproduced in full grammatical form in some languages, 'we have five loaves and two fish'.

39 Then he commanded them all to sit down by companies upon the green grass.

Exegesis: *epetaxen autois anaklithēnai pantas* 'he commanded them all to recline' (the verb 'command' here takes the infinitive 'recline' as direct object, while *pantas* 'all' is the subject of the infinitive; *autois* 'them' is the indirect object).

epitassō (cf. 1:27) 'command', 'order'.

anaklinō (only here in Mark) in the active is causative 'cause to lie down'; in the passive it means 'lie down', 'recline', 'sit' (here equivalent to *anapiptō* in the next verse).

sumposia sumposia 'in groups', 'in parties': for this distributive use cf. *duo duo* 'by twos' in 6:7 and *prasiai prasiai* in the next verse.

sumposion (only here in the N.T.) meant originally 'a drinking party' and then, by extension, the party itself, the guests (cf. Abbott-Smith).

epi tō chlōrō chortō 'upon the green grass': it is generally assumed that this added detail indicates that it was the spring season.

chlōros (only here in Mark) 'green'.
chortos (cf. 4:28) 'grass'.

Translation: *Commanded them* must be followed in many languages by direct discourse, e.g. 'commanded them, You sit down...'

Though Greek has 'reclined', the normal position assumed in eating, one must use whatever is culturally acceptable in the receptor language in question (note the adaptation to English *sit*).

The size of the *companies* is explained in the following verse. Here one may use 'groups' or as in some languages 'parts'. The entire distributive expression may be rendered as 'he commanded them, You sit down, one group here and another group there on the green grass'.

It is not sufficient to ask for the indigenous word for 'green' and then assume that one can say 'green grass', for the color of grass may be designated by another color word, e.g. grass is called 'yellow' in Navajo. That is to say, the word which usually designates yellow also includes chartreuse and grass-color. The word for 'green', used for example in speaking of green trees such as pines, is a different term.

40 *So they sat down in groups, by hundreds and by fifties.*

Exegesis: *anepesan prasiai prasiai* 'they reclined in ranks'.

anapiptō (8:6) 'lie down', 'recline' to eat.

prasia (only here in the N.T.) meant originally 'a garden plot'; when used as here it means 'in orderly groups', 'in rows', 'in ranks' (cf. Moulton & Milligan). The element of *order* is stressed in the use of this word: the multitude formed orderly rows which could be easily and quickly served by the disciples (cf. Rawlinson; E.F.F. Bishop *Expository Times*, 60.192, 1949).

kata hekaton kai kata pentēkonta 'by the hundreds and by the fifties': so most translations and commentaries. Manson, however, has 'a hundred rows of fifty each' (cf. also Moule *Idiom Book*, 59f. "a great rectangle, *a hundred by fifty*...: 'one side of the rectangle was reckoned *at* a hundred, the other *at* fifty'."): this, however, has not commended itself to many (cf. Lagrange "*bien mathématique!*").

Translation: *In groups, by hundreds and by fifties* is a very compact phrase, and one which must in certain languages be somewhat expanded, e.g. 'different groups; some groups had one hundred people and other groups had fifty people' (Subanen); South Toradja expresses it 'in groups there were hundreds, there were fifties'.

41 *And taking the five loaves and the two fish he looked up to heaven, and blessed, and broke the loaves, and gave them to the disciples to set before the people; and he divided the two fish among them all.*

Exegesis: *labōn* (cf. 4:16) 'taking'.

anablepsas eis ton ouranon 'looking up to heaven' in an attitude of prayer.

anablepō (7:34, 16:4) 'look up'; in 8:24, 10:51,52 it means 'to recover sight', 'see again'.

eulogēsen (8:7, 11:9, 10, 14:22) 'he blessed': here and in 8:7 and 14:22 (and parallels in the other Gospels) the word may mean (1) 'invoke God's blessing upon', or (2) 'give thanks (to God)', 'praise (God)' as the equivalent of *eucharisteō* 'give thanks', 'praise'. Arndt & Gingrich reflect lack of finality in the matter by refusing to classify these passages definitely under one or the other heading.

A study of the passages which deal with the two feedings of the multitudes, the Supper, and related passages, shows that *eulogeō* and *eucharisteō* are used interchangeably. In the feeding of the five thousand, *eulogeō* is found in Mk. 6:41 // Mt. 14:19 // Lk. 9:16, and *eucharisteō* in Jn. 6:11,23. In the feeding of the four thousand, *eucharisteō* is used in Mk. 8:6 // Mt. 15:36, and *eulogeō* in Mk. 8:7. In the institution of the Supper *eucharisteō* is used of the loaf Lk. 22:19 // 1 Co. 11:24, and of the cup Mk. 14:23 // Mt. 26:27 // Lk. 22:17; *eulogeō* is used of the loaf Mk. 14:22 // Mt. 26:26 (and of the cup in 1 Co. 10:16). In the Emmaus incident *eulogeō* is used of the bread Lk. 24:30. It would be precarious to try to establish a difference between the actions described by the two verbs in all these passages as though *eulogeō* always meant exclusively 'to call God's blessing upon' and *eucharisteō* 'thank God for'. The conclusion appears inevitable that the two verbs describe the same action of praise or thanksgiving offered in prayer to God.

It should be noticed, however, that in two passages *eulogeō* takes a direct object: the loaves and fish in Lk. 9:16 and the fish in Mk. 8:7. In these two passages it would be natural to assume that the meaning is 'ask God to bless', 'invoke God's blessing upon' (although Taylor, 360, maintains that in Mk. 8:7 no difference is to be established between *eulogeō* [of the fish] and *eucharisteō* in the previous verse [of the loaves]: "The act is one of thanksgiving to God"). In 1 Co. 10:16 'the cup of blessing which we bless' would seem to mean 'the cup of blessing for which we bless (i.e. praise) God' (cf. Robertson and Plummer *I Corinthians in loc.*).

The Vulgate consistently translates *eulogeō* by *benedicere* and *eucharisteō* by *gratias agere*. The Syriac always translates *eulogeō* by *b-r-k* 'bless'; used of God, 'bless God', it means 'praise God' (cf. Koehler). This same verb is also used to translate *eucharisteō* in Mk. 8:6, Jn. 6:11,23, and 1 Co. 11:24. Elsewhere *eucharisteō* is translated by *y-d-ʼ* 'confess', 'give thanks', 'praise' (Hebrew *yadhah*); in Mk. 14:23 both *y-d-ʼ* and *b-r-k* are used, and in Mt. 15:36 *sh-bh-ḥ* 'praise', 'give thanks'. The evidence from the Syriac would seem to indicate that the two Greek verbs are practically synonymous in meaning.

English translations, as a rule, translate *eucharisteō* 'give thanks', and *eulogeō* 'bless'. Weymouth, Moffatt and Goodspeed always have a direct object for 'bless', either the loaves and fish, or the bread and cup of the Supper. RSV has followed ASV by using 'bless' as an intransitive verb, with no object following, meaning (presumably) 'said a blessing'. Brazilian always translates *eulogeō* 'bless' with a direct object (as do Weymouth and others), and *eucharisteō* 'give thanks'; Synodale translates both words 'give thanks' (with the exception of Lk. 9:16 and 1 Co. 10:16 where *eulogeō* is translated 'bless' with a direct object); Zürich translates both words 'say a prayer of thanks for it' (*sprechen das Dankgebet darüber*).

From this it is evident that there exists no uniformity in translating the two terms. That the two are practically equivalent, in these passages, seems to be indicated by the Gospel narratives themselves, and there is good precedent for translating them in this manner.

kateklasen (only here in Mark: cf. *klaō* 8:6,19, 14:22) 'he broke', 'he broke into fragments'.

paratithōsin (8:6, 7) 'that they should set before (them)': though there is no way of determining the question, it would seem probable, in light of the customs of that time, that the Twelve carried the bread and fish and placed them before the various groups of fifty and one hundred, and not before each person individually.

emerisen (cf. 3:24) 'he divided', 'he distributed' (cf. Arndt & Gingrich 2.a).

Translation: *Taking* must in some languages be 'took in his hands', since the instrument or agent of the taking must be specified.

Looked up to heaven is 'looked up toward heaven' not 'looked into heaven', as in some translations.

Blessed involves a number of problems for the translator because of (1) the ambiguous nature of the Greek expression, (2) the tendency to interpret any blessing of an object as involving some magical practices, and (3) the confusion between 'blessing' and 'making taboo'. Where there is an object of the process of blessing, the tendency is to understanding consecration or sanctifying, e.g. 'place holiness on' (Huave) or 'to cause it to be holy'. In some languages there is a more indirect way of dealing with this problem by saying 'gave it his good word' (Chol) and 'prayed about it' (Tarahumara, Subanen). However, in order to avoid a manifestly incorrect interpretation, which presumes that Jesus employed some word ritual to increase the food magically, it may be better to translate 'spoke to God on behalf of the food' or 'gave thanks to God for the food'.

Broke the loaves means breaking them apart in his hands, not, as implied in one translation, smashing them like stones.

Gave them must refer here to the pieces of bread.

To set before, as noted above, probably refers to supplies distributed to the groups which would in turn distribute them among those in the group.

Divided the two fish among them all does not mean that Jesus divided the fish and personally served all the people. In some languages one must say 'divided the fish for all the people' or 'divided the fish so all the people could have some'.

42 *And they all ate and were satisfied.* 43 *And they took up twelve baskets full of broken pieces and of the fish.*

Text: In v. 43 instead of *kophinōn plērōmata* 'basketfuls' of all modern editions of the Greek text, *Textus Receptus* has *kophinous plēreis* 'baskets full'.

Exegesis: *echortasthēsan* (7:27, 8:4,8) 'they were fed', 'they were filled', 'they were satisfied'.

kai ēran klasmata dōdeka kophinōn plērōmata 'and they took up (the) broken pieces, twelve basketfuls'. While it is possible that the subject of 'they took up' is the disciples, it is more probable that the verb is used impersonally, meaning simply 'twelve basketfuls were taken up'.

klasma (8:8,19,20) 'fragment', 'broken piece': it should be made clear in translation that these were pieces that remained uneaten, not crumbs that were dropped in eating (cf. E. F. F. Bishop *Expository Times*, 60.192f. 1949).

dōdeka kophinōn plērōmata literally 'twelve fillings of baskets', 'twelve basketfuls': *plērōma* is 'that which fills', 'complement' (cf. 2:21), and the phrase here indicates the amount (in terms of capacity) of broken pieces of bread which remained (cf. Arndt & Gingrich *plērōma* 1.a; *Expository Times* 60.193, 1949). The strict meaning is rather 'twelve basketfuls' than 'twelve baskets full of...'

kophinos (8:19) 'basket': a stiff wicker basket in which the Jews carried provisions. There is no agreement as to its precise size, nor does it seem that difference in size is what distinguished it from the *spuris* 'basket' of 8:8. It appears that *spuris* was a flexible mat-basket, made of rushes, perhaps, especially used by fishermen for carrying fish or food generally (cf. F. J. A. Hort *Journal of Theological Studies* 10.567-71, 1908-9).

kai apo tōn ichthuōn 'and of the fish', i.e. 'and some of the fish' (BFBS; cf. Black *Aramaic*, 251): for this same kind of construction cf. 5:35 (cf. Arndt & Gingrich *apo* I.6: 'the remnants of the fish').

Translation: *They all* would evidently refer not only to the people but to the disciples and Jesus. One may translate 'everyone ate'.

When the receptor language demands an active construction, specifying who took up the fragments, it is probably justifiable to use 'the disciples took up'. They did not pick up the food from the ground, and hence one may translate as in some languages 'received back from the people pieces of bread and fish, enough to fill twelve baskets'.

Though the Greek term for 'basket' *kophinos* does not indicate the specific size of the container involved, it is entirely legitimate to select in the receptor language a term which would identify a relatively large basket, the type of container that might be carried by people who were out gathering supplies in the fields or who used the baskets for transporting produce.

44 And those who ate the loaves were five thousand men.

Exegesis: *andres* 'men': adult males, as distinguished from the women and children (cf. Mt. 14:21).

Translation: One should not translate this sentence in such a form as to mean that only men ate, and that women and children were excluded (cf. Mt. 14:21). In some languages this requires one to say, 'of those that ate the food there were five thousand men'.

Though *loaves* are specified in this verse, one is not to interpret that the five thousand had some of the loaves, but the fish was entirely too limited to go around. 'Food' is a not unwarranted substitution for *loaves*.

45 *Immediately he made his disciples get into the boat and go before him to the other side, to Bethsaida, while he dismissed the crowd.*

Text: *eis to peran* 'to the other side' is omitted by Taylor and Manson, but retained by all other modern editions of the Greek text.

Exegesis: *ēnagkasen...embēnai...kai proagein* 'he compelled...to enter ...and to go ahead'.

anagkazō (only here in Mark) 'force', 'compel'; Arndt & Gingrich 2, see a weakened meaning 'strongly urge'. The word implies unwillingness on the part of the disciples.

embainō (cf. 4:1) 'get in', 'embark'.

proagō (10:32, 11:9, 14:28, 16:7) 'lead the way', 'go before', 'precede'.

eis to peran (cf. 4:35) 'to the other side': on the difficulties of joining this phrase to *pros Bēthsaida* 'to Bethsaida' see the commentaries. It is generally agreed that this is Bethsaida Julias on the east side of the Lake.

heōs autos apoluei 'while he dismisses'.

heōs 'until': with the present indicative (as here) it means *while* the action indicated by the verb is in process (cf. Arndt & Gingrich I.2.a; for further examples cf. Mt. 5:25, Jn. 9:4).

apoluō (cf. 6:36) 'send away', 'dismiss'.

Translation: *Made his disciples get into the boat* is a verbal, not a direct, instrumental causative, i.e. 'he told his disciples to get into the boat'. One must avoid the impression of Jesus manhandling his disciples, an easy mistake to make at this point.

If a verb of 'speaking' or 'commanding' is used, one may shift this verse to direct discourse, 'he ordered his disciples, Get into the boat and go on ahead of me to the other side, to the town Bethsaida...'

Dismissed the crowd is paralleled in some languages by 'told the crowd to go home' (Subanen), but see also 6:36.

46 *And after he had taken leave of them, he went into the hills to pray.*

Exegesis: *apotaxamenos autois* 'taking leave of them', 'bidding them farewell'.

apotassomai (only here in Mark) 'take leave of', 'say goodbye';

Moulton & Milligan give an example of its use in the papyri with the stronger meaning 'get rid of' (cf. Lk. 14:33).

autois 'them': it is ambiguous in Greek, referring either to the disciples or to the crowd (Mt. 14:23 makes it explicit by saying 'he dismissed the crowds'). The RSV 'them' apparently refers to the disciples, as does BFBS (and others); Vulgate, Goodspeed, Weymouth, Lagrange and Taylor assume that the crowd is meant. If *apotassomai* 'take leave of' differs in meaning from *apoluō* 'dismiss' of the previous verse (as it probably does), then it would seem that *autois* 'them' refers to the disciples rather than to the crowd. If possible, a translation should preserve the ambiguity of the Greek.

eis to oros (cf. 3:13) 'to the hill', 'into the hills'.

proseuxasthai (cf. 1:35) 'to pray': infinitive of purpose, 'in order to pray'.

Translation: As noted above, one should try to preserve the ambiguity in the rendering of *them*. The sequence of events would seem to imply that the disciples left before the crowd, in which case, of course, *them* would refer to the people. On the other hand, he may have ordered his disciples to leave, and while they were getting the boat ready (having possibly drawn it up on the beach), Jesus dismissed the crowd and then turned to say goodbye to the disciples.

Went into the hills is good English but impossible in many languages. One may go 'between the hills', 'to where the hills are', or 'climb among the hills', but 'going into the hills' may be used only of miners.

For *pray* see 1:35.

47 And when evening came, ⎰the boat was out on the sea, and he was alone on the land.

Text: After *ēn* 'was' Soden, Taylor and Kilpatrick add *palai* 'already', which is omitted by all other modern editions of the Greek text.

Exegesis: *opsias genomenēs* (cf. 4:35) 'when evening came': it is to be presumed that nighttime is meant, in light of the 'late hour' (v. 35) before the feeding of the multitude. Cf. Lagrange.

en mesō tēs thalassēs 'in the middle of the sea': the phrase means more than 'out on the sea' of the RSV.

mesos (7:31, 9:36, 14:60; cf. 3:3) 'middle', 'in the midst'.

hē thalassa (cf. 1:16) 'the sea', i.e. the Lake of Galilee.

kai autos monos 'and he (was) alone': *monos* is here an adjective, 'alone', 'by himself'.

Translation: *When evening came* is translatable as 'when it got night' or 'when darkness had come'.

The clause *the boat was out on the sea* may be wrongly interpreted, since it would seem to imply that the boat was there, but not the disciples. Note the contrast in the form of the last clause which specifies Jesus as being alone on the land. Accordingly, one may translate, as required, 'the disciples were in the boat...'

48 *And he saw that they were distressed in rowing, for the wind was against them. And about the fourth watch of the night he came to them, walking on the sea. He meant to pass by them,*

Exegesis: *kai idōn...erchetai* 'and seeing...he comes', 'when he saw... he came': in Greek the complete sentence goes from *kai idōn* 'and seeing' to *epi tēs thalassēs* 'on the sea', the main verb being *erchetai* 'he comes'. The text appears to say that 'he saw them' from *the hill* where he was praying, and so he came, about the fourth watch of the night (cf. Lagrange).

basanizomenous en tō elaunein 'distressed in (their) rowing', 'troubled as they rowed'.

basanizomai (cf. 5:7) here in the sense of 'be troubled', 'be distressed'; perhaps the whole phrase means 'they were straining at the oars' (Goodspeed; cf. Arndt & Gingrich, BFBS; cf. Manson 'labouring at the oars'; Berkeley 'toiling hard at rowing').

en tō elaunein (cf. 4:4 *en tō speirein* 'as he sowed') 'in the rowing', 'as they rowed': the verb occurs only here in Mark.

ho anemos (cf. 4:37) 'the wind'.

enantios (15:39) 'against', 'contrary', 'opposed'.

peri tetartēn phulakēn tēs nuktos 'about the fourth watch of the night': according to the Greco-Roman system the night (6:00 P.M. to 6:00 A.M.) was divided into four watches of three hours each. The fourth watch, the last one, would be from 3:00 to 6:00 A.M.

phulakē (in 6:17 'prison') 'watch'.

peripatōn epi tēs thalassēs 'walking on the sea', 'walking on (top of) the water'.

peripateō (cf. 2:9) 'walk'.

kai ēthelen parelthein autous 'and he was going to pass them by': it is generally agreed that the verb *thelō* here does not mean 'will' or 'wish', but is used in a weakened sense, being the equivalent of an auxiliary (cf. Turner *Journal of Theological Studies* 28.357, 1926-7; Taylor, BFBS, Manson). ASV 'as if intending to pass them by' reads into the text more than is there.

parerchomai (13:30, 31, 14:35) 'pass by', 'pass': this is the meaning most commentators and translators give the verb in this passage; without a direct object it may mean 'come to', 'join' (Lk. 12:37, 17:7) and this is the meaning Goodspeed gives it here, 'and (he) was going to join them', an interpretation which seems quite reasonable in view of the context.

Translation: *Rowing* is not too widely practiced in the world, and even where it is known, there are two principal practices: (1) pulling the oars, and hence going in the direction to which one's back is turned, and (2) pushing the oars, as in the Orient, and thus facing the direction in which the boat is moving. Where rowing is completely unknown, translators have tried to describe the action as 'making the boat move' (Eastern Otomí) and 'pushing the water back with wooden poles' (Trique).

Wind was against them may be translated as 'the wind was blowing against them' or 'the wind was blowing on their back' (i.e. if our Western kind of rowing is understood) or 'the wind was blowing into their faces' (if the Oriental type is generally inferred by the people). One may avoid this problem somewhat by saying 'blowing from the direction in which they were going'.

The fourth watch is variously rendered: 'when it was almost dawn' (Subanen), 'when the cocks had crowed' (Maninka), 'towards dawn' (South Toradja), 'at the very first cock-crow' (Toba Batak), 'when it was already three o'clock at night' (Indonesian).

Walking on the sea is 'walking on top of the lake' (or 'face of the lake' in some instances).

49 *but when they saw him walking on the sea they thought it was a ghost, and cried out;*

Exegesis: *edoxan* (10:42) 'they thought', 'they supposed'.
phantasma (only here in Mark) 'apparition', 'ghost'.
anekraxan (cf. 1:23) 'they cried out', 'they screamed' in terror.

Translation: *Ghost* is usually quite easily translated, for most peoples claim to have seen apparitions of dead people moving in shadowy forms, and for such spectres they usually have a name. In fact, in some languages there are several different names, depending upon the size and definiteness of form of the object in question.

50 *for they all saw him, and were terrified. But immediately he spoke to them and said, "Take heart, it is I; have no fear."*

Exegesis: *etarachthēsan* (only here in Mark) 'they were frightened', 'they were terrified', 'they were troubled'.
elalēsen met' autōn kai legei autois 'he spoke with them and says to them': unlike other constructions in which two almost synonymous verbs are used (one as a participle and the other in a finite form), expressing one idea only, 'said', 'answered', 'spoke' (cf. 1:7, 24, 3:33, 6:37), in the present passage two actions are indicated by the verbs: (1) 'he spoke *with* them' (the only place in Mark *laleō* is used with the preposition *meta* 'with'), and (2) 'he said *to* them'.
tharseite (10:49) is an imperative 'cheer up!', 'courage!', 'take heart!'
egō eimi (13:6, 14:62) 'it is I'.
mē phobeisthe 'quit being afraid' (cf. Burton *Moods and Tenses*, § 165).

Translation: For *terrified* compare 4:40, but in this context the Greek expression is stronger than the one used in 4:40 and implies the active fright of the disciples rather than an intense feeling of awe and latent fear. However, in many languages the same basic idioms are employed, often with qualifiers to indicate the intensity of the emotion.

Take heart is an interesting English idiom, meaning 'have courage', 'don't be afraid', and 'buck up' (to use another figure of speech). This same concept is rendered in other languages in a variety of ways: 'have a hard heart' (Miskito), 'make your heart firm' (Moré), 'strengthen your heart' (Bare'e), 'bring your heart to rest' (Javanese), 'make your heart rest' (Subanen), and 'be strong in your heart' (Zacapoastla Aztec). The basic meaning of the Greek implies the overcoming of fear, and hence any expression—figurative or not—which accurately denotes this experience is valid.

It is I must be recast in many languages to read 'I am Jesus'.

51 And he got into the boat with them and the wind ceased. And they were utterly astounded,

Text: At the end of the verse *Textus Receptus* adds *kai ethaumazon* 'and they marveled', which is omitted by all modern editions of the Greek text.

Exegesis: *anebē pros autous eis to ploion* 'he went up to them into the boat'; Weymouth 'went up to them and entered the boat'.

anabainō (cf. 1:10) 'come up', 'go up': of boats, 'embark, get into' (cf. Arndt & Gingrich 1.a.α).

ekopasen (cf. 4:39) 'abated', 'ceased', 'died down' (of the wind).

lian (cf. 1:35) 'very', 'exceedingly'.

ek perissou (only here in Mark) 'beyond measure', 'exceeding the usual (number or size)' (Arndt & Gingrich). The true force of this prepositional phrase may be appreciated by comparing the cognate words in Mark: verb, *perisseuō* (12:44), noun, *perisseuma* (8:8), comparative adjective, *perissoteros* (7:36, 12:33,40), adverb, *perissōs* (10:26, 15:14).

en heautois existanto 'they were astounded within themselves' (cf. Lagrange *ils étaient tous extrêmement stupéfaits en eux-mêmes*).

existēmi (cf. 2:12) 'be baffled', 'be astounded', 'be puzzled'.

Translation: *The wind ceased* may be rendered quite metaphorically in some languages, e.g. 'the wind healed' (Bolivian Quechua) or 'the wind died'. In Chontal of Tabasco the expression is somewhat more "scientific": 'the wind passed by'.

For *astounded* see 1:22,27. At this point Tzeltal has 'their spirits went straight', implying the kind of astonishment which accompanies emotional relief.

52 for they did not understand about the loaves, but their hearts were hardened.

Exegesis: *ou gar sunēkan epi tois artois* 'for they did not understand about the loaves': i.e. from the multiplication of the loaves, in the feeding of the multitude, they should have gained insight (into the person of Jesus—Arndt & Gingrich).

all' ēn autōn hē kardia pepōrōmenē 'but their heart was hardened'.
kardia (cf. 2:6) 'heart', 'mind', 'thinking'.
pōroō (8:17; cf. *pōrōsis* 3:5) 'harden', 'petrify'; when used of 'heart' it means 'to grow (or, make) dull', 'blind', 'obtuse'.

Translation: Some translations of the expression *they did not understand about the loaves* have meant little more than 'they did not remember about the loaves' or 'they did not think about the loaves'. However, the meaning here is much more. What the Gospel writer implies is that they did not understand the implications of the miracle. If available terms rendering *understand* are inadequate in the receptor language, one may need to expand the clause somewhat, e.g. 'they did not know what it meant when Jesus divided the loaves' or 'they did not recognize the meaning of the feeding the people with the loaves'.

There are relatively few languages in which one can say 'their hearts were hardened' or 'hard' and at the same time preserve the meaning of the original at this point. If translated literally this expression would have the following meanings in various languages: 'endurance' (Popoluca), 'brave' (Tzeltal), 'doubt' (Piro), 'bad character' (Trique) and 'courage' (Shilluk). On the other hand, one can always speak of the characteristic denoted by the phrase *their hearts were hardened*, e.g. 'they have hard heads' (Trique), 'their ears do not have holes' (Shipibo), 'they do not have pain in their hearts' (Tzeltal).

Hardened indicates primarily a state of being resulting from a process, not a specific process requiring the identification of the particular agent. The Greek has reference to the condition of the hearts, not the process by which they become hardened.

53 And when they had crossed over, they came to land at Gennesaret, and moored to the shore.

Text: Instead of *diaperasantes epi tēn gēn ēlthon eis Gennēsaret* 'having crossed over to the land they came to Gennesaret' of all modern editions of the Greek text, *Textus Receptus* has *diaperasantes ēlthon epi tēn gēn Gennēsaret* 'having crossed over they came to the land of Gennesaret'.

Exegesis: *diaperasantes* (cf. 5:21) 'having crossed (the Lake of Galilee)'.
epi tēn gēn 'to land', 'to the land': some take this phrase with *diaperasantes* 'having crossed' (BFBS), but most translations take it with *ēlthon* 'they came' (RSV, Weymouth, Lagrange, Brazilian).
prosōrmisthēsan (only here in the N.T.) 'they came to anchor', 'they came to harbor'.

Translation: For problems involved in *crossed over* see 4:35. In this instance it would appear that a complete crossing is implied, not just from one point of land to another, but the geographical details are not certain.

Land at Gennesaret is the 'region of Gennesaret', probably a fertile plain south of Capernaum.

In some languages the equivalent of *moored to the shore* is 'tied to the shore' or 'drew the boat up on the shore'.

54 ***And when they got out of the boat, immediately the people recognized him,***

Exegesis: *epignontes...periedramon* (next verse) 'recognizing...they ran': the verbs are used in an impersonal sense and the subject 'people' must be supplied. Cf. Turner *Journal of Theological Studies* 25.381f., 1923-4.
epiginōskō (cf. 6:33) 'recognize'.

Translation: Because of the considerable distance of *him* from a noun antecedent, it may be useful to employ 'Jesus'.

55 ***and ran about the whole neighborhood and began to bring sick people on their pallets to any place where they heard he was.***

Exegesis: *periedramon* (only here in Mark; cf. *suntrechō* 6:33) 'they ran about', 'they went throughout'.
holēn tēn chōran ekeinēn (cf. 1:28) 'all that region', 'all that district' (for *chōra* 'region' cf. 1:5).
epi tois krabatois (cf. 2:4) 'upon pallets', 'on (their) sleeping-mats'.
tous kakōs echontas (cf. 1:32) 'those who were sick'.
peripherein (only here in Mark; cf. *pherō* 2:3) 'bring', 'carry'.

Translation: *Whole neighborhood* consists in some languages of 'to the houses of all the people living there'.
Bring sick people would be 'carry sick people' (with careful attention to the specific terms used for 'carrying').
Any place where they heard he was is a somewhat "cut" expression, for it leaves out the fact that the people must have heard other people saying where Jesus was. In some languages (e.g. Kapauku) this must be remedied, if one is to make sense, e.g. 'place where people said that Jesus was there'. In some instances one may wish to be even more precise, 'where people heard others saying, He is there'.

56 ***And wherever he came, in villages, cities, or country, they laid the sick in the market places, and besought him that they might touch even the fringe of his garment; and as many as touched it were made well.***

Exegesis: Most of the words of this verse have already been dealt with: *eisporeuomai* 'enter' (1:21); *kōmē, polis, agros* 'village, city, country-town' (5:14, 6:6); *parakaleō* 'request' (1:40); *hina* of content 'that' (5:10,18); *kan* 'if only', 'at least' (5:28); *himation* 'cloak', 'garment' (2:21); *haptomai* 'touch' (1:41); *sōzō* 'heal', 'cure' (5:23).
en tais agorais (7:4, 12:38) 'in the market places' (perhaps 'in the town squares', 'in the village centers'): not every town and hamlet had its own market place.

tous asthenountas (only here in Mark; cf. the adjective *asthenēs* 14:38) 'those who were feeble', i.e. the sick.

kan tou kraspedou tou himatiou autou hapsōntai 'they might touch at least the fringe of his garment' (cf. Moule *Idiom Book*, 138).

kraspedon (only here in Mark) 'edge', 'border', 'hem'; probably here not in the general sense, but in the specific sense of 'tassel' (in Hebrew *çiçith*) worn by pious Jews on each of the four corners of the cloak (cf. Mt. 23:5).

Lagrange calls attention to the distinction between the aorist *hēpsanto* 'they touched' and the imperfect *esōzonto* 'they were made well' in the last clause: 'And as many as touched it (momentary act) they were being made well (one after the other)'.

Translation: *Came* is probably better rendered as 'went' in most languages, for the point of view of the narrator is that of a companion of Jesus, not of those to whom he was coming.

Villages, cities, or country is paralleled by 'small villages, large towns, and hamlets in the country'. In Latin America *market places* are equivalent to *'plazas'*, the central, open squares of the towns, often used for markets, at least on certain days.

There is a confusion in subject reference in the verb *besought*. Is the meaning here (1) that those who laid the sick in the market places requested Jesus to allow the sick to touch the hem of his garment (probably more accurately the tassel, though this would be difficult to translate in many languages), or (2) that the sick pleaded with Jesus to be able to touch his garment? It may very well be that both would be true, not only would the "sponsors" of the sick try to get Jesus to pay attention to their friends or relatives, but the sick would themselves ask for help. In many languages, however, one cannot preserve such an ambiguity, and hence one must choose between those who brought the sick and the sick themselves, in which case it is probably more in keeping with the context to employ the latter alternative.

Were made well may be translated as 'got well', 'became well', or 'were healed'.

CHAPTER SEVEN

1 *Now when the Pharisees gathered together to him, with some of the scribes, who had come from Jerusalem,* 2 *they saw that some of his disciples ate with hands defiled, that is, unwashed.*

Text: At the end of v. 2 *Textus Receptus* adds *emempsanto* 'they found fault', which is omitted by all modern editions of the Greek text.

Exegesis: *sunagontai pros auton* (cf. 6:30; 2:2) 'they gather together to him'.

hoi Pharisaioi (cf. 2:16) 'the Pharisees'.

tines tōn grammateōn (cf. 1:22) 'some of the scribes': the participial phrase *elthontes apo Ierosolumōn* '(who) came from Jerusalem' modifies 'some of the scribes'.

koinais chersin, tout' estin aniptois 'with unclean hands, that is, unwashed': for the benefit of his readers the author explains what is meant by 'unclean hands'.

koinos (7:5) 'common (to all)', 'communal': from this primary sense the word came to mean (in the N.T.) 'ordinary', 'profane'. Here, then, it would mean 'ceremonially unclean'. Morton Smith (*Tannaitic Parallels*, 31-32) adduces proof from Rabbinical literature to show that *koinos* in the N.T. refers to "objects of which the cleanness or uncleanness is uncertain, and which are therefore a sort of third class, apart from the clean (certainly so) and the (certainly) unclean."

aniptos (only here in Mark) 'unwashed'. As the context shows, the protest of the scribes does not reflect an interest in hygiene: it is a matter of ceremonial laws of purification which the disciples of Jesus have neglected to observe.

Translation: *Now* is to be taken strictly in the transitional sense, not with any temporal meaning.

Gathered together to him is an awkward phrase, even in English. The idea is that they formed a group there where Jesus was. The Greek preposition *pros* indicates their direction of interest and the reciprocal nature of the meeting. This expression is made more complicated by the fact that the scribes are also involved. In some languages this means that one must say 'when the Pharisees, together with some of the scribes (those who had come from Jerusalem), had formed a group there where Jesus was, they saw that...' One may also use the equivalent of 'huddled together' or 'came together as a group'.

For *scribes*, see 1:22.

Because of the considerable distance of the noun *Jesus* from the pronominal forms *him* and *his*, it is often necessary to employ 'Jesus', especially for the first occurrence of the third person pronoun.

It is probably impossible to find an adequate term to designate the neutral concept of *koinos* (see above), and even an equivalent of *defiled* is not readily discoverable in many languages. In some cases one may say 'dirty' (Black Bobo); in others, 'spotted', i.e. by impurities (Zoque). South Toradja says 'with not-pure hands', the word *masero* meaning 'pure, ritually clean, holy'; Bare'e renders 'hands that arouse aversion'. Other possibilities are 'they had not been purified' or 'they had not been made clean'.

That is is equivalent to 'that means' or 'it is also said'.

In following the *Textus Receptus* (something which is required in certain instances—see Introduction), one must render *condemn*, which may be translated as 'sought their sin' (Tzeltal), 'said that it wasn't good' (Chontal of Tabasco), or 'talked against them' (San Blas).

3 *(For the Pharisees, and all the Jews, do not eat unless they wash their hands, observing the tradition of the elders;*

Exegesis: *pugmē* (only here in the N.T.) 'fist': as used in the present passage the word means literally 'with the fist'. There is no agreement on what the phrase means here. The general sense of 'carefully', 'diligently' (cf. Field *Notes*, 30f.) is given the word by ASV, Weymouth, Synodale (*soigneusement*), Brazilian (*cuidadosamente*); 'as far as the wrist' (cf. Black *Aramaic*, 8f.) is preferred by BFBS; Moffatt, and Berkeley have 'up to the elbow' (cf. Turner, *Journal of Theological Studies* 6.353, 1904-5; 29.278f., 1927-8); Zürich has simply *mit der Faust*, and Lagrange *à poing fermé*; Manson and RSV omit the word; Goodspeed has 'in a particular way' adding (*Problems*, 59f.) "though just what that particular way was we cannot as yet determine;" Weis suggests (*New Testament Studies* 3.233-36, 1957) that the word refers to a special vessel supplied for the purpose.

It would seem that the translator may choose to omit the expression since its meaning is not certain and the various alternatives only obscure rather than clarify. If one wishes to employ some equivalent it is probably best to translate 'with the fist' (cf. Arndt & Gingrich; Taylor), if such a phrase carries some intelligible meaning in the language into which he is translating the word.

nipsōntai (only here in Mark) 'they may wash': the verb is used generally with the meaning of washing *some part of the body*, not of taking a bath.

kratountes tēn paradosin tōn presbuterōn 'holding to the tradition of the elders': the participle may be causal, 'because they hold...'

krateō (cf. 1 : 31) 'hold on to', 'keep', 'observe'.

paradosis (7 : 5, 8, 9, 13) 'tradition': i.e. teachings, precepts, handed over, generally in oral form, from generation to generation (from the verb *paradidōmi* 'hand over': cf. v. 13).

presbuteros (7 : 5) 'older (man)', 'elder': in this passage and in v. 5, the word refers to the 'ancient ones', 'the ancestors' from whom had come the traditions; elsewhere in Mark (8 : 31, 11 : 27, 14 : 43, 53, 15 : 1) the word refers to the contemporary 'elders' who with the chief priests and scribes (with whom they are always conjoined) composed the Sanhedrin, the ruling body of the Jews.

Translation: *The Pharisees and all the Jews* poses difficulties for the translator, since this type of expression, if translated literally, would mean in many languages that the Pharisees were not Jews. One must therefore render the phrase in some such form as 'the Pharisees, and in fact, all the other Jews', 'all the Jews, including the Pharisees' or 'all the Jews, and especially the Pharisees'. The use of 'especially' is justified in this inverted order by virtue of the fact that in the original the Pharisees are the focus of the subject expression.

Wash their hands involves certain special aspects which are not clearly understood from the Greek term which means literally 'with the fist'. In some translations it is, however, possible to give something of the meaning without a literal translation (which might be entirely misleading). For example, in Navajo this passage reads 'they wash their hands ceremonially', an expression which is quite understandable within the Navajo religious patterns.

The transliteration of *Jews* may need a classifier, 'the people called Jews'.

Observing should not be translated literally in the sense of 'looking at' or 'watching', but in the meaning of 'keeping', 'living according to', or 'obeying'.

Tradition is essentially the 'customs' of the people, and for this aspect of any people's life there are always some adequate terms, even though the assortment may be rather varied, e.g. 'the old root-trunk', in which the life of a people is likened to a tree (Kekchi), 'to live as the ancients did' (Tarahumara), 'sayings passed down from long-ago times' (Barrow Eskimo), 'what their fathers of old told them to follow' (Navajo), 'the ordinance maintained by the forefathers' (South Toradja), and 'word that has been kept from the ancients' (Tzeltal).

The elders are 'the fathers', 'those who lived long ago', or 'the ancestors'.

4 *and when they come from the market place, they do not eat unless they purify themselves; and there are many other traditions which they observe, the washing of cups and pots and vessels of bronze.)*

Text: Instead of *rantisōntai* 'they may sprinkle', read by Nestle, Westcott and Hort, Vogels, Merk, Lagrange, and Taylor, *baptisōntai* 'they may bathe (themselves)' is read by *Textus Receptus*, Tischendorf, Soden, Souter, and Kilpatrick. The manuscript evidence is fairly evenly divided: *rantizō* 'sprinkle' should be considered the "harder" reading.

At the end of the verse *kai klinōn* 'and of beds' is added by *Textus Receptus*, Soden, Vogels, and Kilpatrick; the majority of modern editions of the Greek text, however, reject it.

Exegesis: As RSV indicates, vv. 3-4 are parenthetical. Unlike RSV, however, v. 2 in Greek is the beginning of a sentence which is left incomplete: instead of v. 5 taking up the sentence and completing it, the incomplete sentence of v. 2 is left hanging, and v. 5 begins another (complete) sentence. It is not necessary in a translation, however, literally to reproduce the Greek grammatical constructions, especially if awkwardness is the result.

kai ap' agoras ean mē rantisōntai 'and from the market-place if they don't sprinkle': there are two main ways in which this admittedly obscure statement may be understood: (1) 'when *they come back* from the market-place they do not eat unless they wash *themselves*': thus Arndt & Gingrich (under *agora*), ASV, RSV, Manson, Synodale, Brazilian (Zürich adds, in brackets, *die Hände*); (2) '*anything* from the market-place they do not eat unless they sprinkle (or, 'wash', depending on the text preferred) *it*': for this use of the phrase *ap' agoras* 'from the market-place' meaning 'something brought from the market-place' cf. Black *Aramaic*, 37; E. F. F. Bishop *Expository Times* 61.219, 1950. This is the translation preferred by Goodspeed, Moffatt, Williams: Lagrange, who argues for it, points out that vv. 3-4 thus refer to the ceremonial purification of the person, of the food, and of the dishes. While dogmatic finality is impossible, especially in light of the textual uncertainty of the main verb, it would appear that Lagrange's arguments offer a reasonable explanation of the text, together with Black's exposition of the Aramaic form underlying the Greek phrase.

It should be noticed that BFBS offers another translation, one which lies between the two discussed above: 'and they do not eat anything from the market place unless they wash themselves' (understanding *ap' agoras* as 'something (brought) from the market-place' and translating *baptisōntai* 'wash themselves').

ha parelabon kratein 'which they received to hold on to': a reference to other traditions, similar to the ones mentioned.

paralambanō (cf. 4 : 36) 'receive': here as the complement of *paradidōmi* 'hand over' of a tradition which is *handed over* by one generation and *received* by another.

krateō (cf. 1 : 31) 'hold on to', 'keep', 'observe'.

baptismous potēriōn kai xestōn kai chalkiōn 'washings of cups and pots and copper vessels'.

baptismos (only here in Mark) 'washing' (of dishes).

potērion (9:41, 10:38,39, 14:23,36) 'cup', 'drinking vessel'.

xestēs (only here in the N.T.) from the Latin *sextarius* 'the sixth part of a modius'; in a general sense, as here, 'pitcher', 'pot', 'jug', without any reference to size.

chalkion (only here in the N.T.) 'copper vessel', or 'kettle'.

Translation: *The market place* is usually not difficult to translate, but in some instances certain local adaptations may be required, e.g. 'the trading post', 'the place of buying and selling', or 'the place where provisions are bought'.

They should refer specifically to the Pharisees (and all the Jews), not to the elders.

Do not eat unless becomes in some languages 'do not eat if they do not', 'do not eat until they', or 'eat only when they have'.

Purify themselves seems somewhat preferable as a base for translating 'wash themselves', since whatever water was used—whether in sprinkling or bathing—had as a primary function the ceremonial purification of the person. Purification is described in various ways, e.g. 'to become really clean' (Mazatec), 'to become not mixed', in the sense of contaminated (Mezquital Otomí), 'to take away pollution' (Loma).

Many other traditions which they observe may be rendered as 'they keep doing many other things which their ancestors told them to do' or 'they follow their fathers in keeping many other customs'.

The washing of cups...is an appositional expression, identifying the content of the traditions. One must frequently reproduce this as a verb expression, especially in languages in which *traditions* may be translated as a verb phrase, e.g. 'they wash cups and pots and bronze vessels'.

Where the people are unacquainted with *bronze* it has been customary to use a word 'metal vessels' or 'metal containers'.

5 And the Pharisees and the scribes asked him, "Why do your disciples not live according to the tradition of the elders, but eat with hands defiled?"

Text: Instead of *kai* 'and' at the beginning of the verse, of the majority of editions of the Greek text, *Textus Receptus*, Soden, and Vogels have *epeita* 'then'.

Instead of *koinais* 'common' of all modern editions of the Greek text, *Textus Receptus* has *aniptois* 'unwashed'.

Exegesis: *eperōtōsin* (cf. 5:9) 'they ask'.

peripatousin (cf. 2:9) 'they walk': here, figuratively, 'they live', 'they proceed'.

kata tēn paradosin 'in accordance with the tradition': this is the only place in Mark in which the preposition *kata* is used with this meaning (cf. Arndt & Gingrich II.5.a.α).

esthiousin ton arton 'they eat bread', i.e. 'they eat', 'they eat *food*' (in general).

Translation: *Asked him* may be 'asked Jesus', if the reference is otherwise not clear in the receptor language.

For *scribes* see 1:22 and for *disciples* 2:15.

Not live...but eat may cause complications, unless translated with care, e.g. 'not live according to what their fathers told them; rather, they eat with hands...'

Defiled is the same word as used in 7:2.

6 *And he said to them, "Well did Isaiah prophesy of you hypocrites, as it is written,*

> *'This people honors me with their lips,*
> *but their heart is far from me;*
> 7 *in vain do they worship me,*
> *teaching as doctrines the precepts of men.'*

Exegesis: *kalōs* (7:9, 37, 12:28, 32, 16:18) 'fittingly', 'rightly': here used ironically. BFBS 'Well... men!'

eprophēteusen Ēsaias 'Isaiah prophesied' (cf. 1:2).

prophēteuō (14:65) 'prophesy': here used in the sense of 'predict', 'foretell' (cf. Arndt & Gingrich 3).

hupokritōn (only here in Mark) 'hypocrites', 'dissemblers': an extension of the original meaning 'stage actors'.

hōs gegraptai (cf. 1:2) 'as it stands written'. The passage quoted is from Isaiah 29:13, the LXX version (which differs significantly from the Hebrew text).

laos (14:2) 'people': here in the special sense of the people of God, Israel.

tois cheilesin me tima 'with the lips they honor me'.

cheilos (only here in Mark) 'lip': by which outward profession is meant, in contrast with the inward thoughts and purposes of the 'heart'.

timaō (7:10, 10:19) 'honor', 'revere'.

hē de kardia autōn porrō apechei ap' emou 'but their heart is far removed from me'.

kardia (cf. 2:6) 'heart' as the center of intellectual activity.

porrō (only here in Mark) adverb 'far away', 'distant from'.

apechō (14:41) here 'to be away', 'to be distant' (cf. Arndt & Gingrich 2).

matēn de sebontai me 'in vain do they worship me'.

matēn (only here in Mark) adverb 'in vain', 'to no purpose', 'to no end'.

sebomai (only here in Mark) 'worship (as God)'.

didaskontes didaskalias entalmata anthrōpōn 'teaching as (divine) teachings the precepts of men'.

didaskalia (only here in Mark) in the passive sense of 'teaching', 'instruction'.

entalma (only here in Mark) 'precept', 'ordinance'.

Translation: For *prophesy* see *prophet*, 1:2. But in this context *prophesy* may need to be taken in quite a special sense, e.g. 'long ago speak the truth about' or 'to declare God's words about' (if *prophesy* is to be understood in the sense of speaking to the people on behalf of God).

You hypocrites is an appositional expression, rendered in some languages as 'about you; and you are hypocrites'; 'about you, as hypocrites', or 'about the hypocrites that you are'.

Hypocrites is one of those metaphorically fascinating terms which exhibits about as wide a variety of different possibilities as exist for any term. Such people exist in all societies and there seems to be no lack of ways in which these persons may be described. However, the different expressions may be classified principally into (1) those which employ some concept of 'two' or 'double', e.g. 'two faced' (Totonac, Mazatec, Lacandon, Cuicatec, Zacapoastla Aztec), 'two hearts' (Tzeltal, Chol), 'two mouths' (Pame), 'two heads' (Mixtec), 'two sides' (Kekchi), 'double (or 'forked') tongue' (Shipibo), 'double talk' (Eastern Otomí); (2) those which make use of some expression of 'mouth' or 'speaking' e.g. 'to talk false' (Tepehua), 'to lie-act' (Zoque), 'to lie' (Kituba, Ifugao, Trukese), 'someone whose lips are fair '(i.e. gracious) (South Toradja), 'to have a sweet mouth' (Moré), 'to have a swollen mouth', from too much speaking (Mazahua), and 'to have a straight mouth and a crooked heart' (Black Thai); (3) those which are based upon some special cultural feature, e.g. 'the bitterness of white' an idiom based on the fact that white-wash looks nice but tastes bitter (Kikongo), 'to spread a clean carpet', an expression used in Madagascar to describe one who covers up the dirt of an unswept floor just before the arrival of guests (Malagasy), and 'to be a priest-heron', based on a fable of a heron who deceived fish into thinking that he was their protector, while actually he was devouring them (Balinese); and (4) those which employ a non-metaphorical phrase, e.g. 'those who make themselves out to be good' (Zanaki) and 'those who deceive' (Tetelcingo Aztec).

As it is written may be in the active form 'as Isaiah wrote'. Some languages, however, may employ 'as the words are written'.

Honors is here often translated as 'praises', e.g. 'say my name' (Tepehua), 'make me great' (Totonac), 'good what is said about me' (Tzeltal), 'speak well of me' (Tarascan), 'lift up my name' (San Blas, Kpelle).

In English we may use *lips* as a figurative substitute for 'voice' or 'speech'. However, in other languages this may not be meaningful. For example, 'mouth' is required in Mazatec and Bolivian Quechua, 'words' (literally, 'they love me with words') is used in Chol, and 'so they say' is the equivalent in Tzeltal.

As in so many instances *heart* may not be rendered literally in many translations. For example, in Popoluca the heart is only 'a blood bowl', and has absolutely no metaphorical significance or usage. One must use in this type of context a borrowing from Spanish *anima*, which is the well-recognized and often-used term for the focus of the personality.

Their heart is far from me is essentially a figurative expression, and may require considerable adaptations: (1) modifications in the word for heart, e.g. liver, abdomen, stomach (see 2:6), (2) shifts from singular to plural, i.e. 'their hearts are...', since each person has a heart, and (3) alteration of the perspective, e.g. 'I have not arrived in their hearts' (Tzeltal).

Terms for *worship* are quite involved (see *Eugene A. Nida, TBT* 6.32-33, 1955; and *God's Word in Man's Language* 24, 163). Words for 'worship' can usually be classified under the following divisions: (1) those based on the physical activity involved in the position assumed in worship, e.g. 'to prostrate oneself before' (Javanese), 'to kneel and bow the head' (Malay), 'to kneel before' (Cakchiquel), 'to drop oneself beneath God's foot' (Loma), 'to cut oneself down before' (Valiente), 'to wag the tail before God', using a verb which with an animal subject means 'to wag the tail', but with a human subject means 'to worship' (Cuicatec), 'to join to' (Tzotzil), (2) those which incorporate some element of 'speaking' or 'declaring', e.g. 'to raise up a blessing to God' (Kpelle), 'to praise as your God' (Kekchi), 'to say one is important' (Cashibo), and (3) those which specify some type of mental activity (whether or not later expressed in words), e.g. 'to think of God with the heart' (San Blas), 'to have one's heart go out to God' (Rincon Zapotec), and 'to holy-remember' (Chontal of Tabasco).

In vain is a phrase giving rise to a number of problems, since it so frequently requires a complete descriptive phrase or clause in order to convey a corresponding meaning, e.g. 'say I am important, but they do not believe it' (Cashibo), 'has no meaning when they praise me' (Kekchi), 'uselessly' (South Toradja, Bare'e), 'uselessly they remember' (Zoque), 'their religion is their mouth' (Gurunse), 'their worship has no meaning' (Subanen), 'they say they love me, but this means nothing' (Tzotzil), 'they worship me but they do not mean what they say' (Black Bobo), 'it is of no value that they honor me' (Mazahua), and 'their thinking is not in their hearts' (San Blas).

Teaching as doctrines the precepts of men must often be recast since *doctrines* and *precepts* more often than not correspond to verb expressions, not nouns. When this modification occurs certain expansions are required in order to identify the participants and the relationships between the processes, e.g. 'teach what men say as though it were what God has said' (Huave), 'teach men's commandments as true teachings', in which 'true teachings' is the regular expression for doctrines (Tzeltal), 'teach as God's words what men have said' (Black Bobo), 'teach rules, which are merely the regulations of men' (Bare'e), 'teach what men have commanded as though it is true' (Ifugao), and 'teach men's commands as though they were the very words of God' (Eastern Otomí).

8 *You leave the commandment of God, and hold fast the tradition of men."*

Text: At the end of the verse *Textus Receptus*, Soden, Vogels, and Merk (in parentheses) add, *baptismous xestōn kai poteriōn, kai alla paromoia toiauta polla poieite* 'washings of pots and cups, and many other such like things you do': the majority of modern editions of the Greek text omit these words.

Exegesis: *aphentes tēn entolēn tou theou* 'leaving the commandment of God'.

aphiēmi (cf. 2:5) 'abandon', 'forsake', 'leave'.

entolē (7:9, 10:5,19, 12:28,31) 'commandment': the singular 'the commandment of God' here represents all the commandments, 'the Law of God' (cf. Arndt & Gingrich 2.a.α).

krateite tēn paradosin tōn anthrōpōn 'you hold on to the tradition of men'.

    krateō (cf. 1:31) 'hold to', 'keep', 'observe'.

    paradosis (cf. 7:3) 'tradition'.

Translation: Without some break at the beginning of this verse, it is quite possible for people to think that these words are likewise from the book of Isaiah. Accordingly, the use of indentation, quotation marks, or special particles or forms to mark such quotations should be employed (e.g. in some languages the limits of quotations are specially marked by some form of the verb, 'says he', e.g.: 'he says....says he'). Some translations have even introduced 'Jesus said', at the beginning of this verse in order to make the transition clear (e.g. Loma).

    Commandment of God may be 'what God commanded' or 'the orders which God spoke'.

    Leave the commandment cannot be translated in some instances simply as 'to abandon', but rather 'to no longer do' or even 'to refuse to do'.

    Hold fast may be rendered as 'you are very careful to do' or 'you do not fail to do'.

9 *And he said to them, "You have a fine way of rejecting the commandment of God, in order to keep your tradition!*

Text: Instead of *tērēsēte* 'you may keep' of the majority of modern editions of the Greek text, Lagrange, Taylor, and Kilpatrick have *stēsēte* 'you may establish'.

Exegesis: *kalōs* (cf. v. 6) 'how well!': ironical. Arndt & Gingrich, 6 suggest 'Are you doing the right thing in rejecting...?'

    atheteite (cf. 6:26) 'you are rejecting', 'you set aside'.

    tērēsēte (only here in Mark) 'that you may keep', 'observe', 'fulfil' (Cf. Arndt & Gingrich 5).

    The reading preferred by Kilpatrick and others, *stēsēte* means 'establish', 'make firm', 'set' (cf. Arndt & Gingrich *histēmi* I.1.b.α); Lagrange *pour établir*.

Translation: The irony of this statement should be made quite clear. A mark of punctuation is often not enough. Note what is done in Chontal of Tabasco by beginning the verse as 'You think you have done well in rejecting...' Cf. also South Toradja 'Your cleverness is without equal, in putting God's commandment out of action'.

    Rejecting may be variously rendered, e.g. 'you say it is of no value to you' (Huave), 'you have changed' (Mazahua), 'you have thrown away' (Kekchi), 'pretty you caused it to be lost' (Zoque), in which the word 'pretty' immediately marks the phrase as ironical.

    The commandment of God in contrast with *your tradition* may be rendered as 'what God has ordered...what your fathers have said'.

10 *For Moses said, 'Honor your father and your mother'; and, 'He who speaks evil of father or mother, let him surely die';*

Exegesis: The first O.T. passage quoted is from Ex. 20:12 (cf. Deut. 5:16); the second is from Ex. 21:17.

tima (cf. v. 6) 'you must honor'.

ho kakologōn (9:39) 'he who reviles', 'he who insults'.

thanatō teleutatō 'with death he is to die', 'he must certainly die': for similar constructions denoting emphasis cf. 4:41, 5:42.

thanatos (9:1, 10:33, 13:12, 14:34,64) 'death'.

teleutaō (9:48) 'come to an end', 'die'.

Translation: *Honor* is in this context primarily 'love' and 'respect' (Popoluca). In some languages the equivalent is 'do good for' (Shipibo).

Speak evil of is not 'to curse' or 'to cast a spell on'. It is simply 'to speak bad words about' or 'to speak bad to'.

Let him surely die must not be translated in the sense of 'permit him to die' (as in some translations) or 'he will certainly die'. It should be rendered to mean 'he must be killed', 'he must certainly be put to death', or 'you must kill the one who speaks evil of his father or his mother'.

11 *but you say, 'If a man tells his father or his mother, What you would have gained from me is Corban' (that is, given to God) —*

Exegesis: *korban* (only here in the N.T.; cf. *korbanas* Mt. 27:16) 'a gift': the Greek transliteration of the Hebrew *karban* 'offering'. The word indicates a gift consecrated to God which could not, therefore, be used for any other purpose. As Black (*Aramaic,* 101) points out, the meaning is not that such things really had been dedicated as an offering to God but were *to be considered as such*; cf. Lagrange; cf. Manson *Teaching,* 315-19.

ho ean ex emou ōphelēthēs 'that of mine which might have been of benefit to you'.

ōpheleō (cf. 5:26) 'profit', 'benefit'; in the passive, as here, 'be benefited', 'be helped'. The construction in the Greek is somewhat difficult, but the sense is clear: literally, 'that of mine, in regard to which you might have been benefited' (cf. Moule *Idiom Book,* 131). The verb is accented as a subjunctive form by all editions of the Greek text, with the exception of Nestle and Kilpatrick, who accent it as an indicative form (in favor of which cf. Goodspeed *Problems,* 60-62).

Translation: There are several structural problems involved in this verse and in what immediately follows: (1) the included direct discourse, consisting of essentially three layers: the two introduced by words of speaking and the explanatory parenthesis, (2) the condition contrary to fact: *what you would have gained* (but did not), and (3) the shift of subjects in the conditional sentence, i.e. 'If a man..., then you...' The double discourse can not be avoided, but in some languages it may be clearer to shift the second one into an indirect form, e.g. 'tells his father or his mother that what they would have gained from him...'

What you would have gained from me is Corban is variously translated, e.g. 'that which I would have given to you is Corban' (Zoque), 'I have now dedicated to God all I could have helped you with' (Mazahua), 'that which should really have been my help for you' (Toba Batak), 'what you could have gotten from me is Corban' (Subanen), 'everything that is mine that could have helped you is Corban' (Chontal of Tabasco), 'earlier I could have given you this gift, but I am not able to do this now, for it is Corban', a rather paraphrastic means of indicating a contrary-to-fact situation (Trique).

That is, given to God should be treated as parenthetical and introduced in the regular manner as all such explanatory additions, e.g. 'as we say, I give it to God' (Zoque).

12 then you no longer permit him to do anything for his father or mother, 13 thus making void the word of God through your tradition which you hand on. And many such things you do."

Exegesis: *aphiete* (cf. 2:5) 'you allow', 'you permit'.

akurountes ton logon tou theou 'annulling the word of God': the participle expresses manner: 'in this way you annul...'

akuroō (only here in Mark) 'make void', 'annul', 'invalidate'.

ho logos tou theou (only here in Mark) 'the Word of God': cf. the absolute use of *logos* 'Word' in ch. 4 (vv. 14, 15, 16, 17, 18, 19, 20, 33).

tē paradosei humōn hē paredōkate 'by means of your tradition which you have handed down'. In saying '*you* have handed down', Jesus refers to the Jews as a whole, not to the particular individuals whom he was addressing then.

paradosis (cf. v. 3) 'tradition'.

paradidōmi (cf. 1:14) 'hand over', 'deliver': when used of tradition, as here, 'hand down'.

paromoia (only here in the N.T.) 'similar', 'like'.

Translation: If, as in some languages, the involved nature of verse 11 (see above) makes the condition quite obscure, one may translate these two verses, as in Black Bobo, 'a man may tell his father or his mother... Then if he does that you do not permit...' The result is essentially the same, but the construction may be more readily understood.

To do anything for may be translated as 'to help' or 'to provide for'.

Thus making void introduces still another clause to an already complex sentence. It may be broken off from what precedes, and still integrally related to it, by translating 'in this way you make void'.

Making void may be translated as 'make without anything' (Subanen), 'cause to be lost' (Popoluca), 'refuse to consider important' (San Blas), 'make powerless' (Javanese), 'break' (Toba Batak), 'annul' (South Toradja), or 'take away its power'.

The word of God should not be confused here with the Bible. This is 'what God has said'.

Your tradition which you hand on implies 'customs which have been handed on to you and which in turn you hand on to others', since these particular persons were part of the Jewish cultural tradition responsible for adherence to these man-made rules. On the other hand, Jesus is, of course, speaking to the larger group of Jewish people and is not assigning the entire responsibility to these particular persons (see above, under *Exegesis*). This meaning can be indicated by saying 'which you as Jews have handed on'.

Hand on is rendered in some languages as 'to speak to others about' or 'to say that your children should do'.

14 And he called the people to him again, and said to them, "Hear me, all of you, and understand:

Text: Instead of *palin* 'again' of the great majority of modern editions of the Greek text, *Textus Receptus* and Taylor have *panta* 'all'.

Exegesis: *proskalesamenos* (cf. 3:13) 'calling to him', 'summoning'.
sunete (cf. 4:12) 'you must understand'.

Translation: *Hear me* is 'listen to me'. *Understand* may be understood figuratively as 'receive it in your hearts'.

15 there is nothing outside a man which by going into him can defile him; but the things which come out of a man are what defile him."

Exegesis: *estin...eisporeuomenon* 'is...going in': although BFBS treats this as a compound verbal phrase meaning simply 'enters' (cf. Kilpatrick *The Bible Translator* 7.8-9, 1956), the majority of translations, like RSV, separate the two, translating *ouden estin* 'there is nothing', and *eisporeuomenon* 'which goes in' as an independent participle modifying *ouden* 'nothing'.

eisporeuomai (cf. 1:21) 'go in', 'enter'.
exōthen (7:18; cf. *exō* 3:31,32) 'from without', 'from the outside'.
koinōsai (7:18,20,23; cf. *koinos* 7:2) 'to make common', 'to defile'.
ekporeuomena (cf. 1:5) 'the things which go out': the reference, of course, is to the passions, sins and evil desires, catalogued in vv. 21-23, which have their origin inside the man, in his heart, and are outwardly expressed in sinful deeds and words.

Translation: *Nothing going into him* must be made somewhat more specific in some languages, for this could be understood as referring to being wounded by a spear, pierced by an arrow, or stabbed by a knife. Obviously the meaning here is 'eating', and hence in Amuzgo the translation is 'nothing that he eats'.

For *defile* see 7:2, but in this context it may be necessary to translate 'make him bad' or 'cause him to sin'.

The phrase *the things which come out of a man* has been grossly misinterpreted in some translations to mean the excretion of body wastes, vomiting, and the discharge of mucus from the nose. In order that these 'things which come out' may be identified as behavior, one may add 'out of the heart' (Tzeltal), or say 'what he does and says'.

16 ["If any man has ears to hear, let him hear."]

Text: This verse is omitted by Tischendorf, Nestle, Westcott and Hort, Souter, and Kilpatrick; ASV, RSV. It is included by *Textus Receptus*, Soden, Vogels, Merk, Lagrange, Taylor; AV, Moffatt.

See 4:23 for **Exegesis** and **Translation**.

17 And when he had entered the house, and left the people, his disciples asked him about the parable.

Exegesis: *eis oikon* (cf. 3:19) literally 'into a house': BFBS 'to His home' (cf. Kilpatrick *The Bible Translator* 7.5-7, 1956); Goodspeed 'home'; Taylor 'indoors'. If the usage here is the same as that in 3:19 and 2:1 the meaning is '(his) home'.

epērōtōn (cf. 5:9) 'they asked'.

parabolēn (cf. 3:23) 'parable'; here in the sense of 'figure', 'illustration' (Gould suggests 'riddle').

Translation: *Entered the house and left the people* poses a problem in some languages if translated literally, for one would assume that Jesus left the people before entering the house, or at least in entering the house he left the people. The Greek text indicates that 'he entered the house, away from the people', meaning 'he went into his home, away from the people'. The equivalent in other languages may be 'when he had gone into his home and the people were no longer with him'.

For *disciples* see 2:15 and for *parable* see 3:23.

18 And he said to them, "Then are you also without understanding? Do you not see that whatever goes into a man from outside cannot defile him,

Exegesis: *houtōs kai humeis asunetoi este*; 'Are you also thus without understanding?' For similar questions and statements cf. 4:13 (not understanding the parable), 4:40 (being fearful), 6:52 (not understanding the miracle of the loaves), and 8:17 (again not understanding about the loaves). The charge, of course, is not that they do not have any sense, but that they are *failing to use* their senses.

asunetos (only here in Mark) 'senseless', 'foolish', 'without understanding'.

ou noeite 'do you not understand?'

noeō (8:17, 13:14) 'perceive', 'understand', 'apprehend'.

Translation: *Without understanding* may be rendered in various ways, e.g. 'do you not understand', 'do you not hear with your hearts' or 'do you not see clearly'.

231

See must often be translated as 'understand', 'realize', or 'know', for this is not literal sight, but mental perception which is involved.

Goes into a man should be relatable to 'eating' (see 7 : 15), e.g. 'enters into a man's mouth' (Kiyaka). For *defile* see 7 : 2, but in this particular verse Mazatec has 'cannot dirty the heart', an expression which, by the use of 'heart', implies moral contamination.

19 *since it enters, not his heart but his stomach, and so passes on?" (Thus he declared all foods clean.)*

Text: Instead of the masculine participle *katharizōn* 'cleansing' (which modifies 'Jesus') of all modern editions of the Greek text, *Textus Receptus* has the neuter participle *katharizon* 'cleansing' (which modifies *pan to exōthen eisporeuomenon* 'everything which goes in from without' of v. 18).

Exegesis: *hoti* 'because'.

koilian (only here in Mark) 'stomach', 'belly'.

kai eis ton aphedrōna ekporeuetai 'and goes on out (of the stomach) into the privy'.

aphedrōn (only here in Mark) 'privy', 'latrine'; where the word may be offensive, synonyms may be used (Manson 'sewer', Moffatt 'drain', Williams 'waste'), or the term be altogether avoided (RSV 'passes on', Goodspeed 'is disposed of', Weymouth 'passes away').

katharizōn panta ta brōmata 'cleansing all foods'. It is conceded by nearly all commentators and translators that this verbal clause is an additional comment by the evangelist himself, explaining the significance of the words of Jesus (cf. Field *Notes*, 31f. and commentaries *in loc.*). In the correct text the masculine participle *katharizōn* 'cleansing' modifies 'he' (i.e. Jesus), and is a participle of manner, '*In this way* he cleansed...'

katharizō (cf. 1 : 40) either 'make clean' or 'declare clean' (cf. Arndt & Gingrich 2.a). '*Make* clean' is a causative, 'to cause to be clean', not in the sense of manufacturing or cleansing, but in the meaning 'declaring clean' or 'establishing as clean'. The comment of the evangelist is: 'In this manner Jesus made clean *for us Christians* all food'.

brōma (only here in Mark) 'food'.

Translation: *It* must in some instances be rendered as 'food', since the indefinite referent would be misinterpreted.

Not...but may be related to two verbs, 'the food does not enter his heart but it enters his stomach'.

This contrast between the 'heart' and the 'stomach' cannot be maintained in some languages, e.g. Gurunse, in which the stomach, not the heart, is the psychological center of the personality and the seat of the affections. Accordingly, one must say 'the food does not enter into his very life, but it goes on through his stomach'.

While in some languages one must be careful so as not to employ some vulgar term in speaking of defecation, in other languages the people will react unfavorably to any apparent prudishness as being either incomprehensible or annoying. Accordingly, in some instances the translation is literally 'goes out of the rectum' or 'goes out when one squats'. In any case the translation must reflect indigenous usage, with sensitivity to normal patterns of expression.

It is most important that translators not follow *Textus Receptus* in the last clause of this verse, for it is not that which goes into the privy which purifies all foods, but Jesus who declared all foods fit to eat. The resulting translations may parallel the following: 'in this way he said, All foods are good to eat' (Subanen), 'by these words he said, 'All food is good' (Gurunse), 'when he said this, he declared that all foods could be eaten' (Black Bobo), 'in saying this he purified all food' (Barrow Eskimo), 'thus he spoke-cleansed all food' (Zoque).

20 *And he said, "What comes out of a man is what defiles a man.*

See verse 15 for **Exegesis** and **Translation**.

21 *For from within, out of the heart of man, come evil thoughts, fornication, theft, murder, adultery,* **22** *coveting, wickedness, deceit, licentiousness, envy, slander, pride, foolishness.*

Exegesis: *esōthen* (7 : 32) 'from within', 'from the inside'.

hoi dialogismoi (only here in Mark; cf. *dialogizomai* 2 : 6) 'thoughts', 'deliberations', 'designs', 'reasoning'.

It is to be noticed in the list of twelve sins which follows that the first six are plural, referring to acts, and the last six are singular, referring more directly to the sin itself.

porneiai (only here in Mark) 'sexual vice', 'unlawful sexual intercourse', 'immoral sexual acts'.

klopai (only here in Mark) 'thefts', 'acts of thievery'.

phonoi (15 : 7) 'murders', 'killings'.

moicheiai (only here in Mark) 'adulteries' (as distinguished from *porneiai* above; sometimes the word may be the equivalent of *porneiai* 'sexual vice').

pleonexiai (only here in Mark) 'avarice', 'greed', 'covetousness', 'cupidity': the word often has a sexual connotation, and so is translated 'lust' by Moffatt (cf. Taylor).

ponēriai (only here in Mark) 'acts of wickedness', 'malicious deeds'.

dolos (14 : 1) 'deceit', 'cunning', 'treachery'.

aselgeia (only here in Mark) 'licentiousness', 'debauchery'; with the connotation of open and flagrant excess, 'wantonness' (Goodspeed, 'indecency').

ophthalmos ponēros (only here in Mark) 'an evil eye': in Jewish thinking 'envy', 'malice' (for other possible meanings see Arndt & Gingrich 1). Synodale *le regard envieux*; Zurich *neidischer Blick*.

blasphēmia (3 : 28) 'blasphemy': here directed not to God but to men, 'slander', 'defamation', 'abusive speech'.

huperēphania (only here in the N.T.) 'haughtiness', 'pride', 'insolence'.

aphrosunē (only here in Mark) literally 'foolishness', 'stupidity': in the Bible not simply to be equated with intellectual stupidity, but rather with 'moral...wrongheadedness of unbelief and sin' (Swete; cf. Gould, 'morally foolish'). Lagrange *hébétude morale*; Synodale *le dérèglement de l'esprit*. Some English translations have it 'recklessness' or 'reckless folly'; BFBS has 'godlessness' (in the *Glossary* this meaning of the word is defended). A translation should convey the moral and spiritual connotation of the word.

Translation: Any passage such as this, in which there are a number of Greek nouns describing processes, e.g. evil thoughts, fornication, theft, murder, adultery, etc., is likely to cause difficulty for translators, since in so many instances the only natural way of speaking about such activities is to employ verbs. If this is done, one cannot easily say that these 'come out of the heart'. Rather, the more usual expression is 'because of what is in the heart people think evil, are immoral . . .' (Amuzgo, Black Bobo) or 'from the heart they think evil, they molest women. . .' (Eastern Otomí, Bolivian Quechua).

For *heart* see 2 : 6.

Evil thoughts in a verbal form may be 'they think evil' or 'they make evil plans'.

Fornication and *adultery* both occur in this list of sins, but even in Greek there is some degree of overlapping. Fornication is the more general term, and specifically denotes sexual relations with prostitutes (*porneia* is the common term for prostitution and *pornē* is a prostitute). Adultery involves some degree of marital infidelity, whether on the part of the man or the woman, but in most contexts this word would refer to the marital status of the woman involved. That is to say, a married man who had sexual relations with a prostitute would be charged with fornication, but if the sex act were with someone else's wife, he would be guilty of adultery. Theoretically the same would be true of women, but in general these terms are employed from the "masculine viewpoint". In many societies there is a more or less parallel distinction between fornication and adultery, but where prostitution does not exist the distinction is between unmarried and married "lovers". The following contrastive sets are interesting of the ways in which this distintion is made:

	Fornication	*Adultery*
Amuzgo	'to be with a woman with a flower' ('woman with a flower' is the name of a prostitute)	'to be with another's wife'
Mazahua	'go around to women' or 'live with unmarried women'	'have women' or 'have two women'
Mazatec	'illicit relations'	'illicit relations in marriage'
Barrow Eskimo	'unmarried people using what is not theirs'	'married people using what is not theirs'
Zoque	'to have lovers'	'men unfaithful to wives and wives unfaithful to husbands'
Shipibo	'to seek a woman'	'to solicit another's spouse'

234

In some languages there are highly specialized idioms for illicit sexual relations, e.g. 'to do something together' (Totonac), which would seem to be quite an "innocent expression," but has a very specific denotation. In Maya one speaks of 'sowing sin', while adultery, on the other hand, is 'pair-sin'. In Valiente fornication is 'robbing self-possession' (that is, to rob what belongs to a person), and adultery is 'robbing another's half self-possession'. In Cakchiquel and Chol adultery is 'to act like a dog', and in Subanen an adulterer is 'one who can't be trusted'. In Loma fornication is described by a euphemism, 'they go out for a purpose', and in South Toradja the equivalent of adultery is somewhat poetic, 'they measure the depth of the river of (another's) marriage'.

Theft may be translated as 'they steal from people'. Note that this is not robbery, which is done by threat of violence, but the unnoticed activity of carrying away other's possessions.

Murder is 'killing', but this should not be a term denoting only killing in war or in defense of clan rights. It should be the most general term which would denote socially unsanctioned killing.

Coveting may be rendered as 'they want what other people have'.

Wickedness may correspond to 'they do bad things' or 'they behave bad'.

Deceit may be 'they deceive people', 'they lie', or 'they trick'.

In some languages it is difficult to distinguish between *wickedness* and *licentiousness*, though the second involves a greater degree of moral abandon. In Barrow Eskimo the term translating *wickedness* covers such a wide area of meaning that *lasciviousness* had to be rendered as 'complete disrespect for commandments', a rather indirect way of denoting moral perversity.

'The evil eye', translated in the RSV as *envy*, cannot be rendered literally in many languages without complete distortion of the meaning. For example, in Shipibo 'evil eye' refers only to sexual designs. The local equivalent of the Greek expression is 'to have a big liver'. In Tzeltal the correct expression is 'sick eye'. In some languages 'evil eye' means the capacity of casting spells upon people, e.g. 'their eyes bite' (Tzotzil), but the fundamental meaning of 'envy' (or 'stinginess') is what should be indicated.

Slander may be rendered as 'they speak evil against' or 'they destroy people's names' (San Blas).

Pride may be 'they are always talking about themselves', 'they think they are big', 'they continually boast' (Ifugao), 'they lift themselves up' (Tzeltal), 'they answer haughtily' (Maya).

Foolishness can sometimes be interpreted as 'they do not think' or 'they do not use their livers', but the meaning is not so much the lack of employment of some faculty, as a kind of perversity and moral failure. The San Blas people say 'they have no livers', that is to say, they are incapable of intelligent, thoughtful behavior.

23 *All these evil things come from within, and they defile a man."*

Exegesis: *ponēra* (as an adjective only here and in v. 22; cf. the noun *ponēriai* in v. 22) 'wicked', 'evil'.

Translation: The translation of this verse, as regards the form of *things come from*...must, of course, follow the pattern of the first part of verse 21. Accordingly, one may need to translate this as 'because of what is within a person he does all these bad deeds'.

For *defile* see 7 : 15.

24 *And from there he arose and went away to the region of Tyre and Sidon. And he entered a house, and would not have any one know it; yet he could not be hid.*

Text: After *Turou* 'of Tyre' *Textus Receptus*, Soden, Vogels, Souter, Westcott and Hort, Merk, RSV, Kilpatrick add *kai Sidōnos* 'and of Sidon'; Tischendorf, Nestle, Lagrange, and Taylor omit the words.

Exegesis: *ekeithen* 'from there': goes with the main verb 'he went away'.

anastas (cf. 1 : 25) 'rising': here not in the specialized sense of rising from bed, but in the general sense of expressing the beginning of an action indicated by another verb, 'he set out', 'he got ready' (Arndt & Gingrich 2.d).

ta horia (cf. 5 : 17) 'boundaries', 'region', 'district'.

eis oikian 'into a house' (cf. *The Bible Translator* 7.5-6, 1956).

kai ouk ēdunasthē lathein 'but he could not be hid'.

lanthanō (only here in Mark) 'escape notice', 'be hidden'.

Translation: *Region of Tyre and Sidon* may be translated as the 'territory of the cities of Tyre and Sidon'. The use of a classifier 'cities' is useful in many instances, since these might be taken as the names of persons, i.e. 'to their land'. In some instances the 'territory of a city' is meaningless, so that one can say 'to the region where the cities Tyre and Sidon were' or 'to a place near the cities of Tyre and Sidon'.

Entered a house does not refer to the simple act of entering into a particular house on one occasion, but to establishing residence in a place, even for a short time. In this context the idea is 'he stayed there in a house, and he did not want anyone to know it'.

He could not be hid does not mean, as it is sometimes translated, that people could not hide Jesus (presumably referring to the efforts of the disciples to keep Jesus in hiding, as though he were trying to escape from the authorities). The meaning is simply that Jesus could not prevent people from discovering where he was.

25 *But immediately a woman, whose little daughter was possessed by an unclean spirit, heard of him, and came and fell down at his feet.*

Exegesis: *euthus* 'immediately': if the word is given its literal meaning it should go with *elthousa prosepesen* 'immediately...she came and fell'.

hēs eichen to thugatrion autēs literally 'of whom the daughter of her had', i.e. 'whose daughter had': here is another example of the redundant personal pronoun *autēs* 'of her' which expresses the same idea as the relative *hēs* 'whose' (for another instance cf. 1 : 7; cf. Moule *Idiom Book*, 176).

thugatrion (cf. 5 : 23) 'little daughter'.
pneuma akatharton (cf. 1 : 23) 'unclean spirit'.
prosepesen pros tous podas autou 'she prostrated herself at his feet'.
prospiptō (cf. 3 : 11) 'fall down (at)', 'prostrate'.
pros tous podas autou (cf. 5 : 22) 'at his feet'.

Translation: For *unclean spirit* see 1 : 26 and for words denoting *possession*, see 1 : 23, 26.

Little daughter would imply a child, certainly before puberty, and perhaps around six or seven years of age—at least this may be as intelligent a guess as any other, if in the receptor language one is required to use one of several age-graded words for 'daughter'.

Fell down at his feet must not be translated literally in some languages. She did not 'fall' (in the sense of accidentally tripping over something), but 'she threw herself down' or 'she spread herself at his feet'.

26 *Now the woman was a Greek, a Syrophoenician by birth. And she begged him to cast the demon out of her daughter.*

Exegesis: *Hellēnis Surophoinikissa tō genei* 'Greek, Syrophoenician by race': thus the evangelist defines her culture and religion (Greek, not Jew: perhaps the equivalent of Gentile, 'pagan'—cf. Lagrange *païenne*) and her nationality (Syrophoenician, as distinguished from the Libyophoenicians in North Africa).

genos (9 : 26) 'nation', 'people', 'race': the use of the word in this passage refers to her national (or racial) origin.

ērōta auton hina to daimonion ekbalē 'she asked him to cast out the demon': all of these words have already been dealt with: *erōtaō* (cf. 4 : 10) 'make a request', 'ask for (something)'; *hina* (cf. 5 : 10, 18) 'that'—indicating content, not purpose; *to daimonion* (cf. 1 : 34) 'the demon'—in this passage, as in the previous one, it is one and the same with 'the unclean spirit'; *ekballō* (cf. 1 : 12) 'cast out', 'drive out'.

Translation: *A Greek, Syrophoenician by birth* is not an easy expression to translate, without at least a little contextual setting, since in many translations the transliterated words *Greek* and *Syrophoenician* will mean absolutely nothing. Since the first of these denotes culture and the latter ethnic origin, one can say 'Greek was her language and Syrophoenicia her tribe' (Tzeltal, Subanen). *Syrophoenician* may also be translated as 'a native of that region', since Tyre and Sidon have already been mentioned in verse 24. The fact that a person of a particular tribal background speaks the language of another group is a very common phenomenon in many parts of the world. Moreover, since language is the most universally recognized symbol of cultural relationship (that is, participation within a cultural group), this usage will properly reflect the meaning of the Greek text. Otherwise, there is an unresolved conflict involving two ethnic groups, and the meaning is often left quite obscure, not to say, entirely misleading. For example, in one language the literal translation really meant that she was born in the city of Syrophoenicia, a place in Greece, and in another rendering she was presumably from a Greek tribe called Syrophoenicia.

For *cast the demon out* see 1 : 26, 32, 34.

27 And he said to her, "Let the children first be fed, for it is not right to take the children's bread and throw it to the dogs."

Exegesis: *aphes* (cf. 2 : 5) 'allow', 'permit', 'let'.

chortasthēnai (cf. 6 : 42) 'be fed', 'be satisfied', 'be filled'.

ta tekna (cf. 2 : 5) 'the children': here figuratively for the Jews (in contrast with the Gentiles, 'the dogs').

kalon (cf. 4 : 8) 'right', 'fitting'.

tois kunariois (7 : 28) 'to the (little) dogs': the word is a diminutive and indicates a house dog, or lap dog, in contrast with the fierce dogs that roamed the streets.

It is, of course, possible that the final clause should be interpreted as a question, perhaps rhetorical, e.g. 'It is not right, is it, to...?'

Translation: *Let the children first be fed* may, in a literal translation, give rise to a wrong interpretation, i.e. 'permit the children to eat first and then the dogs'. The meaning is more accurately conveyed in some languages by 'first of all, the children should eat' or 'first, the children should be given food'.

Though the word *dogs*, in its regular form would be the common term used by Jews in speaking disrespectfully of the Gentiles, Jesus may have softened the term—or perhaps, even here with an understanding smile, have taken all the harshness out of the term, by using the diminutive ending, which may have carried associations of endearment, e.g. 'the puppies'. In some languages there are certain parallel distinctions, e.g. in Spanish (in contrast with the regular *perros* 'dogs'), there are two diminutive forms *perrillos* and *perritos*, the latter of which implies endearment.

28 But she answered him, "Yes, Lord; yet even the dogs under the table eat the children's crumbs."

Exegesis: *nai* (only here in Mark) 'certainly', 'assuredly', 'exactly'.

kurie (in the vocative only here in Mark) 'Sir': a title of respect (cf. Turner *Journal of Theological Studies* 29.348, 1927-8), not the Christian title 'Lord'.

kai ta kunaria 'yet the (little) dogs'.

hupokatō tēs trapezēs 'underneath the table'.

trapeza (11 : 15) 'table'.

esthiousin apo tōn psichiōn 'they eat the crumbs': the phrase *esthiein apo* 'to eat of' indicates the thing of which one partakes (*not* the idea of 'some' of it)—cf. Arndt & Gingrich *esthiō* 1.b.α.

psichion (diminutive) 'crumb', 'bit': perhaps here the word refers to the bits of bread used to clean the hands of the guests and then thrown under the table to the dogs (cf. Rawlinson).

Translation: *Yes* cannot be translated literally in many languages, for there is no direct yes-or-no question. There is simply a negative statement *it is not right*...Moreover, in a high percentage of languages if one is going to show agreement with a negative statement, one must use a negative, not a positive, reply. For example, in Tzeltal the woman's reply must be 'No, sir; but even the dogs...' In some languages, however, one can use the expressions 'you are right' or 'you have said true', to indicate agreement with the preceding statement, whether in a positive or negative form.

Lord is probably not the better rendering at this point. The woman's respect for Jesus is generally regarded as not equivalent to a recognition of his divine status, so much as a very polite means of address.

The children's crumbs cannot be translated as a possessive construction in some languages, since these are not crumbs which belong to the children, but crumbs from the bread which they have been eating. They are therefore 'crumbs from the children' or 'crumbs from the children's bread'. Bare'e translates 'the left-overs of the food', while Javanese has 'the spilt (food)'.

29 **And he said to her, "For this saying you may go your way; the demon has left your daughter."** 30 **And she went home, and found the child lying in bed, and the demon gone.**

Exegesis: *dia touton ton logon* 'on account of this saying (of yours)', 'because of your reply': a word of praise.

exelēluthen 'it has (already) gone out': the verb *exerchomai* 'go out' is used in connection with unclean spirits (or demons) in 1 : 25, 26, 5 : 8, 13, 7 : 29, 30, 9 : 25, 26, 29.

beblēmenon 'lying': either in repose, as an indication of normal health' or exhausted as a result of a final paroxysm caused by the demon's withdrawal (cf. 9 : 20).

epi tēn klinēn (cf. 4 : 21) 'on the bed'.

Translation: *Go your way* may need to be shifted to 'return' or 'go to your home', since a literal translation may imply setting out for a further destination.

Demon has left must be translated in conformity to regular idiomatic ways of describing this type of event (see 1 : 26).

In some languages one must be careful to avoid making *the child lying in bed* parallel with *the demon gone*. The first is a very logical object of the verb 'to find', for she actually found the child in this state. However, she did not 'find the demon', but simply discovered that he had left.

This difference in the nature of the objects of the verb may be rendered as 'saw the child lying in bed and realized (or, 'learned') that the demon had gone'.

One must make certain that the entire clause does not seem to be a rebuke, e.g. 'because you said this, get out', an interpretation which has been implied in a number of translations.

31 Then he returned from the region of Tyre, and went through Sidon to the Sea of Galilee, through the region of the Decapolis.

Exegesis: The route indicated by this verse is difficult to understand (cf. commentaries *in loc.*), but the language itself is clear in its meaning, as the text stands.

horiōn (cf. 5:17) 'boundaries', 'region'.

eis tēn thalassan tēs Galilaias (cf. 1:16) 'to the Sea of Galilee'.

ana meson tōn horiōn Dekapoleōs 'through the middle of the region of the Decapolis'.

ana meson 'through' or 'within' (Arndt & Gingrich *mesos* 2); Moule (*Idiom Book*, 67) suggests 'right through'.

Dekapolis (cf. 5:30) 'the Decapolis'.

Translation: In some languages the combination of 'returned' and 'went' may be impossible. A possible adaptation may be 'went back from the region of Tyre to the Lake of Galilee. In doing this he went through the region of Sidon and the region of the Ten Cities'. (Note that Sidon is to the north of Tyre, and according to this description of the journey Jesus must have made a circuit to the north and then approached the Lake of Galilee from the east.)

32 And they brought to him a man who was deaf and had an impediment in his speech; and they besought him to lay his hand upon him.

Exegesis: *pherousin* (cf. 1:32) 'they bring': an impersonal plural meaning 'people (men) brought'.

kōphon (7:37, 9:25) literally 'dull': it may mean either 'dumb', 'mute', or (as it does here) 'deaf'.

mogilalon (only here in the N.T.) 'speaking with difficulty' (*mogis* 'with difficulty'), 'speaking with an impediment'.

The rest of the words have already been dealt with: *parakalousin* (cf. 1:40) 'they begged'; *hina* (cf. 5:10, 18) 'that', of content; *epithē...tēn cheira* (cf. 5:23) 'he place his hand upon'.

Translation: *They* may need to be more specific, so as not to refer to the disciples, e.g. 'some people' or 'certain persons'.

Either in this verse, or in the preceding, it may be necessary to use 'Jesus' in place of a pronoun, since the closest specific referent is several verses back (note that in the RSV text one has to go back to 6:30).

Deaf may be translated simply as 'he could not hear', though there are always quite adequate terms for 'deaf'.

Impediment in his speech may be equivalent to 'he could not speak well' (Subanen) or 'he had difficulty speaking'. This would seem to imply that the man had either been deaf a long while or was congenitally so, in which case the impediment would have been serious indeed.

The pronouns *they...him...his...him* must be carefully handled, e.g. 'the people asked Jesus to lay his hands on the sick man'. One must avoid any connotations of 'laying on hands' to arrest. This is the 'touching' of healing and mercy.

33 *And taking him aside from the multitude privately, he put his fingers into his ears, and he spat and touched his tongue;*

Exegesis: *apolabomenos auton apo tou ochlou kat' idian* 'taking him aside away from the crowd by himself'.

apolambanō (only here in Mark) 'take aside', 'take away'.

kat' idian (cf. 4:34) 'privately', 'alone', 'by himself'.

ebalen tous daktulous autou 'he put his fingers'.

ballō here means 'put', 'place'.

daktulon (only here in Mark) 'finger'.

eis ta ōta autou 'into his ears': i.e. Jesus placed his fingers in the ears of the deaf man.

ous (cf. 4:9) 'ear'.

ptusas hēpsato tēs glōssēs autou 'spitting he touched his tongue': i.e. Jesus spat and touched the tongue of the deaf man.

ptuō (8:23) 'spit': the text does not say precisely what was the purpose of the action. From the parallel incident narrated in 8:23 it may be deduced that Jesus touched the tongue of the deaf man with the saliva (cf. Moffatt, Goodspeed; cf. Lagrange).

haptomai (cf. 1:41) 'touch'.

glōssē (7:35, 16:17) 'tongue'.

Translation: There are a number of possibilities of misunderstanding in this verse resulting from (1) indefinite pronominal reference in some languages and (2) the relationship of the spitting to the touching of the tongue. In the first place one must make certain that Jesus put his own fingers into the man's ears (this is obscure and misleading in some translations). In the second place, we do not know where Jesus spat. If the interpretation is that Jesus only spat on the ground to indicate the fact that the demon had gone out, that is often one type of expression, but if Jesus spat directly onto the man's tongue (implying some therapeutic value in the spittle), that would often be quite a different way of speaking. There is, of course, still another possibility, namely, that Jesus would spit on his own finger and then touch the man's tongue with his saliva-moistened finger. Translators often feel a certain reluctance in the idea of Jesus either spitting on the man's tongue or touching the tongue with saliva (a feeling of repugnance growing out of quite contemporary concepts of hygiene), but in many parts of the world saliva is still regarded as a means of blessing (Shilluk) or therapy (Kiyaka). There is essentially nothing strange nor unbecoming in this type of healing procedure.

There are several minor problems involved in this verse. For example, one must often specify which finger goes into the ear of the man, since the use of the plural here 'fingers' would in some instances mean a group of fingers in each ear. If, moreover, one means to interpret this verse as 'spitting on the ground and then touching the tongue with a finger', this must imply either that one finger is taken out of the ear, or that another was used (some translations have Jesus' index finger in two places at the same time).

It is impossible to say precisely how one must translate this passage, for there are obvious alternative renderings. The important thing is that the rendering make sense, in keeping with at least one standard interpretation.

34 *and looking up to heaven, he sighed, and said to him, "Ephphatha," that is, "Be opened."*

Exegesis: *anablepsas eis ton ouranon* (cf. 6:41) 'looking up to heaven': in an attitude of prayer.

estenaxen (only here in Mark) 'he sighed', 'he groaned': an expression of deep emotion. Lagrange takes it to be a prayer quickly uttered.

ephphatha (only here in the N.T.) is the Greek transliteration of the Aramaic *'ethpatah* the causative of *phathah* 'open'. Preserving the Aramaic word, the evangelist gives its Greek equivalent for the benefit of his readers.

dianoigō (only here in Mark; cf. *anoigō* next verse) 'open', 'open thoroughly'.

Translation: *Looking up to heaven* may need to be rendered as 'looking up toward heaven', if 'to' would imply 'into' or 'seeing heaven itself'.

Ephphatha must be transliterated, but all such resulting forms must be carefully checked to see to it that they do not have meaning in the indigenous language. For example, in Tzeltal the closest equivalent transliteration (based on Spanish, as the national language of the area) would be *epata*, meaning 'you have found a great deal', a meaning which obviously could not be adjusted to the following explanation. Accordingly, the transliteration was changed slightly to *epjata* (in which the *j* represents a degree of aspiration.), which has no meaning. As a basic principle, therefore, we can say that transliterations should reflect the closest possible correspondence with the source language, except where the resultant forms in the receptor language have meanings of their own.

Be opened is a kind of passive command, a form which is not found in some languages. Moreover, it is presumably relatable to the ears, but is addressed to the man. The closest equivalent in some languages is 'your ears will be open' or 'open up, ears'.

35 *And his ears were opened, his tongue was released, and he spoke plainly.*

Exegesis: *hai akoai* (cf. 1 : 28) 'the ears', i.e. the organs of hearing.

ēnoigēsan (only here in Mark) 'they were opened' (cf. *dianoigō* in previous verse).

eluthē ho desmos tēs glōssēs autou 'the bond of his tongue was loosed'.

luō (cf. 1 : 7) 'loose', 'unbind'.

desmos (only here in Mark) 'bond', 'hindrance', 'fetter'. Deissmann suggests (*Light from the Ancient East*, 306f.) that these words indicate that the man was possessed of a demon (cf. Lk. 13 : 16).

kai elalei orthōs 'and he was speaking clearly', 'he began to speak plainly'.

orthōs (only here in Mark) 'clearly', 'normally', 'correctly'.

Translation: The *ears* must be the inner ear, not the outer ear (many languages make such a distinction, e.g. Spanish *oídos* vs. *orejas*).

Where languages cannot speak of the 'ears being opened', it is still possible to say 'he could hear with his ears' or 'he could hear'.

"Loosing the tongue" seems to us to be quite a universal kind of idiom, but in some languages it is meaningless, for there is obviously no actual cord binding the tongue. In Huave, therefore, one must say 'his tongue was softened', in the sense of made pliable; in South Toradja it is said 'his tongue became supple, mobile'. In other languages one may say 'healed what kept his tongue from moving', and in this way describe the cure.

Spoke plainly introduces a problem in languages which specify whether a particular action represents a new process (something not done previously by the person), or a return to a previous state. This means that one must decide whether the man had ever spoken plainly before. There is no evidence in the Greek text one way or the other. The fact that the man spoke at all would seem to imply that he had not always been deaf (or at least not completely so). Accordingly, it is probably preferable to assume the restoration of ability to speak, rather than miraculous ability to speak after total congenital deafness. On the other hand, the impediment in speech could have been congenital, while the deafness, whether partial or complete, could have come on later in life. One must, of course, make a decision in languages which require certain arbitrary categories expressed, but in making a choice between alternative forms it is well to be on the conservative side, in terms of the extent of the miracle of healing. This does not imply any lessening of the fact of the miracle, only a caution in overdoing what is implied in the originals.

36 *And he charged them to tell no one; but the more he charged them, the more zealously they proclaimed it.*

Exegesis: *diesteilato...hina* (cf. 5 : 43) 'he commanded...that'.

autoi mallon perissoteron ekērusson 'they the more exceedingly proclaimed (it)': in direct proportion to Jesus' commands that they say nothing about it, they persisted in proclaiming the matter far and wide.

mallon (cf. 5:26) 'rather', 'the more'.

perissoteron (12:33,40) 'more abundantly', 'exceedingly': the RSV 'zealously' is more in the nature of an interpretation of the word.

kērussō (cf. 1:4) 'proclaim': as in the parallel case 5:20.

Translation: *Charged them to tell no one* may be shifted to the direct form, 'commanded them, Do not tell anyone'.

*The more...the more...*is not an easy expression to translate, for it is not a comparison, in the sense that one thing is more than something else, but a kind of reciprocal increase, i.e. as one thing increases so does the other. The only equivalents in some instances are 'he commanded and commanded...and they proclaimed and proclaimed...', or 'as he continually commanded them...they continually proclaimed it', or 'as much as he told them not to do so, they just that much more kept proclaiming it'.

37 *And they were astonished beyond measure, saying, "He has done all things well; he even makes the deaf hear and the dumb speak."*

Exegesis: *huperperissōs* (only here in the N.T.; cf. *perissos* 6:51, *perissōs* 10:26) 'exceedingly', 'beyond measure'.

exeplēssonto (cf. 1:22) 'they were amazed', 'they were astounded'.

kalōs (cf. 7:6) 'well', modifying the verb 'he has done'.

kai tous kōphous poiei akouein kai alalous lalein 'he makes both the deaf hear and the dumb speak'.

kai...kai 'both...and'.

kōphos (cf. 7:32) 'deaf'.

alalos (7:14,25) 'dumb', 'mute'.

Translation: For *astonished* see 1:22,27. *Beyond measure* is 'very very much' in some languages.

The deaf hear and the dumb speak may require certain tense contrasts, e.g. 'those who have been deaf to hear now and those who have not been able to speak to speak now'. In other instances this can be handled as 'the deaf to hear again and the dumb to speak again', implying a change of state or capacity. Without this added factor in some languages the meaning is that the people remain essentially deaf, but can still hear—a totally misleading implication.

CHAPTER EIGHT

1 *In those days, when again a great crowd had gathered, and they had nothing to eat, he called his disciples to him, and said to them,*

Exegesis: *en ekeinais tais hēmerais* 'in those days': cf. 1:9 for the identical phrase.

pollou ochlou ontos 'being a great crowd': the participial phrase is probably temporal, 'when there was a great crowd'.

kai mē echontōn ti phagōsin 'and they had nothing to eat': this participial phrase could be causal, '*because* they (the crowd) had nothing to eat' (cf. Manson).

ti phagōsin (cf. 6:36) 'what they should eat' (cf. also Burton *Moods and Tenses*, § 346).

proskalesamenos (cf. 3:13) 'calling to himself', 'summoning'.

Translation: *In those days* cannot be translated literally in some languages, for this would imply that the feeding of the crowd took place on several successive days. The meaning is simply 'at that time', a very general indicator of temporal sequence.

In some languages a 'crowd does not gather', but 'people gather and form a crowd'. Accordingly, one may translate 'many people came together'.

For *disciples* see 2:15.

2 *"I have compassion on the crowd, because they have been with me now three days, and have nothing to eat;*

Exegesis: *splagchnizomai* (cf. 1:41) 'I have pity', 'I feel sorry'.

ēdē hēmerai treis 'already three days', 'three days now': this phrase in the nominative case is called "a nominative in parenthesis," since it is not the subject of the verb that follows. Cf. Lagrange's translation, placing these words between dashes—*voilà déjà trois jours*—.

prosmenousin (only here in Mark) 'they remain with', 'they stay'.

ti phagōsin (cf. v. 1) 'what they should eat'.

Translation: For *compassion* see 6:34.

Have nothing to eat does not mean that they had eaten nothing for three days, but that they now had nothing left to eat.

3 *and if I send them away hungry to their homes, they will faint on the way; and some of them have come a long way."*

Text: *apo* 'from' is omitted by *Textus Receptus*, but included in all modern editions of the Greek text.

Instead of *eisin* 'they are' read by Nestle, Westcott and Hort, Kilpatrick, and Lagrange, *hēkasin* 'they have come' is preferred by Tischendorf, Soden, Souter, Merk, and Taylor; *Textus Receptus* and Vogels have *hēkousi* 'they are come'.

Exegesis: *apolusō* (cf. 6:36) 'I should send away', 'I should dismiss'.
nēsteis (only here in Mark) 'hungry', 'unfed', 'without eating'.
eis oikon autōn (cf. 2:11, 5:19, 7:30) 'to their homes'.
ekluthēsontai (only here in Mark) 'they shall become weary', 'they shall faint', 'they shall give out'.
en tē hodō 'in the road': i.e. 'on the way', 'as they go (home).'
apo makrothen (cf. 5:6) 'from afar', 'from a distance'.
(If *hēkasin* 'they have come' is read—see above—it occurs only here in Mark, and means 'be present', 'have come').

Translation: *Send them away hungry to their homes* may require some realignment of constituent parts, e.g. 'send them to their homes without their having eaten anything' or 'send them to their homes while they are still hungry'.
Faint on the way may be 'collapse along the trail'.

4 And his disciples answered him, "How can one feed these men with bread here in the desert?"

Exegesis: *apekrithēsan* 'they answered': the verb *apokrinomai* 'answer' is used in the aorist passive, with active meaning, here and at 9:6,17, 11:29,30, 12:28,29,34, 14:40, 15:5,9; it appears with *legei* 'he says' in 7:28, and is used in the middle voice in 14:60,61, 15:4 (for its use as a participle with *legei* 'he says' or *eipen* 'he said' cf. 3:33).
hoti 'that': introducing direct speech.
pothen toutous dunēsetai tis hōde chortasai artōn ep' erēmias; 'where can any one here in the desert (get the food to) feed these (people)'; BFBS 'From where shall anyone be able here in a wilderness to satisfy these with bread?'
pothen (cf. 6:2) 'whence', 'from where': it may also be used with the meaning 'how' (cf. Arndt & Gingrich 3) as in 12:37, and that is the meaning assigned to it here by RSV; Lagrange *comment*.
hōde (6:3, 9:1,5, 11:3, 13:2,21, 14:32,34, 16:6) 'here'.
chortasai artōn (cf. 6:42) 'feed with bread', i.e. 'feed', 'satisfy (their hunger)', 'fill'.
ep' erēmias (only here in Mark) 'in (this) uninhabited place', 'in this isolated spot', (cf. *erēmos* 'wilderness' 1:3): this phrase defines the character of *hōde* 'here'.

Translation: *Answered* is not to be understood in reply to a question, though it may have been implied. The basic meaning is 'replied', but in languages which require the introduction of a question by the appropriate verb, one may use 'asked in reply'.

Feed must be carefully translated in instances in which a distinction is made between providing food for people and giving food to animals. *Feed...with bread* may be most naturally rendered in some instances as 'give them bread to eat'.

While the Greek uses an indefinite *tis* 'any one', some languages require either a noun 'any man' or a first person plural 'we'. In this latter instance one must then determine in some languages whether the inclusive or exclusive first person plural must be used, that is to say, were the disciples thinking only of their own inability to feed the people, in contrast with Jesus' presumed ability? It is probably better, however, to use the inclusive form, implying the complete inability, as far as the disciples could determine, to provide food for such a large group in this desert place.

For *desert* see *wilderness* 1:3.

5 And he asked them, "How many loaves have you?" They said, "Seven."

Exegesis: *ērōta* (cf. 4:10) 'he asked', 'he inquired'.
posous (cf. 6:38) 'how many?'

Translation: *Loaves* may require expansion to 'loaves of bread'.
They said may be translated as 'they replied'.
The elliptical elements implied in the reply 'seven' may need some expansion in certain languages, e.g. 'we have seven loaves of bread', 'we have seven loaves' or simply 'seven loaves', for in a number of languages numerals must always be used with the nouns they modify or with some classifier of the noun class to which such objects belong.

6 And he commanded the crowd to sit down on the ground; and he took the seven loaves, and having given thanks he broke them and gave them to his disciples to set before the people; and they set them before the crowd.

Exegesis: Most of the words in this verse have already been dealt with: *paraggellei* 'he commands', 6:8; *anapesein* 'to recline', 'to sit down', 6:40; *labōn* 'taking', 6:41; *paratithōsin* 'they may place', 'they may set before', 6:41.
eucharistēsas (14:23; cf. *eulogeō* 6:41) 'giving thanks (to God)'.
eklasen (8:19, 14:22; cf. *kataklaō* 6:41) 'he broke'.

Translation: *Commanded the crowd to sit...* may be shifted to the direct form as 'commanded the crowd, Sit down...'
In a number of languages 'to give thanks' requires an object. Accordingly, one may translate 'he gave thanks to God' or 'he said to God, Thanks' (Trique, Tzeltal).
For *broke* and *gave to the disciples to set before* see 6:41.
As in all instances of intra-Gospel parallels, one should attempt to

reproduce the identical wording of the Greek text with substantially similar renderings in receptor languages. This may not always be completely possible, for certain minor shifts in wording in the Greek text may call for accompanying adaptations in receptor languages, and hence there cannot be any one-to-one system of exact correspondence. Nevertheless, the degree to which parallelism can be reproduced, whether within a single book or between books, should be a constant concern of the translator. On the other hand, it is not wise to refer to a portion already translated and to take over the wording without examination, for such arbitrary lifting of material out of context may result in very articifial transitions and syntactic relationships, especially in matters of tense sequence, conjunctions, pronominal reference, and aspects of the verb.

7 *And they had a few small fish; and having blessed them, he commanded that these also should be set before them.*

Text: *auta* 'them' is omitted by *Textus Receptus*, but included by all modern editions of the Greek text.

Exegesis: *ichthudia* (only here in Mark) 'little fish': as in the parallel incident in 6:38 these are to be thought of as prepared fish, not fresh.

eulogēsas auta 'blessing them', i.e. 'invoking God's blessing upon them'; 'thanking God for them': here only in Mark with a direct object (cf. the discussion of the verb in 6:41). Probably (cf. Taylor) the phrase means 'thanking God for them': it is highly doubtful that the evangelist meant to draw any distinction between *eulogeō* in this verse, concerning the fish, and *eucharisteō* 'give thanks' in the previous verse, concerning the loaves.

eipen kai tauta paratithenai 'he told (them) to place these also before (the crowd)'.

paratithēmi (cf. previous verse) 'place before'.

Translation: Some languages carefully distinguish between fish when they are alive and swimming about, or just recently caught, and those which are being sold in the market place or prepared as food, (cf. Spanish *pez* vs. *pescado*). The latter meaning is, of course, intended in this verse.

For *bless* see 6:41.

If the receptor language requires an object of the verb 'commanded', one may insert 'disciples'. Often, however, this context does not require the customary verb for 'command', as this may be too strong. Hence, one may render the passage as 'told his disciples to...', 'ordered his disciples to...', or 'said to his disciples, Distribute also the fish to the people'.

8 *And they ate, and were satisfied; and they took up the broken pieces left over, seven baskets full.* 9 *And there were about four thousand people.*

Text: In v. 9 after *ēsan de* 'and there were' *Textus Receptus* adds *hoi* *phagontes* 'those who ate', which is omitted by all modern editions of the Greek text.

Verse Division: RSV ends v. 9 at *tetrakischilioi* 'four thousand'; in most modern editions of the Greek text, and translations, the verse includes, however, also the next sentence *kai apelusen autous* 'and he sent them away'. These notes will follow the RSV division of verses.

Exegesis: *echortasthēsan* (cf. 6:42) 'they were filled'.

perisseumata klasmatōn 'excesses of fragments', 'remaining pieces': as in 6:43 those are pieces of bread left over, uneaten, from the abundance available to the crowd.

perisseuma (only here in Mark) 'that which abounds', 'which is in excess': therefore, 'remaining',. 'left over'.

klasma (cf. 6:43) 'piece', 'broken piece'.

hepta spuridas 'seven baskets': these two words are in apposition to *perisseumata klasmatōn* 'remaining pieces'.

spuris (or *sphuris*; 8:20) 'basket', 'hamper (for provisions)': wherein it differed from *kophinos* 'basket' cf. 6:43.

Translation: *Satisfied* may be translated as 'they had all they wanted'.

Seven baskets full is in an awkward syntactic relationship to what precedes. It is probably better to treat this as 'took up seven baskets full of broken pieces which were left over' or 'they took up the broken pieces that were left over; there were seven baskets full of these pieces'. In other words, the final phrase may be incorporated completely within the preceding clause or it may be expanded into the form of a complete paratactic sentence.

For details of problems involving the manner in which the pieces were taken up and the nature of the baskets, see 6:43.

Note that whereas 6:44 specifically states 'five thousand men', this passage speaks of 'four thousand persons'. Even though the Greek numeral has a masculine declensional ending, this does not mean that only males are to be considered. They are presumably people of all types: men, women, and children.

10 *And he sent them away; and immediately he got into the boat with his disciples, and went to the district of Dalmanutha.*

Exegesis: *apelusen* (cf. 6:36) 'he dismissed', 'he sent away'.

embas eis to ploion (cf. 4:1) 'entering the boat', 'embarking'.

ta merē (only here in Mark) 'the parts': when used of a country, 'region', 'district' in and around a city (cf. Arndt & Gingrich 1.b.γ).

Dalmanoutha (only here in Mark) 'Dalmanutha': as yet unidentified. Presumably (since the incident of feeding the 4000 seems to have taken place on the east side of the Lake) on the west side of the Lake of Galilee.

Translation: As in all instances of the expression *sent them away* one must avoid the connotation of summary dismissal of the crowd, involving emotional overtones of rejection or desire to be rid of them.

249

The boat may have to be in certain receptor languages 'a boat', for the particular boat serving in this context has not been specifically identified previously.

He got into the boat with his disciples must undergo some redistribution of parts in some languages, for both Jesus and the disciples were the subjects of the embarcation. Hence, 'he and his disciples got into a boat'.

District of Dalmanutha may be 'place (or 'region', 'land') called Dalmanutha'. The use of 'called' is to avoid misconstruing Dalmanutha as a person possessing or controlling the area. Some languages treat this relationship as 'went to the Dalmanutha district'.

11 ***The Pharisees came and began to argue with him, seeking from him a sign from heaven, to test him.***

Exegesis: *suzētein* (cf. 1 : 27) 'argue with', 'debate', 'dispute'.

zētountes par' autou sēmeion apo tou ouranou 'seeking from him a sign from heaven'.

zēteō (cf. 3 : 32) 'ask', 'request', 'want'.

sēmeion (8 : 12, 14, 13 : 4, 22, 16 : 17, 20) 'sign', i.e. 'an outward (visible) indication of secret power or truth' (Souter): in this context the 'sign' would be a wonder or miracle clearly of divine origin (*apo tou ouranou* 'from heaven').

peirazontes auton 'testing him', 'putting him to the test': the participle may be understood as indicating purpose (Manson, RSV, Weymouth, Synodale, Zürich), or attempt, '*trying to* test him' (cf. Taylor).

peirazō (cf. 1 : 13) 'test', 'try': here, as in 1 : 13, with a bad intent, and so 'tempt'.

Translation: *Argue* may be 'to exchange words' or 'to speak against what he was saying'.

Seeking from him a sign from heaven may be 'ask him to show them a sign from heaven' or 'wanted him to produce a sign from heaven'.

Though *sign* is used in the sense of 'miracle' or 'mighty work', one should, if at all possible, try to reproduce the essential significance of the Greek term *sēmeion* which points to the meaningful character of an event or object (note the use of the root *sēm-* in the derivatives *semantics* and *semiology*). This then was to be more than a miracle; rather, it was to be a demonstration of power which would have special meaning for the people—in this instance his immediate opponents, the Pharisees. In order to convey this meaning various devices have been used, e.g. 'a thing which shows' (Cuicatec), 'supernatural power which shows', in which 'shows' does not mean 'is visible', but 'that which shows something else' (Navajo), 'events which tell people something' (Uduk), 'happenings which point out' (Zacapoastla Aztec), 'miracles which are to prove', (or 'to demonstrate') (Tarascan), 'how one is going to know' (Shipibo).

From heaven is not always easily related to the preceding expression. If this clause has reference to a portent which shows from heaven (or the sky), that is one thing (and not very difficult to translate), but if the meaning is primarily a demonstration of divine power, then one may be required to say 'wanted him to do a great work with power from heaven' or 'asked him to show that his power was from heaven'.

Test must not be translated in the sense of 'tempt', with the connotation of 'try to make sin'. The meaning is more 'so they could really test him' or 'so they could put him to the test'.

12 And he sighed deeply in his spirit, and said, "Why does this generation seek for a sign? Truly, I say to you, no sign shall be given to this generation."

Exegesis: *anastenaxas tō pneumati autou* 'sighing deeply in his spirit', 'groaning inwardly'.

anastenazō (only here in the N.T.; cf. *stenazō* 7:34) 'sigh deeply', 'groan'.

tō pneumati autou (cf. 2:8) 'in his spirit', 'in himself': Arndt & Gingrich 'to himself'.

ti 'why?': so most translations and commentators. Black (*Aramaic*, 89) takes it to mean 'how?'

genea (8:38, 9:19, 13:30) 'race', 'kind', 'generation': here used of the contemporaries of Jesus.

ei dothēsetai...sēmeion 'if a sign shall be given': a Hebraism indicating strong denial, 'no sign shall be given'. As Arndt & Gingrich *ei* IV, point out, an unexpressed wish, or oath, is implied: 'may this or that happen to me if...' (cf. Moule *Idiom Book*, 179; Burton *Moods and Tenses*, § 272). Only here and in the quotation from Ps. 95:11 in Heb. 3:11, 4:3,5 does this idiom appear in the N.T.

Translation: *Spirit* must not be translated in such a way as to imply (1) the Holy Spirit, (2) the spirit which lives on after death, or (3) a familiar spirit, or demon. (This last meaning has been unfortunately entirely too frequent in translations.) In many languages one can use 'heart', 'liver', 'stomach', or some other emotional center of the personality.

Sighed in his spirit in Huave is 'to let out the air from his heart'. In Zoque the opposite action forms the basis of the figure, 'he drew a breath in his heart'.

This generation is 'the people now' (Chol) or 'those who are in space now' (Tzeltal). In some instances it must be made clear that the Pharisees who posed the question are included in this group, e.g. 'you people now living'.

Truly is often translated with one of two different syntactic relations (1) 'I tell you the truth; no sign shall be...' or (2) 'I tell you, Certainly no sign shall be...' That is to say, the adverb is related to the verb of speaking, as an assertion of the truth of the utterance, or combined with the object of the verb of speaking, namely as a statement about the certainty of the event described. The ultimate results are practically the same, though the receptor languages in question may require one or the other syntactic relationship.

251

13 *And he left them, and getting into the boat again he departed to the other side.*

Exegesis: *apheis* (cf. 2 : 5) 'leaving', 'abandoning'.

embas (cf. 4 : 1) 'entering', 'getting in': although *eis to ploion* 'into the boat' does not belong to the text, the meaning of the verb *embainō* is clear enough—'embarking'.

eis to peran (cf. 4 : 35) 'to the other side (of the Lake)': presumably to the east side of the Lake of Galilee.

Translation: In this instance *left them* should imply a degree of rejection or unfavorable attitude, e.g. 'left them there' or 'went off from them': cf. Bare'e 'He walked away from them'. It must be made clear, however, that the 'them' refers to the Pharisees, and not to the disciples.

For problems involved in translating *to the other side* see 4 : 35.

14 *Now they had forgotten to bring bread; and they had only one loaf with them in the boat.*

Exegesis: *epelathonto* (only here in Mark; cf. *lanthanō* 7 : 24) 'they forgot': the context requires that this aorist be understood as a past perfect, i.e. 'they *had forgotten* (when they set out on the crossing)'—cf. Field *Notes*, 11; Moule *Idiom Book*, 16; Burton *Moods and Tenses*, §§ 48,53.

kai ei mē hena arton ouch eichon meth' heautōn en tō ploiō literally 'and except for one loaf they didn't have (anything) with them in the boat'.

Translation: It is frequently necessary to translate *they* by 'disciples' since the immediately preceding 'they 'must refer to the Pharisees who were left standing there by Jesus.

Had forgotten usually presents no special difficulties, for the concept of forgetting is common enough in all languages. However, some of the idioms used are of interest, e.g. 'to lose from the heart' (Tzeltal), 'to lose from the liver' (Miskito), and 'his insides died' (Kabba-Laka).

A literal translation may imply a contradiction. This is treated in some instances as 'forgotten to bring enough bread; they had only one loaf' or 'they had forgotten to bring bread, except for the one loaf which they had with them in the boat'. However, any minor discrepancy in wording is immediately evident in the following clause, which does not essentially contradict the preceding. The meaning is that they had not procured bread especially for the trip, but they happened to have a loaf with them in the boat.

15 *And he cautioned them, saying, "Take heed, beware of the leaven of the Pharisees and the leaven of Herod."*

Exegesis: *diestelleto* (cf. 5 : 43) 'he ordered', 'he commanded': it would be better literally to translate this verb 'he gave orders' or (in a weakened sense) 'he instructed', 'he enjoined' (BFBS, Zürich; Lagrange; cf. Moulton

& Milligan), than to translate 'he warned' (Goodspeed, Manson, Brazilian), 'he cautioned' (Moffatt, RSV).

horate, blepete apo tēs zumēs 'beware, watch out for the leaven...'
horate (cf. 1:44) 'beware!', 'look out!', 'careful!'
blepō 'look', 'see': in the imperative, 'pay attention!' 'look out!', the verb is used in 4:24, 13:5,9,23,33; with the preposition *apo* 'from' following, 'watch out for!', in 8:15, 12:38.
zumē (only here in Mark; cf. the parallels in Mt. 16:6, 11, 12, Lk. 12:1) 'leaven': used in a figurative sense in these passages in the Gospels and also in 1 Co. 5:6,7,8, and Gal. 5:9, in a bad sense. In general it refers to attitudes (cf. Arndt & Gingrich, 2), teachings, example. Lagrange: "a principle of moral corruption that contaminates all it touches." Gould defines the leaven of the Pharisees as being their blindness to spiritual things, and the leaven of Herod as being his worldliness. Herod is Herod Antipas, referred to in 6:14ff.

Translation: *He* must be changed to 'Jesus' in some languages.

The phrase *take heed, beware*, or as one may also translate in English "beware, watch out for", involves a number of subtle problems: (1) the two related verbs, both implying caution and concern, (2) the need of paying attention only in order to avoid, and (3) the possibility of having the two verbs cancel each other out. In one translation this phrase meant 'beware! take care of...' (in the sense of 'provide what is necessary on behalf of'). The meaning here must sometimes be split between two verbs (as in the RSV), in which the first verb admonishes the disciples to pay attention and the second insists that they they avoid the object in question. From our standpoint, this seems somewhat preferable to the Greek order, which first cautions and then orders one to look out for. The meaning can be conveyed as 'beware, don't become involved with...'

Leaven of the Pharisees and the leaven of Herod are obviously and purposely obscure phrases, designed evidently by Jesus to stimulate his disciples to consider the real implications of the feeding of the multitudes. Accordingly, one must use the word 'yeast' (or 'leaven'), even though within the immediate phrase the meaning is not fully evident.

Leaven is variously rendered, depending upon a number of local cultural factors, e.g. 'that which causes bread to be sour' (Zacapoastla Aztec), 'sour-water' (Maya), 'that which causes bread to swell' (Shipibo), or 'that which causes bread to rise'. In some instances it is the same term as for 'beer foam', for that is precisely what is used by the people in the preparation of bread.

16 *And they discussed it with one another, saying, "We have no bread."*

Text: Instead of *echousin* 'they have' of the majority of modern editions of the Greek text, *Textus Receptus*, Tischendorf, Souter, Kilpatrick and RSV have *echomen* 'we have'.

8:16-18

Exegesis: *dielogizonto* (cf. 2:6) 'they were pondering', 'they were discussing'.

hoti 'that': if *echousin* 'they have' is read (see *Text*, above), *hoti* introduces indirect discourse and may be translated (1) 'that', as is the usual case with indirect discourse; (2) '(it is) because' is preferred by Gould; BFBS takes *hoti* as the equivalent of *ti* 'why?' (cf. Turner *Journal of Theological Studies* 27.59, 1926-7).

echomen 'we have' is adopted by ASV, Moffatt, RSV: in this case *hoti* is not translated, since it introduces direct discourse.

Translation: *It* may here need to be identified as 'what he said'.

17 And being aware of it, Jesus said to them, "Why do you discuss the fact that you have no bread? Do you not yet perceive or understand? Are your hearts hardened?

Text: Before *pepōrōmenēn* 'hardened' *Textus Receptus*, Tischendorf, and Kilpatrick add *eti* 'still', 'yet', which is omitted by the majority of modern editions of the Greek text.

Exegesis: *gnous* 'knowing': better translated '*becoming* aware' than 'being aware'.

hoti 'that' (or BFBS 'why': see previous verse).

oupō noeite oude suniete; 'do you not yet perceive or understand?': for similar questions cf. 7:18.

noeō (cf. 7:18) 'perceive', 'understand', 'apprehend'.

suniēmi (cf. 4:12) 'understand', 'comprehend'.

pepōrōmenēn echete tēn kardian humōn: 'do you have your heart hardened?' i.e. 'is your understanding dull?'. Cf. BFBS 'are you...insensible in mind?' For the meaning of this figure cf. 3:5, 6:52.

Translation: *It* does not have the same referent as in 8:16, where it refers to what Jesus has said. In this verse 17, the third person neuter pronoun *it* refers to what the disciples had just said, and accordingly, one may render this as 'when Jesus became aware of what they were saying' or 'Jesus was aware of what they were saying, and he said to them' (or 'he asked them').

Discuss the fact that may be shifted to the direct form, 'Why do you say, We don't have bread?' or 'Why do you say, It's because we don't have bread?'

Perceive and understand involve two successive steps in understanding, the first involving perception and the second judgment, e.g. 'see and realize', 'perceive and judge', or 'recognize and understand'.

For the figure of speech involving 'hard hearts', see 3:5 and 6:52.

18 Having eyes do you not see, and having ears do you not hear? And do you not remember?

Punctuation: The last three words of v. 18 *kai ou mnēmoneuete* 'and do you not remember' are joined directly to v. 19 (instead of being punctuated as a separate question, as done by RSV) by the Greek texts of Tischendorf, Westcott and Hort, Nestle, Merk, Taylor, and Lagrange; by the Vulgate; and by the following modern translations: Goodspeed, Moffatt, Berkeley, Williams, Zürich, Brazilian.

Exegesis: The first part of the verse reflects such O.T. passages as Jer. 5:21, Ezek. 12:2; there is probably a backward glance at 4:12 where Isa. 6:9,10 is quoted as applying to those "outside," as if to suggest that the verdict there pronounced on them is here being applied to the disciples who, apparently, could not see and could not hear. 'You have eyes, have you not? Can you not see? You have ears, have you not? Can you not hear?'

ophthalmous (8:25, 9:47, 12:11, 14:40) 'eyes'.

ōta (cf. 4:9) 'ears'.

echontes 'having': the participle is concessive, '*though you have* eyes... *though you have* ears...'

mnēmoneuete (only here in Mark) 'you remember', 'recall', 'recollect'.

Translation: *Having eyes do you not see, and having ears do you not hear* may be adapted in some languages to a positive-negative contrast, e.g. 'you have eyes, but do you not see; you have ears, but do you not hear?' The answer to the question implies a 'yes', but it is contextually conditioned in a rather subtle way, implying that they should, but they actually do not.

The separation of the last clause from the following verse 19, may result in a simpler syntactic arrangement, but the relationship seems considerably less meaningful.

19 When I broke the five loaves for the five thousand, how many baskets full of broken pieces did you take up?" They said to him, "Twelve."

Exegesis: This question refers to the first feeding of the multitude, narrated in 6:41-44.

eklasa (cf. 8:6; in 6:41 *kataklaō*) 'I broke'.

kophinous klasmatōn plēreis 'baskets full of pieces'.

kophinos (cf. 6:43) 'basket'.

klasma (cf. 6:43) 'piece', 'broken piece'.

plērēs (cf. 4:28; in 6:43 the genuine text is *plērōmata*) 'full'.

Translation: If the first two clauses of verse 19 are taken as the object of the verb 'remember', it may be necessary to change the order in order to place the principal clause first, e.g. 'do you not remember how many baskets full of broken pieces you took up when I broke the five loaves for the five thousand?'

Terms for *broke, loaves, baskets,* and *take up* should agree with those used in the previous context, 6:41-43.

Five thousand may need to be translated as 'five thousand men', since many languages require such an element with numerals. Similarly, *twelve* may require expansion to 'twelve baskets' or 'we took up twelve baskets'.

20 *"And the seven for the four thousand, how many baskets full of broken pieces did you take up?" And they said to him, "Seven."*

Exegesis: This question refers to the second feeding of the multitude, narrated in 8:6-9.

hote tous hepta literally 'when the seven': as the previous verse shows, this is the concise way of saying, 'When *I broke* the seven loaves...'

poson spuridōn plērōmata klasmatōn ērate; 'how many baskets full of broken pieces did you take up?' The meaning of the question is perfectly obvious but the details of the grammatical relations of the words in Greek should not be overlooked. The verb *ērate* 'you took up' has for its direct object *poson spuridōn plērōmata* literally 'the fillings of how many baskets', 'how many basketfuls' (cf. 6:43 for identical construction, and for the meaning of *plērōma* 'filling', 'complement'); *klasmatōn* 'of broken pieces' is another genitive which indicates the nature of 'basketfuls', i.e. 'basketfuls of broken pieces'.

spuris (cf. 8:9) 'basket'.

Translation: The key words in this verse should be related to those terms employed in 8:6-9.

The seven for the four thousand is a highly elliptical expression, quite regularly employed in many languages, but impossible in others. The expansion may require 'when seven loaves were given to be eaten by the four thousand people' (Subanen), or 'when I broke the seven loaves for the four thousand people', in order to preserve more parallelism with the preceding verse.

Said to him may be 'answered him'.

Seven may require expansion to 'seven baskets' or 'we took up seven baskets'.

21 *And he said to them, "Do you not yet understand?"*

Exegesis: *suniete* (cf. 4:12) 'you understand'.

Translation: The same expression for *understand* should be used here as in verse 17. Otherwise the force of the statement is largely lost.

22 *And they came to Bethsaida. And some people brought to him a blind man, and begged him to touch him.*

Exegesis: *kai erchontai eis Bethsaidan* 'and they come to Bethsaida': this is presumably the same Bethsaida referred to in 6:45.

kai pherousin autō tuphlon 'and they bring a blind man to him': another example of the impersonal plural: '*people* brought...', '*men* brought...'

pherō (cf. 1 : 32) 'bring'.

tuphlos (8 : 23, 10 : 46, 49, 51) an adjective, 'blind', used as a noun: 'a blind man'.

The other words have already been dealt with: *parakaleō* (1 : 40) 'beg', 'plead'; *hina* (5 : 10, 18) 'that', indicating content, not purpose; *haptomai* (1 : 41) 'touch'.

Translation: *They* must be so translated as to refer to Jesus and the disciples. *Him* may require translation by the word 'Jesus' if the reference is to be clear in some languages.

Bring may require a very special type of corresponding form, e.g. 'led', 'directed', or 'showed the way'.

Note that the people are the ones who request Jesus to touch the blind man. *Touch* in this case would probably be either with the finger or the hand. In Mazatec the reference must be quite specific, e.g. 'And Jesus and the disciples arrived at the village of Bethsaida. The people brought to him a man who was blind. They asked Jesus to touch that person'. The problems in Mazatec are especially acute because of a lack of grammatical distinctions in number and gender.

23 *And he took the blind man by the hand, and led him out of the village; and when he had spit on his eyes and laid his hands upon him, he asked him, "Do you see anything?"*

Exegesis: *epilabomenos* (only here in Mark) 'taking hold of', 'grasping': like the verb *krateō* 'grasp', 'seize' (cf. 1 : 31) this verb takes the object in the genitive case *tēs cheiros tou tuphlou* 'the hand of the blind man'.

exēnegken (only here in Mark) 'he took out', 'he led out'.

ommata (only here in Mark) 'eyes': this word is commonly found in poetry (cf. Moulton & Milligan). Cf. 8 : 18 for *ophthalmoi* 'eyes'.

ei ti blepeis: '(if) you see anything?': *ei* 'if' is used as an interrogative particle with direct questions, such as this one. Cf. Arndt & Gingrich V.1; cf. Acts 1 : 6, 7 : 1.

The other words have already been dealt with: *exō* (3 : 31) 'outside of'; *kōmē* (6 : 6) 'village'; *ptuō* (7 : 33) 'spit'; *epitithenai tas cheiras* (5 : 23) 'to lay hands upon'; *eperōtaō* (5 : 9) 'ask', 'inquire'.

Translation: *Out of* may be 'away from' in some languages, since one may go 'out of a house', but only 'away from a village'.

Spit on his eyes may also be rendered 'spit into his eyes' (cf. the Greek preposition *eis* 'into' or 'on'). In some languages one must specify whether the eyelids are closed or not, since different words exist for the eyes closed and open.

Laid his hands upon him may not be sufficiently specific in reference in some languages, since the place on the body where Jesus touched the man is required. In some instances, one may speak of placing the hands on the 'head' or 'face', but it may be best to introduce 'eyes' (compare verse 25), 'again he laid his hands upon his eyes'; cf. South Toradja 'put His hands on his eyes'.

24 *And he looked up and said, "I see men; but they look like trees, walking."*

Exegesis: *anablepsas* (cf. 6 : 41) 'looking up' or, 'recovering sight': either of these meanings is possible. The former is favored by Thayer, Abbott-Smith, Arndt & Gingrich; ASV, RSV, Goodspeed, Weymouth, Williams, Zürich, Taylor; the latter is preferred by Moffatt, Manson, BFBS, Lagrange, Brazilian.

blepō tous anthrōpous hoti hōs dendra horō peripatountas literally 'I see men, for I see (them) walking around like trees'. As the Greek text stands the statement is none too logical: clearly the meaning of the blind man's answer is, 'I see men, because even though the things I perceive look like trees, they are walking around', i.e. the fact that they were in motion told him they were men, not trees. The meaning will be more clearly brought out by a free paraphrase than by a word-for-word translation. Cf. Manson (and Williams) 'I see men: they look to me like trees walking about'; Lagrange *Je vois les hommes, car j'aperçois comme des arbres qui marchent.* Cf. Vincent *Word Studies* I, 206. Black (*Aramaic*, 36f.) conjectures that the underlying Aramaic emphatic form of statement meant 'I see men like trees walking', and the Vulgate and Syriac versions translate a text identical with this, 'I see men like trees that are walking' (omitting the *hoti* 'because' and *horō* 'I perceive' of the critical Greek text).

dendron (only here in Mark) 'tree'.

peripateō (cf. 2 : 9) 'walk', 'walk about'.

Translation: *Looked up* must not be taken in the sense of 'looking up to heaven' or 'looking up at the sky'. Either the man's head was lowered and he looked up, or as is equally possible the Greek verb may mean 'regained his sight' (see above). 'Looking up' should not be, however, any higher than horizontal (in some translations the misunderstanding which follows, in which men are said to look like trees, has been attributed by the readers to the fact that the man looked up toward the sky, and, of course, all he could see would be trees).

Unless one is quite careful the difficult reply of the man is made more complicated by an awkward grammatical arrangement. For example, a number of renderings have meant 'I see men walk like trees'. Of course, trees do not walk, and the meaning of the passage is completely lost. Renderings which have attempted to convey the meaning of the original while remaining as close to the Greek as the receptor languages in question will allow, include 'see men that are walking, they are like trees' (Tzeltal), 'see men like trees, they are walking' (Zoque), 'I see men like they are trees; I see them as they are walking' (Trique).

25 *Then again he laid his hands upon his eyes; and he looked intently and was restored, and saw everything clearly.*

Text: Instead of *dieblepsen* 'he looked intently' of all modern editions of the Greek text, *Textus Receptus* has *epoiēsen auton anablepsai* 'he made him see again'.

Instead of the neuter plural *hapanta* 'all things' of all modern editions of the Greek text, *Textus Receptus* has the masculine plural *hapantas* 'all men'.

Exegesis: For *epethēken tas cheiras* 'he laid his hands upon' cf. 5:23; for *ophthalmous* 'eyes' cf. 8:18.

kai dieblepsen kai apekateste 'and he looked intently and was restored', 'and he saw clearly and was restored'.

diablepō (only here in Mark) 'look intently' (RSV, Arndt & Gingrich) or 'see clearly', 'see properly' (BFBS, Abbott-Smith, Lagrange); others translate the word here 'look hard', 'look steadily', 'stare straight ahead'.

apokathistamai (cf. 3:5) 'be restored', 'be made sound'.

kai eneblepen tēlaugōs hapanta 'and he saw everything clearly'.

emblepō (10:21, 27, 14:67) 'see'.

tēlaugōs (only here in the N.T.) 'plainly', 'clearly'; Moulton & Milligan define it 'clearly from afar' (cf. Taylor, BFBS).

Translation: In many languages, the first occurrence of *he* must be rendered as 'Jesus', since the immediately preceding third person singular subject is the blind man. However, the second *he* must be changed to 'the man', for this marks a change in subject. Of course, the reader can, with some care, determine these shifts from the context, but if in the receptor language it would be normal to mark such changes overtly, they should be so treated in the translation. This procedure is nothing more nor less than having the translation conform to the syntactic requirements of the language into which one is translating.

Restored may be 'regained his sight', 'his eyes were healed', or 'finally he could see'.

Saw everything clearly is rendered in Tzeltal as 'everything far off appeared clear', a normal way of talking about complete vision; cf. South Toradja 'he gained certainty concerning everything when he saw it'.

26 And he sent him away to his home, saying, "Do not even enter the village."

Text: Instead of *mēde eis tēn kōmēn eiselthēs* 'do not even enter the village' of the great majority of modern editions of the Greek text, Taylor and Kilpatrick have *mēdeni eipēs eis tēn kōmēn* 'do not tell anyone in the village'.

At the end of the verse *Textus Receptus* adds *mēde eipēs tini en tē kōmē* 'nor tell (it) to anyone in the village', which is omitted by all modern editions of the Greek text; cf. Taylor and Kilpatrick, however, above.

Exegesis: The words in this verse have already been dealt with: *apostellō* (1:2) 'send', 'send away'; *eis oikon autou* (8:3) 'to his home', 'home'; *kōmē* (6:6) 'village'.

The 'village' is Bethsaida (v. 23): the man did not live in the village, however (v. 22).

Translation: *He sent him away* must be rendered in some instances as 'Jesus sent the man away', since there is again a shift of subjects from the preceding clause.

Sent him away must not contain the connotation of rejection. An equivalent may be 'told him, Go to your home and do not go right back into the village'.

Do not even enter the village must not be translated by a verb form which would imply a permanent prohibition of such an action. What Jesus evidently wished to avoid was the man's immediate return to the waiting crowd.

Negative commands, such as contained in the expression occurring in the *Textus Receptus* and the Kilpatrick text, may contain several negatives, depending of course upon the grammatical constructions of the receptor language in question. The following rendering in Zoque is not unusual, 'nor do not say nothing to nobody', in which the negatives reinforce, rather than cancel out, each other.

27 *And Jesus went on with his disciples, to the villages of Caesarea Philippi; and on the way he asked his disciples, "Who do men say that I am?"*

Exegesis: *eis tas kōmas Kaisareias tēs Philippou* 'to the villages of Caesarea Philippi': i.e. villages surrounding Caesarea, the most important city of the region.

en tē hodō (cf. 8: 3) 'on the way', 'as they went'.

tina me legousin hoi anthrōpoi einai literally 'whom do men say me to be', an indirect form with the infinitive of the verb, rather than the direct form, with the present indicative, *tis legousin hoi anthrōpoi hoti egō eimi* 'Who do men say that I am': it is this indirect form, with the infinitive, which determines the accusative case of 'John the Baptist' and 'Elijah' in the next verse.

Translation: *Caesarea Philippi* should be treated as a unit proper name, referring to a region, e.g. 'the region called Caesarea Philippi', rather than attempting to translate as 'the Caesarea of Philip'.

On the way may be best treated in some languages as a description of a process, e.g. 'as they were walking along' or 'while they were journeying'.

Who do men say that I am is essentially a complex expression, for the predicate complement of the verb *am* is the object of the verb *say*. In some languages such a construction is impossible, but an equivalent may be found in 'Men talk about me. What do they say?', 'When men speak about me, what do they say?', or 'When people talk about me, what person do they say I am?' (this last expression comes closest to the force of the Greek). Cf. Indonesian 'Who am I according to the saying of the people?'

28 *And they told him, "John the Baptist; and others say, Elijah; and others one of the prophets."*

Text: Instead of *eipan autō legontes hoti* 'they told him (that)' of all modern editions of the Greek text, *Textus Receptus* has *apekrithēsan* 'they answered'.

Exegesis: *hoti* (the first one) is recitative, introducing direct speech, and thus not translated.

Iōannēn ton baptistēn, kai alloi Ēlian, alloi de hoti heis tōn prophētōn 'John the Baptist, and others, Elijah, and others, One of the prophets.' Cf. 6: 14-16 for these three estimates of Jesus.

By the use of quotation marks a translation can make clear the nature of the answer given by the disciples: their own words include the whole phrase beginning with 'John the Baptist' and ending with 'prophets'. In their answer they quote three opinions about Jesus held by different people, and these three are separately included in quotation marks as quotations also.

Iōannēn...Ēlian 'John...Elijah': in the accusative case, presupposing the same grammatical construction as of the previous verse, i.e. *hoi legousin se einai Iōannēn* 'some say you are John' *kai alloi legousin se einai Ēlian* 'and others say you are Elijah'.

alloi de hoti heis tōn prophētōn 'but others, One of the prophets': here the direct form is used, and *heis* 'one' is in the nominative case (*Textus Receptus*, wrongly, has the accusative case), presupposing *alloi de legousin hoti su ei heis tōn prophētōn* 'but others say you are one of the prophets'.

hoti is recitative, introducing direct speech ('One of the prophets'), and thus not translated.

Translation: *Told* may be 'answered'.

John the Baptist must in some languages be introduced in such a way that it will not appear that this was the conclusion of the disciples, e.g. 'some men say John the Baptist...'

Baptist, since it is often translated by a verb form, must be carefully treated. In one language, for example, the wrong aspect of the verb was used and the resultant meaning was that John was still baptizing at the time of this conversation—something which was entirely contradictory to the events narrated in Mark 6. In Subanen, for example, this phrase must be 'John who was baptizing'.

Others say Elijah may require expansion, e.g. 'others say, Jesus is Elijah' or 'others say that you are Elijah', depending upon the use of direct or indirect discourse.

Others one of the prophets may likewise need some filling in of elliptical elements, e.g. 'still others say, He is one of the prophets' or 'still others say that you are one of the prophets'.

29 And he asked them, "But who do you say that I am?" Peter answered him, "You are the Christ."

Exegesis: *humeis* 'you' is emphatic: BFBS 'You, who do you say...?' (cf. Weymouth 'You yourselves...'; Manson, Zürich, Synodale, Brazilian).

apokritheis...legei (cf. 3:33) 'answering...he says': 'he answered'.

ho christos (cf. 1:1) 'the Anointed One', 'the Messiah', 'the Christ': here employed as a title, not as a proper name. Most English translations have 'the Christ' (cf. Zürich *der Christus*, Lagrange *le Christ*, Brazilian *o Cristo*); Manson and BFBS, however, 'the Messiah'.

Translation: *Who do you say that I am* is as complex as the parallel question in verse 27. In Tzeltal this may be expressed as 'Who am I, if you should say?'

In general *the Christ* is translated in a form more or less equivalent to a proper name, even though in this instance it is a title. The reasons for this are (1) any expression such as 'the anointed' often involves cultural connotations which are strange and hence difficult to explain, and (2) any such terms as 'the appointed one' or 'the chosen one' must usually be expanded to indicate by whom, e.g. 'the appointed one by God'. Accordingly, a transliterated form of *Christ* is preferred.

30 And he charged them to tell no one about him.

Exegesis: *epetimēsen...hina* (cf. 3:12) 'he commanded...that', 'he warned...that'.

Translation: In the form of direct discourse this verse may be translated as 'he commanded them, Do not tell this about me to any one'. The Greek does not mean, as is translated in some languages, 'Do not speak to anyone about me'; rather the prohibition is to refrain from disclosing this specific information about Jesus as the Christ.

31 And he began to teach them that the Son of man must suffer many things, and be rejected by the elders and the chief priests and the scribes, and be killed, and after three days rise again.

Exegesis: *dei* (9:11, 13:7,10,14, 14:31) 'it is necessary', 'it is needed': the verb denotes compulsion of some sort. What this compulsion is only the total context can indicate. A translation should not convey the idea that an impersonal fate or destiny is the determining factor, as though 'the Son of man is fated to...' Rather this is the God-appointed mission of the Son of man. Lagrange: *une nécessité, imposée d'en haut.*

ton huion tou anthrōpou (cf. 2:10) 'the Son of man'.

polla pathein (cf. 5:26) 'to suffer much' (BFBS) or 'to suffer many things' (RSV).

apodokimasthēnai (12:10) 'be rejected', 'be spurned'.

hupo tōn presbuterōn kai tōn archiereōn kai tōn grammateōn (cf. 7:3) 'by the elders and the chief priests and the scribes': the three groups which composed the Sanhedrin (cf. Lagrange).

hoi presbuteroi (cf. 7:3) 'the elders': these were laymen.

hoi archiereis (10:33, 11:18,27, 14:1,10,43,53,55, 15:1,3,10,11, 31; cf. 2:26) 'the chief priests': high priests, present and past, and members of the high-priestly families in Jerusalem.

hoi grammateis (cf. 1:22) 'the scribes', 'the interpreters of the Law'.
apoktanthēnai (cf. 3:4) 'to be killed'.
meta treis hēmeras (9:31, 10:34; cf. *dia triōn hēmerōn* 14:58; *en trisin hēmerais* 15:29) 'after three days': as Field (*Notes*, 11-13) has abundantly demonstrated *meta treis hēmeras* means 'on the third day after this one', what we should call 'the day after tomorrow', meaning exactly the same thing as *tē tritē hēmera* 'on the third day' in Matthew and Luke.
anastēnai (cf. 1:35) 'rise': here meaning 'rise again', 'rise from the dead'. With this meaning the verb *anistēmi* appears in the active voice further in 9:9, 10, 31, 10:34, 12:23, 16:9 (for *egeirō* 'rise' with this meaning in Mark—7 times—cf. 1:31).

Translation: *Teach them that...* may require adjustment to the direct form, 'teach them, The Son of man...'
For *Son of man* see 2:10, but note also that in languages in which one cannot speak of himself in the third person, it is usually necessary to add 'I', e.g. 'teach them, I who am the Son of man...' Without such an addition the only alternative for the reader is to assume that Jesus was speaking about someone other than himself.
Suffer many things may be, as in Tzeltal, 'go through much trouble'. In other languages the equivalent may be 'endure much pain' or 'hurt much'; cf. South Toradja 'feel much pain'; Indonesian 'taste much suffering'; Toba Batak 'his suffering would be great'.
In some languages there are problems resulting from the fact that the shifts from active (*suffer*) to passive (*be rejected* and *be killed*) and back again to active (*rise again*) cannot be employed within a single sentence. This may mean either changes from passives to actives, with resulting problems of shifts in subject expressions, or the splitting of this sentence into several clause units, e.g. 'he began to teach them, The Son of man must suffer much. The elders and the chief priests and the scribes will repudiate him and kill him. On the third day he will come to life again'.
The *elders* are either 'the old men' or 'the important men'. In most languages there are conventional terms for the elder statesmen—the counselors of the tribes and henchmen of the chief; so South Toradja 'those to whom one says father'.
For *priests* see 1:40. *The chief priests* are 'the important priests', 'the big priests', or 'the priests who have the power'. For *scribes* see 1:22.
Rejected may be translated as 'repudiated', 'denounced', or 'refused', depending upon the closest cultural equivalent.
Rise again cannot be translated literally in many languages, for the meaning is essentially figurative, i.e. 'to come to life again', 'to live again', or 'to arise from among the dead'.

32 And he said this plainly. And Peter took him, and began to rebuke him.

Exegesis: *parrēsia* (only here in Mark) 'freely', 'boldly', 'confidently'

(Moulton & Milligan); 'frankly', 'plainly', 'concealing nothing' (Arndt & Gingrich).

proslabomenos (only here in Mark) 'taking aside' (cf. Arndt & Gingrich 2.a).

epitiman (cf. 1 : 25) 'to reprove', 'to rebuke', 'to censure' (cf. Arndt & Gingrich 1). In this verse and the next one, this meaning seems preferable to BFBS 'check'.

Translation: *Rebuke* in this passage is not easy to translate. In some languages the term used means 'to scold', which is relatively close to the original. On the other hand, some languages require a form of direct discourse, 'he said, This should not be'. Peter was not specifically commanding Jesus to quit talking in this way, so much as condemning his thinking and planning such a course of action as would lead to this result. If this meaning can be conveyed by a rendering such as 'said to him, Don't talk this way', a relatively close equivalent of the Greek will have been found.

33 *But turning and seeing his disciples, he rebuked Peter, and said, "Get behind me, Satan! For you are not on the side of God, but of men."*

Exegesis: *epistrapheis* (cf. 4 : 12) 'turning', 'turning around' as in 5 : 30.

hupage opisō mou 'you get behind me!' is the meaning commonly assigned to the phrase here, as a rebuke, contrary to the usual meaning of *opisō* (cf. 1 : 7) to denote the honored place of the disciple, the follower, of Jesus. Morton Smith (*Tannaitic Parallels*, 30-31) conjectures the Greek should have been *hupage ex opisō mou* meaning 'cease to be my disciple!' Most commentators, however, take the phrase here to mean 'withdraw!' 'retire!' 'go away!' (cf. Arndt & Gingrich *opisō* 2.a, 'get out of my sight!'). C. H. Dodd (*Journal of Theological Studies*, NS 5.246, 1954) translates 'Go backward', i.e. withdraw, and Black (*Aramaic*, 263f.) renders 'away from me that I no longer see thee' (cf. also F. Bussby *Expository Times*, 61.159, 1950).

satana (cf. 1 : 13) 'Satan' (in the vocative case).

hoti ou phroneis ta tou theou alla ta tōn anthrōpōn 'because you are not thinking the things (thoughts) of God but the things (thoughts) of men'. The RSV paraphrase is not very satisfactory.

phroneō (only here in Mark) 'think', 'set one's mind on', 'be intent on' (Arndt & Gingrich 2): the verb refers not simply to intellectual activity but also to direction and purpose of heart (cf. Souter: "moral interest, thought, and study, and not a mere unreflecting opinion").

Translation: *Seeing his disciples* must be in some instances 'seeing his other disciples', for Peter was obviously not in this group, but at that moment at the back of Jesus. In Popoluca the equivalent is 'looking at the disciples', in the sense of facing them.

If possible it would be well to translate *rebuked* in this verse by the same verb as is used in the preceding, but in some instances this cannot be done, since the content of the direct discourse actually follows *said*. Here the context favors 'scolded'.

The literal rendering of *get behind me* has been found in a number of translations to mean 'get behind to assist me'. The possibility of this type of intepretation must of course be carefully avoided. The alternative may be 'get away from me', 'leave me', or 'get away behind me' (Ifugao).

The last clause is almost certain to produce difficulty in a literal rendering, for 'think the thoughts of God' or 'think the things of God' is likely to be relatively meaningless. In some instances one may translate as 'you are not concerned with what God wants but with what men want' or 'you are not thinking as God thinks, but as men think'.

34 *And he called to him the multitude with his disciples, and said to them, "If any man would come after me, let him deny himself and take up his cross and follow me.*

Text: Instead of *elthein* 'come' of the majority of modern editions of the Greek text, *Textus Receptus* and Soden have *akolouthein* 'follow'.

Exegesis: *proskalesamenos* (cf. 3:13) 'summoning', 'calling to himself'.

ei tis thelei 'if any one wants': this meaning is to be preferred over RSV 'if any man would' which may be understood as introducing an element of doubt or contingency not found in the Greek.

opisō mou elthein (cf. 1:20) 'come after me' *as a disciple*.

aparnēsasthō heauton 'he is to deny himself', 'he must renounce himself', 'he must give up all claims upon himself'.

aparneomai (14:30, 31, 72) 'deny': here with the idea of 'renounce', 'abjure'.

aratō ton stauron autou 'he must take up his cross', i.e. 'as a disciple of mine he must share my suffering and death'. Where in current usage among Christians the phrase 'take up one's cross' has come to mean simply to endure a petty burden or an unavoidable irritating inconvenience in daily living, some way should be found, if possible, of restoring the original shock and near brutality of the phrase. 'To take up the cross' meant *to be crucified*, to die in a most painful and shameful manner, as Jesus did.

stauros (15:21,30,32) 'cross': an instrument of punishment and death, usually an upright stake with a cross bar at the top, in the form of a T or †.

Translation: *The multitude with his disciples* is in some languages 'the crowd as well as his disciples' or simply 'the crowd and his disciples'.

Come after me must be understood in the sense of 'follow as disciples' or 'accompany me' (see 1:17).

Deny himself is without doubt one of the most difficult expressions in all of Mark to translate adequately. Unfortunately, too many people have taken this expression to mean 'to deny oneself certain pleasures or objects', while actually the meaning is a denial of one's own presumed prerogatives or personal interests. The different ways of expressing this concept in various languages are highly illuminating, e.g. 'to not accept self' (Tetelcingo Aztec), 'to forget self' (Ifugao, Bolivian Quechua), 'to have no regard for oneself' (Barrow Eskimo), 'not bother oneself about oneself' (South Toradja), 'to cover up oneself' (Mazatec), 'to not worship oneself' (Mixtec), 'to stop doing what one's own heart wants' (Tzeltal), 'to not belong to oneself any longer' (Conob), 'to let go that which he wants to do himself' (Kiyaka), 'says, I will not do just what I want to do' (Cashibo), 'to let him say, I do not serve for anything', in the sense of having no personal value (Tzotzil), 'to not do what is passing through his mind' (Putu), 'to not tåke constant thought for himself' (Mazahua), 'to quit what he himself wants' (Chontal of Tabasco), 'to undo one's own way of thinking' (Totonac), 'to put his own things down' (Gio), 'to despise himself' (Kekchi), 'to refuse himself' (Kituba), 'to turn his back on himself' (Javanese), 'to disobey himself', in the sense of denying one's own wishes (Black Bobo), 'to leave himself at the side' (Huastec), 'to leave his own way' (Trique), 'to take his mind out of himself completely' (Loma), 'to say, I do not live for myself' (Huanuco Quechua), and 'to say No to oneself' (Mitla Zapotec).

Take up is 'to lift up and to carry'. Where languages specify the manner of carrying, one may say 'on the shoulder'.

For *follow* see above, and 1 : 17.

35 *For whoever would save his life will lose it; and whoever loses his life for my sake and the gospel's will save it.*

Exegesis: The use and meaning of *psuchē* 'life', 'soul' in vv. 35-37 is a matter of dispute (cf. 3 : 4). As Lagrange points out, the word has a three-fold meaning, 'life', or 'soul', or 'oneself'. In these verses there is an interplay between natural life, life in the flesh (which is clearly the meaning in v. 35) and true life, spiritual life, future life (which is the sense demanded in vv. 36-37). The Old Testament concept of *nephesh*, which furnishes the basis for the meaning of the New Testament word *psuchē*, bears no resemblance to the Greek idea of *psuchē* 'soul' as the spiritual part of man, distinct and separate from his material make-up, his fleshly body. Rather the basic O.T. concept of *nephesh* (for which LXX *psuchē* generally stands—cf. Hatch *Essays*, 94-108) is that of 'breath', 'life', and is used of the individual (animal or man) in his quality as a breathing, living being. From this the word comes to mean the individual himself, 'person', 'oneself' (cf. Koehler). Passages which speak of killing or destroying *nephesh* mean, of course, to kill a person or persons (cf. Nu. 31 : 19, 35 : 11, 15, 30; Ezek. 13 : 19, 22 : 27; Lev. 7 : 20, 21, 25, 27, 23 : 30, etc.); while, conversely, to save *nephesh* means to save one's life, oneself (cf. Gen. 19 : 17, 32 : 31, Job 33 : 28, Ps. 72 : 13, etc.).

Most English translations (ASV, RSV, BFBS, Weymouth, Manson, Montgomery, Goodspeed, Berkeley) have 'life' in all three verses; some have 'life' in 35 and 'soul' in 36-37 (Moffatt; also Synodale, Lagrange, Brazilian); Zürich has 'life' in all three verses, but in v. 36 introduces 'future' in parentheses before 'life'. The word 'soul' should not be used if it reflects the Greek concept rather than the Hebraic; 'life' adequately represents the word: in vv. 36-37, however, it must mean more than simple physical existence, ordinarily denoted by the word ('true life' or 'real life' is the sense required); perhaps 'oneself', 'himself' or 'true self' would adequately convey the meaning in those two verses (cf. Black *Aramaic*, 76).

sōsai (cf. 3 : 4) 'save', 'preserve', 'keep'.

apolesei (cf. 1 : 24) 'he will lose'.

sōsei (cf. 3 : 4) 'he will save' in the theological sense.

Translation: *Save his life* involves more than merely 'living'. There must be some means of indicating the concern of the man for his continued existence. Otherwise, the whole expression has no special meaning. This problem is met in a number of different ways, e.g. 'he who wants to just keep on living' (Mazahua), 'he who wants to not die' (Cashibo), 'he who wants to make his life safe' (Rincon Zapotec), and 'he who wishes to always keep living' (Tzotzil).

Will lose it is equivalent to 'die', but there is something else also involved,—namely, the loss of the very thing for which he had been concerned. This meaning is suggested in the Tzeltal as follows: 'he who wants his life, all will go to loss, together with his life', implying his total life will be lost. This last phrase adds the necessary elements to make the reader understand that this is not merely existence, but life and all its values.

Loses his life is equivalent to 'dies'.

Will save it may be rendered as 'will really keep it' or 'will really live', in order to indicate that life in this instance involves some degree of qualitative distinction from life as it is used previously in the verse.

36 *For what does it profit a man, to gain the whole world and forfeit his life?*

Exegesis: *ōphelei* (cf. 5 : 26) 'does it profit', 'does it benefit'.

kerdēsai ton kosmon holon 'to gain the whole world', i.e. to acquire the sum total of earthly wealth.

kerdainō (only here in Mark) 'gain'.

kosmos (14 : 9, 16 : 15) 'world': here in the sense of material riches.

zēmiōthēnai tēn psuchēn autou 'to forfeit his life', 'to suffer loss of his life': clearly the meaning is *not* 'to die', as though physical existence were the meaning of *psuchē* 'life' in this context (cf. previous verse).

zēmioō (only here in Mark) in the passive 'suffer loss', 'forfeit', 'pay the penalty of'.

Translation: *Does it profit* may be rendered as 'what advantage is there' or 'how is it better to'.

Gain the whole world may be 'receive the whole world' (Subanen), 'to come to own the whole world' (Navajo), 'to possess everything in the whole world' (Tzotzil), and 'to gain the revenues of the whole world' (Javanese).

Forfeit his life may be 'pay a penalty consisting of his life' (Navajo), 'forfeit his heart', in the sense of life and soul (Mitla Zapotec), or 'lose his real life', in order to emphasize the use of life in the special sense of life and all its values, temporal and eternal.

37 For what can a man give in return for his life?

Exegesis: *antallagma tēs psuchēs autou* 'as an exchange for his life'.

antallagma (only here in Mark) 'purchasing price', 'exchange'. The answer to this rhetorical question is that there is nothing which a man can give to compensate for the loss of his *psuchē* '(real) life', i.e. the loss of his very self. Cf. Lagrange: "a life which is his true life, his soul, himself."

Translation: *Give in return for* is in some languages equivalent to 'pay as a price for keeping' or 'pay to get back', or 'pay in exchange for'.

Life should be translated the same in this verse as in 8:36.

38 For whoever is ashamed of me and of my words in this adulterous and sinful generation, of him will the Son of man also be ashamed, when he comes in the glory of his Father with the holy angels."

Text: Instead of *tous emous logous* 'my words' of all modern editions of the Greek text, Kilpatrick has *tous emous* (omitting *logous*) 'mine', 'my people'. For this deletion of *logous* 'words' which is based more on Marcan usage than on the manuscript evidence, cf. Manson *Teaching of Jesus*, 333f.; Dodd *Parables*, 93 n. 1; Turner *Journal of Theological Studies* 29.25, 1927-8 (of the translations, BFBS and Manson read 'of mine').

Exegesis: *epaischunthē* (only in this verse in Mark) 'he may be ashamed': the meaning is 'ashamed to own me', 'ashamed to confess me publicly', 'ashamed to acknowledge his relation to me'.

en tē genea tautē tē moichalidi kai hamartōlō 'in this adulterous and sinful generation'.

genea (cf. 8:12) 'generation'.

moichalis (only here in Mark) is a noun 'adulteress', used as an adjective, 'adulterous': in the religious sense, as used here, the word means 'irreligious', 'faithless', 'godless', 'irreverent', based on the O.T. concept of God's people being betrothed to God, in the relation of husband and wife (cf. Kennedy *Sources*, 116).

ho huios tou anthrōpou (cf. 2:10) 'the Son of man'.

hotan elthē en tē doxē tou patros autou 'when he comes in the glory of his Father'.

erchomai 'come': the word should be so translated in this passage, and not 'come back' as some translations have it.

doxa (10:37, 13:26) 'glory', 'majesty', 'brightness', 'sublimity' (of God): cf. Kennedy *Sources*, 97.

patēr 'father': used of God in Mark in 11:25-26 ('your Father in heaven'), 13:32 ('the Father') and 14:36 ('Abba, Father').

meta tōn aggelōn tōn hagiōn 'with the holy angels': this phrase is connected with the main verb 'comes': 'when he comes...with the holy angels'.

aggelos (cf. 1:2,13) 'angel'.

Translation: Certain key words have been treated previously: *glory* (2:12), *generation* (8:12), *Son of man* (2:10), *holy* (1:7), and *angels* (1:13).

Ashamed of may be rendered as 'will have nothing to do with', or 'feels shame when I and my words are mentioned' (or 'are remembered').

In this adulterous and sinful generation may require two types of modifications: (1) close relationship to the grammatical subject, e.g. 'whoever in this adulterous and sinful generation' and (2) shift from an abstract to a concrete form, e.g. 'whoever of these sinful and adulterous people living now', or 'adulterers and sinners who are now in the world' (Tzeltal).

Since *adulterous* refers to infidelity to God, this meaning has been brought out in Mixtec as 'to leave one for another against God', in which the expression 'to leave one for another' is a common expression for adultery.

The construction of the three clauses constituting this verse is not an easy one. In some languages this type of arrangement may require some slight modification, e.g. 'if any one...is ashamed..., the Son of man will be ashamed of him, when he comes...'

Compare verse 8:31 for the use of *Son of man* with a possible first person pronoun, e.g. 'I the Son of man'.

Though many instances of the verb *come* must be rendered as 'went', in this instance *comes* must usually be retained in its literal sense, since the meaning is coming from heaven to earth. In some languages, however, one must use 'return'.

In the glory may be more accurately rendered in some instances as 'with the glory', literally 'shiningness' (Tetelcingo Aztec) and 'highness' (Ifugao).

With the holy angels must be more closely connected with 'comes' in many languages, e.g. 'comes together with the holy angels'.

Note that in English the verbs are all present, but these will vary in other languages, e.g. *is ashamed* may be rendered by a tenseless form, implying 'now or ever in the future' and *comes* is generally translated as a remote future tense.

CHAPTER NINE

1 *And he said to them, "Truly, I say to you, there are some standing here who will not taste death before they see the kingdom of God come with power."*

Exegesis: *amēn* (cf. 3:28) 'truly', 'solemnly'.

hoti 'that' is recitative, introducing direct speech.

eisin tines hōde tōn hestēkotōn 'there are some of those standing here', 'some of those here present'.

hōde (cf. 8:4) 'here'.

hoi hestēkotes 'those who are standing': the verb *histēmi* 'stand' is used here in the sense of 'being' or 'existing' rather than the strictly physical sense of 'standing' (cf. Arndt & Gingrich II.2.b.α; Lagrange 'some of those present'; Brazilian 'some of those who are here').

hoitines ou mē geusōntai thanatou 'who certainly will not taste death', 'who will by no means die': the double negative is emphatic, and the statement is a forceful way of saying 'who certainly *will be alive*'.

ou mē (9:41, 10:15, 13:2,19,30, 14:25,31, 16:18) 'not': an emphatic way of making a negative statement.

geuomai (only here in Mark) 'taste': in a figurative sense, as here, 'experience', 'come to know'.

heōs an idōsin 'until they see': the meaning is *not* that they will die as soon as they see the Kingdom of God come with power; the emphasis is on the fact that *during their lifetime* they will see the Kingdom come with power.

heōs an (cf. 6:10) 'until'.

eidein 'see': the word should be translated literally, rather than in a figurative manner, e.g. 'perceive', 'become aware of', 'experience'. The aorist subjunctive should be simply rendered 'see' rather than 'have seen', as some translations have it.

tēn basileian tou theou elēluthuian en dunamei 'the Kingdom of God having come with power': the perfect passive participle *elēluthuian* 'having come' functions as an adjective (in the predicate position) which makes an additional statement concerning the Kingdom. It is not, simply, that in their lifetime they will see the Kingdom of God: it is that they will see the Kingdom *present* ('having come') in power. This 'having come', therefore, lies in the future just as much as *heōs an idōsin* 'until they see': it is said that they will see (in the future, within their lifetime) the Kingdom having arrived—which 'arrival' is also future in relation to the time of the prediction (cf., among others, W. G. Kümmel *Promise and Fulfilment*, 25-29, and references cited). A translation should attempt accurately to convey the meaning of the Greek, which is reasonably clear and precise.

(On the interpretation of the passage, see the commentaries *in loc.*).

hē basileia tou theou (cf. 1 : 15) 'the Reign of God': here spoken of as an 'event' (however interpreted), visible in its coming.

elēluthuia 'having come': regardless of the interpretation of the verse, the force of the perfect participle should be observed. In RSV 'before they see the kingdom of God come', the 'come' is ambiguous: it may mean 'having come', but may also mean 'coming'.

Translation: *Them* should refer to the same group as is identified in 8 : 34, 'the crowd as well as the disciples'.

For this use of *truly*, with double type of attribution, see 8 : 12.

Some standing here, as an expression equivalent to 'now living', may actually be translated in certain languages as 'some sitting here', for 'sitting' is in a number of languages of Africa, for example, the verb which by extension also means 'to live' or 'to exist'.

A literal translation of *taste death* has been understood in some languages to mean 'partake of a cannibalistic meal'. The meaning is, of course, 'to die', though in some languages the negative is shifted to the subject constituent rather than to the verb, e.g. 'not all those here are going to die until they see...' (Zoque). This shift is designed to avoid the tendency to interpret the 'until' clause as designating the point at which such persons are to die. In some languages, one can preserve something of the force of the idiom 'taste death' by using a parallel 'feel death' (Chontal of Tabasco), 'see death' (Navajo; cf. also South Toradja), and 'suffer death' (Zacapoastla Aztec).

In some languages the expression 'see the kingdom' is impossible, because 'kingdom' actually identifies a process of 'rule' or 'ruling' (see *kingdom*, 1 : 15 and 4 : 11). However, one can often speak of 'see God ruling', which would be the closest equivalent to *see the kingdom of God*. In other instances one may be able to translate as 'see that God has now begun to rule with power', though this is not a very close approximate.

Power is generally rendered in this context as 'great authority' (Tzeltal), or 'strength to command', rather than merely 'power' or 'might', if these terms refer primarily to physical prowess or dominance.

It must be recognized that part of the difficulty of translating this verse is the fact that scholars are so divided as to what it actually means. In all fairness to the Scriptures it is best to avoid taking any overly decisive position, or the results may do violence, either to the prediction of Jesus or to the subsequent events of history.

2 And after six days Jesus took with him Peter and James and John, and led them up a high mountain apart by themselves; and he was transfigured before them,

Exegesis: *meta hēmeras hex* (cf. *meta treis hēmeras* 8 : 31) 'after six days', 'six days later'.

paralambanei (cf. 4 : 26) 'he takes', 'he takes along', 'he takes with'.

anapherei (only here in Mark; cf. *pherō* 1 : 32, *ekpherō* 8 : 23) 'he takes up', 'he leads up'.

271

kat' idian monous 'alone by themselves'.

kat' idian (cf. 4 : 34) 'privately', 'apart', 'alone'.

monous (cf. *kata monas* 4 : 10, *autos monos* 6 : 47) 'alone', 'by themselves'.

kai metemorphōthē emprosthen autōn 'and he was transformed in their presence'.

metamorphoō (only here in Mark) 'transform', 'change in form': the context indicates that this is a change outwardly visible in its effects.

emprosthen (cf. 2 : 12) 'before', 'in the presence of'.

Translation: *Jesus took with him Peter and James and John* must be rendered in some languages as 'Peter and James and John went along with Jesus'. A verb such as 'took' may denote either 'led along' (as one does an animal or child) or 'forced to go along' (as one does a prisoner).

Led them up may be 'went ahead of them up' or 'showed them the way up', if 'led' would denote leading of a child, an animal, or a blind or crippled person.

There is no way to know just how high the mountain was on which Jesus was transfigured, but tradition has associated this with Mount Hermon (note the reference to Caesarea Philippi in 8 : 27). However, any expression denoting 'high mountain' will be entirely relative, depending upon the region of the receptor language. For example, a high mountain in some regions of Southeast Asia or the Andean region of South America will be decidedly higher than any mountain which Jesus might have climbed in Palestine. Conversely, 'high mountain' as translated into Maya (an Indian language spoken on the flat peninsula of Yucatan) or Marshallese (the language of some of the low-lying atolls of the South Pacific) will be nothing more than a rather high mound or hill—regardless of the expression used in translating. As in all terms for such geographical objects a translation can only provide a basis for supplementary explanation. It is not possible to incorporate enough data into a translation so as to reconstruct an accurate image of the event.

Apart by themselves must mean that the four were together, not that the three disciples were led off to the side—as is implied in some translations.

Transfigured is not an easy term to translate, for it designates an event which is entirely outside the experience of people. In general, however, it is sufficient to say 'was changed' or 'changed himself', but one must carefully avoid any suggestions of Jesus' becoming a kind of werewolf. In Kizanaki one may say 'changed his likeness' (i.e. 'his appearance'); in Zoque the appropriate expression is 'made himself different'. The meaning here, it should be observed, is passive, not reflexive. In Subanen one must say 'his body was changed', for otherwise the verb would imply some basic change in personality or character.

Before them may be rendered as 'in front of them' or 'there where they were'.

3 and his garments became glistening, intensely white, as no fuller on earth could bleach them.

Text: After *leuka lian* 'exceedingly white' *Textus Receptus* adds *hōs chiōn* 'as snow', which is omitted by all modern editions of the Greek text.

Exegesis: *ta himatia* (cf. 2:21) 'clothes', 'garments'.

stilbonta leuka lian 'glistening, extremely white', 'shining (and) very white'.

stilbō (only here in the N.T.) 'shine', 'be radiant'; Moulton & Milligan, 'glisten'.

leuka (16:5) 'white'; perhaps (cf. Mt. 17:2 and Lk. 9:29) 'shining', 'brilliant', 'bright'.

lian (cf. 1:35) 'very', 'exceedingly'.

hoia gnapheus epi tēs gēs ou dunatai houtōs leukanai literally 'such as a fuller on the earth is not able in this manner to bleach (them)': by means of a construction very common in the N.T., 'any fuller on earth cannot' is the equivalent of saying 'no fuller on earth can'.

hoia (13:19) is a relative pronoun of quality 'what sort of', 'such as': here neuter plural, as its antecedent is *ta himatia* 'the clothes', and in the accusative case as the object of the verb *leukanai* 'to make white'.

gnapheus (only here in the N.T.) 'bleacher', 'fuller': one who cleans woolen cloth (Arndt & Gingrich).

epi tēs gēs 'on the earth': this phrase in Mark appears with the following meanings: (1) 'on the soil' (of sowing) 4:26, 31a; (2) 'on the ground' 8:6, 9:20, 14:35; (3) 'on (the) land' (as opposed to the sea) 4:1, 6:47; (4) 'on the earth', i.e. 'in the world' 2:10, 4:31b. Although it has been suggested that the phrase here means 'on the ground' (in accordance with the way in which clothes are bleached in the East, cf. *The Bible Translator* 4.42, 1953), the overwhelming majority of commentators and translators understand the phrase here 'on the earth', that is, 'no fuller on earth'.

leukainō (only here in Mark) 'to make white', 'to bleach'.

Translation: *Became glistening* may be translated as 'began to shine' or 'became very bright'.

Some languages have two words for 'white', one designating the kind of dull white of chalk and another the brilliant white of crystals. This latter type of color would undoubtedly be the closer equivalent.

If one follows a more accurate Greek text, 'as snow' does not occur, but where it is necessary to conform to a text based on the *Textus Receptus*, the problem of rendering 'snow' naturally arises. Solutions have been quite varied, e.g. 'volcano frost' (Mixtec), in which 'frost' is a well known substance and the snow on the distant volcanoes is regarded as 'volcano frost'. Other renderings are 'frost' (Tzeltal) and 'white rain', though this is the general term for hail (Kituba). In Shipibo the more natural way of speaking would be 'white as peeled cassava' (or 'manioc'). When in a language such as Shipibo there is a traditional term or idiom widely used to express precisely this type of comparison this may be substituted, for the reaction of educated readers (who might later learn about snow as a substance quite different from cassava) would be that 'white as peeled cassava' was simply their traditional way of saying the same thing, as 'white as snow'. However, it is not wise to introduce some comparison which is not within the traditional range of expression, for this would be regarded not as another equally valid means of comparison but an incorrect association. For example, one can translate in some languages 'white as egret feathers' but if 'egret feathers' are not habitually spoken of as a standard of whiteness in this type of idiom, there is no corresponding cultural equivalence between 'white as snow' and 'white as egret feathers'. It is only if the two expressions are both well established similes and would be identified by bilingual speakers as essentially identical that one should substitute one element in a figure of speech for another.

Fuller may be simply 'washer woman' in some languages.

On earth may be 'in all the world' or 'anywhere', e.g. 'no person anywhere who washes (or 'cleans') clothes'.

Bleach is 'make them white', or as in some instances 'make them clean', since bleaching may not be known, and the 'making of clothes white' might be misleading, since it could refer to ruining the dye, rather than bleaching the cloth.

4 *And there appeared to them Elijah with Moses; and they were talking to Jesus.*

Exegesis: *ōphthē* 'was seen': this passive form (from *horaō* 'see') is commonly used with the meaning 'appeared', of beings who make their appearance in a supernatural manner (cf. Lk. 1:11, 22:43, 24:34, Acts 2:3, 7:2 etc.)—cf. Arndt & Gingrich 1.a.δ.

sullalountes (only here in Mark) 'talking with', 'conversing with'.

Translation: *Elijah with Moses* must be rendered in some languages as 'Elijah and Moses'.

The transliteration of Old Testament proper names should correspond to the form which they have (or will have) in any Old Testament translation.

If a direct form of expression is required, *appeared to them* may be rendered either 'came into their view' or 'they saw'.

In some languages (e.g. Zapotec) special grammatical forms are required in speaking of persons who have died. Accordingly, Elijah and Moses must be so designated, regardless of the account of Elijah's miraculous ascent to heaven. In other languages all such patriarchs must be addressed or spoken of with honorific language.

5 *And Peter said to Jesus, "Master, it is well that we are here; let us make three booths, one for you and one for Moses and one for Elijah."*

Exegesis: *apokritheis...legei* (cf. 3:33) 'answering...says', 'he answered'.

rabbi (11:21, 14:45) 'Rabbi', 'Teacher': cf. *rabbouni* 'Rabbi' 10:51 (cf. *didaskale* 'Teacher' 4:38).

kalon estin (cf. 4:8) 'it is good', 'fitting', 'advantageous'.

hōde (cf. 8:4) 'here'.

poiēsōmen treis skēnas 'let us make three booths': we are to understand by 'us' the three disciples, not Peter and Jesus.

skēnē (only here in Mark) 'tent', 'booth': a temporary construction like those built during the celebration of the Feast of Tabernacles (or, Booths).

Translation: The Greek term *apokritheis*, often translated 'answered', may also designate the action of a person who breaks into a conversation or who introduces something new into the discourse—this is its use here, for Peter had not been asked any questions.

Master is probably better taken in the sense of 'teacher' or 'my teacher' (in languages which may demand a possessive in such a construction). However, if there is a title of respect which also designates one's 'boss', 'leader', and/or 'respected guide', this can certainly be used, for the term *rabbi* implied more than merely 'teacher'.

For languages employing contrasts between inclusive and exclusive first person plurals, this verse presents certain complications. When Peter says to Jesus 'It is well that we are here' does he mean that it is good (1) that all six persons are present (or that at least the disciples and Jesus are there) or (2) that the three disciples are on hand to make some shelters for the three important personages: Jesus, Elijah, and Moses. In other words, is Peter describing the blessedness of the experience for all those present or only saying that it is fortunate that the three disciples are present to help provide shelter. The first alternative has been preferred by many, and accordingly the inclusive first person plural should be used. However, in the next clause *let us make three booths* can scarcely be taken as 'inclusive', for it would seem out of place for Peter to be asking Jesus to assist in the preparation of the three shelters. In this instance the exclusive first person plural is no doubt better.

The *booths* are 'leaf shades' (Shipibo), 'lean-tos' or 'thatch shelters'. What is implied is a very temporary type of construction designed primarily to protect one from the sun or rain. Some translators have resorted to borrowings at this point, e.g. *pabellón*, borrowed from Spanish, but more often than not such borrowings have had wrong denotations. For example, in the case of several Indian languages in Latin America the Spanish word *pabellón* meant only a 'mosquito net'.

6 *For he did not know what to say, for they were exceedingly afraid.*

Exegesis: *ou gar ēdei ti apokrithē* 'for he did not know what he should answer' (or 'say') (for this grammatical construction cf. *ti phagōsin* 'what they should eat' 6:36; *ti aiteisthe* 'what you are asking for' 10:38; *ouk ēdeisan ti apokrithōsin autō* 'they did not know what they should answer him' 14:40).

ekphoboi gar egenonto 'for they became terrified', or 'for they had become terrified' (rather than 'were').

ekphobos (only here in Mark) 'terrified', 'very afraid'.

Translation: The syntactic problems of this verse are complex because of the two uses of *for*. The first introduces the reason for the preceding action, namely, Peter's remark, and the second indicates why Peter did not know what to say. In some languages this distinction may be indicated only by expanding the first causal conjunction, e.g. 'the reason he said this was that he really didn't know what to say, for they...' In Navajo the sequence of clauses is shifted 'since they were exceedingly afraid, he did not know what to say'.

They must be translated in such a way as to refer to the disciples, not to the entire group nor to the immediately preceding third person plural pronoun, *they* in verse 4, which refers to Elijah and Moses.

7 *And a cloud overshadowed them, and a voice came out of the cloud, "This is my beloved Son; listen to him."*

Exegesis: *egeneto nephelē episkiazousa* 'there came a cloud, overshadowing', 'there appeared a cloud, covering': it is generally agreed that *egeneto* 'came', 'appeared' here has an independent force of its own and does not function as an auxiliary to *episkiazō* 'overshadow' (as RSV translates it): cf. ASV, Weymouth, Moffatt, Goodspeed, Manson, BFBS, Synodale, Zürich; Black *Aramaic*, 94.

nephelē (13:36, 14:62) 'cloud'.

episkiazō (only here in Mark) 'overshadow' (from *skia* 'shadow'), 'cover' (cf. Arndt & Gingrich, 2).

houtos estin ho huios mou ho agapētos 'this is my Son, the Beloved': cf. the Voice from Heaven at the baptism of Jesus, 1:11. Notice that at the baptism the Voice addresses itself to Jesus; here, to the disciples.

Translation: *Overshadowed* may be rendered as 'passed over them', 'came between them and the sun' or 'covered up the sun for them'.

As noted in Mark 1:3 in some languages one cannot speak of a 'voice speaking', much less one 'coming out of a cloud', as in this verse. People may speak, but not 'voices come'. In Tarahumara, for example, the only way to translate this passage is to say 'God spoke out of the cloud'. Some translators have tried to make the reference less specific by rendering the passage as 'they heard someone speaking in the cloud', but this suggested a person, not God. In certain instances, however, it is possible to say 'they heard words coming from somewhere in the cloud' (cf. Indonesian and Javanese 'and a voice out of the cloud was heard'), a rendering which conserves something of the indefinite form of the original.

For *my beloved Son* see 1:11. In Navajo this phrase becomes 'this is the Son I love', but it is nonrestrictive. That is to say, this passage must not be translated in such a way as to suggest that Jesus is the Son God loves, while other sons he does not love. The correct meaning may be conveyed in some languages by translating 'this is my Son; I love him'.

8 *And suddenly looking around they no longer saw any one with them but Jesus only.*

Text: Instead of *ei mē* 'except' of Westcott and Hort, Souter, Nestle,

Lagrange, and Taylor, *alla* 'but' is read by *Textus Receptus*, Tischendorf, Soden, Vogels, Kilpatrick, and Merk.

Instead of *ei mē* (or *alla*) *ton Iēsoun monon meth' heautōn* 'except (or, but) Jesus alone with them' of Nestle, Souter, *Textus Receptus*, Tischendorf, Soden, Vogels, and Merk, the order of words is changed to *meth' heautōn ei mē ton Iēsoun monon* 'with them except Jesus alone' in Westcott and Hort, Lagrange, Taylor (cf. Kilpatrick).

Exegesis: *exapina* (only here in the N.T.) 'suddenly', 'unexpectedly', 'abruptly'.

periblepsamenoi (cf. 3:5) 'looking around'.

monon 'only', 'alone': an adjective, modifying *Iēsoun* 'Jesus' (cf. Arndt & Gingrich 1.a.γ), not an adverb modifying *eidon* 'they saw'.

Translation: *They* must be translated to refer to the disciples.

In some languages, the dependent participial construction *suddenly looking around* must be made into an independent or at least coordinate phrase, for it is obviously a more important aspect of the process than the negative statement which follows. Accordingly, one may translate 'they suddenly looked around and could no longer see any one...'

But Jesus only may be translated as 'no one except Jesus; there was no one else'.

9 ***And as they were coming down the mountain, he charged them to tell no one what they had seen, until the Son of man should have risen from the dead.***

Exegesis: *katabainontōn autōn* 'while they were coming down' (cf. *embainontos autou* 'as he was entering' 5:18).

For *katabainō* 'come down' cf. 1:10; *diastellō...hina* 'command... that' cf. 5:43; *diēgeomai* 'narrate', 'relate' cf. 5:16; *ek nekrōn* 'from the dead' cf. 6:14; *anistēmi* 'rise' cf. 8:31.

ei mē hotan 'except when': in this context the meaning is 'until after'. As Arndt & Gingrich *hotan* 1.b. point out, in such a construction as this the action of the subordinate clause (in this case *anastē* 'should rise') precedes that of the verb of the main clause (here *diēgēsōntai* 'they should say'): therefore, not until *after* the Son of man should rise from the dead were they to narrate what they had seen on the mountain.

ei mē 'except': introduces a condition, or exception, to a statement or command (cf. Arndt & Gingrich *ei* VI.8.a; Burton *Moods and Tenses*, § 471).

hotan (cf. 2:20) 'when'. For a similar construction cf. 12:25 *hotan gar ek nekrōn anastōsin* 'for when they rise from the dead'.

Translation: The pronominal referents of *they*, *them* and *they* must be made clear. The first *they* refers to Jesus and the disciples, while the following *them* and *they* denote the disciples. In many languages it is not necessary to be so careful about pronominal reference, as would seem to be implied in this and other notes with regard to pronouns, since the context seems to "sort out" the referents adequately. However, in some languages one may be completely misled by inexact pronominal elements, since the language requires very specific identification in any potentially ambiguous situation.

Charged them to tell must be shifted into direct discourse in many languages, e.g. 'commanded them, Do not tell anyone...'

Some languages do not have a syntactic construction corresponding closely to the negative exception implied in the relationship *no one... until.* This can only be rendered by a paraphrastic construction, e.g. 'he commanded them not to tell anyone what they had seen, but he said they could tell when he, the Son of man, had risen from the dead' (Kekchi).

Rise from the dead is in Greek literally 'arise from among the dead'. A literal rendering is not always possible, for it might very well imply (as it has in some translations), 'to stand up in the cemetery'. The idea is of course 'come back to life', 'live again after being dead', or 'to regain life'.

10 *So they kept the matter to themselves, questioning what the rising from the dead meant.*

Text: Instead of *to ek nekrōn anastēnai* 'the rising from the dead' of all other editions of the Greek text, Lagrange and Taylor, based on the evidence mainly of some Western mss. and some of the early versions, prefer *hotan ek nekrōn anastē* 'when he should rise from the dead'.

Exegesis: *ton logon ekratēsan* 'they kept the word', i.e. 'they obeyed the command', 'they observed the recommendation': for this use of *krateō* 'hold' in the sense of observing or keeping an instruction, cf. 7:3, 4, 8 (cf. Lagrange, Rawlinson). Others, however, understand it differently: Arndt & Gingrich *krateō* 2.e.δ take it to mean that they kept the saying in order to occupy themselves with it later (so RSV). Taylor combines the two: 'they kept it in mind and observed the charge'. BFBS has 'They seized on the saying, discussing among themselves...'

pros heautous 'to themselves', 'with themselves': although some (RSV and others) take this phrase with the verb *ekratēsan* 'they kept', others take it with the participle *suzētountes* 'discussing' (cf. ASV, Goodspeed, Moffatt, Weymouth, BFBS, Brazilian, Zürich, Lagrange). From the use of the verb *suzēteō* in vv. 14, 16, it would appear that the verse here should be read, "They observed the command, questioning among themselves..."

suzētountes (cf. 1:27) 'questioning', 'discussing', 'debating'.

ti estin to ek nekrōn anastēnai 'what is the to rise from the dead'. Depending on the use of the definite article *to* 'the', this phrase may be understood in two different ways: (1) 'what is the rising from the dead', 'what is the resurrection from the dead': in this case *to anastēnai* 'to rise' is understood as a verbal noun 'the rising', 'the resurrection'; this is the position of Arndt & Gingrich *ho* II.4.a; (2) 'what is the meaning of the saying, To rise from the dead': in this case *to* 'the' is used to introduce the following words which are taken as a saying, the equivalent in many modern languages to quotation marks, "what is 'To rise from the dead' " (cf. 9:23; cf. Moule *Idiom Book*, 110). The context would seem to favor the second interpretation: it is hardly conceivable that the disciples—Jews all—should not know what was meant by the resurrection from the dead, since it was a well-known article in Jewish faith; rather, they would be puzzled by what Jesus meant in saying that the Son of man should rise from the dead. Their question would have to do with *this* 'to rise from the dead'.

Translation: Depending primarily upon the variety of ways in which this verse may be interpreted (see above), the renderings may be quite diverse, e.g. 'they did what they were told', 'they obeyed what he had said', or 'they kept to themselves the knowledge of what had happened'.

Questioning may be two quite different verbs in some languages, depending upon whether one assumes that this questioning was reciprocal among the three or entirely within the thinking of each person. If the first interpretation is taken, then the translation would be 'asked each other' or 'talked about to each other'. If the second meaning is assumed, then one may translate 'they thought about it in their hearts' (Subanen).

In rendering *what the rising from the dead meant* it is rare that one can conserve as much of the ambiguity as the RSV has done, for in general one must choose distinctly between the first or the second interpretation (see above). In the first instance, one must often translate 'questioned what was meant by the fact that a person may rise from the dead' or 'questioned how people might rise from the dead'. The second interpretation, which seems distinctly preferable, could be rendered as 'questioned what Jesus meant when he spoke of rising from the dead', thus relating Jesus' statement to a specific occurrence, not to the general belief.

11 *And they asked him, "Why do the scribes say that first Elijah must come?"*

Text: Before *hoi grammateis* 'the scribes' Tischendorf and Soden have *hoi Pharisaioi kai* 'the Pharisees and', which is omitted by all other editions of the Greek text.

Exegesis: *hoti* 'why?': interrogative, as in 2:16 (cf. Arndt & Gingrich *hostis* 4.b; Field *Notes*, 33; Moule *Idiom Book*, 159; Burton *Moods and Tenses*, § 349).

For *hoi grammateis* 'the scribes' cf. 1:22; *dei* 'it is necessary' cf. 8:31.

Translation: For *scribes* see 1:22.

First must in some languages be grammatically related to the subject Elijah, rather than to the verb, e.g. 'that Elijah will be the first to come'. The only alternative in certain languages is to say 'Elijah will come

279

before anything else happens'. Whichever expression is employed there is a degree of obscurity, even as there is in the Greek text itself.

12 *And he said to them, "Elijah does come first to restore all things; and how is it written of the Son of man, that he should suffer many things and be treated with contempt?*

Exegesis: Some expositors attempt to alleviate the difficulties of the text by rearranging the clauses in vv. 11-13 (cf. C. C. Oke *Expository Times* 64.187f., 1953); others, however, by a device available also to the translator, make a question out of the first phrase in v. 12: 'Does Elijah come first and restore all things?' (cf. *Expository Times* 64.239, 1953; cf. Rawlinson *in loc.*). The resultant meaning of the whole statement would then be: 'If—as the scribes claim—Elijah is to come first and restore all things, how then is it written that the Son of man should suffer much and be despised?' For another punctuation of the clauses cf. BFBS.

Elias men elthōn prōton apokathistanei panta 'Elijah comes first and restores all things': on the role of Elijah as precursor to the Messiah, cf. Malachi 4:5-6.

elthōn...apokathistanei 'coming...he restores': the time element of the two verbs is determined by the tense of the main verb, 'he comes and restores'. The present tense is not to be understood as meaning 'he is coming and restores'; it is a statement of fact in which the time element does not appear: 'Elijah, in fact, comes and restores'—as the scribes say.

apokathistēmi (cf. 3:5) 'restore', i.e. to its original condition or order.

pōs gegraptai epi ton huion tou anthrōpou hina 'how does it stand written concerning the Son of man that'.

graphō (cf. 1:2) 'write'.

epi 'about', 'with reference to' (cf. Arndt & Gingrich *graphō* 2.d.)

hina 'that' of content, not of purpose.

polla pathē kai exoudenēthē 'he should suffer much and be treated with contempt'.

polla paschō (cf. 8:31) 'suffer much', 'suffer many things'.

exoudeneō (only here in Mark) 'treat with contempt', 'count as of no value'.

Translation: *Said to them* may be rendered as 'answered them', depending upon receptor language usage.

Does come first introduces certain problems because of the tense form, which is present in English, but generally understood in this sequence as future. However, in verse 13, Jesus makes it quite clear that this present tense form (with future implications), is really not to be understood in the strictly temporal sense at all, but as a required event, which is entirely relative in time. In some languages the closest equivalent is 'must come'.

Restore may be rendered as 'to make everything new again' (Ifugao), 'to return it', implying to its former condition (Ilocano), 'to make all things sure', in the sense of establishing or rectifying (Subanen), and 'to set everything up' (Javanese).

As in other instances of the use of *the Son of man* the pronominal reference may need to be first person when Jesus is speaking, 'written of me the Son of man, that I must suffer...'

Suffer many things may be 'suffer much'.

Treated with contempt may be translated as 'scorn', 'deride', 'count as nothing', 'be said that he is nothing'.

13 *But I tell you that Elijah has come, and they did to him whatever they pleased, as it is written of him."*

Exegesis: *hoti* 'that' is recitative, introducing direct speech.

hosa (cf. 3:8) 'all things', 'as many things (as)'.

gegraptai ep' auton (cf. previous verse) 'it is written concerning him'.

Translation: The impersonal use of *they* in the expression *they did to him* is difficult to render in many languages. In general one can translate *they* by some such expression as 'the people', but in this instance obviously the opposition to John the Baptist was not prompted by the populace in general but by certain persons. This will require 'some people' or 'certain persons'.

As it is written of him is generally equivalent to a paratactically combined clause, 'that is just the way the Scriptures speak of him' or 'that is the way it is told about him in the Writings'.

14 *And when they came to the disciples, they saw a great crowd about them, and scribes arguing with them.*

Text: Instead of *elthontes...eidon* 'they came and saw' of the majority of editions of the Greek text, *Textus Receptus*, Soden and Vogels have *elthōn...eiden* 'he came and saw'.

Exegesis: All the words of this verse have already been dealt with: for *ochlos polus* 'a great crowd' cf. 5:24; *grammateis* 'scribes' cf. 1:22; *suzēteō* 'dispute' cf. 1:27.

Translation: The *they* of this verse is the same as the first *they* of verse 9. However, in order to make the reference clear one must in some cases translate *the disciples* as 'the other disciples', since Peter, James, and John had accompanied Jesus.

A great crowd around them may be rendered as 'a great many people gathered around them' (referring to the other disciples, not to Jesus and those accompanying him).

For *scribes* see 1:22.

15 *And immediately all the crowd, when they saw him, were greatly amazed, and ran up to him and greeted him.*

Exegesis: *exethambēthēsan* (14:33, 16:5,6) 'they were amazed': there are differences of opinion on what is the exact significance of the word here. Arndt & Gingrich take it to mean 'they were alarmed'; Lagrange 'very surprised'; Gould 'joyous surprise'. It would appear that the context indicates surprise at the unexpected appearance of Jesus: the idea of fear would not fit in very well with their immediate reaction in running up to him and greeting him.

prostrechontes (10:17; cf. *suntrechō* 6:33; *trechō* 5:6) 'running to'.

ēspazonto (15:18) 'they greeted', 'they welcomed': the imperfect tense aptly indicates the action of the people as they came to Jesus and greeted him in turn.

Translation: One should not attempt to reproduce the rather awkward syntax of the English construction *immediately all the crowd, when they saw him, were greatly amazed.* A much more usual expression would be 'right then when the crowd saw him, they were amazed and ran...'

Words which designate *greeting* are quite varied, depending upon local usage. For example, among some of the Nilotic people of the Sudan the regular expression is 'to meet snapping fingers'; among the Kapauku of New Guinea one says 'they grasped fingers'. Among the San Blas 'they shook hands'. One may legitimately ask if this would be the way a crowd would behave. Actually, that is not the right question to ask, for the actual behavior of a crowd is not the point; what matters is how the people describe the action of a crowd which greets a visitor. Whether or not each member of the crowd personally salutes (i.e. snaps fingers, shakes hands, grasps fingers, or rubs noses with the guest) is not what counts. What is important is how such people regularly speak of the behavior of such a crowd. Even though the people may not actually shake his hand, nevertheless the standard idiom for greeting may be 'they shook his hand'. In Tzotzil, for example, one must translate as 'they spoke to him', for this is the way to formalize greetings, which are of two types: (1) 'Are you still alive?', a question invariably asked if a person has been gone for more than two weeks, and (2) 'Are you really there?' the normal greeting to anyone who has made a shorter trip. The problem then is not what the people actually do or are likely to do in such circumstances, but the ways in which people speak about such actions.

16 *And he asked them, "What are you discussing with them?"*

Text: Instead of (the first) *autous* 'them' of all modern editions of the Greek text, *Textus Receptus* has *tous grammateis* 'the scribes'.

Exegesis: *autous* 'them': to whom did Jesus direct his question? The text allows two or possibly three alternatives: (1) the disciples: inasmuch as in v. 14 it is said that Jesus came to his disciples, around whom there was a great crowd and with whom scribes were arguing, it would seem natural that Jesus should ask them the question (so Bengel); (2) the scribes: copyists who introduced into some manuscripts the words *tous* *grammateis* 'the scribes' (see *Text*, above), understood them to be the ones to whom Jesus spoke (so F. C. Grant); (3) the crowd: since one of the crowd answers (next verse), the majority of commentators (Gould, Swete, Lagrange, Taylor and others) assume that the crowd was being addressed. If so, the question 'What are *you* discussing with them?' must be taken in a general sense, since it was not the crowd but the scribes who were discussing with the disciples. Of the three alternatives the context favors the first one: Jesus would be more likely to question his disciples than the scribes (or the crowd).

The majority of translations have simply 'he asked them', undefined, carrying over the same ambiguity that exists in the Greek text.

pros autous 'with them': who is referred to here depends on the interpretation given *autous* 'them'. If 'them' refers to the crowd or to the scribes, 'with them' refers to the disciples; if, on the other hand, 'them' refers to the disciples, as is probable, 'with them' refers to the scribes. For this second *autous* Kilpatrick has *heautous*, translated 'among yourselves'.

Translation: The fact that one person in the crowd should respond to the question of Jesus does not seem to be particularly strange, even though Jesus may have directed his words to the disciples, for obviously the action of the man in question was what had prompted the discussion with the scribes. One can, of course, attempt to reproduce the ambiguity of the Greek text, though in some languages this is not possible.

17 *And one of the crowd answered him, "Teacher, I brought my son to you, for he has a dumb spirit;*

Exegesis: *heis* (cf. 5:22) 'one': the equivalent of the indefinite *tis* 'a certain one', 'somebody' (cf. Black *Aramaic*, 249).

The other words have already been dealt with: for *didaskale* 'Teacher' cf. 4:38; *pherō* 'bring' cf. 1:32; *pneuma* 'spirit' cf. 1:23; *alalon* 'mute' cf. 7:37.

echonta pneuma alalon 'having a dumb spirit'; the participle is causal, '*because* he has a dumb spirit'. The spirit is called dumb (or mute) because the boy whom it possessed was mute (and deaf, as well, v. 25), presumably as a result of being possessed by the unclean spirit; cf. South Toradja 'into whom a spirit has entered, so that he is dumb'.

Translation: For *teacher* see 2:15 and 9:5.

Brought should be rendered probably in the sense of 'led' or 'brought along' (as one would a small child).

Dumb spirit would be rendered in many languages 'a spirit which makes him dumb', 'a demon which keeps him from speaking' or 'a spirit which makes him so that he cannot speak'. In some languages, however, *dumb* is rendered by an idiomatic phrase, e.g. 'his heart is closed' (Tzeltal), in which case it would be the spirit which causes this condition.

For *spirit* in the sense of 'demon', see 1:26, 32.

18 *and wherever it seizes him, it dashes him down; and he foams and grinds his teeth and becomes rigid; and I asked your disciples to cast it out, and they were not able."*

Exegesis: *hopou ean auton katalabē* 'wherever it seizes him', i.e. wherever the boy might be when the spirit seizes him.

hopou ean (*hopou an* 6:56) 'wherever', 'whatever place'.

katalambanō (only here in Mark) 'take hold of': with hostile intent, as here, 'seize' (cf. Arndt & Gingrich 1.b).

rēssei auton kai aphrizei kai trizei tous odontas kai xērainetai 'it throws him to the ground, and he foams at the mouth and grinds his teeth and grows rigid'.

rēssō (cf. *rēgnumi* 2:22) 'throw down', 'dash to the ground' (cf. Arndt & Gingrich 2.a).

aphrizō (9:20) 'foam at the mouth'.

trizō (only here in the N.T.) 'gnash', 'grind', 'grit'.

xērainō (cf. 3:1) 'dry up', 'wither', therefore (as in 3:1), 'grow rigid', 'become stiff' (cf. Arndt & Gingrich 2.b.; cf. Lagrange, Manson, Moffatt, Synodale). This meaning of the word suits the context better than 'waste away', 'pine away' (ASV, Goodspeed, Weymouth, Brazilian). BFBS has 'becomes parched'.

The other words have already been dealt with: *hina* 'that' of content, not of purpose, cf. 3:9; *ekballō* 'cast out' cf. 1:12, 34; *ischuō* 'be strong', 'be able' cf. 2:17, 5:4.

Translation: As in all expressions of demonic seizure (cf. RSV *seizes him*), one must make certain of the way in which one can speak of such events in the receptor language (see 1:23). In some instances it may be necessary to speak of 'entering into', 'taking hold of him', or 'being captured by'.

Dashes him down is equivalent in some languages to 'causes him to to fall down', especially if the demon is regarded as being within the person. However, whenever possible this strong figure should be used, but the idiom must be applicable to persons, and not exclusively to things (as has been the case in certain translations).

He may need to be changed to 'the boy', since the pronominal reference may not clearly indicate the shift between the dumb spirit as the subject and the boy.

Foams may be easily translated in most languages by finding out how people describe the actions of demented persons, epileptics, or those suffering from rabies. In Subanen one says literally 'his mouth fills with bubbles'.

Becomes rigid is translatable as 'his body becomes stiff' (Subanen) and 'he becomes bone' (Conob).

For *cast it out* see 1:34.

Were not able is translatable as 'could not do so' or 'could not cast the demon out'. In some languages one says 'they did not have the strength to do so'.

19 *And he answered them, "O faithless generation, how long am I to be with you? How long am I to bear with you? Bring him to me."*

Text: Instead of *autois* 'them' of all modern editions of the Greek text, *Textus Receptus* has *autō* 'him'.

Exegesis: *genea* (cf. 8:12) 'generation': here also refers to the contemporaries of Jesus.

apistos (only here in Mark) 'unbelieving', 'not having faith', 'faithless' (rather than 'unfaithful').

heōs pote 'until when?' 'how long?'

heōs (6:23, 13:19,27, 14:25,34,54, 15:33,38) 'until', 'till'.

pote (13:4,33,35) 'when'.

anexomai (only here in Mark) 'I will endure', 'bear', 'put up with'.

Translation: For *generation* see 8:12.

Faithless is to be understood in an active sense 'you people who do not believe' (Zoque, Zacapoastla Aztec). For *faith* see 1:15.

How long am I to be with you is equivalent in some languages to 'how long must I remain with you', in the sense of how long must I remain with you in order for you to have faith.

Bring should be translated by the same word as *brought* of verse 17.

20 *And they brought the boy to him; and when the spirit saw him, immediately it convulsed the boy, and he fell on the ground and rolled about, foaming at the mouth.*

Exegesis: *kai ēnegkan auton pros auton* 'and they brought him (the boy) to him (Jesus)'.

kai idōn auton 'and when he saw him': this phrase can be understood in three ways: (1) 'when Jesus saw the boy': although grammatically possible, this is improbable; (2) 'when the boy saw Jesus': among others, this is the interpretation of Bengel, Lagrange, Montgomery, Synodale, and Brazilian; in its favor it should be noticed that *idōn* 'seeing' is masculine, agreeing in gender with *auton* 'him' of the previous verse (which goes back to *ton huion mou* 'my son' of v. 17); (3) 'when the spirit saw Jesus': although *idōn* 'seeing' is masculine and does not agree in gender with *to pneuma* 'the spirit', neuter, in light of the masculine participles *kraxas* 'shrieking' and *sparaxas* 'convulsing' in v. 26 which are masculine and refer to the unclean spirit, it is probable that the subject of *idōn* 'seeing' is 'the spirit' (cf. also in 5:7-9, 11-12, the case of the Gerasene demoniac); this is the interpretation given by most commentators and translators, and probably should be preferred.

sunesparaxen (only here in Mark; cf. *sparassō* 1:26) 'he pulled about', 'he tore', 'he convulsed'.

kai pesōn epi tēs gēs ekulieto aphrizōn 'and he fell to the ground and rolled about, foaming (at the mouth)'.

piptō (cf. 4:4) 'fall', 'fall down'.

epi tēs gēs (cf. 9:3) 'on the ground'.

kuliomai (only here in the N.T.; cf. *kulismos* 2 Pet. 2:22) 'to roll oneself', 'twist about', 'wallow'.

aphrizō (cf. 9:18) 'foam at the mouth'.

Translation: For *spirit* see 1:26, 32.

Note that it is the spirit which is said to see Jesus.

For *convulsed* see 1:26.

Fell...rolled...foaming may be treated as three coordinate verb expressions if the receptor language construction so requires, e.g. 'he fell on the ground, he rolled about; he foamed at the mouth'. For *rolled* South Toradja has a vivid expression referring to the wobbling to and fro of a sun hat that has been put down in a sloping position, hence 'turning and tossing restlessly'.

21 *And Jesus asked his father, "How long has he had this?" And he said, "From chidhood.*

Exegesis: *posos* (cf. 6:38) 'how long'.

chronos (cf. 2:19) 'time'.

hōs 'as', 'when': here it is a temporal conjunction meaning 'since' (cf. Arndt & Gingrich, IV.1.b). The question asked by Jesus, literally translated, is: 'How long a time is it since this (first) happened to him?' (cf. BFBS).

paidiothen (only here in the N.T.) 'from childhood'.

Translation: *His father* is 'the father of the boy'.

The expression *has...had this*, though quite intelligible to us as English speaking persons, is not translatable literally into many other languages. These may require such renderings as 'has he suffered this way', 'has he been afflicted', or 'has he had the demon in his heart'.

From childhood is an elliptical expression which may require different degrees of expansion in various languages, 'he has suffered since he was a child' or 'even when a little child he suffered and still does'.

22 *And it has often cast him into the fire and into the water, to destroy him; but if you can do anything, have pity on us and help us.*

Exegesis: *pollakis* (cf. 5:4) 'often'.

kai eis pur...kai eis hudata either 'both into fire...and into water' or 'even into fire...and into water'.

ebalen (cf. 2:22) 'he threw', 'he hurled', 'he cast'.

hina 'in order to', 'so that': expresses purpose.

apolesē (cf. 1:24) 'he might destroy', 'he might kill'.

all' ei ti dunē 'but if you can do anything', 'but if you are at all able'. Cf. the leper's *ean thelēs* 'if you will' 1:40.

boētheson (9:24) 'help', 'aid': the imperative expresses a petition, not a command.

splagchnistheis (cf. 1:41) 'being merciful', 'having pity'. The participle

286

takes its mode from that of the main verb, and so is here imperatival: 'Be merciful and help!' (cf. similar case in 6:11).

Translation: *Cast him into* is to an extent a figurative expression, equivalent in some languages to 'caused him to fall into'.

Into the water must be translated in Zoque as 'under the water', since just throwing him into a small puddle of shallow water would not kill him. The purpose was obviously to drown him, and hence 'under' is required.

See *pity* 1:41 and *mercy* 5:19. In this type of context Huastec reads 'suffer with me' and Piro has 'see me with sorrow'. The essential ingredient of this type of pity is genuine empathy.

23 And Jesus said to him, "If you can! All things are possible to him who believes."

Text: After *dunē* '(if) you can' *Textus Receptus* adds *pisteusai* 'to believe', which is omitted by all modern editions of the Greek text.

Exegesis: *to ei dunē* 'the if you can': here the definite article *to* 'the' is the equivalent of quotation marks in modern writing (cf. 9:10). In effect, Jesus takes the phrase 'if you can' which the father applied to him and applies it to the father: 'Jesus said to him, (This saying of yours) *If you can...*' Cf. BFBS; Arndt & Gingrich *ho* II.8.a: "as far as your words 'If you can' are concerned". Cf. Moule *Idiom Book*, 110.

dunata (10:27, 13:22, 14:35, 36) 'possible'.

tō pisteuonti (cf. 1:15) 'to him who has faith', 'to him who believes': if an object is to be supplied, it will be faith *in God*.

Translation: *If you can* is a highly elliptical expression and is likely to be badly misunderstood unless the contextual setting is more evident. In many instances people interpret this phrase as meaning 'if you can do so, then all things are possible...' However, this is not the meaning of the passage and in order to make clear what the intent of this expression is, one can translate 'why do you say, If you can? Why, all things are possible to him who believes'. Indonesian and South Toradja translate 'What about: if you can take it on you'. In Putu the rendering is 'why do you ask if I fit?', in which the direct form is shifted to the indirect and 'fit' is the idiomatic term expressing capacity for a particular action.

Possible is interpreted in two different ways: (1) anything can happen with respect to one who believes (i.e. the one who has faith can be the recipient of any and all kinds of miraculous benefits) and (2) the one who has faith can do anything. It is this second meaning which should be reproduced here, in which case some languages require the direct, rather than the indirect statement, e.g. 'the one who has faith can do all things'.

For *faith* see 1:15.

24 *Immediately the father of the child cried out and said, "I believe; help my unbelief!"*

Text: Before *elegen* 'he said' *Textus Receptus* adds *meta dakruōn* 'with tears', which is omitted by all modern editions of the Greek text.

After *pisteuō* 'I believe' *Textus Receptus* adds *kurie* 'Sir', which is omitted by all modern editions of the Greek text.

Exegesis: The words in this verse have already been dealt with: for *krazō* 'cry out' cf. 3:11; *paidion* 'child' cf. 5:39; *boētheō* 'help' cf. 9:22; *apistia* 'unbelief' cf. 6:6.

boēthei mou te apistia 'you help my unbelief!': the meaning, of course, is 'help (*me because of*) my lack of faith', or 'help me (*to overcome*) my unbelief'. It was not, properly, his lack of faith which needed help, but the man himself for being unbelieving.

Translation: *Help my unbelief* has been incorrectly rendered in scores of translations. In fact, in many instances the words mean nothing more than 'help me believe less', for if one is going to assist one's lack of faith, it would logically follow that the result would be still less faith. But certainly the plea here is not 'to strengthen my unbelief' or 'to increase my lack of faith', as is specifically stated in a number of translations. Rather, the meaning is 'cast out my unbelief (Marathi), 'help me that I believe' (Villa Alta Zapotec), 'help me where I lack in belief' (Ilocano), 'help because I have a need of faith (Subanen), 'in my not believing, help me' (Shipibo), 'help my unbelieving heart' (Cashibo), 'help me when I don't believe' (Tzeltal), and 'help me in that which is lacking in this faith' (Toba Batak).

25 *And when Jesus saw that a crowd came running together, he rebuked the unclean spirit, saying to it, "You dumb and deaf spirit, I command you, come out of him, and never enter him again."*

Exegesis: *episuntrechei ochlos* 'a crowd was coming together'; perhaps, 'a mob was gathering' (cf. Berkeley).

episuntrechō (only here in the N.T.; cf. *prostrechō* 9:15) 'come together', 'run together': there may be an indication of mob action of one sort or another (cf. Manson 'the crowd closing in upon them'; cf. Black *Aramaic*, 85 n. 3, who suggests the verb may mean 'attack', the boy being the object of the crowd's hostile mood).

The other words in this verse have already been dealt with: for *epitimaō* 'rebuke' cf. 1:25; *to pneuma to akatharton* 'the unclean spirit' cf. 1:23; *alalon* 'dumb' cf. 7:37; *kōphon* 'deaf' cf. 7:32; *epitassō* 'command' cf. 1:27.

Translation: *A crowd* refers to a still larger group of people, or at least additional persons, not merely the ones identified in verse 14.

Rebuked should here be translated in the sense of 'scold' or 'speak very sternly to'.

For *unclean spirit* see 1 : 26.

Dumb and deaf spirit, on the analogy of dumb spirit (verse 17), may be translated as 'spirit (or 'demon') which causes a person not to be able to speak or hear'.

For expressions equivalent to *come out* and *enter*, see 1 : 23, 34.

26 And after crying out and convulsing him terribly, it came out, and the boy was like a corpse; so that most of them said, "He is dead."

Exegesis: *kraxas kai polla sparaxas* 'crying out and convulsing (him) much': though masculine, the two participles refer to the unclean spirit (cf. v. 20).

krazō (cf. 3 : 11) 'cry out', 'shriek'.

sparassō (cf. 1 : 26) 'convulse'.

polla is adverbial 'much'; here it indicates number, or frequency, 'many times' (cf. Moule *Idiom Book*, 35 'fit after fit'; some translations have 'convulsion after convulsion').

nekros (12 : 26, 27; cf. 6 : 14) 'dead': here, 'a corpse', 'a dead body'.

hostē...legein 'so as to say', 'so that they said': indicates result (for this construction cf. 1 : 27).

tous pollous 'the many': most translations take it to mean 'most (of them)', 'many (of them)'; Arndt & Gingrich (*polus* I.2.a.β) take it to mean '*all* of them' (cf. 6 : 2).

hoti is recitative, introducing direct speech.

apethanen (cf. 5 : 35) 'he died', 'he is dead'.

Translation: For *convulsing* see 1 : 26.

Like a corpse is translatable in Subanen as 'looked like a dead body', but in other languages the use of the equivalent of 'corpse' is questionable. Hence, a somewhat different idiom may be required, e.g. 'seemed to remain dead' (Tzeltal).

Most of them should be related here to the people in general, e.g. 'most of the people there'.

He is dead must in some languages be translated as 'he has died', for death is regarded as a process, or event, and not a state, as is implied in a verb such as *is*.

27 But Jesus took him by the hand and lifted him up, and he arose.

Exegesis: The words in this verse have already been dealt with: for *krateō* 'seize' and *egeirō* 'raise' cf. 1 : 31; for *anistēmi* 'rise' cf. 1 : 35.

Translation: *Took him by the hand* seems to us such a perfectly normal way of speaking that we do not realize that there are various alternative ways of describing this type of activity: 'took his hand', 'grasped the hand of the boy', 'put the boy's hand in his hand', 'took hold of the boy by grasping his hand'—all variants of the activity of grasping by the hand.

Lifted him up must not be translated in such a way as to be contradictory to the following expression 'he arose'. In some languages 'lifted him up' has been so rendered as to imply that Jesus literally lifted the child up off the ground by the arm. This is not what is implied by the following phrase. Obviously, Jesus assisted the boy to arise by taking hold of his hand. The resultant translation in some languages is 'helped him rise up and he stood up' (Chontal of Tabasco).

28 *And when he had entered the house, his disciples asked him privately, "Why could we not cast it out?"*

Punctuation: Instead of the punctuation adopted by the majority, in which *hoti* is understood as the interrogative 'why?', Souter takes *hoti* as introducing direct discourse and the phrase that follows as a statement of fact, "We couldn't cast it out": Field (*Notes*, 33), however, calls such a construction "intolerable".

Exegesis: *eis oikon* (cf. 3:19, 7:17) 'in a house': probably with the same meaning 'home' as in 3:19, 7:17 (cf. Goodspeed, BFBS, Brazilian; cf. Kilpatrick *The Bible Translator* 7.5, 1956); Moffatt and Manson take it simply 'indoors'; Lagrange translates *à la maison*.
    kat' idian (cf. 4:39) 'privately', 'alone'.
    hoti (cf. 9:11) 'why?': cf. Field *Notes*, 33; Turner *Journal of Theological Studies* 27.58-59, 1925-6.
    ekbalein (cf. 1:12, 34) 'to cast out', 'to drive forth'.

Translation: Since the immediately preceding third person singular referent is the boy, it is necessary in a number of languages to use 'Jesus' as the subject of 'entered the house', otherwise, the passage means that after the boy went home, the disciples made their inquiry of Jesus.
    Privately may be translated as 'when there was no one else there'.
    Could is often translatable as 'have the power to' or 'have enough strength', though obviously the capacity is not physical, but spiritual.
    For *cast out* see 1:34.

29 *And he said to them, "This kind cannot be driven out by anything but prayer."*

Text: After *proseuchē* 'prayer' *Textus Receptus*, Soden, Vogels, and Merk (in brackets) include *kai nēsteia* 'and fasting', which is omitted by the majority of modern editions of the Greek text.

Exegesis: *genos* (cf. 7:26) here 'class', 'kind' (cf. Arndt & Gingrich, 4): 'this kind' probably refers to demons or unclean spirits considered as a whole, rather than to the particular kind of unclean spirit which possessed this boy.
    exelthein (cf. 7:29) 'go out', i.e. 'be driven out', 'be cast out'.
    proseuchē (11:17) 'in prayer', 'by means of prayer': this means prayer to God.

Translation: *This kind* is an elliptical expression which may require some expansion in certain languages, either by the addition of the referent, e.g. 'this kind of spirit' (or 'demon'), or by the shifting of the relationship of referent to qualifier, e.g. 'demons like this one'. In some languages there is no word indicating 'type', 'kind', or 'class' which can be applied to such spirits, and hence one can use 'this spirit' or 'a spirit like this one' (Kekchi).

The passive construction must often be shifted to active, e.g. 'you cannot cast out demons like this one except...'

For *driven out* see problems discussed under *cast out*, 1:34. In this instance it is usually possible to employ a causative, 'to cause to come out', 'to cause to go out' or 'to cause to leave'.

By anything but prayer must be altered if *prayer* is translatable only by a verb expression. In such instances the change is generally from an instrumental to a conditional expression, 'you cannot...if you do not pray'. Though it would seem most natural for Jesus to reply using the second person plural, e.g. 'you cannot...unless you...', in some languages truths which are generally applicable can only be expressed with the first person plural, 'we cannot..., unless we...' (Zoque); cf. South Toradja 'except then only when we pray'.

Fasting, which occurs in the *Textus Receptus*, and certain other derived translations, must not be rendered by a word meaning merely 'to be hungry' (see 2:18). In many languages one must indicate the purposeful abstinence from food, e.g. 'to hold back from eating' (Bolivian Quechua).

30 **They went on from there and passed through Galilee. And he would not have any one know it;**

Exegesis: *pareporeuonto* (cf. 2:23) 'they went along', 'they went by': with *dia* 'through' the verb means 'go through', 'pass through'.

ouk ēthelen hina (cf. 6:25, 10:35) 'he did not want that': the clause that follows, 'any one should know it', defines the content of what Jesus did not want.

Translation: *Went on from there*, as an indicator of the point of departure, is equivalent in some languages to 'left that place'. *Passed through* would imply 'went right on through the region of Galilee', implying that Jesus did not stop along the way to preach or minister to the people in the various cities and towns.

Not in the English sentence *he would not have any one know it* is a negative of the first verb, expressing the intention of Jesus. However, the logical structure is different from the grammatical pattern, for the negation actually applies to the fact that the people should not know about Jesus' presence. Many languages, therefore, require a shift in the place of the negative, e.g. 'Jesus wanted that people would not know it'. This tendency in English (and Greek) to shift the negative from the secondary or subordinate expression (where it may logically belong) to the primary or principal constituent (where it is grammatically "attracted") must be carefully noted and the proper adjustments made. Otherwise the resulting renderings may be entirely misleading to speakers of the receptor languages.

31 *for he was teaching his disciples, saying to them, "The Son of man will be delivered into the hands of men, and they will kill him; and when he is killed, after three days he will rise."*

Exegesis: For the whole verse see 8 : 31.

edidasken gar 'for he was teaching': this clause should receive the necessary emphasis as explaining the reason why Jesus did not want anyone to know of his trip through Galilee.

Most of the words in this verse have already been dealt with: for *ho huios tou anthrōpou* 'the Son of man' cf. 2 : 10; *apokteinō* 'kill' cf. 3 : 4; *meta treis hēmeras* 'after three days' cf. 8 : 31; *anistēmi* 'rise' cf. 1 : 35, 8 : 31.

paradidotai eis cheiras anthrōpōn 'he is delivered into the hands of men': with most commentators (cf. Taylor; Moule *Idiom Book*, 7; Burton *Moods and Tenses*, § 15) it is reasonable to presume that the present tense of the verb in this instance has a future force, *'will be delivered* into the hands of men' (see Lagrange, however, for arguments against this position, and cf. BFBS 'is being delivered').

paradidōmi (cf. 1 : 14) 'hand over', 'deliver', 'arrest'.

eis cheiras anthrōpōn (cf. 14 : 41) 'into the hands of men', i.e. 'into the power of men' who are to be regarded as hostile (cf. Arndt & Gingrich *cheir* 2.b).

Translation: *Was teaching...saying* may be translated as a single verb expression in introducing indirect or direct discourse, e.g. 'he was teaching...that the Son of man...' or as two verbs, often in paratactic arrangement, e.g. 'he was teaching his disciples; he was saying, The Son of man...' The choice between a single or double verb expression must depend upon the requirements of the receptor language.

For *Son of man* see 2 : 10, and for other syntactic problems refer to 8 : 31. Translations should consistently reflect whatever degree of parallelism there is in the original texts—making sure to translate in the same way what is the same in Greek and at the same time not to force conformity in the translation, where the original is not identical.

Into the hands of men is an idiom standing for men's power or control. In some languages *hands* become 'arms', 'power', 'control', or 'beneath', e.g. 'he will be put beneath men', in the sense of under their power.

32 *But they did not understand the saying, and they were afraid to ask him.*

Exegesis: *ēgnooun* (only here in Mark) 'they did not know', 'they were ignorant (about)': in this context, 'they did not understand' (cf. Arndt & Gingrich 3).

to rēma (14 : 72) 'word', 'saying', 'expression', with the special meaning in this context of 'prophecy', 'prediction' (cf. Arndt & Gingrich 1).

ephobounto auton eperōtēsai 'they were afraid to ask him': the infinitive *epērōtēsai* 'to ask' completes the meaning of the main verb *ephobounto* 'they were afraid', while *auton* 'him' is the direct object of the infinitive.

Translation: It is rarely that one can find a noun expression equivalent to the Greek *rēma* or English *saying*. Usually, the only corresponding expression is 'what he was saying' or 'what he meant when he was saying', for the men were not ignorant of the words which Jesus used, but of the implications of what he was trying to communicate to them.

To ask him may require expansion in some languages by the addition of the direct object (or second object, as it is sometimes called), e.g. 'to ask him what he meant' or 'to ask him what his words meant'.

33 *And they came to Capernaum; and when he was in the house he asked them, "What were you discussing on the way?"*

Text: Instead of *ēlthon* 'they came' of the majority of modern editions of the Greek text, *Textus Receptus* and Soden have *ēlthen* 'he came'.

Before *dielogizesthe* 'you were discussing' *Textus Receptus* adds *pros heautous* 'among yourselves'; Kilpatrick adds *pros heautous* after *dielogizesthe*; all other modern editions of the Greek text omit the two words.

Exegesis: *en tē oikia* 'in the house': perhaps Peter's house, which, it would seem, had become Jesus' "home" in Galilee.

dielogizesthe (cf. 2:6) 'you were discussing', 'debating (with one another)'.

Translation: *Came* must often be changed to 'arrived at', because of the problem of narrative perspective. However, in some languages, e.g. Villa Alta Zapotec, there are two words for 'arriving': one is used when one arrives at a destination other than one's home and another when the point of arrival is at home (though in Villa Alta Zapotec there is an additional complication in that in this particular passage the point of arrival must also be related to the home of the narrator). In this passage Jesus was evidently arriving at his "home".

On the way must be rendered in some languages by an expression containing a verb, 'as you walked along the path' (or 'along the road'), since *on the way* implies a process of journeying, not simply a position.

34 *But they were silent; for on the way they had discussed with one another who was the greatest.*

Exegesis: *hoi de esiōpōn* (cf. 3:4) 'but they kept silent' (cf. Lagrange *ils gardaient le silence*).

dielechthēsan (only here in Mark) 'they discussed'; more expressly 'they had an argument', 'they had entered into controversy'. The aorist of the verb, in this context, is to be translated as a past perfect, 'they *had argued*'.

tis meizōn 'who is greater?' i.e. 'who is the greatest?' For the use of the comparative form with the superlative meaning cf. 4:31,32, and see Moule *Idiom Book*, 97.

Translation: *Were silent* is often rendered as 'said nothing', 'did not reply'.

On the way, as in the preceding verse, should be translated in many languages as 'when they were going along the road' or 'as they were walking along'.

Discussed may require the introduction of direct discourse, in which case the pronouns must be changed, e.g. 'discussed with one another, Which one of us is the greatest', or 'asked one another, Which of us, do you think, is the greatest' (in the sense of 'most important').

Superlative expressions have a variety of forms, e.g. 'surpasses all in being...' (as in many Bantu languages), 'finds more...' (Zoque), and 'is the first in being...'

35 **And he sat down and called the twelve; and he said to them, "If any one would be first, he must be last of all and servant of all."**

Exegesis: *kathisas* (10:37,40, 11:2,7, 12:36,41, 14:32, 16:19) 'sitting down'—perhaps, as a teacher.

tous dōdeka (cf. 3:14,16, 6:7) 'the Twelve': a title, not simply a number.

ei tis thelei (cf. 8:34) 'if any one wants': as in 8:34, this translation is to be preferred to RSV 'if any one *would*'.

prōtos (cf. 6:21) 'first', with idea of rank and position (cf. also 10:31, 44, where the word is used with this same meaning).

estai pantōn eschatos kai pantōn diakonos 'he shall be the last of all and the servant of all'. This statement is not in the nature of a threat against the selfseekers, as though it meant, "This is what will happen if anyone wants to be first!" It is rather Jesus' teaching on how really to be 'first': 'If you want to be first, become the last, become the servant of all' (cf. Gould). The future *estai* 'shall be' has the force (as often) of an imperative 'must be'.

eschatos (10:31, 12:6,22) 'last' in rank or position, as in the case of *prōtos* 'first'; therefore, 'least', 'most insignificant' (cf. Arndt & Gingrich 2).

diakonos (10:43) 'servant'.

Translation: *Called the twelve* must be carefully translated, for 'calling' may imply shouting to, which obviously is not the meaning here. Rather, the meaning is that Jesus told his disciples to gather around him or to come to him to listen to what he had to say.

The twelve must be expanded in many languages to 'the twelve disciples', since numerals cannot be used as substantives in this type of construction.

If any one would be first may require some more specific delimitation, since 'first' may not imply rank or relative position among persons, as it does in Greek and English. For example, in Tzeltal one must translate, 'if any one wishes to raise himself up to the first place' (implying relative height), but in other languages, e.g. Yipounou, one may say 'if any one wishes to be at the face', meaning the front of the line of men going down a trail; cf. South Toradja 'when someone wants to be in the forefront'; Javanese 'leading-man'. Still another ordering is found in some languages 'if any one wishes to be the elder', employing age grading as a basis for rank in any group. It makes no difference whether a language employs space or time as a basis for distinction—the important thing is the ranking of members within a group.

Last of all must be translated in contrast with 'first'. For example, in Yipounou one may say 'he must return to the back of all', thus preserving the figure of the trail.

Servant of all may need some cultural adaptation, e.g. 'do errands for everyone' (Zoque).

36 *And he took a child, and put him in the midst of them; and taking him in his arms, he said to them,*

Exegesis: Most of the words in this verse have already been dealt with: for *lambanō* 'take', 'receive' cf. 4:16; *paidion* 'child' cf. 5:39; *en mesō* 'in the midst' cf. 3:3.

estēsen auto 'he stood him': this is the only place in Mark where the verb *histēmi* (cf. 3:24) 'stand' takes a direct object.

enagkalisamenos (10:16) 'taking into (his) arms', 'embracing'.

Translation: *Took a child...taking him in his arms* must be translated so as not to be contradictory or redundant. In some renderings of this passage the first expression actually means to take up into one's arms, and hence the repetition in the latter part of the verse seems confusing. If we attempt to reconstruct, on the basis of the Greek text, what probably happened, we can say that first he took a child by the hand and led him over in front of the disciples, there in the midst of the group as they crowded around Jesus. Then he took the child up in his arms and put him on his lap. This would seem to be the normal procedure, and the translation should suggest this type of sequence, rather than being a literal translation of *took...taking*, using the same verb, and implying either a contradiction in the order of events or a redundancy in the passage.

37 *"Whoever receives one such child in my name receives me; and whoever receives me, receives not me but him who sent me."*

Text: Instead of *hen tōn toioutōn paidiōn* 'one of such children' of most modern editions of the Greek text, Tischendorf and Soden have *hen tōn paidiōn toutōn* 'one of these children'.

Exegesis: *dexētai* (cf. 6:11) 'he should receive', 'welcome', 'accept'.

epi tō onomati mou (cf. v. 39; 13:6; cf. *en onomati* 11:9; *en tō onomati* v. 38, 16:17) 'on my name', 'on account of my name'. Vincent *Word Studies* I, 103 (on Mt. 18:5) 'on the ground of', 'on account of', 'for the sake of'. Lagrange translates 'because of my name'; Arndt & Gingrich *onoma* I.4.c.ε explain, 'when someone's name is mentioned or called upon', 'receive (a child) when my name is confessed, when I am called upon'. Most English translations have simply 'in my name'; Goodspeed has 'on my account' and Weymouth 'for my sake'.

ton aposteilanta me 'him who sent me', i.e. God. This saying reflects the familiar Jewish idea that a man's messenger is the same as the man himself, in that particular charge or mission.

Translation: *Receives* involves a problem of translation in many languages because of the variety of terms used, depending upon the type of object which is received. In the case of a 'child', as the object of 'receiving', the problem is made even more difficult, and in some languages requires special usage, e.g. 'to take under one's care' (Tzeltal), 'to say, Come into my house' (Cashibo), 'to say Welcome to' (Navajo), 'to help' (Kiyaka), and 'to treat well' (Gio). However, if the idiom is too highly specialized, there are of course problems in adjusting the form of the second clause (in which case some of the force of the expression may be lost). However, one can say, for example, 'whoever helps a child like this helps me', 'whoever says welcome to a child says welcome to me', or 'whoever asks this child into his home, asks me into his home'. When, however, one must use an idiom such as 'to take under one's care', then obviously some adjustment in form must be made.

In my name involves a very complex problem (see *Bible Translating*, 178-79), since in so many languages 'name' cannot be used as a substitute for the person. In such instances one must use a direct reference to the person, rather than employing the indirect reference of 'name', e.g. 'for my sake', 'because of me' (Tarahumara), or 'out of regard for me'. But note that this usage of *in my name* is somewhat different in many translations from what it is in the next verse.

38 *John said to him, "Teacher, we saw a man casting out demons in your name, and we forbade him, because he was not following us."*

Text: There are three different ways in which the last part of this verse is read by modern editions of the Greek text: (1) the RSV reading *kai ekōluomen auton hoti ouk akolouthei hēmin* 'and we were forbidding him because he does not follow us' is the text preferred also by Westcott and Hort, Vogels, and Souter; (2) *hos ouk akolouthei hēmin, kai ekōluomen auton, hoti ouk ēkolouthei hēmin* 'who does not follow us, and we were forbidding him, because he was not following us' is the text preferred by *Textus Receptus* (with slight differences noted in Appendix), Tischendorf, Nestle, Kilpatrick, Merk, and Taylor; (3) *hos ouk akolouthei hēmin, kai ekōluomen auton* 'who does not follow us, and we were forbidding

296

him' is preferred by Soden and Lagrange. The choice seems to lie between (1) and (2), the majority of editors preferring (2).

Exegesis: *Iōannēs* 'John': presumably the apostle, son of Zebedee and brother of James (cf. 1:19, 3:17).

en tō onomati sou (cf. v. 37; 16:17) 'in your name', 'using your name': cf. Arndt & Gingrich *onoma* I.4.c.γ 'with mention of the name, while naming or calling on the name'.

ēkoluomen (9:39, 10:14) 'we were hindering', 'preventing', 'forbidding': the imperfect tense in this case expresses attempt 'we tried to stop him' (cf. Swete; Moulton *Prolegomena*, 129; Moule *Idiom Book*, 9; cf. Weymouth, Montgomery, Manson).

The other words in this verse have already been dealt with: *didaskale* 'teacher' cf. 4:38; *ekballein daimonia* 'cast out demons' cf. 1:12, 34; *akoloutheō* 'follow (as a disciple)' cf. 1:18.

Translation: For *teacher* see 2:13.

For *casting out demons* see 1:34.

In your name has a somewhat different meaning here from that in verse 9:37, for here the usage is more technical—more related to the concepts of "word magic", in the sense that the man was evidently invoking the name of Jesus, whose reputation as an exorcist had attracted considerable attention, and had acquired evident "power". One may translate this passage merely as 'by using your name' or 'by calling out your name'. However, even this use of 'name' may be utterly meaningless in a receptor language and in such instances one can use a more paraphrastic equivalent 'as though on orders from you' (Zacapoastla Aztec). It is not possible to say merely 'on your orders', for obviously the man had not been commissioned by Jesus, and the use of Jesus' name was evidently a prerogative assumed by the man without warrant. In Tzeltal the equivalent is 'by your authority, so he said'.

Forbade him may be translated as 'said, Don't do that' (Navajo).

Not following us involves unsuspected difficulties, for if translated literally, it would mean that the man was not coming along behind the other disciples, obviously not what was meant. The equivalent in many languages does not involve the use of a verb 'to follow', but an identification of the adherence of the man to the group, e.g. 'he was not one of us' (Subanen) or 'he was not with us'.

39 But Jesus said, "Do not forbid him; for no one who does a mighty work in my name will be able soon after to speak evil of me.

Exegesis: *oudeis gar estin hos poiēsei...kai dunēsetai* literally 'for there is no one who will do...and will be able': instead of one verb in the present tense and the other in the future tense (as in RSV), it is preferable to have them both in the present tense, or in the future tense (ASV, Goodspeed, BFBS, Manson; Weymouth 'who will perform a miracle...and be able').

poiēsei dunamin (cf. 5:30) 'will do a mighty work', 'will perform a miracle'.

epi tō onomati mou (cf. v. 37) 'in my name': it would be hazardous to try to establish a hard and fast distinction between *en tō onomati* 'in the name' and *epi tō onomati* 'on the basis of the name' in these passages (cf. Silva New *The Beginnings of Christianity*, vol. V, p. 123, n.2).

tachu (only here in Mark) 'soon afterward', 'quickly', 'suddenly': cf. Manson 'in the same breath', Synodale *en même temps*.

kakologēsai (cf. 7:10) 'to speak evil of', 'to revile'.

Translation: *Do not forbid* may be translated as 'Do not tell him he should not' or 'Do not say to him, You must not' (Huave).

Some languages may require the shift of the negative from the person to the capacity to speak against Jesus, e.g. 'anyone who does...will not be able to...' or 'if a person does...he will not be able to...' In both instances the verb forms should indicate the most general circumstances. In certain languages, this type of tense-aspect would be expressed by essentially tenseless forms of the verbs.

For *mighty work* see *miracles* 6:2. In many instances this type of context leads to the choice of words expressing the response of the viewer, e.g. 'things people are astonished at' (Tzotzil) and 'big things, not (customarily) seen' (San Blas).

In my name should be translated the same as in the preceding verse.

40 *For he that is not against us is for us.*

Exegesis: *kata* with the genitive meaning 'against' (3:6, 11:25, 14:55, 56, 57).

huper (14:24) with the genitive 'for', 'in behalf of' (cf. Moule *Idiom Book*, 64).

Translation: *Against us...for us* would seem to be simple enough, but prepositions such as 'against' and 'for' do not exist in some languages, and the entire concept must be shifted into verb constructions, e.g. 'the man who does not fight against us is on our side', 'the man who does not work against us is helping us', 'for he goes with us, who is not against us' (Toba Batak), or 'he who does not look mean at us is ours' (Kekchi).

41 *For truly, I say to you, whoever gives you a cup of water to drink because you bear the name of Christ, will by no means lose his reward.*

Exegesis: Apparently for stylistic reasons RSV has changed *amēn legō humin* 'truly I say to you' from the position it occupies in the Greek text to the beginning of the verse.

potisē humas potērion hudatos 'he should give you to drink a cup of water': the verb *potisē* 'should give to drink' takes two direct objects in Greek, *humas* 'you' and *potērion hudatos* 'a cup of water'.

potizō (15:36) 'give to drink', 'make to drink'.

potērion (cf. 7:4) 'a cup'.

en onomati hoti 'in the name that': the phrase means 'on the ground that' (Moule *Idiom Book*, 79; Moulton & Milligan quote a papyrus in which the phrase *onomati eleutherou* means 'in virtue of being freeborn'; Goodspeed, 'on the ground that you belong to Christ'); *onoma* 'name' is used with the meaning 'title', 'category': cf. Arndt & Gingrich II, 'under the category that you belong to Christ', 'in your capacity as a follower of Christ'. Most translations use 'because' (ASV, Moffatt, Montgomery, Weymouth, Manson; Lagrange *pour la raison que vous êtes au Christ*); the RSV 'because you bear the name of Christ' is more interpretive in character. BFBS has 'in the Name, for you are Messiah's'.

misthon (only here in Mark) 'pay', 'wages', 'reward'.

For *ou mē* 'not' cf. 9:1; *apollumi* 'lose' cf. 1:24.

Translation: For syntactic problems involving *truly* see 8:12.

The order adopted in the RSV with respect to the expression *truly, I say to you* is generally better in most languages, since the direct discourse is not interrupted.

In some languages *cup* must be translated in terms of the closest equivalent, e.g. 'little calabash' (Black Bobo). In other instances one cannot say 'cup of water', but 'water in a cup' (Barrow Eskimo).

The verb *give* must always be treated with care, for there are many implications involved in some languages. For example, there may be two entirely different terms, depending upon whether (1) the gift is one in which an equivalent gift is expected in return (known as exchange gifts, and constituting a highly formalized type of indigenous barter) or (2) the object is one given without any regard for compensation. It is this latter meaning which should be indicated here. On the other hand, languages also distinguish between gifts which are prompted by evident need and those which are wholly without reference to such circumstances. Something of this point of view is suggested in the Zoque rendering, 'whoever lets you ask for a cup of water', implying that the man responds to the need.

Bear the name of Christ may be translated as 'are called by the name of Christ' (literally, 'have the name of being Christian' Ifugao). On the other hand, Greek *onomati* 'name' would seem to be used more in the sense of 'because of' or 'on the basis that', and hence one may translate as 'because you belong to Christ' (Tzeltal).

Lose his reward is often badly mistranslated, implying that after the man has received his reward he will not forthwith lose it by misplacing it. The more idiomatic way of saying this in some languages is 'he will certainly get what is to be given to him' (Amuzgo) or 'he will certainly receive the pay for his hand' (Tzeltal). In this latter expression 'pay for his hand' is the compensation which is gained for anything which a man has done with his hands. If it were an errand he had run, then he would receive 'the pay for his feet'.

42 *Whoever causes one of these little ones who believe in me to sin, it would be better for him if a great millstone were hung round his neck and he were thrown into the sea.*

Text: After *tōn pisteuontōn* 'those who believe' *Textus Receptus* and Kilpatrick add *eis eme* 'in me', which is omitted by all other modern editions of the Greek text.

Exegesis: *skandalisē* (cf. 4:17) 'he should cause to stumble' (Montgomery, Manson, Brazilian); 'cause to fall' (Goodspeed; BFBS 'cause to fall away'; Weymouth 'occasion the fall of'); 'is a hindrance' (Moffatt). 'Cause to (fall into) sin' (Synodale, RSV) is too specific a translation of *skandalizō*.

hena tōn mikrōn toutōn tōn pisteuontōn 'one of these little ones who believe': perhaps, 'one of the least of these who believe'. The RSV addition 'in me' is not part of the genuine text, in the opinion of most editors of the Greek text.

kalon estin (cf. 4:8) 'it is good': the use of the absolute form 'good' for the comparative 'better' appears to be thoroughly Semitic (cf. Black *Aramaic*, 86).

mallon (cf. 5:26) 'rather', 'instead'.

ei perikeitai...kai beblētai 'if it had been placed...and he had been thrown': the two perfects (the verb *perikeimai* is itself a perfect, meaning 'to have been placed'—cf. Souter) are here used with the force of past perfects: it would be better if, *before causing a little one to stumble*, he had had a millstone hung around his neck and had been thrown into the sea.

mulos onikos (only here in Mark) 'a large millstone', i.e. the large upper millstone that required an ass to turn it, instead of being hand-turned, as in the case of the small mills.

Translation: Clauses introduced by *whoever* must be shifted to conditional clauses in some languages, e.g. 'if a man does...it would be better...'

Little ones is 'little children', to be understood in this context as being a reference to the child of verses 36 and 37.

Though the better texts all have only 'believe', it is necessary in many languages to have some object to the verb of believing, and hence 'in me' is a very natural addition (cf. *Textus Receptus* and the RSV).

Causes...to stumble is only rarely translatable in a literal manner. In one instance this was done, and the people were utterly surprised that Jesus would speak of such a dire penalty for anyone playing a practical joke. In this particular language the translation had to be changed to read 'to cause his heart to be spoiled', for only this type of expression would convey the idea of moral offense. In Tzeltal the appropriate equivalent is 'to cause to go wrong' and in Totonac one must say 'to show such little children the wrong road'. In Chontal of Tabasco the correct idiom is 'to cause them to leave the way'; in South Toradja the translation is 'whoever causes that one of these little ones come into misfortune through sin'.

Great millstone is more meaningfully translated in many languages than in English, for so few English speaking people really know from personal experience what millstones are. In Tzeltal the equivalent expression is 'large *metate*' (*metate* is the name for the indigenous type of grinding stone). In some languages, however, grinding stones are not used, and hence one must say simply 'a big rock' (Barrow Eskimo). South Toradja must render 'large stone which is placed under the piles on which the house rests', while Toba Batak has 'stone block in which the rice is beaten' (to remove the husks).

One must make certain that the stone is not literally 'hung round his neck', for in one language the people were intrigued by this kind of stone, which could be put as a wreath around a person's neck. An appropriate equivalent may be 'tied round his neck' or 'tied to him, with a rope around his neck'.

43 *And if your hand causes you to sin, cut it off; it is better for you to enter life maimed than with two hands to go to hell, to the unquenchable fire.*

Exegesis: *apokopson* (9 : 45) 'cut (it) off'.

kullon (only here in Mark) 'maimed', 'crippled', 'deformed'.

eiselthein eis tēn zōēn (9 : 45) 'to enter into life': i.e. future life, eternal life, the blessed life with God (cf. *zōē aiōnios* 'eternal life' 10 : 17, 30).

apelthein eis tēn geennan 'go away to Gehenna', 'go off into hell' (for *aperchomai eis* 'go away to' cf. 6 : 32, 36, 46, 7 : 24, 30, 8 : 13).

apelthein 'to go off': in light of the use of *exelthein* 'to go out' in 7 : 29 with the meaning 'to be cast out', and of the passive verb *blēthēnai* 'to be thrown' in the parallel passages in vv. 45, 47, it is probable that *apelthein* here means simply 'to be cast', 'to be thrown', as synonym of *blēthēnai* 'to be thrown' in vv. 45, 47.

geenna (9 : 45, 47) in the New Testament is 'hell', the eschatological place of final punishment.

asbeston (only here in Mark) 'unquenchable', 'inextinguishable', 'which cannot be put out'.

Translation: As suggested in the previous verses 'causes to stumble' (which is the literal meaning of the Greek text) must be modified in various translations. In this particular verse a literal rendering might be entirely misleading, i.e. 'to stumble over one's hands' or 'to be tripped up because of one's hands'. Accordingly, one must use some other equivalent expression, e.g. 'if your heart is spoiled because of your hand' (Kekchi). In Zoque the appropriate expression for this passage is 'if your hand causes you to be lost'.

In languages in which comparative expressions cannot be formed by the ready use of certain special forms or idioms (there are a number of languages which have no such morphological or syntactic devices), a number of adjustments may be required. For example, in Tzeltal one may say 'it is good if you enter...with just one hand, but if you have

301

two hands and go to hell..., poor you!' The comparative is only implied, not specifically stated. However, the ultimate effect of the communication is just as positive as it is in English, Greek, or any other languages which have specific comparative constructions such as *better...than.*

Enter life cannot be said in many languages, for the concept of 'life' may be translatable only as a verb. In Kekchi, for example, one must translate 'enter into heaven and live'. It is quite true that in the Greek text 'enter life' is not restricted specifically to going to heaven, but in contrast with going to Gehenna the parallelism does support such an addition.

Hell (reflecting the use of Greek *Gehenna*) is rendered in three principal ways: (1) by borrowing a term from a trade or national language (this is done in a number of Indian languages in Latin America, which have borrowed Spanish *infierno*), (2) by using an expression denoting judgment or punishment, e.g. 'place of punishment' (Loma), 'place of suffering' (Totonac, San Blas), or 'place of destruction', and (3) by describing a significant characteristic: (a) the presence of fire or burning, e.g. 'place of fire' (Kipsigis, Moré), 'the large bonfire' (Shipibo), or (b) the traditionally presumed location, e.g. 'the lowest place' (a well-known term in Valiente), 'the place inside' long used to designate hell, as a place inside the earth (Aymara).

In choosing a word for *hell* it is equally important to study possibilities for translating *hades* (see *Bible Translating*, 231-32). This latter term is transliterated (not too common a practice) or described as 'the place of the dead' (though distinguished clearly from 'cemetery').

If *hell* is translated as 'the place of fire', then the added expression *to the unquenchable fire* may be combined as 'to the place of fire which cannot be put out'.

44 *[, where their worm does not die, and the fire is not quenched.]*

Text: Only *Textus Receptus* includes this verse: it is omitted by all modern editions of the Greek text (it is genuine as v. 48).

Exegesis and **Translation:** see verse 48.

45 *And if your foot causes you to sin, cut it off; it is better for you to enter life lame than with two feet to be thrown into hell.*

Text: After *geennan* 'hell' *Textus Receptus* adds *eis to pur to asbeston* 'into the unquenchable fire', which is omitted by all modern editions of the Greek text.

Exegesis: Most of the words in this verse have already been dealt with in v. 43.

duo podas 'two feet', 'both feet'.

chōlon (only here in Mark) 'lame', 'crippled'.

blēthēnai 'to be cast', 'to be thrown'.

Translation: Many languages do not distinguish 'foot' from 'leg', in speaking of a person's lower limbs. Either term is quite acceptable, for the emphasis here is upon one's ability to walk, not the possession of a particular part of the anatomy. The important thing is that the resulting loss would make one lame, translatable in some instances as 'having just one foot' or 'having just one leg'.

46 *[, where their worm does not die, and the fire is |not quenched.]*

Text: Only *Textus Receptus* includes this verse: it is omitted by all modern editions of the Greek text (it is genuine as v. 48).

Exegesis and **Translation:** See verse 48.

47 *And if your eye causes you to sin, pluck it out; it is better for you to enter the kingdom of God with one eye than with two eyes to be thrown into hell,*

Text: After *geenan* 'hell' *Textus Receptus* adds *tou puros* 'of fire', which is omitted by all modern editions of the Greek text.

Exegesis: Most of the words in this verse have already been dealt with in v. 43; for *ekballō* 'throw out', 'pull out' cf. 1:12.
   monophthalmon (only here in Mark) 'one-eyed'.
   eiselthein eis tēn basileian tou theou 'to enter into the Kingdom of God' (cf. 10:15, 23, 24, 25): in such a phrase *hē basileia tou theou* (cf. 1:15) 'the Kingdom of God' is thought of as a realm (or state, or condition) that one enters, into which one comes. Here it is identical with 'the life' (i.e. 'eternal life') of vv. 43, 45. It is, therefore, eschatological, with reference to the future life which follows the resurrection from the dead.

Translation: In so far as possible the translation of this verse should parallel the treatments of verses 43 and 45, but note that there are some significant differences, especially in the use of *the kingdom of God*.
   Pluck it out must be translated in such a way as to make it applicable to eyes, e.g. 'gouge it out', 'push it out', or 'dig it out'.
   For *kingdom of God* see 1:15 and 4:11. In this particular context *kingdom* as a place fits very well, since the introductory verb *enter* implies movement into a space. However, 'enter' in a receptor language may denote moving into an enclosure, and this may not be acceptable in speaking of the kingdom. What is more, if, as in so many instances, *kingdom* must be treated as 'rule' or 'governing' (a process, rather than a place or state), some adaptation may be required, e.g. 'enter where God rules' or 'go where you are under the rule of God'.

48 *where their worm does not die, and the fire is not quenched.*

Exegesis: This verse is a free quotation from Isa. 66:24.
   ho skōlēx autōn ou teleuta 'their worm does not die': in the context of

303

Isaiah 66 : 24, 'their' refers to the men who rebelled against God. 'Their worm' means 'the worm *that feeds upon* them'.

skōlēx (only here in the N.T.) 'worm': the singular 'the worm' is used generically for 'the worms'—it does not mean a single worm. The reference is to worms which feed upon decaying bodies.

teleutaō (cf. 7 : 10) 'die': a 'worm that does not die' is a figure of unending decay.

to pur ou sbennutai 'the fire (of hell) is not quenched': a figure of unending suffering and torment.

sbennumi (only here in Mark) 'quench', 'extinguish', 'put out' (cf. *asbestos* v. 43).

Translation: Many languages distinguish clearly between two types of worms: (1) intestinal parasites and (2) worms which feed on carrion and refuse. By translating literally 'their' the meaning of intestinal parasites has often been given, but of course this is entirely wrong. The pronoun (in the possessive form in Greek) is by no means possessive. The rotting corpse certainly does not possess the worms—if anything, it is the reverse. Accordingly, one must employ a word which clearly refers to worms feeding on dead flesh and indicate the specific relationship, e.g. 'where the worms feeding on the bodies' or 'worms eating their flesh'. More often than not a plural rather than a singular for 'worms' must be used (for one thing they are seldom seen alone), and 'their' implies a plural.

Is not quenched is a negative expression of continuous time, hence translatable in some languages as 'never put out'.

49 *For every one will be salted with fire.*

Text: At the end of the verse *Textus Receptus* adds *kai pasa thusia hali halisthēsetai* 'and every sacrifice will be salted with salt', which is omitted by all modern editions of the Greek text.

Exegesis: The translation of this verse offers no insurmountable difficulties: concerning its interpretation, however, at least 15 different explanations of the meaning of the verse have been proposed.

halisthēsetai (only here in Mark) 'will be salted', 'will be seasoned': it is generally assumed that the figure 'to salt with fire' is in some way related to Lev. 2 : 13, salt denoting preservation, and fire, purification (cf. commentaries *in loc.*). Goodspeed translates 'must be seasoned'.

Moffatt attempts a meaningful translation by rendering: 'Everyone has to be consecrated by the fire of the discipline', in a footnote explaining his translation by reference to Lev. 2 : 13.

Translation: The real problem of translation in this verse is that we do not know exactly what is meant. Moreover, it is not easy in some languages to say 'be salted', for the only equivalent would be 'have salt added to', but then how can one add to this 'with fire' or 'by means of fire'. Many suggestions have been made, and some noted in *The Bible*

Translator (5.143-44, 1954) are valuable: 'everyone shall be seasoned with fire', 'everyone shall be purified with fire', and 'everyone shall be tempered by fire' (the last of which departs from the Greek metaphor, but certainly conveys a significant meaning). In Tzeltal the rendering is 'everything becomes salty by means of fire', but this admittedly does not mean much though it carefully adheres to the original. In Loma, the expression is expanded considerably, e.g. 'fire will be put on everyone just as salt is placed on food', which is probably as meaningful as a translation can be, without involving complete recasting of the expression.

50 *Salt is good; but if the salt has lost its saltness, how will you season it? Have salt in yourselves, and be at peace with one another."*

Exegesis: *ean de to halas analon genētai* 'if the salt becomes saltless', 'if the salt lose its saltness': it is explained (cf. Arndt & Gingrich) that the coarse salt from the Dead Sea would dissolve, from excessive dampness or other causes, and leave savorless salt-like crystals as a residue. On the other hand, this may be an instance of oriental hyperbole in which 'salt losing its salt' is equivalent to something losing its reason for existence.

en tini auto artusete; 'how will you season it?', 'with what will you restore its flavor?', i.e. restore its saltness, its capacity to season, its distinguishing characteristic *as salt*.

echete en heautois hala 'have salt in yourselves': the majority take *echete* 'have' as imperative; Manson, however, takes it to be indicative, 'there is salt between you'. A reasonable explanation of the figure is offered by Lagrange who understands it to mean affability and agreeableness in social relations.

kai eirēneuete en allēlois 'and be at peace among yourselves', 'and keep peace with one another'.

eirēneuō (only here in Mark) 'to be at peace'.

Translation: *Good* must be understood in the sense of 'valuable', 'good for something' or 'useful'—not 'good', in the sense of moral or beneficent.

Salt has lost its saltness is translated in Ifugao as 'if salt has lost its salt flavor'; in Javanese it is 'if its being-salty has disappeared'. One could also say 'if salt is no longer salty'. There is, of course, a problem here in that pure sodium chloride cannot lose its saltiness, but as noted above, this passage refers evidently to a highly impure substance from which the sodium chloride could be leached out. Similar kinds of salt are found in many parts of the world, and hence the statement does not seem so "impossible" as it might to those who are acquainted only with more refined products.

How will you season it is in some languages equivalent to 'how can you put the salt flavor (or 'taste') back again'; cf. Javanese 'what shall then be done so that its flavor is made to return?'

There are two principal meanings conveyed by the word *peace*: (1) inward attitudes of tranquillity and contentment and (2) lack of strife between persons. The first type of meaning is expressed in such idioms as 'a song in the body' (Baouli), 'heart coolness' (Maninka), 'to sit down in the heart' (Bolivian Quechua), and 'quietness of heart' (Chol). The second meaning, which is the one occurring in this context, relates to the capacity for unruffled social intercourse and for sympathetic and thoughtful consideration of others (in addition, of course, to the actual absence of strife—whether on a local or national level). In this type of context idioms such as 'quiet goodness' (Kekchi) and 'having your hearts feel oneness for one another' (Tzeltal) fit quite well, for Jesus is speaking not merely of the absence of strife, but of the positive quality of social adjustment.

CHAPTER TEN

1 *And he left there and went to the region of Judea and beyond the Jordan, and crowds gathered to him again; and again, as his custom was, he taught them.*

Text: Instead of *kai* 'and' before *peran tou Iordanou* 'beyond the Jordan' of the great majority of the modern editions of the Greek text, *Textus Receptus* and Soden have *dia tou* 'through the', so that the whole clause reads 'through the other side of the Jordan'.

Exegesis: *anastas erchetai* (cf. *anastas apēlthen* 7:24) 'rising, he comes', i.e. 'leaving that place (*ekeithen* 'thence') he went'.

horia (cf. 5:17) 'boundaries', 'region': the phrase *eis ta horia* does not mean 'to the boundaries' but 'into the region'. The route indicated by the words of the text goes through Judea, across the river Jordan into Perea (cf. Goodspeed).

peran tou Iordanou (cf. 3:8, 4:35) 'beyond the Jordan', 'Perea'.

sumporeuontai palin ochloi pros auton 'again crowds come together to him'.

sumporeuomai (only here in Mark) 'go along with'; with reference to many people, as here, 'come together', 'flock', 'gather'.

ochloi 'crowds': here only, in Mark, is the plural used.

eiōthei (only here in Mark) 'he was accustomed': the form *eiōtha* is the perfect of *ethō* but has a present sense 'to be accustomed'; the pluperfect *eiōthei*, therefore, has an imperfect sense. The meaning here is not 'as he had been accustomed', but 'as he was accustomed', 'as his custom was'.

Translation: *Beyond the Jordan* identifies 'the region on the other side of the Jordan' (or 'Jordan river', if a classifier is required).

Crowds involves certain difficulties, since in many languages there are two types of plurals, aggregates and distributives. In Greek, however, it is not certain whether the plural actually denotes different crowds or whether it is a so-called augmentative plural, i.e. a plural which emphasizes the extent or size rather than the actual number of objects or occurrences. If, therefore, the Greek term *ochloi* is taken to mean simply the size of the crowd, then 'many, many people' or 'very large crowd' may be used. However, the use of the Greek form may indicate a distributive plural, implying that Jesus met with crowd after crowd wherever he went, in which case, of course, a distributive—whether of time or space— may be used. One must, however, avoid the mistake made in some languages of using an aggregate plural, for Jesus would not be addressing himself to several crowds at the same time.

As his custom was is translatable in many languages by a habitual, or customary, aspect of the verb. However, in some languages the idea of customary action can only be expressed by a separate verb phrase, e.g. 'he was accustomed to teach; he began to teach again' (Tzeltal).

2 *And Pharisees came up and in order to test him asked, "Is it lawful for a man to divorce his wife?"*

Text: The words *proselthontes Pharisaioi* 'Pharisees coming' are omitted by Taylor and Kilpatrick, but retained by all other editions of the Greek text.

Exegesis: Most of the words in this verse have already been dealt with: for *proserchomai* 'approach', 'come to' cf. 1:31; *Pharisaioi* 'Pharisees' cf. 2:16; *exestin* 'it is lawful', 'it is permitted' cf. 2:24; *apoluō* 'send away', 'dismiss', 'divorce' cf. 6:36; *peirazō* 'test', 'tempt' cf. 1:13.

Pharisaioi 'Pharisees': here, without the article, the meaning is 'some Pharisees' (cf. Moffatt, Goodspeed).

ei exestin 'if it is lawful': may be understood either as a direct question, as does RSV (also ASV, Weymouth, Arndt & Gingrich *ei* V.1; cf. 8:23)— 'Is it lawful...?'; or it may be taken as an indirect question (Moffatt, Lagrange, Goodspeed, BFBS, Manson; cf. 3:2)—'...if it is lawful...' The meaning is not vitally affected by this matter.

peirazontes auton 'testing him', 'tempting him': the majority of translations (cf. ASV, Goodspeed, Montgomery, Manson, Lagrange, Synodale, Brazilian) translate 'test', 'try' (cf. Gould); Moffatt, however, has 'tempt' and Weymouth 'entrap'. The force of the participle is taken by the majority to express purpose, 'in order to test him'; Weymouth, however, understands it as indicating attempt, 'seeking to entrap him'. The identical phrase is found, in connection with the Pharisees, in 8:11, and the meaning is probably the same in both passages.

Translation: *Came up* should not be translated literally as 'ascending'. The meaning is 'approached' or 'came to where he was'.

Test may require in some languages a very specific limitation in order to make it applicable to this context, since in a receptor language 'testing' must be distinguished on the basis of proving one's physical prowess, resisting temptation, or trying one's intelligence or knowledge. In Barrow Eskimo it was necessary to translate 'trying to make him say the wrong words'. In Tzotzil the equivalent expression is 'to hear his intelligence', in the sense of trying to discover a fault in what he would say.

Lawful often provides trouble for the translator, since in so many societies there is no body of codified law—only well-recognized customs. Moreover, the customs are so taken for granted that they are scarcely recognized as "rules"—only as implicitly accepted norms of behavior. For example, in Zoque, one must translate 'is it permitted to...', a generalized phrase representing the broadest possible relationship to norms of customary behavior. In other areas particular reference may be made to 'the law', e.g. 'does the law say that a man can'.

Divorce may be translated, either by some formal legal term, where such may exist, or by some descriptive expression, normally used for more or less permanent separation or abandonment, e.g. 'to leave his wife' (Cashibo) or 'to send his wife back' (Tzeltal).

3 *He answered them, "What did Moses command you?"*

Exegesis: *eneteilato* (13:34) 'he commanded', 'ordered'. Freely translated, the meaning of the question is: "What commandment (*entolē*) did Moses give you?"

Translation: *Answered* may be easily mistranslated in languages which require certain types of verbs introducing direct discourse. What follows is of course a question, even though it is given in response to another question. Accordingly, in some languages this must be adapted as 'he asked them in turn'.

Command may be rendered as 'tell you to do' or 'order you to do'. Often some complementary verb must be added, for Moses was not actually commanding the people but enjoining a particular order upon them.

4 *They said, "Moses allowed a man to write a certificate of divorce, and to put her away."*

Exegesis: *epetrepsen...grapsai kai apolusai* 'he allowed...(a man) to write and to divorce (her)': by law a Jewish husband had to write a divorce certificate in the presence of witnesses, sign it and deliver it to his wife, saying, "Here is your bill of divorce" (cf. the tractate *Gittin* in the Mishnah).

epitrepō (cf. 5:13) 'allow', 'permit': the Pharisees cannot quote a Mosaic *commandment* concerning divorce, but only what Moses allowed (Deut. 24:1).

biblion apostasiou (only here in Mark) 'a document of divorce', 'a certificate of divorce': in the LXX the word *apostasion* 'putting away' is always used in the sense of divorce (cf. Kennedy *Sources*, 121).

Translation: *Certificate of divorce* is translatable as 'paper concerning sending his wife away' (Ifugao), 'write her a paper when he puts her out' (Zacapoastla Aztec), or 'write a paper and she no longer will be his wife' (Piro).

Put her away must not be translated literally in most languages, for this would imply 'storing her' or 'placing her in a position away from people', a not uncommon mistake in translating. As in all such instances the receptor language idiom should be the one commonly used for a man getting rid of or abandoning a wife.

309

5 *But Jesus said to them, "For your hardness of heart he wrote you this commandment.*

Exegesis: *pros tēn sklērokardian humōn* 'on account of your hardness of heart'.

pros 'because of', 'with reference to' (Arndt & Gingrich III.5.a); 'in view of' (Moule *Idiom Book*, 53); 'having regard to' (BFBS).

sklērokardia (16:14) 'hardness of heart', 'obstinacy', 'stubbornness': Lagrange is probably right in referring the word to the lack of docility on the part of the Israelites in their relation *to God*, their unwillingness to accept his will in the matter. Cf. *pōrōsis kardias* 3:5; *pōroō kardia* 6:52.

entolēn (cf. 7:8) 'commandment', 'legislation'.

Translation: For *hardness of heart* see 6:52. In this particular phrase, however, the idiom may require a verbal form, e.g. 'because your hearts are hard' or 'since you do have hard hearts.'

Wrote you this commandment must not be taken in the sense of 'wrote this commandment to you', but rather, 'wrote this commandment for your sake'.

6 *But from the beginning of creation, 'God made them male and female.'*

Exegesis: *apo de archēs ktiseōs* 'but from the beginning of creation': so most translations. Manson, however, translates: 'From the beginning of the creation-story we learn that...' (cf. Rawlinson).

archē (cf. 1:1) 'beginning'.

ktisis (13:19, 16:15) 'creation': the meaning here may be (1) 'the sum total of everything created, *creation, world*' (Arndt & Gingrich 1.b.β) or (2) the act of creation (Swete). The use of the identical phrase in 13:19 (*ap' archēs ktiseōs*) would favor the first meaning.

arsen kai thēlu epoiēsen autous 'male and female he made them': a quotation of Gen. 1:27 (cf. also Gen. 5:1). On the meaning of this passage, in light of Jewish interpretation of it, cf. Daube *New Testament and Rabbinic Judaism*, 71-83.

Translation: For certain problems involved in translating *beginning* see 1:1. In many languages *beginning* can be translated only as an adverbial expression of time sequence, e.g. 'when God first made the world' (Huave, Bolivian Quechua) or as a verb of beginning, e.g. 'when God began in creating the world'.

Creation indicates a process which is translatable in most languages only by a verb for 'making' and an object, for 'the world' or 'everything'. However, in some languages creation may be referred to in somewhat different ways, e.g. 'when life began' (Eastern Otomí).

Them must usually be more specific, e.g. 'people' or 'human beings'.

Male and female constitutes a generic phrase. capable of including not only humans, but animals as well. In many languages, however, this type of classification is not possible. One may have to say, for example, 'God made men and women', or as in Tzeltal 'God made man with woman'.

7 *'For this reason a man shall leave his father and mother, and be joined to his wife,* **8** *and the two shall become one.' So they are no longer two but one.*

Text: The clause *kai proskollēthēsetai pros tēn gunaika autou* 'and he shall be joined to his wife', is omitted by Tischendorf, Nestle, Westcott and Hort, Lagrange, and Taylor, but included by *Textus Receptus*, Soden, Vogels, Souter, and Merk.

Exegesis: *heneken toutou kataleipsei* 'on account of this (he) will leave', 'because of this (he) will forsake'.

heneken 'on account of', 'because' (at 8:35, 10:29 it has the specific meaning 'for the sake of', 'in behalf of').

kataleipō (12:19, 21, 14:52) 'leave behind', 'forsake'.

The quotation is from Gen. 2:24, Adam's statement that because the woman was made from his bone and his flesh, *on this account* a man will leave his father and mother, etc.

proskollēthēsetai (Eph. 5:31) 'shall be joined to': the verb *proskollaō* means literally 'to glue to'.

kai esontai hoi duo eis sarka mian 'and the two shall become one flesh'. The rather unusual construction *esontai...eis* 'shall be...into' is the LXX literal translation of the Hebrew *hayah lᵉ* and means simply 'shall become', 'shall be' (cf. Arndt & Gingrich *eis* 8.a.β; Moule *Idiom Book*, 203).

sarx (13:20, 14:38) 'flesh': the phrase 'one flesh' denotes a relationship more intimate and binding than any other (cf. Lagrange, Rawlinson). In the O.T. when appeal is made to loyalty springing from family relationships the phrase 'my bone and my flesh' is used (cf. Gen. 29:14, 37:27, Judges 9:2).

Translation: *For this reason* is often translatable simply as 'because of this', referring back to the previous statement.

Leave must not be understood as 'abandoning' or 'forsaking', but as 'leaving the house of his father and mother' or 'no longer living with his father and mother'.

Joined to his wife should be translated with care or the connotations of sexual intercourse are likely to be introduced. Though of course this relationship is implicit in the statement, any explicit reference is likely to be regarded as vulgar. In some translations the equivalent expression is merely 'will live with his wife'.

Two shall become one, if rendered literally, is an impossible expression in many languages. For example, in most Bantu languages the element 'two' requires a plural prefix and the unit 'one' in the predicate of the expression would need to have this same prefix, but a plural prefix simply

311

cannot be used with the numeral one. There are, however, quite proper ways of saying essentially the same thing, e.g. 'the two different people shall be just as though they are one person'. This introduces noun expressions (required in many languages) and changes the metaphor to a simile, but in many languages this is a distinct gain in intelligibility—in fact, the only type of expression which can convey the meaning of the original.

In some translations attempts have been made to render the Greek term *sarx* literally. In certain instances the results have been ludicrous. For example, in one language the meaning was literally 'beefsteak'. In other instances, the use of 'body' has been attempted, but in certain cases even this has proved awkward, and at times vulgar. Sometimes the bare numeral 'one' can be used, e.g. 'become just one' (Zoque, Huave). In other cases the languages already possess an idiomatic equivalent, e.g. 'become one blood' (Mitla Zapotec) and 'become the complement of each other's spirit' (Tzeltal).

9 *What therefore God has joined together, let not man put a-sunder."*

Exegesis: *ho* 'that which': i.e. 'that condition', 'that state of affairs', 'that union (which God has effected)'.

sunezeuxen (only here in Mark) 'he yoked together': both in classical Greek (Arndt & Gingrich) and in non-literary *koiné* Greek (cf. Moulton & Milligan) the word is used of the marital relationship.

anthrōpos mē chōrizetō 'man is not to separate': as Rawlinson points out 'man' here indicates not judicial authority, but the husband, for it was he who actually dissolved the marriage relationship by writing a certificate of divorce and giving it to his wife, without recourse to legal authorities.

chōrizō (only here in Mark) 'divide', 'separate': Moulton & Milligan point out that the word was "almost...a technical term in connection with divorce" (cf. references in Arndt & Gingrich also). Daube (*New Testament and Rabbinic Judaism*, 74) translates: "What therefore God hath married into one, let not man divorce."

Translation: *Joined together*, as in the case of *joined* in verse 7, must be treated with care to avoid vulgar connotations. In some instances the most satisfactory equivalent is 'therefore, if God has made two people man and wife'.

Put asunder must not be taken in the purely literal sense of physical separation, a rendering which has likewise led to certain vulgar associations. The meaning here is often translatable as 'cause to be divorced' or 'abandon'. If the first clause is made conditional, the second may follow quite normally, e.g. 'If God has made them man and wife, then no one should cause abandonment', referring here to the actual participants in the marriage, not to outside authorities.

10 *And in the house the disciples asked him again about this matter.*

Exegesis: *eis tēn oikian* (cf. 7:17, 24, 9:33) 'in the house' (RSV, Goodspeed); 'indoors' (Moffatt, Weymouth, Montgomery); 'back home' (Manson; cf. Brazilian *em casa*, Zürich *zu Hause*).

palin 'again': practically all commentators and translations connect 'again' with 'the disciples asked'; Gould, Manson and BFBS, however, connect it with *eis tēn oikian* 'in the house', 'indoors'.

epērōtōn 'they were asking': Weymouth and Montgomery translate 'began questioning'.

Translation: *In the house* is not only a locative phrase, but a transitional one as well, for it points out a contrast in location. The equivalent in some languages is 'when they were back in the house'.

This matter may be specified as 'what he said' or 'divorce', if the receptor language has no generic term such as 'matter'.

11 *And he said to them, "Whoever divorces his wife and marries another, commits adultery against her;*

Exegesis: *kai gamēsē allēn* 'and he should marry another': the meaning is, naturally, 'another *woman*' (*nct* 'another wife'). ˙

gameō (cf. 6:17) 'marry'.

moichatai ep' autēn 'he commits adultery with reference to her': the great majority of commentators and translators understand *autēn* 'her' to refer to the first woman, whom the husband divorced (not the second, whom he married). Lagrange: "with regard to her: for it is with respect to her and to her rights that the second act is (an act of) adultery" (cf. Arndt & Gingrich, Taylor). BFBS and N. Turner, however (*The Bible Translator* 7.151-52, 1956), understand it to mean 'commits adultery with her' (i.e. the second woman); Turner appeals to LXX Jer. 5:8 *chremetizō epi* 'neigh after': he cannot, however, cite any instance of Mark's using *epi* with the accusative meaning 'with'.

epi 'upon', 'with reference to': in a hostile sense, 'against' (cf. its use with this meaning in 3:24, 25, 26, 13:12, 14:48).

Translation: The clause introduced by *whoever* may be shifted to a conditional clause, as is required by many languages, 'if any one does..., he...'

Against her is not only a difficult expression for exegesis, but also a complicated phrase to translate. In some languages the reference must be made more specific, to be meaningful at all, e.g. 'commits adultery against the first woman' (Ifugao). In Huastec one may say 'commits sin against her'. In Conob an idiomatic phrase is commonly used 'did evil against her eyes', but in some languages (e.g. Kiyaka, Tzeltal) the phrase is best omitted, since 'adultery' is understood with reference to the first woman, and any attempt to translate this phrase is either highly redundant or is understood as applying somehow to the second woman.

313

12 *and if she divorces her husband and marries another, she commits adultery."*

Text: Instead of *autē apolusasa* 'she divorcing' of the majority of modern editions of the Greek text, *Textus Receptus*, Lagrange, and Kilpatrick have *gunē apolusē...kai* 'a woman should divorce...and'; Taylor has *gunē exelthē apo tou andros kai* 'a woman should abandon her husband and'.

Instead of *gamēsē* 'she should marry' of all modern editions of the Greek text, *Textus Receptus* has *gamēthē* 'she should be married'.

Exegesis: As the commentators point out, this saying has in view Graeco-Roman customs: in Jewish law only the husband could get a divorce.

kai ean autē 'and if she': in the general sense of 'and if a woman' (*not* 'she' the woman in v. 11 who has been divorced by her husband).

Translation: *She* may be translated as 'a woman' or 'any woman'.

For *divorces* see 10:4.

Commits adultery may need to be translated as 'is guilty of adultery' or 'is guilty of sin', since the previous clause may describe quite clearly what she has done, e.g. 'leaves her husband and lives with another man'.

Marries is always translatable, but in a variety of ways, depending upon such factors as (1) whether a man or a woman is spoken of, (2) the consent or agreement of the clan (in this type of context clan consent would not be likely), and (3) whether or not a previous marriage has been contracted.

13 *And they were bringing children to him, that he might touch them; and the disciples rebuked them.*

Exegesis: *prosepheron* (cf. 2:4) 'they were bringing to': another example of the impersonal plural, 'people were bringing' (cf. Moule *Idiom Book*, 28).

paidia 'children': these are not necessarily infants, babes in arms (Luke 18:15 uses *brephē* 'infants'). As Lagrange points out the term includes children from the age of eight days to twelve years (cf. Mk. 5:39ff. where it is used of the twelve year old daughter of Jairus).

hina autōn hapsētai 'that he might touch them'.

haptomai (cf. 1:41) 'touch': here the equivalent of *epitithenai tas cheiras* 'lay hands upon', with the purpose, of course, of blessing (cf. Arndt & Gingrich 2.b.).

epetimēsan (cf. 1:25) 'they rebuked', 'reproved' (so most translations); Moffatt and BFBS, however, 'checked'.

autois 'them' i.e. the people who were bringing the children.

Translation: *Bringing* had better be interpreted in the sense of 'leading', rather than 'carrying', where languages make such a distinction.

Touch may require some further specification in some languages, e.g. 'touch with the hand'.

Rebuked may be translated as 'told them not to do so', or in instances where a clear reference to the people is required, 'the disciples told the people who were leading the children, Don't do that'.

14 But when Jesus saw it he was indignant, and said to them, "Let the children come to me, do not hinder them; for to such belongs the kingdom of God.

Exegesis: *ēganaktēsen* (10:41, 14:4) 'he grew indignant', 'he got angry', 'he was aroused'.

aphete (cf. 2:5) 'allow', 'permit', 'let'.

mē kōluete auta 'stop forbidding them', 'quit hindering them'.

kōluō (cf. 9:38) 'hinder', 'forbid', 'restrain'.

tōn gar toioutōn estin hē basileia tou theou 'for of such as these is the Kingdom of God' (cf. BFBS).

ho toioutos 'one of this kind', 'one of this sort', 'one such as this' (cf. Arndt & Gingrich 3.a.α): the proper force of this correlative demonstrative pronoun of quality should be observed, and not be reduced simply to a demonstrative, as though it meant only 'this one'. Cf. Goodspeed 'such as they'; Moffatt 'such as these'; Manson 'such as them'; Synodale *ceux qui leur resemblent*. As seen in the next verse *hōs paidion* 'as a child', Jesus is speaking of the characteristics or qualities of children, not of the children themselves (so most commentators; Lagrange, however, supposes that both meanings *à ceux qui resemblent aux enfants*, and *à ces enfants eux-mêmes* are not mutually exclusive).

eimi 'to be' with the genitive may mean 'belongs to', indicating possession (cf. Arndt & Gingrich *eimi* IV.1), or quality.

hē basileia tou theou (cf. 1:15) 'the Kingdom of God'.

Translation: *It* is in some languages 'what had happened' or 'what they were doing'.

Said to them refers to the statement to the disciples, e.g. 'said to the disciples'. In some languages this third person plural object tends to be related to the immediately preceding pronoun of the same type, which refers to those bringing the children to Jesus.

For *kingdom of God* see 1:15 and 4:11.

To such belongs implies a very difficult relationship in some languages, especially where *kingdom* is translated as 'rule' or 'government', as a process rather than an object. In such instances one cannot speak of a person possessing such a process. In Zoque the entire construction is recast as 'God will rule over such as these'. In Tzeltal an entirely different perspective is employed, e.g. 'persons like these will reach God's government'.

It is possible to interpret the Greek expression *tōn...toioutōn estin* 'of such is' as referring to the quality of the participants, rather than to possession. In this case, the relationship of the kingdom to the participants becomes somewhat easier to express, especially in languages in

315

which kingdom is translated as 'rule' or 'government' (i.e. as a process rather than an object). For example, in Barrow Eskimo this passage is rendered as 'the kingdom of God is full of people who are as children', a close equivalent of one possible meaning of the Greek expression.

15 *Truly, I say to you, whoever does not receive the kingdom of God like a child shall not enter it."*

Exegesis: *dexētai* (cf. 6:11) 'should receive', 'should accept'.
ou mē (cf. 9:1) 'in no way', 'by no means': an emphatic negative.

Translation: For *truly* as an introductory adverb see 8:12.

Receive the kingdom of God is not an easy expression to translate, and its literal rendering has often resulted in misunderstanding. For example, in one language it meant that a person had taken over the kingdom upon the death of God. In another language the literal rendering meant that one man had agreed to guard God's property for him. Moreover, a kingdom (even as a territory, rather than a rule) cannot be received as some portable object can be received. The result of all these problems leads to a number of necessary adaptions, e.g. 'receive God as king' (Conob), 'like God to rule over' (Zoque), 'agree to God reigning over' (Mixtec), 'welcome God as ruler' (Huastec), 'be happy to have God rule over' (Popoluca), and 'be happy to have God be your chief' (Tzotzil).

Like a child must be added to the first expression in such a way as to characterize the activity of a child, e.g. 'welcome God as ruler as a child welcomes him' (Huastec) and 'wish for, as a little child does, where God rules' (Huave).

Enter it must be translated in such a way as to correspond with the immediately preceding clause, e.g. 'will not have God as ruler' (Popoluca).

16 *And he took them in his arms and blessed them, laying his hands upon them.*

Exegesis: *enagkalisamenos* (cf. 9:36) 'embracing', 'taking into (his) arms'.

kateulogei titheis 'he blessed laying': most translations have it simply, 'he laid (his hands upon them) and blessed'. The participle *titheis* 'laying' may indicate means 'by laying (his hands upon them)', or accompanying circumstances 'as he laid (his hands upon them)' (cf. Williams, Zürich).

kateulogeō (only here in the N.T.; cf. *eulogeō* 6:41) 'bless': in accordance with the customs of the time, we are to understand that Jesus invoked God's blessings upon them ('May God bless you') rather than pronounced a blessing himself ('I bless you'). Some commentators and translators understand the preposition *kata* in this compound verb to have the meaning 'tenderly', 'warmly', 'lovingly'. The imperfect of the verb describes Jesus blessing the children one by one, not all at the same time.

tithenai tas cheiras (cf. 5:23 for *epitithenai tas cheiras*) 'to lay hands', 'to place (his) hands': as Lagrange points out, this imposition of hands is the mode of the benediction.

Translation: *Them* must refer specifically to the children.

In his arms probably refers to a position on his lap rather than to his simply lifting them up from the ground while he was in a standing position (as a Rabbi he was probably teaching in a seated position). This difference is important in some languages.

For *bless* see 6:41, but in this instance persons are the object of the blessing, and hence certain adjustments may be required.

17 And as he was setting out on his journey, a man ran up and knelt before him, and asked him, "Good Teacher, what must I do to inherit eternal life?"

Exegesis: *ekporeuomenou autou eis hodon* 'as he was setting out on the journey', 'as he was leaving for the trip'.

ekporeuomai (cf. 1:5) 'go out', 'proceed'.

eis hodon (cf. 6:8) 'in the road', 'on the way'.

prosdramōn heis kai gonupetēsas auton 'a man running up and kneeling before him'.

prostrechō (cf. 9:15) 'run to'.

heis 'one': here is the same as the indefinite pronoun *tis* 'a certain one', 'someone' (cf. Moule *Idiom Book*, 125).

gonupeteō (cf. 1:40) 'kneel'.

didaskale agathe 'good teacher': the word 'good' here means 'kind', 'beneficent', 'generous', *not* 'efficient' or 'capable', as though the man were complimenting Jesus on his ability as a teacher; neither does it refer to the moral character of Jesus in the sense of 'holy' or something similar (cf. Lagrange).

hina zōēn aiōnion klēronomēsō; 'in order that I inherit eternal life?'

klēronomeō 'inherit': although the word may mean simply 'obtain', 'acquire', 'possess', the literal meaning 'to receive by lot', 'to come into the inheritance of', better fits in with the Jewish concept of the people of Israel as God's lot and eternal life as a gift, an inheritance, that man receives from God (cf. Ps. 37:11; Lagrange refers to Ps. Sol. 14:5, 10, which speak of Israel as the lot and inheritance of God, and of the just inheriting life; cf. also Dalman *Words*, 125-27).

zōē aiōnion (10:30) 'eternal life' (cf. 3:29 for *aiōnion* 'age-long', 'eternal'). It should be observed that the question is eschatological, from the point of view of Jewish theology of that time: "What must I do that in the resurrection from the dead eternal life be my lot?" The earliest expression of this eschatological concept is to be found in Dan. 12:2.

Translation: Since this verse often begins an entirely new section, the use of 'Jesus' in place of 'he' may be required.

Where required by the cultural patterns, *knelt before him* may be expressed as 'stooped down before' or 'bowed down before' leaving implicit the exact position of the knees.

317

For *teacher* see 2:13.

Good Teacher as a phrase of direct address may not be permitted, since—though nouns as titles may be so used—they are often restricted in such a way that attributive adjectives cannot be used with them as modifiers. However, an expanded, attributive clause can often be employed, 'Teacher, you who are good'.

Inherit cannot be translated literally in many languages since it would imply that someone has died and that the life which is inherited is the one which has just been given up, which has given some readers the impression that the Bible is talking about metempsychosis. In such instances one must use a verb meaning 'receive', 'come to possess', or 'have'.

For certain problems related to *eternal* see 3:29, but in this context the difficulties are somewhat different because *eternal* is combined with *life*. Often *eternal* is translated as 'lasting' or 'continuing', or by some idiomatic equivalent which indicates some type of continuity, e.g. 'day with day' (Kabba-Laka) or 'of all the years' (Kiyaka). However, there are certain problems in this usage. For example, in Navajo the expression 'continuous life', which had seemed for some time to be satisfactory, proved entirely erroneous, for the Navajos believe that all people possess 'continuing life', in the sense that each succeeding generation is a demonstration of this continuing stream of life within the family unit. Accordingly, in Navajo it was necessary to translate 'life without end'. The same type of expression is used in Barrow Eskimo, Zacapoastla Aztec, Maya, Amuzgo, and Bare'e.

Inherit eternal life must undergo certain changes in languages in which *life* must be translated as a verb, e.g. 'do in order to be able to live without end'.

18 **And Jesus said to him, "Why do you call me good? No one is good but God alone.**

Exegesis: *agathos* 'good': as the word is used by Jesus it refers to moral attributes, and here, with reference to God, is the equivalent of 'perfect' (cf. Arndt & Gingrich 1.b.α and examples there quoted).

heis ho theos (cf. 2:7) 'one, (that is) God': cf. in 2:7 the suggestion that the phrase means 'the One God'. If, in a given language, the translation of *oudeis agathos ei mē heis ho theos* 'no one (person) is good except God alone', implies that God is thereby classified as a human being, the error may be avoided by translating 'no man is good: only God is good', or, simply, 'God alone is good'.

Translation: *Said* may need to be changed to 'asked' because of the following question.

Even apart from the problem of confusing God with human beings, the construction *no one...but...* is rendered in some languages as a paratactically combined set of clauses, e.g. 'no one can be good; only God is good', meaning precisely what the Greek says, but expressing the idea in a somewhat different form.

318

19 *You know the commandments: 'Do not kill, Do not commit adultery, Do not steal, Do not bear false witness, Do not defraud, Honor your father and mother.' "*

Exegesis: The commandments quoted (from Ex. 20:12-16; cf. Deut. 5:16-20) are, with the exception of 'Do not defraud', numbers VI, VII, VIII, IX, V, in that order, from the Decalogue.

mē phoneusēs 'you shall not kill', 'you shall not murder' (the verb is found only here in Mark; cf. the noun *phonos* in 7:21).

mē moicheusēs 'you shall not commit adultery' (cf. *moichaomai* in 10 : 11-12, and *moicheia* in 7:21).

mē klepsēs 'you shall not steal'.

mē pseudomarturēsēs (cf. 14:56, 57) 'you shall not bear false witness', 'you shall not give false testimony'.

mē aposterēsēs 'you shall not defraud': the verb has the specialized meaning of 'defraud', 'deprive of' (cf. Field *Notes*, 33-34). By some it is taken to refer to commandment X ('you shall not covet'); others see it as another aspect of commandment VIII ('you shall not steal').

tima (cf. 7:6) 'you must honor'.

Translation: *Commandments* is translatable in some languages only by a verb, in which case a subject must be introduced, e.g. 'what God commanded' (or 'ordered'), or 'what God said people should do' (or 'not do', depending upon the requirements of following sequence).

Kill should be interpreted here in the sense of *murder*, but it should not be restricted merely to ingroup killing (in some tribes the murder of a member of the outgroup—whether of a hostile or foreign clan or tribe—is a heroic deed, while the murder of a member of the ingroup, i.e. the immediate social unit, is condemned).

For *adultery* see 7:21. Note, however, that in languages in which adultery is described in terms of either the man's taking another woman or a woman's taking another man, one must choose the first of these alternatives in this passage since Jesus is addressing himself specifically to a man, e.g. 'don't take another woman' (Cashibo) or 'don't be unfaithful to your wife' (Zoque).

False witness is 'do not lie about people' (Huave), and 'say he is guilty, while lying' (Totonac).

Defraud is translated as 'do not take from others by cheating' (Tzeltal).

For *honor* see 7:6, but in this context the meaning is not primarily one of 'praise', but of 'obedience', translated sometimes as 'show respect for' and 'demonstrate obedience to'.

20 *And he said to him, "Teacher, all these I have observed from my youth."*

Exegesis: There is no evidence, either in the man's statement, or in Jesus' reply, that these words are an exaggeration or a falsehood (cf. Lagrange).

ephulaxamēn (only here in Mark) 'I kept', 'I guarded': with reference

319

to a commandment, as here, the verb means 'observe', 'follow' (cf. Arndt & Gingrich 2.b).

ek neotētos 'from youth (up to now)', 'ever since I was young'.

Translation: *Said* may need to be translated as 'replied'.

For *teacher* see 2: 13.

All these I have observed must be translated carefully, for obviously this must not be translated literally in the sense of 'looked at' or 'regarded'. The meaning here is 'I have obeyed these commandments'. In some translations the rendering has been 'have done all these things', with exactly the wrong meaning, for though the last commandment is a positive one, the previous ones are in a negative form, and to say 'I have done these' might be entirely in error. Accordingly, one may translate in some cases as 'I have done just what I should' or 'I have obeyed these words'.

Youth would imply approximately thirteen years of age, at which time Jewish boys were regarded as having reached the age of accountability and hence moral responsibility for their actions.

21 *And Jesus looking upon him loved him, and said to him, "You lack one thing; go, sell what you have, and give to the poor, and you will have treasure in heaven; and come, follow me."*

Text: At the end of the verse *Textus Receptus*, Soden, Vogels, and Merk add *aras ton stauron* 'taking up the cross', which is omitted by the majority of modern editions of the Greek text.

Exegesis: *emblepsas autō ēgapēsen auton* 'looking on him he loved him'.

emblepō (cf. 8: 25) 'see', 'look at', 'look on'.

agapaō (12: 30, 31, 33) 'love': here Field (*Notes*, 34) suggests that perhaps it means 'he caressed him', and gives examples of the verb used with this meaning (cf. Arndt & Gingrich 1.b.α).

hen se husterei literally 'one thing lacks you': the verb *hustereō* means 'fail', 'lack' and is here used impersonally; the numeral *hen* 'one thing' is the subject, and the personal pronoun *se* 'you' is the object.

hosa echeis pōlēson 'whatever you have sell'.

hosa (cf. 3: 8) 'everything that', 'as many things as'.

pōleō (11: 15) 'sell'.

kai dos tois ptōchois 'and give (the proceeds from the sale) to the poor' (cf. Weymouth).

thēsauron en ouranō 'treasure in heaven': Arndt & Gingrich comment, "which is, as it were, deposited there and becomes available to men after death" (*thēsauros* 2.b.α). Or, as Taylor comments, 'treasure in heaven' means 'treasure with God'.

ouranos (cf. 1: 10) 'heaven' where God dwells.

deuro (only here in Mark; cf. *deute* 1: 17) is an adverb 'hither' used as an imperative 'come!'

akolouthei (cf. 1 : 18) 'you follow', 'become my disciple'.

Translation: *Loved* should be translated in such a way as to indicate Jesus' profound admiration and regard for this young man, but one must carefully avoid any suggestion of emotional attitude which would imply amorous instincts of homosexuality. In speaking of love, whether divine or human, there are a number of idiomatic expressions used in various languages, e.g. 'his heart burned for' (Amuzgo), 'he hurt in his heart' (Tzeltal), 'his heart went away with' (Mitla Zapotec), 'his abdomen died for him' (Conob), 'his thoughts were toward him' (Cashibo), and 'put him in his heart' (Habbe).

A literal rendering of *you lack one thing* may be quite misleading, if it refers essentially to the lack of possessions. The meaning here is that there is still one thing which he should do, e.g. 'you still fail in one thing' (in the sense of 'action' or 'activity').

Give to the poor must be understood in the sense of 'distribute the proceeds (i.e. 'the money') to the poor people'.

And come must be rendered in some languages as involving some transitional element, since the last two imperative verbs are not completely coordinate with the first three. That is to say, the commands to *go, sell and give* represent one stage, followed by the commands, *come, follow*. Accordingly, one must sometimes translate as 'then come, follow me'.

For *follow* see 1:17.

22 At that saying his countenance fell, and he went away sorrowful; for he had great possessions.

Exegesis: *stugnasas* (only here in Mark) 'becoming gloomy': Arndt & Gingrich suggest possibly 'shocked' or 'appalled'.

epi tō logō 'at the word', 'with the saying'.

epi 'upon': after verbs which express feeling the preposition means 'at', 'because', 'with' (cf. 1:22, 3:5; see Arndt & Gingrich II.1.b.γ).

lupoumenos (14:19) 'sorrowing', 'sad', 'distressed'. Manson translates 'in annoyance'.

ktēmata (only here in Mark) in general means 'property', 'possessions'; specifically it means 'lands', 'estates' (cf. Moulton & Milligan; Swete).

Translation: *Countenance fell* can only rarely be translated literally. In Navajo one must say 'his face drew together' and in Ifugao the equivalent is 'his feeling changed'.

At that saying may be translated as a verb expression in the form 'when Jesus said that'.

Sorrowful must in some languages be carefully handled in order to avoid the meaning of 'sorrow' as an emotional response to death or bereavement. In this passage the meaning is one of emotional distress and disturbance, and as in so many instances of such psychological reactions the ways of speaking about these experiences are quite varied and often highly metaphorical, e.g. 'his stomach died' (Mezquital Otomi), 'he was heavy in his stomach' (Uduk), 'his heart was pained' (Kpelle), 'he was sick in his mind' (Ifugao), 'his heart hung' (Loma), and 'his heart was spoiled' (Moré).

The cultural equivalent of *great possessions* is in many languages 'many farms' and in others 'many houses'. In some languages the closest corresponding expression is 'he was very rich'.

23 *And Jesus looked around and said to his disciples, "How hard it will be for those who have riches to enter the kingdom of God!"*

Exegesis: *periblepsamenos* (cf. 3 : 5) 'looking around'.
duskolōs (10 : 24) 'with difficulty'; *pōs duskolōs* 'with what difficulty!'
chrēmata (only here in Mark) 'wealth', 'property', 'riches'.
eiseleusontai 'they shall enter': the Kingdom of God is here referred to in eschatological terms.

Translation: *Looked around* implies 'looked around at the people'.
How hard introduces an exclamatory expression, which in some languages can only be stated as 'very hard' or 'exceedingly difficult', e.g. 'those who have riches will have a very difficult time to enter...'
Have riches may be either 'have much property' or 'are very rich'.
For problems involved in expressions for *the kingdom of God* see 1 : 15, 4 : 11, and 10 : 15.

24 *And the disciples were amazed at his words. But Jesus said to them again, "Children, how hard it is to enter the kingdom of God!*

Text: After *pōs duskolon estin* 'how hard it is' *Textus Receptus*, Soden, Vogels, Souter, and Merk add *tous pepoithotas epi toi chrēmasin* '(for) those who trust in riches', with considerable support from Greek mss. and early versions; Tischendorf, Westcott and Hort, Nestle, Lagrange, Taylor, and Kilpatrick do not include the words.

Exegesis: Most of the words of this verse have already been dealt with: for *thambeomai* 'be amazed' cf. 1 : 27; *epi* 'at' cf. 10 : 22; *teknon* 'child' cf. 2 : 5.

Translation: For *amazed* see 1 : 22 and 27. *His words* may be rendered as 'what he said'.
Children must often be adapted to the cultural framework of such an utterance, for otherwise this would seem to be a reference by Jesus to the children whom he had blessed (verse 16) and who were still standing by listening to his words. (Compare the use of *my son* in 2 : 5). In such instances one may need to use 'young men', as a culturally applicable term to designate the disciples (cf. the English usage 'my dear young man', especially in a context in which one wishes to raise an objection to a statement or an inference).
Trust in riches, though not in the better Greek texts, is found widely in traditional translations. The meaning is rendered as 'think their riches are important' or 'think their riches will save them' (Tzeltal).

25 *It is easier for a camel to go through the eye of a needle than for a rich man to enter the kingdom of God."*

Exegesis: The words of this verse are clear and precise in their meaning: there is no doubt as to how they are to be translated. The camel was the largest animal in Palestine and the eye of a needle the smallest opening: the metaphor of a camel going through the eye of a needle vividly defines an *impossibility.*

eukopōteron (cf. 2:9) 'easier'.

tēs trumalias tēs raphidos (only here in Mark) 'the eye of the needle'. For the fanciful conjecture that there was a small gate into Jerusalem with the name 'eye of a needle' in the time of Jesus, cf. the commentaries.

plousion (cf. 12:41) 'a rich man'.

Some details of the syntax of the Greek should not be overlooked: the subject of the main verb *esti* 'is' is the infinitive *dielthein* 'to go through', with *kamēlon* in the accusative case as the subject of the infinitive (according to normal Greek construction; some grammarians call this "the accusative of general reference"); *eukopōteron* 'easier' is the predicate, and is neuter because *eiselthein* 'to enter', the subject of the verb *esti* 'is', is neuter. In the second clause the same construction prevails: *plousion* 'a rich man' is the subject of the infinitive *eiselthein* 'to go in' (while the main verb and the predicate of this second clause, *esti eukopon* 'is easy', are implied).

Translation: A number of problems all seem to conspire to make this verse a very difficult one to translate: (a) the form of the comparative, (b) the use of *camel*, (c) the idiom *eye of a needle*, and (d) the phrase *enter the kingdom of God.*

Neat comparative expressions, applicable to the comparison of activities (rather than merely objects), are not too common in languages throughout the world. Very frequently one must use paratactically combined expressions, often with a positive-negative contrast and frequently with some more limited form of comparison, involving 'more', 'surpassing', 'beyond', or 'very much'. For example, in Tzeltal this verse reads 'it is difficult to thread the eye of a needle with a camel, but it is beyond difficult that rich men enter God's government' (this latter phrase does not refer to participation in the government, only to their entrance within the realm of his rule). In Navajo this passage is translated as 'it is not hard for a camel...; it is hard for a rich man...' In Trique one says 'it is hard to pass...; it is more hard...' (For related problems of comparison see 1:7).

Easier may be translated in some languages as 'less hard' or 'not difficult', since such qualities are often paired by positive-negative terms using different poles of meaning from those with which we may be accustomed. (For example, in Maya the word for 'good' is literally 'not bad'.)

Camel is most often rendered by a borrowed word, with or without a classifier, e.g. 'animal called *camello*', using a borrowing from Spanish (Cashibo). In some instances, however, 'llama-like animal' has been used in the Andean area of South America (see 1 : 6). In Barrow Eskimo a descriptive term has been employed, e.g. 'big-humped animal'.

Eye of a needle is rendered variously in different languages: 'foot of a needle' (Mitla Zapotec), 'hole in the foot of the needle' (Amuzgo), 'nostril of a needle' (Piro), 'mouth of a needle' (Haka Chin), 'ear of a needle' (Tiddim), 'nose of a needle' (Lahu), 'channel of a needle' (Rawang).

For *kingdom of God* see 1 : 15, 4 : 11, and 10 : 15.

26 And they were exceedingly astonished, and said to him, "Then who can be saved?"

Text: Instead of *pros heautous* 'to one another' of the majority of modern editions of the Greek text, Westcott and Hort, and Taylor (and RSV) have *pros auton* 'to him'.

Exegesis: *perissōs* (15 : 14) 'beyond measure', 'exceedingly' (cf. *perissoteron* 7 : 36).

exeplēssonto (cf. 1 : 22) 'they were astonished', 'they were amazed'.

kai tis 'and who': in this context *kai* has the meaning of *ara* 'therefore'. Lagrange translates *Mais alors?*, classifying this use of *kai* as classical and giving further examples from the N.T.

sōthēnai (cf. 3 : 4) 'to be saved': in the theological sense. In the context of this incident all these theological terms have an eschatological reference.

Translation: For *astonished* see 1 : 22, 27.

For a discussion of problems related to the rendering of *save* see *The Bible Translator*, 1.90, 94 (1950), 2.112 (1951), 3.228-29 (1952), 4.73 (1953), 5.93 (1954), and 8.84 (1957), *Bible Translating*, 222; and *God's Word in Man's Language*, 139-40. In general there are three types of expressions used in translating *save*: (1) those meaning 'to help, assist, aid, care for', (2) those signifying 'to rescue' or 'to deliver (from danger, or from confinement, e.g. a jail)', and (3) those which imply 'healing' or 'restoration to health'. The Greek term involves essentially the latter two meanings, since the same word may be translated either as 'to heal' or 'to save' depending upon the context. For the most part, words which mean only 'to help' have been regarded as inadequate, but as in the case of the Conob, the word which means essentially 'to help' may also be used in contexts involving the rescuing of a person from danger. Accordingly, not only by its indigenous association, but by biblical context, the word has acquired certain significant qualities which make it acceptable. In Shipibo the term rendering *save* means literally 'to make to live', which is in many regards very good, for it combines not only the meaning of 'to rescue' and 'to deliver from danger', but also the concept of 'to heal' or 'restore to health'—precisely what is involved in the Greek term. In some languages certain metaphorical expressions have been used: 'to help the heart' (San Blas), 'to take by the hand' in the meaning of 'rescue' or 'deliver' (Kabba-Laka), 'to lift out on behalf of' (Mazatec), 'to have life because of' (Anuak), 'to be healed in the heart' (Mazahua), 'to save his head', meaning to rescue a person in the fullest sense (Baouli), 'to come out well' (Amuzgo), and 'to be helped as to his breath' (or 'life') (Ngok Dinka).

Though the construction *be saved* is passive in form, one must not automatically change this to an active in languages which have no passive, for if this is done and God is made the subject, e.g. 'Whom can God save', this would imply a doubt as to God's capacity rather than the unlikelihood of any person attaining salvation. In such instances one must adjust the rendering so that 'saved' will denote a state, rather than the passive of the process.

27 *Jesus looked at them and said, "With men it is impossible, but not with God; for all things are possible with God."*

Exegesis: *emblepsas* (cf. 10 : 21) 'looking at', 'looking on'.

para anthrōpois...para theō 'with men...with God': *para* with the dative has, in this construction, the force of the dative—'for men...for God' (cf. Arndt & Gingrich *para* II.2.c). The implied subject is *touto* 'this' (i.e. *to sōzesthai* 'the being saved').

adunaton (only here in Mark) 'impossible'.

"All things are possible with God" is an O.T. phrase (Gen. 18 : 14; cf. Job 42 : 2, Zech. 8 : 6).

dunata (cf. 9 : 23) 'possible'.

Translation: *With men it is impossible* is a highly elliptical phrase, quite understandable, but quite difficult to reproduce in certain languages, where it is impossible to use an indefinite pronoun such as 'it' referring to a process of being saved and to employ 'impossible' without specifically stating what is impossible. Accordingly, one must translate in some instances 'people cannot cause saving' or 'people cannot save themselves' (in which case a reflexive may be necessary if an object of the verb 'save' is required). The following clause is then combined with the first as 'but God can save them'.

In some languages a generic type of verb can be used, e.g. 'men cannot do this, but God can do so', in which case 'do' is a type of substitute verb for 'save', employed in the previous verse.

All things are possible with God must often be changed, as in the case of Tzeltal, to a direct active expression, e.g. 'God can do anything' (or 'all things').

28 *Peter began to say to him, "Lo, we have left everything and followed you."*

Exegesis: *ērxato legein* 'he began to say'. RSV is probably justified in giving full force to *archomai* 'begin' in this verse, rather than regarding it as a virtually meaningless auxiliary (cf. 1 : 45), as does BFBS.

idou hēmeis 'behold we': the pronoun 'we' is probably emphatic, in

325

contrast with the rich man who was not willing to leave anything (cf. Gould).

For *aphiēmi* 'leave' cf. 2:5, and *akoloutheō* 'follow' cf. 1:18. Gould and Taylor call attention to the use of the aorist *aphēkamen* 'we left', describing the decisive act of renunciation, and the perfect *ēkolouthēkamen* 'we have followed', describing the permanent role of discipleship.

Translation: *Lo* in some languages is equivalent to 'look here' or 'mind you'. It is an emphatic element, designated to call special attention to what is said. It does not imply literal 'looking'.

Left everything may require expansion to 'left all that we had', in order for it to be understood in the sense of renunciation rather than merely of getting up and departing, or of inadvertently leaving things behind.

For *follow* see 1:17.

29 ***Jesus said, "Truly, I say to you, there is no one who has left house or brothers or sisters or mother or father or children or 1s, for my sake and for the gospel,***

Text: After *patera* 'father' *Textus Receptus* and Kilpatrick add *ē gunaika* 'or wife', which is omitted by all other modern editions of the Greek text.

Exegesis: The words of this verse have already been dealt with: for *aphiēmi* 'leave' cf. 2:5; *agros* 'field' cf. 5:14; *heneken* 'for the sake of' cf. 10:7; *euaggelion* 'gospel' cf. 1:1.

Translation: For *truly* as an emphatic introductory particle see 8:12.

The construction *no one who...who will not...* is difficult to reproduce as such in many languages. Frequently a conditional construction must be substituted, e.g. 'if any one does..., he will...' (Huave). In other languages it is advisable to break this long sentence (consisting of verses 29 and 30) as 'a man may...; he will certainly receive...' or 'those who have left..., they will receive...' The difficulty with the Greek construction is not only its length but the double negative.

House refers to a man's own home, translatable in some languages as 'home village', rather than literally his 'hut', for a man may leave one house for another, but this passage refers to a more permanent separation from the close village and family ties.

In languages which have special distinctions for 'brothers and sisters' this verse becomes somewhat more complex. For example, there may be special words for younger versus older brothers and sisters. Also, brothers and sisters may be classed not as two groups, but as one, namely, siblings. Accordingly, if in some languages one wishes to include all possibilities, the corresponding phrase must be somewhat altered, e.g. 'older siblings and younger siblings', 'older brothers and older sisters and younger siblings', in which older siblings are distinguished as to sex, but not younger ones (Tzeltal, Zoque), or 'older and younger brothers and older and younger sisters' (Tzotzil).

326

For my sake may be treated either as causal 'because of me...' or purposive 'for the benefit of' or 'for the sake of...' In some instances *for my sake and for the gospel* may be combined as 'to help me and the good news'.

30 *who will not receive a hundredfold now in this time, houses and brothers and sisters and mothers and children and lands, with persecutions, and in the age to come eternal life.*

Exegesis: *ean mē labē* 'unless he receive', 'except he receive': this construction goes back to the beginning of v. 29, *oudeis estin hos aphēken... ean mē labē* 'there is none who left...unless he receive'. The phrase can be freely translated, 'Whoever left...will receive'.

en tō kairō toutō 'in this time': the word *kairos* (cf. 1:15) is here equal in meaning with *aiōn* 'age' and 'this time (age)' is contrasted with 'the coming age' in the next clause.

meta diōgmōn 'with persecutions': that is, among or accompanied by persecutions (cf. Moule *Idiom Book*, 61).

diōgmos (cf. 4:17) 'persecution'.

en tō aiōni tō erchomenō 'in the coming age', 'in the future age'.

aiōn (cf. 3:29) 'age'.

ho erchomenos 'the coming one', 'the future one' (for this use of the participle of *erchomai* 'come' cf. Arndt & Gingrich II.1.b.β).

zōēn aiōnion (cf. 10:17) 'eternal life'.

Translation: *Hundredfold* is often not easily translated, but in some languages one can say 'if he leaves a home, a brother, a sister ..., he will receive one hundred homes, brothers, sisters,...'

Receive must not be translated in the sense of 'take into his hands'. The equivalent expression in many languages is 'will come to possess' or 'will come to have'.

With persecutions must in some languages be translated as a separate clause, e.g. 'and at the same time he will be persecuted' (or 'treated bad').

Age is a highly abstract concept which does not exist in some languages. The equivalent is 'day' or 'time'. *In the age to come* may be 'the far off time' (Tzeltal) or 'in the future' or 'then later', in which case 'now' contrasts with 'then later'.

For *eternal life* see 10:17.

31 *But many that are first will be last, and the last first."*

Exegesis: *de* 'but', 'and': as Taylor says, it is impossible to dogmatize whether the particle is here adversative 'but' or explanatory 'for'. The interpretation of the saying is vitally affected by the question. Almost without exception commentators and translations adopt the adversative meaning 'but'; Lagrange, however, understands it to mean 'for' and thus interprets the saying.

prōtoi 'first' and *eschatoi* 'last' probably refer, not to time, but to rank, as in 9:35.

Translation: *First* and *last* in such a context as this are highly abstract terms (compare the usage in 9 : 35). In Mazatec *first* and *last* must be shifted to the figure of a line of men, e.g. 'he who wants to be placed first will follow'. A similar figure exists in Trique 'those in front will go to the rear'. In Zoque the same figure is employed 'first ones go behind and the behind ones go ahead'. In some instances, however, the contrast must be related to importance, e.g. 'the greatest' (Zacapoastla Aztec).

32 *And they were on the road, going up to Jerusalem, and Jesus was walking ahead of them; and they were amazed, and those who followed were afraid. And taking the twelve again, he began to tell them what was to happen to him,*

Text: Instead of *hoi de* 'but those' before *akolothountes* '(who) were following' of most modern editions of the Greek text, *Textus Receptus* and Kilpatrick have *kai* 'and'. Thus the meaning is changed to '...and following (they were afraid)'.

Exegesis: There is general agreement that the subject of 'they were going up to Jerusalem' is 'Jesus and his disciples'; that the subject of 'they were amazed' is 'the disciples'; and that 'but those (others) who were following were afraid' refers to people other than the disciples.

Most of the words of this verse have already been dealt with: for *anabainō* 'go up' cf. 1 : 10; *proagō* 'precede', 'go ahead' cf. 6 : 45; *thambeomai* 'be amazed' cf. 1 : 27; *akoloutheō* 'follow' (here in a physical sense) cf. 1 : 18; *phobeomai* 'be afraid' cf. 4 : 41; *paralambanō* 'take along', 'take aside' cf. 4 : 36; *hoi dōdeka* 'the Twelve' cf. 3 : 16.

ēsan de en tē hodō anabainontes eis Ierosoluma 'they were on the road going up to Jerusalem': it is probable (with RSV) that *ēsan* 'they were' is the main verb, and *anabainontes* 'going up' is an independent participle, modifying 'they'.

en tē hodō (cf. 8 : 3, 27) 'in the road', 'on the journey'.

anabainontes eis Ierosoluma 'going up to Jerusalem': cf. 'those who came down from Jerusalem' in 3 : 22.

ta mellonta autō sumbainein 'the things that were to happen to him'.

mellō (13 : 4) 'about to be (or, happen)', 'coming', 'future': the verb denotes something in the future which is about to take place; often, however (as here), more than mere time is implied: there is the quality of "compulsion, necessity or certainty" (Abbott-Smith), so that the participial form *to mellon* does not mean simply 'the thing that will happen (in the future)' but 'something that must take place', 'something that is bound to happen'. Cf. Arndt & Gingrich l.c.δ: "an action that necessarily follows a divine decree, *is destined, must, will certainly.*"

sumbainō (only here in Mark) 'happen', 'come about'.

Translation: *Were on the road* must often be rendered 'traveling on the road'.

They must be so translated as to identify Jesus and those with him, not the immediately preceding third person plural 'the many' of verse 31, or those who will receive the hundredfold. Accordingly, one may translate 'Jesus and those with him were journeying along'.

Going up to is generally used of traveling to Jerusalem because of the greater height of Jerusalem relative to the surrounding region, especially Jericho (see verse 46). However, at this point they were not evidently in the ascent from the Jordan valley, for the episode described as near Jericho occurs later in the chapter.

Ahead of them may actually be 'ahead of the rest' in some languages, for Jesus is contrasted with the disciples and the following crowd.

They, as the subject of *were amazed*, may be translated as 'the disciples', if a more specific subject is required.

For *amazed* see 1:22, 27.

Taking the twelve refers to 'going aside with the twelve disciples' or 'leading aside the twelve disciples' (cf. 3:14, 4:10).

Happen to him may in some languages be translated as active, from the perspective of the person undergoing the events, e.g. 'what he would experience'. In other languages *what would happen to* is best translated as 'what men would do to'.

33 saying, "Behold, we are going up to Jerusalem; and the Son of man will be delivered to the chief priests and the scribes, and they will condemn him to death, and deliver him to the Gentiles;

Exegesis: This is the third prediction of the Passion (cf. 8:31, 9:31).

Most of the words of this verse have already been dealt with: for *ho huios tou anthrōpou* 'the Son of man' cf. 2:10; *paradidōmi* 'deliver up' cf. 1:14; *hoi archiereis* 'the chief priests' cf. 8:31; *hoi grammateis* 'the scribes' cf. 1:22.

katakrinousin (14:64, 16:16) 'they will condemn'.

tois ethnesin (10:42, 11:17, 13:8, 10) 'to the nations', i.e. 'to the Gentiles'. The modern equivalent of this word on the lips of the Jews would be "pagans", "heathen". All non-Jews were considered "pagan". In this context the specific reference is to the Roman authorities.

Translation: *Saying* may be translated as a coordinate or independent verb of speaking, e.g. 'and he said,...'

Behold is not a command to look, but to pay attention.

For *the Son of man* see 2:10, and note especially the problems of a third person referent applicable to the speaker, hence translated in some instances as 'I the Son of man'.

Will be delivered, as a passive, would normally be shifted to the active form in many languages, but this is made difficult by the fact that the one who delivered up Jesus was Judas, and Jesus does not make this known at this time. An equivalent form of expression can, however, usually be found, e.g. 'the Son of man will come under the control of', 'will come into the hands of', or 'the chief priests...will get the Son of man in their hands'.

329

For *chief priests* see 2:26 and 8:31, and for *scribes* see 1:22.

Condemn him to death is translatable in some instances as 'declare, You must die' (or 'be killed'), depending upon the normal way of speaking about the execution of criminals.

Deliver is 'hand him over', 'turn him over to', or 'lead him to'.

Gentiles is often rendered by transliteration, but this is not very satisfactory, since it conveys no meaning. A better, but not entirely adequate, alternative is to use the local equivalent of 'foreigners', e.g. 'the people of other lands' (Amuzgo), 'people of other towns' (Tzeltal), 'people of other languages' (Mixtec), and 'strange peoples' (Navajo).

34 *and they will mock him, and spit upon him, and scourge him, and kill him; and after three days he will rise."*

Exegesis: *empaixousin* (15:20, 31) 'they will ridicule', 'they will make fun of', 'they will mock'.

emptusousin (14:65, 15:19; cf. *ptuō* 7:33, 8:23) 'they will spit on'.

mastigōsousin (only here in Mark; cf. *mastix* 3:10, 5:29, 34) 'they will scourge', 'they will flog': here the verb refers to the whipping given those who were condemned to death (Latin *verberatio*)—cf. Arndt & Gingrich 1.

The other words have already been dealt with: for *apokteinō* 'kill' cf. 3:4; *meta treis hēmeras* 'after three days' cf. 8:31; *anastēnai* 'to rise (from the dead)' cf. 8:31.

Translation: *They* refers to the Gentiles.

In some languages the equivalent of *and* connecting a series of events is 'then', e.g. 'they will mock him; then they will spit on him; then they will...'

In some parts of the world spitting is regarded as a symbol of blessing, e.g. among the Shilluk. In this instance one must translate so that the people will understand that spitting among the people of ancient Palestine had a different meaning, e.g. 'spit on him to show they hate him' (or 'despise him').

35 *And James and John, the sons of Zebedee, came forward to him, and said to him, "Teacher, we want you to do for us whatever we ask of you."*

Text: Before *huioi* 'sons' Nestle, Westcott and Hort, Kilpatrick, and Taylor include *duo* 'two', which is omitted by the majority of editions of the Greek text.

After *aitēsōmen* 'we ask (of)' *Textus Receptus* omits *se* 'you' which is retained by all modern editions of the Greek text.

Exegesis: *prosporeuontai* (only here in the N.T.) 'they come near', 'they approach'.

thelomen hina (cf. 6:25, 9:30) 'we want that' with the request following: 'you should do for us whatever we ask of you'.

aitēsōmen (cf. 6 : 22) 'we should ask for', 'we should request'.

Translation: The appositional expression *the sons of Zebedee* may be treated in some languages as a kind of relative modifier, e.g. 'who were the sons of Zebedee' or as a paratactically combined sentence 'these were Zebedee's sons'.

To him may require in some languages the use of the noun, e.g. 'to Jesus'.

For *teacher* see 2 : 13.

Whatever we ask of you may be adapted to a conditional clause in some languages, e.g. 'if we ask something of you, we want you to do it for us'.

36 And he said to them, "What do you want me to do for you?"

Text: After *thelete* 'you want' Westcott and Hort, Lagrange, Kilpatrick, and Taylor omit *me* 'me', which is included by the majority of modern editions of the Greek text.

Exegesis: The construction of the Greek is rather uncommon (with the omission of *me* 'me' the construction is more nearly normal), but the sense is clear enough: RSV 'What do you want me to do for you?' accurately translates the Greek.

Translation: In some instances *said* must be rendered as 'asked' because of the following question.

37 And they said to him, "Grant us to sit, one at your right hand and one at your left, in your glory."

Exegesis: *dos hēmin hina* 'grant us that', 'allow us that': as commonly in Mark (cf. 5 : 10, 18) *hina* 'that' gives the content of the request rather than its purpose.

ek dexiōn stands for *ek dexiōn merōn* 'from the parts of the right' and means, simply, 'on the right' (cf. Arndt & Gingrich *dexios* 2.b).

dexios (10 : 40, 12 : 36, 14 : 62, 15 : 27, 16 : 5, 19) 'right'.

ex aristerōn (only here in Mark) 'on the left', similar in construction and meaning to *ek dexiōn* 'on the right'. The two places 'on the right' and 'on the left' were the places of honor.

kathisōmen en tē doxē sou 'we may sit in your glory': the thought behind the request is eschatological. 'The glory' is that which the Son of man will share with his Father, in his coming (8 : 38), and in this final triumph (cf. Goodspeed 'in your triumph') the two disciples want the preeminent places of honor and authority.

kathizō (cf. 9 : 35) 'sit': in this context the verb refers to sitting in chairs, or thrones, next to the king on his throne.

doxa (cf. 8 : 38) 'glory', 'majesty', 'sublimity'.

Translation: *Grant us* may be translated as 'permit' or 'give us the honor'.

331

Your right hand may of course be 'your right side' or 'your strong arm'. Similarly the *left* may be known by a number of figurative expressions.

For *glory* see 8 : 38. In Eastern Otomí the only equivalent is 'greatness' and in Mazahua a phrase 'where you are in command' has been used. At first thought this latter term would not seem to be adequate, but a man's glory or distinction is generally spoken of in terms of his commanding position or authority, in which case the phrase seems to fit the context quite well.

38 But Jesus said to them, "You do not know what you are asking. Are you able to drink the cup that I drink, or to be baptized with the baptism with which I am baptized?"

Exegesis: *ti aitesthe* 'what you are asking for' (rather than RSV 'what you are asking'—cf. v. 35; see Goodspeed).

piein to potērion 'to drink (the contents of) the cup': here a symbol of suffering, as often in the O.T. (cf. Ps. 75 : 9, Isa. 51 : 17-22, Jer. 25 : 15).

pinō (10 : 39, 14 : 23, 25, 16 : 18) 'drink'.

potērion (cf. 7 : 4) 'cup', 'drinking vessel'.

to baptisma ho egō baptizomai 'the baptism with which I am baptized'. The use of the noun and the verb 'baptism' and 'baptize' in the metaphorical sense of sufferings and tribulations which "overwhelm" one is well attested by the papyri (cf. Moulton & Milligan). For the two words cf. 1 : 4, 5.

The two presents *pinō* 'I drink' and *baptizomai* 'I am baptized' may be understood in one of three ways: (1) as "punctiliar" presents, without any time reference at all, so that the statements are the equivalent of: 'Are you able to drink *my cup*, or undergo *my baptism?*'; (2) as futuristic presents, as quite commonly used in the N.T.: 'the cup which I am to drink' and 'the baptism with which I am to be baptized'; (3) as linear presents the words would mean: 'the cup which I am (now) drinking' and 'the baptism which I am (now) undergoing'. Most translations reflect the first possibility (ASV, Montgomery, Berkeley, Manson, RSV, BFBS, Brazilian), while others prefer the second (Moffatt, Weymouth, Lagrange; cf. Swete); the third interpretation is adopted by Goodspeed (cf. also Taylor). The whole context of the disciples' request and Jesus' answer would seem to favor the second interpretation.

Translation: *Drink the cup* cannot be translated literally in many languages. People say 'to drink from a cup', but not 'drink a cup'.

An additional problem exists in this verse because of the fact that there is no clue to indicate that these expressions about drinking and being baptized are figurative statements. As straight literal statements, e.g. 'are you able to drink from the cup that I drink from', they would not seem to be very meaningful. Accordingly, in some languages the introduction of a linguistic clue to the fact that these are figures is legitimate—in fact, necessary, e.g. 'are you able, as it were, to drink from the cup...' Any such expression, e.g. 'as it were', 'like', 'as though', may indicate to the reader the figurative, and hence, more meaningful significance of the passage.

For *baptize* see 1:4, but in this context there is usually a simplification of wording which is required, e.g. 'can you be baptized as I will be baptized' (Putu), for *baptized with the baptism* is often a quite impossible expression, expecially in languages in which *baptism* must be translated as a verb, not as a noun.

39 *And they said to him, "We are able." And Jesus said to them, "The cup that I drink you will drink; and with the baptism with which I am baptized, you will be baptized;* **40** *but to sit at my right hand or at my left is not mine to grant, but it is for those for whom it has been prepared."*

Exegesis: *to de kathisai ek dexiōn mou ē ex euōnumōn* 'but to sit at my right or at my left'.

euōnumos (15:27) literally 'well-named': an euphemism for 'the left' to avoid the sinister connotation of the word.

ouk estin emon dounai, all' hois hētoimastai 'is not mine to give, but (it is) for those for whom it has been prepared'.

all' 'but' modifies the whole preceding phrase 'to sit...is not mine to give', representing a denial on the part of Jesus that it is he who will decide who shall occupy the places of honor. The word is *not* to be translated 'except' as though Jesus were saying that he could not give the places of honor to the two brothers but *only* to those for whom these places had been prepared (as does Manson, following Turner: 'I am not free to give to any but those for whom it is already destined'): on this interpretation cf. Swete.

hetoimazō (cf. 1:3) 'prepare', 'keep in readiness': the passive 'has been prepared' presupposes God as the subject, 'God has prepared' (cf. Dalman *Words*, 128f.). As Lagrange says, the word here reflects the concept of the predestinating action of God (which several translations convey by the use of 'it is destined': cf. Goodspeed, Moffatt, Manson; others, 'it is reserved': cf. Weymouth, Montgomery, Berkeley).

Translation: *Said* may need to be rendered as 'replied'.

We are able requires in certain languages expansion by some complementary verb, e.g. 'we are able to do that'.

The clause *to sit at my right hand...is not mine to grant* must be recast in some languages, for one cannot use a possessive such as *mine* to describe a particular capacity to do something. For example, in Tzeltal one must change the clause to read 'but I cannot give that you sit...'

It in the final clause (ocurring twice) refers to the prerogative to sit on the right and the left. In some instances one must substitute a verb expression 'to do that' or a noun phrase 'this position'.

41 *And when the ten heard it, they began to be indignant at James and John.*

Exegesis: *aganaktein* (cf. 10:14) 'to be indignant', 'to be angry': the

333

preposition *peri* 'about' indicates the object of the indignation—'to be angry *at*'.

Translation: *The ten* is often translatable as 'the ten other disciples', since in many instances a numeral cannot be used as a substantive, and 'other' must contrast the two sets of disciples: the ten versus the two.

42 And Jesus called them to him and said to them, "You know that those who are supposed to rule over the Gentiles lord it over them, and their great men exercise authority over them.

Exegesis: *proskalesamenos* (cf. 3:13) 'calling to him', 'summoning'.

hoi dokountes archein tōn ethnōn 'those appearing to rule the Gentiles': the exact force of *hoi dokountes* 'those who seem' (cf. 6:49) is not certain. Moffatt's 'so-called rulers' would seem too extreme: it does not appear that Jesus was intending to deny the fact of their authority in this case. Arndt & Gingrich (*dokeō* 2.b) have 'those who are reputed to be rulers'; Manson 'those who claim to be rulers'; Weymouth 'those who are deemed rulers'; BFBS has 'those who consider themselves to be rulers' and, in a footnote, the alternative 'are considered to be rulers'. Perhaps best of all is 'those who are regarded as rulers' (cf. Montgomery, Swete).

archō (only here in the active voice in Mark; elsewhere always middle *archomai* 'begin'; cf. also the participle *ho archōn* 'ruler' in 3:22) 'to rule'.

ta ethna (cf. 10:33) 'the nations', 'the foreigners', 'the Gentiles'.
katakureuousin (only here in Mark) 'they have the mastery over'.
katexousiazousin (only here in Mark) 'they exercise authority over'.

Translation: *Called them* must refer here to all the disciples, though in many translations the reference is erroneously understood to apply only to the two immediately preceding disciples, at whom the rest were angry.

To rule is translatable as 'to command', 'to boss', or 'to govern'.

For *Gentiles* see 10:33.

Lord it over may be rendered as referring to exorbitant demands 'make them run back and forth' in the sense of constantly running errands (Zoque) or to self-exaltation, e.g. 'raise themselves up' (Tzeltal).

Great is usually interpreted in terms of (1) physical strength, with metaphorical extensions: 'strong', 'mighty', 'powerful' or (2) authority or position to command: 'with much authority' or 'who says strong commands'.

Exercise authority may be rendered as 'tell them exactly what to do' or 'constantly boss them'.

43 But it shall not be so among you; but whoever would be great among you must be your servant,

Text: Instead of *estin* 'is' of all modern editions of the Greek text, *Textus Receptus* has *estai* 'shall be'.

Exegesis: *ouch houtōs de estin en humin* 'but it is not thus among you': as the Greek stands this is a statement of fact, not a command or a statement concerning the future.

megas 'great': some (cf. Rawlinson) understand it to mean, in accordance with Semitic usage, 'greatest'.

estai humōn diakonos 'shall be your servant': as in the similar saying in 9:35 this is a volitive future, a command: '*must be* your servant' (so RSV).

diakonos (cf. 9:35) 'servant'.

Translation: *It* refers to the pattern of life described in the previous verse. However, some scholars, e.g. Goodspeed, have taken this present as referring to the future, e.g. 'but it is not to be so among you'. Luther has *aber also soll es unter euch nicht sein* 'but it should not be so among you'. This type of pronoun may not occur in some languages, and hence a recasting of the clause may be required, e.g. 'you should not do like that', if the meaning is exhortatory; or 'you do not lord it over each other', if the meaning is purely descriptive of their relationships to each other.

Whoever would be great must be your servant may require certain syntactic adjustments, e.g. 'if a man wishes to be great he must be ...' or 'a man who wishes to be... must become...'

Would be great means 'desires to have authority' or 'wants to be in command'. In Tzeltal this is rendered as 'has a heart to receive strong authority', meaning 'desires to have much power'. In Tzotzil the equivalent is 'whoever wants to tell everybody else what to do'.

Must be your servant can be translated as 'must do errands for you' or 'must serve you'.

In some translations the force of this verse is lost because *among you* is mistranslated, for if it refers only to the position of greatness among the disciples, it can mean that if a person wants to come in from the outside, (i.e. originally not one of the disciples) and desires to be the greatest of the group, he must get to be such by being the servant of the disciples. This is the meaning attached to this passage by those who cite the actions of a novitiate in an order who wants to end up by being head of an order. The meaning, however, must be made clear that it is 'whoever among you wants to be great among you, must be the servant of all of you'.

44 *and whoever would be first among you must be slave of all.*

Exegesis: *prōtos* (cf. 6:21) 'first': as in 9:35 and 10:31 the word indicates rank.

doulos (12:2, 4, 13:34, 14:47) 'slave', 'bond-slave' (as distinguished from *diakonos* 'servant' and *misthōtos* (1:20) 'hired man': cf. Goodspeed *Problems*, 77-79).

Translation: For translations of *first* see 10:31 and 9:35. In this

335

context, however, *first*, in the sense of the first in a line, may not be applicable, for in this passage 'strongest to command' may be a closer correspondence in meaning.

Where a term for *slaves* is not known, there are sometimes different grades of servants. For example, among the Tzotzil a *servidor* (borrowed from Spanish) is 'one who works for hire', but a *mozo* (likewise from Spanish) is one who is working off a debt, and for all practical purposes is a slave, for the chances of his ever paying off the debt are rather remote, unless he can obtain some legal help.

45 *For the Son of man also came not to be served but to serve, and to give his life as a ransom for many."*

Exegesis: The following words have already been dealt with: for *ho huios tou anthrōpou* 'the Son of man' cf. 2:10; *ēlthen* 'came' in a profoundly theological sense, cf. 2:17 (cf. J. M. Robinson *The Problem of History in Mark*, 37, 79); *diakoneō* 'serve', 'be a servant (*diakonos*)', cf. 1:13.

kai gar 'for even' (cf. Montgomery, BFBS, Manson): ASV and RSV 'for...also' could be misunderstood as meaning that *someone else* also came not to be served, etc. Weymouth 'for indeed'; Moffatt, Goodspeed, Brazilian 'for the Son of man himself'.

dounai tēn psuchēn autou 'to give his life': which is to say, 'to give himself' (cf. discussion of *psuchē* in 3:4, 8:35).

lutron (only here in Mark; elsewhere in the N.T. only in the parallel Mt. 20:28; cf. *antilutron* I Tim. 2:6) 'ransom', 'price of release'. As Deissmann (*Light from the Ancient East*, 327-30; cf. also Moulton & Milligan) points out, the word in *koiné* Greek signified the money paid for the release of slaves. In his discussion of the Biblical use of *lutron* and its cognates, however, Westcott (*Hebrews*, 297-99) shows that in the Bible the word loses its idea of the purchase price paid someone, and means rather 'redemption', 'release', as a theological term, based upon the experience of Israel's release from the Egyptian bondage. There is, therefore, no connotation of someone to whom the price of release is paid, as would be the case if *lutron* were to be literally understood as 'ransom'. While the word 'ransom' correctly translates *lutron*, it must not be pressed to mean more than is justified by Biblical usage of the term.

anti (only here in Mark) 'instead of', 'in behalf of', 'for': this preposition is the object of debate. The majority of translations have simply 'for' (and its equivalents in other languages: *pour, por, pro, für*). Arndt & Gingrich 3 classify its meaning here as being 'in behalf of'. Taylor, however, contends that it means 'in the place of', 'instead of' (cf. his *Jesus and his Sacrifice*, 99-105), quoting Moulton & Milligan to the effect that the simple 'instead of' is by far the commonest meaning of the word. Certainly 'in the place of', 'in exchange for' is the usual meaning of the preposition in the N.T. (cf. Mt. 2:22, 5:38 (*bis*), Lk. 11:11, Jn. 1:16, Rom. 12:17, I Thess. 5:15, I Pet. 3:9 (*bis*), I Co. 11:15, Heb. 12:16, Jas. 4:15).

Robertson, in his discussion of *anti* (*Grammar*, 572-74) and *huper* (*ibid.*,

630-32), points out that it is the action involved in the passage in which the preposition is used, which determines whether *anti* (and *huper*) indicates 'in the place of' or 'in behalf of'. With this Taylor (*Jesus and his Sacrifice*, 103) agrees, saying that it is the meaning of *lutron* which determines the meaning of *anti* in this passage.

In light of these considerations (and of the similar phrase *antilutron huper pantōn* in I Tim. 2 : 6), it would seem that the majority of translations are justified in rendering *lutron anti pollōn* 'a ransom for many'.

pollōn 'of many': it is generally agreed that 'many' here is not to be taken strictly in the sense of 'some but not all', but in the general sense of 'many' as contrasted with the single *psuchē* which is given for their *lutron*.

Translation: As noted above *also* must be translated with care, since it may imply that Jesus, along with others, came to serve. The interpretation of 'Son of man himself' is much to be preferred.

For *Son of man*, especially in connection with a first person pronoun, see 2 : 10.

Not to be served but to serve may be rendered quite explicitly as 'did not come to have servants but to give himself to be a servant' (Tzeltal). One may also translate as 'not to have servants but rather to be a servant'.

In many languages *give his life* cannot be rendered literally. The meaning here, of course, is 'to die', but the implication is that he surrenders himself to death, rather than being forced by others.

A ransom is easily translated in those parts of the world which employ such a term, e.g. as a ransom for someone captured, whether in fighting or in kidnapping. However, in some regions *ransom* is translated by a descriptive phrase meaning 'to pay for something'. For example, in Amuzgo one may say 'he died in order to pay for many', but this does not really convey the meaning of the original, for the implication of the Greek text is that by this payment many were 'released'. This is indicated in Amuzgo by saying 'paid for the sins of many', in which case the expression fits the religious context, but does obviously introduce an added factor. In Huastec the rendering has been 'he will die in order to make many live'. This translation has the advantage of showing the purpose of the dying in terms of the rescuing of those who are given life. In Mitla Zapotec the release is made explicit in 'die to pay for many being released', the implied result of a ransom payment.

46 *And they came to Jericho; and as he was leaving Jericho with his disciples and a great multitude, Bartimaeus, a blind beggar, the son of Timaeus, was sitting by the roadside.*

Exegesis: The use of *erchontai eis* 'they come to' and *ekporeuomenou autou apo* 'as he was leaving from' indicates that Jesus and his disciples passed *through* the city on the way to Jerusalem.

ochlou hikanou 'a large crowd', 'a sizeable multitude'.

hikanos (cf. 1 : 7) here means 'large', 'considerable' (cf. Moulton & Milligan).

prosaitēs (only here in Mark) 'beggar'.

The other words have already been dealt with: for *tuphlos* 'blind' cf. 8:22; *kathēmai* 'be seated' cf. 2:6; *para tēn hodon* either 'alongside (by) the road' (Arndt & Gingrich III.1.b.α) or 'on the road' (Arndt & Gingrich III.d): cf. 4:4.

Translation: *They*, as subject of the first verb, is contextually clear, but syntactically confusing in many languages. Since, however, *they* refers to the same group as are indicated later in the verse, namely, 'Jesus...with his disciples and a great multitude', it may be possible to change the order of elements so that the passage may be less misleading, e.g. 'Jesus with his disciples and a great crowd of people arrived at Jericho town, and as they were leaving, Bartimaeus...'

Beggar may be rendered 'a man who was always asking for money', for though beggars are common enough in most parts of the world, one must simply describe their activities in those regions where such activity is not known.

The double appositive expressions, i.e. *a blind beggar, the son of Timaeus*, must in some languages be recast as dependent descriptive clauses, e.g. 'who was a blind beggar and the son of Timaeus' or as paratactically combined statements, e.g. 'Bartimaeus was sitting along the road; he was a blind beggar; he was the son of Timaeus'. The choice of syntactic forms is dependent upon the requirements of the receptor language.

47 *And when he heard that it was Jesus of Nazareth, he began to cry out and say, "Jesus, Son of David, have mercy on me!"*

Exegesis: *Nazarēnos* (1:24, 14:67, 16:6) 'of Nazareth', 'Nazarene'.
krazein (cf. 3:11) 'to cry'.
huie Dauid (10:48, 12:35) 'Son of David': a messianic title.
eleēson (cf. 5:19) 'have mercy', 'be merciful'.

Translation: *It was*...may require readjustment, e.g. 'when he heard that Jesus of Nazareth was there'.

Cry out is in this context 'shout'.

Son of David can usually be translated literally, since 'son' often permits expansion in the sense of anyone's belonging to the lineage of such and such a person. However, in some languages an alternative term, roughly equivalent to our *grandson* may be necessary, so as to avoid a serious misunderstanding. On the other hand, there are often generic terms such as 'offspring' or 'descendant', which can be used in such instances, if 'son' includes entirely too narrow a range of meaning.

For *mercy* see 5:19.

48 *And many rebuked him, telling him to be silent; but he cried out all the more, "Son of David, have mercy on me!"*

Exegesis: *epetimōn...hina siōpēsē* 'they were rebuking...that he be silent': the *hina* gives the content of the rebuke, not its purpose.

epitimaō (cf. 1:25) 'rebuke', 'stop', 'command'.
siōpaō (cf. 3:4) 'be silent', 'be quiet'.
pollō mallon 'the more instead', 'rather much more'.
polu 'much': as an adverb elsewhere in Mark it is always used in the neuter accusative plural form *polla* (cf. 1:45, 3:12, 5:10, etc.): here in the dative singular it means 'the more'.
mallon 'more', 'rather'.

Translation: *Rebuked* is here used in the sense of 'scolded'.
All the more is sometimes translatable as 'the more they told him, Be quiet, that much more he kept shouting out'.

49 And Jesus stopped and said, "Call him." And they called the blind man, saying to him, "Take heart; rise, he is calling you."

Exegesis: *stas* 'standing', 'standing still': only here in Mark is *histēmi* used with the meaning 'standing still', 'stopping', (cf. Arndt & Gingrich II.1.a); elsewhere it means simply 'to stand'.
tharsei (cf. 6:50) 'Cheer up!' 'Courage!' 'Take heart!'
egeire (cf. 1:31) 'rise', 'stand up'.

Translation: *Said* must in some languages occur with an object specifying to whom he spoke. The most likely object would be 'the disciples'.
Call him implies 'call him to come' or 'summon him', not just 'shout at him'.
For *take heart* see 6:50.

50 And throwing off his mantle he sprang up and came to Jesus.

Exegesis: *apobalōn* (only here in Mark) 'throwing off', 'taking off': so as to run faster (Lagrange; cf. Rawlinson).
to himation (cf. 2:21) 'the cloak', 'the mantle'.
anapēdēsas (only here in the N.T.) 'jumping to his feet', 'springing up'.

Translation: *Mantle* is the outer garment, equivalent in other cultures to 'coat', 'blanket', 'poncho', or 'cloth'.
Came to can usually be translated literally, since the center of focus in the story is Jesus.

51 And Jesus said to him, "What do you want me to do for you?" And the blind man said to him, "Master, let me receive my sight."

Exegesis: *rabbouni* (only here in Mark; cf. *rabbi* 9:5) 'my teacher', 'my master': the Aramaic *raboni*, as Lagrange says, may mean *Monseigneur* or, simply *Monsieur*.
hina anablepsō 'that I regain sight', 'that I may see': either *hina* is imperatival and the phrase means 'Let me see' (so Moule *Idiom Book*,

145), or else it stands for *thelō hina* 'I want that' in which *hina* denotes the content of the request.

anablepō (cf. 6:41) 'recover sight': the word may imply, but *not* necessarily so, that at one time the man had been able to see (in Jn. 9:11, 15, 18 it is used of the man born blind; cf. Arndt & Gingrich 2.a.β).

Translation: *Said to* in the first clause may be rendered as 'asked', in conformance with receptor language requirements.

For *master* see discussion under 9:5. In this context there seems to be more than merely 'teacher' involved. Bartimaeus is evidently recognizing Jesus as an important personage, and an equivalent title in the receptor language should be found.

One cannot always translate literally 'receive sight'. For example, in Totonac one receives 'light' and in Zoque the equivalent expression is 'permit my eyes to shine'.

52 And Jesus said to him, "Go your way; your faith has made you well." And immediately he received his sight and followed him on the way.

Exegesis: *hē pistis sou sesōken se* 'your faith has made you well': cf. 5:34 where the identical phrase is used in an identical context.

pistis (cf. 2:5) 'faith'.

sōzō (cf. 3:4) 'make well', 'heal', 'cure'.

ēkolouthei (cf. 1:18) 'he was following': in the context this refers to a physical following, without precluding the possibility that the man became a "follower" in the deeper sense of the word.

en tē hodō (cf. 10:32) 'in the road', 'on the way'.

Translation: *Go your way* should not be translated as an abrupt dismissal. The meaning is 'you may go'.

For problems involved in words for *follow* see 1:17. In this particular context the meaning is essentially 'accompany', i.e. 'went along with'.

CHAPTER ELEVEN

1 *And when they drew near to Jerusalem, to Bethphage and Bethany, at the Mount of Olives, he sent two of his disciples,*

Exegesis: For the geographical details cf. Dalman *Sacred Sites and Ways,* 249-58. Bethany was about two miles from Jerusalem, while Bethphage was closer, probably less than one mile from the city; Dalman (*op. cit.,* 252) calls it "a suburb, but not a separate unit" of the city of Jerusalem.

eggizousin (cf. 1:15) 'they approach'.

to oros tōn elaiōn (13:3, 14:26) 'the Mount of Olives'.

apostellei (cf. 1:2) 'he sends'.

Translation: *To Jerusalem, to Bethphage and Bethany* has been translated in some instances in such a way as to suggest that the crowd approached three different cities all at the same time. Actually, *to Bethphage and Bethany* is a kind of appositional explanation of the previous prepositional phrase, meaning 'that is to say, to the outlying towns of Bethphage and Bethany', which were considered as essentially a part of the larger city unit. To make this clear one can sometimes use 'that is' as an introductory phrase. As a classifier for the small towns of Bethphage and Bethany, one may be able to employ some term which indicates small dependent towns on the outskirts of a larger city.

As in all instances of transliteration, one must check for possible meanings in strange words. For example, in one language in Mexico the normal transliteration of Bethphage turned out to mean 'a debt tomorrow'. By a slight modification in the transliterated form all possibility of misinterpretation was eliminated.

At as a preposition used with *the Mount of Olives* is so indefinite that it is often not readily translatable, especially in languages which require somewhat more precise indications of locations. In this instance one can say 'on the slope of the Mount of Olives' or 'on the side of the Mount of Olives', or as in some languages 'on the skirt of the Mount of Olives'.

Olives refers to the 'olive trees', not to the fruit. In most instances the practice is to transliterate *Olives*, and use it strictly as a proper name, though in some instances a classifier such as 'trees' is employed, e.g. 'high hill on which there were olive trees' or 'Mount of Olive trees'. In some translations, however, the local equivalent of the olive tree is employed, though olive trees do not have a very wide geographical distribution. *Mount* should not be translated in such a way as to give the impression of a high mountain, for in comparison with the surrounding terrain it is only a high hill, even though it does rise somewhat higher than the surrounding hills.

2 *and said to them, "Go into the village opposite you, and imme-diately as you enter it you will find a colt tied, on which no one has ever sat; untie it and bring it.*

Exegesis: Most of the words of this verse have already been dealt with: for *eisporeuomai* 'enter' cf. 1:21; *deō* 'bind' cf. 3:27; *kathizō* 'sit' cf. 9:35; *luō* 'loose' cf. 1:7; *pherō* 'bring' cf. 1:32.

tēn kōmēn tēn katenanti humōn 'the village which is opposite you', i.e. 'the village which lies before you' (cf. Arndt & Gingrich *katenanti* 2.a). By most of the commentators this is held to refer to Bethphage; Dalman (*Sacred Sites and Ways*, 255), however, and Gould (who omits the words *Bēthphagē kai* 'Bethphage and' from v. 1 as a later addition) understand it to mean Bethany.

kōmē (cf. 6:6) 'village'.

katenanti (12:41, 13:3) 'opposite', 'over against', 'before'; BFBS 'facing'.

pōlon...eph' hon oudeis oupō anthrōpōn ekathisen 'a colt...upon which no man ever sat': this description of the animal is perhaps suggested by Zech. 9:6.

pōlon (11:4, 5, 7) 'colt', 'young donkey', 'the foal of an ass'.

Translation: *Go into* may need to be 'go to' or 'arrive at', since 'into' may not be applicable to anything but enclosures such as houses or stockades.

Opposite you has been interpreted by some to refer to a village on the opposite side of a small ravine or valley, a very possible meaning for such a relatively unusual expression.

Colt must be the young of an ass—not of a mule, as was done in one translation, and as a result the people were appalled, not only because mules only very rarely have been known to give birth, but because according to local legend such an event would herald the end of the world. Where donkeys are completely unknown one can employ one of these three alternatives: (1) use a descriptive phrase such as 'the young of a beast of burden', (2) use a classifier, 'the young of an animal called ass', employing a transliteration based on the prestige language from which most borrowings are taken, or (3) use a borrowed term without classifier. One must beware, however, of descriptive phrases. For example, one translator in Latin America, in an area where donkeys were unknown, used 'a long-eared animal', but the people interpreted this in terms of the only long-eared animal they knew, namely, a rabbit. They thought that it must have been a very large rabbit to have carried Jesus.

Sat must be clearly distinguished in some languages between 'sitting in a chair or on a stool' and 'mounted on an animal'. The latter meaning is, of course, necessary here.

Bring must be used in the sense of 'lead'.

3 *If any one says to you, 'Why are you doing this?' say, 'The Lord has need of it and will send it back here immediately.'"*

Text: After *apostellei* 'he sends' *Textus Receptus* omits *palin* 'again', which is retained by all modern editions of the Greek text (this omission sensibly alters the meaning of the phrase: cf. AV and *Exegesis*, below).

Exegesis: *ho kurios autou chreian echei* 'the Lord has need of it': the majority of translations thus render the phrase, understanding *ho kurios* as meaning 'the Lord', in the Christian sense of the word. Commentators, however, call attention to the fact that in Mark (and Matthew also) this would be the only place in the narrative of Jesus' ministry where the title is applied to him (cf. Arndt & Gingrich *kurios* II.2.c.β; cf. 1:2 for *kurios* in Mark). Some have tried to meet this difficulty by taking *ho kurios* as 'the Master' (cf. Goodspeed, Weymouth, Manson; Lagrange *le Maître*, but in his translation *Le Seigneur*). This would hardly seem correct in view of the use of the terms *ho didaskalos* (cf. 4:38 and references) and *rabbi* (cf. 9:5 and references) 'the Teacher' throughout the Gospel. Taylor, therefore, suggests that *ho kurios* is the *owner* of the animal, and the phrase means 'the owner needs it'. This interpretation has been further expanded by the suggestion that Jesus himself was the owner of the animal (*Expository Times* 64.93, 1952; cf. *The Bible Translator* 4.52, 1953). McNeile (*Matthew*, 294) points out that some Syriac versions and Ephraim join *autou* to *ho kurios* "as though Jesus claimed to be the real master of the animal." So BFBS translates, 'Its owner needs it'.

If *ho kurios* in the sense of 'the Lord' be taken as the exact equivalent of what Jesus said to the two disciples, in the historical context of the incident the phrase could only mean, '*God* needs the animal'. Commentators point out, however, that here, as often, we may not have the very words spoken by Jesus.

kai euthus auton apostellei palin hōde 'and immediately he sends it back here': part of the reply the disciples were to give to any who might raise objections to their taking the animal. The subject of *apostellei* 'he sends' is *ho kurios* of the preceding clause. The AV translation is based on the *Textus Receptus* omission of *palin* 'again', with the meaning 'and he (i.e. the man who might object) will send him here' (Field *Notes*, 34-35 defends this interpretation of the text).

apostellei palin 'he sends again', i.e. 'sends back', 'returns'.

Translation: *Doing this* may require a more specific reference, rather than this generic substitute, e.g. 'untying the animal'.

The Lord is admittedly a difficult expression, but it is probably best to take this as a third person reference to Jesus. One difficulty is involved in the fact that this is put in the form of a direct statement, which in some languages would require 'I, the Lord', as spoken by Jesus. However, Jesus is stating what the disciples should say, not what he himself is declaring to them. This problem can be resolved somewhat in certain languages by shifting the form into indirect discourse, e.g. 'say that the Lord has need of it . . .' In languages which require a possessive of 'Lord', one can translate as 'our Lord' or 'our Master' (in the direct form) or as 'your Lord' or 'your Master' (in the indirect form of discourse).

343

Has need of it is translatable as 'must use the animal' or 'has need to ride it'.

Send it back should not be translated with the connotation of letting the donkey come back alone, but 'cause it to be led back'.

4 And they went away, and found a colt tied at the door out in the open street; and they untied it.

Exegesis: *pros thuran* 'at the door' (cf. Arndt & Gingrich *pros* III.7).

exō epi tou amphodou 'outside in the street': so most commentators and translations (cf. Arndt & Gingrich *amphodon*).

amphodon (only here in the N.T.) 'a city quarter' (cf. Moulton & Milligan): by extension of meaning 'the street (or, road) around (the quarter)' —cf. Vincent *Word Studies* I, 214.

kai luousin auton 'and they loose it', i.e. 'and they untie it'.

Translation: *Found a colt tied at the door out in the open street* may require a division into two or possibly three paratactically combined sentences, because of the change in subject, e.g. 'they found the young donkey; it was tied by the door; it was standing out in the street'. Where the passive *it was tied* must be changed to active one may say 'men had tied it'.

Some translations have taken *amphodon* in the sense of 'cross-roads', e.g. 'where roads come together' or 'where roads separate', but this is not the meaning of the Greek. This term has reference to the larger streets which encircled smaller quarters of a town, through which led only small passageways, often completely covered over.

5 And those who stood there said to them, "What are you doing, untying the colt?"

Exegesis: *tines tōn ekei hestēkotōn* 'some of those who were standing there', i.e. "some bystanders" (cf. 9:1 and 15:35).

ti poieite luontes ton pōlon 'what are you doing untying the colt?': the burden of the question, of course, is '*Why* are you untying the colt?', 'What do you mean by untying the colt?' (cf. Moffatt, Manson, Gould).

Translation: *Said to* must often be translated as 'asked' because of the following question.

The periphrastic construction...*doing, untying*...must be changed to 'why are you untying...' in many languages.

In some instances *untying* must be translated by a somewhat expanded expression, e.g. 'untying the rope which is around the neck of the colt' or 'loosing the rope which is holding the colt'.

6 And they told them what Jesus had said; and they let them go.

Exegesis: *kai aphēkan autous* 'and they gave them leave', 'and they allowed them'; BFBS 'and the men let them do it'.

aphiēmi (cf. 2 : 5) 'allow', 'permit', 'give leave'.

Translation: *They told them* contrasts in subject-object relationships with *they let them go*. In some languages this must be made somewhat more definite or confusion is inevitable in such closely combined sentences, e.g. 'the disciples told the men (or 'those there') what Jesus had said; and the men let them (or 'the disciples') go'.

7 And they brought the colt to Jesus, and threw their garments on it; and he sat upon it.

Exegesis: *epiballousin* (cf. 4 : 37) 'they throw upon'.
ta himatia autōn (cf. 2 : 21; for the plural cf. 9 : 3) 'their cloaks' (cf. Goodspeed, Montgomery, Manson), or, in general, 'their clothes' (without meaning, of course, *all* their clothes).
ekathisen (cf. 9 : 35) 'he sat'.

Translation: *Brought* should be understood in the sense of 'led'.
Threw must be translated in the sense of 'put their garments on' or 'threw them over the animal' (in the form of a saddle), not in the sense of 'threw away' or 'threw at'. (In some translations the literal rendering has been ridiculous.)
Sat upon it must be altered in some languages to read 'sat upon them', i.e. the clothing—otherwise it would mean that the garments were draped over the head and tail of the animal, but not as a kind of saddle. However, this problem can be avoided in some instances by using 'mounted the animal'.

8 And many spread their garments on the road, and others spread leafy branches which they had cut from the fields.

Text: Instead of *kopsantes ek tōn agrōn* '(which) they cut from the fields' of most modern editions of the Greek text, *Textus Receptus* and Kilpatrick have *ekopton ek tōn dendrōn, kai estrōnnuon eis tēn hodon* 'they were cutting from the trees and spreading on the road'.

Exegesis: *estrōsan* (14 : 15) 'they spread'.
alloi de stibadas 'and others (spread) leafy branches': the verb is supplied from the preceding clause.
stibas (only here in the N.T.) is specifically a litter or a kind of mattress made of straw, leaves, and so forth: here it obviously means 'leaves', 'leafy branches' (Goodspeed 'straw', BFBS 'foliage'), probably branches from olive trees (Dalman *Sacred Sites and Ways*, 256). (It should be noticed that the 'palm leaves' are from John 12 : 13.)
kopsantes (only here in Mark; cf. *katakoptō* 5 : 5) 'having cut'.
agrōn (cf. 5 : 14) 'fields'.

Translation: *Spread their garments on the road* must not be translated

345

so as to imply that the folks completely undressed and put their clothes in the road. The meaning is, of course, that they put their outer cloaks down on the road in front of the donkey on which Jesus rode.

Leafy branches are 'branches of trees with leaves', not dead sticks.

Cut from the fields may require expansion as 'cut from the trees in the fields', for in some languages one cannot 'cut from fields', but only 'cut from trees'.

The type of action described here, in which the crowd tried to honor Jesus by casting their garments and branches in his path, is regarded by some peoples as utterly incomprehensible. For example, in most of Africa the arrival of a government official or local chief is prepared for by scrupulous cleaning of all paths leading into the village or town. Anyone who casts any object in the way of the arriving dignitary is guilty of the worst sort of disrespect. However, it is impossible and unwarranted to rewrite the Gospel narrative. What may be required, on the other hand, is a brief note of explanation indicating that this was designed to show honor to Jesus.

9 *And those who went before and those who followed cried out, "Hosanna! Blessed is he who comes in the name of the Lord!*

Exegesis: *hoi proagontes kai hoi akolouthountes* 'those going before and those following', 'those who were in front and those who were behind (Jesus)'.

proagō (cf. 6:45) 'go before', 'precede', 'lead'.

akoloutheō (cf. 1:18) 'follow': here in a physical sense.

ōsanna· eulogēmenos ho erchomenos en onomati kuriou 'Hosanna! Blessed the one coming in the name of the Lord!': the words are from Ps. 118:25-26.

ōsanna (11:10) represents the Aramaic *hosha'-na'*, the Hebrew of Ps. 118:25 being *hoshi'ah-na'* 'save Thou now!', a petition addressed to God, which the LXX translates *sōson dē*. As used in the passage here, it may be taken in two ways: (1) in its literal O.T. meaning, 'save (us)!' as a prayer addressed to God (cf. Gould, 'be propitious!'); (2) as a shout of welcome and praise, 'Hail!', 'Welcome!' in which the original meaning of the phrase is forgotten. Goodspeed (*Problems*, 34-35), in support of this interpretation, instances modern usage of 'God save the King!', or *Vive le roi*! It appears probable that this is the correct interpretation, particularly in light of the parallel in Matthew 21:9 'Hosanna to the Son of David!' which Dalman (*Words*, 220-23) takes to mean, "Glory (hail) to the Son of David!" (cf. likewise W. C. Allen *Matthew*, 221; A. H. McNeile *Matthew*, 296; Rawlinson).

Where modern translations (most English translations; cf. also Synodale, Zürich, Brazilian) have simply transliterated the word, the meaning is, without a doubt, 'Hail!', 'Welcome!' (Goodspeed has 'God bless him!', and Williams, 'Welcome Him!').

eulogēmenos (cf. 6:41) 'blessed': either (1) 'blessed *is*' (ASV, RSV, BFBS, Manson, Gould, Brazilian), or (2) 'blessed *be*' (most translations and commentators). The latter is probably to be preferred: *'may God bless him who comes...'*

ho erchomenos (as an independent participle only here in Mark; cf. *hoi erchomenoi* 6:31) 'he who comes': in the historical context of the Marcan narrative the phrase applies to Jesus, with the meaning *'he who is coming'* (not, as in v. 10, with a future connotation).

en onomati kuriou 'in the name of the Lord': i.e. as his represent-ative, with his authority (cf. Gould), as vicegerent of Yahweh. For the phrase 'in the name of' cf. 9:38.

Translation: *Cried out* has the sense of 'shouted'.

Hosanna may be transliterated, as in the case of most translations, or translated as a shout of 'welcome' or an expression of intense joy at the arrival of such a person. It is almost equivalent to English 'Hurrah!', but with religious connotations which are absent from the English term. In Mitla Zapotec one may say 'great thanks' (as an exclamation of thanks-giving) and in Huave the closest parallel is 'it is very wonderful now'.

For a discussion of problems related to *bless* see 6:41, but note that in this context the meaning must be applied to a person, not to a thing. Moreover, the syntactic problem is difficult because of either (1) a third person imperative 'blessed be...' or (2) a third person declarative 'he is blessed...' There is actually no verb in the Greek and either the imperative or declarative may be understood. In the case of a straight declarative the rendering is often much easier, e.g. 'he is blessed' (with the addition of 'by God', in languages which may require the agent in such passive expressions) or 'God has blessed him'. Another possibility of a direct active form is 'The Lord has blessed him who comes in his name'.

In this particular context the word *blessed* provides a number of problems of equivalence. In Barrow Eskimo the closest equivalent is 'let him be praised'; the same is true of Mazahua and Cashibo. In Tzeltal the most satisfactory form seems to be 'very great is his goodness', a statement of fact—but one which by its form indicates an intense degree of acclamation and praise. In Kituba one may say 'joy is with him who...', an indication of his blessed state rather than an expression of praise on the part of the worshiper.

10 *Blessed is the kingdom of our father David that is coming! Hosanna in the highest!"*

Text: After *basileia* 'kingdom' *Textus Receptus* adds *en onomati kuriou* 'in the name of the Lord', which is omitted by all modern editions of the Greek text.

Exegesis: *hē erchomenē basileia* 'the coming kingdom': the context demands that the participle be understood in a future sense, 'the kingdom which is coming'.

tou patros hēmōn Dauid 'of our father David': only in Acts 4:25 is the phrase 'our father David' found elsewhere in the N.T.

347

ōsanna en tois hupsistois 'Hosanna in the highest!'

ōsanna 'hosanna!': the meaning of the word in this verse becomes even more difficult to define by the addition of the phrase 'in the highest'. In English the phrase 'Hosanna in the highest!' is virtually devoid of meaning, since 'hosanna' conveys no meaning, other than as a shout of praise, while 'in the highest', as Goodspeed (*Problems*, 35) points out, may be misunderstood as signifying 'in the highest *degree*'. If, on the other hand, it be more correctly understood as meaning 'in the highest places', i.e. 'in heaven', what does 'Hosanna in heaven!' mean?

If 'Hosanna' here is understood in its literal sense 'save Thou!' the phrase means 'grant salvation (thou who art) in the highest heavens' (Arndt & Gingrich, Gould, Swete, Grant). It would appear improbable, however, that the word in this verse means something different from what it means in v. 9. If in v. 9 the word is simply a shout of praise or welcome, 'Hail!', 'Praise (him)!', that must be the meaning in this verse also.

en tois hupsistois 'in the highest places', i.e. 'in heaven'. Connected with the previous *ōsanna* 'hosanna!' as a shout of praise, the phrase may be understood in two ways: (1) 'Hail him who lives on high!'—that is, God (Dalman *Words*, 221); (2) 'let those who are in the heights of heaven (i.e. the angels) say 'Hail!' (cf. Allen *Matthew*, 221; McNeile *Matthew*, 296: "the angels are invoked to shout Hosanna to God").

On the whole it appears that the Greek, and the O.T. phraseology it represents, is not to be taken in its literal sense, and that the phrase is to be understood as meaning 'Praise be to God!' as a shout of acclaim and thanksgiving. Lagrange: "the acclamation rises as far as heaven, as though to thank God for inaugurating his salvation, and to ask him his help."

Translation: *Blessed is* should be interpreted in a manner parallel with the form of the preceding verse, in which there are obvious problems, not only in syntactic construction but in lexical content of the words, especially *blessed*. Compare some of the following typical renderings: 'let us praise the government...' (Popoluca), 'it is good that people praise...', in which 'it is good' is the idiomatic way of indicating the equivalent of a third person imperative (Zoque), 'let us talk well of the government...' (Trique), 'how good it will be...' (Tzotzil), 'very great the goodness of the government...' (Tzeltal), and 'holy is the rule of ...' in which 'holy' is a term with a wide area of meaning involving many phases of religious attitudes and activities (Huave).

Our father David must in some languages be 'our grandfather David' or 'our ancestor David'. In some languages, however, there is a manifest difficulty in speaking of the rule of one's ancestor coming in the future. In Trique the rendering has been 'government which David had and which will exist again'. This is not, however, such an elaborate paraphrase as it might at first appear, since 'government which David had' is roughly equivalent to 'kingdom of David', and 'which will exist again' parallels 'that is coming'. In Popoluca the problem of past and future is obviated by 'the government that is coming; it will be like the one our father David had', which is essentially a substitution of a simile for a metaphor. In Zoque the metaphor is retained in 'it is good that the people praise when our father David will rule over us', in which case the clause introduced by 'when' is not the time of the praising, but the object of the praise.

One must make certain to avoid the common mistake of speaking about 'our father David who is coming', for what is coming is not David but the kingdom of David.

Is coming must be rendered as 'exist' or 'be', since though persons can 'come', institutions such as 'governments', 'rule', and 'power' must in many languages 'become', 'exist', or 'be'.

Hosanna in the highest may be translated as 'praise be to God', 'let God be praised', 'let praise be in heaven', or as in Shipibo 'let hosanna be shouted in heaven'.

11 And he entered Jerusalem, and went into the temple; and when he had looked round at everything, as it was already late, he went out to Bethany with the twelve.

Exegesis: *hieron* (11:15, 16, 27, 12:35, 13:1,3, 14:49) 'temple': the whole area of the Temple in Jerusalem.

periblepsamenos (cf. 3:5) 'looking around'.

opse ēdē ousēs tēs hōras 'since the hour was already late'.

opse (11:19, 13:35; cf. *opsia* 4:35) 'late': presumably late afternoon, toward sunset (in 13:35 *opse* used as a noun stands for the first watch of the night—according to the Roman system—from 6:00-9:00 P.M.).

ēdē (cf. 6:35) 'already', 'by now'.

ousēs tēs hōras 'the hour being': the participle is causal, *'because* the hour was...' (cf. 6:35 for a similar construction *ēdē hōras pollēs genomenēs*).

Translation: *Entered* may need to be translated 'arrive at', while 'went into the temple' may be quite satisfactory, since the object in this case is a building.

Temple is quite generally translated as 'God's house', though there is in Greek a distinction between *hieron* including the entire temple area and *naos*, the sanctuary itself. In some instances, however, the temple is called 'the big house of worship' (Bambara), in order to contrast this with 'the small houses of worship', which is the designation of 'the synagogue'. In some languages it is sufficient to designate the temple as 'the holy place' (Loma) or 'the sacred house' (Futa-Fula).

As it was already late may be placed after the main clause, e.g. 'he went out to Bethany with the twelve, since it was already late'.

For the translation of *the twelve* see 3:14.

12 On the following day, when they came from Bethany, he was hungry.

Exegesis: *tē epaurion* (only here in Mark) 'on the morrow', 'on the following day' (the word *hēmera* 'day' is implied).

349

exelthontōn autōn apo Bēthanias 'when they came out from Bethany', 'after they had left Bethany' (Weymouth).
epeinasen (cf. 2:25) 'he hungered', 'he was hungry'.

Translation: *They* must refer back to Jesus and the twelve disciples.
Came is rendered better in some languages as 'traveling along, having left', in order to preserve the perspective of the narrative.

13 *And seeing in the distance a fig tree in leaf, he went to see if he could find anything on it. When he came to it, he found nothing but leaves, for it was not the season for figs.*

Exegesis: *apo makrothen* 'from a distance': this adverbial phrase modifies the verb *idōn* 'seeing', 'when he saw'.
sukēn (11:20, 21, 13:28) 'a fig tree'.
echousan phulla 'having leaves': the participle functions as an adjective in the predicate position, 'which had leaves'.
phulla (13:28) 'leaves': at this season of the year (the week before Passover) it was not uncommon for a tree already to be covered with leaves (cf. the commentaries).
ēlthen ei ara ti heurēsei en autē 'he went (to see) if perchance he will find anything on it'.
ei...heurēsei 'if he shall find', 'whether he would find': for another example of this form of indirect question (with the verb in the future indicative) cf. 3:2.
elthōn ep' autēn 'coming to it', 'when he got there': for this use of *epi* 'upon', 'to' cf. Arndt & Gingrich III.1.a.β.
kairos (cf. 1:15) 'time', 'season': the season for ripe figs started about the first of June.
sukōn (only here in Mark) 'of figs', i.e. 'for figs'.

Translation: *Fig tree* may be (1) transliterated, e.g. 'a tree called fig' or 'a fig tree', borrowing *fig* from the prestige language of the area, or (2) translated, using the local equivalent.
Anything may need to be translated as 'fruit', for obviously he was not looking for animals or birds—as some translations have implied.
It was not the season may need to be made somewhat more specific, for some languages require a verb indicating that the season had passed or that the season had not as yet begun, in which case the latter is correct.

14 *And he said to it, "May no one ever eat fruit from you again." And his disciples heard it.*

Exegesis: *apokritheis eipen* (cf. 3:33) 'he said': a literal translation 'he answered and said' (AV, ASV) is highly incongruous (yet cf. Swete's ingenious interpretation).
Notice the emphatic form of the statement, which Moule (*Idiom Book*, 136) calls "most vehemently prohibitive": *mēketi* 'no longer', *eis ton aiōna* 'eternally', 'forever' (cf. 3:29), *mēdeis* 'no one'.

phagoi 'may eat': the optative is used for command (here, of course, a prohibition).

Translation: *May no one ever eat* is a special form of utterance which has parallels in some languages in a simple future 'no one will ever' or with a somewhat more emphatic introductory expression 'it will be very so that no one will ever'. The form is that of a curse upon the fig tree.

Heard it is translatable in some languages 'heard what he said'.

15 **And they came to Jerusalem. And he entered the temple and began to drive out those who sold and those who bought in the temple, and he overturned the tables of the moneychangers and the seats of those who sold pigeons;**

Text: Before *agorazontas* 'buying' *Textus Receptus* omits *tous* 'the ones', 'those', which is retained by all modern editions of the Greek text.

Exegesis: *hieron* (cf. 11:11) 'Temple': here specifically the Court of the Gentiles where all this traffic was carried on.

tous pōlountas (cf. 10:21) 'those who sold': the merchants who sold the animals, as well as oil, wine, and salt, for the Temple sacrifices.

tous agorazontas (cf. 6:36) 'those who bought': pilgrims who came to offer sacrifice and worship in the Temple.

tas trapezas (cf. 7:28) 'the tables' on which the money changers displayed their coins; 'banks' (cf. Arndt & Gingrich 4).

tōn kollubistōn (only here in Mark) 'of the money changers': many of the worshipers, Jews of the Dispersion, would not have the half shekel coins required for the payment of the Temple tax (cf. Rawlinson).

tas kathedras (only here in Mark) 'the chairs', 'seats', 'stools'.

tas peristeras (cf. 1:10) 'the doves' used in sacrifices, according to the requirements of the Law (cf. Lev. 12:6, 8, 14:22, 15:14, 29).

katestrepsen (only here in Mark) 'he upset', 'he overturned'.

Translation: *Came to* may require alteration to 'arrived at'.

Drive out may be rendered in a form parallel to what is used in other Gospels where the action is described as accomplished—at least in part—by the use of a whip. Where languages require a distinction between driving out as a group, or singly (as, for example, in Navajo), the former is probably preferable.

Sold and...bought is in some languages best rendered as 'exchanged' (or in some cultures as 'bartered').

Pigeons, which are very widespread,—at least in some relatively similar form—may be translated by the closest local parallel, even though the relationship may not be exact.

16 **and he would not allow any one to carry anything through the temple.**

Exegesis: *ēphien* (cf. 2:5) 'allowed', 'permitted'.

hina 'that': as so often in Mark *hina* plus the subjunctive of the verb is equivalent to the complementary infinitive, indicating the content rather than the purpose of the action contained in the verb (cf. Arndt & Gingrich *hina* II.1.a.ζ).

tis dienegkē skeuos dia tou hierou 'any one should carry a vessel through the temple': many would walk through the Court of the Gentiles using it as a short cut between the city and the Mount of Olives (cf. Swete).

diapherō (only here in Mark) 'carry through', 'take through'.

skeuos (cf. 3:27) 'a vessel': here, as Arndt & Gingrich observe, any sort of object used for any purpose.

Translation: *Would not allow anyone to...* may be changed in some languages to a form of direct discourse, 'he said, You cannot...' and in others to a paratactic form, 'he stopped people; they could not carry...' Where the negative *not allow* does not exist, it is sometimes possible to translate as 'he prohibited them from...'

17 *And he taught, and said to them, "Is it not written, 'My house shall be called a house of prayer for all the nations'? But you have made it a den of robbers."*

Text: *autois* 'to them' is omitted by Westcott and Hort, and Taylor, but retained by all other editions of the Greek text.

Exegesis: *gegraptai* (cf. 1:2) 'it is written', 'Scripture says': the quotation, from Isa. 56:7, represents Yahweh speaking, so that 'My house' of the quotation is '*God's* house' (not as though Jesus were claiming the Temple was his own house).

proseuchēs (cf. 9:29) 'of prayer'.

klēthēsetai 'shall be called': a Hebraism for 'shall *be*' (cf. Lagrange; Arndt & Gingrich *kaleō* 1.a.δ).

pasin tois ethnesin (cf. 10:33) 'for all peoples', 'for all nations'.

spēlaion lēstōn 'a den of robbers', 'a cave of bandits': the phrase is a reference to another O.T. passage, Jer. 7:11.

spēlaion (only here in Mark) 'cave', 'den'.

lēstēs (14:48, 15:27) 'robber', 'highwayman', 'bandit'.

Translation: *Taught* may require an object, as it does in so many languages, in which case one may have 'taught the people'.

Is it not written anticipates a positive answer, but the form may be quite varied, e.g. (1) 'Is it written...; it surely is so written'; (2) 'it is written, is it not, of course,...' and (3) 'is it not written, no...' or 'is it not written, yes...' It should be noted that in some languages agreement with a sentence introduced by a negative must also be a negative, while in other languages agreement is introduced by a positive—forms which are anticipated in some languages in the very form of the question.

Is it...written involves an awkward passive which because of the anticipatory *it*, referring to the following direct discourse, must be altered in many languages, e.g. 'the writings contain, do they not, My house shall...'

House of prayer may be rendered as 'house where they talk to God' (Zoque, Amuzgo). In some instances, however, 'all the nations' must be made the subject of the praying, for the prayers are not to be uttered on behalf of all the nations, but the temple is a place where all people may pray, e.g. 'a house in which people of all the nations may pray'.

Den is a cave, but one with a special purpose, namely, to hide in. In order for the full meaning to be conveyed, in Shipibo this added feature must be introduced, e.g. 'cave....to hide in', otherwise one might assume that this was only a providential provision for travelers caught in a rainstorm.

Robbers are not thieves, but those who take away possessions by force.

18 *And the chief priests and the scribes heard it and sought a way to destroy him; for they feared him, because all the multitude was astonished at his teaching.*

Exegesis: Most of the words of this verse have already been dealt with: for *hoi archiereis* 'the chief priests' cf. 8:31; *hoi grammateis* 'the scribes' cf. 1:22; *apollumi* 'destroy', 'kill' cf. 1:24; *phobeomai* 'be afraid of' cf. 4:41; *pas ho ochlos* 'the whole crowd' cf. 2:13; *ekplēssomai epi* 'be astonished at' cf. 1:22; *didachē* 'teaching' (here in the passive sense of that which was taught, 'doctrine') cf. 1:22.

ēkousan 'they heard': not meaning, necessarily, that they were present and heard Jesus making the statement; the meaning may be, 'they heard of it'.

ezētoun pōs 'they were seeking how': here the verb *zēteō* (cf. 3:32) means 'seek a way' implying deliberation, study, consideration (cf. Arndt & Gingrich l.c.). Cf. the identical phrase in 14:1, 11.

ephobounto gar auton 'for they were afraid of him' explains the reason why the chief priests and scribes had to consider ways and means of putting Jesus to death and find the best possible way.

pas gar ho ochlos exeplēsseto 'for the whole crowd was amazed' explains the reason why the chief priests and scribes feared Jesus.

Translation: *Heard it* may be rendered in some languages 'they heard about what had happened'.

Destroy him is 'kill him'.

In some languages causal clauses must precede main clauses, e.g. in Navajo. This requires a double shift in order, e.g. 'Because the crowds were astonished at his teaching, they feared him; therefore, they sought to kill him'. Jesus' popularity with the crowds caused the chief priests and scribes to fear Jesus, and this fear caused them to seek some means of getting rid of him (note the double use of *gar* 'for' in the Greek text).

19 *And when evening came they went out of the city.*

Text: Instead of *exeporeuonto* 'they went out' of Westcott and Hort,

353

Nestle, Kilpatrick, and Merk (and RSV), *exeporeueto* 'he went out' is read by *Textus Receptus*, Tischendorf, Soden, Vogels, Souter, Lagrange, and Taylor.

Exegesis: *hotan opse egeneto exeporeuonto* 'when it was evening they left' (or *exeporeueto* 'he left'): this is the meaning assigned the phrase by RSV, Moffatt, Manson, BFBS, Brazilian, Zürich, Synodale (for which cf. Moulton *Prolegomena*, 248; Robertson *Grammar*, 973; Field *Notes*, 35). It is possible, however, that the conjunction of *hotan* in the first clause (which properly means 'whenever') with the imperfect *exeporeuonto* (or *exeporeueto*) 'they were leaving' of the second clause, means 'whenever it was evening they used to leave', indicating an action which took place every evening (cf. ASV, Weymouth, Goodspeed, Montgomery; Gould, Swete; Arndt & Gingrich *hotan* 2.d; C. S. Emden *Expository Times* 65.147, 1954).

In Mark *hotan* appears 21 times, in 14 of which it is used with the aorist subjunctive: in all 14 a single action is indicated, usually definite; where indifinite, as required by the context, the meaning is 'whenever' (*hotan* with aor. subj.: 2:20, 4:15, 16, 29, 31, 32, 8:38, 9:9, 12:23, 25, 13:7, 14, 28, 29). Four times *hotan* appears with the present subjunctive, of which a single action is indicated in two (13:4, 14:25) and repeated action in two (13:11, 14:7). It appears with the indicative mode three times: with the present tense (11:25) repeated action is indicated, likewise with the imperfect (3:11), while its use with the aorist tense is the passage under discussion (11:19). The conclusion seems inevitable that *hotan opse egeneto* means 'when evening came', indicating a single, definite occurrence.

As for the imperfect *exeporeuonto* (or *exeporeueto*) it is possible that repeated action is indicated, 'they used to leave' (or, 'he used to leave'): Marcan usage, however, and the context (cf. next verse) appear decisive in favor of 'they went out', a single action.

    opse (cf. 11:11) 'late', 'evening': presumably towards sunset.

    ekporeuomai (cf. 1:5) 'go out', 'leave', 'go forth'.

Translation: *Evening* refers to the first quarter of the night, indicating after sundown.

    In many languages 'evening' cannot 'come'; it may, however, 'descend' or 'become' or 'be'.

20 ***As they passed by in the morning, they saw the fig tree withered away to its roots.***

Exegesis: Most of the words of this verse have already been dealt with: for *paraporeuomai* 'pass by' cf. 2:23; *prōi* 'early', 'in the morning' cf. 1:35; *xērainō* 'dry up', 'wither' cf. 3:1.

    ek rizōn 'from the roots (up)': indicates that the *whole tree* was withered, not simply the branches.

Translation: *Passed by* implies the place where the fig tree was. Perhaps, however, the most satisfactory equivalent is 'passed along the road'.

Saw the fig tree withered away may require the combination of two paratactically united clauses, e.g. 'saw the fig tree; it was withered away'.

To the roots may be translated as 'even the roots were withered'.

21 And Peter remembered and said to him, "Master, look! The fig tree which you cursed has withered."

Exegesis: *anamnēstheis* (14:72) 'being reminded', 'recalling', 'remembering'.

rabbi (cf. 9:5) 'Master', 'Teacher'.

katērasō (only here in Mark; elsewhere in N.T., Mt. 25:41, Lk. 6:28, Rom. 12:14, Jas. 3:9) 'you cursed'.

Translation: In languages in which 'remembered' is a transitive verb, one may translate as 'remembered what had happened'.

Him may require substitution by 'Jesus', depending upon the receptor language usage.

In most languages there is a technical term meaning 'to curse', but many translators have hesitated to employ this term because it usually implies the use of black magic and the motivation would be almost inevitably a case of jealousy. In Barrow Eskimo, for example, rather than use the technical term a substitute is found in the expression 'punished with his words'. In Navajo a rather generic expression 'to speak against' has been employed.

22 And Jesus answered them, "Have faith in God.

Exegesis: *echete* is the imperative (not the indicative) 'you must have'.

pistin theou 'faith in God' in which the genitive *theou* 'of God' indicates the object of faith, not its subject.

Translation: For *faith* see 1:15.

The imperative form of Jesus' statement does provide certain difficulties for the translator, especially in languages in which there are no corresponding forms of this verb. In such instances one may render the passage as 'you should believe in God', 'you must trust in God', or 'it is necessary that you have confidence in God'.

23 Truly, I say to you, whoever says to this mountain, 'Be taken up and cast into the sea,' and does not doubt in his heart, but believes that what he says will come to pass, it will be done for him.

Text: At the end of the verse *Textus Receptus* adds *ho ean eipē* 'whatever he may say', which is omitted by all modern editions of the Greek text.

Exegesis: *arthēti kai blēthēti* 'you be taken up and cast': although passive in form, these two verbs probably have the force of middles:

355

'take and throw yourself' (so most English translations; cf. also Synodale, Brazilian, Zürich).

eis tēn thalassan 'into the sea'.

kai mē diakrithē (only here in Mark) 'and he should not doubt': the verb in the New Testament means 'to become undecided', 'to waver', 'to vacillate' (cf. Arndt & Gingrich 2.b).

hoti ho lalei ginetai 'that what he says comes to pass': *ginetai* is used here with a futuristic force, 'will come to pass', 'will happen'.

estai autō 'it shall be to him', i.e. what he says shall be done for him, shall be granted him (Weymouth): for this use of *eimi* cf. Arndt & Gingrich I.4.

Translation: For *truly* in this type of construction see 8:12.

Whoever says...it will be done for him must in many instances be adapted to a conditional construction, involving 'if', e.g. 'if anyone says...it will be done for him'.

Part of the syntactic problem in this verse is the fact that so many clauses intervene between the principal condition (the clause introduced by *whoever*) and the final result *it will be done for him*. These intervening clauses are complex because of (1) the direct discourse, with its own subject, (2) the negative-positive contrast *does not doubt...but believes*, and (3) the involved indirect discourse *believes that what he says will come to pass*. This type of complexity necessitates in some languages a division of the sentence into several basic units and with a somewhat altered order, e.g. 'if a man says to this mountain, Be taken up and cast into the sea, this will be done for him, provided he does not doubt in his heart but believes that what he says will happen', or 'if anyone says to this mountain, Be removed from here and be thrown into the sea, this is just what will be done for him; it will happen for him only if he does not doubt in his heart; he must believe that what he says will come to pass'. This last alternative is a typical paratactically combined series of sentences which convey essentially the same meaning as the hypotactically arranged group in the Greek construction.

Be taken up and cast into the sea, as noted above, may be taken in the reflexive sense, e.g. 'get up and throw yourself into the sea' or 'remove yourself from here and hurl yourself into the sea'. The reflexive is a much easier and often more meaningful form of expression than the passive.

Though *doubt* is usually a much easier term to translate than *faith* or *believe*, it is represented by a variety of idiomatic renderings, and in the majority of instances the concept of duality is present, e.g. 'to make his heart two' (Kekchi), 'to be with two hearts' (Yipounou), 'to stand two' (Juarez Zapotec), 'to be two' or 'to have two minds' (Navajo), 'to think something else' (Chontal of Tabasco), 'to think two different things' (Shipibo), and 'to have two thoughts' (Kiyaka). In some languages, however, *doubt* is expressed without reference to the concept of 'two' or 'otherness', e.g. 'to have whirling words in one's heart' (Chol), 'his thoughts are not on it' (Baoule), 'to have a hard heart' (Piro), and 'to repeatedly spread out in order', implying the process of arranging and rearranging of material as one wavers back and forth over varying possibilities (Chokwe).

24 *Therefore I tell you, whatever you ask in prayer, believe that you receive it, and you will.*

Text: Instead of *elabete* 'you received' of all modern editions of the Greek text, *Textus Receptus* has *lambanete* 'you receive'.

Exegesis: *panta hosa* (cf. 6 : 30, 12 : 44) 'all things whatsoever'.

proseuchesthe kai aiteisthe 'you pray and ask for': as Lagrange points out, this is a Semitic construction meaning simply 'you ask in prayer', 'you ask for as you pray'.

proseuchomai (cf. 1 : 35) 'pray'.

aiteō (cf. 6 : 22) 'ask for', 'request'.

pisteuete hoti elabete 'believe that you received it': ASV and RSV 'you receive it' is obscure because of the tense forms. Most translations accurately give the sense of the aorist *elabete*: cf. especially Moffatt and Manson 'you have got it'.

kai estai humin 'and it shall be done for you': the phrase is identical in construction and probably parallel in meaning to *estai autō* of the previous verse, though in this context it could mean 'it will be yours' (cf. Goodspeed and Moffatt).

Translation: *Ask in prayer* may require expansion into two verb constructions, e.g. 'ask as you talk to God' or 'ask for when you talk to God'.

There is a subtle use of the aorist tense of *elabete* 'received', which cannot always be indicated in another language. Where possible, however, it is well to translate this as 'believe that you have surely got it and it will be yours'. On the other hand, such an idiom is not always possible, and one must settle for an emphatic future in the first clause, e.g. 'believe that you will indeed receive it, and it will be yours'.

25 *And whenever you stand praying, forgive, if you have anything against any one; so that your Father also who is in heaven may forgive you your trespasses."*

Exegesis: *hotan* (cf. 11 : 19) 'whenever': here with the present indicative denoting repeated action.

stēkete proseuchomenoi 'you stand up praying', 'you stand in prayer': this was the normal mode of prayer, among the Jews, with face lifted up to heaven.

stēkō (cf. 3 : 31) 'stand'.

aphiete (cf. 2 : 5) 'forgive': if in a given language the verb requires an object, the Greek may be translated 'forgive him against whom you have something'.

paraptōmata (only here in Mark) 'transgressions', 'trespasses' (from *parapiptō* 'fall alongside', 'fall on the way').

Translation: *Stand praying* may require a translation involving a subordinate or coordinate relationship, e.g. 'stand up to pray', 'stand up and speak to God'.

For *forgive* see 1 : 4.

If you have anything against any one is translatable from two points of view: (1) what the offending person may have done, e.g. 'if anyone has sinned against you' (Kekchi), or (2) the attitude of the offended person as the result of the wrong comitted, e.g. 'if you are angry at anyone' (Amuzgo).

So that must be directly related to the verb 'forgive', which, however, may be so far separated from the purpose clause that the meaning is lost, in which case one may use a transitional verb expression, e.g. 'do this so that...' or 'forgive him so that...'

Also must be related to the 'father' or to the process of 'forgiving'; it should not imply 'also your father', meaning that God is also the father of you as well as the other person. To avoid this meaning *also* may be related to the verb 'may also forgive you', even as you have forgiven the person in question. It is most important that *also* not be connected with 'in heaven', as is done in some translations.

In this type of context it is often difficult to distinguish between 'trespasses' and 'sins'. In fact, in many languages one must use one and the same type of expression in all passages such as this (see 1 : 4 for words designating *sin*). In some languages, however, there are ways of making this distinction, e.g. 'missing the commandment' (Kipsigis) and 'to step beyond the law' (Navajo).

26 ["But if you do not forgive, neither will your Father who is in heaven forgive your trespasses."]

Text: This verse, introduced into manuscripts from the parallel Mt. 6 : 15, is omitted by all editions of the Greek text, save *Textus Receptus* and Kilpatrick.

Translation: The problems of translation in this verse are almost identically the same as in the preceding, except for the negative form of the constructions. Most languages, however, do not employ the highly specialized idiom '*not...neither*', but use only a parallel negative series, 'do not forgive, your Father...will not forgive'.

27 And they came again to Jerusalem. And as he was walking in the temple, the chief priests and the scribes and the elders came to him,

Exegesis: *palin* 'again': points back to v. 15.

peripatountos (cf. 2 : 9) 'walking'.

hoi archiereis kai hoi grammateis kai hoi presbuteroi (cf. 8 : 31 for all three groups) 'the chief priests and the scribes and the elders': it is not necessary to suppose that *all* of them were there, in formal meeting as the Sanhedrin (as is true of 14 : 53 and 15 : 1).

Translation: *Came* may be rendered 'went'. *He* may require substitution by 'Jesus'.

For *chief priests* see 2:26 and 8:31; for *scribes* see 1:22; and for *elders* see 8:31.

If in the receptor language a distinction is made between (1) the sanctuary and (2) the temple, including the sanctuary and grounds (Greek *hieron*), the latter meaning is the one to use at this point.

28 *and they said to him, "By what authority are you doing these things, or who gave you this authority to do them?"*

Exegesis: *en poia exousia* 'in what sort of authority', 'by what authority'.

poios (11:29, 33, 12:28) is a qualitative interrogative pronoun meaning properly 'of what kind', 'of what sort': in usage, however, it is often weakened to mean simply 'what' (cf. 12:28), and that is the meaning most commentators and translations give it here. Arndt & Gingrich, however, suggest that the dative *poia* 'by what' here is equivalent to the genitive of the indefinite pronoun, *tinos* 'of whom', and the phrase means 'by whose authority' (Arndt & Gingrich 2.a.γ).

exousia (cf. 1:22) 'authority'.

tauta 'these things' is undefined. Most commentators take it to refer to the cleansing of the Temple, narrated in vv. 15-16.

hina tauta poiēs 'that you should do these things': in this phrase *hina* indicates result, 'so that you do these things' (cf. Black *Aramaic*, 62), or else *hina...poiēs* 'that...you should do' is simply equivalent to *poiein* 'to do', as RSV has it (cf. Arndt & Gingrich *hina* II.1.e; Burton *Moods and Tenses*, § 216).

Translation: *Said* may be rendered by 'asked', in view of the following question.

By what authority is not easy to translate literally in some languages, but the meaning can be conveyed, even though a somewhat paraphrastic expression may be required, e.g. 'what permission do you have to do these things' (Eastern Otomí), 'by whose power do you do these things', or 'because of what sort of right do you do these things'.

The last clause shifts the question from the abstract 'authority' to the specific source of the authority, e.g. 'who told you that you could do these things' or 'who gave you the right to do these things'.

29 *Jesus said to them, "I will ask you a question; answer me, and I will tell you by what authority I do these things.*

Exegesis: *eperōtēsō humas hena logon* 'I will ask you one question': Lagrange insists that the proper force of *hena logon* is '*just one* question'.

eperōtaō (cf. 5:9) 'ask (a question)'.

logos 'word', 'statement' in this context means 'question' (cf. Arndt & Gingrich 1.a.β).

apokrithēte (cf. 8:4) 'you answer': the subjunctive here is volitive, with the force of the imperative.

359

Translation: *Said* may need to be translated 'replied'.

Answer me, and in this type of construction may be treated as a conditional, 'if you answer me, then I will tell...'

By what authority in this verse can be most satisfactorily treated in many languages as personal, rather than impersonal, e.g. 'I will tell you who gave me the right to do these things'.

30 *Was the baptism of John from heaven or from men? Answer me."*

Exegesis: *to baptisma to Iōannou* (cf. 1:4, 5) 'the baptism (that) of John': the reference is to the whole ministry of the Baptist, and, if necessary, the phrase may legitimately be expanded to read 'the baptism which John preached and administered'.

ex ouranou 'from heaven': of divine origin, as opposed to 'from men' (cf. Manson 'by divine appointment').

Translation: *The baptism of John* must be translated as subjective, not objective (as has been done in a number of translations). That is to say, this phrase must often be rendered as 'the baptism that John performed' (Eastern Otomí) or 'the baptism which John gave' (Zoque).

However, if one uses a verb in translating 'baptize', then the problem of adding 'heaven' may become a problem. For example, if translated literally in Popoluca this expression would mean 'throw water on him from heaven'. To avoid this and to translate *heaven* in its proper meaning as a substitute for 'God', the passage was rendered as 'who sent John to baptize, God or men?'

In Mazahua, however, one can say 'was John's baptizing one which belongs to heaven'. In Huave much the same kind of expression may be used in speaking of heaven, but the last phrase must be translated as 'or did people tell him to do it'.

31 *And they argued with one another, "If we say, 'From heaven,' he will say, 'Why then did you not believe him?'*

Text: Instead of *dielogizonto* 'they debated' of the majority of editions of the Greek text, *Textus Receptus* and Soden have *elogizonto* 'they reasoned'.

After *legontes* 'saying' Soden, Taylor, and Kilpatrick add *ti eipōmen*; 'what shall we say?' which is omitted by the majority of modern editions of the Greek text.

Exegesis: *dielogizonto pros heautous* 'they were debating among themselves', 'they were arguing with one another'.

dialogizomai (cf. 2:6) 'discuss', 'debate'.

pros heautous (cf. 9:10) 'among themselves'.

dia ti 'why?' (also in 2:18, 7:5).

episteusate (cf. 1:15) 'you believed': not in the Christian sense of 'to have faith' by means of which God's grace effects salvation, but in the sense of *believing* John, i.e. accepting his message as true.

autō 'him': grammatically this could be 'it', i.e. John's baptism, the subject of the question (v. 30). There is nothing in Marcan usage of *pisteuō* 'believe' to compel decision one way or the other: 'him', however, is the almost unanimous choice of translators (Synodale has *à sa parole* 'in his message').

Translation: *Argued* may be rendered 'talked back and forth', a good description of what must have taken place among the men gathered to trap Jesus.

From heaven, as a highly elliptical expression, may require some contextual expansion, e.g. 'the baptism was from heaven'. Otherwise 'from heaven' might be related to the immediately preceding verb of speaking.

If we say may need to be translated as 'if we reply' and similarly *he will say* may require a rendering such as 'he will ask', verbs which give some clue to the following forms.

Believe him carries the meaning of 'believe what he said' or 'trust his words'.

32 But shall we say, 'From men'?"—they were afraid of the people, for all held that John was a real prophet.

Text: Instead of *ochlon* 'crowd' of all modern editions of the Greek text, *Textus Receptus* has *laon* 'people'.

Exegesis: *alla eipōmen* 'but (if) we say': with identically the same meaning as *ean eipōmen* 'if we say' in v. 31, with *ean* 'if' implied, although RSV "shall we say?" is possible. It is not, however, a question that is raised, 'shall we say?', but a possibility, 'if we say', the result of which is clearly stated in the words that follow. The sentence as it stands is unfinished, but the meaning is clear.

ephobounto (cf. 4:41) 'they feared': with *ton ochlon* 'the crowd' as the object, as here, cf. 12:12.

hapantes gar eichon ton Iōannēn ontōs hoti prophētēs ēn 'for all held that John was really a prophet'. Most translations and commentators, as RSV, join *ontōs* 'truly' to the verb *ēn* 'was': Swete, however, joins it to *eichon*—'they really held' (cf. ASV).

echō 'have': here in the sense of 'consider', 'look upon', 'view' (cf. Arndt & Gingrich I.5; Moulton & Milligan).

ontōs (only here in Mark) 'truly', 'really', 'in fact'.

prophētēs (cf. 6:4) 'a prophet'.

ēn 'was': in the historical setting of the narrative the meaning is 'had been'.

Translation: The more usual practice is to take the initial clause as a condition, parallel with the preceding, e.g. 'if we say, From men'. The

main clause of the condition (sometimes called the *apodosis*) is lacking,
for Mark shifts immediately and gives the reason for the men's unwillingness to even give such an answer, since they would have immediately
exposed themselves to the hostility of the crowd for whom John had
become a popular hero. However, as in the RSV, it is possible to assume
that the first clause is a question, but without any answer, in which case
it is essentially a conditional expression.

From men, as in the case of *from heaven*, may require some expansion,
e.g. 'his baptizing was from men' or 'men told him to baptize'.

Held that John was is equivalent in some languages to 'considered John
to be', 'regarded John as', or 'thought of him as'.

For *prophet* see 1 : 2.

33 *So they answered Jesus, "We do not know." And Jesus said to
them, "Neither will I tell you by what authority I do these things"*

Exegesis: *apokrithentes...legousin* (cf. 3 : 33) 'they answered'.

en poia exousia (cf. v. 28) 'by what authority'. For a discussion of this
phrase cf. Daube *New Testament and Rabbinic Judaism*, 217-23.

Translation: *So* is equivalent to 'therefore', 'because of this', or 'accordingly'.

In Tzeltal there is an interesting idiomatic way of disclaiming knowledge, namely, 'What shall we say!'—an expression which fits this context perfectly, for it was not ignorance but unwillingness to answer which
dictated the reply of the authorities.

Neither will I...is equivalent in some languages to 'in that case I will
not tell you...' or 'then I will not tell you...'

For other problems in this verse see 11 : 28.

CHAPTER TWELVE

1 *And he began to speak to them in parables. "A man planted a vineyard, and set a hedge around it, and dug a pit for the wine press, and built a tower, and let it out to tenants, and went into another country.*

Exegesis: *en parabolais* (cf. 3:23) 'in parables', 'by means of parables': here the phrase is adverbial, referring to the manner of teaching; "parabolically" (Rawlinson).

The beginning of this parable is modelled after Isa. 5:1-2, and contains eight words appearing for the first time in Mark (four of which occur only here in Mark), from the LXX version of Isa. 5:1-2. They are the following:

ampelōn (12:2, 8, 9) 'vineyard'.

phuteuō (only here in Mark) 'to plant'.

peritithēmi (15:17, 36) 'to place around'.

phragmos (only here in Mark) 'fence', 'wall', 'hedge': in this case, probably a wall of unmortared stones (cf. Rawlinson).

orussō (only here in Mark) 'to dig'.

hupolēnion (only here in the N.T.; the LXX of Isa. 5:2 is *prolēnion*) properly the 'pit for the wine press', dug into the rock, in which was placed the 'vat' or 'vessel' (the *prolēnion* of Isa. 5:2) into which the liquid would run. Arndt & Gingrich, however, take it to be the *vat* or *trough* itself into which the wine would run (cf. also Liddell & Scott). It should be noticed that AV 'winefat' is 'wine vat' today.

oikodomeō (12:10, 14:58, 15:29) 'build', 'erect'.

purgos (only here in Mark) 'tower' which was built in a vineyard from the top of which men could keep watch over the vineyard.

The parable follows Isa. 5:1-2 up to this point. From here on the parable is independent of the Old Testament passage.

kai exedoto auton geōrgois, kai apedēmēsen 'and he leased it to vinedressers and went away'.

ekdidomai (only here in Mark) 'let out for hire', 'lease'.

geōrgos (12:2, 7, 9) 'a tiller of the soil', 'a farmer', 'a vinedresser'; by extension (as here) 'a tenant farmer' (cf. Arndt & Gingrich).

apodēmeō (only here in Mark) 'leave on a journey', 'go abroad': RSV (following ASV) 'go into another country' appears to be too literal a rendering of the word. The papyri (cf. Moulton & Milligan) use the verb in the general sense of 'going away', rather than in the strict etymological sense of leaving one's country (cf. Manson, 'went away').

Translation: For *parables* see 3:23, but the combination *speak in* *parables* may require two verbs of speaking, e.g. 'as he spoke, he told them likenesses' or 'he told them stories as he spoke'.

Vineyard immediately causes difficulty for the translator in many parts of the world, especially the tropics, where grapes cannot be grown, except under very special circumstances. In such instances one may use a descriptive phrase, 'planted many plants which bore fruit' or 'planted many vines which gave a fruit called grape', in which case 'grape' would be borrowed from the most appropriate prestige language of the area.

Hedge is often translated as 'a stone wall', but any general word for 'fence' or 'enclosure' can be used, if 'stone walls' are completely unknown.

It is very possible that this winepress consisted of a large trough cut into the stone in which the grapes were squeezed by the process of men walking on them. From the bottom of the vat would be a small opening through which the juice could flow out into vessels. In most translations one must attempt to describe such an object, e.g. 'pit where they squeezed the juice' (Zacapoastla Aztec), 'hole for squeezing out grapejuice' (Tarahumara), or 'place to take juice out of the fruit' (Barrow Eskimo).

The *tower* in this passage is not a 'bell-tower' or 'church tower', as some translations have implied. It is only an elevated platform, usually built up of stone, with a temporary brush shelter on top, from which one could watch the crop to protect it from prowlers and birds.

Let it out must refer to the entire vineyard, not just to the tower, as some translations seem to imply. In general, however, there is no difficulty in expressing the meaning of letting out property to tenant farmers, for this practice is so widespread. However, in some regions this practice is not known, and hence one must describe the process briefly in order for the parable to make sense, e.g. 'arranged to have men take care of the vineyard in exchange for part of the produce' or 'contracted with men to take care of the fruit plants in exchange for some of the fruit'.

Another country may be translated as 'another region' or 'another land', but it should be sufficiently far as to preclude easy return, close supervision, or quick communication. The essential meaning here is not related to the distance which the man went on his journey but that he was out of close touch. Where, for example, a translation implies only that the owner went over into another valley, the reader will not realize just why he didn't take care of the matter himself.

2 **When the time came, he sent a servant to the tenants, to get from them some of the fruit of the vineyard.**

Exegesis: *tō kairō* (cf. 1 : 5, 11 : 13) 'at the season', 'at the (right) time': in this case, the 'right time' would be the fifth year after planting (cf. Lagrange).

apo tōn karpōn 'from the fruits', 'some of the fruit': a Semitism, as in the similar construction in 5 : 35 (cf. Black *Aramaic*, 251). Under the terms of the lease the tenants were to turn over to the owner of the vineyard a certain portion of the yield.

karpos (cf. 4 : 7) 'fruit'.

For *apostellō* 'send' cf. 1:2; *doulos* 'slave' cf. 10:44.

Translation: *The time* must in some languages be rendered as 'the time of harvest' or 'the time that the fruit was ripe'. Otherwise, 'time' is entirely too ambiguous.

Tenants may usually be translated by a very well-known local equivalent, but where such a term does not exist a descriptive phrase, paralleling the one used in the previous verse, may be employed, e.g. 'the men who took care of the vineyard in exchange for part of the fruit' or simply 'the men who were taking care of the vineyard', since the previous verse would describe the terms of their contract.

To get must imply a legitimate receipt of payment, not a forced exaction.

3 And they took him and beat him, and sent him away empty-handed.

Exegesis: *edeiran* (12:5, 13:9) 'they beat', 'they flogged', 'they whipped'.

kenon (only here in Mark) 'empty', 'empty-handed'.

Translation: *Empty-handed* may be translated in some languages simply as 'without anything'. In one instance it is idiomatically rendered as 'holding his own hands', i.e. without anything in them.

4 Again he sent to them another servant, and they wounded him in the head, and treated him shamefully.

Text: Before *ekephalaiōsan* 'they wounded in the head' *Textus Receptus* adds *lithobolēsantes* 'having stoned', which is omitted by all modern editions of the Greek text.

Instead of *ētimasan* 'they dishonored' of all modern editions of the Greek text, *Textus Receptus* has *apesteilan ētimōmenon* 'they sent away dishonored'.

Exegesis: *ekephalaiōsan* (only here in the N.T.) means 'they summed up' (from *kephalaion* 'a summary', 'a resumé' which, in turn, is from *kephalē* 'head'): in this passage, however, it is the consensus that the word means 'they wounded (him in) the head', a meaning found nowhere else. Field (*Notes*, 35-36) discusses the word and its use, concluding that the Vulgate *in capite vulneraverunt* 'they wounded (him) in the head' is probably the only meaning to be attributed to the verb in this passage. Burkitt's suggestion (*American Journal of Theology*, April, 1911, 173ff.) that the reading of the text may be a palaeographical blunder for *ekolaphisan* 'they buffeted', has not been widely accepted (cf. Taylor, in favor, and Lagrange, against).

ētimasan (only here in Mark) 'they dishonored', 'they insulted', 'they treated shamefully'.

Translation: *He* may require the use of 'the owner', since in some languages *he* would refer back to the immediately preceding third person singular referent, namely, the servant who was beaten.

Treated him shamefully is sometimes expressed in a negative form, e.g. 'they treated him as they should not have done', which in some languages conveys quite accurately the meaning of insult and disrespect. In other instances, however, the closest equivalent is 'they were very mean to him'.

5 *And he sent another, and him they killed; and so with many others, some they beat and some they killed.*

Exegesis: *apekteinan* (cf. 3:4) 'they killed'.

kai pollous allous 'and many others': in the accusative case, as the direct object of a verb which is implied, perhaps 'they mistreated'.

hous men derontes, hous de apoktennontes 'beating some and killing others': the two participial clauses denote manner, indicating the manner in which the tenants mistreated the many other servants who were sent.

Translation: *He* must in some languages be rendered 'the owner'.

And so with many others may require some expansion since certain of the semantic components are omitted, e.g. 'the same thing happened to many others' or 'many others suffered in this same way'.

Some they will require more precise identification in certain languages, e.g. 'the men beat some of the servants and killed others'.

6 *He had still one other, a beloved son; finally he sent him to them, saying, 'They will respect my son.'*

Text: After *agapēton* 'beloved' *Textus Receptus* adds *autou* 'his', which is omitted by all modern editions of the Greek text.

Exegesis: *hena* 'one': in the nature of the case either 'man' or 'messenger' is to be understood, rather than 'slave' (vv. 2, 4, 5), to which, grammatically, the pronoun refers.

huion agapēton (cf. 1:11) 'a beloved son', 'an only son'.

eschaton (cf. 9:35) 'last', 'at last' as an adverb, with reference to time, not to rank.

hoti is recitative, introducing direct speech.

entrapēsontai 'they will reverence', 'they will respect': the verb *entrepō* (only here in Mark) in the active means 'to make ashamed', and in the passive 'to be put to shame', 'to be ashamed'; here, 'have regard for', 'respect' (cf. Arndt & Gingrich 2.b).

Translation: *He had still one other* has been wrongly translated as 'another servant', which, as noted above, is not the meaning of the

366

passage. However, to avoid this difficulty one may translate as 'there was still another person with him' or 'he had with him still one other man'.

For *beloved son* see 1:11.

They will respect must refer to the action of the tenants, translatable in some languages as 'show honor to'.

7 But those tenants said to one another, 'This is the heir; come, let us kill him, and the inheritance will be ours.'

Exegesis: *klēronomos* (only here in Mark; cf. *klēronomeō* 10:17) 'heir'. *deute* (cf. 1:17) 'come!'
klēronomia (only here in Mark) 'inheritance'.

Translation: *Heir* is a term which corresponds to widespread cultural patterns and so is usually quite easily translated. However, the practice of passing on inheritance is not known in some societies, and hence a descriptive expression may be necessary, e.g. 'this one will eventually be the owner' (Shipibo) or 'he will receive his father's land' (Cashibo).

Come as an exhortation for group activity may be more idiomatically rendered as 'let's get together' or 'let's unite', for this is not the 'come' of travel, but of cooperation.

The inheritance may be literally 'what he would receive' or 'what he will later own'; or one may use a more generic phrase, e.g. 'the property' or 'this planted land'.

Will be ours may require transposition, e.g. 'we will possess what he would get'.

8 And they took him and killed him, and cast him out of the vineyard.

Exegesis: *exebalon auton exō tou ampelōnos* 'they threw him out of the vineyard': the words indicate that they did not bury the body but threw it out unburied, a final indignity. (If the cultural context of the language requires it, 'cast him out' may be read 'cast the body out' with no violence being done the Greek.)

Translation: *Took him* is equivalent to 'grabbed him'.

Cast him out may require a change to 'threw his corpse out', for the use of the pronoun 'him' might imply that he was not actually dead.

9 What will the owner of the vineyard do? He will come and destroy the tenants, and give the vineyard to others.

Exegesis: *ho kurios* (cf. 11:3) 'the owner'.
apolesei (cf. 1:24) 'he will kill', 'he will destroy', 'he will put to death'.
allois 'to others': either generally 'to other men', or specifically 'to other tenants'.

Translation: *Come* may usually be translated as 'come' in this type of context since the story centers on the vineyard, but the shift of subject may in some languages require 'go'.

Some translations have rendered *destroy* merely as 'to ruin the business of the tenants', but this is not the meaning of the passage, as is indicated above.

Give must not be interpreted in the sense of 'give as a gift', but 'to rent it out', likewise on a commission basis. This must be rendered in some cases as 'arrange to have other tenants take care of the vineyard'.

10 *Have you not read this scripture:*

> *'The very stone which the builders rejected*
> *has become the head of the corner;*
> 11 *this was the Lord's doing,*
> *and it is marvelous in our eyes'?"*

Exegesis: *oude tēn graphēn tautēn anegnōte*; 'have you not read even this scripture?': in such a context *oude* means 'not even' (cf. Lagrange 'at least this scripture') rather than 'not' (cf. Moffatt). The scripture quoted is Ps. 118:22-23, quoted exactly as the LXX translates it.

graphē (only here in singular; in 12:24, 14:49 in plural) 'writing', '(passage of) scripture': the singular refers to a particular passage in the O.T., in accordance with normal use of the word in the N.T.

anaginōskō (cf. 2:25) 'read'.

lithon (cf. 5:5) 'stone': RSV 'the very stone' carries somewhat more emphasis than the Greek allows; 'the stone' or, at the most, 'that stone', is an accurate translation. The word *lithon* is in the accusative case, by attraction to the case of the relative pronoun *hon* 'which', the object of the verb *apedokimasan* 'they rejected', a construction common in Greek.

apedokimasan (cf. 8:31) 'they rejected', 'they considered worthless'.

hoi oikodomountes (cf. 12:1) 'the builders'.

egenēthē eis kephalēn gōnias 'was the cornerstone', 'became the head of the corner': *egenēthē eis* is the literal LXX translation of the Hebrew phrase *hayah lᵉ* and means simply 'was', 'became' (cf. 10:8).

kephalē gōnias (only here in Mark) is either 'the cornerstone' which holds together the walls, or 'the keystone', 'the capstone' which is placed above the door (cf. Arndt & Gingrich *kephalē* 2.b). Most translations have 'cornerstone'. RSV (following ASV) 'the head of the corner', here and elsewhere in the N.T. where the passage is quoted (//s Mt. 21:42, Lk. 20:17; Acts 4:11, 1 Pet. 2:7), is inconsistent with its translation of the O.T. passage (Ps. 118:22), which appears as 'chief cornerstone'. The cognate *akrogōniaios*, the LXX translation in Isa. 28:16, is found in Eph. 2:20 and 1 Pet. 2:6, the RSV translation in all three passages being 'cornerstone'. If a distinction is to be maintained between *kephalē gōnias* and *akrogōniaios* in the N.T., 'chief cornerstone' should be used for the former and 'cornerstone' for the latter. 'The head of the corner' may be virtually meaningless.

para kuriou egeneto hautē 'this came from the Lord', 'this was the Lord's doing' (cf. Arndt & Gingrich *para* I.2).

kuriou 'of the Lord', i.e. 'of Yahweh', 'of God' (cf. 1:3).

hautē 'this': the feminine gender is due to the LXX literal translation of the Hebrew feminine demonstrative *zo'th* which is used for the neuter, and means, in this passage, 'this thing', 'this matter' (cf. Moule *Idiom Book*, 182; Field *Notes*, 15, gives other LXX passages where the same thing occurs). Gould, with little probability, refers *hautē* to *kephalē gōnias* 'cornerstone' (cf. Lagrange, Swete, Taylor).

thaumastē (only here in Mark) 'marvelous', 'wonderful'.

en ophthalmois hēmōn 'in our sight', i.e. 'in our judgment' (cf. Arndt & Gingrich *ophthalmos* 2).

Translation: For the treatment of a question implying a positive answer, as for example, *have you not read this scripture*, see 11:17, but in this particular context the problem is somewhat more difficult because of the long direct discourse which follows and which cannot be combined in some languages with the question. Accordingly, one may need to employ certain close equivalents, e.g. 'Have you read this scripture; I am sure you have' (which implies the same as the negative form in English which anticipates a positive answer and as such is really a strong affirmation of the statement), or 'You have read this scripture surely?', or 'Have you not read this scripture—yes?' (or 'no', depending upon patterns of agreement). Whether the punctuation of the question should be placed at the end of the direct discourse will depend entirely upon the syntactic patterns of the receptor language and the traditional practices.

Scripture may be translated as 'the writing' (Maya), 'the sacred writing', in which 'sacred', as a kind of classifier, is required in order to indicate the religious nature of the writing (Valiente), and 'this writing of God', without implying that God literally wrote out the document (Tzotzil, San Blas, Eastern Otomí).

Builders may be translated in some languages as 'house-makers' (Barrow Eskimo).

Rejected may be objective in the sense of 'cast aside', but the more accurate rendering is a subjective one 'regarded as worthless' or 'thought was not of value' (or 'was useless').

Head of the corner should not be translated literally, unless by some strange coincidence it is a meaningful expression. As noted above, the meaning is either corner stone or cap stone. As the first meaning one may have 'ear of the house' (Conob) or 'the strongest stone in the corner' (Tzotzil). In other instances, translators have chosen the meaning of cap stone or keystone, and translated this as 'the top stone' or 'the high stone'. However, an ambiguous expression, which at the same time conveys the significance of the passage, may emphasize the relative importance of the stone, e.g. 'the most important stone' (Huastec), 'surpasses in importance to hold up the house' (Kiyaka), 'most valued stone', with the meaning of 'most useful' (Eastern Otomí).

Many languages distinguish two words for 'corner', an inside and an outside corner, e.g. Spanish. Here the outside corner is the one involved.

This was the Lord's doing is a relatively difficult expression to translate literally into other languages, but it may be transformed into a direct construction, 'the Lord has done this'.

For the use of *Lord* see 1:3. Despite the fact that this is a reference to Lord as God, it is important to preserve the ambiguity of the N.T. in using a word which is also the common designation of Jesus as Lord.

Marvelous in our eyes must usually be changed to a direct construction, e.g. 'as we see it we are amazed' (Navajo) or 'we see it as a big thing' (Eastern Otomí). *Eyes* is only an indirect way of speaking about 'seeing'.

12 *And they tried to arrest him, but feared the multitude, for they perceived that he had told the parable against them; so they left him and went away.*

Exegesis: The words in this verse have already been dealt with: for *zēteō* 'seek', here meaning 'attempt', 'try' cf. 3:32; *krateō* 'seize', 'arrest' cf. 1:31; *ephobēthēsan ton ochlon* 'they feared the crowd' cf. 11:32; *aphiēmi* 'leave', 'forsake' cf. 2:5.

egnōsan 'they knew' here means 'they perceived', 'they understood' (cf. Arndt & Gingrich 3.c).

pros 'with reference to' (Arndt & Gingrich II.5.a); in the context, almost 'against' (cf. Moule *Idiom Book*, 53).

Translation: *They* is obscure, for it refers back to the 'chief priests and the scribes and the elders' of 11:27. However, rather than repeat this expression one can remove the ambiguity (in which the pronouns might refer to the tenants, referred to in the preceding parable, or to the people in general), by saying 'those to whom Jesus addressed his words' or 'those to whom Jesus was speaking'. In Tzotzil one may say 'his opponents' to distinguish this group.

Arrest may require an indirect causative in some languages 'cause him to be seized', since the authorities would not themselves take him in hand but would order soldiers to do it.

Against them must refer back to the authorities.

The relationship of ideas in this verse may require in some languages a recasting of the order, since the causal clause introduced by *for* does not give the reason for the immediately preceding event, namely, 'the fearing of the multitude' but for the desire on the part of the authorities to arrest Jesus. The Greek order of clauses, 1, 2, 3, 4 is shifted for example in Navajo to 3, 1, 2, 4, e.g. 'perceiving that he was speaking against them, they sought to...; but because they feared the multitude, they left him...'

13 *And they sent to him some of the Pharisees and some of the Herodians, to entrap him in his talk.*

Exegesis: *apostellousin* is probably impersonal 'they send', i.e. '(some of the Pharisees and some of the Herodians) *were sent*'. It is not likely that the subject of the verb is the 'they' of the previous verse (which, in the Marcan context, goes back to 'them' in 12 : 1 and eventually to 'the chief priests and the scribes and the elders' in 11 : 27).

agreusōsin (only here in the N.T.) 'they may catch', 'they may take': used in the papyri (cf. Moulton & Milligan) literally of hunting and fishing.

logō 'in a word', 'by means of a statement' (cf. Arndt & Gingrich 1.a.γ).

Translation: *Herodians* are 'the henchmen of Herod' or 'the followers of Herod'.

To entrap him in his talk has been idiomatically rendered in Shipibo as 'having headed him off to catch him' (a metaphorical expression derived from the practice of tracking down animals). In Zoque this same expression is rendered 'to cause him to fall because of his words' and in Tzotzil one may say 'to catch him because of what he said'.

14 *And they came and said to him, "Teacher, we know that you are true, and care for no man; for you do not regard the position of men, but truly teach the way of God. Is it lawful to pay taxes to Caesar, or not?*

Verse Division: RSV (following ASV and AV) ends the verse in accordance with the verse division of *Textus Receptus* (and Souter); most modern translations, however, follow the majority of editions of the Greek text by including in v. 14 the next sentence *dōmen ē mē dōmen*; 'Should we pay, or should we not?' These notes will follow the RSV division.

Exegesis: *didaskale* (cf. 4 : 38) 'Teacher', 'Master'.

alēthēs (only here in Mark) 'true': of persons, 'truthful', 'honest'.

ou melei soi peri oudenos literally 'you have no concern for any one' (cf. 4 : 38 for the same idiom): this literal rendition, however (and RSV 'you care for no man'), may appear to be a charge of indifference and heartlessness, which is certainly not the case. Various translations are given: 'you pay no special regard to any one' (Weymouth; cf. Lagrange, Brazilian); 'you court no man's favor' (Arndt & Gingrich *melei* 2); 'you are not afraid of any one' (Montgomery); 'fearless' (Moffatt); 'impartial' (Manson). The meaning is that Jesus, as a teacher, taught with strict justice and impartiality, neither afraid of wounding anyone's sensibilities by the rigor of his teaching, nor seeking to curry any man's favor by making casuistic distinctions in applying his principles. Weymouth's translation more nearly approximates the actual wording of the Greek; Arndt & Gingrich's 'you court no man's favor', however, probably better represents the meaning of the original.

ou gar blepeis eis prosōpon anthrōpōn 'for you do not look at men's

371

face': this is a Hebraism meaning 'you do not consider men's outward appearance' (Weymouth; cf. Synodale, Brazilian, Swete; Arndt & Gingrich *blepō* 5 suggest 'you do not regard men's opinions'). 'Outward appearance', of course, has to do with social, economic, or religious status, not with physical appearance.

ep' alētheias 'on the basis of truth', 'in accordance with truth' (cf. Arndt & Gingrich *epi* I.1.b.β).

tēn hodon tou theou 'the way of God', i.e. 'religion' simply stated (cf. Rawlinson; perhaps, as one Jewish teacher to another, "The Faith").

exestin (cf. 2:24) 'it is permitted', 'it is lawful'.

dounai kēnson 'to pay the tax', 'to pay taxes'.

kēnsos (only here in Mark) is a loanword from the Latin *census* and means 'tax', 'poll-tax' (cf. Moulton & Milligan) which was paid to the Roman government. The word is here probably used in the general sense of 'taxes' without specific reference to any one tax (cf. Lagrange).

Kaisari (12:16, 17) is another loanword, from the Latin *Caesar*, used here as a title 'Emperor' or the equivalent (at that time Tiberius was Emperor).

Translation: For *teacher* see 2:13.

You are true may require some metaphorical modification, e.g. 'you are straight', 'you always speak true words', or 'you always speak straight words' (Eastern Otomí).

Care for no man, as noted above, must be translated with close attention to possible misinterpretation. For example, in the Chontal of Tabasco one must say 'you say the same thing to everyone' and in Shilluk an equivalent is 'you show the same respect to everyone'. In Shipibo, however, the same meaning is conveyed in quite a different way 'in your mind no one is anything' and in Chol one must say 'your heart is equally straight in the presence of all men', while in Tzeltal the corresponding expression is 'it does not matter who—all of us are equal as far as you are concerned'.

Do not regard the position of men has reference to respect for external symbols of position, rank, or status, translatable as 'you do not look at what is on the surface' (Shipibo), and 'you do not just see a man's face' (Zoque).

Truly may be rendered as 'with true words'.

The way of God may often be rendered literally as 'the road of God', i.e. the road God has prescribed for men. In some languages, however, the idiom cannot be used, but a descriptive equivalent must be employed, e.g. 'the way God has said people should live' or 'what God wants men to do'.

Lawful may be rendered as 'in accordance with the law', 'right', 'proper', or even 'good', in the sense of the correct thing to do, not in the meaning of moral worth.

Caesar may require some type of classifier, e.g. 'chief Caesar' or 'ruler Caesar'.

Is it lawful . . . or not may need a somewhat fuller treatment in the second clause, e.g. 'is it right that we should pay taxes to Caesar or shall we not pay taxes to him', but see the following verse.

15 *Should we pay them, or should we not?" But knowing their hyprocrisy, he said to them, "Why put me to the test? Bring me a coin, and let me look at it."*

Exegesis: *dōmen ē mē dōmen*; 'are we to pay, or not?': an example of what is called the deliberative subjunctive (Moule *Idiom Book*, 22).

ho de eidōs autōn tēn hupokrisin 'but he, perceiving their hypocrisy': cf. Goodspeed (and Lagrange) 'but he saw through their pretense'.

hupokrisis (only here in Mark; cf. *hupokritēs* 7:6) 'dissimulation', 'outward show', 'hypocrisy'.

ti me peirazete; 'why do you put me to the test?': cf. the similar use of the verb in 8:11, 10:2.

pherete moi dēnarion hina idō 'bring me a denarius that I may look (at it)': the *hina* clause expresses purpose (cf. Moule *Idiom Book*, 145); Rawlinson and RSV, however, understand it as being imperatival 'let me look at it'.

dēnarion (cf. 6:37) 'denarius': a silver coin, minted by the Roman government.

Translation: *Should* implies the concept of obligation, which is equivalent in some languages to 'must we pay'. This is a question of obligation, not of mere future possibility.

Knowing may be rendered either as 'being acquainted with' or 'recognizing'; either meaning would fit this context.

For *hypocrisy* see 7:6. In this particular context the Huave language employs an interesting idiom 'he could see that they were talking just with their mouth', that is to say, 'not with the heart', which would have implied sincerity.

16 *And they brought one. And he said to them, "Whose likeness and inscription is this?" They said to him, "Caesar's."*

Exegesis: *eikōn* (only here in Mark) 'image', 'likeness'.

epigraphē (15:26) 'inscription', 'legend (on a coin)'.

The silver denarius bore, on the obverse, the likeness of the emperor's head, in high relief, with the following inscription surrounding: TI CAESAR DIVI AVG F AVGVSTVS ('Tiberius Caesar Augustus, son of the divine Augustus'): cf. Hastings *Dictionary of the Bible* III, 428; on the plates between pp. 424 and 425, the denarius is coin no. 13, with both sides shown.

Translation: *Likeness* is translated as 'picture' (Subanen, Ifugao), or 'written mark' (Tzeltal). In some languages engraving is referred to as 'cutting'. *Caesar's* may require expansion to 'these belong to Caesar'.

17 *Jesus said to them, "Render to Caesar the things that are Caesar's, and to God the things that are God's." And they were amazed at him.*

Exegesis: *ta Kaisaros* 'the things that are Caesar's'; 'what belongs to the emperor' (Arndt & Gingrich).

apodote (only here in Mark) 'give back', 'return', 'pay', 'render'.

exethaumazon ep' autō 'they marvelled greatly at him'.

ekthaumazō (only here in N.T.; cf. *thaumazō* 5:20) 'to wonder greatly', 'to marvel much'.

epi 'at': for this use of the preposition cf. 1:22.

Translation: *Render to* is equivalent in many languages to 'pay to' or 'give back to', in the sense that the coin had been minted by Caesar's government. Accordingly, one can translate this passage as 'pay back to Caesar the things that belong to Caesar and pay back to God the things that belong to God'.

For *amazed* see 1:22, 27. However, *at him* may require adaptation in the form of a causal statement, e.g. 'because of him' or 'because of what he said', in instances in which one cannot say 'amazed at a person', but only 'amazed at what a person does' or 'because of a person'.

18 *And Sadducees came to him, who say that there is no resurrection; and they asked him a question, saying,*

Exegesis: *Saddoukaioi* (only here in Mark) 'Sadducees': as in the similar case in 10:12, the meaning here is 'some Sadducees'. They were not so much a religious party (as the Pharisees), but more of a social class, or elite, composed mostly of the priests (cf. Acts 5:17). The traditionalists of their day, they rejected all "innovations," including the idea of the resurrection, angels, etc. (cf. Acts 23:8).

hoitines legousin 'who say', 'who affirm': this is said of the Sadducees as a party, not just of the individuals who came to Jesus.

anastasin mē einai 'resurrection not to be': the indirect form, with the verb in the infinitive and the subject in the accusative case (cf. 8:27). The equivalent, in the direct form, is 'there is no resurrection'.

anastasis (12:23; cf. *anistēmi* 8:31) 'resurrection': this, of course, is eschatological, referring to the resurrection on the last day (cf. Arndt & Gingrich 2.b).

epērōtōn (cf. 5:9) 'they asked (a question)'.

Translation: *Who say there is no resurrection* must usually be brought closer to the subject expression, either as a relative clause, e.g. 'the Sadducees, who say there is no resurrection, came to him' or as a paratactically combined statement, e.g. 'the Sadducees say there is no resurrection; they came to him'.

In view of the fact that *resurrection* is a process, it is very commonly translated as a verb expression: 'to rise from the dead is not' (Sediz), 'the dead will never rise' (Subanen), 'people do not rise from the dead' (Ifugao).

Saying, as an extra verb of speaking, may not be required in some languages; in fact, it may be entirely misleading after a statement of 'asking' or 'questioning'. It should be noted, however, that the immediately following sentences are not questions. The question does not come until verse 23, and hence the introductory verb should agree with receptor-language usage.

19 *"Teacher, Moses wrote for us that if a man's brother dies and leaves a wife, but leaves no child, the man must take the wife, and raise up children for his brother.*

Exegesis: *didaskale* (cf. 4 : 38) 'teacher'.

hēmin 'for us (Jews)'—not simply 'for us Sadducees'.

hoti 'that': may be taken as introducing indirect discourse (as done by RSV) and so translated 'that'; it is more probable, however, that it serves here to introduce a quotation as direct discourse (represented in English by colon and quotation marks; cf. Arndt & Gingrich *hoti* 2, Lagrange, BFBS). The passage quoted is a free rendering of Deut. 25 : 5f.

apothanē (cf. 5 : 35) '(if) he die'.

katalipē (cf. 10 : 7) '(if) he leave'.

kai mē aphē 'but (if) he not leave': *kai* here is adversative. The verb *aphiēmi* (cf. 2 : 5) 'leave' is here equivalent to *kataleipō* of the previous clause.

teknon (cf. 2 : 5) 'child': here used generically, 'children', 'offspring'.

hina 'in order that': may be taken as dependent upon *egrapsen* 'he wrote...that', giving the content of what Moses wrote (cf. Arndt & Gingrich II.1.a.δ), or else simply as imperatival, *hina labē* 'he must take' (equivalent to the LXX volitive future *lēmpsetai* 'he shall take').

labē...tēn gunaika 'he take...the woman': the phrase here and in vv. 20-21 indicates marriage, and not simply sexual possession, and means 'take a wife' (cf. Arndt & Gingrich *lambanō* 1.c).

ho adelphos autou 'his brother', that is, the brother of *the dead man* (and not the brother of the 'someone', *tinos*, referred to in the previous clause, in which case it would be the dead man himself, or a third, unnamed, brother: that is why instead of 'his brother' in the Greek text, RSV has 'the man' which makes for clarity and accuracy).

exanastēsē sperma tō adelphō autou 'raise up seed for his brother', 'produce descendants for his brother': under the regulations of Levirate marriage, the child born to the marriage of a man with his brother's widow would be accounted the son of the dead man. It is to be noticed that this clause in Mark is not an exact transcription of the Deuteronomic Law (Deut. 25 : 5f.) but recalls the language of Gen. 38 : 8-9.

exanistēmi (only here in Mark) 'raise up': not in the ¦modern sense of 'rearing' or 'bringing up' children, but with the meaning of 'causing to rise (or, appear)', in the sense of begetting children.

sperma (cf. 4 : 31) 'seed': here figuratively and generically for 'children', 'offspring'.

Translation: *For us* should not be interpreted as an exclusive first person plural reference, as some translators have done, for though the Sadducees had a particular purpose in asking this question, as related to their interpretation of the law, certainly Jesus was included by the Sadducees in the group who were the recipients of the law of Moses.

Wrote...that if...but...the man must take...and raise up... is a very complex form of indirect discourse. In some instances it is wise to simplify the structure in accordance with the regular patterns of the receptor language, e.g. 'wrote for us these words, If a man's brother dies...' or 'wrote for us, If a man's brother dies...', thus adapting the form to direct discourse.

Man's brother must often be 'man's older brother', since so many languages make a distinction between older and younger, especially in this type of context.

Leaves a wife may be changed in perspective to read 'his wife is alone and has no children' or 'leaves his widow without any children'.

The man must be translated as 'the younger brother' in languages in which a clear distinction between younger and older brother must be preserved. Of course, it was not absolutely necessary that the levirate relationship be between brothers of successive ages, but that would be the more normal relationship, and in this context this is obviously the order.

Must take the wife must be translated in such a way as to avoid any concept of improper relations, e.g. 'must marry the widow' or 'must marry the woman'. In most languages the technical term for 'wife' must be avoided, since in many societies she is no longer legally the wife of the deceased.

Raise up children is a very specialized kind of idiom which must be changed in most languages, e.g. 'have children', 'produce children'. The use of 'raising up seed' (which is the literal translation of the Greek) must generally be avoided, since it is likely to be either meaningless (any meaning it might have would refer to plants) or be very vulgar, as a reference to sexual intercourse.

For his brother is neatly expressed in Cashibo as 'for the name of his brother', indicating that the children would bear the name of the dead brother. In the Chontal of Tabasco the precise relationship must be expressed as 'to produce children by his sister-in-law for his older brother'.

20 *There were seven brothers; the first took a wife, and when he died left no children;*

Exegesis: *ho prōtos* 'the first': probably, though not necessarily so, the oldest of the seven.

apothnēskōn ouk aphēken 'dying he did not leave': the participle is temporal, 'when he died'. In English the proper relation between the two verbs will be established by translating 'he died without leaving...'

Translation: *The first* is 'the oldest brother'.

Took a wife may be quite wrongly understood if translated literally, e.g. 'took away someone else's wife'. A more common idiom is 'married a woman'.

21 and the second took her, and died, leaving no children; and the third likewise;

Exegesis: *mē katalipōn* 'not leaving': the participle may be that of manner or accompanying circumstances.

hōsautōs (14:31) 'in like manner', 'similarly', 'in the same way'. The third brother married the woman and died childless also.

Translation: *The second* is 'the second brother' or 'the younger brother'. *Took her* is 'married her' (see the preceding verse).

Leaving no children may often be placed after the verb 'died' if the meaning is quite clear. In some instances, however, it is necessary to say 'without leaving any children'. In other languages one must say 'the younger brother married the woman; they did not have children; and he died'.

The third likewise may require some expansion to fill out the elliptical expression, e.g. 'the same thing happened to the third brother' or 'the third brother did the same'.

22 and the seven left no children. Last of all the woman also died.

Text: Instead of *kai hoi hepta* 'and the seven' of most modern editions of the Greek text, *Textus Receptus* and Kilpatrick have *kai elabon autēn hoi hepta kai* 'and the seven took her and'.

Exegesis: *kai hoi hepta* 'and the seven': this phrase summarizes the whole story, meaning 'and thus all seven' (cf. Brazilian *de sorte que*, Lagrange *ainsi*).

eschaton is an adverb 'lastly', 'last of all'.

Translation: The shift to *the seven left no children* may not convey all the meaning, since in the previous verse what happened to the third brother is stated, though elliptically, but there is no specific indication that all seven were married to the woman. This is implied, but not stated. Because of the fact that the levirate practice may seem exceptionally strange—if not downright immoral to some peoples—it is important that the details be at least correctly stated. Accordingly, in Tzeltal this verse contains 'she passed from one to another, the seven, and none of them had children by her'.

Last of all is translated as 'after all the rest had died, the woman died'.

23 In the resurrection whose wife will she be? For the seven had her as wife."

Text: The clause *hotan anastōsin* 'when they rise' following *anastasei* 'resurrection', is omitted by Westcott and Hort, Souter, and RSV, but retained by all other modern editions of the Greek text. (For the textual evidence, strong in favor of omission, cf. Taylor.)

Exegesis: *en tē anastasei* (cf. v. 18) 'in the (Day of) resurrection'.

hotan anastōsin is impersonal 'when they rise', i.e. 'when men are raised (from the dead on the resurrection Day)'. Cf. v. 25.

hotan (cf. 11:19) 'when', referring to a single definite event.

eschon 'they had': for the use of this verb with the meaning of 'have' or 'possess' cf. 6:18. The phrase 'had her as wife' means 'married her'.

Translation: For *resurrection* compare 12:18, and note also the expressions for *rise again* 9:9.

The first clause may be variously translated, e.g. 'when people rise from the dead to whom will she be a wife' or '...who will have her for a wife', or '...to whom will she belong'.

The seven, as a numeral substitute for a noun expression (compare the use of *the Twelve*), may require a noun complement, e.g. 'the seven men' or 'the seven brothers'.

24 *Jesus said to them, "Is not this why you are wrong, that you know neither the scriptures nor the power of God?*

Exegesis: *ou dia touto...*; 'is it not on account of this...?', 'is this not the reason why...?'

planasthe (12:27, 13:5, 6) 'you err', 'you are mistaken': the verb may be read as a middle, 'you deceive yourselves', but is probably to be taken as passive, 'you are misled' (cf. Arndt & Gingrich 2.c.γ).

mē eidotes 'not knowing': the participle is causal, '*because* you do not know'.

tas graphas (cf. 12:10) 'the Scriptures': by this, of course, the Hebrew Scriptures are meant.

tēn dunamin (cf. 5:30) 'the power'.

Translation: *Why you are wrong* refers to their mistake in judgment and speech, not to "wrong" in the moral sense. In Tzeltal this meaning is brought out nicely by 'you go off the wrong road in speech'.

Since the final clause introduced by *that* states the cause of the wrong judgment (grammatically anticipated in the words *this why*), one may substitute a causative conjunction, 'is not this the reason why you are wrong, because you know...'

Know the power of God may give rise to two quite different meanings: (1) to experience the power of God, which is obviously not the meaning of this passage, and (2) to know about the power of God, e.g. 'to know how God has power' (Tzeltal).

25 *For when they rise from the dead, they neither marry nor are given in marriage, but are like angels in heaven.*

Exegesis: *hotan gar ek nekrōn anastōsin* 'for when they rise from the dead': as in v. 23, the verb is impersonal, meaning 'when the dead rise', and not simply 'when the seven brothers and the woman rise'. As the context indicates, the meaning is 'in the resurrection life *after* the dead are risen'.

ek nekrōn (cf. 6:14) 'from the dead'.

oute gamousin oute gamizontai 'neither do they (the men) marry nor are they (the women) given in marriage'. The present tense of the two verbs may be translated either as the present of general truth (as is done by RSV) or as future, 'neither shall they marry nor shall they be be married'.

gameō (cf. 6:17) 'marry': used of men.

gamizō (only here in Mark) 'give (a woman) in marriage'; in the passive, as here, it is used of women 'be given in marriage'.

aggeloi en tois ouranois 'angels in heaven'. For *aggeloi* 'angels' cf. 1:13; for *en tois ouranois* (13:25) cf. *en ouranō* 13:32 and *en tois hupsistois* 11:10. Cf. also 1:10.

Translation: *They* is better translated as 'people' in order to avoid reference to the specific seven brothers and the common wife.

The distinction between *marry* and *given in marriage* cannot always be conveniently made. Hence, one can say 'men and women do not get married' or 'they do not marry one another'.

Are like must be carefully translated to avoid the impression that people are to resemble angels in appearance. Where necessary one may use 'live like' or 'exist like', so as to specify behavior, at least in this respect of marriage, rather than appearance.

For *angels*, see 1:13.

26 And as for the dead being raised, have you not read in the book of Moses, in the passage about the bush, how God said to him, 'I am the God of Abraham, and the God of Isaac, and the God of Jacob'?

Exegesis: *peri de tōn nekrōn hoti egeirontai* 'but concerning the dead that they are raised': the second clause, beginning with *hoti* 'that', further explains the thought of the first clause, beginning with *peri* 'concerning'.

egeirō (cf. 1:31) 'rise'; in the passive, as here, 'to be raised'. The present tense defines a general truth, being known as a "gnomic" present (cf. Burton *Moods and Tenses*, § 12). It could, however, have the force of a future tense (cf. v. 25).

ouk anegnōte...; 'have you not read...?' As in other similar cases (cf. 2:25, 12:10), the question is not a request for information, but is meant as an accusation.

en tē biblō Mōuseōs 'in the book of Moses', that is, in the Pentateuch. The accusation is all the more telling in light of the fact that for the Sadducees the Torah, the five books of Moses, was supremely *the* Scriptures, of greater authority than other Scriptures. The passage quoted is from Ex. 3:2-6.

biblos (only here in Mark; cf. *biblion* 10:4) 'book'.

epi tou batou 'upon the bush': there is general agreement that the phrase means 'in the passage concerning the bush' (cf. Abbott-Smith *batos*; Arndt & Gingrich *epi* I.1.a.γ).

batos (only here in Mark) 'bush', 'thornbush'.

pōs 'how?': cf. 2:26 for the same type of question.

Translation: *As for the dead being raised* is a very loosely connected phrase which constitutes a real problem for a translator who wants to make sense. This may be done in some instances by a slight expansion, e.g. 'if it is a question about whether the dead rise again' or 'if you are really asking about whether the dead rise again'.

For the treatment of questions expecting a positive answer see 11:17, and 12:10.

The book of Moses is not the 'book that Moses possessed', as is to be inferred from many translations, but 'the book that Moses wrote' or 'the book Moses gave' (cf. 12:19).

In the passage about the bush is 'in the part about the bush' or 'in the words that tell about the bush'.

God said to him must be so translated as to refer clearly to God's speaking to Moses.

Am, as a copulative verb indicating identity, is not used in some languages. Rather, one simply puts the subject and the predicate together without any verb, even as in the case of the Greek itself, 'I the God of Abraham...'

27 He is not God of the dead, but of the living; you are quite wrong."

Exegesis: *nekrōn...zōntōn* 'of dead people...of living people'.

zaō (cf. 5:23) 'to live': in Mark only here is the participle used.

polu planasthe 'you are very much mistaken' (cf. Arndt & Gingrich *planaō* 2.c.γ). For *polu* as an adverb 'much', 'very' cf. 10:48; for the verb cf. v. 24.

Translation: This verse is mistranslated and misinterpreted about as much as any other verse in the New Testament, since a literal rendering is frequently understood to mean that God has no relationship to the dead. Such literal translations need to be abandoned in many instances, with a resultant complete recasting of the sentence, e.g. 'These dead persons, for whom God is their God, are really living'; 'He is the God of living people, including those who are regarded as dead, but they are living'; or 'If God is the God of certain people, that means that they must have life, even though they have died'. These alternatives are admittedly extreme "paraphrases", in the general sense of this term, but the only alternative in many languages is to state categorically that God has nothing to do with people after they are dead and that his only concern is for the living—an obvious untruth, but one which has been emphatically stated in numerous literal translations.

28 *And one of the scribes came up and heard them disputing with one another, and seeing that he answered them well, asked him, "Which commandment is the first of all?"*

Text: Instead of *eidōs* 'knowing', 'perceiving' of the great majority of modern editions of the Greek text, Taylor, Turner and (apparently) RSV have *idōn* 'seeing'.

Exegesis: Some of the words in this verse have already been dealt with: for *proserchomai* 'come to', 'approach' cf. 1 : 31; *grammateus* 'scribe' cf. 1 : 22; *suzēteō* 'dispute' cf. 1 : 27; *kalōs* 'well', 'fittingly' cf. 7 : 6; *entolē* 'commandment' cf. 7 : 8; *prōtē* 'first' (of rank, or importance, not of time) cf. 6 : 21.

heis 'one': as in 5 : 22 the numeral is equivalent to the indefinite pronoun *tis* 'a certain one'. The whole phrase *heis tōn grammateōn* means simply 'a scribe'.

akousas 'hearing': the participle here is practically in the nature of a relative clause, 'who heard'.

poia (cf. 11 : 28) 'what', 'which': although some (cf. Swete, Lagrange) hold that the pronoun has here the qualitative force 'of what sort', 'of what kind', most commentators and translations take it to be simply interrogative, equivalent to *tis* 'what?', 'which?'

prōtē pantōn '(the) first of all': it is to be noticed that *pantōn* 'of all' is not feminine, in agreement with *prōtē* 'first (commandment)', but is either masculine or neuter. It probably is to be taken in a general way "first of all *commandments*" even though there is no concordance of genders (in which Taylor sees Semitic influence); Field, however (*Notes*, 36), takes it to mean *omnium rerum* "of all things" (cf. also Lagrange *le premier de toutes choses*).

Translation: *Them disputing with one another* may have one of two different meanings: (1) Jesus is included in the group disputing, and hence it is a case of the Sadducees disputing with Jesus, or (2) the Sadducees may be regarded as disputing among themselves on the basis of Jesus' answer. Where the ambiguity of the Greek may be preserved, one should attempt to do so. Otherwise, one can choose either of the alternative meanings and translate the clause in such a way as to relate it meaningfully to the following.

Because of the series of verbs, involving three different subjects, (*came up...heard...disputing...seeing...answered...asked*), it is often necessary to break the sentence up into smaller units, e.g. 'a scribe came up and heard them disputing with one another; he saw that Jesus was answering them well; he asked Jesus'.

First must be understood in terms of importance or value, not with reference to time or position, except as these elements may also imply importance. One may translate accordingly, 'what is the most important commandment?'

29 *Jesus answered, "The first is, 'Hear, O Israel: The Lord our God, the Lord is one;*

Exegesis: *hoti* 'that' introduces direct speech and is thus not translated.

akoue, Israël 'hear, o Israel': this passage (Deut. 6 : 4), known as the *Shema‘* (the first word in the Hebrew text, 'hear!'), was repeated twice daily by pious Jews, as the essence of their faith.

kurios ho theos hēmōn kurios heis estin 'the Lord our God, the Lord is one' (RSV). There is no general agreement as to the precise meaning of this saying, for two reasons: (1) it may be that there are two clauses, with the verb 'is' implied in the first one, thus—'The Lord (is) our God'; (2) the verb *estin* 'is' at the end of the saying does not define precisely the relation of (the second) *kurios* 'Lord' to *heis* 'one', which may be understood either, 'is one Lord', or, 'the Lord is one'. Nor are matters settled by referring to the Hebrew of Deut 6 : 4 since that passage, as seen below, is also variously translated.

The majority of translations translate the first four words *kurios ho theos hēmōn* 'the Lord our God'; it is on the last three, *kurios heis estin*, that there is wide disagreement: 'the Lord is One' (ASV, RSV; Gould, Taylor); 'is one Lord' (AV, Moffatt, Goodspeed, Weymouth, Williams, Montgomery, BFBS, Berkeley; Lagrange); 'is the only Lord' (Manson, Synodale, Brazilian; cf. Zürich 'only He is Lord'). The Vulgate *Dominus Deus noster, Deus unus est*, may be equally ambiguous.

The Hebrew *YHWH ʾelohenu YHWH eḥadh* may be translated: 'The Lord (i.e. Yahweh) our God is one Lord' (AV, ASV, RSV, Zürich); 'The Lord our God the Lord is One' (Jewish Publication Society); 'The Lord is our God, the Lord alone' (Lagrange, Moffatt). The difficulty lies essentially in the question as to whether the declaration has to do with the nature of Yahweh—'he is One'—or to his relation to Israel—'he alone is our God'. The difficulty is still further compounded by the possibility that the saying originally meant one thing and later was taken to mean another.

Where such diversity of possibilities exists, it may be that the best decision is to side with the majority, although any one of the possibilities mentioned above is almost equally defensible from the point of view of the Greek and/or the Hebrew.

Translation: *The first* may require the addition of 'commandment', i.e. 'the first commandment'.

O is only a particle to indicate direct address. The equivalent in other languages may be 'you', e.g. 'you people of Israel'.

Israel may be rendered merely as a transliterated form or with a classifier, 'people', e.g. 'people of Israel' or 'Israel people'.

In some languages the phrase *the Lord our God*, which is essentially an appositional expression, requires the use of (1) a copulative: 'the Lord is our God' or (2) a paratactic construction: 'the Lord; he is our God'.

The use of *one* as the predicate after a copulative verb such as *is* is a relatively rare type of construction since it would be applied only to expressions in which several different objects are described as being one and the same, a meaning which does not apply to this passage. Accordingly, where that is the likely meaning of 'is one', it is preferable to adopt some other rendering such as 'one Lord' or 'only Lord', for *One* occurs in the passage not as a symbol of the unity of the Lord but as an expression of his exclusiveness and uniqueness. Hence, 'only' is often a more satisfactory translation.

30 *and you shall love the Lord your God with all your heart, and with all your soul, and with all your mind, and with all your strength.'*

Exegesis: *agapēseis* (cf. 10:21) 'you shall love': the future tense is volitive, expressing a command.

ex holēs tēs kardias sou 'with all your heart': cf. 2:6 for the Hebrew concept of 'heart' as the center of man's intellectual activity.

ek 'from': indicates "the inner source from which something proceeds" (Arndt & Gingrich 1.g.γ).

ex holēs tēs psuchēs sou 'with all your soul': cf. 3:4 for the Hebrew concept of 'soul' as 'the seat of the will, desires and affections' (Abbott-Smith).

ex holēs tēs dianoias sou 'with all your understanding': this clause has no equivalent in the O.T. passage quoted (Deut. 6:5), which speaks only of *lebhabh* 'heart', *nephesh* 'soul', and *me'odh* 'might'.

dianoia (only here in Mark) 'mind', 'understanding', 'intelligence': often, in the LXX, it is used interchangeably with *kardia* 'heart' as a translation of the Hebrew *lebhabh* (cf. Hatch *Essays*, 104).

ex holēs tēs ischuos sou 'with all your strength': it is to be noticed that the passage in Mark does not follow the LXX here, which translates the Hebrew *me'odh* 'might' by *dunamis*. The two Greek words, *ischus* and *dunamis*, however, are close enough in meaning to become synonymous in certain contexts, as is the case here.

ischus (12:33) 'strength', 'might', 'power'.

Translation: For *love* see 10:21.

Lord your God, an appositional construction, must in some languages be changed to a type of dependent expression, consisting of a relative clause, e.g. 'the Lord, who is your God'.

In many languages one cannot 'love with the heart'. For example, in Kabba-Laka one must love with the liver; in Conob the equivalent expression is 'abdomen'; in the Marshallese one can love with the throat. The heart is thus translated by a number of other terms which represent the emotional center or focus of the personality.

Soul is generally translated in two ways: (1) by means of words which identify that part of the personality which lives on after death, often called the 'shadow' or 'the counterpart' and (2) by means of terms for 'life', 'insides', or 'person'. In this context the latter meaning is involved, e.g. 'love the Lord your God with all your heart and with all your life' (Kiyaka). In Navajo the living soul is 'that which stands inside of one'.

Mind may be translatable in some languages only as 'thoughts', since the mind as separate from thoughts is not recognized.

383

31 *The second is this, 'You shall love your neighbor as yourself.' There is no other commandment greater than these."*

Exegesis: The commandment quoted is from Lev. 19:18, and follows the LXX literally.

plēsion (12:33) is an adverb used as a noun, meaning 'neighbor'. In this context it does not indicate simply the person who lives next door, but represents the Hebrew *re'a* 'fellow citizen', or, in a more general way, 'the other man', 'fellow-man' (cf. Arndt & Gingrich 1.b).

hōs seauton 'as yourself': in the same way a man loves himself he is to love his fellow-man.

Translation: *The second* may require the addition of the noun 'commandment', sometimes with a shift in order of subject and predicate elements, e.g. 'this is the second commandment'.

The form of this command is in the singular, including not only the subject *you* but the object *neighbor*. In many languages, however, this use of the singular would be understood to mean that Jesus was telling the particular man that he should love his one neighbor. In order for this to be generic, many languages require plurals, e.g. 'you (plural) should love your neighbors'.

The English form employs the future auxiliary *shall* but the meaning is obligatory, which in many languages must be rendered as 'must', 'ought to', or 'should'.

For *love* see 10:21.

Neighbor is usually quite easily translated, but there are sometimes certain idiomatic forms which are employed, e.g. 'a person outside of your building' (Barrow Eskimo), 'your back and side', implying position of the dwellings (Tzeltal), 'younger-brother-older-brother', a compound which means all one's neighbors in a community (Kekchi).

As yourself may require the repetition of the verb in order to show the parallelism, e.g. 'feel hurt for your neighbors as you feel hurt for yourselves' (Tzeltal).

For constructions involving comparison see 1:7. In this instance one can sometimes translate as 'no other commandment surpasses these two commandments' or 'these two commandments are really big; no other commandment is big' (where a paratactic positive-negative statement is the normal construction).

32 *And the scribe said to him, "You are right, Teacher; you have truly said that he is one, and there is no other but he;*

Text: After the words *heis estin* 'he is one', *Textus Receptus* adds *theos* 'God', which is omitted by all modern editions of the Greek text.

Exegesis: *kalōs* 'well', 'rightly': here used absolutely, as an exclamation. 'Quite right'; 'That is true'; 'Well said' (cf. Taylor, BFBS).

didaskale (cf. 4:38) 'teacher'.

ep' alētheias (cf. 12:14) 'truly', 'in accordance with truth'.

heis estin kai ouk estin allos plēn autou 'he is one and there is no other except him': this statement represents two O.T. passages, Deut. 6:4 (quoted in v. 29) and Deut. 4:35. This may be taken to represent an interpretation of the saying 'The Lord (i.e. Yahweh) is One' as meaning that only he is God, and no other.

plēn (only here in Mark) is an adverb 'only', 'except that': used as an "improper" preposition with the genitive, as here, it means 'except' (cf. Arndt & Gingrich 2).

Translation: For *scribe* see 1:22.

Because of other third person referents it may be necessary to employ 'Jesus' rather than 'him' as the object of 'said'.

For *Teacher* see 2:13, but compare the usage of 12:19.

He is one may be difficult to translate in this form, primarily because of the indefinite third person reference, in which case one may need to translate as 'God is one'. However, the use of 'one' in the predicate may provide little or no meaning, and hence one may be forced to adjust this to a more equivalent expression 'there is only one God', which is the essential meaning of the passage.

No other but he is equivalent in some languages to saying 'and no other god exists'.

33 *and to love him with all the heart, and with all the understanding, and with all the strength, and to love one's neighbor as oneself, is much more than all whole burnt offerings and sacrifices."*

Text: After *suneseōs* 'understanding', *Textus Receptus* includes *kai ex holēs tēs psuchēs* 'and with all the soul', which is omitted by all modern editions of the Greek text.

Exegesis: *to agapan* literally 'the to love': the infinitival phrase is used as a noun, and is the subject of the sentence. The infinitive is timeless, indicating simply the action involved in the verb without any reference to the time aspect (cf. Burton *Moods and Tenses*, § 96).

It is to be noticed that the three clauses 'heart', 'understanding', and 'strength' do not follow literally either v. 30 or LXX Deut. 6:5.

ex holēs tēs kardias 'with all the heart', following v. 30 and the LXX of Deut. 6:5.

ex holēs tēs suneseōs 'with all the understanding', which follows neither v. 30 nor the LXX of Deut. 6:5. It is the equivalent of *ex holēs tēs dianoias sou* 'with all your mind' of v. 30, which, as noticed, is added to the three clauses of Deut. 6:5.

sunesis (only here in Mark; cf. *suniēmi* 4:12) 'comprehension', 'understanding'.

ex holēs tēs ischuos 'with all the strength', following v. 30 (but not the LXX of Deut. 6:5, which has *dunamis*).

perissoteron (cf. 7:36) 'much more (than)', 'more abundant (than)': in the neuter, agreeing with the subject *to agapan* 'the to love', which is also neuter.

385

holokautōmatōn (only here in Mark) 'whole burnt offerings': these were the offerings in which the animal was entirely consumed by fire.

thusiōn (only here in Mark) 'sacrifices', 'offerings': refers to all offerings and sacrifices of the Jewish religion, whether animal or vegetable. (Carefully to be avoided is any rendering which might convey the idea of "sacrifice" as the personal element of cost and hardship with which one may accomplish certain tasks or perform certain duties.)

Translation: For problems involved in translating *love with...the heart* see 12:30.

Understanding may be translated in the same way as 'mind' in 12:30.

The basic problem of translation in this verse is the use of the infinitive constructions which in many languages cannot be used, especially not when the infinitive constructions are so involved and include two different expressions for 'love'. In this passage there are often two alternative ways of treating the construction: (1) by means of a conditional clause, e.g. 'if you love him...and if you love your neighbor..., that is much more than...' or (2) through the use of paratactic constructions, in which the first is a statement of obligation, e.g. 'you should love him... and you should love your neighbors...; that is much more than...'

General obligations or a truth of universal import may be stated in terms of second person 'you' or of first person 'we', usually in the inclusive form, if the inclusive-exclusive contrast exists. The use of these persons is seemingly more widespread than an indefinite third person singular, as in the Greek and English.

Much more than all is a difficult comparative expression since two complex processes, 'loving God' and 'loving one's neighbors', are compared with two other processes 'providing burnt offerings' and 'making sacrifices'. This is treated in Tzeltal as 'great the goodness this becomes past the goodness of burned gifts for God and killed gifts'.

Where there is no special designation, *burnt offerings* are often treated as 'gifts that are burned', sometimes with 'to God' added in order to imply their religious significance. *Sacrifices* are frequently rendered as 'killed gifts' or 'gifts that one kills'.

34 *And when Jesus saw that he answered wisely, he said to him, "You are not far from the kingdom of God." And after that no one dared to ask him any question.*

Exegesis: *idōn auton hoti* 'seeing him that': by a construction fairly common in Greek, the subject of the clause which begins with *hoti* (in this case *autos* 'he') is drawn into the main clause as its object. Therefore, *idōn auton hoti* 'seeing him that' is the equivalent to *idōn hoti autos* 'seeing that he' (cf. Arndt & Gingrich *hoti* 1.b.ζ). As Black (*Aramaic*, 36) points out, this lends emphasis to the displaced word.

nounechōs (only here in the N.T.) 'wisely', 'thoughtfully', 'discreetly'.

ou makran ei apo tēs basileias tou theou 'you are not far from the Kingdom of God': here the Kingdom of God is thought of as a condition, or relationship, into which one enters here and now. Lagrange: "he almost has the necessary disposition to receive the Gospel." Cf. Arndt & Gingrich (*makran* I.a.β): "you are almost ready to enter it."

makran (only here in Mark) is an adverb 'far (away)'.

oudeis ouketi 'no one any longer', 'no one any more' (for similar phrases cf. 5:3, 9:8).

etolma (15:43) 'dared', 'had the boldness', 'ventured'.

Translation: *Saw* is a normal type of verb from the standpoint of Greek and English, but in other languages one may be required to translate 'realized' or 'recognized', to imply a mental reaction, not just a visual perception.

The rendering of *he* must refer to the scribe mentioned in verse 32. In some instances a noun will need to be substituted for this pronoun.

Wisely is translatable in some languages only by relating 'wise' to the person, e.g. 'he was wise when he answered' or to the words, e.g. 'he answered with wise words'.

For *kingdom of God* see 1:15, 4:11, and 10:15.

No one dared to ask is equivalent in some languages to saying 'everyone was afraid to ask' (Tzeltal, Bolivian Quechua).

35 *And as Jesus taught in the temple, he said, "How can the scribes say that the Christ is the son of David?*

Exegesis: *didaskōn* 'teaching': the participle is probably temporal, 'while he was teaching'. It is to be noticed that the text does not say that Jesus was addressing the scribes: it is to be inferred that he was speaking to a group of people (whether there were scribes present or not is of no moment).

hoi grammateis (cf. 1:22) 'the scribes', 'the teachers of the Law'.

ho christos (cf. 8:29) 'the Christ': a title, 'The Anointed One', and not a proper name.

huios Dauid (cf. 10:47) 'son of David', 'descendant of David', 'David's offspring'. As a Messianic title, 'son of David' indicated that the Messiah would be of the lineage of David.

Inasmuch as a faulty interpretation may influence the translation of this incident, it is well to notice that Jesus, in raising the question and quoting Ps. 110:1, is not denying the fact that the Messiah, indeed, would be a descendant of David (as attested in many passages in the O.T.). Implicit in the title 'son of David', however, was the concept that the Messiah would be somewhat less than David, or, at the most, one like unto David: so Jesus says, in effect, "not only David's son, but David's Lord" (Rawlinson). The purpose of the argument, as Taylor points out, "is not to deny the Davidic descent of the Messiah, but to suggest that a much higher view of his origin is necessary since David calls him 'lord'."

Translation: For *taught* see 2:13, and for *temple* see 11:11.

A rendering of *taught* may require an object, since in many languages it is a transitive verb, e.g. 'taught the people'.

For *scribes* see 1:22.

Son must in some instances be rendered 'descendant' or 'offspring'. In certain languages one must use 'grandson' so as to avoid the interpretation that the Christ was to be regarded as the immediate biological son of David.

The basic problem of this verse, however, as suggested above, is that the form would seem to deny the fact that Jesus was the offspring of David. To avoid this implication, which may be much stronger in some languages than in the Greek or English, one may be obliged to insert 'merely' or 'just', e.g. 'the Christ is just the son of David', implying inferiority of status.

36 *David himself, inspired by the Holy Spirit, declared,*

> *'The Lord said to my Lord,*
> *Sit at my right hand,*
> *till I put thy enemies under thy feet.'*

Text: *hupokatō* 'under' is read by Westcott and Hort, Lagrange, Nestle, Kilpatrick, and Taylor, while *hupopodion* 'footstool' is read by *Textus Receptus*, Tischendorf, Soden, Vogels, Souter, and Merk. The genuine reading in the O.T. passage quoted (Ps. 110:1) is *hupopodion* (the LXX translation of *hadhom* 'footstool'): this fact, besides the manuscript evidence, makes it probable that the genuine reading here is *hupokatō* 'under' (as well as in the parallel Mt. 22:44; in Lk. 20 : 43, however, the true reading is *hupopodion* 'footstool').

Exegesis: *autos Dauid* 'David himself': in accordance with normal Greek usage the pronoun is emphatic (cf. Lagrange); Black (*Aramaic*, 71), however, sees Semitic influence and translates 'He, David'.

en tō pneumati tō hagiō 'in the Holy Spirit', 'under the influence of the Holy Spirit' (cf. Arndt & Gingrich *en* I.5.d; cf. 1:23).

to pneuma to hagion (cf. 1:8) 'the Holy Spirit'.

The passage quoted (Ps. 110:1) is the O.T. passage most often quoted in the New Testament. It is here reproduced exactly as the LXX translates the Hebrew, with the single exception of the omission of the definite article *ho* before *kurios* 'Lord'. This does not, however, affect the meaning of the passage.

eipen kurios tō kuriō mou 'the Lord said to my Lord': the Greek is a translation of the Hebrew *ne'em YHWH la'dhoni* 'said Yahweh to my Lord'. As quoted here *Kurios* (*YHWH*) is God, while the second *kurios mou* ('adhoni) 'my Lord', is the Messiah. If language allows, the translation should be equivalent to the Greek, 'the Lord said to my Lord'. If, however, ambiguity arises from this double use of 'Lord', the meaning may be conveyed by 'The Lord (or, God) said to my Messiah', or, 'God said to my Lord'. By no means, however, should a translation read 'God said to Christ', in which 'Christ' is a proper name: such a translation would altogether mar the allusiveness of the quotation on the lips of Jesus.

kathou ek dexiōn mou 'sit at my right hand': the 'right hand' is the place of authority and power.

kathēmai (cf. 2:6) 'to sit'.

ek dexiōn mou (cf. 10:37) 'at my right'.

heōs an 'until': this phrase may mean 'until that time—*and no longer*' (as it does in 6:10; cf. also *heōs* alone in 6:45 and 14:32), but not necessarily so. It is the context which determines the particular force of the phrase, and here, as well as in 9:1, it is not to be inferred that the action of the verb ('sit') is to last only until the point indicated by the *heōs an* clause ('until I put your enemies under your feet'), and is then terminated. Cf. 9:1 for a similar instance of this usage.

hupokatō tōn podōn sou 'underneath your feet': as indicated in *Text* (above), the LXX reading here is *hupopodion* 'footstool'. No great difference in meaning is involved: it may be that *hupokatō* 'underneath' is to be derived from *hupokatō tōn podōn autou* 'underneath his feet' of Ps. 8:7, a passage also often quoted in the N.T. The figure is that of subjection of enemies, in which the victors placed their feet upon the necks of their defeated enemies (cf. Joshua 10:24).

Translation: *Inspired by the Holy Spirit* is an RSV rendering of the secondary agency, indicated in Greek by the use of the preposition *en* 'in' or 'by' and the dative case of the following noun phrase 'the Holy Spirit'. In some languages one can use a preposition such as 'by' or 'through', but in other languages one must employ a kind of paratactic construction, e.g. 'David said; the Holy Spirit caused him to say it' (Popoluca).

The Lord must often be adapted to the requirements of possession, since 'Lord' cannot occur in some languages without some possessive, e.g. 'our Lord'. In Tzeltal, for example, 'our Lord' is commonly used of God, and hence in the passage 'our Lord said to my Lord' the meaning is relatively clear, despite the generally allusive character of the passage.

At my right hand (cf. usage in 10:37) may require a marginal note in some languages in order to indicate that this is the preferred or honored position, since in some cultures the right hand is regarded as the place of less honor than the left.

Put should not be rendered in a grossly literal manner. The meaning is better conveyed in some languages by a causative, e.g. 'cause your enemies to be'.

Since a position 'under the feet' is generally regarded as one of inferiority or defeat, such an idiom is almost always quite acceptable and does not require any marginal explanation.

37 *David himself calls him Lord; so how is he his son?" And the great throng heard him gladly.*

Exegesis: *kai pothen* 'how, then...?' For this use of *pothen* 'whence cf. 8:4. 'In what way?' (Arndt & Gingrich 3; cf. also Lagrange, who equates it with *pōs* 'how?').

By many editors and translators the second part of this verse is made the initial sentence of the following paragraph, rather than the closing one of this paragraph (cf. Nestle, Westcott and Hort, Lagrange, Taylor, Swete, Goodspeed, Moffatt).

ho polus ochlos 'the great crowd', 'the crowd of people': on the basis of classical Greek usage Field (*Notes*, 37) defends and supports the AV and ASV reading 'the common people'. Marcan usage, however (cf. 5:21, 24, 6:34, 9:14), favors the RSV translation (cf. Vincent *Word Studies* I, 220).

Translation: *Calls him Lord* can be quite easily mistranslated and hence misinterpreted by the reader, if the referent of *him* is not clear. For example, in some translations the meaning has been 'David calls God Lord', since 'him' is understood as referring to God. In such cases one may say 'calls this person Lord', in which case the reference would be to 'the offspring of David', who is also spoken of as 'my Lord'.

A further ambiguity of reference may occur in *he his son*. In Tzeltal these problems are resolved as 'the same David called him his Lord; how then is his Lord his son'.

The great throng is translatable in some languages as 'the very great crowd' or 'the many, many people there'. If one adopts the interpretation of 'the common people' (see above), the equivalent often is 'the masses' or 'the poor people', or as in Tzeltal, 'the people without offices'.

38 And in his teaching he said, "Beware of the scribes, who like to go about in long robes, and to have salutations in the market places

Exegesis: *en tē didachē autou* 'in his teaching', 'while he was teaching': *didachē* has here the active meaning of 'act of teaching' (cf. 1:22).

blepete apo (cf. 8:15) 'watch out for', 'be on the lookout against'.

tōn grammateōn tōn thelontōn 'the scribes who like': the participle *thelontōn* 'liking' having the article before it, is attributive, and so defines and particularizes the noun ('the scribes') it modifies. In essence Jesus is warning his disciples to watch out for those (particular) scribes who like to walk about, etc.: he is not, according to the wording of the text, accusing *all* scribes of ostentation and hypocrisy.

thelō (only here in participial form in Mark) 'wish', 'want': here with the meaning 'like' (cf. Arndt & Gingrich 4; Moulton & Milligan; Lagrange *qui aiment*).

en stolais (cf. 16:5) 'in robes': here refers to a long flowing robe, the *ṭallith*, "denoting scholarship and piety" (Daube *New Testament and Rabbinic Judaism*, 125).

peripatein (cf. 2:9) 'to walk', 'to walk about'.

aspasmous (only here in Mark) 'greetings', 'formal salutations' given them in their quality as religious leaders, including, perhaps, a low obsequious bow (cf. Lagrange). It is to be noticed that *aspasmous* is in the accusative case, the direct object of the participle *thelontōn* 'liking'.

agorais (cf. 6:56) 'market places', 'town squares'.

Translation: *In his teaching* (see 2:13) is often rendered as a verb expression, 'as he taught' or 'when he was teaching', with 'the people' as object of 'teaching' if one must use a transitive verb requiring an object.

He or *his* may require the substitution of 'Jesus'.

Long robes may be translated as 'long clothes' or 'long coats' (Navajo).

To have salutations usually requires a shift of subject expression, e.g. 'they enjoy to have people greet them' or 'they like to have people give them a greeting'. In Tzeltal this is rendered as 'a strong greeting' to indicate the obsequious nature of the salutation.

39 *and the best seats in the synagogues and the places of honor at feasts,*

Exegesis: *prōtokathedrias en tais sunagōgais* 'the chief seats in the synagogues', 'the places of importance in the synagogues': it is explained that in the synagogue such seats were to be found in front of the Ark (which contained the sacred scrolls), facing the people, reserved for the scribes and other dignitaries (cf. Edersheim *Jesus the Messiah*, I, 436).

sunagōgē (cf. 1:21) 'synagogue'.

prōtoklisias en tois deipnois 'the chief couches at the banquets', 'the places of honor at the banquets': these were next to the host (for an instance of this cf. Lk. 14:7).

deipnon (cf. 6 : 21) 'reception', 'formal dinner', 'banquet'.

Translation: This verse is a continuation of the construction begun in 12:38, but it is often not possible to employ a series of relative clauses. Accordingly, one must generally break the sentence at this point and reintroduce the subject, e.g. 'they like the best seats'. 'Best', however, should not refer to the quality of the seats, but to the distinction and prestige accompanying the position, e.g. 'the most important seats'.

For *synagogues* see 1:21.

At feasts may require expansion to 'when they attend banquets', or 'when they are feasting', since *feasts* may be translatable only by what is a verb, not a noun.

40 *who devour widows' houses and for a pretense make long prayers. They will receive the greater condemnation."*

Exegesis: *hoi katesthontes* 'the ones devouring': there is lack of syntactical concordance, inasmuch as the participle here is in the nominative case, in apposition to *houtoi* 'these' of the last clause, and not in the genitive, in agreement with *tōn grammateōn* 'the scribes' to which it refers. The difficulty may be resolved by making this a relative clause, 'who devour' (RSV), or by starting a new sentence, as BFBS, 'They who devour...' RSV, however, makes for greater clarity and intelligibility.

katesthō or *katesthiō* (cf. 4 : 4) 'devour': here, figuratively, meaning 'rob', 'exploit', 'consume', 'destroy'. Arndt & Gingrich 2 suggest 'appropriate illegally', and give examples. Lagrange suggests that they despoiled the widows by their knowledge of the law.

tas oikias tōn chērōn 'the houses of widows': a summary way of saying 'their belongings', 'their fortunes' (cf. Lagrange *les biens*).

chēra (12 : 42, 43) 'widow'.

kai prophasei makra proseuchomenoi 'and for a pretense make long prayers'. The exact force of *prophasis* (only here in Mark) is not clear: (1) it may be connected with what precedes, meaning 'and *to cover it up* make long prayers' (Goodspeed; cf. also Brazilian; cf. Gould); (2) it may modify the subject ('the scribes') and mean 'for a pretense' (RSV), 'for show' (Berkeley, BFBS), 'for appearance' sake' (Arndt & Gingrich 2); (3) it may modify the object ('the long prayers' implied in the clause *makra proseuchomenoi* 'praying long'), 'offer long, unreal prayers' (Moffatt), make long but insincere prayers' (Manson). Grammar alone cannot decide the question: it would appear, however, that the context favors the second possibility.

prophasis 'pretense', 'pretext', 'ostensible reason'.

makra is adverbial (neuter accusative plural of the adjective *makros* 'long'; cf. the adverb *makran* 12 : 34) 'lengthily', 'extensively'.

proseuchomai (cf. 1 : 35) 'pray'.

lēmpsontai perissoteron krima 'they shall receive greater condemnation': the meaning is eschatological, 'they shall receive from God on the day of Judgment a more severe sentence'.

perissoteron (cf. 7 : 36) 'greater': here it is an adjective, modifying *krima*.

krima (only here in Mark) 'condemnation', 'judgment', 'sentence'.

Translation: *Devour widows' houses* is a metaphor which is quite meaningless in many languages. In some, however, it would convey an entirely wrong idea. For example, in one language *scribes*, which was rendered by a transcribed borrowing from a trade language (and hence was not fully understood), was thought to be the name of a special kind of animal which could consume the thatch and cornstalk houses so often used as shelters by the poor widows. When, however, 'devour widows' houses' does not convey the proper meaning, one can shift the metaphor to a nonmetaphor in any one of several ways, e.g., 'cause houses to come to nothing' (Piro), 'take away all the widows have' (Subanen), 'eat up what widows have' (Zoque), 'take away what belongs to poor women and use it up', in which 'poor women' is the usual term for 'widow' (Tzeltal), and and 'eat up the money of the houses of widows' (Chontal of Tabasco).

In line with the second possible interpretation of *for a pretense* (see comments above), one may translate in a number of different ways, e.g. 'only with their lips they pray very much' (Huave), 'so that they may deceive they pray a long time' (Bolivian Quechua), 'they make long prayers but do not mean them' (Tzeltal), and 'try to show they are good by making long prayers' (Amuzgo).

Receive the greater condemnation may be translated in terms of the sentence or judgment passed, e.g. 'receive a bigger judgment' (Tarahumara), or as in some languages by means of a reference to the punishment which results from the condemnation, e.g. 'they will have greater pain' (Zoque), and 'they will pay greater hurt' (Amuzgo).

41 *And he sat down opposite the treasury, and watched the multitude putting money into the treasury. Many rich people put in large sums.*

Exegesis: Some words in this verse have already been dealt with: for *kathizō* 'sit' cf. 9:35; *katenanti* 'opposite', 'in front of' cf. 11:2; *chalkos* 'copper', 'money' cf. 6:8; *plousios* 'rich' cf. 10:25.

gazophulakeion (12:43) 'treasury': presumably one of the thirteen contribution boxes, or receptacles, in the form of trumpets, with broad bases and narrow openings at the top, which were placed under the colonnade in the Court of the Women (cf. Edersheim *Temple*, 48-49). It may be that the particular area, in which the thirteen boxes were placed, was known popularly as the 'treasury'.

etheōrei pōs 'he was watching how': for similar constructions cf. 5 : 16 *diēgēsanto...pōs* 'they explained...how'; 11:18, 14:1 *ezētoun pōs* 'they were seeking how'; 14:11 *ezētei pōs* 'he was seeking how'.

eballon polla 'they were putting in much (money)': Burton (*Moods and Tenses*, § 56) calls attention to the imperfect here, describing the repeated acts, and the aorist *ebalon* 'they put' in v. 44, a summary statement of the incident.

Translation: The *treasury* is often translatable as 'the place where the money was received (or 'kept')', or 'the place where the people put in the money'.

Watched the multitude putting...must in some languages be broken up into two clauses, e.g. 'watched while the crowd of people put their money...' or 'watched the many people; they were putting money...'

Rich people may often be rendered as 'those who possess much money' and in this context, therefore, one may translate as 'those who had much money put in a lot of money'.

42 *And a poor widow came, and put in two copper coins, which make a penny.*

Exegesis: *mia* 'one': the pronoun is here equivalent, as often in Mark, to the indefinite pronoun *tis* 'a' (only here, however, does it function as an adjective: elsewhere it is a pronoun—cf. 5:22, 9:17, 10:17, 12:28).

ptōchē (cf. 10:21) 'poor'.

lepta duo 'two small copper coins': the *lepton* was the smallest coin in circulation. It is impossible precisely to determine the actual value of the coin. Manson (*A Companion to the Bible*, 498) estimates it to have been worth 1/96 of a denarius (cf. 6:37 for the denarius).

393

ho estin kodrantēs 'which is a quadrans': this is added for the benefit of Graeco-roman readers, who would not have been acquainted with the *lepton*. The word *kodrantēs* is a Latin loan word *quadrans*, i.e. 'one-fourth' of an *assarion* (the *assarion* was estimated to be one-sixteenth of a denarius: cf. Arndt & Gingrich). As may be seen, the equivalence between two *lepta* and one *kodrantēs* is not exact.

Translation: The relationship between the *two copper coins* and a *penny* is described in Barrow Eskimo as 'put in two little copper pieces of money which is equal to only the cheapest kind of money'. In Cashibo one may say 'two little pieces of money which have the value of a *centavo*', in which case *centavo* is borrowed from Spanish.

43 *And he called his disciples to him, and said to them, "Truly, I say to you, this poor widow has put in more than all those who are contributing to the treasury.*

Exegesis: *proskalesamenos* (cf. 3:13) 'calling to him', 'summoning'.

pleion pantōn ebalen tōn ballontōn 'she put more than all those who are putting': the strict, literal meaning of the Greek is that she put in more than all others *together* put in.

pleion 'more' is an adverb modifying *ebalen* 'she put': 'she contributed more'.

Translation: *Called* must not be understood as 'calling out to', but as 'called the attention of' or 'told them to note what was happening', for no doubt the disciples were grouped close enough to Jesus, so as to have readily heard his statement. (What one must avoid in the translation of *call*, which occurs so often in the Gospels, is the impression that Jesus was constantly shouting to his disciples like some army sergeant—an impression which has been given by some translations.)

For *truly* in this type of construction see 8:12.

For the analysis of problems involved in comparative constructions such as *more than* see 1:7. In this particular context one may say in some languages 'what this poor widow has put in surpasses all that...' or 'what this poor widow has put in is much, what all the rest have put in...is not much'.

44 *For they all contributed out of their abundance; but she out of her poverty has put in everything she had, her whole living."*

Exegesis: *ek tou perisseuontos autois* 'from that which abounds to them', 'from their abundance': the participle is the genitive of the neuter form *to perisseuon* 'that which abounds'.

perisseuō (only here in Mark; cf. *perisseuma* 8:8) 'to abound', 'to be present in abundance' (cf. Arndt & Gingrich 1.a.β).

husterēseōs (only here in Mark; cf. *hustereō* 10:21) 'lack', 'need', 'poverty'.

panta hosa (cf. 6:30, 11:24) 'everything', 'everything as much (as)'.

bion (only here in Mark) 'life': here in terms of 'livelihood', 'means of living', 'subsistence', 'property' (cf. Arndt & Gingrich 3).

Translation: *Out of their abundance* is neatly translated in the Chontal of Tabasco as 'they gave money which they didn't need'. In Tzeltal this is 'the left-over money'.

In Bali the last of this verse is idiomatically rendered as 'but she, being wholly destitute, has cast in all her money and has shaken out her house' (as one shakes out a bag so that nothing is left in it), implying that all the money she had was given.

The idea of *her whole living* can also be translated as 'all she had; this was her food' (Chontal of Tabasco) and 'all she was going to eat' (Zoque).

CHAPTER THIRTEEN

1 *And as he came out of the temple, one of his disciples said to him, "Look, Teacher, what wonderful stones and what wonderful buildings!"*

Exegesis: *ekporeuomenou autou* 'as he was coming out': cf. 10:17 for another identical use of the present participle denoting action in progress.

ekporeuomai (cf. 1:5) 'go out', 'leave'.

potapoi (only here in Mark) 'of what sort': here as an exclamation, 'how great!' 'how wonderful!' (cf. 1 Jn. 3:1).

lithoi (cf. 5:5) 'stones': these are the sculptured and worked stones of which the Temple was made.

oikodomai (13:2) 'buildings': the plural refers to the various buildings in the Temple area (cf. Arndt & Gingrich *oikodomē* 2.a).

The other words in this verse have already been dealt with: for *hieron* 'temple' cf. 11:11; *heis* 'one' as an indefinite article cf. 5:22; *didaskale* 'teacher' cf. 4:38; *ide* 'see!' cf. 2:24.

Translation: *He* may require substitution by 'Jesus'.

For *temple* see 11:11, and for *teacher* see 2:13.

Said may require translation by 'exclaimed' or 'spoke with amazement' in order to agree properly with the following sentence.

Wonderful must frequently be rendered by reference to (1) size, e.g. 'how big' or (2) appearance, e.g. 'how beautiful' or 'how impressive'. It is best to avoid the implications of value, or people may think that the stones were gems. More often than not the category of size is the most acceptable equivalent.

2 *And Jesus said to him, "Do you see these great buildings? There will not be left here one stone upon another, that will not be thrown down."*

Text: Before *lithos* 'stone' Westcott and Hort, Souter, Soden, Vogels (in brackets), Lagrange, and Taylor add *hōde* 'here', which is omitted by *Textus Receptus*, Tischendorf, Nestle, Merk, and Kilpatrick.

Exegesis: *ou mē aphethē* 'will not be left': the double negative is emphatic. For *aphiēmi* 'leave' cf. 2:5.

ou mē kataluthē 'will not be torn down': also emphatic. The sense of the two clauses is, 'No two stones will be left standing together'—so thorough will the destruction of the Temple be.

kataluō (14:58, 15:29) 'destroy', 'demolish', 'tear down'.

Translation: *Said* may be 'replied', if the point of view in the receptor language is the previous exclamation, or 'asked', if what follows governs the form of the verb introducing direct discourse.

Great is to be understood in terms of size, not importance.

The Greek text does not mean that no two stones will be left one on top of another (that is to say, Jesus did not prophesy that the stones would all be spread out singly on the ground), but that no two joining stones would be left together. In Zoque this is well rendered by 'will not remain a stone on stone's companion'. One may also translate this prophecy as 'no two stones will be left together; they will all be thrown down'. In Tzeltal the relationships of the stones in the first part of the expression is made somewhat more explicit by the phrase 'these stones that are built up'.

3 And as he sat on the Mount of Olives opposite the temple, Peter and James and John and Andrew asked him privately,

Exegesis: *kathēmenou autou* 'while he was sitting' (cf. v. 1).

eis to oros tōn elaiōn 'on the Mount of Olives': here *eis* 'into' is clearly equivalent to *en* 'in' (cf. Arndt & Gingrich *eis* 9.a), with the meaning 'at', 'on' (cf. Arndt & Gingrich *en* I.1.b). (Though this use of *eis* might have some bearing on the meaning of *eis* in 1:10, it should be noticed that the verb there denotes motion, while here it denotes rest.)

to oros tōn elaiōn (cf. 11:1) 'the Mount of Olives'.

For *katenanti* 'opposite', 'in front of' cf. 11:2; *kat' idian* 'privately' cf. 4:34.

Translation: For *Mount of Olives* see 11:1.

Opposite the temple is translatable in many instances as 'facing the temple' or 'on the opposite side of the ravine from the temple'.

Privately may be rendered as 'when they were alone with him'.

4 "Tell us, when will this be, and what will be the sign when these things are all to be accomplished?"

Exegesis: *pote* (cf. 9:19) 'when?'

tauta 'these things': refers back to the statement that not one stone of the Temple would be left standing on another. In the next clause *tauta...panta* 'all these things' would appear to include more than the single *tauta* of the first clause. A reasonable explanation is offered by Lagrange who takes 'all these things' to refer to everything connected with the destruction of the Temple, the destruction itself being only one of a series of events. The second question, then, represents an expansion of the first one, in normal Semitic style.

sēmeion (cf. 8:11) 'sign': here in the sense of a 'token' or 'indication' pointing to the events referred to. In this context the 'sign' asked for would be an indication that the events were about to take place.

hotan mellē tauta sunteleisthai panta 'when all these things are about to be accomplished'.

hotan (cf. 11:19) 'when': indicates one single event.

mellō (cf. 10:32) 'about to be', 'on the point of' (cf. Arndt & Gingrich 1.c.α).

sunteleō (only here in Mark) 'to fulfil', 'accomplish': the meaning 'come to an end' is suggested as possible here by Arndt & Gingrich 1.

Translation: *Tell us* may require a shift to 'answer us', since questions follow.

This, which is an ambiguous or obscure reference, may require a translation by 'what you said' (Tzeltal) if the meaning is to be intelligible.

For *sign* see 8:11.

Accomplished is translatable only as 'happen' in some languages.

5 And Jesus began to say to them, "Take heed that no one leads you astray.

Exegesis: *blepete* (cf. 8:15) 'beware!' 'caution!' 'watch out!' Moulton & Milligan give examples from the papyri showing that this use of the verb *blepō* 'see' was not purely Semitic, but was Greek as well.

mē tis humas planēsē 'lest any one deceive you', 'that no one lead you astray'.

planaō (cf. 12:24) in the active, as here, 'cause to err', 'lead astray', 'deceive'.

Translation: *Leads you astray* is equivalent to 'deceive', or as in some languages 'cause you to believe a lie'.

6 Many will come in my name, saying 'I am he!' and they will lead many astray.

Exegesis: *epi tō onomati mou* (cf. 9:37) 'in my name': some difficulty arises from the fact that the phrase ordinarily means 'on my account', 'for my sake', 'in my behalf'; here, however, it seems to demand the meaning, 'representing to be me', 'as though they were I', since they will say, "I am he." Arndt & Gingrich (*onoma* I.4.c.ε) suggest 'using my name'; 'in my name' is the reading of most English translations (cf. Vulgate *in nomine meo*); Lagrange has *sous mon nom*. Notwithstanding the difficulty, some such translation as RSV 'in my name', or 'under my name', will probably convey the meaning without involving the statement in any contradiction.

hoti 'that' introduces direct statement.

egō eimi literally 'I am' or 'It is I' (cf. 6:50); here, clearly, a claim to be the Messiah—'I am He' (cf. 14:62), or, in accordance with Marcan language, 'I am the Son of man' (cf. v. 26).

Translation: For the use of *in my name* see 9:37, but in this context a special rendering is often required, e.g. 'making use of my name', 'calling themselves by my name', or 'applying my name to themselves'.

I am he is sometimes very ambiguous, especially as this expression is spoken by Jesus. Hence, 'I am the Christ' or 'I am the Son of man' is a much closer equivalent. In languages which generally prefer an indirect form of discourse, this statement may be less ambiguous, e.g. 'they will say that they are I', or 'they will say that they are what I am'.

A further complication may be found in the shift from plural to singular in the form of the direct discourse, e.g. 'many will come..., each will say, I am he'. Moreover, the plural of 'many' must be interpreted as distributive, not as collective, for each person claims for himself the Messiahship.

For *lead many astray* see the previous verse.

7 *And when you hear of wars and rumors of wars, do not be alarmed; this must take place, but the end is not yet.*

Text: After *dei* 'it is necessary' *Textus Receptus*, Soden, Vogels, Merk add *gar* 'for', which is omitted by the majority of modern editions of the Greek text.

Exegesis: *polemous kai akoas polemōn* 'wars and reports of wars': *akoas* is probably not to be taken in the sense of '*false* rumors', but rather with the meaning of 'reports', 'news'. Manson translates 'sounds of battles close at hand and news of battles far away' (cf. Lagrange *les guerres prochaines et les guerres éloignées*).

polemos (only here in Mark) 'war', 'battle'.

akoē (cf. 1:28) 'report', 'message'.

mē throeisthe 'do not be alarmed': the verb *throeō* (only here in Mark) appears in the N.T. only in the passive, meaning 'be disturbed', 'be frightened'.

dei genesthai 'it is necessary (that these things) happen', 'it must be'.

dei (cf. 8:31) 'it is necessary'.

to telos (cf. 3:26) 'the end': in this context it refers to the end of the age (cf. Arndt & Gingrich 1.b, "the final act in the cosmic drama").

Translation: Many translators have distinguished between *wars and rumors of wars* as wars now in progress and rumors about wars that threaten, e.g. 'wars that have started and wars that shall come, so they shall say'. However, the word *rumors* is to be understood more in the sense of 'report' or 'information about' rather than in the meaning of 'rumor' or 'gossip'; hence 'wars near and far' is a closer equivalent of the Greek text.

This must take place involves a generic use of *this* to refer to all the wars, but in other languages 'wars' may require a plural reference, e.g. 'these must happen'.

The end is an extremely difficult expression to translate. In the first place, it is impossible in many languages to talk about 'the end'. One can only speak of 'the end of something'. In other languages *end* must be translated as a verb, since in this passage one is not speaking of a point of an object, e.g. 'the end of a stick' or 'the end of one's finger', but of a process of termination. The equivalent expression in such a language may be 'everything has not yet come to an end' (or 'terminated'). Where, however, one can use 'end' as a noun, though with obligatory possession, it is possible to say 'the end of everything', or 'the end of all happenings', or 'the end of the age'.

8 *For nation will rise against nation, and kingdom against kingdom; there will be earthquakes in various places, there will be famines; this is but the beginning of the sufferings.*

Text: After *limoi* 'famines' *Textus Receptus* adds *kai tarachai* 'and tumults' which is omitted by all modern editions of the Greek text.

Exegesis: The first sentence of this verse recalls the language of Isa. 19:2, but is not a quotation of that passage.
  egerthēsetai (cf. 1:31) 'shall be raised', 'shall arise' in war or hostility.
  ethnos (cf. 10:33) 'people', 'nation'.
  basileia (cf. 3:29) 'kingdom'. In both clauses *epi* 'upon' has a hostile sense, 'against' (cf. 3:24-26; Arndt & Gingrich III.1.a.ε).
  seismoi (only here in Mark) 'earthquakes'.
  kata topous 'in various regions', 'in different places' (cf. Arndt & Gingrich *kata* II.1.a, and *topos* 1.d).
  limoi (only here in Mark) 'famines'.
  archē ōdinōn 'a beginning of birth-pangs', 'the beginning of travail'.
    archē (cf. 1:1) 'beginning', 'start'.
    ōdin (only here in Mark; cf. //Mt. 24:8; cf. Acts 2:24, 1 Thess. 5:3) 'birthpang', 'pain (the mother suffers) in childbirth'. As a technical phrase in apocalyptic literature, 'the beginning of birth-pangs' are the terrors and torments that precede the coming of the Messianic age.

Translation: *Nation* is translatable as 'tribe' or 'people', the largest group which is recognized by the people as an in-group, that is, as having mutual bonds of responsibility; the size of such groups will differ greatly in different areas.
  Kingdom may be rendered as 'government' in some languages, or as 'rulers' in others, since an abstract entity such as a 'kingdom' or 'government' cannot be spoken of as participating in such a process as 'rising up against'. On the other hand, people can be so described.
  Rise against means 'to make war against' or 'to fight against'.
  In most places there are quite adequate terms for *earthquakes*. Where necessary, however, one can always describe such an event as 'the earth shakes' or 'the ground moves violently'.
  Famines are of frequent enough occurrence in most parts of the world, but the term can always be rendered as a phrase, e.g. 'people will not have food to eat'.
  This must be translated as 'these' in some languages or the reader will understand that only the last event, namely, the famines, is involved. Hence, one may render this phrase 'these are just the beginning...'

In some languages *beginning* cannot be treated as a noun (cf. 1:1), and hence the entire sentence may require recasting, e.g. 'these sufferings are just the first'.

9 *"But take heed to yourselves; for they will deliver you up to councils; and you will be beaten in synagogues; and you will stand before governors and kings for my sake, to bear testimony before them.*

Exegesis: *blepete de humeis heautous* (cf. v. 5) 'but you watch out for yourselves'. The personal pronoun *humeis* is emphatic (cf. Gould).

paradōsousin (cf. 1:14) 'they will deliver up *to trial*'.

eis sunedria kai eis sunagōgas 'to councils and in synagogues': the majority of commentators and translations divide these two clauses as does RSV, joining 'to councils' with the verb 'deliver up', and 'in synagogues' with the verb 'beat'. Some, however (cf. Gould, Rawlinson), join both clauses to the first verb, thus: 'they will deliver you up to councils and synagogues', and take *darēsesthe* 'you shall be beaten' independently.

sunedria (here only in plural in Mark; in 14:55, 15:1 the singular refers to the Sanhedrin of the Jews in Jerusalem) 'councils': the local councils of the various Jewish cities (cf. Arndt & Gingrich 3).

sunagōgē (cf. 1:21) 'synagogue'.

darēsesthe (cf. 12:3) 'you shall be beaten'.

epi hēgemonōn kai basileōn stathēsesthe 'before rulers and kings you shall stand'.

epi 'upon' means here 'before', in the language of law courts (cf. Arndt & Gingrich I.1.a.δ).

hēgemones (only here in Mark) 'rulers', 'governors': in the Roman system the word was used of the imperial governors of provinces.

basileis (cf. 6:14) 'kings': in a general sense, such as used in 6:14 of Herod Antipas.

histēmi (cf. 3:24) 'stand' on trial, in judgment.

heneken (cf. 10:7) 'on account of', 'because': in this verse *heneken emou* is to be understood as 'on my account', 'because of me', and not 'on my behalf' (as RSV 'for my sake' may be understood).

eis marturion autois (cf. 1:44, 6:11) 'for a witness to them', 'for a testimony before them'.

G. D. Kilpatrick (*Studies in the Gospels: Essays in Memory of R. H. Lightfoot*, 145-58), following earlier suggestions made by Burkitt and Turner, proposes a change in punctuation and re-arrangement of the clauses in vv. 9-11, as follows:

> "But take heed to yourselves;
> For they will deliver you up to councils and synagogues,
> and you will be beaten before governors and kings,
> for my sake you will stand for a testimony to them and
>   among all the Gentiles.
> The gospel must first be preached, and then when they
>   bring you to trial and deliver you up, etc."

As seen, the greatest difference between this punctuation and that normally followed, is that v. 10 is so completely altered as to say nothing about the gospel being preached in all nations. The other changes affect in a smaller measure the traditional reading of these verses. Kilpatrick's proposal has been subjected to analysis and rejected by Austin Farrer (*Journal of Theological Studies* NS. 7.75-79, 1956).

Translation: *Take heed to* is likely to be mistranslated since in some languages there are two quite different ways of translating such an expression: (1) 'watch out for', in the sense of being solicitous for yourselves and watching out for your own interests, and (2) 'be aware of the danger to which you will be exposed'. The latter meaning is, of course, the correct one here, but a number of translations have used the former, with obvious contradiction with what occurs in the following verse.

They is an indefinite subject, meaning 'persons' or 'some people', not 'the people', as referring to the masses, who maintained a relative sympathy for the followers of Christ.

Deliver you up is equivalent to 'hand you over to' or 'grab you and turn you over to trial'.

Councils is translatable in Zoque as 'where the rulers are'; in Piro a rather involved term meaning 'where judgments are heard' is employed. However, 'councils', whether formal or informal, are known in all societies.

For *synagogues* see 1:21.

You will be beaten may be made active as 'they will beat you'.

Governors and kings cannot be easily distinguished in some languages where the different classes of rulers are not parallel to classical usage. However, in some instances *governors* has been translated as 'rulers' (who are appointed by some central government or authority) and 'chiefs' (who are hereditary rulers).

Bear testimony may be rendered 'to tell the truth' (Barrow Eskimo) or 'to tell what has happened'.

10 *And the gospel must first be preached to all nations.*

Exegesis: *eis panta ta ethnē* 'in all nations', 'among all peoples', 'to all the Gentiles'.

eis 'in', 'to' (cf. Arndt & Gingrich 1.d.β). Moule (*Idiom Book*, 69) calls the use of *eis* in this verse equivalent to a pure dative.

ta ethnē in a general sense 'all nations'; it could, however, have the meaning 'all the Gentiles'.

prōton 'first' is an adverb, modifying the verbal phrase *dei kēruchthēnai* 'it is necessary (that) be preached'. It is generally taken to indicate time, 'first', that is 'before' (something happens: in this case, before the End comes): so most translations (cf. also Arndt & Gingrich *prōtos* 2.a); by some, however, it is taken to indicate degree of rank or importance: cf. Manson, "the first essential"; Synodale *tout d'abord*; Lagrange "*avant tout, tout d'abord.*"

For *dei* 'it is necessary' cf. 8:31; *kērussō* 'proclaim', 'preach' cf. 1:4; *euaggelion* 'the gospel' cf. 1:1.

Translation: For *gospel* see 1:1, and for *preached* see 1:4. A typical rendering is 'the good news must first be announced'.

All nations may be 'all peoples' or 'the people of all different places'. In the first instance the point of view is the diversity of kinds and in the second the distinction in place, differences which must be carefully observed in some languages.

In the active form, as required by some languages, one may translate as 'people must announce the good news to...'

11 *And when they bring you to trial and deliver you up, do not be anxious beforehand what you are to say; but say whatever is given you in that hour, for it is not you who speak, but the Holy Spirit.*

Text: After *ti lalēsēte* 'what you should say' *Textus Receptus* adds *mēde meletate* 'nor be anxious', which is omitted by all modern editions of the Greek text.

Exegesis: *hotan agōsin humas paradidontes* 'and whenever they arrest you and deliver you up to trial'.

hotan (cf. 11:19) 'whenever': here the sense is probably 'whenever' (rather than 'when'), indicating repeated events and not simply one single event (cf. Moule *Idiom Book*, 133; Arndt & Gingrich 1.a).

agō (cf. 1:38) 'cause to go', 'lead', 'bring': in a specialized use, 'lead away', 'take into custody', 'arrest' (cf. Arndt & Gingrich 2).

paradidōmi (cf. 1:14) 'deliver up (to trial)', 'turn over to the court'.

mē promerimnate 'do not be concerned beforehand': only here does the verb appear in the N.T.

ho ean dothē humin 'whatever may be given you (*by God*)'.

to pneuma to hagion (cf. 1:8) 'the Holy Spirit'.

Translation: The first clause may be accurately translated as 'arrest you and hand you over to the authorities to be tried'.

For *anxious* see under *cares* 4:18. In this context words for 'worry' or 'concern' must be specifically applicable to the special anxieties involved, e.g. 'don't let your stomach rise up' (Gurunse), 'don't let your mind kill you' (Navajo), 'don't be driven hard', a reference to animals being chased in the hunt (Piro).

Is given is a very indefinite passive, requiring in some languages an agent, e.g. 'God gives you'.

Hour is more idiomatically rendered as 'at that time' or 'on that occasion', since 'hour', as a precise unit of time may be quite strange and completely inapplicable to this type of context.

For *Holy Spirit* see 1:7.

403

12 *And brother will deliver up brother to death, and the father his child, and children will rise against parents and have them put to death;*

Exegesis: *epanastēsontai tekna epi goneis* 'and children will rise against their parents': the clause recalls the language of Micah 7:6.

epanistēmi (only here in Mark) 'raise up against': in the middle, as here, 'rise up against'.

goneis (only here in Mark) 'parents'.

thanatōsousin (14:55) 'they will put to death', 'they will hand over to be killed'.

Translation: *Deliver up...to death* means 'hand them over in order to have them killed' or 'hand them over so that they will be killed'.

Brother...brother gives rise to certain problems of translation when there are various terms for 'brother'. One may, for example, use a generic term such as 'siblings will hand over siblings'. On the other hand, where 'older brother' and 'younger brother' must be distinguished, one may say, 'an older brother will hand over a younger brother and a younger brother will hand over an older brother'. In some languages, however, this doubling of the expression is not necessary, since general truths about reciprocal activities may be expressed as 'older brothers will hand over younger brothers'. Note, however, that in many instances one must use plural rather than singular forms, in order for the statement to be generally applicable and not merely restricted to a particular event.

Because of the necessity for plural forms, and in some instances for a filling out of the elliptical expressions, one may translate the clause as 'fathers will hand over their children to be killed and children will be angry with their parents and cause them to be killed'.

13 *and you will be hated by all for my name's sake. But he who endures to the end will be saved.*

Exegesis: *misoumenoi* (only here in Mark) 'hated', 'detested'.

dia to onoma mou 'because of my name', i.e. 'on account of me' (cf. v. 9). 'Because you bear my name' (Goodspeed; cf. Arndt & Gingrich *onoma* I.4.c.α); 'because of your allegiance to me' (Manson); 'because you are called by my name' (Weymouth).

ho...hupomeinas (only here in Mark) 'he who endures', 'he who perseveres', 'he who remains firm'.

eis telos 'to the end', 'until the end': either in a general sense, 'until the persecution and hatred are ended', or, in a special sense, 'until one's life is ended'. The context would seem to favor the second alternative. Swete and Taylor take it adverbially, 'finally', 'completely'.

sōthēsetai (cf. 3:4) 'shall be saved' in the theological sense (cf. Taylor, who compares it to 10:26; Lagrange; Arndt & Gingrich 2.b).

Translation: *You will be hated by all* is easily shifted to the active when necessary, e.g. 'all people will hate you'.

To the end must generally be made somewhat more specific, e.g. 'to the end of his life'.

Endures is equivalent in some lang~~ges to 'has patience' or 'bears the suffering'.

For *save* see 10:26, but where a subject is required for active, transitive verbs, 'God' may be used, e.g. 'God will save him'.

14 But when you see the desolating sacrilege set up where it ought not to be (let the reader understand), then let those who are in Judea flee to the mountains;

Text: After *tēs erēmōseōs* 'of desolation' *Textus Receptus* adds *to rēthen hupo Daniēl tou prophētou* 'that was spoken by the prophet Daniel', which is omitted by all modern editions of the Greek text.

Exegesis: *hotan de idēte* 'but when you see': refers to a single definite event.

to bdelugma tēs erēmōseōs 'the abomination of desolation': the Greek phrase is the LXX translation of the Hebrew *shiquç shomem* in Dan. 11:31, 12:1 (cf. also 9:27) 'the detested thing causing horror' (Brown, Driver and Briggs). It is generally held that the phrase in Daniel referred to the heathen altar erected in the Temple in Jerusalem by Antiochus Epiphanes in 168 B.C. (cf. 1 Macc. 1:54). In the O.T. *shiquç* refers generally to a heathen idol or false god, or any other symbol of heathenism. The verb *shamem* means 'to appal', 'to cause horror'.

The Greek phrase means literally 'the detested thing causing desolation'. The cryptic language of Mark does not make clear what is desolated by the 'abominable thing'. Various translations are proposed for the phrase: 'the dreadful desecration' (Goodspeed), 'the appalling Horror' (Moffatt), 'the destructive desecration' (Williams).

hestēkota 'standing': the accusative case of the masculine participle *hestēkōs*, meaning properly 'he who stands'. Whereas *to bdelugma* 'the detestable thing' to which the participle refers is neuter, either 'the detestable thing' is personified (cf. Swete), or else it is thought of as being a man (the Antichrist—so many commentators). Against RSV it would be preferable to translate 'standing where *he* should not' rather than 'it'.

histēmi 'stand': as in 9:1 the emphasis here is more on the idea of 'being' or 'existing' than on 'standing' as such (cf. Arndt & Gingrich II.2.b.α).

hopou ou dei 'where (he) ought not to be': for *dei* 'it is necessary', 'it is fitting' cf. 8:31.

ho anaginōskōn noeitō 'he who reads is to understand': as RSV parentheses indicate, this is a note added by the author (cf. a similar instance in 7:19) calling the reader's attention to what he is reading. It is probable that 'the reader' is the man who would be reading the passage aloud to the assembled congregation, not to the individual reading alone. It is not agreed what is the specific thing to which the author calls the reader's attention: many take it to refer to the enigmatic phrase 'the abomination of desolation', admonishing the reader to understand the phrase in light of its use in the O.T., while others take it to refer to the vague designation of the place where 'the abomination of desolation' would stand. It has also been suggested that the note, possibly a marginal note at first, called the reader's attention to the masculine *hestēkota* 'standing' which the reader would be tempted to read as a neuter, agreeing with *to bdelugma* 'the abomination' (H. A. Guy, *Expository Times*, 65.30, 1953).

anaginōskō (cf. 2:25) 'read', 'read aloud'.

noeō (cf. 7:18) 'understand', 'comprehend'.

hoi en tē Ioudaia pheugetōsan eis ta orē 'those who are in Judea are to flee to the mountains': in the hill country to the west of the Jordan they would find refuge from the desolation sweeping Judea.

pheugō (cf. 5:14) 'flee'.

eis ta orē (cf. 3:13) 'to the hills', 'to the hill country'.

Translation: *Desolating sacrilege* is not an easy expression to translate, for the words include complex concepts which are not clearly defined, either in their immediate forms or in the larger context. The only alternative in most languages is to attempt to use some descriptive phrase which will approximate the meaning of the Greek, but not reproduce it in any word-for-word relationship, e.g. 'the hated (thing) which does terrible destruction' (Maya), 'the foul object which desolates the town', in which 'desolate' must occur with a direct object (Trique), 'that which is bad which destroys' (Mazahua, Tzeltal), 'fearful thing which destroys' (Kiyaka), and 'loathsome thing which destroys' (Huave).

See the desolating sacrilege set up involves a construction which requires two clauses in many languages, since the object of the first verb *see* is also the subject of the second verb *set up*, e.g. 'see the desolating sacrilege; it will be set up where it ought not to be'.

If the interesting shift in the Greek from the neuter to the masculine, implying evidently a personification of the desolating sacrilege, can be reproduced in another language, this should be done, but in most instances this cannot be accomplished without considerable confusion to the reader.

Let the reader understand is in the form of a third person imperative, which is paralleled in other languages by a statement of obligation, e.g. 'the one who is reading should understand'. The same type of adaptation may be required in the case of the last clause, e.g. 'those who are in the Judea country should flee to the mountains'.

15 let him who is on the housetop not go down, nor enter his house, to take anything away;

Text: After *mē katabatō* 'he is not to go down' *Textus Receptus*, Soden, Vogels, and Taylor add *eis tēn oikian* 'into the house', which is omitted by the majority of modern editions of the Greek text.

Exegesis: *ho epi tou dōmatos* 'he who is on the roof': on the flat roofs the people spent much of their leisure time, especially in the cool of the evening, at the close of the day's work, and here they would get the news, good or bad, passed from roof top to roof top. The roof was reached by outside steps (cf. 2:4).

dōma (only here in Mark) 'housetop', 'roof'.

mē katabatō mēde eiselthatō 'he is not to go down or enter': as Lagrange points out, the two clauses do not prohibit two actions, as though they meant 'he is neither to go down, nor is he to enter', but designate a single action, 'he is not to go down and enter'. In effect it is an order for the man to go down and flee at once to the hills, without taking the time to go into the house and get some of his belongings.

katabainō (cf. 1:10) 'go down', 'come down'.

Translation: *Not go down*, as the result of literal translating, has implied in many instances that the person was instructed to remain on the housetop indefinitely. As noted in *The Bible Translator*, 3.88, 1952, this problem, which is confronted in a number of translations, may be solved by shifting the negative in accordance with the requirements of the activity described, e.g. 'when he comes down from the housetop, he should not enter the house to take anything' (Chontal of Tabasco). Compare also 'the man on the housetop in going should not enter...' (Subanen).

In some parts of the world flat roofs are carefully distinguished from peaked ones. It is quite essential that as much of the meaning as can be conveyed in this passage be implied by the right choice of words. For example, not only should a word applicable to a flat roof be used, but the translation of 'take anything away' should imply, if possible, his own possessions. It should not, as in some instances, connote the stealing of someone else's property which the thief has failed to obtain by trying to break through the roof and so proposes to take (as assumed by the reader) by entering boldly into the house.

16 **and let him who is in the field not turn back to take his mantle.**

Exegesis: *ho eis ton agron* 'the man (working) in the field'.

eis here equals *en* 'in' (cf. 1:9).

agros (cf. 5:14) 'field', 'plot of ground'.

mē epistrepsatō eis ta opisō 'he is not to go back (to the house)': the man working in the field is enjoined to flee at once without taking time to go back to the house and get his cloak.

epistrephō (cf. 4:12) 'turn around', 'turn back': here, with *eis ta opisō* (literally, 'to the places behind'), it means 'go back', 'return'.

himation (cf. 2:21) 'outer garment', 'cloak', 'mantle'.

Translation: *Turn back* is often rendered as 'return to his home'.

Let him...not turn back may be translated as a statement of obligation, e.g. 'a man who is in the field should not return to his home to get his cloak'.

17 And alas for those who are with child and for those who give suck in those days!

Exegesis: *ouai* (14:21) 'woe!' 'alas!': an interjection expressing pain or displeasure.

tais en gastri echousais 'for those who are pregnant', 'for those who are with child'.

tais thēlazousais 'for those who are nursing (children)', 'for those who suckle': for mothers with small nursing children, and for expectant mothers, flight would be difficult and perilous.

Translation: *Alas* is translatable in one of three different ways: (1) by a similar exclamative particle, indicating pity and sympathy (but such particles are not too frequent in languages), (2) by a verbal expression of 'suffering', e.g. 'those who are pregnant...will suffer' (Zoque), and (3) by an adjectival expression denoting the state of the persons involved, e.g. 'poor those who are pregnant...' (Tzeltal).

Are with child is rarely translatable in a literal form. In fact, literal translations usually imply women who are carrying children in their arms and is hence a more or less redundant expression of what occurs in the following phrase. However, there are always expressions for pregnancy in all languages. The trouble is that there are so many, some of which are regarded as vulgar, others as humorous, and still others as proper, though in this latter instance propriety may be dictated by whether a man or a woman is speaking.

In those days should be so construed as to be applicable to both 'those who are pregnant' and 'those who are nursing'.

Give suck must be translated with care in order to avoid possible vulgar expressions and also so as to make certain that the words of Jesus are those which are fitting for a man to utter, since often distinctions are made between men's and women's speech at this point.

18 Pray that it may not happen in winter.

Text: After *genetai* 'happen' *Textus Receptus* adds *hē phugē humōn* 'your flight', which is omitted by all modern editions of the Greek text.

Exegesis: *proeuchesthe* (cf. 1:35) 'you must pray'.

hina 'that': as often in Mark it here denotes the content of the prayer, not its purpose.

mē genētai 'it may not happen': if a subject is needed, the word *thlipsis* 'affliction', 'tribulation' of the next verse may be supplied, or else 'flight' from v. 14.

ginomai 'become': here in the sense of 'happen', 'come about', 'occur' (cf. Arndt & Gingrich I.1.a.β).

cheimōnos (only here in Mark) 'of a winter': the genitive here expresses time—'in winter-time'. At such time flight would become difficult and dangerous because of the torrential rains, and inclement weather in general.

Translation: Contrary to what might seem to be the case, there are numerous difficulties in translating *winter*. If, for example, one employs a term which identifies a particular time of the year, e.g. from December to March, this may prove to be precisely the best time to travel, as in the case of Zoque. In tropical areas in the southern hemisphere it is usually possible to speak of 'the rainy season', for this is often a difficult period in which to travel, but again this often depends upon the mode of travel. Some translators, accordingly, have rendered *winter* as 'the cold time', employing for 'cold' a word which would imply a difficult, inclement season. In other languages it has been possible to use 'the bad months' or 'the hard season', as an indirect means of describing the difficulties involved.

19 *For in those days there will be such tribulation as has not been from the beginning of the creation which God created until now, and never will be.*

Exegesis: *esontai gar hai hēmerai ekeinai thlipsis* literally 'for those days shall be affliction'.

thlipsis (cf. 4:17) 'affliction', 'tribulation', 'distress'.

hoia...toiautē 'of such kind...as', 'the like of which' (Weymouth, Moffatt): the order of the two qualitative pronouns in Greek is unusual, the normal order being *toiautē...hoia*; the meaning, however, is clear. Only here, in Mark, are the two used together.

hoios (cf. 9:3) 'of what sort'.

toioutos (cf. 4:33) 'such as'.

ap' archēs ktiseōs (cf. 10:6) 'from the start of creation', 'from the beginning of the world'. The description in this verse of the 'tribulation' recalls the language of Dan. 12:1 (cf. also Joel 2:2).

hēn ektisen ho theos 'which God created': the relative *hēn* which' refers to the immediately preceding *ktiseōs* 'creation'.

ktizō (only here in Mark) 'create'.

heōs tou nun 'until the present time': *nun* 'now' 'is an adverb, used here with the definite article as a noun meaning 'the present' (cf. Arndt Gingrich 3.b).

kai ou mē genētai 'and will never happen': at no time in the past, present, or future, has there been, or will there be, such a 'tribulation' as that one described here.

Translation: *Tribulation*, as a noun describing a process, must be translated often as a verb, e.g. 'people will suffer'.

From the beginning of creation which God created is a highly complex literal rendering of the Greek text. The equivalent in some languages is simply 'from the time that God first made the world'. *Beginning* in this context does not mean to specify the start of the creation in contrast with later processes in creation. It is only a somewhat redundant way of speaking about the beginning of the world.

This entire verse may be rendered as 'in those days people will suffer (or 'be afflicted') as they never have since first God created the world;

and they never will again suffer so much'. The phrase *until now* is adequately rendered in some languages by the form 'as they never have since'. However, one can incorporate 'until now' either into the clause itself, or emphasize the meaning by setting up a paratactic expression, e.g. 'they have not suffered that way until now'.

20 *And if the Lord had not shortened the days, no human being would be saved; but for the sake of the elect, whom he chose, he shortened the days.*

Exegesis: *ei mē ekolobōsen kurios tas hēmeras* 'if the Lord had not shortened the days', 'unless the Lord had cut short those days'.

koloboō (only here in Mark) 'amputate', 'curtail', 'shorten': the phrase 'shorten the days', means, of course, to *reduce the number of days* (of the 'tribulation' referred to in the previous verse). It is to be noticed that the whole verse speaks of the matter as though it were past, in conformance with Hebrew prophetic style.

kurios (cf. 1 : 3) 'the Lord': here, of course, God.

tas hēmeras 'those days' better fits the context than 'the days'.

ouk an esōthē pasa sarx literally 'all flesh would not have been saved': the Hebrew idiom *lo'*...*kol* (Greek *ouk*...*pas*) 'not all' means 'none', 'not one', so that the clause means, 'no flesh would have been saved'.

sōzō (cf. 3 : 4) 'save': here with the meaning 'escape', 'survive', 'live (through it)' (cf. Arndt & Gingrich 1.a; of the translations, Weymouth, Goodspeed, and Montgomery have 'escape'; Moffatt 'be saved alive'; Berkeley 'survive'). Lagrange and Taylor, however, understand the word in its eschatological sense, 'to be saved', as in v. 13. This depends, of course, upon the interpretation given the events described in the context. Other considerations aside, the plain meaning of the events in vv. 14-23 connected with the 'tribulation' (*thlipsis*, v. 19) is that they are of a temporal and temporary nature which none would survive unless the Lord had 'shortened the days': it seems difficult, therefore, to understand the verb *sōzō* in the theological sense of "salvation unto eternal life."

pasa sarx 'all flesh': here with the meaning 'every human being', 'every man' (for this meaning of the Hebrew *basar* 'flesh' cf. Arndt & Gingrich *sarx* 3).

tous eklektous hous exelexato 'the chosen ones whom he chose', 'the elect whom he elected'.

eklektos (13 : 22, 27) 'chosen one', 'elected one': in the context the word refers to the Christians, the followers of Jesus.

eklegomai (only here in Mark) 'choose', 'select', 'prefer': the verb, in accordance with Jewish theology, indicates the predestinating activity of God.

Translation: *Shortened the days*, if translated literally, may imply quite a wrong meaning, namely, reduce the length of each day. One may therefore have to speak of 'reducing the time' or 'cutting off the days' (Tzeltal) or 'cutting the time' (Cashibo).

In some languages the problem of tense in this verse is extremely difficult, to the point of making the passage meaningless. For example, the reduction in time is spoken of as past, while the salvation is obviously future. This problem may be resolved in some instances by translating 'if the Lord had not decided to cut off the days'. That is to say, the decision is past (as determined in the counsel of God), but the actual event is still future.

No human being ('no one', or 'no person') is a necessary translation of the Greek phrase which means literally 'no flesh'. Translated word-for-word in some languages, this phrase has meant nothing more than 'no meat'. On the basis of such a translation as 'no flesh', the people in question concluded that this was in some way related to the tendency for carcasses to spoil after a period of time, and that for this reason the time was reduced.

Be saved is generally interpreted on the basis of (1) continued existence or life, e.g. 'remain living' (Chontal of Tabasco), or (2) escape from destruction, e.g. 'nobody would escape' (Tzotzil).

The elect, whom he chose is a redundant expression which is frequently translated with only a single reference to the process of choosing, e.g. 'those whom he chose' or 'the people whom he chose'. The obvious reason for this is the fact that *elect* is translatable in many languages only as 'those whom he chose', and to repeat 'those whom he chose' would be completely tautological.

21 ***And then if any one says to you, 'Look, here is the Christ!' or 'Look, there he is!' do not believe it.***

Exegesis: *ide* (cf. 2:24) 'look!' 'see!'

ho christos (cf. 1:1, 12:35) 'the Messiah', 'the Christ'.

mē pisteuete 'do not believe it' or 'do not believe him' (i.e. the one who says such a thing).

pisteuō (cf. 1:15) 'believe', 'have faith'.

Translation: The syntactic problem in this verse is a rather subtle one, but nevertheless one which can give rise to misunderstanding—namely, the fact that all the direct discourse is not necessarily actually uttered by the same person. In some translations this verse is interpreted to mean that one person says that the Christ is in one place and that another declares him to be in another place. In other translations the first part may be intelligible, but after the 'or' the reader becomes confused as to whether the 'or' is part of the direct discourse or provides an alternative kind of statement. In order to avoid misunderstanding and to conform to the syntactic requirements of the receptor language, one may translate as 'If any one says to you Look, here is the Christ! or, if he says, Look, there he is! do not believe it'. This shows clearly that the alternative consists of two entirely different statements, and is not a sign of hesitation

411

or uncertainty on the part of the speaker as to precisely where the Christ is.

Do not believe it may be rendered as 'do not believe him' or 'do not believe what he says'. The Greek text employs simply the verb *pisteuō*, without object, but some languages require some direct object, whether personal or nonpersonal.

22 *False Christs and false prophets will arise and show signs and wonders, to lead astray, if possible, the elect.*

Text: Before *sēmeia* 'signs' Tischendorf, Nestle, and Kilpatrick have *poiēsousin* 'they will perform'; all other editions of the Greek text, however, have *dōsousin* 'they will give' (presumably RSV 'show' translates *dōsousin*).

Exegesis: *egerthēsontai* (cf. 1 : 31) 'they will arise', i.e. 'will appear', 'will arrive on the scene' (cf. Arndt & Gingrich 2.e).

pseudochristoi (only here in Mark) 'false Christs', 'pseudo Messiahs'.

pseudoprophētai (only here in Mark) 'false prophets': the saying about false prophets and their signs and wonders recalls the language of Deut. 13 : 2.

dōsousin sēmeia kai terata 'they will give signs and wonders', in the sense of '*causing* (signs and wonders) *to appear*' (cf. Arndt & Gingrich *didōmi* 1.b.γ).

sēmeion (cf. 8 : 11) 'sign'.

terata (only here in Mark) 'wonders', 'portents', 'prodigies': in the N.T. used only in the plural and always with *sēmeia* 'signs'.

pros to apoplanan 'for the purpose of deceiving', 'with a view to leading astray'.

pros here means 'with the purpose of', 'in order to' (cf. Arndt & Gingrich III.3.a).

apoplanaō (only here in Mark; cf. *planaō* 13 : 5) 'deceive', 'lead astray'.

ei dunaton (14 : 35) 'if possible': for *dunatos* 'possible' cf. 9 : 23.

Translation: *False* is often translatable only by some verb phrase which describes the activity of the person in question, e.g. 'those who pretend to be Christ' (Ifugao, Zoque), 'deceiving christs' (Tzeltal), 'christs who really are not' (Zacapoastla Aztec), 'men who say they are Christ' (Huave), and 'people will come, one will say, I am Christ; another will say, I am a prophet' (Kiyaka). In Mitla Zapotec *false prophet* has to be completely recast because of the phrasal form of the expression for *prophet*, e.g. 'speak lies as if speaking for God'. In all these expressions the concept of falseness, pretence, and deceit are clearly indicated, despite the rather radical syntactic and lexical divergencies from the Greek expression. Such adaptations are quite common in languages in which activities or behavior implied by Greek (and English) adjectives plus nouns are describable only by verbs, which require a full complement of subject and object components.

Will arise may be 'will stand', 'will come into existence', 'will appear', or 'will become'. It is only rarely that *arise* can be translated literally.

For *signs* see 8:11.

Wonders are different from miracles in that they usually involve some unusual phenomena in nature which are a portent of dire woe or extraordinary blessing. In Huichol these are 'awe-inspiring things'. In Maya they are 'things which show what is coming', but in Eastern Otomí the expression must be cast into the form of a verb phrase 'they will amaze the people'.

Lead astray is sometimes translated in such a way as to reflect this same English metaphor, but usually one must employ some other more generic term as 'deceive' or 'cause to believe a lie'.

If possible may require some expansion because of the essentially elliptical form, e.g. 'if they can do so' or 'if they are able'.

The elect are 'the chosen ones' or where an agent is required, 'the ones God has chosen' (see 13:20).

23 But take heed; I have told you all things beforehand.

Exegesis: *humeis* 'you yourselves': the pronoun is emphatic (cf. Raw-linson).

blepete (cf. v. 5) 'beware!' 'watch out!'

proeirēka (only here in Mark) 'I have foretold', 'I told (it) beforehand'.

Translation: *Take heed* does not refer to the people's paying close attention to what Jesus was saying at that time, but to their being aware of what was going to happen in the future, i.e. 'be on your guard against', 'be careful', or 'watch out for what will happen'.

Beforehand may require expansion into the form of a clause, e.g. 'before these things happen' or 'before these events take place'.

24 But in those days, after that tribulation, the sun will be darkened, and the moon will not give its light,

Exegesis: *en ekeinais tais hēmerais* (cf. 1:9) 'in those days': a vague definition of time (cf. v. 17, where it is more definite).

meta tēn thlipsin ekeinēn 'after that tribulation': in the context, this refers to the *thlipsis* 'tribulation' in v. 19. The preposition *meta* 'after' in no way indicates the length of time intervening between the two events, whether great or small: it simply denotes the temporal succession of the events described.

The rest of the verse is patterned after the language of Isa. 13:10.

skotisthēsetai (only here in Mark) 'shall be darkened': the verb *skotizō* 'to darken', 'to lose (its) light' appears only in the passive in the N.T.

to pheggos (only here in Mark) 'the light', 'the radiance'.

Translation: *In those days*, as a general reference to time, is translated in some languages as 'at that time', 'then', or 'then later'.

Tribulation, which is a noun of process, must often be translated as a verb, e.g. 'after the people have suffered', 'after they have had great troubles', or 'after they have been greatly troubled'.

Will be darkened is in some languages equivalent to 'will not shine' or 'will become dark'.

Give its light is usually translatable by some verb meaning 'to shine', 'to be brilliant', or 'to glow'. A literal rendering of 'give light' is often quite misleading.

25 *and the stars will be falling from heaven, and the powers in the heavens will be shaken.*

Text: Instead of *ek tou ouranou* 'from heaven' of all modern editions of the Greek text, *Textus Receptus* has *tou ouranou* 'of heaven'.

Exegesis: *hoi asteres* (only here in Mark) 'the stars'.

esontai...piptontes 'shall be falling': the verbal phrase is perhaps linear, denoting a succession of stars falling from heaven (cf. Moule *Idiom Book*, 18).

piptō (cf. 4:4) 'fall'.

hai dunameis hai en tois ouranois 'the powers which are in the heavens': in accordance with Hebrew parallelism, these heavenly 'powers' may be simply the stars themselves, this second clause being synonymous with the first (as is probably the case in Isa. 34 : 4, whose language is reflected in this passage in Mark); or these 'powers' might be the evil spirits which, in Jewish thought, were supposed to rule the heavenly bodies. For the attributive phrase *hai en tois ouranois* 'the ones in the heavens' cf. a similar instance in 11:25.

saleuthēsontai (only here in Mark) 'they shall be shaken': i.e. they will be driven out of their normal course.

Translation: It must be noted that the differences of exegesis (and exposition) of this passage (verses 24-25) may be quite pronounced, for though some persons believe that this description refers to extraordinary astronomical phenomena, others are certain that this description applies not to celestial bodies but to the collapse of earthly governments, which are often described in apocalyptic literature by these figures of speech. However, regardless of the ultimate exposition of the passage, the translation should preserve the wording as closely as possible, leaving this wider interpretation to commentaries.

Heaven is best translated as 'sky', if the language in question distinguishes between words for 'sky' and 'heaven' (as the abode of God).

Powers in the heavens is translatable in some languages as the 'authorities in the sky'. One must avoid implying that God's own authority is to be shaken by translating *heavens* as 'the abode of God'. However, 'authorities' (or 'powers') is not very meaningful even at best, since this type of expression is quite alien to the concepts of most people. In Navajo an alternative expression 'that which holds things firm in the sky' has been employed, but this is a phrase which would imply literal rearrangement of heavenly bodies.

26 *And then they will see the Son of man coming in clouds with great power and glory.*

Exegesis: The language of this verse is patterned after Dan. 7:13.

opsontai 'they will see': this is an impersonal plural, meaning 'people will see', or, as the equivalent of the passive form, '(the Son of man) will be seen...'

ton huion tou anthrōpou (cf. 2:10) 'the Son of man'.

en nephelais (cf. 9:7) 'in clouds' (cf. 14:62 'with the clouds of heaven'): in the O.T. the Presence of God manifested itself *en nephelē* 'in a cloud' (cf. Ex. 34:5, Lev. 16:2, Num. 11:25).

For *dunamis* 'power' cf. 5:30; *doxa* 'glory' cf. 8:38.

Translation: The occurrence of the "pivot construction," in which *the Son of man* serves as the object of one verb, namely, *see*, and as subject of another, namely, *coming*, may require two clauses, paratactically combined: 'the people will see the Son of man; he will be coming in clouds...' Strictly speaking, the object of the verb *see* is not merely *the Son of man*, but the entire following dependent clause *the Son of man coming in clouds with great power and glory*, for what is seen is not just a person, but the entire event. However, in many languages this type of construction requires the use of two closely combined, but syntactically independent clauses.

With great power is not usually translatable as mere accompaniment, a meaning usually implied in the preposition *with*. Rather, one must use an expression of possession, e.g. 'he will have power' (Tzotzil).

For *glory* see 8:38. In this context it is often possible to use a term which implies great 'beauty', e.g. 'be very beautiful' (Tzotzil) and 'having much beauty' (Mazahua). In other languages *glory* may be more readily relatable to 'light' and 'brilliance', but usually with the connotation of permanent, glowing light, rather than flashing brilliance, as in the case of lightning.

27 *And then he will send out the angels, and gather his elect from the four winds, from the ends of the earth to the ends of heaven.*

Text: After *aggelous* 'angels' *Textus Receptus* and Kilpatrick add *autou* 'his', which is omitted by all other modern editions of the Greek text.

There is considerable doubt concerning the authenticity of *autou* 'his' after *eklektous* 'elect': it is omitted by Tischendorf and Soden; placed in brackets by Westcott and Hort, Nestle, and Taylor; included by *Textus Receptus*, Vogels, Souter, Lagrange, Kilpatrick, and Merk.

Exegesis: *apostelei* (cf. 1:2) 'he will send': in the context, the subject is 'the Son of man' of the preceding verse.

415

tous aggelous (cf. 1:2) 'the angels', 'the heavenly messengers'.

The rest of the verse reflects O.T. concepts and language such as found in Zech. 2:10 and Deut. 30:4.

kai episunaxei (cf. 1:33) 'and he will gather', 'and he will bring together (into one group)'.

tous eklektous (cf. v. 20) 'the elect', 'the chosen ones'.

ek tōn tessarōn anemōn 'from the four winds': this phrase indicates the four points of the compass, meaning (in popular language) 'from the four corners of the earth' (cf. in 1 Chr. 9:24, in the LXX, the description of the four sides of the Temple, *kata tous tessaras anemous ēsan hai pulai* 'the gates were on the four sides'—literally, 'according to the four winds'). The phrase appears not only in the Bible but in the papyri as well (cf. Deissmann *Bible Studies*, 248, and Moulton & Milligan). RSV's literal translation 'from the four winds' is likely to be misleading, since in current English the idiom does not denote the four points of the compass (cf. Weymouth 'from north, south, east and west'; Williams 'from the four points of the compass').

ap' akrou gēs heōs akrou ouranou 'from the extremity of the earth to the extremity of heaven'. This phrase is unique and offers some difficulty. It appears to be a combination of two phrases often used in the O.T.: *ap' akrou tēs gēs heōs akrou tēs gēs* 'from one extremity of the earth to the other' (Deut. 13:8, Jer. 12:12), and *ap' akrou tou ouranou heōs akrou tou ouranou* 'from one extremity of heaven to the other' (Deut. 4:32, 30:4, Ps. 18 (19):7; cf. Mt. 24:31). It would mean, therefore, 'from one end of the world to the other' (cf. Bengel: "*from the uttermost part of* the heaven (sky) and *earth* in the east, *even to the uttermost part of the heaven* and earth in the west"). Manson confesses ignorance of the precise meaning of the phrase and conjectures it originally meant 'from one end of earth to the other'.

The concept of the universe which underlies this idiom, in conformance with Jewish cosmogony, was that of the heaven as a half circle overarching the earth, the two meeting at the two extremes, thus:

Some, however, take the phrase to mean, 'he will gather the elect... from the highest (or 'lowest', according to others) point of earth *and carry them to* the heights of heaven' (to which I Thess. 4:17 lends some support).

Translation: for *angels* see 1:13.

Gather should be rendered by an expression applicable to persons, not to things, e.g. 'he will cause to come together' or 'he will cause to be led together'. Literally, the angels are the ones which evidently are to perform this task of bringing the elect together, but the syntactic form of the expression would indicate that the Son of man is the cause, since the third person singular subject of the verb is the same as for the verb *send*.

His elect are 'his chosen ones' or 'the people he has chosen'.

Four winds provides no end of trouble, especially since only rarely can this idiom be translated literally. In Ifugao, for example, one speaks only of two winds, and 'winds' are never used as reference points for directions. Accordingly, one must say 'from north, east, south, and west'. In Cashibo one may translate 'from all parts'. In San Blas the equivalent is 'from the four directions', and in Piro one may use 'from the four sides'.

From the ends of the earth to the ends of heaven is admittedly one of the most difficult idioms to translate in the entire Gospel of Mark, for frankly, as noted above, we do not know precisely what is meant, since we do not know exactly how this expression is relatable to the cosmogony underlying Scriptural usage. It is impossible to translate *end* as a 'point' or 'projection'. In some instances this passage has been rendered as 'from wherever they are, all over the earth and all over heaven' and 'from all over earth to all over heaven'. However, these translations imply gathering the elect together from heaven, a meaning which is not in the original. A more accurate rendering would be 'from the limit of the earth in one direction to the limit of the earth in the other direction'.

28 **From the fig tree learn its lesson: as soon as its branch becomes tender and puts forth its leaves, you know that summer is near.**

Exegesis: Most of the words of this verse have alrady been dealt with: for *sukē* 'fig tree' cf. 11:13; *parabolē* 'parable', here in the sense of 'lesson' (RSV, Goodspeed, Weymouth), cf. 3:23; *hotan* 'when', indicating a definite event, cf. 11:19; *ēdē* 'already' cf. 6:35; *klados* 'branch' cf. 4:32; *phulla* 'leaves' cf. 11:13.

mathete (only here in Mark; cf. the cognate noun *mathētēs*, 2:15) 'you are to learn', 'you must learn'.

hapalos (only here in Mark) 'tender': in the springtime the sap, rising through the limbs, makes tender the branch which has been stiff and dry through the winter, causing the leaves to sprout (cf. Lagrange). Montgomery's translation is vivid: 'as soon...as her branches are full of sap and bursting into leaf...'

ekphuē (only here in Mark) 'it puts forth', 'it causes to grow': as accented in the Nestle text, the verb is a present subjunctive active having as subject *ho klados* 'the branch' of the previous clause, and as object *ta phulla* 'the leaves'. Some (cf. Howard II, 264; Field *Notes*, 38) prefer to accent it as a second aorist subjunctive passive with *ta phulla* 'the leaves' as subject—'the leaves sprout' (cf. Arndt & Gingrich). Lagrange accepts the present active accentuation, but regards *ta phulla* as the subject: *les feuilles ont poussé*.

theros (only here in Mark) 'summer'.

Translation: *Lesson* is not easily translated in this context except as an integral part of the verb phrase, e.g. 'learn from what happens to the fig tree' or 'learn from what the fig tree does'. The RSV *its* seems to be especially awkward, even in English; and since it does not reflect any element in the Greek text, it need not be translated.

The big problem in this verse is the matter of the season, for in the tropical areas of the world the distinction between 'summer' and 'winter' as the growing and the dormant seasons simply does not exist. In such parts of the world (where most Bible translating and revising is being done) the two seasons are the 'rainy season' and the 'dry season', which correspond roughly to the calendar 'summer' and 'winter' respectively in the northern hemisphere, but are reversed in the southern hemisphere. Moreover, there have been some "strange" borrowings of terms in certain languages. For example, in the Maya language of Yucatan, Mexico, the Spanish word *verano* (usually regarded as equivalent to English *summer*) has been used to identify the winter and spring months, that is to say, the dry season, which is actually quite hot, especially toward the end. It would certainly not make sense to say that when the fig tree puts forth its branches, the *verano* is near, for this would be in the fall of the year. Moreover, trees which lose their leaves each year, do so usually during the dry season and only put forth buds and new leaves after the beginning of the rainy season. Accordingly, even if one uses 'rainy season' for *summer*, the analogy is not quite right, for if one says that 'as soon as its branch becomes tender and puts forth its leaves, you know that the summer is near', a Mayan Indian is likely to be perplexed, for this type of budding and coming out in leaf is proof that the rainy season has already come, not that it is merely near. Nevertheless, despite such lack of complete agreement in details, it is generally preferable to translate *summer* as the rainy season, since this is usually the period of budding and growth.

Summer is near must be recast in some instances as 'soon it will be the rainy season', 'summer will be soon', or 'summer has almost come'.

29 **So also, when you see these things taking place, you know that he is near, at the very gates.**

Exegesis: *hotan idēte tauta ginomena* 'when you see these things happening': in the context 'these things' refers primarily to the events described in vv. 24-27, but would include also those described in vv. 14-23.

ginōskete 'you are to know': probably here an imperative form (in v. 28 the identical form is clearly indicative).

eggus estin 'it is near': the majority of English translations have '*he* is near', with obvious reference to 'the Son of man' in v. 26 (Synodale actually translates *le Fils de l'homme est proche*). Others, for example Lagrange, regard the saying as "mysterious and veiled," in the style of v. 14, and they believe that one should not attempt to supply any definite subject, e.g. *que c'est proche* (cf. Brazilian *que está próximo*; Luther has *es* 'it'; BFBS 'it is near').

epi thurais 'at the door': this figure of speech denotes immediate nearness (cf. Arndt & Gingrich *thura* 2.a).

Translation: Though in English the present tense forms *see* and *know* are applicable to a future condition, in many languages this type of condition must have special tense forms applicable to such a future event, 'when you will see..., then you will know...' This future usage also requires the use of the future in the dependent clause, e.g. 'that he will be near'.

At the very gates may be quite meaningless in some languages, for it has no possible relationship to a temporal context. In fact, its use may completely distort the meaning of the passage in such a way as to cause people to think of the Son of man as standing at the gate of the corral or by the roadside. On the other hand, if the subject of 'is near' refers to a general event, then the meaning is even more difficult, for 'happenings' cannot be spoken of as being 'at the very gates', unless one is to assume that all these apocalyptic happenings are to take place at the gates. Accordingly, in languages in which the metaphor 'at the very gates' is going to be inevitably misunderstood, one may employ 'is come very near indeed' (Chontal of Tabasco).

30 **Truly, I say to you, this generation will not pass away before all these things take place.**

Exegesis: For *amēn* 'truly' cf. 3:28; *ou mē* emphatic 'in no way' cf. 9:1 (in ch. 13 cf. vv. 2 (twice), 19).

ou mē parelthē hē genea hautē 'this generation will not in any way pass away', i.e. 'this generation will assuredly be alive'. This saying is of the same kind as 9:1, and, like that one, nothing is to be inferred here as to *when* this generation 'will pass away': the emphasis here lies on the fact that 'all these things will happen' during the lifetime of this generation.

parerchomai (cf. 6:48) 'pass by', 'pass away': here in the sense of 'disappear', 'come to an end' (cf. Arndt & Gingrich 1.b.α).

hē genea hautē (cf. 8:12) 'this generation': the obvious meaning of the words 'this generation' is the people contemporary with Jesus. Nothing can be gained by trying to take the word in any sense other than its normal one: in Mark (elsewhere in 8:12, 9:19) the word always has this meaning (cf. Lagrange).

mechris hou (only here in Mark) 'until', 'until which time': a succinct way of saying *mechris ekeinou tou chronou en hō* 'until that time in which' (cf. Moule *Idiom Book*, 82, 85).

tauta panta 'all these things': in the context this can only refer to all the events described in the discourse. (Notice that *tauta* 'these things' of v. 29, and *tauta panta* 'all these things' of v. 30, correspond to the *tauta* and *tauta...panta* of the disciples' question in v. 4.)

Translation: For *truly* employed in this type of construction and for *generation* see 8:12. By far the most common translation of *generation* in this passage is 'those living now' or 'people who are now alive'.

Pass away cannot be translated literally in most languages. The closest equivalent is generally 'die', but if a term parallel to the use of

419

pass away in the following verse can be employed, this should be done.

Take place is translatable as 'occur', 'happen', or 'become' (Greek *genetai*), often in the future tense or its equivalent, since these events followed the statement of Jesus.

31 *Heaven and earth will pass away, but my words will not pass away.*

Exegesis: *ho ouranos kai hē gē* 'heaven and earth', 'the whole created universe'.

hoi...logoi mou 'my words': although in the context this refers to the discourse, it is better literally to translate 'my words', 'my teachings' (cf. *hoi emoi logoi* 'my words' in 8:38).

Translation: *Heaven* in this context is to be understood as the 'sky', not the abode of God. Hence, one may translate 'the sky and the earth will come to an end' (Tzeltal, Zoque), or 'the sky and the earth will exist no more'.

Some translators have interpreted this verse as 'even though the sky and the earth should pass away, my words would not pass away', but though this may be implied, it is not a necessary or recommended rendering.

Depending upon the expression used in the first clause, one may translate the second clause as 'my words will not come to an end' or 'my words will not cease to exist'. On the other hand, the mere continuation of words may not clearly indicate the meaning of this passage, which denotes the fact that the statements of Jesus will have eternal validity. Accordingly, in some languages one must translate as 'my words will always have their power' or 'my words will never stop being strong' (in the sense of true, dependable prophecy).

32 *But of that day or that hour no one knows, not even the angels in heaven, nor the Son, but only the Father.*

Exegesis: In such statements as these the translator must consciously refrain from making the saying any more definite or explicit than the original, as it stands in Mark.

peri de tēs hēmeras ekeinēs ē tēs hōras 'but concerning that day or that hour': this, of course, refers to the *time* when that day or hour will come (not, as Moffatt has it, 'no one knows anything of that day or hour'). No great significance is to be attached to the phrase 'day or hour': it is simply a way of saying that no one knows the precise moment when 'the time will come' (v. 33).

oudeis...oude...oude...ei mē 'no one...not even...nor...except only' (cf. Gould). For *ei mē* 'except', 'but only' cf. 2:7.

hoi aggeloi en ouranō (cf. 12:25) 'the angels in heaven'.

ho huios 'the Son': only here in Mark is the phrase used absolutely: elsewhere it is always defined by a following genitive (cf. 1:1).

ho patēr (cf. 8:38) 'the Father', that is, God.

Translation: *That day and that hour* is a difficult phrase to translate for two reasons. First, there is the problem of the indefinite nature of the reference (implied in the use of *that*), whether, for example, to the days of the tribulation (verse 19) or the time of the coming of the Son of man (verse 26) or the lesson from the fig tree (verse 28); (the one thing we are sure of is that it does not refer to the immediately preceding verse dealing with the passing of heaven and earth). Secondly, a problem arises over the use of *day* and *hour* without some further designation as to how they are related to any specific event. In order to make some sense of this passage some translators have rendered the first part of this verse 'no one will know the day or the hour when these things will happen', using a phrase occurring at the end of verse 30.

The phrases introduced by *not even...nor...but* may require the filling in of the elliptical elements, e.g. 'the angels in heaven do not know this, the Son does not know this; only the Father knows this'.

In many languages one basic problem in the translation of *the Son* and *the Father* is that the corresponding words 'son' and 'father' must be possessed, for, after all, persons cannot be 'sons' or 'fathers' without being the sons or fathers of someone. In this passage, for example, one must translate in Zoque 'the Son of God does not know, but only my Father...' The use of 'my' is required because of the fact that Jesus is speaking. In languages in which one cannot speak of himself in the third person, it would be necessary to say 'I who am the Son'.

33 Take heed, watch; for you do not know when the time will come.

Text: After *agrupneite* 'watch' *Textus Receptus*, Soden, Vogels, and Souter add *kai proseuchesthe* 'and pray', which is omitted by the majority of modern editions of the Greek text.

Exegesis: *blepete* (cf. v. 23) 'watch out!', 'beware!'

agrupneite (only here in Mark) 'keep awake!', 'be alert!'

ho kairos (cf. 1:15) 'the time': here, of course, as an eschatological term, it refers to the last time, the time of crisis (cf. Arndt & Gingrich 4); BFBS 'the appointed time'.

Translation: For *take heed* see verse 23.

The *time* is here to be understood in terms of 'an occasion', in other words, a point of time, not duration of time. This meaning is translatable as 'occasion', 'occurrence', or 'this happening'.

Watch is translatable in some languages as 'keep on looking' (Tzotzil) or 'wait and see' (Tzeltal).

34 It is like a man going on a journey, when he leaves home and puts his servants in charge, each with his work, and commands the doorkeeper to be on the watch.

Exegesis: *hōs anthrōpos apodēmos* '(It is) like a man (who is going) away on a trip'.

421

apodēmos (only here in the N.T.; cf. *apodēmeō*, 12:1) is an adjective meaning 'away on a trip', 'away from one's country'.

apheis (cf. 2:5) 'leaving': the participle is equivalent to the relative phrase *hos aphēken* 'who left'.

doulois (cf. 10:44) 'slaves'.

tēn exousian (cf. 1:22) 'the authority', 'the power': here, as RSV has it, to give the authority to the slaves means to put them in charge (cf. Arndt & Gingrich 3; Goodspeed, Moffatt). Lagrange comments that 'the authority' given the slaves is a certain degree of autonomy: "each one will be free to do his job in his own way."

hekastō (only here in Mark) 'to each one', 'to every one'.

to ergon (14:6) 'the work', 'the task', 'the job': Arndt & Gingrich 2, 'assigned to each one his task'. The word *ergon* is in the accusative case, the object of the participle *dous* 'giving'.

tō thurōrō (only here in Mark) 'to the doorkeeper', 'to the gate guard'.

eneteilato hina grēgorē 'he commanded that he be on watch', 'he ordered (him) to remain alert'.

entellomai (cf. 10:3) 'command', 'order'.

hina 'that' denotes the content of the order, not its purpose (cf. 3:9).

grēgoreō (13:35, 37, 14:34, 37, 38) 'be awake', 'watch', 'be alert': the verb is formed from the perfect form of *egeirō* 'rise'.

Translation: *It is like* is a very indefinite type of transitional phrase from the preceding verse, and as such must in some languages be adapted to other syntactic and lexical requirements, e.g. 'in the same way a man went on a journey...' (Bolivian Quechua), or 'all this is like what happens when a man...', or 'this is just like the experience of a man who...'

Because of the relative complexity of the subject-predicate constructions in this verse, some major breaks are often required, e.g. 'this is just like what happens when a man goes on a journey; he leaves home and gives special authority to his servants. Each has his own work. He commands the man who guards the door to be on the look-out continually'.

Puts his servants in charge is often equivalent to 'gives his servants responsibility for everything', i.e. for everything about the estate.

Each with his work is translatable as 'he gives each servant a special work to do'.

35 Watch therefore—for you do not know when the master of the house will come, in the evening, or at midnight, or at cockcrow, or in the morning—

Exegesis: For *grēgoreō* 'watch' cf. the preceding verse; *ho kurios* 'the master', 'the owner' cf. 1:3.

Listed here are the four watches of the night, according to the Roman system, of three hours each, running from 6:00 P.M. to 6:00 A.M.

opse (cf. 11:11) 'the evening', 'late': here, the first watch, from 6:00-9:00. P.M.

mesonuktion (only here in Mark) literally 'the middle of the night': here, the second watch, from 9:00 P.M. to 12:00 midnight.

alektorophōnias (only here in the N.T.) 'at the crowing (*phōnē*) of the rooster (*alektōr*)': here, the third watch, from 12:00 midnight to 3:00 A.M.

prōi (cf. 1:35) 'early', 'at dawn': here, the fourth watch, from 3:00-6:00 A.M. (cf. 6:48 where 'the fourth watch' is referred to).

Translation: *Watch* is variously translated in this context, e.g. 'be on the look-out', 'keep a close watch', 'be constantly alert', or 'wait, look'.

The paraphrastic expression included within dashes in the RSV text combines quite well with the introductory verb *watch*. Where the difficulty arises is the connection of this sentence with the following verse, which expresses a negative purpose. This latter expression cannot be combined with the last of verse 35. There are usually three different types of solutions: (1) punctuation as a parenthetical expression, either within parentheses or dashes—a solution which is quite acceptable to rather literate people; (2) the repetition of 'watch' at the beginning of verse 36, so that the proper syntactic relationship may be preserved; or (3) an alteration in order in which the clause within dashes in the RSV is placed first in the verse, followed by the imperative, 'watch', e.g. 'since you do not know when the owner of the house will come, whether in the evening, or at midnight, or at cockcrow, or in the early morning, therefore watch, lest he come suddenly and find you sleeping'.

Many languages have highly developed expressions for periods of the night, some of which rather closely parallel the series occurring in this verse. For example, the evening is 'the sun is lost' (Tzotzil) and 'the sitting together time' (Mende). The period around midnight is 'the stomach of the night' (Uduk). A *cockcrow* is 'when the 'owls make a noise', 'when the cock screams' (Piro), and 'rooster-cry-time' (Maninka). The period in the morning before sun-up may be described as 'when the world begins to get white' (Tzeltal), and 'before the sky-opens-door' (Maninka).

36 *lest he come suddenly and find you asleep.*

Exegesis: *mē elthōn...heurē* 'lest coming...he should find', 'lest he come...and find'.

exaiphnēs (only here in Mark) is an adverb 'suddenly', 'unexpectedly'.

katheudontas (cf. 4:27) 'sleeping', 'asleep'.

Translation: For the syntactic connections of this verse to the preceding, see under 13:35.

He must refer to the owner of the house.

Suddenly is interestingly translated 'as lightning' in Piro.

37 *And what I say to you I say to all: Watch."*

Exegesis: *grēgoreite* (cf. v. 34) 'you must watch'.

Translation: *Say* is used in this verse in two different meanings: (1) addressing particular persons and (2) uttering something which is universally applicable. This may require two different verbs in another language, e.g. 'what I am saying to you I mean for everyone', 'what I am now talking to you about includes everyone' or 'what I am telling you I am also saying for the benefit of everyone'.

For *watch* see verse 33.

CHAPTER FOURTEEN

1 *It was now two days before the Passover and the feast of Unleavened Bread. And the chief priests and the scribes were seeking how to arrest him by stealth, and kill him;*

Exegesis: *to pascha* (14:12, 14, 16) 'the Passover': the Greek word is the transliteration of the Aramaic *pasha'* (Hebrew *pesaḥ*), the Hebrew festival of Passover, commemorating the day when the Lord 'passed over' (Hebrew *pasaḥ*) the homes of the Hebrews in the slaughter of the first-born of Egypt (cf. Ex. 12:13, 23, 27). The pascal lambs were slain on the afternoon of 14th Nisan (March-April) and the meal eaten that evening, between sundown and midnight (by Jewish reckoning 15th Nisan, since the day began at sundown).

ta azuma (14:12) '(the feast of) Unleavened Bread': this feast lasted from the 15th to the 21st Nisan, and during the time unleavened bread was eaten (cf. Ex. 12:8, 15-20). The two religious feasts, running together, were celebrated as one (cf. Arndt & Gingrich *pascha*).

meta duo hēmeras 'after two days': in accordance with Jewish reckoning this could mean 'the next day' (so Bengel). Cf. in 8:31 the phrase *meta treis hēmeras* 'after three days'.

en dolō (cf. 7:22) 'by deceit', 'by cunning', 'by stealth'.

The other words in this verse have already been dealt with: for *zēteō... pōs* 'seek...how', 'consider...how' cf. 3:22, 11:18; *hoi archiereis* 'the chief priests' cf. 8:31; *hoi grammateis* 'the scribes' cf. 1:22; *krateō* 'seize', 'arrest' cf. 1:31; *apokteinō* 'kill' cf. 3:4.

Translation: *Now* is translatable as 'then', 'by that time', or 'the time was'. In Kiyaka the introductory expression is translated as 'it was two days and then the feast for...'

Passover is usually translated as 'the passing over', but this expression has little or no meaning except as it is placed in an adequate context. For example, 'the passing over' may be rendered as 'feast to remember the passing over' (Kiyaka), 'day to commemorate the passing over', or 'feast concerning the passing over' (Subanen). In some languages there is a term already used to designate Easter. For example, in Tzeltal the word *cuxibal*, meaning literally 'instrument of living' or 'instrument of life' is the long-employed word for Easter, having been introduced by early Roman Catholic missionaries. Because of its traditional use and its basic acceptability in meaning, it has been incorporated into the Tzeltal New Testament.

Feast of Unleavened Bread usually involves a distinctly idiomatic treatment of the relationship indicated by the English preposition *of*, e.g. 'feast at which the people ate unleavened bread', 'feast at which was eaten unleavened bread', or 'feast where there was unleavened bread'.

425

One should not, of course, do as some translators have done—namely, make the 'unleavened bread' the possessor of the feast.

Unleavened Bread is 'the bread which has not risen', 'the bread without yeast', or 'unswollen bread' (Shipibo). In some languages yeast is 'beer foam', 'wine froth' or 'sour water' (Maya), but in many instances a term is borrowed from the dominant language of the area.

By stealth is not always easily translated, for the noun *stealth* must often be rendered by a verb, in which case one must determine precisely who is the object of the deceit or trickery. Some translators have rendered this phrase so as to mean that the chief priests and scribes sought to have Jesus arrested in such a way that 'the crowds would not know about it' (cf. Mark 12:12 and 14:2). Others have interpreted the passage to mean that the officials sought to trick Jesus into committing some act which would provide an excuse for his arrest (cf. the numerous questions which had been asked Jesus in order to snare him into giving some treasonable answer), e.g. 'were trying to find a way to deceive Jesus and thus to arrest him'.

2 *for they said, "Not during the feast, lest there be a tumult of the people."*

Exegesis: *elegon gar* 'for they were saying': this explains the reason why the chief priests and scribes were looking for a way to arrest and kill Jesus by stealth.

mē en tē heortē 'not during the feast': so most commentators and translations. Jeremias (*Eucharistic Words*, 47-49), however, argues for the meaning 'not in the presence of the festal crowd', referring to Jn. 7:11 for this meaning of *heortē* 'feast', and to Lk. 22:6 'in the absence of the multitude'. This gives excellent sense to the words and may be the meaning intended.

thorubos (cf. 5:38) 'uproar', 'tumult': here not simply a vocal disturbance but a riot (cf. Goodspeed, Moffatt, Manson, Weymouth; Vulgate *tumultus*).

tou laou (cf. 7:6) 'of the people', 'of the populace': the word here is equivalent to *ochlos* 'crowd' more commonly used by Mark. Arndt & Gingrich (*laos* 1.c.α) see here 'the people' in contrast to their leaders.

Translation: *Not during the feast* must often be expanded so as to include the implied, but not specifically stated elements, e.g. 'we must not arrest him during the feast' (or 'in the presence of the crowd attending the feast').

Tumult is a 'riot', translatable in some instances as 'in order that the people do not start to fight us'.

3 *And while he was at Bethany in the house of Simon the leper, as he sat at table, a woman came with an alabaster jar of ointment of pure nard, very costly, and she broke the jar and poured it over his head.*

Exegesis: *ontos autou en Bēthania* 'while he was at Bethany', 'during his stay in Bethany' (cf. 11:1 for Bethany).

Simōnos tou leprou 'of Simon the Leper': commentators suggest, with considerable probability, that this Simon was by now cured, but still retained the name of 'the Leper' (so Jerome, quoted by Swete).

lepros (cf. 1:40) 'leper'.

katekeimenou autou (cf. 1:30) 'while he was reclining at the table'.

gunē 'woman': here she remains anonymous; in John 12:3 she is identified as Mary, sister of Martha and Lazarus.

echousa 'having', i.e. 'having with her' (cf. Arndt & Gingrich I.1.a).

alabastron (only here in Mark) 'alabaster': by extension 'a flask made of alabaster', described as "a vessel with a rather long neck which was broken off when the contents were used" (Arndt & Gingrich). Lagrange suggests that the vase was perhaps made of oriental onyx, popularly called alabaster.

murou (14:4, 5) 'of ointment', 'of unguent': the genitive defines the contents of the flask, not the material of which it was made.

nardou (only here in Mark) 'of nard': this genitive defines the kind of ointment in the flask. The oil was extracted from the root of the nard, a plant native to India.

pistikēs (only here in Mark) 'pure', 'genuine', 'unadulterated': the genitive further defines the ointment. The meaning of this word has been a source of speculation and disagreement. Most commentators take it to mean here 'pure', 'genuine': others, however, take it to refer to a plant whose name, being misunderstood, was simply transliterated into Greek. Black (*Aramaic* 159-61) surmises that it was the oil of the pistachio nut, which in Aramaic would have been *piṣtaka'*.

polutelous (only here in Mark) 'expensive', 'costly'.

suntripsasa (cf. 5:4) 'breaking', 'smashing'.

katecheen (only here in Mark) 'she poured', 'she poured on': the woman broke the flask, presumably its neck, and poured the ointment on the head of Jesus.

Translation: *He* must be clearly identified, whether in this verse or in one of the two preceding verses. In some instances it is best to use 'Jesus'.

For *leper* see 1:40.

There is an awkward syntactic problem in this verse because of the double dependent temporal clauses *while he was...*, *as he sat...* In some languages these must be separated, since two such clauses cannot precede the main clause, e.g. 'Jesus was at Bethany in the house of Simon the leper. While he was sitting there,...'

Sat at table is equivalent to saying 'sat eating' or even 'was eating'.

Alabaster jar may be translated as 'a jar made of stone called alabaster' or 'an alabaster stone jar'. 'Stone' must often be added in order that the borrowing 'alabaster' may have some significance.

Ointment is equivalent in many languages to 'oil' or simply 'liquid'.

Nard must usually be borrowed, e.g. 'a liquid called nard' (Ifugao) or 'ointment, very fragrant, *nardo* its name' (Tzeltal), in which *nardo* has been borrowed from Spanish. 'Very fragrant' has been used in order to help explain the significance of the type of ointment, for otherwise the Tzeltal term would be understood to mean 'medicine'. In Huastec, the translation is 'stone container of perfume, called *nardo*, very expensive'. In Ifugao one may say 'stone jar with a liquid called nard, smelling like flowers', in which the last phrase is a usual designation for any kind of perfume.

Very costly must constitute an entirely separate sentence in some languages, e.g. 'it was very expensive' or 'this had cost a great deal'.

One must be very careful of the syntactic relationship of the phrase 'over his head', which in some languages has been related to the breaking of the jar, implying that the jar was crushed on Jesus head.

It must refer to the liquid, not the jar, e.g. 'poured the liquid on his head' or 'poured the perfume onto his head'.

4 But there were some who said to themselves indignantly, "Why was the ointment thus wasted?

Exegesis: *aganaktountes* (cf. 10:14) 'indignant', 'angry'. The Greek verbal phrase *ēsan...aganaktountes* 'were...angry' must be given some sense such as RSV gives it, 'were *saying* indignantly'.

pros heautous (cf. 9:10, 10:26, 11:31, 12:7, 16:3) literally 'to themselves', meaning 'to one another', 'among themselves', as in the other passages where the phrase occurs. Black (*Aramaic*, 77) suggests this represents the Aramaic ethical dative, meaning 'some were *indeed* vexed'.

eis ti (15:34) 'for what reason?', 'for what purpose?', 'why?' (cf. Arndt & Gingrich *eis* 4.f).

hē apōleia (only here in Mark) 'destruction', 'waste'.

gegonen 'has happened', 'took place' (cf. Arndt & Gingrich I.3.a). Literally the question reads: 'For what purpose did this waste of the ointment occur?'

Translation: *To themselves* must be understood as reciprocal, not reflexive, e.g. 'they were saying to each other'.

Indignantly must often be treated as a separate verb expression, e.g. 'some of the people there were angry and they said to each other'.

Wasted may be translatable in terms of (1) discard, i.e. 'thrown away' or 'used for no good purpose', or (2) failure to use properly, e.g. 'not used for a good purpose'.

5 For this ointment might have been sold for more than three hundred denarii, and given to the poor." And they reproached her.

Text: *to muron* 'the ointment' is omitted by *Textus Receptus* and Kilpatrick, but included by all other modern editions of the Greek text.

Exegesis: *ēdunato gar touto to muron prathēnai* 'for it would be possible for this ointment to be sold', 'for this ointment could have been sold'.

pipraskō (only here in Mark) 'sell'. The syntax of the Greek sentence should be noticed: the subjects of the sentence are the two verbal infinitives *prathēnai* 'to be sold' and *dothēnai* 'to be given'; *to muron* 'the ointment' is the subject of the infinitives and, as Greek sentence construction requires, is in the accusative case (called by some grammarians "the accusative of general reference").

epanō (only here in Mark) 'over', 'above', 'beyond'.

dēnariōn triakosiōn 'three hundred denarii': the genitive is known as the genitive of price. For *dēnarion* 'denarius' cf. 6:37.

kai dothēnai tois ptōchois: as in the similar case in 10:21, 'and *the proceeds* be given to the poor'.

enebrimōnto autē (cf. 1:43) 'and they were indignant with her', 'and they scolded her': the word indicates indignation which was outwardly expressed by gestures and murmurs (cf. Lagrange).

Translation: *Might have been sold* can be shifted, where necessary, into an active form, e.g. 'a person might have sold this ointment'.

For the treatment of *denarius*, with some adequate marginal note or by reference to a *Table of Weights and Measures*, see 6:37.

When there is more than one system of numerals, e.g. an indigenous method of counting and another borrowed from some trade or national language, there is usually a distinct preference, one way or another, for expressing higher numbers. One should employ the generally preferred system.

Given to the poor is often translated in such an ambiguous manner that readers understand that the ointment is to be given directly to the poor. In languages in which the context does not completely clarify such an ambiguity or obscurity, one may translate 'and give the money to poor people'.

6 But Jesus said, "Let her alone; why do you trouble her? She has done a beautiful thing to me.

Exegesis: *aphete autēn* (cf. 2:5) 'leave her alone': Arndt & Gingrich *aphiēmi* 4 suggest 'let go', 'tolerate', while Lagrange prefers the meaning 'let her do it'. In light of the context, however, the RSV is to be preferred (cf. Swete).

ti autē kopous parechete; 'why are you causing her trouble?' 'why are you giving her difficulty?': Moulton & Milligan give examples from the papyri of the use of this phrase meaning 'cause trouble', 'bother'.

kopos (only here in Mark) 'trouble', 'difficulty', 'toil'.

parechō (only here in Mark) 'to present', 'to furnish', 'to cause'.

kalon ergon 'a good work', 'a beautiful deed', 'a noble thing': the adjective here indicates "what is morally good, with a nuance of nobility and beauty" (Lagrange); cf. Arndt & Gingrich *ergon* 1.c.β.

kalos (cf. 4:8) 'beautiful', 'fine', 'fitting'.

ergon (cf. 13:34) 'deed', 'task', 'action'.

429

ērgasato (only here in Mark) 'she worked', 'she performed', 'she accomplished'.

en emoi 'to me': the preposition here indicates the object to whom something is done (cf. Arndt & Gingrich *en* I.2).

Translation: *Let her alone* is sometimes translated rather concretely, e.g. 'do not touch her' (Cashibo), an expression which implies avoidance of molestation or disturbance.

Beautiful thing requires recasting in some languages, e.g. 'what she has done to me is beautiful' or 'it is very good what she has done to me'.

7 *For you always have the poor with you, and whenever you will, you can do good to them; but you will not always have me.*

Exegesis: *pantote* (only here in Mark) 'all times', 'always'.

hotan (cf. 11 : 19) 'whenever', indicating here more than one definite occasion.

eu poiēsai (only here in the N.T.; cf. *agathopoiēsai* 3 : 4) 'to do good'.

Translation: The expression *have...with* may require recasting in some such form as 'the poor people are always with you' or 'there are always poor people where you are'.

In contrast with the Greek and English of the two clauses *whenever... to them,* some languages require the first of the two clauses to be the full one and the second one the elliptical one, e.g. 'whenever you want to do good to them, you can' or 'if ever you want to do good to such people, you are able to'.

Have me must be recast in much the same way as the first clause of this verse, e.g. 'I will not always be here with you' (Tzeltal) or 'I will not always be here where you are'.

8 *She has done what she could; she has anointed my body beforehand for burying.*

Exegesis: *ho eschen epoiēsen* 'what she had she did': it is generally agreed that the meaning of the phrase is 'she did what she was able (to do)', the verb *echō* 'have' being equivalent to *dunamai* 'be able' (cf. Field *Notes*, 14). Arndt & Gingrich *echō* I.6.a call attention to the fact that the full phrase would include the infinitive, *ho eschen poiēsai epoiēsen* 'what she was able to do she did'. Cf. Lagrange, *Ce qui était en son pouvoir*; Brazilian, *Ela fêz o que pôde.*

proelaben (only here in Mark) 'she did beforehand', 'she anticipated': the verb *prolambanō* means to do something before the usual time (so Moulton & Milligan, quoting examples from the papyri).

murisai (only here in the N.T.) 'to anoint'.

entaphiasmon (only here in Mark) 'preparation for burial': this is the meaning assigned the word by Field (*Notes*, 98) and Moulton & Milligan; Arndt & Gingrich, however, state the word can also signify the burial itself. In the context the meaning 'preparation for burial' is to be preferred.

Translation: Where there is no contrast in genders between pronouns, it may be necessary to render *she* by 'this woman' (Bolivian Quechua).

The concept of *beforehand* is not always easy to translate, since the time sequence is never absolute, but merely relative to more normal activities. This meaning has been quite neatly expressed in Zacapoastla Aztec, e.g. 'she has already come to anoint my body to prepare to bury it'. By the use of 'already' and 'to prepare to bury', the idea of *beforehand* is quite adequately conveyed. The meaning is more directly expressed in Chontal of Tabasco, e.g. 'she made me smell good ahead of time for my burial'. In Tzeltal this concept must be stated even more explicitly, e.g. 'I have not yet been buried, but she came to anoint my body for death'.

9 *And truly, I say to you, wherever the gospel is preached in the whole world, what she has done will be told in memory of her."*

Exegesis: *hopou ean* (cf. 6:10, 9:18, 14:14; cf. *hopou an* 6:56) 'wherever', 'wheresoever'.

kēruchthē (cf. 1:4) 'be preached', 'be proclaimed'.

to euaggelion (cf. 1:1) 'the Gospel'.

holon ton kosmon (cf. 8:36) 'the whole world', 'all the world'.

kai ho epoiēsen hautē 'what she did will also (be told)': *kai* 'and' here means 'also' and should be included in translation.

mnēmosunon (only here in Mark) 'memory', 'memorial'.

Translation: For *truly* as employed in this verse see 8:12.

Wherever may be translated in some instances as 'in all the places that'.

The gospel is preached can be recast in the active form as 'wherever they will preach the good news' (Kapauku).

Is preached, though present in form, must usually be translated by some form which can refer to the future.

Wherever and *in the whole world* may need to be more closely combined in some languages, e.g. 'wherever in the whole world the good news is preached' or 'in all the places in the whole world in which the good news will be announced'.

Will be told can be rendered in an active form 'people will tell'.

In memory of her may be recast as a verb phrase, e.g. 'tell so that people will remember her' or 'tell so that her name shall be remembered' (Tzeltal), in which 'name' can be employed as a kind of substitute for 'reputation'.

10 *Then Judas Iscariot, who was one of the twelve, went to the chief priests in order to betray him to them.*

Exegesis: *ho heis tōn dōdeka* literally 'the one of the Twelve': this "peculiar expression," as Arndt & Gingrich (*heis* 1.a.β) call it, has had several explanations. Field (*Notes*, 38f.) protests that the phrase, thus read (it appears only here in the New Testament), can only mean, in Greek, "the first (Number 1) of the twelve," which he calls absurd. It would appear from the evidence of the papyri, however (cf. Moulton & Milligan *heis*; Moulton *Prolegomena*, 97), that the phrase means simply 'one of the Twelve', no special importance being attached to the definite article *ho* 'the'. Lagrange compares it to the French use of *l'un*.

hoi dōdeka (cf. 3:14) 'the Twelve': a title, not simply a number.

tous archiereis (cf. 8:31) 'the chief priests'.

hina 'in order that': here indicates purpose.

paradoi autois 'he might deliver (him) to them': for *paradidōmi* 'hand over' cf. 1:14; in relation to Judas Iscariot, cf. 3:19; elsewhere in connection with the arrest of Jesus the verb occurs in 9:31, 10:33, 14:11, 21, 41, 42, 44.

Translation: See 3:14 for the rendering of *the Twelve*.

For *chief priests* see 1:40, 2:26, and 8:31, and for *betray* see 3:19.

11 ***And when they heard it they were glad, and promised to give him money. And he sought an opportunity to betray him.***

Exegesis: *echarēsan* (15:18) 'they were glad', 'they rejoiced'.

epēggeilanto (only here in Mark) 'they promised': this is the normal meaning of the middle form of the verb *epaggellō* 'announce', 'proclaim'.

argurion (only here in Mark) 'silver', i.e. 'money'.

ezētei pōs (cf. v. 1) 'he was seeking how', 'he was considering in what way'.

eukairōs (only here in Mark; cf. *eukairos* 6:21; *eukaireō* 6:31) 'conveniently', 'opportunely'.

Translation: *Heard it* gives rise to certain difficulties in translating, since some languages do not possess such a general third person neuter pronoun. In Greek there is no pronoun at all, but some languages cannot use a verb such as 'hear', without specifying an object, e.g. 'heard what he said' or 'heard his offer'.

Money, which is entirely indefinite in Greek and English, may need some additional qualifier in another language, e.g. 'some money' or 'an amount of money'.

Sought an opportunity may be rendered 'was looking for a good way to' or 'was trying to find a good chance to'.

12 ***And on the first day of Unleavened Bread, when they sacrificed the passover lamb, his disciples said to him, "Where will you have us go and prepare for you to eat the passover?"***

Exegesis: *tē prōtē hēmera* 'on the first day': in the strictest sense the Passover lambs were not slain 'on the first day of the Unleavened Bread', which was 15th Nisan (cf. v. 1), but on the day preceding, i.e. the afternoon of the 14th Nisan. It has been suggested by commentators, therefore, that the phrase be taken to mean 'on the day before the Unleavened Bread' (cf. Black *Aramaic*, 100 n.3). It would appear probable, however, that here the word 'day' is used in a general sense, and not in the precise meaning of the twenty-four hour period running from sundown to sundown. On Thursday afternoon, 14th Nisan, the lambs were slain, and at sundown that evening began the first day of the Unleavened Bread, 15th Nisan. In Lk. 22 : 7 a similar indication of time is found.

hote to pascha ethuon 'when they slew the Passover (lamb)': the verb is used in an impersonal sense, meaning 'when the Passover lamb was slain'. The imperfect *ethuon* 'they were slaying' indicates here a customary action: 'when it was customary for them to kill'.

to pascha (cf. v. 1) 'the Passover lamb': here the animal is referred to, not the Feast, as in v.1. The singular 'passover lamb' is used generically for all the lambs slain that afternoon.

thuō (only here in Mark) 'slaughter', 'kill', 'sacrifice'. The Greek word in the LXX translates both *shahaṭ* 'slay' and *zabhah* 'sacrifice', and may mean either one in this passage.

pou theleis apelthontes hetoimasōmen...; 'where do you want us to go and prepare...?'

hetoimazō (cf. 1:3) 'prepare', 'make ready'.

hina phagēs 'in order that you may eat', 'for you to eat'.

to pascha here is 'the Passover meal' (as in v. 14), in contrast with the Passover feast in v. 1, and Passover lamb in the first part of this verse.

Translation: *Day of Unleavened Bread* often requires some type of more precise definition of the relationship between 'day' and 'unleavened bread', e.g. 'day of the festival of unleavened bread' or 'day of the time when unleavened bread was eaten'. Certainly one must not use a typical possessive construction, 'unleavened bread's day', as has been done in so many languages.

Sacrificed in this context must often be translated merely as 'killed'.

Passover lamb has not infrequently been translated as 'the passing-over lamb', a phrase which was interpreted to mean that the lamb in question passed over something. In order that the relationships between the component parts may be clear one may render this phrase as 'lamb to remember the passing over' (Ifugao), 'lamb of the passing-over day' (Tchien), or 'lamb for the *pascua* day', in which *pascua* has been borrowed from Spanish (Zoque).

Eat the passover may be completely meaningless in a literal translation, e.g. 'eat the passing-over'. Hence, one may need to employ a phrase such as 'eat the meal that reminds people of the passing over'.

13 *And he sent two of his disciples, and said to them, "Go into the city, and a man carrying a jar of water will meet you; follow him,*

433

Exegesis: For *apostellō* 'send' cf. 1:2; *hupagō* 'go' cf. 1:44; *akoloutheō* 'follow' cf. 1:18.

tēn polin 'the city' is Jerusalem, wherein the Passover feast must be celebrated (Deut. 16:5-7).

apantēsei (only here in Mark) 'he will meet'.

keramion hudatos 'a jar of water', i.e. 'a jar filled with water' (cf. *alabastron murou* in v. 3).

keramion (only here in Mark) 'jar' or 'jug' made of earthenware.

bastazōn (only here in Mark) 'carrying', 'bearing'.

Translation: *Sent* is often rendered by two quite distinct terms: one which means 'to be sent away' without destination and another which means 'to be sent to accomplish a particular task'. The latter meaning is, of course, appropriate at this point.

Carrying may require some specific indication of the manner employed. Where meaningful, 'carried on the head' would be appropriate.

Meet corresponds to two different terms in many languages: (1) meet by accident or without intention and (2) meet by design or advance planning. The Greek text does not specify, but many translators have chosen the first alternative.

Follow here bears the meaning of 'accompany' or 'go along with', not 'track down'.

14 *and wherever he enters, say to the householder, 'The Teacher says, Where is my guest room, where I am to eat the passover with my disciples?'*

Text: *mou* 'my' after *kataluma* 'guest room' is omitted by *Textus Receptus*, but included by all modern editions of the Greek text.

Exegesis: *hopou ean* (cf. 14:9) 'wherever': the phrase 'wherever he enters' refers, of course, to whatever *house* he should enter.

oikodespotē (only here in Mark) 'master of the house', i.e. the owner of the house (cf. Lagrange *proprietaire*).

ho didaskalos (cf. 4:38) 'the teacher'.

to kataluma (only here in Mark) 'the lodging', 'the guest room' (cf. Moulton & Milligan); possibly 'the dining room'.

to pascha 'the Passover meal' as in 14:12b.

Translation: *Wherever he enters* must not be translated as a generic or distributive expression, meaning that the man was likely to enter a number of places and that the disciples should inquire of each householder. The equivalent expression in some languages is 'when he goes into a house, then say to the householder there'. Unless this clause is translated with care, the impression will be given that the disciples were to follow the servant about town, begging a place from one householder after another.

My guest room must not be rendered as a straight possessive in some languages or it will imply that Jesus himself owned a part of the house. The meaning is rather 'a guest room for me', 'a room where I may be a guest', or 'a room where I am to eat' (see above).

Am to eat is rendered as a type of future. One must not interpret *am to eat* in the sense of 'destined to eat', as some translators have done.

15 And he will show you a large upper room furnished and ready; there prepare for us."

Exegesis: *deixei* (1:44) 'he will show'.

anagaion (only here in Mark) 'a room upstairs', 'an upper room'.

estrōmenon (cf. 11:8) 'strewn', 'spread out': by most commentators this is taken to mean 'spread with carpets and couches', ready for the meal (cf. Field *Notes*, 39; Lagrange *fournie de tapis et de divans*). Though improbable, the word could mean 'paved' (cf. Arndt & Gingrich). Taylor is of the opinion that the participle is used in a general sense, meaning simply 'prepared', and suggests it may have been simply "a bare attic."

hetoimon (only here in Mark; cf. the verb *hetoimazō* in v. 12 and here) 'ready', 'prepared'.

Translation: *Upper room* is not easy to translate in languages in which one-roomed huts are about the size of dwelling to which the people are accustomed. However, some such expression as 'high room' or 'room high in the house' will at least be descriptive of what the people may see in urban centers.

Furnished must be rendered in such a way as to make it meaningful, but not so detailed as to specify more than is included in the Greek term. Accordingly, 'with what was needed' or 'having what they required' may be adequate.

Prepare must often be translated with an object, e.g. 'prepare the meal there for us' or 'there prepare the food for us'.

16 And the disciples set out and went to the city, and found it as he had told them; and they prepared the passover.

Text: After *mathētai* 'disciples', *Textus Receptus*, Soden, Vogels, Lagrange, and Kilpatrick add *autou* 'his', which is omitted by the majority of modern editions of the Greek text.

Exegesis: It should be noticed that 'it' in RSV does not refer to 'the city', but is used in the general sense of 'the situation', 'the conditions'

Translation: *It* creates a problem in some languages, since any indefinite pronoun would refer to the 'city' of the previous clause. Where a specific noun must be introduced, 'room' is probably the most satisfactory.

For *prepared the passover* see 14:12, e.g. 'prepared the meal to remember the passing-over'.

17 *And when it was evening he came with the twelve.*

Exegesis: *opsias genomenēs* (cf. 4:35) 'when it was evening', i.e. after sunset on Thursday, and by now (according to Jewish reckoning) the 15th Nisan.

meta tōn dōdeka (cf. 3:16) 'with the Twelve': a title, not a number.

Translation: Because of the distance of *he* from the closest specific noun antecedent, it may be necessary to translate 'Jesus came with the twelve disciples'.

18 *And as they were at table eating, Jesus said, "Truly, I say to you, one of you will betray me, one who is eating with me."*

Exegesis: *kai anakeimenōn autōn kai esthiontōn* 'and while they were reclining at table and eating'.

anakeimai (cf. 6:26) 'recline at table', 'recline at meal'.

heis ex humōn 'one from you' means simply 'one of you', 'a certain one of you' (cf. Arndt & Gingrich *ek* 4.a.α).

paradōsei (cf. v. 10) 'will hand over', 'will deliver'.

ho esthiōn met' emou 'he who eats with me', 'the one eating with me': the definite article with the participle does not particularize the designation as though it meant 'the *only one* who is eating with me', 'that *particular man* who is eating with me', but simply designates the man as a table companion, as a table guest. Several commentators and translations agree with RSV in taking the phrase to mean 'the one who is *even now* eating with me'. Though possible (and perhaps probable) this meaning is not necessarily intended: the phrase may mean simply 'one who eats with me' with no reference to time.

The turn of the phrase, in Mark, may have been influenced by Ps. 41:10.

Translation: *At table* need not be translated literally, since it is only implied in the Greek, which reads literally 'reclining and eating'. The equivalent in some languages is 'sitting there eating'.

For *truly* in this type of construction see 3:28 and 8:12.

As noted above, there is considerable difference of opinion as to the precise meaning of the clause *one who is eating with me*. Some have interpreted this in a strictly temporal manner, indicating that Judas was at that moment eating with Jesus, while others have assumed that it meant that Judas, who might have been reclining next to Jesus, was one dipping into the same bowl. However, the meaning did not seem to be particularly evident to the disciples, for they all seemed to regard themselves as being included in this possibility.

For *betray* see 3:19.

In order to reflect the type of appositional construction of clauses in the Greek text, one may wish to follow a rather paratactic type of arrangement in some languages, e.g. 'one of you will betray me; he will be one who is eating with me'. Such an adaptation may be necessary if, the construction 'one...one...' is not possible.

19 *They began to be sorrowful, and to say to him one after another, "Is it I?"*

Text: At the end of the verse *Textus Receptus*, Soden, Vogels, and Kilpatrick add *kai allos, Mēti egō*; 'and another, Is it I?', which is omitted by the majority of modern editions of the Greek text.

Exegesis: *ērxanto* (cf. 1:45) 'they began'.
lupeisthai (cf. 10:22) 'to be sad', 'to be sorrowful'.
heis kata heis 'one after the other' (cf. Arndt & Gingrich *heis* 5.a).
mēti egō; 'Is it I?': the interrogative *mēti* expects a negative answer (cf. 4:21), and the question is not a request for information, but a protest of loyalty, 'Surely it is not I?' a question requesting confirmation —'No, it is not!'

Translation: For *sorrowful* see 10 : 22. *Began to be* is equivalent in many languages to 'became'.
To say...one after another is rendered in some languages by a distributive form of the verb 'to say'. In other languages one must translate, 'one said, Is it I, and another said, Is it I, and so all said the same'.
The form of the question should definitely anticipate a negative reply, e.g. 'I am not the one, am I?' or 'I will not do it, will I?'

20 *He said to them, "It is one of the twelve, one who is dipping bread in the same dish with me.*

Text: Before *trublion* 'dish' *Textus Receptus*, Tischendorf, Soden, Vogels Souter, Lagrange, and Merk omit *hen* 'one'; it is included, in brackets (with some doubt as to its genuineness, therefore), by Westcott and Hort, Nestle, and Taylor; Kilpatrick includes it without brackets; RSV also includes it, translating 'same'.

Exegesis: *heis tōn dōdeka* (cf. v. 10) 'one of the Twelve'.
ho embaptomenos met' emou 'he who dips with me', 'the one dipping with me': what is said in v. 18 concerning the force of the definite article *ho* 'the' with the participle, and concerning the time involved in the designation, is applicable here as well.
embaptō (only here in Mark) 'to dip in', 'to plunge in': here it is used with reference to the bread which was held in the hand and dipped into the bowl containing the designated sauce for the meal.
to hen trublion 'the one bowl', i.e. 'the same bowl'.
trublion (only here in Mark) 'dish', 'bowl': placed in the center of the table, it contained the sauce into which the bread was dipped for eating.

437

Translation: *The twelve* must be modified in two ways in some languages: (1) by the addition of a substantive, e.g. 'disciples' or 'men', and (2) by a shift to a second person form, or identification, e.g. 'one of you twelve disciples'. Without the addition of 'you', the clause may be interpreted as referring to another twelve persons rather than to those being addressed, since in certain languages one cannot speak to a person in the third person, any more than in some languages it is possible to speak of oneself in the third person.

Dipping does not mean complete submersion of the bread, but only the dipping of it into a sauce.

One of the twelve must in some languages be 'one with the eleven' (Chol).

21 *For the Son of man goes as it is written of him, but woe to that man by whom the Son of man is betrayed! It would have been better for that man if he had not been born."*

Exegesis: *ho huios ... tou anthrōpou* (cf. 2:10) 'the Son of man'.

hupagei 'he goes': here the verb is used with obvious reference to death (cf. Arndt & Gingrich 3).

kathōs gegraptai (cf. 1:2; 9:12) 'as it is written', 'even as Scripture says'.

ouai (cf. 13:17) 'woe!' 'alas!': not a curse, but a cry of commiseration.

di' hou 'by whom', 'through whose instrumentality' (cf. Arndt & Gingrich *dia* III.2.b.α).

kalon (cf. 4:8) 'good' here used in the comparative sense, 'better'. Though the verb *eimi* 'to be' is not part of the genuine text, it is clearly implied: the whole conditional clause *ei ouk egennēthē ho anthrōpos ekeinos* 'if that man had not been born' is the subject of the sentence, and *kalon* is the predicate nominative, in the neuter gender, agreeing with the gender of the subject. The comparative 'better 'implies, 'It were better that that man had not been born *than that he had been born!*'

egennēthē (only here in Mark) 'he was born'.

Translation: *Goes* can be very badly translated, since in some instances it has been found to mean nothing more than 'goes away' or 'goes on a journey'. If there is no other alternative one can translate as 'goes to his death' (Tzeltal).

For the use of the *Son of man* as a first person reference, see 2:10.

It is written is in many languages an obscure type of construction which would have no implication of 'the Scriptures'. Accordingly, one may translate 'as the Scriptures say about him' or 'as the words are written about him' (or 'me').

For the rendering of passages beginning with *woe* see the translation of *alas* 13:17. In Ifugao this type of idiom is rendered as 'that man will suffer'.

By whom the Son of man is betrayed may, where necessary, be recast as an active, e.g. 'who betrays the Son of man'.

The construction *better for that man if...* is quite complex in many languages. This is especially true in those languages which do not have a closely parallel type of comparative construction. As a result, a number of alternatives must be employed: 'that man would have an advantage if he had not been born', 'that man would have a better lot if he had not been born', or 'it would be counted good for that man if he had not been born'.

22 *And as they were eating, he took bread, and blessed, and broke it, and gave it to them, and said, "Take; this is my body."*

Exegesis: The narrative portion of this verse is built upon a succession of three participles and three finite verbs: *esthiontōn...labōn...eulogēsas eklasen kai edōken...kai eipen* 'while (they) were eating...(he) taking... blessing he broke and gave...and said'.

labōn (cf. 6:41, 8:6, 14:23) 'taking': from the table, where it would be with the food.

eulogēsas (cf. 6:41) 'blessing': as noticed in the study of the verb in 6:41, *eulogeō* and *eucharisteō* (next verse) both refer to the same action of 'blessing God', i.e. praising God, being both the equivalent of the Hebrew *barak*. The Jewish "blessing" which was spoken over the bread was, "Blessed be thou, O Lord our God, king of the world, who causest bread to come forth from the earth" (Jeremias *Eucharistic Words*, 107).

eklasen (cf. 8:6) 'he broke (into pieces)'.

labete '(you) take (it)', i.e. the piece of bread which Jesus gave to each of them.

touto estin to sōma mou 'this is my body': whatever interpretation be given to this saying, the translation must faithfully represent the plain meaning of the words. Such translations as 'this means my body' (Moffatt), or 'this represents my body' (Williams) are not to be recommended.

Translation: *He* should be rendered as 'Jesus' in a number of languages since the immediately preceding third person singular referent is the one who is to betray the Son of man.

For *bless* see 6:41 and 11:9, 10.

Take may require an object, e.g. 'take this' or 'take these pieces of bread'.

Body must not be translated as 'corpse'. The closest equivalent in some languages is 'my meat and bones' (which is equivalent to body) or 'myself', also used to identify the living body in which one dwells.

23 *And he took a cup, and when he had given thanks he gave it to them, and they all drank of it.*

Text: Before *potērion* 'cup' *Textus Receptus* and Kilpatrick add *to* 'the', which is omitted by all other modern editions of the Greek text.

Exegesis: *potērion* (cf. 7:4) 'cup' containing the wine.

439

eucharistēsas (cf. 8:6, 6:41) 'giving thanks': as already seen, the same as *eulogēsas* 'blessing'. Jeremias (*Eucharistic Words*, 108, 119, 121) calls the verb *eucharisteō* a "Graecising" of the Semitic term *eulogeō*. Bengel (on Mt. 26:26) says of the two: "Each verb explains the other."

epion ex autou pantes 'they all drank from it', i.e. 'they all drank some of its contents': the cup was passed from disciple to disciple until they had all drunk of the wine.

Translation: *Had given thanks* may require an object, e.g. 'gave thanks to God'.

Gave it means 'he gave the cup'.

24 And he said to them, "This is my blood of the covenant, which is poured out for many.

Text: After *mou* 'my' *Textus Receptus* adds *to* 'the', which is omitted by all modern editions of the Greek text.

Before *diathēkēs* 'covenant' *Textus Receptus* adds *kainēs* 'new', which is omitted by all modern editions of the Greek text.

Exegesis: *to haima mou tēs diathēkēs* 'my blood of the covenant': the phrase is perhaps consciously modelled after Ex. 24:8 "Behold the blood of the covenant (LXX *to haima tēs diathēkēs*) which the Lord has made with you." "The blood of the covenant" is the blood which *ratifies*, or *seals*, the covenant God made with his people.

diathēkē (only here in Mark) 'will', 'testament', 'compact', 'covenant': it is agreed that the meaning of the word in the New Testament is to be derived from the use and meaning of *berith* in the O.T., with reference to the 'covenant' which God made with the people of Israel. Rather than translate the Hebrew word by *sunthēkē*, the normal Greek word for 'agreement', 'covenant', the LXX uses *diathēkē*, perhaps with the purpose of avoiding the implication in *sunthēkē* of an agreement reached by a settlement between two parties who stand as equals; for in the O.T. God's *berith* with his people is, so to speak, drawn up, proposed and executed by God alone (cf. Arndt & Gingrich 2).

to ekchunnomenon (only here in Mark) 'the (blood) poured out': several commentators translate the present participle '(the blood) which is *now* being poured out', as though in the mind of Jesus his blood were already being shed. It is better, however, to take the participle as having a future force, in accordance with Aramaic usage (cf. Jeremias *Eucharistic Words*, 122), '(the blood) which will be poured out' (cf. Weymouth, Goodspeed).

huper pollōn 'in behalf of many', 'for many' (cf. the discussion on *anti pollōn* in 10:45).

Translation: There are a number of expressions used to signify *covenant*, some of which closely resemble the force of the Greek *diathēkē*, while others are simply general terms for a contract or agreement, e.g. 'to put mouths equal', signifying complete assent on the part of all (Conob);

'helping promise' (Moré); 'a thing-time-bind', that is to say, an arrangement agreed upon for a period of time (Vai); 'an agreement' (Loma); 'agreement which is tied up', i.e. secure and binding (Ngok Dinka); 'a word which is left' (Chol); 'a broken-off word', based on the concept of 'breaking off a word' and leaving it with the person with whom an agreement has been reached (Huastec); 'a death command', a special term for testament (Tetelcingo Aztec); 'a promised word' (Piro); 'a word between' (Tchien); and 'promise that brings together' (Kiyaka).

Perhaps a more difficult problem than finding a term for *covenant* is relating this expression to the preceding, namely, 'blood', for the *of* in English cannot be reproduced by any possessive construction, as some translators have tried to do. The covenant does not possess the blood; it is only that the covenant is established or ratified by means of the blood. This relationship must be made explicit in some languages, e.g. 'blood which establishes the promise...' (Kiyaka), 'blood which arranges...' (Pame), 'blood that makes the word between us strong' (Tchien), and 'blood which confirms the covenant' (Mitla Zapotec). In Gbeapo the entire construction is recast as 'agreement made by shedding my blood'.

Poured out must be carefully translated to make sure that this does not refer to the pouring of blood from a glass or other type of receptacle. This is not a reference to the pouring out of animal's blood, but the shedding of Jesus' own blood, translated in some languages as 'running out', 'coming out', and 'gushing out'.

25 ***Truly, I say to you, I shall not drink again of the fruit of the vine until that day when I drink it new in the kingdom of God."***

Exegesis: *amēn* (cf. 3:28) 'truly'.

ouketi ou mē piō 'no longer will I drink', 'I will not drink again'. On the double negative *ou mē* cf. 9:1.

tou genēmatos tēs ampelou 'the fruit of the vine', 'the produce of the (grape) vine': a designation, of course, of wine.

genēma (only here in Mark) 'fruit', 'yield', 'produce': the noun (from *ginomai*) is used of vegetable products.

ampelos (only here in Mark; cf. *ampelōn* 12:1) 'vine', 'grapevine'.

kainon (cf. 1:27) 'new': either (1) the neuter accusative of the adjective, used adverbially, modifying the verb *pinō* 'drink', meaning thus 'drink in a new way' (or, perhaps, 'drink in a new sense'); or (2) the masculine accusative, modifying *oinos*, 'wine', which is to be supplied, meaning thus 'drink new wine' (cf. Weymouth, Goodspeed, Lagrange).

en tē basileia tou theou (cf. 1:15) 'in the Kingdom of God': the Kingdom of God, as an eschatological reality, is here referred to in the familiar Rabbinical fashion as the great Messianic banquet.

Translation: For *truly* employed in this type of construction see 3:28 and 8:12.

In some languages it is quite impossible to talk about 'drinking... fruit'. The only equivalent is 'drink...the juice of the fruit'.

Vine must be translated in such a way as to refer to a fruit-bearing plant. In some languages this was referred to by a term designating typical jungle vines, which were never known to produce fruit.

New should not be translated merely as 'again'. The emphasis here is either upon the new manner of drinking or the 'new wine'.

For *kingdom of God* see 1:15.

26 And when they had sung a hymn, they went out to the Mount of Olives.

Exegesis: *humnēsantes* (only here in Mark) 'having sung a hymn': at the end of the Jewish Passover, Psalms 115-18 were sung (cf. Goodspeed *Problems*, 62f.).

to oros tōn elaiōn (cf. 11:1) 'the Mount of Olives'.

Translation: *Hymn* has been translated as 'prayer song' in Barrow Eskimo. In other languages it is rendered as 'song of praise' or 'singing of thanks'.

For *Mount of Olives* see 11:1.

27 And Jesus said to them, "You will all fall away; for it is written, 'I will strike the shepherd, and the sheep will be scattered.'

Text: After *skandalisthēsesthe* 'you will stumble' *Textus Receptus* adds *en emoi en tē nukti tautē* 'in me in this very night', which is omitted by all modern editions of the Greek text.

Exegesis: *hoti* 'that' is recitative, introducing direct speech.

skandalisthēsesthe (cf. 4:17) 'you will be scandalized', 'you will be offended', 'you will be ensnared': the precise meaning of the verb here is difficult to determine. This difficulty is reflected by the various translations given: 'desert me' (Goodspeed); 'be disconcerted' (Moffatt); 'stumble' (Montgomery); 'turn against me' (Weymouth); 'lose confidence in me' (Manson); 'take offence' (Zürich). RSV and BFBS 'fall away', with a possible note of finality and irrevocableness, seems rather too strong. Lagrange points out that in the present passage the sense of the word is defined by the following quotation from Zech. 13:7, and means not that the disciples will lose their faith in their Master, but that their courage will fail and they will abandon him. In light of this, unless a literal translation 'be ensnared' or 'stumble' is possible, either Manson's or Weymouth's translation seems to convey best the meaning of the word.

hoti gegraptai (cf. 1:2) 'for it is written', 'for it stands on Scriptural record'.

pataxō (only here in Mark) 'I will smite', 'I will strike': here with the meaning 'slay' (cf. Arndt & Gingrich 1.c). The 'I' refers, of course, to God.

ton poimena (cf. 6:34) 'the shepherd'.

ta probata (cf. 6:34) 'the sheep'.

diaskorpisthēsontai (only here in Mark) 'they will be scattered', 'they will be dispersed'.

Trans lation: As noted above, *skandalizō* is extremely difficult to translate, especially in this passage. A number of idioms are used, e.g. 'you shall begin to have something in your hearts against me', in the sense of losing confidence in (Tzeltal), 'ashamed to see me' (Huave), and 'shall abandon me' (Chontal of Tabasco).

For some of the problems involved in the phrase *it is written* see 14:21.

Strike is not merely 'to hit', but 'to kill'.

The shepherd may be 'the one who takes care of the sheep'.

Will be scattered does not necessarily imply an active agent. In some instances the closest parallel to the passive construction is 'the sheep will run in all directions' (or 'shall flee away').

28 *But after I am raised up, I will go before you to Galilee."*

Exegesis: *meta to egerthēnai me* 'after I am risen (from the dead)': for the preposition *meta* 'after' with the infinitive, cf. 1:14.

egeirō (cf. 1:31) 'raise', 'rise': if possible, the passive form of the verb should be carried over into translation, 'I am raised (*not* 'I rise'), as in the other places where the passive refers to rising from the dead (cf. 6:14, 16 of John the Baptist; 12:26 of the dead in general; 16:6 of Jesus).

proaxō (cf. 6:45) 'I will go before', 'I will precede': so most commentators and translations who (comparing with 16:7) refer the saying to a Resurrection appearance of Jesus to his disciples. It has been suggested, however (*Journal of Theological Studies*, NS 5.3-18, 1954), that the meaning here is 'I will lead you into Galilee', 'I will go at your head to Galilee'.

Translation: *Am raised up* is equivalent to 'caused to live again' or 'caused to come back to life'. As noted above, the passive should be retained, if at all possible. Where the agent must be explicitly noted, one may translate, 'God has raised me up' or 'caused me to live again'.

Before you is probably better taken in the temporal sense, e.g. 'ahead of you' or 'before you do'.

29 *Peter said to him, "Even though they all fall away, I will not."*

Exegesis: *ei kai* 'even though': this refers to a supposition "conceived of as actually fulfilled or likely to be fulfilled" (Burton *Moods and Tenses*, §280; cf. §§281, 285).

pantes 'all': here, of course, 'all *others*'.

On *skandalizō* 'stumble' cf. v. 27.

Translation: *I will not* may require expansion of the elliptically implied elements, e.g. 'I will not fall away' or 'I will not abandon you'.

30 *And Jesus said to him, "Truly, I say to you, this very night, before the cock crows twice, you will deny me three times."*

Exegesis: *su* 'you' is emphatic: 'you yourself', 'even you'.

sēmeron tautē tē nukti 'today, in this very night': the 'today' of the phrase would last until sunset the following day; 'this very night' defines even more precisely the period of 'today' in which the denial would occur—it would be before sunrise.

prin (14:72) 'before'.

dis alektora phōnēsai 'the cock to crow twice'. At least three explanations are given of this phrase: (1) the words are to be taken literally of the crowing of a cock, before dawn, with the suggestion that 'twice' refers to a second crowing of a cock in response to the first one; (2) the phrase refers to the bugle call, known as the *gallicinium*, which sounded the end of the third watch of the night (the 'cock-crowing' watch which ended at 3:00 A.M.—cf. 13:35), when the guard was changed (cf. *Journal of Theological Studies* 22.367-70, 1920-21); (3) the expression simply means 'before dawn' (for which there is support in classical usage—cf. Rawlinson). On the other hand, F. C. Grant suggests that the words are a proverbial expression indicating not time, but readiness to betray, 'before the cock can crow twice'. From vv. 68 and 72, however, it appears certain that the author intends that the words be taken literally (cf. Branscomb).

aparnēsē (cf. 8:34) 'you will deny', 'you will disown': here with the sense of refusing to admit knowledge of, or relation to, Jesus.

Translation: For *truly* in this type of construction see 3:28 and 8:12.

This very night should be related to what follows, not to what precedes. This may require an adjustment in order, e.g. 'before the cock crows twice, you will this very night deny me three times'.

In some translations the Greek phrase has been rendered literally as 'today, this night', resulting in obvious difficulties in languages in which the words for 'day' and 'night' are mutually exclusive in meaning. Note, however, that in the N.T. the word *sēmeron* refers to the twenty-four hour period, and hence there is no contradiction. In other languages the equivalent can be expressed by 'this very night', 'just on this night', or 'during exactly this night'.

Since chickens are widely distributed throughout the world, there is very little difficulty in obtaining satisfactory terms for 'cock' and 'crowing'. However, 'when the fowl called cock makes an early noise' can suffice where chickens are not known.

Deny is most commonly translated as 'say that you do not know me'. Tzeltal renders the expression as 'cover in your heart that you know me'. In instances in which direct discourse is required, one may translate 'say, I do not know him'.

31 **But he said vehemently, "If I must die with you, I will not deny you." And they all said the same.**

Text: After *elalei* 'he said' *Textus Receptus* and Kilpatrick add *mallon* 'the more', which is omitted by all other modern editions of the Greek text.

Exegesis: *ekperissōs* (only here in the N.T.; cf. *perissōs* 10:26, *huper-perissōs* 7:37) 'exceedingly', 'vehemently', 'emphatically'.

ean deē 'even if it be necessary', 'even if it must be': for *dei* 'it is necessary' cf. 8:31.

sunapothanein (only here in Mark; cf. *apothnēskō* 5:35) 'to die with', 'to die together with'.

hōsautōs (cf. 12:21) 'in the same way', 'in like manner'.

Translation: *Said* may need to be translated by some term which implies a response to a previous statement, e.g. 'replied', or 'said in return', or 'spoke back'.

Vehemently is as strong a statement of assertion as can be used, e.g. 'said hard hard' (Zoque). In combination with the verb one may render this expression as 'insisted strongly', 'declared with strength', or 'said very strong words'.

Die with you may imply in some languages only natural death. Accordingly, as in Kekchi, one must render the passage as 'be killed with you', implying violent death.

If *deny* is translated as 'say that one does not know', it may be impossible to use a double negative, e.g. 'not say...not know'. In this case the double negative *not deny* must be rendered as 'I will always say that I know' (Zoque).

32 And they went to a place which was called Gethsemane; and he said to his disciples, "Sit here, while I pray."

Exegesis: *chōrion* (only here in Mark) 'place', 'plot of land', 'field', 'estate': it is from John 18:1 that we get the designation 'garden' (*kēpos*).

Gethsēmani (only here in Mark) 'Gethsemane': the word is derived from *gath-semane*', 'oil-press'.

kathisate (cf. 9:35) 'you sit here'.

heōs proseuxōmai 'until I pray': the aorist of the verb may be taken here to refer to the action as completed, i.e. 'until I finish praying'; the meaning, therefore, is 'while I pray' (cf. Burton *Moods and Tenses*, § 325).

proseuchomai (cf. 1:35) 'pray'.

Translation: The word employed to render *place* must be capable of indicating a small area such as a garden. In some languages, however, there is no equivalent of the generic term *place*, and one must use a more specific designation, e.g. 'grove of trees', implying an area which is planted and cared for.

They must include not only the disciples, the immediately preceding third person plural referent, but also Jesus. In some languages one can only overcome this syntactic problem by saying 'Jesus and his disciples went'. Otherwise, the implication is that the disciples went off to the garden of Gethsemane without Jesus.

For *pray* see 1:35.

445

33 *And he took with him Peter and James and John, and began to be greatly distressed and troubled.*

Exegesis: *paralambanei* (cf. 4:36) 'he takes', 'he takes with him'.

ērxato (cf. 1:45) 'he began': the verb here has its proper force, and should be included in translation (as done by RSV).

ekthambeisthai kai adēmonein 'to be extremely distressed and troubled': the two verbs together describe an extremely acute emotion, a compound of bewilderment, fear, uncertainty and anxiety, nowhere else portrayed in such vivid terms as here. Rawlinson: 'shuddering awe, amazement, deep distress'; Swete: 'amazed awe... overpowering mental distress'. Cf. the following translations: 'distress and dread' (Goodspeed); 'appalled and agitated' (Moffatt); 'full of terror and distress' (Weymouth, Montgomery); 'dismay and distress' (Manson); 'appalled and sorely troubled' (BFBS); 'surprised and terrified' (Lagrange); 'fright and anguish' (Synodale, Brazilian).

ekthambeō (9:15; cf. *thambeomai* 1:27) 'to amaze', 'to alarm': the word denotes a distress which is the result of surprise, i.e. a dread caused by something unexpected. 'Dismay', 'distress' or 'dread' would seem best to characterize the emotion indicated by the verb here.

adēmoneō (only here in Mark) 'be in anxiety', 'be troubled': the emphasis of this verb seems to be on the element of anguish caused by uncertainty and bewilderment as to what to do. Moulton and Milligan give examples from the papyri in which the word indicates distress and bewilderment. Therefore, 'anguish', 'anxiety', or perhaps 'despondency' (cf. Lagrange) would convey the meaning here.

Translation: There is almost inevitably a minor problem of interpretation in verses 32 and 33, namely, the identity of the persons to whom the command of sitting down was directed. Did Jesus, for example, tell all the disciples to sit down, and then ask the three disciples to arise and go with him? There is no way of knowing and, moreover, it does not seem particularly necessary to try to resolve such an obscurity, since the overall meaning is quite certain.

Took with him must be translated with care or the results may imply that Jesus was leading the disciples along like children. A proper equivalent in some languages is 'caused them to go along with him' or 'had them accompany him'.

Distressed and troubled is not easily translated, for unless one is quite careful, the rendering will seem to refer only to purely physical trouble and hardship. However, any terms which are used to express such severe mental distress will in many instances be expressed in ways which suggest other kinds of symptoms or activity e.g. 'began to groan and began to suffer' (Tzeltal) or 'began to feel trouble in his heart and his stomach'.

34 *And he said to them, "My soul is very sorrowful, even to death; remain here, and watch."*

Exegesis: *perilupos estin hē psuchē mou* 'my soul is very sorrowful': the statement is reminiscent of the phrase which appears in Ps. 41(42):6, 12, 42(43):5.

perilupos (cf. 6:26) 'very sad', 'extremely grieved'.

hē psuchē mou (cf. 3:4) 'my soul': here either the equivalent of 'myself', 'my whole being', or, in a more specialized sense, the 'soul' as the center of the 'inner life', the seat of the emotions. Inasmuch as the phrase is Biblical, it would appear that the first meaning prevails here.

heōs thanatou 'unto death', 'to the point of dying': the phrase recalls the LXX of Jonah 4:9, "I am exceedingly sorrowful, unto death" (*heōs thanatou*). As Swete says, it is "a sorrow which well-nigh kills."

meinate (cf. 6:10) 'you are to stay': the definite act.

grēgoreite (cf. 13:34) 'you must keep on watching': the abiding attitude (cf. Lagrange, Taylor).

Translation: It may be quite impossible to translate *soul* without doing violence to the meaning of this passage. In many languages, of course, one can render *soul* as 'heart', 'liver', or 'stomach', depending upon what may be the psychological center of the personality. However, in other instances one may employ simply 'I'. The danger in using a term which designates the part of the personality which lives on after death (the meaning of *soul*, as often understood in English) is that people may assume that Jesus was already dying in his soul and that the crucifixion was relatively meaningless.

For *sorrowful* see 10:22.

Even to death poses real problems for the translator, since this expression must be understood in a strictly figurative way. This may be clearly indicated in several ways; 'as if I would die' (Zoque), 'my soul has gone over it so that it is like that it kills me' (Navajo), and 'I am very much counting my heart; I die because of it, it seems' (Tzotzil).

Watch must not be translated in such a way as to imply that the disciples were to watch Jesus pray (a not infrequent mistake). Their task was to remain awake in order to watch out for anyone who might be coming with hostile intent.

35 *And going a little farther, he fell on the ground and prayed that, if it were possible, the hour might pass from him.*

Exegesis: *proselthōn mikron* 'going ahead a little', 'going forward a bit'.

proserchomai (cf. 1:31) 'approach', 'advance', 'go (or, 'come') forward'.

mikron (14:70) 'a little': here used adverbially, of space.

epipten epi tēs gēs (cf. 9:20) 'he fell upon the ground', 'he prostrated himself on the ground': an attitude of supplication and prayer (cf. Arndt & Gingrich *piptō* 1.b.α.ב).

proseucheto hina (cf. 13:18) 'he prayed that': the *hina* clause indicates the content of the prayer which follows, in indirect form.

ei dunaton (cf. 13:22) 'if possible', 'if it could be done'.

parelthē ap' autou hē hōra 'the hour might pass from him': the verb

447

parerchomai (cf. 6:48) here means to pass by, or away (without affecting him; cf. Arndt & Gingrich 1.b.γ). Lagrange: 'make it pass far away from me'.

hē hōra (14:41) 'the hour': not simply an indication of time, but supremely of the content, or nature, which makes it critical. 'The hour' is the approaching Passion. The word has, as Lagrange says, "a nuance of divine predestination."

Translation: *Fell on the ground* must not be translated so as to imply that Jesus stumbled and fell, but rather that he 'caused himself to fall' or 'prostrated himself on the ground', e.g. 'lay down flat on the ground'.

The idiom *the hour might pass from* is an extremely complex and unusual expression, especially in those parts of the world which do not speak of 'hours'. Moreover, one may often speak of people passing a time, but rarely of a time passing from a person. Furthermore, it is often necessary to specify the relationship of the person to the period of time in a some-what more specific manner. The following translations are typical of the adaptations which may be made: 'allow me to pass this time' (Mazahua); 'that pass which would happen to him in that hour' (Zoque); 'might not experience that hour' (Zacapoastla Aztec); and 'that this hour might change' (Navajo).

36 And he said, "Abba, Father, all things are possible to thee; remove this cup from me; yet not what I will, but what thou wilt."

Exegesis: *abba ho patēr* (Rom. 8:15, Gal. 4:6) 'Abba, Father': *abba* represents the Aramaic *'aba'*, 'Father', used in prayer. From its occurrence in Romans and Galatians, it would appear that this bi-lingual expression was used in prayer, as an address to God: 'O my Father!' (cf. Arndt & Gingrich *abba*).

panta dunata (cf. 9:23, 10:27) 'all things are possible', '(you) can do all things'.

parenegke (only here in Mark) 'take away', 'remove': Field (*Notes*, 39) defines it, 'turn aside, cause to pass by'.

to potērion touto 'this cup': in a figurative sense, of impending affliction (as in 10:38f.). In the context, 'this cup' and 'the hour' (in the previous verse) refer to the same experience.

egō...su 'I...you': the pronouns are emphatic.

Translation: *Abba, Father* tends to cause a number of difficulties in translating. First, a transliteration of *abba* may, by coincidence, already have a meaning which would make it impossible in combination with 'Father' or it may, as in some instances, actually mean 'father'. For example, in Tchien, a language of Liberia, the correct transliteration of *abba* is *aba*, but this is a word meaning 'our father'. It cannot, however, be used with the following 'my Father' (the word 'father' should be possessed). The only solution in this instance is to drop the expression *Abba* and translate simply 'my Father'. A similar problem exists in

Barrow Eskimo, where the transliteration of *abba* would be *aappa*, which actually means 'father', but in this type of context Jesus would have to say 'my father' (*aappaang*), or the expression would be a denial of his own sonship. Moreover, it is impossible to use *aappa, aappaang*, literally 'father, my father'. Again, the only solution is to drop the transliteration.

In most languages, of course, it is possible to use the transliterated expression equivalent to *Abba*, but it may not be possible to use it in an appositional expression with much meaning, and it is scarcely warranted to put in an explanatory phrase, as though this would be a part of the prayer of Jesus to his Father. Accordingly, the best which can be done is to reproduce the *Abba*, despite its relative meaninglessness and add 'father' or 'my father', immediately following.

All things are possible to thee must usually be shifted to a more direct form of expression, e.g.'you can do anything' or 'you are able to do everything'.

Remove this cup from me may be badly misunderstood if translated literally, e.g. 'remove this cup which is stuck to me' or 'take away this cup which I have'. In some instances, where the figure of 'cup' is utterly meaningless (and in fact quite misleading) a phrase has been added to indicate the figurative nature of the expression. For example, in Chol, immediately following the use of *vaso* (borrowed from Spanish), the phrase 'which is the picture of *wocol*' has been employed (see *The Bible Translator*, 8.110-11, 1957). The Chol word *wocol* has a wide range of meaning, including affliction, trial, punishment, and retribution. It is particularly important that in any word for 'cup' one avoid the connotations of 'cup of intoxicating liquor' (a not infrequent mistake).

Not what I will, but what thou wilt is only very tenuously connected with the preceding. The ellipsis must sometimes be filled in as 'but do not do what I want...' or 'but do not let it happen just as I want...' In Tzeltal the contrast in desire is neatly expressed as 'not the desire of my heart, but the desire of your heart'.

37 *And he came and found them sleeping, and he said to Peter, "Simon, are you asleep? Could you not watch one hour?"*

Exegesis: For the same combination of the three verbs *erchesthai... heuriskein...katheudein* 'come...find...sleep' cf. 13:36 and 14:40.

ouch ischusas...; 'were you not able...?' 'could you not...?': either (as RSV) 'be able' (as in 9:18), or, literally 'have the strength' (as in 5:4), which Taylor prefers.

ischuō (cf. 2:17) 'be strong', 'be able'.

mian hōran 'one hour': here a period of time. Perhaps the sense is '*even* (as little as) one hour?'

grēgorēsai (cf. 13:34) 'to watch', 'to stay alert', 'to keep awake'.

Translation: Since the perspective of the previous section has been the activity of Jesus, it may be necessary to translate *came* as 'went back'.

Said may require rendering by 'asked'.

For *watch* see verse 34.

Where there is no equivalent for *hour* in the strict sense of a precise period of time, one can often translate as 'for even a short period of time' or 'for even a while'.

38 *Watch and pray that you may not enter into temptation; the spirit indeed is willing, but the flesh is weak."*

Exegesis: *grēgoreite kai proseuchesthe hina* 'you (plural) must watch and pray that': RSV takes 'that' to refer to the content of the prayer (as in v. 35, and 13:38); if, however, both verbs be taken with *hina*, it could indicate purpose—'watch and pray, in order that...' (so BFBS; cf. Moffatt "so that").

peirasmon (only here in Mark; cf. *peirazō* 1:13) 'temptation': the context seems to demand the meaning of 'temptation' leading to sin, and not merely the idea of 'trial' or 'testing'.

pneuma (cf. 2:8)...*sarx* (cf. 10:8) 'spirit...flesh': here presented as distinct and antithetical elements of man's nature. The contrast between the two, say Arndt & Gingrich (cf. *pneuma* 3.b), is between the will as opposed to inferior feelings such as fear, anxiety, etc., which are attributed to the 'flesh'.

prothumon (only here in Mark) 'ready', 'willing', 'eager'.

asthenēs (only here in Mark; cf. *astheneō* 6:56) 'weak', 'powerless'.

Translation: *Watch* would seem to be best translated as 'stay awake' or 'stay alert'.

Enter into temptation is an awkward idiom in most languages, for one does not literally 'enter into' such an experience. In Tzeltal this concept is expressed as 'end by being tempted', and in Zoque one must say 'fall when Satan tries you'. In Sierra Aztec one may 'enter into sin', but not 'enter into temptation'.

The spirit...the flesh is a fundamental contrast, but one which is variously expressed in different languages. Often, however, *spirit* is equivalent to 'heart' (Eastern Otomí, Loma, Amuzgo, Sierra Aztec), and *flesh* may be rendered as 'body' (Amuzgo, Sierra Aztec, Tzeltal), 'you yourself' (Tarahumara). The following translations are illustrative of the contrastive expressions: 'your hearts are ready but your bodies are weak' (Sierra Aztec), 'your heart is strong but you yourselves are not strong' (Tarahumara), 'your heart has strength, but your body does not have strength' (Tzeltal), 'your heart desires to do good, but your heart is weak', in which 'heart' must be used in both clauses since it not only stands for the center of the personality, but is also the symbol of typical human nature (Loma).

39 *And again he went away and prayed, saying the same words.*

Exegesis: *apelthōn* 'going away': i.e. from the three disciples.

ton auton logon 'the same word': in this context, 'the same prayer' or 'the same petition' (cf. similar use of *logos* in 5:36, 7:29, 8:32, 9:10, 10:22, 11:29, 12:13).

Translation: *Saying the same words* must refer to the previous prayer, not to the immediately preceding words uttered by Jesus, e.g. 'he spoke to God with the same words with which he had spoken to God' or 'he talked to God just as he had done before'.

40 **And again he came and found them sleeping, for their eyes were very heavy; and they did not know what to answer him.**

Text: Instead of *palin elthōn heuren autous katheudontas* 'coming again he found them sleeping' of the majority of modern editions of the Greek text, *Textus Receptus*, Tischendorf, Soden, and Vogels have *hupostrepsas heuren autous palin katheudontas* 'returning he found them sleeping again'.

Exegesis: *ēsan...katabarunomenoi* (only here in the N.T.) 'they were... weighted down', 'they were...heavy' (from *barus* 'heavy').
ouk ēdeisan ti apokrithōsin autō (cf. 9:6 for a similar statement) 'they did not know what they should answer him', 'they did not know what to say to him': as in 9:6 the verb *apokrinomai* (cf. 8:4) does not always have the meaning 'answer' with a previous question implied, but may mean simply 'say'.

Translation: For the translation of *came* as 'went back' see verse 37.
Their eyes were very heavy is merely an idiom meaning 'they were very sleepy', translatable in some instances as 'they could scarcely open their eyes'.

41 **And he came the third time and said to them, "Are you still sleeping and taking your rest? It is enough; the hour has come; the Son of man is betrayed into the hands of sinners.**

Exegesis: *to triton* 'the third time': an adverbial phrase modifying the verb *erchetai* 'he comes'.
katheudete to loipon kai anapauesthe· How this sentence is to be taken is subject to wide differences of opinion. Most Greek texts punctuate it as a statement, either as a command ('you are to sleep...and rest') or as a simple statement ('you are sleeping...and resting'); Kilpatrick, however, punctuates it as a question. Though the verb forms may be read either as imperative or indicative, with a semi-colon following, and in the context, the Greek would normally be read as an imperative—and presumably that is what the majority of editors of the Greek text assume it to be. The words have been translated in three ways: (1) as a statement, indicating surprise, 'You are still sleeping and resting!' (Synodale); (2) as a command, intended either seriously or ironically, 'Sleep on now and rest' (Vulgate; AV, ASV, Weymouth; Zürich, Brazilian; Gould,

Swete, Lagrange); (3) as a question, 'Are you still sleeping and resting?' (RSV, Moffatt, Goodspeed, Berkeley, Manson, BFBS, Williams; Rawlinson, Taylor). The context would seem to favor the third alternative. However, if we interpret this as a question, it must be admitted that *to loipon*, in this case, assumes a meaning it does not ordinarily have, since, as an adverbial phrase indicating time, it means 'henceforth', 'from now on', 'for the future'. Arndt & Gingrich (*loipos* 3.a.α) suggest various interpretations, including the interrogative sense, which they state thus, 'Do you intend to sleep on and on?' or, possibly, 'You are sleeping in the meantime?' On the whole it would seem that the words should be taken as a question.

anapauō (cf. 6:31) 'to rest'.

apechei. On this single word, used nowhere else in the New Testament in an absolute sense, as here, Vincent says, with some justification: "Expositors are utterly at sea as to its meaning" (*Word Studies* I, 228). The meaning 'it is enough', favored by most translations and commentators, goes as far back as the Vulgate, which has *sufficit* (for evidence in favor of this meaning cf. Field *Notes*, 39). By most this is taken to refer to the sleeping and resting of the disciples: 'enough of that!' 'no more of that!' Lagrange, however, translates *C'en est fait* with reference to Jesus himself and his thrice-repeated prayer concerning his approaching Passion: 'sleep, I am now ready'. Montgomery seems to assume some such meaning by translating, 'it is over'.

The form *apechei* is normally used of receipting bills, with the meaning 'paid in full' (cf. Moulton & Milligan). Following this meaning, J. de Zwaan (quoted by Rawlinson) suggested that the verb here has a personal sense and is to be referred to Judas, as the subject: 'He did receive (the promised money)'. Thus Manson translates 'the money has been paid!' and E. K. Simpson (*Words Worth Weighing in the Greek New Testament*, 16-17) paraphrases, 'It is settled! The deed of infamy is done! He pockets his reward'.

Another translation has been suggested by G. H. Boobyer (*New Testament Studies* 2.44-48, 1955): he proposes the meaning 'take possession of', and refers the verb to Judas, as the subject, 'He is taking possession of (me)!' BFBS translates 'Is he far away?'

Emendation, the last resource of the translator, has also been proposed. Black (*Aramaic*, 161f.), following the variant reading (found in the sixth century uncial manuscript D) *apechei to telos kai hē hōra*, suggests that there was a mistranslation of the underlying Aramaic which meant, 'The end and the hour are pressing'. It should be noted that the Peshitto version of the Syriac has 'the end has come' (reading *to telos* as the subject of the verb and apparently translating the Greek *ēggiken* 'has come' rather than *apechei*). Otherwise it has been proposed (*Expository Times* 46.382, 1935) that the original Marcan phrase was *to telos apechei* meaning, 'the end is holding off', to be taken as a question: 'The end is far away?' (cf. Taylor).

Although these proposed variant readings and their emendations offer a reasonable explanation of what is otherwise quite an obscure saying (cf. Taylor, who inclines to accept either one of the proposed emendations), so long as the accepted text can be made to bear some intelligible meaning it should be followed and translated. In the present case it would seem best to go along with the majority (Arndt & Gingrich 1; cf. Moule *Idiom Book*, 27).

ēlthen hē hōra (cf. v. 35) 'the hour has come', 'the hour is here'.

idou (cf. 1:2) 'see': should not be omitted (as in the RSV) here, even though repeated in the next verse.

paradidotai (cf. 1:14; cf. 9:31) 'is delivered': the ordinary meaning of the verb should be observed here, as in the identical phrase in 9:31. It is to be doubted that 'deliver' is to be understood in 9:31 and 'betray' here (as done by RSV).

ho huios tou anthrōpou (cf. 2:10) 'the Son of man'.

eis tas cheiras tōn hamartōlōn 'into the hands of sinful men', 'into the power of sinners': *hoi hamartōloi* here presumably has the moral and theological connotation of 'sinners' who transgress God's will, rather than the specialized sense in which it is used in 2:15f.

For similar statements concerning the Son of man cf. 9:31, 10:33.

Translation: For the translation of *came* as 'went back' see verse 37.

Said may be in some languages better rendered as 'asked', because of the following question.

The form of the question 'Are you still sleeping and resting?' should not imply that Jesus was actually asking for information. This is a rhetorical question implying a certain amount of surprise and irony. Hence, if in the receptor language special forms of questions are used for this type of expression, one should make certain that the appropriate equivalent is employed.

The problems involved in the translating of *it is enough* depend largely upon the exegesis. However, even then one will find that the closest equivalent is likely to be relatively idiomatic, e.g. 'it is over', 'it has happened', and 'that is all'.

The hour has come is translatable as 'the time has come' or 'now is the time'.

For the use of *the Son of man* as a third person reference in a first person relationship, see 2:10.

In many languages *is betrayed* must be translated as an immediate future, rather than present, e.g. 'is going to be betrayed' or 'is about to be betrayed'.

The hands of sinners cannot be translated literally in many languages, since 'hands' do not always stand for 'power' or 'control'. The closest equivalent in some instances is 'into the power of evil men' or 'under the authority of sinful men'.

42 Rise, let us be going; see, my betrayer is at hand."

Exegesis: *egeiresthe* (cf. 1:31) 'rise', 'get up', 'rouse yourselves'.

agōmen (cf. 1:38) 'let us go': not in the sense of running away, but of meeting the approaching group.

453

ho paradidous me 'he who delivers me' (for the verb *paradidōmi* used with reference to Judas Iscariot cf. v. 10).

ēggiken (cf. 1 : 15) 'has come', 'is here': the meaning 'is near', 'is at hand' would not seem to fit the context quite so well as 'has arrived', since the following verse states that while Jesus was still speaking Judas arrived.

Translation: *My betrayer* consists of an object-action relationship, not a possessor-object relationship as might be assumed from the use of the so-called possessive pronoun *my*. Accordingly, one must usually translate this as 'the one who is going to betray me'.

43 *And immediately, while he was still speaking, Judas came, one of the twelve, and with him a crowd with swords and clubs, from the chief priests and the scribes and the elders.*

Text: After *ochlos* 'crowd' *Textus Receptus* and Kilpatrick add *polus* 'great', which is omitted by all other modern editions of the Greek text.

Exegesis: *eti autou lalountos* 'while he was speaking': cf. 5 : 35 for the identical phrase.

paraginetai (only here in Mark) 'he is present', 'he comes', 'he arrives'.
heis tōn dōdeka (cf. 14 : 10, 20) 'one of the Twelve'.
ochlos 'crowd': here, in the nature of the case, 'mob' (Moffatt), 'rabble' (Taylor).
meta machairōn kai xulōn 'with swords and clubs': the *machairai* (14 : 47, 48) were not necessarily swords, in the usual or technical sense of the term; they might have been knives (cf. Field *Notes*, 76f.). The *xula* (14 : 48) would be clubs, or cudgels (cf. Arndt & Gingrich 2.b).
para 'from' (cf. 8 : 11, 12 : 2, 21 for other places in which the preposition is used in this sense): here 'from' goes back to the main verb *paraginomai* 'arrive' (cf. Arndt & Gingrich *para* I.1), or else something like *apestal-menos* 'sent' is to be understood (cf. Lagrange *envoyée*).
tōn archiereōn kai tōn grammateōn kai tōn presbuterōn 'the chief priests and the scribes and the elders', all three groups of the Sanhedrin (cf. 8 : 31).

Translation: The syntax of this verse is deceptively simple, for there are a number of difficulties which, if not treated properly, result in mis-understanding. In the first place *immediately* should be related to the coming of Judas. This often requires a shift of order, e.g. 'and while Jesus was still talking, Judas came right up' or '...Judas came up immediately'.

One of the twelve is in apposition with Judas, and as such may be treated (1) as a paratactically combined expression, e.g. 'He was one of the twelve' or as in many languages 'he was one with the eleven', or (2) as a dependent relative clause, e.g. 'Judas, who was one of the twelve, came right up'.

The phrase *with him a crowd with swords and clubs* must frequently be made a separate clause, with two entirely different treatments of the preposition *with*, since in the first instance the meaning is accompaniment and in the second, possession, e.g. 'a crowd who had (or 'carried') swords and clubs accompanied Judas'.

From the chief priests and the scribes and the elders is sometimes wrongly translated in such a way as to imply only that the swords and the clubs came from the three groups of the Sanhedrin. In still other instances, the rendering has implied that the crowd consisted of these groups. However, the real meaning is that Judas and the crowd came from these authorities, in the sense of having been sent out by them. This meaning can be conveyed in some languages by a pronominal usage 'these came from...' or 'they came from...' This verse, consisting of a single sentence in Greek, must often be translated by at least three in other languages because of the radical shifts in participants and the fact that the Greek prepositions imply a complex relationship which cannot be duplicated by corresponding phrases in other languages.

For certain lexical problems, the following references are useful: *chief priests* (2:26, 8:31), *scribes* (1:22), and *elders* (8:31).

44 *Now the betrayer had given them a sign, saying, "The one I shall kiss is the man; seize him and lead him away safely."*

Exegesis: *dedōkei* 'he had given': the pluperfect has here its full force.

ho paradidous auton (cf. v. 10) 'he who delivered him'.

sussēmon (only here in the N.T.) a prearranged 'sign', 'signal'.

philesō (only here in Mark) 'I shall kiss' (cf., for this meaning of *phileō* 'love', Arndt & Gingrich, 2; Moulton & Milligan).

kratēsate auton (cf. 1:31) 'you are to seize him', 'you arrest him'.

apagete (14:53, 15:16) 'you are to lead (him) away': the verb is used of prisoners or condemned men being taken away under guard (cf. Arndt & Gingrich).

asphalōs (only here in Mark) 'safely'.

Translation: *The betrayer* is often rendered as 'the one who was going to betray Jesus'.

Given them a sign may need to be shifted to 'given the crowd a sign', for otherwise *them* will refer to the immediately preceding third person plural referents, namely, the chief priests, the scribes and the elders.

In most languages there are ways of describing a secret sign which is given to persons in advance of an event. However, in some cases one must simply describe the circumstance, e.g: 'he had already told them how he was going to do' (Chontal of Tabasco).

Kiss constitutes a problem, not only because kissing is not practiced in many parts of the world, but even where it is, there is a tendency to associate kissing with strictly sexual practices. In order to avoid a wrong connotation one may add a classifying expression, e.g. 'shall greet by kissing'.

Part of the difficulty with the word *kiss* may be avoided if one does

455

not imply the necessity of kissing on the mouth, for undoubtedly the kiss by Judas was on the cheek, since this would be the normal manner of greeting. In one early translation the rendering 'kiss (literally 'suck') on the mouth' was very offensive, but a shift which meant only 'to suck' was considered quite acceptable, when it was accompanied by a classifying phrase 'greeted him by sucking'. In Ifugao a solution has been found in the expression 'the one I shall greet by smelling his face'. The Ifugao people do not themselves kiss, but they call foreign kissing 'smelling the face'.

Safely is surprisingly difficult to render literally. Certainly, the safety implied was not a matter of Jesus' own safety, as some translations have declared. Rather, it was a caution for the men to guard Jesus carefully lest he do something which would thwart their purposes. In Tzeltal this type of action is described as 'lead him away between persons', that is, guarded on all sides. In other instances, 'guard him carefully' would be an equivalent of the Greek term *asphalōs*.

45 *And when he came, he went up to him at once, and said, "Master!" And he kissed him.*

Text: After *rabbi* 'Master' *Textus Receptus* and Soden add another *rabbi*, which is omitted by all other editions of the Greek text.

Exegesis: *proselthōn* (cf. 1:31) 'approaching', 'drawing near'.

rabbi (cf. 9:5) 'Rabbi', 'Teacher'.

katephilēsen (only here in Mark) 'he kissed': this would seem to be the normal way in which a Rabbi was greeted. Lagrange cites a passage which speaks of one Rabbi greeting another affectionately by kissing him on the forehead. As distinguished from the simple *phileō* of the preceding verse, *kataphileō* is taken to mean 'kiss warmly', 'kiss affectionately' (cf. Weymouth, Goodspeed). The meaning 'kiss much' (ASV margin) is styled "very doubtful" by Moulton & Milligan, on the basis of the papyri evidence. It has been suggested (*Expository Times* 64.240, 1953) that the "sense of intense emotion" present in the verb is to be identified, in this passage, as that of repentance, on the part of Judas.

Translation: The pronouns *he...he...him* are not always clear in reference. Therefore, one may have to make certain substitutes, e.g. 'Judas...he...Jesus'.

Master, as a translation of *rabbi*, means much more than merely 'teacher'. The irony of this event is brought out more forcibly and accurately if some term meaning 'master', 'honored leader', or 'respected teacher' is employed.

For *kiss* see verse 44.

46 *And they laid hands on him and seized him.*

Exegesis: *epebalan* (cf. 4:37; with direct object, 11:7) 'they placed',

'they laid on': here in the sense of 'they laid hold of him', 'they grabbed him'.
ekratēsan (cf. v. 44; 1:31) 'they seized', 'they arrested'.

Translation: *They* may be rendered as 'the men there' or 'the people',
if the literal translation of *they* is misleading.

47 *But one of those who stood by drew his sword, and struck the*
slave of the high priest and cut off his ear.

Exegesis: *heis...tis* (cf. 5:22) 'a certain one': Lagrange thinks this
indicates that this person was known to the author.

tōn parestēkotōn (4:29) 'of those standing by', 'of those present' (for
this use of the perfect participle *hoi parestēkotes* 'bystanders', cf. 14:69,
70, 15:35). The vague language does not identify the man as a disciple,
and seems to exclude, perhaps purposely, such identification.

spasamenos (only here in Mark) 'drawing (his sword)': this does not
necessarily mean, strictly, 'drawing out of a scabbard'. It may mean
generally 'pulling' or 'brandishing'.

epaisen (only here in Mark) 'he struck', 'he hit': here with the resultant
meaning 'he wounded'.

ton doulon (cf. 10:44) 'the slave'.

tou archiereōs (cf. 2:17) 'of the high priest': here, of course, *the* high
priest of the time (identified in the other Gospels as Caiaphas).

apheilen (only here in Mark) 'he took away', 'he cut off'.

ōtarion (only here in Mark; the diminutive of *ous* 4:9) 'ear': though
the diminutive of *ous*, it is equal in meaning to it. Taylor suggests that
the lobe of the ear may be intended by the word here.

Translation: *Drew his sword* may be rendered as 'pulled out his sword'
or 'showed his sword'. In some languages, of course, *sword* is merely
'a huge knife' or *machete*.

It is not necessary to make a distinction between the attributives
employed in 'chief priests' and 'high priest'. (In Greek the terms are the
same; the only difference is the plural and singular contrast). In many
languages therefore chief priests are merely 'the big priests' and high
priest is 'the big priest'. In some instances, one may say 'the biggest priest'
for 'the high priest', since there was technically only one high priest at
a time. Of course, instead of 'big' one may use an equivalent of 'great',
'important', 'head', or 'high'.

Many societies distinguish carefully between servants and slaves, but
where this is not done, one may often employ certain descriptive terms,
e.g. 'one compelled to work without wages' or 'man who was owned by'.
In some languages the term used for the lowest grade of servants seems
to be a fitting equivalent of slave.

48 *And Jesus said to them, "Have you come out as against a rob-*
ber, with swords and clubs to capture me?

Exegesis: *apokritheis...eipen* (cf. 3 : 33) 'he answered', 'he said'.

hōs epi lēstēn 'as against a bandit', 'as (though you were coming out) against a robber'.

epi 'upon': here with hostile intent, 'against' (cf. Arndt & Gingrich III.1.a.δ,ε).

lēstēs (cf. 11:17) 'robber', 'bandit'.

exēlthate meta machairōn kai xulōn 'you came out (armed) with swords and clubs' (cf. v. 43).

sullabein (only here in Mark) 'to seize', 'to take', 'to apprehend': used of a prisoner, 'to arrest' (cf. Arndt & Gingrich 1.a.α).

Translation: *Said* may be rendered as 'asked'.

With swords and clubs must not be related to the word 'robber', as is sometimes done in literal translations. Moreover, in many languages one cannot say 'come out with swords and clubs', for this would mean 'accompanied by swords and clubs'. The only way to render this passage in some instances is 'have you come out carrying swords and clubs, as though you were going to capture me, just as you would a robber'.

Capture is equivalent to 'arrest', translatable in some languages as 'grab and tie'.

It is of interest that the Greek term *lēstēs* was often used in a technical sense of a rebel, one who defied the Roman power and was hence an outlaw, dependent upon robbery for existence. This makes all the more significant the contrast between Jesus and Barabbas, who was under condemnation as a *lēstēs*.

49 Day after day I was with you in the temple teaching, and you did not seize me. But let the scriptures be fulfilled."

Exegesis: *kath' hēmeran* 'daily', 'every day': the preposition *kata* has here the distributive force (cf. Arndt & Gingrich II.2.c). It has been suggested, however (*Expository Times* 63.354, 1951), that the phrase here means 'by day', 'in the day-time', as opposed to the night-time hour of the arrest.

pros humas 'with you', 'in your company': the preposition *pros* here indicates position, rather than motion (cf. 6:3, 9:19a; Arndt & Gingrich III.7; Moule *Idiom Book*, 52).

all' hina plērōthōsin hai graphai 'but (this has happened) in order that the Scriptures be fulfilled': by all translations this saying is punctuated as having been spoken by Jesus. Instead of taking *hina* here to indicate purpose (as do Arndt & Gingrich III.1), some commentators and translations (like RSV) take it to be imperatival: 'The Scriptures must be fulfilled!' (cf. Goodspeed; Moule *Idiom Book*, 144).

plēroō (cf. 1:15) 'fulfill'.

hai graphai (cf. 12:10; for the plural cf. 12:24) 'the Scriptures'.

Translation: *Day after day* is probably best taken as a distributive, translatable as 'many days' or 'on successive days', literally 'days, days' in some languages.

For *temple* see 11:11, and for *scriptures* see 12:10.

Let...be fulfilled should not be translated as a request for permission. The meaning is either 'the holy writings must be fulfilled' or 'this has happened so that the holy writings may be fulfilled'.

Fulfilled is an extremely difficult concept to translate in some languages. Actually, 'fulfilling writing' is quite impossible in certain instances, and one is obliged to render this passage as 'so that what is spoken of in the holy writings may happen' (or 'may occur').

50 And they all forsook him, and fled.

Exegesis: *aphentes* (cf. 1:18, 2:5) 'leaving', 'abandoning', 'forsaking'. *ephugon* (cf. 5:14) 'they fled'. *pantes* 'all', i.e. 'all *the disciples*'.

In this verse is to be found the meaning of *pantes skandalisthēsesthe* of v. 27.

Translation: While in many instances languages tend to render what is a subordinate construction in Greek by coordinate verbs implying sequence of action, there are times in which coordinate verbs must be incorporated into a subordinate type of construction, if, as in this case, the relationship is not one of sequence of events but of incorporated events; that is to say, the forsaking of Jesus was accomplished by the flight of the disciples. Accordingly, in Tzeltal this meaning is given as 'fleeing, they left him'.

51 And a young man followed him, with nothing but a linen cloth about his body; and they seized him,

Text: At the end of the verse *Textus Receptus*, Soden, and Vogels add *hoi neaniskoi* 'the young men', which is omitted by the majority of modern editions of the Greek text.

Exegesis: *neaniskos* (16:5) 'a young man'.

sunēkolouthei (cf. 5:37; cf. *akoloutheō* 1:18) 'he was following with (him)'.

peribeblēmenos sindona epi gumnou 'clothed with a linen (sheet) about his naked (body)'. Arndt & Gingrich (*periballō* 1.b.α) translate: 'who wore (nothing but) a linen cloth on his naked body'.

periballō (16:5) 'to place around': the verb is used of clothing 'to put on', 'to clothe with', and in the passive, as here, it means 'to be clothed with', 'to wear'. Field (*Notes*, 40) takes the word in its literal sense, 'with a sheet *wrapped about* his naked body'.

sindōn (14:52, 15:46) 'linen cloth': here either a 'sheet', or else a garment, the *chitōn* 'under garment' (cf. 6:9), made of the material (cf. Arndt & Gingrich). Lagrange conjectures that it was a flimsy sleeping garment.

epi gumnou 'on his naked body': here *to gumnon*, as a substantive, means 'naked *body*' (cf. Abbott-Smith; Arndt & Gingrich, 1). Moulton

& Milligan show, from the papyri, that the word may mean 'wearing only the *chitōn* [tunic]'. The meaning in this passage may be that the young man was wearing nothing except a linen tunic.

kratousin (cf. 1:31) 'they seize'.

Translation: *Followed him* should be understood in the sense of 'followed along with'.

Linen cloth is variously translated, either as 'a sheet' or 'a piece of white cloth' (Subanen, Barrow Eskimo), 'one layer of clothing' (Tzeltal), and 'a cloth' (Navajo).

They must refer to the men of the group who came out against Jesus, not to the immediately preceding third person plural pronoun which designates the disciples. Accordingly, this clause may be translated as 'some men there grabbed him'.

52 *but he left the linen cloth and ran away naked.*

Text: At the end of the verse *Textus Receptus*, Soden, Vogels, Merk, and Kilpatrick add *ap' autōn* 'from them', which is omitted by the majority of modern editions of the Greek text.

Exegesis: *katalipōn* (cf. 10:7) 'leaving', 'leaving behind'.

gumnos 'naked': here it is an adjective, modifying the subject of the verb.

ephugen (cf. v. 50) 'fled', 'ran away'.

Translation: *Left* must not be understood in the sense of 'laying the cloth down', as some translations imply. In Navajo the rendering is accurate and idiomatic, 'he ran out of the cloth red', in which 'red' is a term meaning 'naked'.

53 *And they led Jesus to the high priest; and all the chief priests and the elders and the scribes were assembled.*

Text: After *sunerchontai* 'they come together', *Textus Receptus*, Soden, Vogels, Souter, and Kilpatrick add *autō* 'to him', which is omitted by the majority of modern editions of the Greek text.

Exegesis: *sunerchontai* (cf. 3:20) 'they come together', 'they assemble', 'they gather': the verb here expresses the act of coming together, rather than describes the gathering as having taken place. Therefore, 'they came together' or 'they assembled themselves' is a better translation than RSV 'were assembled' (which is the meaning of *sunēchthēsan* in the parallel passage Mt. 26:57).

The other words in this verse have already been dealt with: for *apagō* 'lead off' cf. v. 44; for *ho archiereus* 'the high priest' cf. v. 47; for *hoi archiereis kai hoi presbuteroi kai hoi grammateis* 'the chief priests and the elders and the scribes' cf. 8:31.

Translation: For *high priest* and *chief priests* see verse 47; for *elders* see 8:31, and for *scribes* see 1:22.

Were assembled may be rendered as 'came together into an assembly', 'got together in a council', or 'came together to decide on the matter'.

54 And Peter had followed him at a distance, right into the court-yard of the high priest; and he was sitting with the guards, and warming himself at the fire.

Exegesis: *heōs esō eis tēn aulēn* literally 'until within into the courtyard'.

aulē (14:66, 15:14) 'inner court', 'courtyard': the enclosed area, open to the sky, and surrounded on the sides by buildings or porches. AV 'palace' is misleading (cf. Gould).

ēn sugkathēmenos (only here in Mark; cf. *kathēmai* 2:6) 'he was sitting with'.

tōn hupēretōn (14:65) 'the servants', 'the helpers': in all probability these were members of the Temple guard; therefore, as RSV has it, 'the guards'.

thermainomenos (14:67) 'warming himself': the auxiliary *ēn* 'he was' goes with this participle as well as with the previous one, 'he was sitting... and warming himself'.

pros to phōs literally 'at the light': here, however, the phrase means 'at the (light of the) fire' (cf. Moulton & Milligan for this use of *phōs* 'light', and see also Arndt & Gingrich 1.b.α). It has been suggested (*Expository Times* 68.27, 1956), that 'light' is here a mistranslation of the unpointed Hebrew word *'wr* which could be pointed *'or* 'light' or *'ur* 'fire'.

For *apo makrothen* 'from afar' cf. 5:6; *akoloutheō* 'follow' cf. 1:18.

Translation: *Followed him* must not be rendered so as to indicate Peter's favorable intent, but his evident distance from Jesus. In general one cannot use the same verb as may be employed, for example, in the words of Jesus *follow me* (1:17). At this point Peter was following along after the crowd, not in accompaniment with Jesus.

Right into... may be rendered as 'he went right on into', for 'at a distance' and 'right into' may be difficult to combine in a single clause in a receptor language.

In some languages one cannot speak of 'courtyard of the high priest', but only of 'courtyard of the buildings of the high priest', since the area surrounded by buildings is essentially relatable only to the buildings and they, in turn, to the high priest.

In most languages there is no problem involved in the description of Peter's being with the guards and warming himself, for it is implied that the guards were also warming themselves. In some languages, however, the contrast of pronominal construction is so great that Peter's action would be interpreted as being in contrast with the others. Hence, in Isthmus Zapotec one must say 'he with them was warming', thus including Peter.

461

55 *Now the chief priests and the whole council sought testimony against Jesus to put him to death; but they found none.*

Exegesis: *holon to sunedrion* (15:1; cf. the plural *sunedria* 13:9) 'the whole Sanhedrin', 'the entire (High) Council': the Sanhedrin was the supreme governing body of the Jews, presided over by the current high priest, possessing both spiritual (ecclesiastical) and juridical (political) powers.

ezētoun kata (cf. 3:22) 'they were seeking against'.

marturian (14:56, 69) 'witness', 'testimony'.

eis to thanatōsai auton 'to put him to death': the preposition *eis* 'into' with the infinitive of the verb, indicates here purpose—'they were seeking (adverse) testimony against Jesus in order to put him to death'.

thanatoō (cf. 13:12) 'put to death', 'hand over to be killed'.

kai ouch hēuriskon 'but they were not finding (it)': the *kai* is adversative.

Translation: *The whole council* is in some languages 'all the men who decided things' or 'all the important men', another way of designating the membership of the council.

Sought testimony against is a very compact phrase involving two quite separate processes: (1) the seeking of persons who might testify and (2) the testimony of the men against Jesus. Moreover, the preposition *against* implies the statements made by Jesus' accusers. Accordingly, in some languages this succinct expression must be somewhat expanded, e.g. 'looked for men who would accuse Jesus' (Zacapoastla Aztec) and 'sought testimony as to the sin of Jesus' (Tzeltal). In the first instance *testimony* is rendered as 'men who would accuse', supplying what is essentially a subject-verb expression for the event noun of Greek and English. In the second case, *against* is expanded so as to indicate the hostility of the testimony.

56 *For many bore false witness against him, and their witness did not agree.*

Exegesis: *epseudomarturoun* (cf. 10:19) 'they gave false testimony', 'they bore false witness'.

isai (14:59) 'equal', 'alike': the adjective is in the feminine nominative plural form, agreeing with *hai marturiai* 'the testimonies'. In the context the adjective means 'consistent', 'coherent': the accusations brought against Jesus by the witnesses were not consistent one with the other.

Translation: *Bore false witness against* may be rendered as 'spoke against him but they were lying' or 'they told lies about him' (Zacapoastla Aztec).

Their witness did not agree may be quite simply translated as 'they did not say the same thing' (Tepehua) or idiomatically as 'they did not mate their words' (Tzeltal).

57 *And some stood up and bore false witness against him, saying,*

Exegesis: *anastantes* (cf. 1:35) 'rising': here (as in 14:60) 'standing up'.

58 *"We heard him say, 'I will destroy this temple that is made with hands, and in three days I will build another, not made with hands.'"*

Exegesis: *hoti...hoti* 'that...that': both times the *hoti* is recitative, introducing direct speech.

katalusō (cf. 13:2) 'I will tear down', 'I will demolish', 'I will destroy'. On this saying, cf. further 15:29.

ton naon (15:29, 38) 'the sanctuary': it is generally assumed that *naos* refers to the central area of the Temple, the holy of holies, as distinct from the whole Temple area as such, referred to as the *hieron* (cf. 11:11).

cheiropoiēton (only here in Mark) 'hand made', 'built by men', i.e. material.

dia triōn hēmerōn (cf. 2:1 *di' hēmerōn*) 'after three days': cf. the similar phrase *meta treis hēmeras* (8:31, 9:31, 10:34).

acheiropoiēton (only here in Mark) 'not made by hand', 'built not by men', i.e. spiritual.

oikodomēsō (cf. 12:1) 'I will build', 'I will construct'.

On the use and meaning of the two adjectives 'hand made' and 'not hand made', cf. Lightfoot *Colossians*, commentary on 2:11.

Translation: *We heard him say* must in some languages be shifted to a paratactic construction of two subject-predicate constructions: 'we heard him; he said'.

For *temple* see 11:11, but note that in this context the central building is designated. Accordingly, one may often use 'this house of God', 'this dwelling of God', or 'this place of God', since all of these expressions may give rise to a double meaning, including not only the temple itself but Jesus' own person.

Made with hands is most often translated as 'built by men' or 'built by men's hands'. *Hands* is a figurative substitute for 'men'. *Not made with hands* may be rendered as a modifying clause, 'which men will not make .

59 *Yet not even so did their testimony agree.*

Exegesis: 'And not even in this manner was their witness consistent': for *isē* 'alike', 'the same' cf. v. 56; *marturia* 'witness', 'testimony' cf. v. 55.

Translation: In instances in which *testimony* must be translated as a verb, one may need to recast the sentence as 'but even in what they said they didn't say the same thing' or 'even these men who spoke did not say the same words'.

60 *And the high priest stood up in the midst, and asked Jesus, "Have you no answer to make? What is it that these men testify against you?"*

Verse punctuation: The majority of editions of the Greek text, commentaries, and translations, divide the words of the high priest into two questions, as does RSV; some editions of the Greek text (Tischendorf, Nestle) and some translations (Vulgate, Berkeley, Zürich, Synodale, Brazilian) read the same words as one single question, thus: "Have you no answer to give to what these men are testifying against you?"

Exegesis: *anastas...eis meson* 'standing up...(and going) to the center'; cf. Weymouth, 'stood up, and, advancing into the midst of them all...'; Manson, 'stood up in the presence of the council...'

anistēmi (cf. 1:35) 'rise': as in v. 57, 'stand up'.

eis meson (cf. 3:3, 9:36) 'in the center', 'in the presence of everybody'.

ouk apokrinē (cf. 8:4) 'do you not answer...?'

ti 'what?': as the first word in the second question of the high priest, the interrogative has the meaning 'What is it that (these men testify against you)?' Instead of *ti* Kilpatrick has *hoti*, translated, 'why...?' (BFBS).

katamarturousin (only here in Mark) 'they are bearing witness against', 'they testify against'.

Translation: For *high priest* see 14:47.

No answer to make may be rendered as 'are you unable to answer' or 'have you no words with which you can answer'.

Testify against may be, as noted in verse 55, 'accuse you of', 'speak words against', or 'talk about your sin'.

61 *But he was silent and made no answer. Again the high priest asked him, "Are you the Christ, the Son of the Blessed?"*

Exegesis: *esiōpa* (cf. 3:4) 'he remained silent', 'he maintained silence'.

ouk apekrinato ouden literally 'he did not answer nothing': in Greek the double negative is emphatic (and not, as in some languages, equivalent to an affirmative).

su ei ho christos...; 'are you the Messiah?': the personal pronoun *su* 'you' is emphatic (cf. Synodale *C'est toi qui es le Christ...?*). Taylor suggests it may be also contemptuous.

ho christos (cf. 1:1) 'the Messiah', 'the Anointed One': here, as in 8:29, 12:35, 13:21, a title.

As Moule remarks (*Idiom Book*, 158), no indication is given in the question of the answer expected.

ho huios tou eulogētou 'the Son of the Blessed (One)'.

ho huios (cf. 1:1) 'the Son'.

ho eulogētos (only here in Mark; cf. *eulogeō* 6:41) 'the Blessed One': this is a familiar Jewish way of referring to God, avoiding reference to

464

the holy, unpronounceable name of God by using a title. The whole phrase usually employed was 'the Holy One, Blessed is He' (cf. Dalman *Words*, 200). In the New Testament *eulogētos* is always used of God (Lk. 1:68, Rom. 1:25, 9:5, 2 Cor. 1:3, 11:31, Eph. 1:3, 1 Pet. 1:3).

Translation: *He was silent and made no answer* is in a sense repetitious, but the redundancy is purposeful and emphatic, and hence should be treated as such in any translation, e.g. 'he kept silent; he did not speak' or 'he did not open his mouth; he did not answer with a single word'.

The Son of the Blessed is an extremely complex phrase and subject to ready misinterpretation. For example, in many languages this passage has been understood to be a reference to the blessed Virgin (see *The Bible Translator*, 2.133, 1951). In such instances one may be required to add the word 'God', e.g. 'Son of God, who is blessed'.

For a discussion of some of the problems involving the translation of *bless* see 6:41 and 11:9-10, but note that in this passage *bless* refers to an activity of a lower personage to a higher one, namely, man's blessing of God. Blessing in this type of context is often rendered (1) by a term such as 'praise' or 'honor', or (2) by direct discourse, e.g. 'say: he is very good'. The following translations of this expression are typical, e.g. 'Son of the honored one' (Ifugao), 'Son of God whom people worship' (Putu), 'Son of one very much his goodness is said about him by us' (Tzeltal), 'Son of the one whom we praise' (Cashibo, Tarahumara), and 'Son of the one people say, He is very good' (Tzotzil).

62 And Jesus said, "I am; and you will see the Son of man sitting at the right hand of Power, and coming with the clouds of heaven."

Exegesis: *egō eimi* (cf. 13:6) 'I am': it is probable that the words carry a meaning that goes beyond a simple affirmative answer to the question (cf. BFBS 'I am He'). As a set phrase (cf. their use in 13:6) the words carry an overtone of Messianic and divine self-identification.

opsesthe 'you shall see': this is addressed directly to the whole council as a statement of fact (in 13:26 *opsontai* is impersonal, 'they shall see', i.e. 'men shall see'). As in the parallel statement in 9:1 so here the verb 'see' should be translated unequivocally to indicate an actual experience on the part of those addressed.

ton huion tou anthrōpou ek dexiōn kathēmenon tēs dunameōs 'the Son of man sitting at the right hand of the Power': as in 12:36, the words are a reference to Ps. 110:1.

ho huios tou anthrōpou (cf. 2:10) 'the Son of man'.

ek dexiōn (cf. 10:37, 12:36) 'at the right (hand)': as in both other passages, this is the place of authority and power.

hē dunamis (cf. 5:30) 'the Power': as in the case of 'the Blessed One' in the previous verse, this is a title for God (cf. Dalman *Words*, 200-202).

erchomenon meta tōn nephelōn tou ouranou 'coming with the clouds of heaven': as in 13:26, these words are a reference to Dan. 7:13 (the

Hebrew has 'with the clouds of heaven' while the LXX has 'upon the clouds'; in 13:26 the expression is 'in clouds').

Translation: Though the words *I am* may imply a subtle allusion to the divine self-revelation (cf. Exodus 3:14), it is difficult, if not impossible, to reproduce this type of allusion in a receptor language. In most languages Jesus' reply must be either (1) an affirmative such as 'yes' or 'that is right' or (2) a declaration such as 'I am the Christ'. In most instances it is quite impossible to translate literally 'I am' because the copulative verb requires some type of so-called predicate complement.

As in other instances of the use of *the Son of man* in this first person relationship, it may be necessary to say 'me who am the Son of man' or 'me as the Son of man'.

Power cannot be used as a substitute for God in some languages since not only is the figure 'right hand of the Power' unintelligible, but 'power' does not exist apart from a possessor, e.g. 'God who has power' (Tzeltal) or 'the one who has power' (Mazahua).

Where there are two processes (namely, 'sitting' and 'coming') as objects of the verb 'see', it may be necessary to repeat the verb in order to avoid the implication that the Son of man comes in a seated position. Hence, the rendering may be 'see the Son of man; he will be sitting at the right hand of God who has power. And you will see him coming...'

With the clouds of heaven implies the position of the Son of man, not the fact that he will be coming, having in his possession the clouds of heaven. Moreover, one must not render *with* in merely the sense of accompaniment, i.e. that Jesus will be accompanying the clouds of heaven. In many instances 'in' is a more correct translation of the Greek *meta* than a presumably more literal rendering which may, however, have quite different denotations in such a context.

63 And the high priest tore his mantle, and said, "Why do we still need witnesses?

Exegesis: *diarēxas tous chitōnas autou* 'tearing his (own) garments'.
diarēssō (only here in Mark) 'rend', 'burst', 'tear'.

hoi chitōnes (cf. 6:9) 'the tunics': as Arndt & Gingrich remark the word is here probably used in a general way for 'clothes', 'garments', rather than strictly with reference to the under-garments (the parallel Mt. 26:65 has *ta himatia* 'the garments'). RSV 'mantle' is inaccurate: cf. 'clothes' (Moffatt, Williams, BFBS, ASV), 'vestments' (Montgomery), 'garments' (Weymouth, Manson), 'clothing' (Goodspeed). The gesture of tearing one's garments was indicative of sorrow or horror and, in the case of judicial proceedings, such as this one, in tearing his garments the high priest indulged in a formal ceremonial act, minutely prescribed by tradition.

chreian echomen (cf. 2:17) 'we have need of'.
marturōn (only here in Mark) 'witnesses'.

Translation: For *high priest* see 14:47.

Tore must not imply some accidental tearing, but a deliberate, planned tearing as a gesture of consummate indignation. Such an action may not be readily understandable to people in other cultures, but the context is such as to prevent any very wrong interpretation of the action.

Mantle should be translated by the most generic term for 'clothes'.

Still need witnesses is equivalent in some languages to 'need more people to speak against him' or 'require more men to say what they know about him'.

64 *You have heard his blasphemy. What is your decision?" And they all condemned him as deserving death.*

Exegesis: *tēs blasphēmias* (cf. 3:28) 'the blasphemy': impious speech against God.

ti humin phainetai; 'what does it seem to you?', 'how does it appear to you?' (cf. Arndt & Gingrich *phainō* 2.g).

katekrinan (cf. 10:33) 'they condemned'.

enochon (cf. 3:29) 'liable of', 'worthy of', 'deserving of': here the word denotes the punishment (cf. Arndt & Gingrich 2.b.α).

Translation: For *blasphemy* see 2:7, but note that in this passage it is not necessary to interpret *blasphemy* in the technical sense of 'making oneself equal with God'. It is quite enough to render this passage as 'the evil words he has spoken' or 'you have heard him speak against God'. In Tzeltal this is rendered as 'you have heard him, he's against God'.

What is your decision is often translatable either as 'what do you think' or 'what do you say?'

Condemned him as deserving death involves a number of complex relationships of events, rendered in some instances by paratactic combinations, e.g. 'condemned him, they said, He should be killed', or 'condemned him and decided that he should be killed'. *Death* must be interpreted usually in the sense of 'be killed', not merely as 'to die'.

65 *And some began to spit on him, and to cover his face, and to strike him, saying to him, "Prophesy!" And the guards received him with blows.*

Text: Instead of *elabon* 'they received' of all modern editions of the Greek text, *Textus Receptus* has *eballon* 'they struck'.

Exegesis: *emptuein* (cf. 10:34) 'to spit upon'.

perikaluptein (only here in Mark) 'to cover', 'to cover over'.

kolaphizein (only here in Mark) 'to strike', 'to beat': this verb is used of beating with the closed fist, or the back of the hand (cf. Lagrange).

prophēteuson (cf. 7:6) 'prophesy!', 'guess!', 'reveal it!': the meaning, of course (as the parallels Mt. 26:68, Luke 22:64 make explicit), is 'reveal who it is that struck you!'

hoi hupēretai (cf. v. 54) 'the servants', 'the guards'.

rapismasin auton elabon 'treated him to blows': this is a Latin collo-quialism, *verberibus eum acceperunt* (cf. Moule *Idiom Book*, 192), describing the way in which the guards dealt with Jesus.

rapisma (only here in Mark) 'blow': although it may mean a blow with a club or whip (cf. Arndt & Gingrich), here it would almost certainly mean a blow with the open hand, a slap (cf. Field *Notes*, 105-6; Moulton & Milligan).

Translation: *Cover his face* could have been either with a cloth or with their hands; the text does not specify.

Prophesy must in this text be understood in a very specific sense, e.g. 'tell who hit you' (Tzeltal) or 'say who did it' (Ifugao). The technical meaning of prophesy must generally be avoided in this context or the real meaning of the passage is likely to be lost.

Only rarely can the phrase *received him with blows* be translated literally. The meaning is 'beat him up', a common enough practice among bullies, whether in or out of military uniform.

66 *And as Peter was below in the courtyard, one of the maids of the high priest came;*

Exegesis: *kai ontos tou Petrou* (cf. 14:3) 'and while Peter was': the participial clause indicates time.

katō (cf. 15:38) 'down', 'below', 'beneath': from this word it is to be inferred that the interrogation of Jesus was taking place in a room above the courtyard; Lagrange suggests the great hall on the second level.

aulē (cf. v. 54) 'courtyard'.

mia 'one': as often in Mark, the numeral has the indefinite sense, 'some-one'. The expression *mia tōn paidiskōn* means merely 'a maid'.

paidiskē (14:69) 'servant girl', 'female slave', employed in domestic service (cf. Swete).

Translation: *Maids of the high priest* should not be translated in such a way as to imply any illicit relationship, as is sometimes the case. The problem may be resolved in some languages by saying 'a maid who worked for the high priest'.

67 *and seeing Peter warming himself, she looked at him, and said, "You also were with the Nazarene, Jesus."*

Exegesis: *thermainomenon* (cf. v. 54) 'warming himself'.

emblepsasa (cf. 8:25) 'looking on (him)', 'looking closely at (him)', 'fixing her gaze upon (him)': this participle, in contrast with the first one (*idousa* 'seeing'), indicates a more prolonged scrutiny (cf. the use of the verb in 10:21, 27).

kai su 'you too', 'you also'.

tou Nazarēnou (cf. 10:47) 'the Nazarene': it is probable that in the other three places in Mark where the word occurs (1:24, 10:47, 16:6)

468

it should be translated as here, 'the Nazarene', and not simply as a geographical designation, 'of Nazareth'. Here, in conjunction with *tou Iēsou* 'Jesus', the meaning is 'the Nazarene, (even) Jesus'; cf. Montgomery 'that Nazarene, Jesus'; Lagrange *avec le Nazaréen, avec Jésus*.

Translation: It is essential that the two verbs *seeing* and *looked* are not translated as mere repetitions of the same action. In the first instance the maid saw that Peter was there warming himself. In the second case, 'she looked very closely at him' or 'she examined him'.

Though it is true that *Nazarene* probably implies more than mere geographical origin, in most languages there is no way in which a derivative adjectival form such as 'Nazarene' can carry the implications of the Greek text. Accordingly, 'that man from Nazareth, that Jesus' may be the only equivalent. In some languages, however, the appositive elements must be reversed, 'with Jesus, that man from Nazareth', or if a relative clause is required, 'with Jesus, who is that man from Nazareth'. In the use of 'that man from' or 'the one from' one may attempt to approximate something of the articular construction in Greek 'the Nazarene', whereas merely 'Jesus from Nazareth' would not carry quite the same range of meaning.

68 *But he denied it, saying, "I neither know nor understand what you mean." And he went out into the gateway.*

Text: At the end of the verse *kai alektōr ephōnēsen* 'and a cock crowed' is included by the great majority of editions of the Greek text; it is omitted, however, by Nestle, Westcott and Hort (and RSV), on the not inconsiderable witness of codices Vaticanus and Sinaiticus, other uncial manuscripts, and some early versions. Internal evidence also favors the omission of the phrase.

Exegesis: *ērnēsato* (14:70; cf. *aparneomai* 8:34) 'he denied'; here, as for *aparneomai* in v. 30, the meaning is 'repudiate', 'disown' (cf. Arndt & Gingrich 3.a). BFBS understands the verb to have reference to Jesus, translating, 'But he disowned Him...'

oute oida oute epistamai 'I neither know nor understand': it is to be doubted whether any distinction is to be made between the two verbs, *oida* (cf. 4:13) 'I know', the verb commonly used in Mark, and *epistamai* 'I understand', used only here in Mark (cf. Lagrange). Some commentators suggest the meaning to be 'I neither know *him*, nor understand *what you mean*': while this makes good sense it requires reading into the verse the personal pronoun 'him' which is not there, nor is necessarily implied. Some translations (Moffatt, Montgomery, Weymouth) divide the words into two separate affirmations, 'I do not know. I do not understand...'

oute...oute (cf. 12:25) 'neither...nor'.

su ti legeis 'what you are saying', 'what you mean'. In the margin of their text Westcott and Hort suggest this may be taken as a separate question, 'What are you saying?' 'What do you mean?', a suggestion

Moffatt and Weymouth have incorporated into their translations (cf. also Rawlinson). Black (*Aramaic*, 61) supports Torrey's conjecture that instead of *ti* 'what' the correct rendering of the underlying Aramaic *di* would have been *tis* 'who', i.e. 'I neither know nor am I acquainted *with him of whom you speak*'. This conjecture, however, has been contested on the ground that the Greek text as it stands, vividly reflects the uncertainty and confusion of the apostle (cf. *Expository Times* 67.341, 1956).

exēlthen exo eis to proaulion 'he went out (of the courtyard) into the passageway (leading to the gate)'.

proaulion (only here in the N.T.) is the 'forecourt' or 'passageway' leading from the gateway (*pulōn*) to the courtyard (*aulē*).

[*kai alektōr ephōnēsen* 'and a cock crowed': cf. v. 30.]

Translation: *Denied it* must refer to the immediately preceding statement made by the maid. In some languages the proper equivalent is merely 'he said, No'. In others one may translate 'he said that was not true'.

Know and understand what you mean may be variously translated, depending primarily upon one's exegesis of the passage in question (see above). *What you mean* may be 'what you are saying' or 'what you are trying to say', depending upon receptor language usage.

69 **And the maid saw him, and began again to say to the bystanders, "This man is one of them."**

Exegesis: *hē paidiskē* 'the (same) maid': this is the same one referred to in v. 66; cf. Synodale *cette servante*.

tois parestōsin (cf. v. 47) 'to the bystanders', 'to those present'.

hoti 'that' is recitative, introducing direct speech.

Translation: Though *one of them* might be a little ambiguous, the context is generally quite sufficient to make the reference clear, and thus to avoid the necessity of saying 'one of the disciples' or 'one of Jesus' men'. However, in some instances one must employ 'his companion' or 'his associate' (Tzeltal).

70 **But again he denied it. And after a little while again the bystanders said to Peter, "Certainly you are one of them; for you are a Galilean."**

Text: At the end of the verse *kai hē lalia sou homoiazei* 'for your speech is like (the speech of Galileans)' is added by *Textus Receptus* and included in brackets by Soden and Taylor; it is omitted, however, by the majority of modern editions of the Greek text.

Exegesis: *ērneito* (cf. v. 68) 'he was denying': the imperfect tense here, in contrast to the aorist tense in v. 68, may portray the denial as being repeated; cf. Weymouth, 'he repeatedly denied it'. BFBS (again cf. v. 68), 'But he disowned Him again.'

meta mikron (cf. 14:35) 'after a little (while)' (cf. Arndt & Gingrich *mikros* 3.e).

kai gar Galilaios ei 'for you also are a Galilean': the *kai* 'also' should not be omitted (as done by RSV).

Galilaios (only here in Mark) 'a Galilean', 'a man from Galilee'.

Translation: *Again he denied it* may be rendered as 'again he said it was not so' or 'again he declared that it was not true'.

One of them is rendered as 'one with them' in some languages, since association is described as being 'with' a group rather than 'of' it.

Galilean is generally rendered as 'a man from Galilee' or 'Galilee is your land'.

71 **But he began to invoke a curse on himself and to swear, "I do not know this man of whom you speak."**

Exegesis: *anathematizein* (only here in Mark) 'to invoke anathema', 'to devote to destruction', 'to put under the curse': the verb means to pronounce *anathema* (Hebrew *ḥerem*), i.e. 'devoted to destruction', upon someone, in this case on the speaker himself. 'May I be accursed if (what I say is not true)!' For instances of this cf. 1 Sam. 20:13, 2 Sam. 3:9, Acts 23:12.

omnunai (cf. 6:23) 'to swear', 'to put oneself on oath': neither one of the two verbs here employed would suggest vulgarity or profanity on the part of Peter (cf. Gould); they are rather, on his part, expressive and solemn protestations of the truth of his assertion.

Translation: In most societies there is some means whereby a person may put himself under a curse if his statement is not true, e.g. 'said that he wanted God to punish him if it were not so' (Pame). However, in some languages the description of such a process would take a paragraph, since curses are not normally invoked as proof of one's veracity. In these instances, 'declare with solemn words' or 'say with very strong words' may be the closest parallel.

Curse and *swear* are distinct processes, even though the witness of God or supernatural sanctions are invoked in both instances. In the first case, God is asked to punish one for not telling the truth, and in the second, God is asked to be a witness of the truth, e.g. 'God truly sees me that I don't know the one you say' (Tzeltal).

72 **And immediately the cock crowed a second time. And Peter remembered how Jesus had said to him, "Before the cock crows twice, you will deny me three times." And he broke down and wept.**

Text: *Textus Receptus* and Soden omit *euthus* 'immediately', which is included by all other editions of the Greek text.

Instead of *hōs* 'how' of the majority of modern editions of the Greek text, *Textus Receptus* has the relative *hou* 'which' (agreeing with *tou rēmatos* 'the saying', in the genitive case, instead of *to rēma* 'the saying' in the accusative case, of the genuine text), and Soden has *ho* 'which' (agreeing with *to rēma*).

Exegesis: *ek deuterou* 'for the second time', 'again' (cf. Arndt & Gingrich *deuteros* 4).

alektōr ephōnēsen 'a cock crowed': here and in v. 68 (if genuine) the words are meant quite literally (cf. v. 30; see Rawlinson).

anemnēsthē (cf. 11:21) 'he was reminded', 'he remembered'.

to rēma (cf. 9:32) 'the word', 'the saying'.

hōs (cf. 4:27) 'how': indicates the thing which Peter remembered, being thus, in a general way, equivalent to *hoti* (cf. Arndt & Gingrich IV. 4); as Thayer notes, however (*hōs* I.6), the emphasis is not on the thing remembered itself, but on the mode or quality of it. BFBS gives it a temporal sense, *'when* Jesus had said...'

hoti 'that' is recitative, introducing direct speech: for the saying of Jesus, here repeated, cf. v. 30.

kai epibalōn eklaien 'and he broke down and cried' (cf. 5:38 for *klaiō* 'cry'): there is no agreement on the meaning of *epibalōn*. (1) *'He began to cry'* is a meaning supported by the early versions, and preferred by Arndt & Gingrich (*epiballō* 2.b): cf. Vulgate, Luther, Synodale; (2) in a stronger sense, *'he set to* and wept', *'he burst* into tears,' is supported by an example from the papyri quoted by Moulton *Prolegomena*, 131f. (cf. Moulton & Milligan), and is preferred by RSV, Moffatt, Manson, BFBS, Lagrange (cf. also *Expository Times* 61.160, 1950, where another passage is quoted which supports this meaning of the word); (3) *'he thought on it* and wept', is a sense which assumes that an object, such as 'mind' ('he set *his mind* to it') is implied: this meaning is adopted by AV, ASV, Weymouth, Montgomery, Berkeley, Brazilian, Williams (cf. Gould and cf. also Liddell and Scott); (4) 'he *covered his head* and wept' is strongly defended by Field (*Notes*, 41-43) with his usual impressive array of supporting evidence; it is accepted by Rawlinson, and has been adopted by Zürich, *Und er verhüllte sich und weinte*; (5) 'he threw himself on the ground' is Turner's understanding of the phrase; (6) 'he dashed out' is Black's conjecture (*Aramaic*, 78f.). Before such a display of different translations no final certainty can be reached. The most one can say for RSV is that it has as much to commend it as some, and more than others.

Translation: *A second time* must not be translated to mean that the cock crowed twice at that time, but for the second time the cock crowed, implying that the first time preceded this particular moment. The problem is entirely parallel to *crows twice*, where the meaning is not of a cock which crows twice in immediate succession, but which for the second time during the night undertakes to crow.

Deny me is often rendered as 'say that you do not know me' or 'say, I do not know him'.

The rendering of *broke down and wept* is dependent entirely upon the exegesis which is adopted in the case of *epibalōn*. The one caution to observe is not to attempt to translate literally such phrases as 'broke down' and 'burst into'.

CHAPTER FIFTEEN

1 *And as soon as it was morning the chief priests, with the elders and the scribes, and the whole council held a consultation; and they bound Jesus and led him away and delivered him to Pilate.*

Text: Instead of *sumboulion hetoimasantes* 'reaching a decision' of Tischendorf, Nestle, Soden, Kilpatrick, and Merk, the majority of editions of the Greek text have *sumboulion poiēsantes* 'holding a counsel', which is the text of RSV. The external evidence does not seem decisive either way (some mss. and versions have *epoiēsan*); internal evidence would prefer *poiēsantes* as the "harder" reading, more likely, therefore, to be original.

Exegesis: *prōi* (cf. 1:35) 'early', 'in the morning': apparently it is meant to indicate here the sunrise.

sumboulion poiēsantes 'holding a counsel', 'holding a consultation': so the majority of the Greek texts (see *Text*, above). The Nestle reading *sumboulion hetoimasantes* means 'reaching a decision', 'formulating a plan' (cf. Arndt & Gingrich *sumboulion* 1).

sumboulion (cf. 3:6) 'counsel', 'consultation'.

hoi archiereis meta tōn presbuterōn kai grammateōn (cf. 8:31) 'the chief priests with the elders and scribes'.

holon ton sunedrion (cf. 14:55) 'the whole Council', 'the entire Sanhedrin'.

dēsantes...apēnegkan 'binding...they took away', 'they bound...and took away'.

deō (cf. 3:27) 'bind', 'tie', 'fasten'.

apopherō (only here in Mark; cf. *pherō* 1:32) 'lead away', 'take away': Moulton & Milligan cite the use of the verb in the papyri of forcible removal (cf. Arndt & Gingrich 1.a.β).

paredōkan Pilatō 'they delivered (him) to Pilate': for *paradidōmi* 'hand over', 'deliver' cf. 1:14. Pontius Pilate was the Roman procurator of Judea A.D. 25/6-36, governing under the *legatus* of Syria. His official residence was in Caesarea, on the sea coast.

Translation: Translation notes are to be found on several of the key words: *chief priests* (2:26, 8:31, and 14:47), *elders* (8:31), and *scribes* (1:22).

And the whole council may constitute a problem in some languages since the use of *and* in the meaning of 'with' or 'in company with' may imply that the chief priests, elders, and scribes were not themselves members of the council. To correct this meaning of the conjunction, one may translate as 'and all the rest of the members of the council'.

Council is not usually difficult to translate since such institutions exist in almost all societies. Some typical renderings are 'officials who gather together' (Tzeltal), 'those who think together' (Zoque), and 'those who take charge of the affairs' (Ifugao).

Held a consultation may be either 'thought about the matter together' or 'talked about the matter'.

Delivered him may be equivalent to 'turned him over to' or 'put him in the custody of'.

Led him away must be translated in such a manner as to be applicable to prisoners, and not as in some translations connoting the leading of children.

2 And Pilate asked him, "Are you the King of the Jews?" And he answered him, "You have said so."

Exegesis: *epērōtēsen* (cf. 5:39) 'he asked', 'he inquired'.

su ei...; 'are you...?': the personal pronoun is emphatic, indicating either surprise or disdain (cf. Gould).

ho basileus tōn Ioudaiōn (15:9, 12, 18, 26; cf. *ho basileus Israēl* 15:32) 'the King of the Jews'.

su legeis literally 'you are saying (it)'. By many commentators and translators this is taken to be an unequivocal affirmative, 'Yes', 'Certainly', 'I am' (Goodspeed, Moffatt, Weymouth, Williams, Berkeley, Montgomery; Zürich translates 'You say it' and adds, in a footnote, "This means: Yes, I am"). Goodspeed (*Problems*, 64-68) argues that a comparison between Jesus' answer to the high priest in Mark 14:62 'I am', and in Matthew 26:64 'You said (it)', proves that the expression *su legeis* (in Matthew *su eipas*) must mean 'I am (as you say)'. This, however, is to argue in a circle, on the unproved assumption that Mt. 26:64 is meant to convey the same meaning as Mk. 14:62 (which immediately raises the question, "Why, then, did not Matthew use the same expression as Mark?").

These and other considerations (cf. Moulton *Prolegomena*, 86; Morton Smith *Journal of Biblical Literature*, 64.506-10, 1945; Swete, Rawlinson, Taylor) would indicate that a literal translation, 'You said it', 'The statement is yours', is perhaps better. Notwithstanding efforts to the contrary, it has not been established that the Greek phrase represents a Jewish form of assent (cf. Rawlinson, who thus paraphrases: "The assertion is yours. I neither affirm nor deny it"). Thus the early versions (Vulgate *Tu dicis*—which Knox translates 'Thy own lips have said it'; Syriac Peshitto) and later translations (Luther, Synodale, Brazilian, ASV, BFBS, Manson) agree with RSV's 'You have said so' (Arndt & Gingrich *legō* II.1.e translate, 'That is what you maintain').

Translation: Where a technical term for *King* does not exist, one may use a descriptive substitute, based on function, e.g. 'one who rules over', 'one who bosses', or 'one who is the big chief of'.

Jews may require in a receptor language a classifier, e.g. 'Jew people'.

You have said so is variously translated, depending upon one's exegesis of the clause. In some instances, however, 'that is what you say' has seemed to translators to be entirely too evasive, if not disrespectful. Accordingly, some have attempted to combine possible meanings in some such form as 'I am as you say', an interpretation of affirmative assent with somewhat more of the literal form of the Greek clause.

3 And the chief priests accused him of many things. 4 And Pilate again asked him, "Have you no answer to make? See how many charges they bring against you."

Text: In v. 4 instead of *katēgorousin* 'they bring charges against' of the modern editions of the Greek text, *Textus Receptus* has *katamarturousin* 'they are witnessing against'.

Exegesis: *katēgoroun* (cf. 3:2) 'they were bringing charges against': this is a technical term used of bringing charges in court against someone.

polla (cf. 1:45) may be adverbial 'much', 'strongly', 'insistently', or adjectival 'many things' (RSV), 'many accusations' (Moffatt).

ouk apokrinē ouden; (cf. 14:60) 'do you answer nothing?', 'do you not answer anything?'

ide (cf. 2:24) 'see!', 'look!'

posa (cf. 6:38) 'how many (things)', 'how many (charges) they bring against you': *posa* parallels *polla* of v. 3.

Translation: *Accused him of many things* may be translated as 'said that he had done many bad things'.

In some instances one may not speak of 'having...an answer', but rather 'being able...to answer'. Accordingly, one may say, 'Are you not able to reply to these accusations' or 'are you unable to defend yourself against what they say'.

See cannot be translated literally in many languages since what occurred was 'heard', not 'seen'. Hence, one may render this passage as 'hear how many accusations...'

5 But Jesus made no further answer, so that Pilate wondered.

Exegesis: *ouketi ouden apokrithē* 'no longer did he answer anything', 'he did not answer anything any more'.

apokrinomai (cf. 8:4) 'answer', 'reply'.

hōste thaumazein 'so as to marvel', 'so that he marvelled': for this construction, indicating result, cf. 1:27.

thaumazō (cf. 5:20) 'marvel', 'wonder'.

Translation: *Made...answer* may refer either to the accusations or to Pilate's question. In the first instance, an equivalent may be 'he did not say another word to defend himself'; in the second, one may translate as 'he did not answer Pilate anything further'.

Wondered implies surprise on the part of Pilate at such unusual behavior, almost equivalent to 'Pilate was dumbfounded'.

6 *Now at the feast he used to release for them one prisoner whom they asked.*

Exegesis: *kata de heortēn* 'now at every (Passover) feast', 'now at each feast (of the Passover)': the preposition *kata* is distributive (cf. *kath' hēmeran* 'every day' 14:49), indicating *every* feast, and not just this particular one (cf. Lagrange; cf. Arndt & Gingrich *kata* II.2.c).

heortē (cf. 14:2) 'feast'.

apeluen (cf. 6:36) 'he released': RSV correctly gives the force of the imperfect 'he used to release', indicating habitual action (cf. also *epoiei* in v. 8).

hena desmion 'one prisoner', 'any prisoner': the cardinal 'one' is here used as an indefinite pronoun, 'any one' or 'some one'.

desmios (only here in Mark; cf. *deō* 3:27) 'prisoner'.

parētounto (only here in Mark; cf. *aiteō* 6:22) 'they asked (for)', 'they requested'.

Translation: *Now* is not to be interpreted as a temporal adverb, but as a transitional particle, equivalent in many languages to 'but' or 'however'.

At the feast must not be translated in such a way as to mean that Pilate released a person at the place where the people were gathered together eating. It is better to treat this as a temporal reference, e.g. 'at the time when the people feasted' or 'at that time when the people were feasting'. When, however, *feast* is translated as a verb, it should agree in aspect (or tense) with the verb 'used to release', for the meaning here is an habitual, repeated action, which occurred each year.

Release... one prisoner is translatable in some languages as 'to make go free... one person in jail' or 'to let go out from jail... a person'.

Whom they asked may require some expansion, e.g. 'whom they asked Pilate for' or 'whom they asked Pilate to set free'.

7 *And among the rebels in prison, who had committed murder in the insurrection, there was a man called Barabbas.*

Exegesis: *ho legomenos Barabbas* 'the one called Barabbas': only here is the passive present participle of *legō*, with the meaning 'called', 'named', used in Mark (cf. Arndt & Gingrich *legō* II.3).

Barabbas 'Barabbas': the Greek name represents the Aramaic *baraba'* 'son of Abba', or 'son of the father'.

ēn... dedemenos 'was bound': in accordance with Marcan style (cf. *ēn... endedumenos* 'was clothed' 1:6), this is to be taken as a verbal phrase and not to be split up into two verbs indicating two different actions (as done by RSV). Cf. C. H. Turner *Journal of Theological Studies* 28.350 (1926-7). The clause would then read, 'Now the man called Barabbas was bound with the insurrectionists, those who in the insurrection had committed murder'.

stasiastōn (only here in the N.T.) 'rebels', 'revolutionaries', 'insurrectionists'.

en tē stasei (only here in Mark) 'in the rebellion', 'in the uprising', 'in the insurrection': the event is referred to in a definite way as though known to the readers, without being further identified.

phonon (cf. 7:21) 'murder'.

pepoiēkeisan 'they had committed': the full force of the pluperfect is to be observed here, referring to an action terminated in the past (cf. *dedōkei* 14:44).

Translation: *Rebels* may be translated in some languages as 'men who fought against the government' (Ifugao).

Committed murder is often equivalent merely to 'killed a man', or 'killed some people'.

Insurrection is usually quite easily translated since such events are common enough in various parts of the world. However, there are various ways of rendering such a term 'beating the government's mouth' (Putu), 'fighting against rulers' (Navajo), and 'riot' (Zoque).

The position of the logical subject *Barabbas* at the end of the verse is not easily reproduced in many languages. Accordingly, one may have to recast the sentence as 'a man called Barabbas was in prison among the rebels, who had killed people in an uprising against the government'.

8 *And the crowd came up and began to ask Pilate to do as he was wont to do for them.*

Text: Instead of *anabas* 'coming up' of the modern editions of the Greek text, *Textus Receptus* has *anaboēsas* 'crying out'.

After *kathōs* 'even as' *Textus Receptus* and Merk add *aei* 'on every occasion', which is omitted by the majority of modern editions of the Greek text.

Exegesis: *anabas* (cf. 1:10) 'coming up', 'going up': the verb describes the movement of the crowd up to Pilate, in the praetorium (v. 16). The exact location of Pilate's residence, in Jerusalem, is a matter of dispute.

ērxato aiteisthai kathōs epoiei autois '(the crowd) began to ask (Pilate to do) as he (always) did for them': in order to fill out the meaning of the Greek, which is concisely stated, it is necessary to add the words in parentheses. The imperfect *epoiei* indicates habitual action, 'he always did', 'he was in the habit of doing' (cf. *apeluen* in v. 6).

Translation: *Came up* may be rendered literally, implying that the crowd ascended into the palace, or may be translated as 'approached' or 'came up to'.

Ask Pilate to do...must sometimes be shifted into the form of direct discourse e.g. 'asked Pilate, Do for us what you always do at this time of year'. 'At this time of year' may be required in order to indicate that the action requested was not habitual throughout the year. However, such an addition may not be required if the rendering of 'at the feast' sufficiently clarifies the context.

9 And he answered them, "Do you want me to release for you the King of the Jews?"

Exegesis: *thelete apolusō*...; 'do you want (that) I should release...?', 'do you want me to release...?': for another example of this construction see 10:36.

humin 'for you', i.e. in accordance with their request (v. 8).

ton basilea tōn Ioudaiōn (cf. v. 2) 'the King of the Jews'.

Translation: *Answered* is in some languages rendered as 'asked them in return', since a question follows.

For *release* see verse 6, and for *King* see verse 2.

10 For he perceived that it was out of envy that the chief priests had delivered him up.

Exegesis: *phthonon* (only here in Mark) 'envy', 'jealousy'.

paradedōkeisan 'they had handed over', 'they had delivered': another pluperfect (cf. v. 7), of an action completed in the past.

hoi archiereis (cf. 8:31) 'the chief priests'.

Translation: The pronominal referents in this verse may be somewhat obscure, thus requiring the substitution of 'Pilate' for *he* and possibly 'Jesus' for *him*.

There is a tendency to mistranslate *envy* as 'jealousy', which may be applicable only to jealousy over women. Hence, in some languages the closest equivalent is 'because they were angry with him' (Zoque). In some instances, however, in order to avoid misinterpretation, the particular nature of this envy must be described, e.g. 'they hated Jesus because everybody liked him' (Chontal of Tabasco).

11 But the chief priests stirred up the crowd to have him release for them Barabbas instead.

Exegesis: *aneseisan* (only here in Mark) 'they stirred up', 'they incited' (cf. Vulgate *concitaverunt*).

hina 'in order that', indicating purpose: the chief priests stirred up the crowd in order that (*at their request*) he should release, instead, Barabbas for them. Cf. Moffatt, 'to get him to release'.

mallon (cf. 5:26) 'rather', 'instead', 'on the contrary'.

Translation: *Stirred up* may be rendered simply as a causative, e.g. 'caused the crowd to have Pilate release...' On the other hand, some languages may express this relationship more elaborately, e.g. 'the head priests gave strength to the crowd so they would ask...' (Zoque), and 'the chief priests the crowd, Barabbas we want, you will say to him, they said to them' (Navajo). It is of interest to note how in Navajo no indirect discourse may be employed, but all expressions of speaking, whether explicit or implied, require the form of direct discourse.

12 *And Pilate again said to them, "Then what shall I do with the man whom you call the King of the Jews?"*

Text: Before *poiēsō* 'I shall do' *Textus Receptus* and Kilpatrick add *thelete* 'you wish', which is omitted by all other modern editions of the Greek text.

Exegesis: *ti oun poiēsō hon legete...*; 'what then shall I do with him whom you call...?': the relative *hon* serves both as the object of *poiēsō* 'I shall do' and as the object of *legete* 'you call'. The proper translation is (as RSV has it) 'what shall I do *with* him...' and not 'what shall I do *to* him...' (cf. Lagrange); but in many languages it is quite impossible to reproduce such a fine distinction.

Translation: *Said* may need to be shifted to 'asked', because of the following question.
    Shall...do with must often be recast, e.g. 'cause to happen to' or 'decide how this man...will fare'.

13 *And they cried out again, "Crucify him."*

Exegesis: *palin* 'again': the ordinary meaning 'again' seems out of place here since this is the first time, according to the narrative, that the crowd shouted to Pilate. Black (*Aramaic*, 82) suggests 'thereupon', while Lagrange refers to 2:13 as an example of *palin* used in a more general sense than 'again' with its implication of a repetition of an act done before. Arndt & Gingrich 5 suggest that a previous outburst is implied in v. 11, or else (which seems more probable) that *palin* here carries the idea of 'back'—'they shouted back'—as in 11:3 *apostelein palin* means 'to send back' (cf. Goodspeed).
    ekraxan (cf. 3:11) 'they shouted', 'they cried out'.
    staurōson (15:14, 15, 20, 24, 25, 27, 16:6) 'you must crucify!'

Translation: *Cried out again* may be translated as 'yelled back at him' or 'shouted back'.
    For a discussion of the form of the cross see 8:34. The verb *crucify* should in some way be related to execution by means of a cross. It is not enough merely to translate 'kill him'. However, the particular way in which Jesus was executed by being put on the cross is differently described in various languages, e.g. 'fasten him to a spread-back-stick' (Loma) and 'nail him on a cross' (Zoque), and 'nail on the cross wood' (Mongolian). However, since Pilate would not himself nail Jesus to the cross, it is necessary in some languages to use a causative, e.g. 'cause him to be nailed on a cross'.

14 *And Pilate said to them, "Why, what evil has he done?" But they shouted all the more, "Crucify him."*

Exegesis: *ti gar epoiēsen kakon*; 'why, what evil (thing) has he done?':

479

in such a question *gar* means 'why!' 'how so!' (cf. Arndt & Gingrich *gar* 1.f).

kakos (cf. 7:21) 'evil deed', 'bad thing'.

perissōs (cf. 10:26) 'exceedingly', 'all the more'.

Translation: *Said to them* may require modification to 'asked them'.

Why may be expanded slightly in order to be an equivalent expression of concern, e.g. 'why so' or 'why say that'.

What evil has he done may be paralleled by 'what sin has he committed' or 'what bad deed has he done'.

All the more is a kind of comparative, indicating at the same time a high degree of activity, e.g. 'yelled more, more' or 'shouted so much greater'.

15 So Pilate, wishing to satisfy the crowd, released for them Barabbas; and having scourged Jesus, he delivered him to be crucified.

Exegesis: *boulomenos* (only here in Mark) 'desiring', 'wishing', 'wanting'.

to hikanon poiēsai is a Latinism, *satisfacere*, 'satisfy' (cf. Arndt & Gingrich *hikanos* 1.c; Moule *Idiom Book*, 192; Moulton & Milligan).

phragellōsas (only here in Mark) 'having flogged', 'having scourged' (cf. Latin *flagellare*). The aorist participle here indicates action antecedent to that of the main verb *paredōken* 'he delivered'. The word should not be translated in such a way as to imply that Pilate personally flogged Jesus: instead of 'having scourged Jesus' (of RSV) the proper sense is achieved by 'having Jesus scourged' (cf. Goodspeed). This flogging, or scourging, was extremely severe, inflicted only on slaves or provincials, never on Roman citizens, and applied to those who were condemned to death (cf. Swete).

Translation: *Satisfy the crowd* may be translated as 'make the crowd happy' or 'give the crowd what they wanted'.

For *released* see verse 6.

Scourged Jesus is better rendered in many languages 'caused Jesus to be whipped' or 'caused Jesus to be beaten with whips'.

Delivered him to be crucified is a highly condensed expression, requiring some more specific identification of participants and events in some languages, e.g. 'handed Jesus over to the soldiers in order that they would nail him to a cross'. In many languages one can not 'hand a person over' without specifying to whom. Moreover, the following expression of 'crucify' may require an identified grammatical subject.

16 And the soldiers led him away inside the palace (that is, the praetorium); and they called together the whole battalion.

Exegesis: *stratiōtai* (only here in Mark) 'soldiers': these are probably soldiers of Pilate himself (as Mt. 27:27 has it).

apēgagon (cf. 14:44) 'they led away', 'they took off'.

esō tēs aulēs(cf. 14:54) 'inside the court': here *aulē* is the 'court' of a prince, from which the sense 'palace' derives (cf. Arndt & Gingrich 4). By Suidas the word was defined as 'the house of the king' (cf. Moulton & Milligan).

esō 'within', 'inside': only here in the N.T. does *esō* function as a preposition (cf. Moule *Idiom Book*, 85).

praitōrion 'praetorium' is a Latin loanword *praetorium*, the governor's official residence (cf. the many examples in Moulton & Milligan; for an extensive study of the word see Lightfoot *Philippians*, 99-102).

sugkalousin (only here in Mark) 'they call together', 'they summon'.

holēn tēn speiran (only here in Mark is *speira* used) 'the whole cohort', 'the entire contingent (of men)', 'the whole detachment': *speira* is the Greek word which translates the Latin *cohors*, normally composed of 600 men (i.e. one-tenth of the legion). It is not necessary to suppose, however, that anywhere near that number of soldiers were there present or took part in the mockery.

Translation: *Palace* is often 'the house of the ruler' or 'the governor's building'.

That is, the praetorium may be treated as an explanatory phrase, involving a transliteration of *praetorium*, but this may not be very meaningful, for explanatory additions are supposed to elucidate, while in this instance *praetorium* would mean much less than a translation of *palace*. Accordingly, some translators have rendered the passage as 'that is the place called praetorium', in order that the word may be readily identified as a borrowing.

The whole battalion may be 'the rest of the group of soldiers', for the soldiers mentioned as subject of the sentence also belonged to this same battalion.

17 *And they clothed him in a purple cloak, and plaiting a crown of thorns they put it on him.*

Exegesis: *endiduskousin* (only here in Mark; cf. *enduō* 1:6) 'they clothe', 'they dress' (after having taken off his own clothes—cf. v. 20).

porphuran (15:20) 'purple cloth', 'purple robe'; Souter defines it as a red-colored cloak, such as common soldiers wore, which Rawlinson identifies as the *paludamentum* or the *sagum*.

perititheasin (cf. 12:1) 'they place around': here of the 'crown' or, better, 'wreath' placed on the head.

plexantes (only here in Mark) 'having woven', 'having plaited'.

akanthinon (only here in Mark) 'thorny': the *akantha* (cf. Mt. 27:29) was a thorn bush.

stephanon (only here in Mark) 'wreath', 'crown': probably an imitation of the laurel wreath worn by the Emperor (cf. Rawlinson).

Translation: In verse 16 or 17, it may be necessary to make the third person singular reference clear by using 'Jesus' in place of 'him'.

The color of *purple* is treated in a number of ways, of which the following are the most common: (1) an indigenous term which is approximately the color of purple (or dark red, as some believe the Greek term implies); (2) an approximation of the color, employing other terms which identify colors which are reasonably near in the spectrum, e.g. 'a kind of blue' (Ifugao), 'dark red' (Tzeltal), 'burnt red' (Huastec), 'a kind of red' (the choice of one or another such expression depends upon the way in which people in a receptor language actually speak of purple); (3) the identification of the color by some bird or flower, e.g. 'cloth of the color of...', at which point the name of some commonly employed object is used, provided, of course, this is a normal way of speaking about the color in question; and (4) the use of a phrase identifying the process of dyeing cloth, e.g. 'cloth like that dyed in...', with the introduction of the proper plant used as dye stuff (Piro).

Crown is difficult to translate in the sense of a circular object worn by royalty, for this type of artefact is not very common. However, the object may be described as 'put a circle of thorns on his head' (Tzeltal) or 'wove thorn branches together into a wreath (or 'circle') and put them on his head'.

Put it on him must in many instances be amplified so as to specify where the thorns were placed, namely, 'on his head'.

18 And they began to salute him, "Hail, King of the Jews!"

Exegesis: *aspazesthai* (cf. 9:15) 'to salute', 'to hail'.

chaire (as a salutation only here in Mark; in form it is the imperative of *chairō* 'rejoice'—cf. 14:11) 'hail!' 'welcome!' (cf. Arndt & Gingrich *chairō* 2.a). The Latin of the soldiers' mock salute would be *Ave, rex Judaeorum!*

Translation: *Salute* implies formal address or greeting, as offered to a dignitary, translated in Amuzgo as 'greeting him as though honoring'.

Hail can be translated by the indigenous equivalent of 'Long live the King', e.g. 'live long' (Ifugao), 'we wish you have a long life' (San Blas), 'viva', borrowed from Spanish (Zoque).

19 And they struck his head with a reed, and spat upon him, and they knelt down in homage to him.

Exegesis: The force of the three imperfects *etupton, eneptuon, proskunoun*, 'they were beating', 'they were spitting', 'they were doing homage', is that of actions repeated by several soldiers.

tuptō (only here in Mark) 'strike', 'beat'.

emptuō (cf. 10:34) 'to spit on'.

proskuneō (cf. 5:6) 'to worship', 'to reverence', 'to do homage': here in mockery, as to a king (cf. Gould, Rawlinson).

kalamō (15:36) 'with a stalk', 'with a reed', 'with a staff'.

tithentes ta gonata (only here in Mark; cf. *gonupeteō* 1:40, 10:17) 'bend the knees', 'kneel down': perhaps the Greek equivalent of the Latin *genua ponere* (cf. Arndt & Gingrich *tithēmi* I.1.b.α; Moule *Idiom Book*, 192).

Translation: The reed was evidently used as a flail with which to beat Jesus over the head, thus pounding the crown of thorns deeper into his flesh. One may have to translate 'beat him on the head with a reed' (or 'stick' or 'staff') or 'flailed him on the head...'

The imperfect form of the Greek verbs translated *struck, spat*, and *knelt* justify the translation of 'repeatedly struck...spat...and knelt' or 'one after another struck,...spat...and knelt'.

Knelt down in homage may require the addition of a qualifier so as not to lead to misinterpretation, e.g. 'knelt down as though honoring' or 'got down on their knees, pretending to show respect'.

20 And when they had mocked him, they stripped him of the purple cloak, and put his own clothes on him. And they led him out to crucify him.

Exegesis: *enepaixan* (cf. 10:34) 'they ridiculed', 'they made fun of', 'they mocked': the aorist here indicates the action as completed, 'when they had finished mocking him' (cf. Burton *Moods and Tenses*, § 48).

exedusan (only here in Mark) 'they stripped off', 'they undressed'.
tēn porphuran (cf. v. 17) 'the purple cloak'.
enedusan (cf. 1:6) 'they put on', 'they dressed'.
ta himatia autou (cf. 2:21) 'his own clothes'.
exagousin (only here in Mark; cf. *agō* 13:11) 'they lead out': primarily, 'out of the praetorium', though the further sense 'out of the city' may also be implied.

hina staurōsōsin auton 'that they should crucify him', 'in order to crucify him'. For *stauroō* 'crucify' cf. v. 13.

Translation: For *purple cloak* see verse 17.
Stripped him is translatable as 'took away' or 'grabbed off of him'. For *led him* see 15:1 and for *crucify* see 15:13.

21 And they compelled a passer-by, Simon of Cyrene, who was coming in from the country, the father of Alexander and Rufus, to carry his cross.

Exegesis: *aggareuousin* (only here in Mark) 'they impressed (into service)', 'they forced': the verb is a Persian loanword, and refers to the right enjoyed by the occupation troops of impressing people into service for the purpose of carrying loads or performing other services (cf. Hatch *Essays*, 37-38, and cf. further use of the verb in the N.T.,//Mt. 27:32, and Mt. 5:41). Cf. Moulton & Milligan.

paragonta tina Simōna Kurēnaion 'a passerby, a certain Simon of Cyrene' (cf. Goodspeed, Weymouth, Manson).

paragō (cf. 1:16) 'to pass by', 'to go along' (cf. Arndt & Gingrich 2.a.α).
Simōna Kurēnaion 'Simon Cyrenean': the name indicates the man

483

was a Jew, from Cyrene, the capital city of the North African district of Cyrenaica.

erchomenon ap' agrou (cf. 5:14) 'coming in from the country', and not 'coming from the field' (cf. Arndt & Gingrich *agros* 2).

hina arē ton stauron autou 'that he should carry his cross': *hina* indicates the content of the command implied in the verb *aggareuō* (cf. Arndt & Gingrich *hina* II.1.a.ε).

airō (cf. 8:34) 'carry', 'lift up and carry along': a man condemned to die by crucifixion was forced to carry the cross-piece (the *patibulum*) to the place of execution.

Translation: This verse, despite its clear meaning in English, includes a number of syntactic problems when translated into some languages. In the first place, between the object *a passerby* and the verb expression with which it goes, namely, *to carry his cross*, it is often quite impossible to interpose so much which is explanatory: (1) an appositive construction consisting of the man's name; (2) a description of what he was doing; and (3) his relationship to Alexander and Rufus, men who were evidently well known to the Christian community to which this Gospel was being addressed. Because of the syntactic difficulties imposed by this type of arrangement, some languages require considerable recasting of the word order, e.g. 'Simon, a man from Cyrene country, was passing along as he came in from the fields. He was the father of Alexander and Rufus. The soldiers forced Simon to carry Jesus' cross'. In Navajo the verb *compel* must be translated by an explicit description of what happened, e.g. 'they said, Carry this cross; and they pushed him to it'.

22 *And they brought him to the place called Golgotha (which means the place of a skull).*

Exegesis: *pherousin* (cf. 1:32) 'they take', 'they conduct', 'they bring' (cf. Arndt & Gingrich 4.b.β).

Golgothan 'Golgotha': the Greek equivalent of the Aramaic *golgolta'* 'skull'.

ho estin methermēneuomenos (cf. 5:41) 'which, translated, is'.

kranion (only here in Mark) 'skull'.

Translation: *Brought* may also be 'caused to go' or 'led', in the sense employed in verse 20.

Place of a skull may require expansion by means of some verb in certain languages, e.g. 'place where there was a skull' or 'place like a skull'. The phrase used in this instance will depend upon the interpretation which one follows as to the origin of this place name, for which there is no universally accepted explanation.

23 *And they offered him wine mingled with myrrh; but he did not take it.*

Text: After *autō* 'to him' *Textus Receptus* adds *piein* 'to drink', which is omitted by modern editions of the Greek text.

Instead of the masculine *hos* 'he' of the majority of modern editions of the Greek text, *Textus Receptus*, Soden, Vogels, and Souter have the neuter *ho* 'it'.

Exegesis: *edidoun* 'they were giving': the imperfect indicates an unsuccessful attempt (what is called a "conative" imperfect: cf. *Expository Times* 65.147, n.3, 1954), correctly translated by RSV 'they offered'. The plural is probably impersonal, meaning 'he was given', 'he was offered'. Who 'they' were is a matter of conjecture: certainly not the soldiers, so perhaps one of the women.

esmurnismenon oinon 'wine flavored with myrrh': it is ordinarily assumed that the mixture would act as a narcotic, but there is no clear proof of this.

smurnizō (only here in the N.T.) 'be like myrrh', 'mingle with myrrh'.

oinos (cf. 2:22) 'wine'.

Translation: *Offered* is sometimes translatable as 'tried to give' or 'held out for him to take'.

Wine mingled with myrrh may be 'wine in which myrrh had been mixed'. *Myrrh* is, of course, unknown in most parts of the world, thus necessitating a borrowed word, which may be identified satisfactorily in several ways, e.g. 'something called *myrrh*' (Barrow Eskimo), 'a mirra herb', in which *mirra* is borrowed from Spanish (Tzeltal), and 'mir resin', in which myrrh in a borrowed form is classified as a kind of resin and thus presumed to have certain medicinal or helpful qualities.

Take it may also be translated as 'drink it'.

24 *And they crucified him, and divided his garments among them, casting lots for them, to decide what each should take.*

Exegesis: *diamerizontai ta himatia autou* 'they divide his garments among themselves', 'they distribute his garments among themselves': only here in the N.T. is *diamerizō* used.

ballontes klēron ep' auta 'casting lots over them': the participial clause is of manner, indicating the way in which they divided the clothes among themselves. This was accomplished by means of pebbles or a small stick (cf. Arndt & Gingrich).

klēros (only here in Mark) 'lot'.

tis ti arē 'who should take what', i.e. what each one should get (cf. Field *Notes*, 43f.).

The language of this verse is patterned after Ps. 22:19.

Translation: For *crucified* see verse 13.

Since in some languages the temporal sequence must be followed in a series of events such as are described in *divided...casting...decide*, a recasting of the order is required, e.g. 'they cast lots in order to decide who should get which piece of Jesus' clothing and in this way they divided his garments'. If this order is not followed, people may interpret the action as first dividing the garments equally and then gambling in order to see which soldier would end up with the most garments.

Casting lots is a quite common practice in many parts of the world, but it is not universally known. Accordingly, in some areas one may need to employ some sort of descriptive equivalent, e.g. 'tossed little marked pebbles in order to know' or 'decided by playing with little stones'. In Shipibo the passage is rendered as 'they shook little things to get his clothes, in order to know who would get what'. And in Tzeltal the usage is 'made play to see who would get what clothes'.

25 And it was the third hour, when they crucified him.

Exegesis: *hōra tritē* 'the third hour': this is the equivalent of the modern 9:00 A.M., being the 'third hour' from sunrise (cf. Goodspeed *Problems*, 68f.). It appears that in this chapter Mark means to divide the day into four three-hour periods: *prōi* (15:1), sunrise (i.e. 6:00 A.M.); *hōra tritē* (15:25), 9:00 A.M.; *hōra hektē* (15:33), 12:00 noon; *hōra enatē* (15:34), 3:00 P.M.; *opsia* (15:42), sunset (i.e. 6:00 P.M.).

kai 'and' is here used according to Semitic fashion, and should be translated 'when' (cf. Arndt & Gingrich 2.c).

Translation: The indigenous equivalents of the *third hour* are quite varied, e.g. 'yoking up time' (Bolivian Quechua), 'sun half way up' (Zoque), 'when the sun is raising itself up' (Shipibo), 'the sun is not very high' (San Blas), and 'middle of the morning' (Piro). Of course, where time is reckoned by hours one can do one of two things: (1) use the equivalent expression such as 'nine o'clock' or (2) follow the Greek expression somewhat more closely, e.g. 'three hours after sunrise'.

26 And the inscription of the charge against him read, "The King of the Jews."

Exegesis: *epigraphē* (cf. 12:16) 'inscription', 'superscription' (Latin *titulus*).

aitias (only here in Mark) 'charge': a legal technical term, indicating the charge for which the death sentence was passed (cf. Latin *causa capitalis* 'reason for capital punishment').

ēn...epigegrammenē 'was...inscribed', 'was...written on': it is not necessary to suppose, with Arndt & Gingrich (*epigraphō* 1), that the verb here indicates 'written *over* Jesus', i.e. affixed to the cross above his head. Rather the verb *epigraphō* means simply 'written on *the tablet*', and is thus rendered by RSV (cf. Gould).

HO BASILEUS TŌN IOUDAIŌN (cf. v. 2) 'THE KING OF THE JEWS'.

Translation: *The inscription of the charge* is often a difficult expression to translate, since though an actual object is referred to, the phrase includes two distinct processes: (1) the writing of the accusation and (2) the charge which was made against Jesus. In Tzeltal this phrase is translated as 'thus written what said he had done'. In Chontal of Tabasco the charge can only be described in terms of the reasons for the crucifixion, e.g. 'writing as to why they crucified him'. In Zoque the phrase is 'paper which accused him', a more or less technical reference to any written type of charge.

It is quite easy for us to understand *read* in this specialized sense of the content of a writing, but in other languages one must say 'said' or 'these were the words'.

For *King of the Jews* see 15 : 2.

27 And with him they crucified two robbers, one on his right and one on his left.

Exegesis: *duo lēstas* (cf. 11 : 17) 'two bandits', 'two robbers': perhaps, like Barabbas, insurrectionists.

ek dexiōn (cf. 10 : 37) 'on the right'.

ek euōnumōn (cf. 10 : 40) 'on the left'.

Translation: *With him* must be translated spatially, but with caution, e.g. 'at the same place'. A literal rendering of 'with him' might imply three men on one cross.

One on his right and one on his left is somewhat elliptical, therefore requiring some additions in certain languages, e.g. 'they crucified one man at Jesus' right side and another man was crucified at Jesus' left side'. In some instances, however, a much more natural and meaningful translation would be 'one on each side of Jesus'.

[28 And the scripture was fulfilled which says, "He was reckoned with the transgressors."]

Text: This verse is omitted from the Greek editions ot Tischendorf, Westcott and Hort, Souter, Nestle, and Taylor; included in brackets in the editions of Vogels, Lagrange, and Merk; added by *Textus Receptus*, Soden, and Kilpatrick. Omitted by the best manuscripts and many of the early versions, it is not in keeping with Mark's use of O.T. Scriptures. The scripture quoted is Isa. 53 : 12 (cf. Lk. 22 : 37 where it is quoted).

Exegesis: *eplērōthē* (cf. 1 : 15, 14 : 49) 'it was fulfilled'.

hē graphē (cf. 12 : 10) 'the scripture', 'the passage of Scripture'.

anomōn (not used in Mark) 'transgressors', 'lawless ones'.

elogisthē (not used in Mark) 'he was reckoned', 'he was counted'.

Translation: For *scripture* see 12 : 10, and for *fulfilled* see 14 : 49.

He was reckoned, if changed into an active form, may be rendered as 'they counted him with' or 'they thought of him as with'.

Transgressors are those who 'break the law', 'kill the law', or 'do what is bad'. In Zoque this last clause is rendered as 'they saw him among the bad men'.

487

29 *And those who passed by derided him, wagging their heads, and saying, "Aha! You who would destroy the temple and build it in three days,*

Text: The preposition *en* (before *trisin hēmerais*) 'in' is omitted by Tischendorf, included in brackets by Nestle, Westcott and Hort, Taylor; the majority of editions of the Greek text include it.

Exegesis: *hoi paraporeuomenoi* (cf. 2:23) 'the transients', 'the passers-by'.

eblasphēmoun (cf. 2:7, 7:22) 'they were blaspheming': here in the sense of 'insult', 'slander', 'derision' directed against man (not 'irreverent speech' directed against God).

kinountes tas kephalas autōn 'shaking their heads', 'wagging their heads': a gesture of derision (cf. Ps. 22:8 for the phrase).

kineō (only here in Mark) 'move', 'shake'.

oua (only here in the N.T.; not to be confused with *ouai* 13:17, 14:21) 'aha!': an exclamation of scornful wonder, of mocking amazement (cf. Moulton & Milligan).

ho kataluōn ton naon kai oikodomōn en trisin hēmerais (cf. 14:58) 'the one who tears down the sanctuary and builds it (again) in three days': the whole phrase is in the nature of a title, and to be taken as a vocative, in apposition to the subject of the verb 'save thou' in the next verse.

en trisin hēmerais (cf. *dia triōn hēmerōn* 14:58; *meta treis hēmeras* 8:31) 'in three days'.

Translation: *Derided him* is perhaps most accurately translated in many languages as 'insulted him'.

One must be careful in translating *wagging their heads*, for though we would assume that such derisive attitudes would be expressed by wagging the head back and forth, in many languages one must translate by terms which imply raising the head up and down. What counts here is not the precise manner in which the head was moved, but the cultural implications of the action.

Aha should not be transliterated, but rather rendered by an equivalent term of contempt, of which there are usually plenty.

The clause *you who...in three days* is sometimes impossible as a subject of the following verb *save*, and hence it must be rendered as a separate sentence, e.g. 'you are that person who said he would destroy the temple and build it in three days; you save yourself...'

Would destroy, if translated literally, is quite ambiguous or obscure in some languages. The closest equivalent may be 'said that you would'. One should avoid translating *would* as 'wanted to'.

30 *save yourself, and come down from the cross!"*

Exegesis: *sōson* (cf. 3:4) 'you must save (yourself)': the verb here is used in the sense of rescuing or delivering from death.

katabas (cf. 1:10) 'coming down': the participle here is to be taken as indicating means, 'by coming down (from the cross)', rather than as an additional imperative. Cf. Lagrange *en descendant*.

For *stauros* 'cross' cf. 8:34.

Translation: *Save yourself* is translatable as 'rescue yourself', 'prevent yourself from dying', 'cause yourself to escape', or 'cause yourself not to suffer'.

Come down may not be translatable in a literal form, since it would imply 'walk down' or 'travel down'. Hence, one may need to employ an expression such as 'get down from', 'climb down from', or 'descend from'.

31 *So also the chief priests mocked him to one another with the scribes, saying, "He saved others; he cannot save himself.*

Exegesis: The words in this verse have already been dealt with: for *homoiōs* 'in like manner' cf. 4:16; *hoi archiereis* 'the chief priests' cf. 8:31; *empaizō* 'mock' cf. 10:34; *pros allēlous* 'among themselves', 'to one another' cf. 4:41; *hoi grammateis* 'the scribes' cf. 1:22; *sōzō* 'save', 'rescue', 'help' cf. 3:4.

Translation: The logical subject includes both *the chief priests* and *the scribes*. In many languages this full logical subject must also be the formal grammatical subject, e.g. 'the chief priests together with the scribes mocked him...'

Mocked him to one another is not always easy to translate, for a double type of object is involved: (1) Jesus is actually the one mocked but (2) the chief priests and scribes direct their speech, not to Jesus, but to each other. In some instances this may be translated as 'made fun of Jesus, speaking to each other'.

For *save* see 10:26.

32 *Let the Christ, the King of Israel, come down now from the cross, that we may see and believe." Those who were crucified with him also reviled him.*

Exegesis: *ho christos* (cf. 8:29) 'the Messiah', 'the Christ'.

ho basileus Israēl (only here in Mark) 'the King of Israel'.

katabatō (cf. v. 30) 'he must descend', 'let him come down'.

hina here indicates purpose, 'in order that', 'so that'.

idōmen kai pisteusōmen 'we may see (it) and believe (that he is the Messiah)'.

pisteuō (cf. 1:15) 'have faith', 'believe'.

hoi sunestaurōmenoi (only here in Mark) 'those who had been crucified with'.

ōneidizon (16:14) 'they were reviling', 'they were insulting'.

Translation: *Let the Christ*...is a kind of third person command, not an expression of permission, as some translators have taken it. However, a third person imperative is rather rare in languages and hence some paraphrastic equivalent must be employed. These are generally of two types: (1) a shift to second person, e.g. 'you who claim to be the Christ, the King of Israel, come down...so that we may...' and (2) a statement of obligation, e.g. 'the Christ, who is the King of Israel, should come down ...so that we may...' In general the latter method is preferred, for it eliminates the necessity of relating 'you' to 'the Christ' by some phrase which would be out of keeping with the attitudes of the chief priests and scribes. 'You who are the Christ' would be entirely out of harmony with the context.

Christ, the King of Israel, which is an appositive phrase, must be made a relative clause in some languages, e.g. 'Christ who is the King of Israel', and a paratactically combined explanation in others, e.g. 'Christ, he is the King of Israel'.

For *the King of Israel* see comments under *the King of the Jews* (15:2).

See is often a transitive verb in various receptor languages, thus requiring an object, e.g. 'see you (or 'him') do it'. Likewise *believe* may be translatable only as transitive, e.g. 'believe in you' (or 'him').

Reviled him may be rendered as 'heaped insults on him', 'denounced him', or 'said bad things about him'.

33 And when the sixth hour had come, there was darkness over the whole land until the ninth hour.

Exegesis: *genomenēs hōras hektēs* (cf. 6:35 *hōras pollēs genomenēs*) 'when the sixth hour came', 'at mid-day'.

skotos (only here in Mark; cf. *skotizomai* 13:24) 'darkness'.

egeneto eph' holēn tēn gēn 'came upon the whole country', rather than RSV 'was' (cf. Arndt & Gingrich *ginomai* I.1.b.α).

holē hē gē 'the whole earth' or 'the whole land': most commentators and translators prefer the second meaning.

heōs hōras enatēs 'until the ninth hour', 'lasting to 3:00 P.M.'

Translation: In general *the sixth hour* is translated by some equivalent for noon, which, however, is expressed by a variety of idiomatic expressions, e.g. 'middle day' (Zoque, Tzeltal), 'sun reaches the top of my head' (Maninka), 'sun is on the middle of the head' (Mende), and 'sun in the stomach head' (Uduk). *The ninth hour* is also usually translatable by indigenous means of reckoning time, e.g. 'the sun has turned over on its side' (Tzeltal) or 'the sun is in the middle of the afternoon'. In some languages, the three hour period may be expressed as 'from noon until three hours later' (Gio).

In many languages one cannot speak of an hour as 'coming'. The time may 'arrive', 'be at', or 'sit', but 'coming' may be excluded as a possibility. If this is the case, one may translate this verse as 'from noon until the middle of the afternoon there was darkness over the whole land'.

Darkness may be best rendered in some languages as 'it did not shine' or 'there was no light'.

34 *And at the ninth hour Jesus cried with a loud voice, "Eloi, Eloi, lama sabachthani?" which means, "My God, my God, why hast thou forsaken me?"*

Exegesis: *tē enatē hōra* (cf. *tē prōtē hēmera* 14:12) 'at the ninth hour', 'at three o'clock'.

eboēsen (cf. 1:3) 'he cried out', 'he shouted'.

phōnē megalē (cf. 1:26, 5:7) 'with a loud voice', 'with a great cry'.

elōi elōi lama sabachthani 'My God, my God, why hast thou forsaken me?' It is debated whether the cry was uttered in Hebrew or Aramaic. The Hebrew of Ps. 22:2 reads, transliterated, *'eli 'eli lamah 'azabhtani*. The reaction of the bystanders—'He calls for Elijah!'—is more intelligible if the cry was uttered in Hebrew (cf. Lagrange, Taylor).

ho estin methermēneuomenon (cf. v. 22) 'which, translated, is'.

ho theos mou 'my God': this is to be understood as a vocative, the case of address.

eis ti 'why?': cf. Arndt & Gingrich *eis* 4.f.

egkatelipes (only here in Mark; cf. *kataleipō* 10:7) 'you forsook', 'you abandoned', 'you left'.

Translation: *Cried* is to be understood in the sense of 'shouted', not 'cried', as in tears or weeping.

In translations into so-called primitive languages one must transliterate *Eloi, Eloi, lama sabachthani*, using as a basis for the pronunciation the form in which this expression is uttered in the dominant language of the area, e.g. French, Spanish, Portuguese, Thai, Indonesian, etc. It is not recommended in these cases that one go to the Greek, Hebrew, or Aramaic form as a basis for the transliteration since any further acquaintance which people will have with such an expression will be in the form which it has already been given in Bibles published in languages of greater prestige.

Forsaken is to be understood in the sense of 'left', 'deserted', or 'gone away from me' (Navajo).

35 *And some of the bystanders hearing it said, "Behold, he is calling Elijah."*

Exegesis: *tines tōn parestēkotōn* (cf. 14:47) 'some of the bystanders', 'certain of those standing there'.

ide (cf. 2:24) 'look!', 'see!', 'notice!'

Translation: *Hearing it said* may require some recasting as 'when some of those standing by heard what he said, they said,...'

Behold must often be changed to 'listen', 'hear'.

Calling may be understood as 'calling to' or 'calling for', not merely 'calling out the name of'.

36 *And one ran and, filling a sponge full of vinegar, put it on a reed and gave it to him to drink, saying, "Wait, let us see whether Elijah will come to take him down."*

Exegesis: *dramōn de tis* 'and a certain one running': again it is impossible to identify the man. He is simply a 'bystander' or 'spectator'.

trechō (cf. 5:6) 'run'.

gemisas spoggon oxous peritheis kalamō epotizen auton 'filling a sponge (full) of vinegar (and) placing (it) on a reed gave (it) to him to drink': the three aorist participles (*dramōn, gemisas, peritheis,* 'running', 'filling', 'placing') precede the action of the main verb *epotizen* 'he gave to drink', while the present participle *legōn* 'saying' is simultaneous with the action of the main verb.

gemizō (cf. 4:37) 'fill', 'fill up'.

spoggos (only here in Mark) 'sponge'.

oxos (only here in Mark) 'sharp', i.e. *'sour* wine', 'vinegar': generally identified as the *posca,* a cheap wine of the Roman soldiers.

peritithēmi (cf. 12:1) 'place around', 'place on'.

kalamos (cf. v. 19) 'reed', 'staff'.

potizō (cf. 9:41) 'give to drink': the imperfect *epotizen* is probably conative, 'he tried to give to drink' (cf. *edidoun* in v. 23). So BFBS 'offered it to Him to drink'.

aphete idōmen 'let us see': the verb *aphiēmi* 'let', 'allow' (cf. 2:5) is taken here as an auxiliary (cf. Moulton & Milligan; Arndt & Gingrich 4; Moulton *Prolegomena,* 175). Some, however, do not agree with this, rendering *aphete* 'allow me!' 'let me do it' (cf. Rawlinson; Burton *Moods and Tenses,* § 161): so RSV 'wait'.

kathelein (15:46) 'to take down', 'to bring down (from the cross)': Field (*Notes,* 44) calls this the technical word for the removal of a body from the cross.

Translation: *Sponge* is rendered either by (1) a borrowing, which is the most common procedure, especially where such objects have been introduced to some extent—in which case they often are known by a foreign term; or (2) a descriptive term, e.g. 'something which takes up liquid' (Barrow Eskimo), 'something with holes-holes', a phrase used to designate anything of the nature of a sponge (Shipibo), 'something which drank up the vinegar' (Tzeltal). In some languages the closest equivalent to a sponge is the fibre of a gourd, which is used for almost the same purposes as marine sponges and hence is quite an acceptable substitute.

Vinegar is 'sour wine' or 'sour juice of a fruit'.

Drink cannot be translated literally in some languages, since one would not speak of 'drinking from a sponge', but rather 'sucking' (Zoque, Mitla Zapotec).

In a number of languages the series of verbs: *ran...filling...put... gave...drink...saying,* must be broken up into more than one sentence, especially since the subject of *drink* is different from the subject of the other verbs, e.g. '...gave it to him to drink. He said, Wait...'

Wait is directed toward the crowd standing about. *Let us see* is rendered in some languages as a declarative 'we shall see' and in others as a question 'shall we see whether Elijah...?' *Let us see* is a type of hortatory first person plural which has no close grammatical parallel in some languages. The nearest equivalents may be (1) an imperative introductory statement, e.g. 'come and we shall see', (2) a simple future statement, 'we shall see', and (3) in rare instances a question, with the same function as the Greek hortatory, e.g. 'shall we see whether'.

Take him down may require a more specific translation such as 'take him down from the cross', 'take him off the cross', or 'unnail him from the cross'.

37 And Jesus uttered a loud cry, and breathed his last.

Exegesis: *apheis* (cf. 2 : 5) 'letting out', 'letting loose': for this use of *aphiēmi* cf. Arndt & Gingrich 1.a.β.

phōnēn megalēn (cf. v. 34) 'a loud cry'.

exepneusen (15 : 39) 'he expired', 'he died'.

Translation: *Uttered a loud cry* may be translated 'shouted loud' or 'cried out hard'.

Breathed his last is a good idiomatic equivalent of the Greek, but it is not literally translatable into many languages. 'He died' is a more frequent parallel.

38 And the curtain of the temple was torn in two, from top to bottom.

Exegesis: *to katapetasma tou naou* 'the veil of the sanctuary', 'the curtain of the temple': it is generally assumed that the *katapetasma* (only here in Mark) was the veil separating the holy place from the holy of holies. This curtain is described by Edersheim (*Life and Times of Jesus* II, 611) as being sixty feet long, thirty feet wide, and of the thickness of the palm of a man's hand.

naos (cf. 14 : 58) 'sanctuary'.

eschisthē (cf. 1 : 10) 'was rent', 'was torn'.

ap' anōthen heōs katō 'from top to bottom' (cf. Arndt & Gingrich *anōthen* 1).

Translation: *Curtain* is not always easily translated, since in many societies such objects are not known. In Zoque the closest equivalent is 'cloth-closure', literally equivalent to 'cloth door'. In a number of languages *curtain* has been rendered by a borrowed form. It is important, however, to avoid a literal translation of *veil*, since this may apply only to veils worn by women, and accordingly the veil of the temple would be quite meaningless.

Was torn is a passive construction without the mention of a specific agent; nor would it be justifiable to introduce a specific grammatical

493

subject of a transitive expression, e.g. 'God tore the curtain'. Accordingly, it is best, in such instances, to shift the verb expression to an intransitive equivalent, e.g. 'the curtain split into two pieces', or 'divided into two parts'.

From top to bottom is a highly elliptical expression, requiring some fuller statement in some languages, e.g. 'the curtain began to split first at the top and then continued to split to the bottom'.

39 *And when the centurion, who stood facing him, saw that he thus breathed his last, he said, "Truly this man was the Son of God!"*

Text: After *houtōs* 'thus' *Textus Receptus* adds *kraxas* 'crying out', which is omitted by all modern editions of the Greek text.

Exegesis: *ho kenturiōn* (15:44, 45) 'centurion' (Latin *centurio*), commander of one hundred soldiers (Matthew, Luke and Acts use the Greek term *hekatontarchēs* 'ruler of one hundred').

ho parestēkōs ex enantias autou 'who stood by opposite him', 'who stood facing him'.

ho parestēkōs (cf. 14:47) 'the one standing by'.

ex enantias (only here in Mark; cf. *enantios* 6:48) 'opposite', 'against': here, in the nature of the case, 'facing (him)'.

exepneusen (cf. v. 37) 'he expired', 'he died'.

alēthōs (cf. 14:70) 'truly', 'certainly'.

houtos ho anthrōpos huios theou ēn 'this man was the (a) Son (son) of God': commentators and translators are divided over whether the words are to be taken as an expression of awe and admiration on the part of a pagan, 'a son of God', meaning 'a hero', 'a superhuman being', or whether they are to be understood in a Christian sense 'the Son of God'. In favor of the former are Goodspeed, Moffatt, BFBS, Manson; Gould, Swete, Rawlinson, Taylor; for the latter cf. ASV, RSV, Weymouth, Synodale; Berkeley and Williams have 'God's Son' (cf. also Zürich, Brazilian, Lagrange), while Knox, Douay, and Confraternity translate the Vulgate *Filius Dei* by 'the Son of God'.

It should be made clear that grammar is not decisive since the Greek may be just as correctly translated 'a son of a god' as 'the Son of God': here it is the context, which is to say one's interpretation of the incident, which will determine the translation. The precisely identical Greek construction occurs in nine other passages in the Gospels (Mt. 4:3, 6, Lk. 4:3, 9, Mt. 14:33, 27:40, 43, 54, Jn. 10:36; similar phrases in Lk. 1:32, Jn. 19:7): in all of these passages RSV translates 'the Son of God'.

There is good evidence for understanding *huios theou* here as 'the Son of God' (cf. *Expository Times* 68.27-28, 1956 where there is a full discussion of the question).

Translation: *Centurion* is usually translated as (1) the local equivalent

of 'captain' or (2) by a descriptive phrase 'leader of one hundred soldiers'.
For *breathed his last* see verse 37.

Truly, though in initial position, is usually related to the verb or the predicate, e.g. 'this man was really the (or 'a') Son of God'.

The son of God may involve difficulties quite apart from the exegetical problems cited above. For example, in Tarahumara 'a son of God' refers only to a Tarahumara person. All other people are classed as 'sons of the devil'. Accordingly, in the Tarahumara language one must say 'the only Son of God', or the comment of the centurion becomes quite meaningless.

40 *There were also women looking on from afar, among whom were Mary Magdalene, and Mary the mother of James the younger and of Joses, and Salome,*

Exegesis: *gunaikes* 'women': here 'some women' as in the similar case (*Saddoukaioi* 'some Sadducees') in 12:18.

apo makrothen (cf. 5:6) 'from a distance', 'from afar'.

ēsan...theōrousai (cf. 3:11) 'they were...observing', 'they were... watching'.

Maria hē Magdalēnē 'Mary the Magdalene', i.e. Mary of Magdala, a town near Tiberias on the west shore of the Lake of Galilee. The only thing the Gospels say about her is that she had seven demons driven out of her by Jesus (cf. Lk. 7:2): there is nothing at all to support the past history commonly attributed to her.

Maria hē Iakōbou tou mikrou kai Iōsētos mētēr 'Mary the mother of James the younger and of Joses': in v. 47 she is identified as 'the mother of Joses' and in 16:1 as 'the mother of James'.

Iakōbos ho mikros either 'James the small (in stature)' or 'James the younger': cf. Arndt & Gingrich *mikros* 1.a,b. Deissmann (*Bible Studies*, 144f.) adduces evidence in support of understanding the epithet as refering to age, not to size.

Iōsēs 'Joses': where possible, by use of a different form of the name, this man should be distinguished from *Iōsēph* 'Joseph' (vv. 43, 45). If only one form of the name is available for both (cf. Brazilian) there may arise the possibility of 'Mary the mother of *Iōsētos*' in v. 47 being thought of as being the mother of Joseph of Arimathea (v. 45): cf. the Roman Catholic translations in English which have 'Joseph' for both names.

Translation: *Looking on from afar* may require a division into two expressions, e.g. 'some women were standing at a distance; they were watching'.

Among whom were... is in some languages an awkward expression to try to render as a relative clause. Hence, one may need to break the sentence and translate as 'among these women were Mary Magdalene and...' or 'Mary Magdalene...and Salome were among these women'.

Mary Magdalene is translatable as 'Mary from Magdala town'.

495

James the younger provides certain difficulties, not only with regard to exegesis, whether this is a matter of age or stature, but with respect to the comparative. In some languages 'James who was young' (Subanen) is used. In Tzeltal the equivalent is 'James who grew up after'.

And Salome has been a source of considerable syntactic difficulty, since often Salome is combined with James and Joses as another child of Mary. To avoid this difficulty, without beginning an entirely new sentence, e.g. 'Salome was also there', translators have shifted the order of the women's names, e.g. 'Mary of Magdala, Salome, and Mary the mother of James the younger and Joses'.

41 **who, when he was in Galilee, followed him, and ministered to him; and also many other women who came up with him to Jerusalem.**

Exegesis: *ēkolouthoun autō kai diēkonoun autō* 'they followed him and ministered to him', 'they used to follow him and minister to him'.

akoloutheō (cf. 1:18) 'follow': here, as disciples.

diakoneō (cf. 1:13, 1:31) 'serve', 'wait on', 'minister to'.

kai allai pollai 'and many other (women) also'.

hai sunanabasai (only here in Mark; cf. *anabainō* in 10:32, 33) 'who came up with', 'who accompanied (him) on the way up'.

Translation: This sentence, which began with verse 40, is so complex that in many instances one must start another sentence with the beginning of verse 41, e.g. 'these women followed...'

When he was in Galilee may be preposed or postposed to the verb expressions with which it is associated, e.g. 'when Jesus was in Galilee, these women followed him and ministered to him' or 'these women followed Jesus and ministered to him when he was in Galilee'.

Since Jesus has not been specifically identified in the context since verse 37, the introduction of 'Jesus' in this verse may be required so as to avoid grammatical confusion with references to the centurion.

Followed is to be understood in the sense of 'accompany' (see 1:17).

Ministered to him must be translated with care so as to indicate clearly the degree to which they provided for Jesus' needs, since in some languages expressions have been used which would imply illicit relationships. To avoid such a difficulty, some translations have used rather explicit statements, e.g. 'prepared food for him' (Tzeltal).

The final clause *and also many other women... to Jerusalem* is also part of the logical subject of verse 40. As the clause now stands there is no verb, and the grammatical relationship may be quite obscure when translated into other languages. Therefore, one may need to introduce a verb, e.g. 'and also many other women...were there'.

42 **And when evening had come, since it was the day of Preparation, that is, the day before the sabbath,**

Exegesis: *ēdē opsias genomenēs* 'evening having already arrived', 'when evening had now come': ordinarily the phrase *opsias genomenēs* in Mark (cf. the references in 4:35) would indicate sunset or after, especially with the addition of *ēdē* (cf. 6:35, 11:11) 'already', 'by now'. Here, however, it seems that all that Joseph of Arimathea did took place between the ninth hour (3:00 P.M.), when Jesus died, and sunset, which would mark the beginning of the sabbath (cf. Lagrange). Jeremias (*Eucharistic Words*, 3) points out that Mark has a habit of using a second time reference precisely to define the first one, and refers to 1:32, 1:35, 4:35, 13:24, 14:12, 14:30, 16:2: here, therefore, evening is approaching, but it is still the day of Preparation, before sabbath begins at 6:00 P.M.

epei (only here in Mark) 'since', 'because'.

paraskeuē (only here in Mark; cf. Mt. 27:62, Lk. 23:54, Jn. 19:14, 31, 42) 'day of preparation' (from *paraskeuazō* 'prepare'), i.e. Friday, the day the Jews made preparation for the sabbath. Josephus (*Antiquities* XVI. 6. 2) indicates that preparation for the sabbath usually began after the ninth hour (3:00 P.M.) on Friday afternoon.

prosabbaton (only here in the N.T.) 'before the sabbath'.

Translation: *Evening had come* is probably best translated as 'late in the afternoon' or 'becoming dusk'.

Day of Preparation may be 'day for preparing', but if the verb 'preparing' is only transitive, one may need to add 'the feast', i.e. 'day for preparing the feast'.

For *sabbath* see 1:21.

43 *Joseph of Arimathea, a respected member of the council, who was also himself looking for the kingdom of God, took courage and went to Pilate, and asked for the body of Jesus.*

Exegesis: *Iōsēph ho apo Harimathaias* 'Joseph who (was) from Arimathea', 'Joseph of Arimathea': the man is identified by the name of the town from which he hailed. Arimathea was a city in Judea which Dalman (*Sacred Sites and Ways*, 225-26) locates to the northwest of Jerusalem.

euschēmōn (only here in Mark) 'prominent', 'of repute', 'noble': perhaps, 'wealthy' (cf. Mt. 27:57).

bouleutēs (only here in Mark) 'counsellor', i.e. a member of the Sanhedrin (cf. Lk. 23:50-51).

ēn prosdechomenos (only here in Mark) 'he was waiting for', 'he was expecting'.

tēn basileian tou theou (cf. 1:15) 'the Kingdom of God': Joseph is spoken of as awaiting its arrival, its coming, as in 1:15, 9:1.

tolmēsas (cf. 12:34) 'being bold': here, as RSV has it, 'he took courage' (cf. Field *Notes*, 44).

The action of Joseph of Arimathea in requesting the body of Jesus was probably motivated by the requirement in the Jewish law (Deut. 21:23) that prohibited leaving the bodies of executed men exposed overnight.

497

Translation: The sentence which begins with verse 42 and extends through verse 43 is relatively difficult to translate, not primarily because of its length, but because of the shifts in subject and the included explanatory expressions. In some languages, it is preferable to make verse 42 a separate sentence, e.g. 'it was already evening, since it was the day of Preparation, that is the day before the sabbath'. Verse 43 can then begin, 'Joseph of Arimathea, who was a respected member...and who was looking..., took courage...'

Of Arimathea may be translated in some languages as 'from the town of Arimathea'.

Respected member of the council involves two concepts: (1) the respect with which Joseph was regarded and (2) his function as a member of the Sanhedrin. These two ideas are variously combined: 'one of the members of the council and noble' (Maya), 'a true man among the older men' (Chontal of Tabasco), 'a fixer of affairs who was respected' (Huastec), 'a big honorable official' (Tzeltal).

Looking for must not be understood in the sense of 'out searching', but rather waiting for with hope and expectancy, e.g. 'waiting for the time when God would rule' (Zoque) and 'wait, hoping for God's rule'.

For *the kingdom of God* see 1:15 and 4:11.

Took courage may be translated in a manner similar to *take heart* (6:50.) In Zoque one may say 'took strength and went to Pilate'. In Tzeltal the expression is rendered in a negative form 'was not afraid to go to Pilate'.

Body is often translated by two quite different words, depending upon whether the person is alive or dead. In this case one would use the equivalent of 'corpse'.

44 *And Pilate wondered if he were already dead; and summoning the centurion, he asked him whether he was already dead.*

Text: Nestle and the majority of editions of the Greek text have *palai* 'for some time' (before *apethanen* 'he died'); Westcott and Hort, Lagrange, Taylor, Kilpatrick (and RSV), however, read *ēdē* 'already'.

Exegesis: *ethaumasen ei* 'he marvelled that' (and not RSV 'he wondered if'; cf. BFBS 'was astonished that'): *ei* after *thaumazō* 'to marvel', 'to wonder at' (cf. 5:20) is to be translated 'that', indicating the cause of the wonder or admiration (cf. Arndt & Gingrich *ei* II; Moule *Idiom Book*, 154; Burton *Moods and Tenses*, §277; cf. 1 Jn. 3:13 which RSV correctly translates 'wonder...that'). The verb *thaumazō* here does not mean 'to wonder' in the sense of 'to conjecture', 'to be undecided about': it means 'to wonder at', 'to marvel'.

ēdē tethnēken 'he had already died', 'he was by now dead'.

thnēskō (only here in Mark; cf. *apothnēskō* 5:35) 'to die'.

proskalesamenos (cf. 3:13) 'summoning', 'calling to himself'.

epērōtēsen auton ei 'he asked him if': *ei* 'if' used in indirect questions (cf. 3:2) has the sense of 'whether' (cf. Arndt & Gingrich V.2.a).

palai apethanen (Nestle text) 'a long time (ago) he died': although *palai* usually means 'for a long time' it can mean (as it probably does here) 'already', as a virtual synonym of *ēdē* 'already', 'by now' (cf. Arndt & Gingrich *palai* 2.a,b; RSV margin translates *palai* 'some time').

Translation: *Wondered if...* is translatable in some languages only as direct discourse, e.g. 'Pilate said in his mind, Is it really true that he has died?' (Chontal of Tabasco).

Were already dead identifies a state, but in some languages the process must be specifically mentioned, e.g. 'had already died'.

Summoning is rendered in some languages as 'sent for the centurion to come' or 'sent servants to say to the centurion to come'. *Summoning* should not be rendered as 'yelled at'.

Asked him whether..., if shifted into the form of direct discourse, may be translated as 'asked him, Is Jesus already dead?' If the indirect discourse is retained one must make certain that the proper referent for *he* is understood; otherwise the reader may be confused with what is grammatically a reference to the centurion or even to Pilate.

45 *And when he learned from the centurion that he was dead, he granted the body to Joseph.*

Text: Instead of *ptōma* 'corpse' of the modern editions of the Greek text, *Textus Receptus* has *soma* 'body'.

Exegesis: *gnous* (cf. 6: 38, 8 : 17) 'finding (it) out', 'learning (it)'. RSV adds 'that he was dead' for clarity: there are no equivalent words in the Greek text.

edōrēsato (only here in Mark) 'he bestowed', 'he presented', 'he gave'.

to ptōma (cf. 6: 29) 'the corpse', 'the (dead) body'.

Translation: *Learned from the centurion that...* may require adjustment to direct discourse, e.g. 'when the centurion had told him, Jesus is dead'.

Granted must not be translated in such a way as to imply that Pilate literally handed over to Joseph the body of Jesus. A more meaningful rendering is often 'told him that he could take' or 'allowed him to have'.

46 *And he bought a linen shroud, and taking him down, wrapped him in the linen shroud, and laid him in a tomb which had been hewn out of the rock; and he rolled a stone against the door of the tomb.*

Text: Instead of *katethēken* 'he deposited' of the majority of editions of the Greek text, Westcott and Hort, Souter, Lagrange, and Taylor have *ethēken* 'he placed'.

Exegesis: *agorasas* (cf. 6: 36) 'buying': according to normal usage of the aorist participle, 'he bought' indicates here an action which followed the actions in the preceding verses (and preceded the action of the main verb in this verse). It is not, therefore, to be translated 'he had bought'.

sindona (cf. 14: 51) 'a linen cloth', 'a linen sheet': RSV 'linen shroud'

is derived, of course, from the use to which the cloth was put.
kathelōn (cf. v. 36) 'taking down (from the cross)'.
auton 'him', i.e. Jesus, and not 'it' (the body).
eneilēsen (only here in the N.T.) 'he wound in', 'he wrapped in'.
katethēken (only here in Mark) 'he deposited', 'he placed'.
en mnēmati (cf. 5:3) 'in a tomb'.
ēn lelatomēmenon (only here in Mark) 'it had been hewn out': here this verbal phrase has its proper meaning as a pluperfect, indicating an action completed in the past.
ek petras (only here in Mark; cf. *petrōdēs*, 4:5) 'out of the rock': as further details indicate, this is to be thought of as an artificial cave or cavern dug out from the side of the rock, and not a grave dug into the ground, below the surface of the earth.
prosekulisen lithon epi tēn thuran 'he rolled a stone against the entrance'. *thura* here is not to be thought of as a 'door' or 'gate', its normal meaning; it is the entrance to the tomb (cf. Arndt & Gingrich *thura* 1.b).
For *mnēmeion* 'tomb' cf. 5:2.

Translation: *Linen shroud* is generally 'linen cloth', or where linen is quite unknown 'good white cloth' is used as a functional equivalent.

Though the Greek text refers to 'him', rather than the body, as being taken down from the cross, in translations it is often necessary to specify the body, since 'him' would refer only to a living person or to his ghost. Hence, 'took the body down, wrapped it in a linen cloth, and laid it in a tomb' is the only correct equivalent expression for the Greek text.

Tomb may be described as 'a small cave which was cut (or 'dug') out of the rock'.

Rock may be translated as 'rock cliff', so as to indicate that the cave was dug into a rock cliff, rather than excavated out of the ground.

Rolled a stone against the door has very often been mistranslated in such a way that people assume that a door was used to close the tomb and then that a large stone was rolled up in front of the door so as to prevent easy entrance. Rather the meaning is that a large stone was 'rolled up to cover the entrance to the tomb'.

In some languages distinctions must be made between various kinds of stone, e.g. 'limestone' vs. 'sandstone' (Shipibo). It is more likely that the tomb was hewn out of limestone.

47 Mary Magdalene and Mary the mother of Joses saw where he was laid.

Exegesis: *etheōroun* (cf. 3:11) 'they were observing', 'they were watching'.
pou (cf. 14:12) 'where'.
tetheitai 'he has been placed', 'he has been put'.

Translation: *Mary Magdalene and Mary the mother of Joses* may be translated as 'Mary who was from Magdala town and Mary who was Joses' mother'.

He was laid, if changed into an active form, may be translated as 'they put him' (or 'the body').

CHAPTER SIXTEEN

1 *And when the sabbath was past, Mary Magdalene, and Mary the mother of James, and Salome, bought spices, so that they might go and anoint him.*

Exegesis: *diagenomenou tou sabbatou* 'the sabbath having passed': this would be any time after 6:00 P.M. on Saturday, when the first day of the week would begin. In the context, it would have been Saturday evening when the women bought the spices.

diaginomai (only here in Mark) 'to go through': of time, 'to pass', 'to elapse'.

For Mary Magdalene and Mary the mother of James cf. 15 : 40.

ēgorasan (cf. 6:36) 'they bought'.

arōmata (only here in Mark) 'spices', 'aromatic oils (or, 'salves')': used in the Jewish practice of anointing the dead, for burial.

aleipsōsin (cf. 6:13; cf. *murizō* in 14:8) 'they might anoint': it is to be noticed that this is an anointing, and not the (Egyptian) art of embalming. Therefore Synodale *pour embaumer* and Brazilian *para... embalsamá-lo* may be misleading.

Translation: The phrase *and Salome* may require a transposition in order to avoid the meaning of Mary being the mother of both James and Salome, e.g. 'Mary from Magdala, Salome, and Mary the mother of James'.

Spices must not be translated in such a way as to refer only to spices used as condiments, a not infrequent error. In Tzeltal the proper equivalent is 'fragrant medicines', in which 'medicines' is a general term for any kind of ointment or salve, regardless of its function. In Navajo, the only phrase which may be employed is 'herbs for anointing', in which 'herbs' covers all types of substances derived from plants. In Ifugao a descriptive equivalent is 'sweet-smelling things'.

Evidently the buying of the spices took place in the evening after the sabbath had ended at sundown, but the actual going to the tomb was early the following morning.

Anoint him is 'anoint his body' in many languages; otherwise there is an implicit reference to Jesus as still living.

2 *And very early on the first day of the week they went to the tomb when the sun had risen.*

Exegesis: *lian prōi tē mia tōn sabbatōn...anateilantos tou hēliou* 'very early on the first day of the week...when the sun had risen': this is Sunday morning (following the Saturday evening of the previous verse) at or soon after sunrise.

lian prōi (cf. 1 : 35) 'exceedingly early'.

tē mia tōn sabbatōn (only here in Mark; cf. Mt. 28 : 1, Lk. 24 : 1, Jn 20 : 1, 19, Acts 20 : 7, 1 Co. 16 : 2) 'the first (day) of the week': for this Semitism cf. Black *Aramaic*, 90. For the plural *sabbata* (cf. 1 : 21) 'sabbaths' meaning 'week', cf. Arndt & Gingrich *sabbaton* 2.b.

anatellō (cf. 4 : 6) 'come up', 'rise': the aorist participle indicates that the sun had risen.

erchontai epi to mnēma 'they come to the tomb': for this use of *epi* meaning 'to' cf. Arndt & Gingrich III.1.a.γ.

mnēma (cf. 5 : 3) 'tomb'.

Translation: *Week* is not usually difficult to translate since the division of the month into four units, representing different phases of the moon, is widely employed. However, where a term for week is not known, one can say 'the first of the seven days'. There is, however, a further difficulty with the phrase 'first day of the week' in that in many parts of the world Monday is regarded as the first day of the week. Nevertheless, the only solution seems to be to translate the phrase as it stands and depend on explanation to correct any local usage.

It is important that a translation of *very early* does not contradict the meaning of *when the sun had risen*, for in many languages, 'very early in the morning' means well before sunrise.

3 And they were saying to one another, "Who will roll away the stone for us from the door of the tomb?"

Exegesis: *pros heautas* (cf. 10 : 26, 12 : 7) 'to themselves', i.e. 'to one another' (as in 11 : 31, 14 : 4).

For the words in the question, 'Who will roll away the stone for us from the door of the tomb?' cf. 15 : 46.

apokuliō (only here in Mark; cf. *proskuliō* 15 : 46) 'roll away'.

Translation: A translation of the question in some languages may have to be 'who will roll away the stone which blocks the entrance to the tomb', for *door* is 'doorway' or 'entrance', not 'door' in its more usual sense.

4 And looking up, they saw that the stone was rolled back; for it was very large.

Exegesis: *anablepsasai* (cf. 6 : 41) 'looking up': Lagrange suggests that here the verb means 'look closely', 'look attentively'.

theōrousin (cf. 15 : 47) 'they notice', 'they observe'.

anakekulistai (only here in the N.T.; cf. *apokuliō* in previous verse) 'it has been rolled back'.

ēn gar megas sphodra 'for it was exceedingly large': this explanatory clause would seem logically to belong to v. 3, explaining the women's discussion as to who should roll away the stone for them. As it stands, at the end of this verse, it seems to explain why the women noticed it had been rolled away. Several translations circumvent the difficulty by disregarding *gar* 'because', 'for', a procedure which is not to be recommended.

sphodra (only here in Mark) 'very much', 'extremely', 'greatly'.

Translation: The women may have looked at the tomb from some little distance, and hence, because of the size of the stone, they could see that it had been rolled away. This at least provides some basis for the interpretation of *gar* as 'for', 'because'.

Was rolled back is not technically a passive, in that the women saw the stone actually being rolled back. What they saw was the state of the stone in a rolled-back position. This means that in some languages one must translate either as a pluperfect passive of process, e.g. 'had been rolled back' or as a past state, e.g. 'was in a rolled-back position'.

5 *And entering the tomb, they saw a young man sitting on the right side, dressed in a white robe; and they were amazed.*

Exegesis: *eiselthousai eis to mnēmeion* (cf. 5:2) 'going into the tomb': cf. 15:46, and see Lagrange for a description of the tomb as it probably was.

eidon neaniskon kathēmenon en tois dexiois peribeblēmenon stolēn leukēn 'they saw a young man sitting on the right, wearing a white robe': the description and the circumstances would imply that the 'young man' was, in fact, an angel, and Lagrange refers to 2 Macc. 3:26, 33 for a similar description. A translation should have, however, 'young man', and not 'angel'. For *neaniskos* 'young man' cf. 14:51; *kathēmai* 'sit' cf. 2:6; *en tois dexiois* 'on the right (side)' cf. 10:27 (elsewhere in Mark always *ek dexiōn*); *periballō* 'to clothe', 'wear' (cf. 14:51); *stolē* 'robe' cf. 12:38; *leukē* 'white' cf. 9:3.

exethambēthēsan (cf. 9:15) 'they were astonished'; perhaps (cf. Arndt & Gingrich) 'they were alarmed'. It should be noticed that this compound verb, indicating strong emotion, is used only by Mark in the New Testament.

Translation: *Entering the tomb* may be treated as a dependent clause of time, e.g. 'when they had entered the tomb, they saw...' or as a coordinate event in prior sequence, e.g. 'they entered the tomb and saw...'

Saw a young man sitting is a type of construction which requires two clauses in many languages, e.g. 'saw a young man; he was sitting'.

On the right side must be related to the orientation of the tomb or to the position of the women, not to the right side of Jesus, as some translations have implied, thus giving the impression that Jesus was still in the tomb, though unseen.

Dressed in a white robe would imply a garment which was both long and white, e.g. 'wearing clothing, long and white' (Zoque).

For *amazed* see 1:22, 27.

6 *And he said to them, "Do not be amazed; you seek Jesus of Nazareth, who was crucified. He has risen, he is not here; see the place where they laid him.*

Exegesis: *Iēsoun zēteite ton Nazarēnon ton estaurōmenon* 'you seek Jesus the Nazarene the crucified (one)': by some this is taken as a question (cf. Moffatt, Montgomery), but the majority translate it as a statement.

zēteō (cf. 3:32) 'look for', 'seek'.

ho Nazarēnos (cf. 14:67) 'the Nazarene': here, as in 14:67, more of a title than a geographical description.

ho estaurōmenos (cf. 15:13) 'he who has been crucified', 'the crucified one': in apposition to 'the Nazarene', this perfect passive participle with the definite article is probably to be taken as a title, and not simply translated as a relative clause (as done by RSV and the majority of translations). Cf. its use in 1 Co. 1:23, 2:2, Gal. 3:1. Cf. Weymouth 'the crucified one', and Zürich *den Gekreuzigten*.

egerthē (cf. 1:31) 'he was raised': in conformance with the uniform use of the passive form of the verb in Mark, in speaking of resurrection (cf. 14:28), the verb should be translated here as a passive, 'he has been raised' or even (in English) 'he is risen', rather than as an active, 'he has risen' (RSV).

ide ho topos hopou ethēkan auton 'look! (this is) the place where they placed him', 'here (is) the place where they laid him': it should be noticed that *ide* (cf. 2:24) is an exclamation, and *ho topos* 'the place' is not the direct object (as RSV's 'see the place' would make it appear).

ho topos 'the place': not the grave or tomb itself, but inside the tomb (v. 5) the shelf or alcove where Jesus' body had been placed (cf. Taylor).

ethēkan 'they placed', 'they laid': this is clearly an impersonal plural; 'they placed him' is equivalent to 'he was placed'.

Translation: *You seek* may be rendered as 'you are looking for' or 'you are trying to find'.

Though *of Nazareth* is probably more correctly conceived of as a title, it is rare that such a connotation can be given to this type of place name (see 14:67).

For expressions relating to *rising from the dead* see 8:31 and 9:9.

7 *But go, tell his disciples and Peter that he is going before you to Galilee; there you will see him, as he told you."*

Exegesis: *hupagete* (cf. 1:44) 'off with you!', 'go!', 'depart!'

tois mathētais autou (cf. 2:15) 'his disciples'.

kai tō Petrō 'and Peter': whatever may have been the reason why Peter was thus distinguished from the rest (most commentators think there is an allusion to his denial), it is fairly certain that Peter was not hereby classified as not being one of the disciples (cf. the similar case in Acts 1:14 'with the women *and Mary*'). If in a given language the connective 'and' should be exclusive, something like 'including also Peter' will fairly well convey the sense of the Greek.

hoti 'that': most commentators take *hoti* here to be recitative, introducing direct speech (so the translations of Goodspeed, Moffatt, Montgomery, Manson, Williams, BFBS, Zürich), and not declarative, introducing indirect speech (as RSV has it).

proagei humas eis tēn Galilaian (cf. 14:28) 'he goes before you into Galilee': the statement should be translated exactly the same here as it is in 14:28. The present *proagei* here probably has the force 'he *is* going ahead', 'he is *on his way* before (you)'.

ekei auton opsesthe kathōs eipen humin 'there you will see him, as he said to you': since the words 'there you will see me' are not in 14:28, C. H. Turner (*Journal of Theological Studies* 26.155-56, 1924-5) proposes that 'there you will see him' be placed in parentheses (so also Rawlinson). This seems overly subtle, however.

Translation: For *disciples* see 2:15, but in this context *his disciples and Peter*, if rendered literally, can be very misleading (see above), implying that Peter was no longer a disciple. A more correct equivalent of this expression in some languages is 'his disciples, including Peter' or even 'Peter and the other disciples'.

Whether *before you* is to be taken as temporal or spatial see the discussion under 14:28. The likelihood, however, is that *before* should be understood in the temporal sense, e.g. 'going on ahead of you' or 'going on before you do'.

8 ***And they went out and fled from the tomb; for trembling and astonishment had come upon them; and they said nothing to any one, for they were afraid.***

Exegesis: *exelthousai* 'going out (of the tomb)'.

eichen gar autas tromos kai ekstasis 'for trembling and astonishment had taken hold of them': for this use of *echō* 'have' cf. Arndt & Gingrich I.1.d; Field *Notes*, 44-45.

tromos (only here in Mark) 'trembling', 'quivering'.

ekstasis (cf. 5:42) 'confusion', 'astonishment', 'terror'.

ephobounto gar 'for they were afraid': for *phobeō* cf. 4:41. C. F. D. Moule suggests (*New Testament Studies* 2.58-59, 1955) their fear kept them from saying anything to any person they might have encountered, as they hurried straight to the disciples with the message.

Translation: The rendering of *from the tomb* may need to be related more closely to 'went out', since some languages require an indication of what was 'gone out of', e.g. 'went out of the tomb and fled away'.

Trembling and astonishment had come upon them is a form of expression which cannot be easily translated literally in many languages. In the first place *trembling* and *astonishment* are normally rendered by verbs, 'they were trembling and were astonished' (or 'amazed'). *Had come upon them* really means in many languages 'began to...' Hence, this clause may be translated as 'they began to tremble and to be astonished' (or 'terrified'). For *astonish* see 1:22, 27.

Here ends the Gospel of Mark, as it has been transmitted to us by the most reliable manuscripts. What is conventionally printed as vv. 9-20 of chapter 16 is a "Longer Ending" which early was appended to manuscripts and versions of the Gospel (cf. the Additional Note in the Appendix for reasons for not accepting this ending as Marcan); there exists also a "Shorter Ending," appended to other manuscripts and versions of the Gospel. By most scholars it is held that the Gospel is not complete, and various solutions to the problem are proposed: the ending was never written; the ending was lost; the ending, for some reason, was suppressed. The position which raises the least formidable counter arguments is that, for some reason or other, the Gospel was never completed. Some, however, hold that the author did in fact purposely end his Gospel with v. 8: cf. the references in Taylor, and among recent writers see especially R. H. Lightfoot *The Gospel Message of St. Mark*, 80-97, 106-16; Austin Farrer *A Study in St. Mark*, 172-81. Cf. also Arndt & Gingrich *phobeō* 1.a.

THE LONGER ENDING

The Longer Ending, conventionally printed as vv. 9-20 of chapter 16, is found in most manuscripts and versions. It is omitted by the two most ancient Greek Uncial manuscripts of the New Testament, Codex *Vaticanus* and Codex *Sinaiticus*, both of the 4th century. It is also omitted by the Old Latin manuscript *k* (4th or 5th century), by the oldest Syriac version of the Gospels, the Sinaitic Syriac (4th or 5th century), and by important codices of the Armenian, Ethiopic and Georgian versions.

Whether it existed as an independent document, or was the ending of a longer document, before being appended to the Gospel of Mark, is a matter of conjecture. It is a concise statement of the appearances of Jesus, his final command to the disciples, his ascension to the right hand of God, and the preaching of the gospel throughout the whole world.

It was early appended to the Gospel of Mark, probably between A.D. 100 and 140. Verbal similarity between v. 20 and a statement by Justin Martyr in *Apol.* I. 45 (c. A.D. 148) makes it possible (though not conclusively so) that he knew the passage. Tatian had the Longer Ending to Mark in his harmony of the four Gospels, the *Diatessaron* (c. A.D. 170). Ireneus (c. A.D. 180) is the first writer expressly to quote any part of this section as being from the Gospel of Mark: in his work *Adv. Haer.* III. x. 6 he says, "Also, towards the conclusion of his Gospel Mark says..." and quotes v. 19.

Since this ending was in the late manuscripts used by Erasmus (his oldest manuscript was of the 10th century, and the most important one for his edition of the Gospels was of the 15th century), it was included in his Greek New Testament (first edition 1516), and from then on was reprinted in all successive editions of the Greek New Testament, including the *Textus Receptus* (which, on the Continent, is Elzevir's 2nd edition, 1633, and in Britain is Stephanus' 3rd edition, 1550: both are substantially the same). Thus it was included in the Authorized Version of 1611 and all other translations based on the *Textus Receptus*.

In modern editions of the Greek New Testament the Longer Ending is generally printed in brackets, with a space separating it from Mark 16:8, as an appendix. They still follow, however, the traditional verse division (vv. 9-20 of chapter 16) of the *Textus Receptus*. Cf. the editions of Tischendorf, Soden, Vogels, Westcott and Hort, Souter, and Nestle.

Most modern translations continue to print it as part of Mark. Some, however, indicate its non-Marcan nature. ASV adds a footnote to the beginning of v. 9: "The two oldest Greek manuscripts, and some other authorities, omit from ver. 9 to the end. Some other authorities have a different ending to the Gospel." Synodale adds a footnote to v. 8: "The Gospel of Mark ends here in the two most ancient manuscripts," and includes vv. 9-20 in brackets. Zürich adds a footnote to the paragraph: "This paragraph is a supplement from a later hand." RSV prints the whole section in the margin, ending the Gospel at v. 8 (cf. V. Taylor: "The RSV is fully justified in placing the passage in the margin instead of, as in the RV, in the text after a wide space").

Any modern translation should indicate, by such means as these, that the Longer Ending is not part of the Gospel of Mark.

9 **Now when he rose early on the first day of the week, he appeared first to Mary Magdalene, from whom he had cast out seven demons.**

Exegesis: *anastas* (cf. Mk. 8:31) 'having risen (from the dead)'. The aorist masculine participle has as its implied subject 'he', i.e. Jesus. In Mk. 16:8, however, the subject throughout the whole verse is 'they', i.e. the women.

prōi (cf. Mk. 1:35) 'early': presumably before sunrise.

prōtē sabbatou 'on the first day of the week': the construction of the phrase here differs from the phrase used in Mk. 16:2, *tē miᴗ tōn sabbatōn*.

ephanē 'he was manifested', 'he appeared': the verb is used in Mk. 14:64 in a different sense.

Maria tē Magdalēnē par' hēs ekbeblēkei hepta daimonia 'to Mary the Magdalene from whom he had cast out seven demons': Mary is here introduced as though she had not been referred to before.

par' hēs 'from whom': nowhere else in the N.T. is this preposition used in connection with demon expulsion.

ekbeblēkei 'he had cast out': the pluperfect has its full force, describing an action completed in the past.

The statement that seven demons had been cast out of Mary of Magdala is from Lk. 8:2.

Translation: *He* must generally be changed to 'Jesus' in order to make clear the proper subject constituent.

A number of the lexical units in this verse have already been treated: *rose* (8:31 and 9:9), *first day of the week* (16:2), *Mary Magdalene* (15:40), *cast out* (1:34), and *demons* (1:26, 32).

Appeared may be rendered as 'showed himself to' or 'caused her to see him'.

10 *She went and told those who had been with him, as they mourned and wept.*

Exegesis: *ekeinē* 'that one', i.e. 'she': the demonstrative pronoun is used here and in vv. 11, 13, 20, in a way different from that in which it is used in Mark, who never uses it to refer to the disciples.

poreutheisa (vv. 12, 15) 'going', 'proceeding': this verb is not used by Mark.

apēggeilen tois met' autou genomenois 'she announced (it) to those who had been with him'. For the verb *apaggellō* cf. Mk. 5:14.

hoi met' autou genomenoi 'those who had been with him': this description of the disciples, which is not used by Mark, is translated by Arndt & Gingrich (*ginomai* II.4.a) 'his intimate friends'; Goodspeed translates 'his old companions'.

penthousi kai klaiousin 'while they were mourning and weeping': the two present participles describe the state the disciples were in.

pentheō (not in Mark) 'be sad', 'grieve', 'mourn'.

klaiō (cf. Mk. 5:38) 'cry', 'weep'.

Translation: *Told* requires in some receptor languages not only an object specifying what was said, but also an object indicating who was addressed, e.g. 'told those who had been with him what had happened', or 'told the news to those who had been with him'. On the other hand, it is often possible to choose a verb of speaking which requires only an indication of those spoken to, e.g. 'spoke to those who had been with him'.

11 *But when they heard that he was alive and had been seen by her, they would not believe it.*

Exegesis: *kakeinoi* (= *kai ekeinoi*; cf. v. 10) 'and they'.

etheathē (not in Mark; cf. v. 14) 'he had been seen'.

ēpistēsan (not in Mark; cf. v. 16) 'they were unbelieving', 'they disbelieved (it)'. Cf. *apistia* in Mk. 6:6.

Translation: *Had been seen by her* may be transposed into an active form as 'she had seen him'.

He was alive must be very carefully rendered, for in some translations the form of this phrase has been such as to deny that Jesus ever died. To avoid such a misinterpretation the rendering in Zoque is 'that Jesus just existing one', thus avoiding the use of the verb 'to live' which would imply continued living and that Jesus had merely suffered a coma when he was put into the tomb.

Not believe it may be equivalent to saying 'they doubted it'.

12 *After this he appeared in another form to two of them, as they were walking into the country.*

Exegesis: *meta...tauta* 'after this': this temporal phrase is not used by Mark.

dusin ex autōn peripatousin...poreuomenois eis agron 'to two of them as they were walking...going to the country': this appearance would seem to be that one which is described in Lk. 24:13-35.

peripateō (cf. Mk. 2:9) 'walk', 'walk about'.

poreuomai (cf. v. 10) 'go'.

eis agron (cf. *ap' agrou* Mk. 15:21) 'to the country': the context implies a journey from Jerusalem out to the neighboring rural region.

ephanerōthē en hetera morphē 'he was manifested in another form', 'he appeared in a different fashion': the statement seems to be that this appearance was in a form different from that in which he appeared to Mary.

phaneroō (not used with this meaning in Mark; cf. v. 14) 'to make manifest'; in the passive, as here, 'to be made manifest', 'to appear' (in Mk. 4:22 of a hidden matter, 'to be revealed'). BFBS translates here 'He was revealed'.

en hetera morphē 'in a different form': what is meant, apparently, is that in manifesting himself to these two Jesus took on a different form or appearance from that in which he appeared to Mary. The adjective *heteros* 'another', 'different' is not in Mark, nor is *morphē* 'form', 'shape', 'appearance' (elsewhere in the N.T. it appears only in Phil. 2:6, 7). In the Transfiguration story in Mark the change which Jesus underwent is described by Mark by the verb *metamorphoō* (Mk. 9:2).

Translation: *Appeared in another form* may be rendered as 'came to two of them in a different appearance' or 'he looked different as he came to two of them'. In Tzeltal this is rendered as 'looking like another'.

Into the country identifies the open country away from the city, roughly equivalent to 'out into the fields' in some languages.

13 And they went back and told the rest, but they did not believe them.

Exegesis: *kakeinoi* (cf. v. 11) 'and they'.

apelthontes 'going away', 'going off': apparently, from the context, the meaning here is that 'they went *back*' to the city of Jerusalem, where the others were. (Of the twenty-one times Mark uses the verb *aperchomai*, only once—in 7:30—can it be taken to mean 'go back', 'return').

tois loipois (cf. Mk. 4:19) 'to the remaining ones', 'to the rest': that is, the other disciples, 'those who had been with him' of v. 10.

oude ekeinois episteusan 'neither did they believe them'.

pisteuō (cf. Mk. 1:15) 'believe', 'have faith'.

Translation: *The rest* must very often be translated with a more specific referent, 'the rest of the disciples' or 'the rest of those that had been with him'.

14 Afterward he appeared to the eleven themselves as they sat at table; and he upbraided them for their unbelief and hardness of heart, because they had not believed those who saw him after he had risen.

Text: See below, at the end of the exegesis of this verse.

Exegesis: *husteron* (not in Mark) 'later', 'thereafter' (cf. Arndt & Gingrich 2.a); here, perhaps 'finally', 'lastly' (cf. Lagrange, who translates *enfin*).

anakeimenois autois tois hendeka 'to the Eleven themselves, while they were eating'.

anakeimai (cf. Mk. 6:26) 'recline at table'.

hoi hendeka 'the Eleven': as in the case of 'the Twelve' in Mark (cf. 3:16), a title, not a number.

ōneidisen (cf. Mk. 15:32) 'he reproached', 'he rebuked'.

apistian (cf. Mk. 6:6) 'unbelief', 'lack of faith'.

sklērokardian (cf. Mk. 10:5) 'hardness of heart', 'obtuseness', 'obstinacy'.

hoti tois theasamenois auton egēgermenon ouk episteusan 'because they did not believe those who had seen him risen'.

theaomai (cf. v. 11) 'see'.

egeirō (cf. Mk. 1:31) 'rise': in the passive, as here, 'be raised'. The perfect passive participle here can be translated 'resurrected'.

In manuscript *W* (the Greek uncial manuscript "Freer"), of the fourth or fifth century, at the end of the verse the following passage is added (Moffatt's translation): "But they excused themselves, saying 'This age of unbelief lies under the sway of Satan, who will not allow what lies under the unclean spirits to understand the truth and power of God; therefore,' they said to Christ, 'reveal your righteousness now.' Christ answered them, 'The term of years for Satan's power has now expired, but other terrors are at hand. I was delivered to death on behalf of sinners, that they might return to the truth and sin no more, that they might inherit that glory of righteousness which is spiritual and imperishable in heaven.' "

Until the discovery of *W* (otherwise called the "Washington" manuscript) in Egypt in 1906, the first part of this passage (from the beginning until the words "...reveal your righteousness now") was known from its quotation by Jerome, who said it was found "in certain copies [of the Gospel], and especially in Greek codices" (*Adv. Pelag.* ii. 15).

Translation: *Appeared* may be 'showed himself', 'presented himself where they were', or 'caused himself to be seen by'.

The eleven, as with the phrase *the twelve*, must often be supplemented with a substantive, e.g. 'the eleven disciples'.

Sat at table is usually better rendered as 'were eating'.

Upbraided may be rendered in some languages as 'scolded', 'criticized', or 'denounced them because of...'

Their unbelief is frequently translated as a clause containing a verb, e.g. 'because they did not believe' (for *believe* see 1:15).

For *for their hardness of heart* see 6:52, but note that in a plural construction the pronominal referents and plural forms of substantives must agree, e.g. 'because they did not have pain in their hearts' (Tzeltal).

If the phrase *for their unbelief and their hardness of heart* is rendered as 'because they did not believe and because their hearts were hard' it may then be impossible to employ the following clause 'because they had not believed...' since such a postposed causal clause would seem to give the reason for the hard hearts, not the reason why Jesus rebuked the disciples. Accordingly, one may have to end the first sentence with 'hardness of heart' and begin over again, e.g. 'he rebuked them because they had not...'

15 And he said to them, "Go into all the world and preach the gospel to the whole creation.

Exegesis: *poreuthentes* (cf. v. 10) 'going', 'proceeding': in connection with the main verb, which is in the imperative, the participle also has imperatival force, 'you go!'

eis ton kosmon hapanta kēruxate to euaggelion 'into all the world preach the gospel': nearly all the words in this clause are found in Mk. 8:36. For *hapas* 'all' cf. Mk. 1:27.

pasē tē ktisei 'to the whole creation': it is probable that *ktisis* here means 'mankind' (cf. Arndt & Gingrich 1.b.β), i.e. that which is created, and not the act of creation itself (as it is used in Mark: cf. 10:6). As Gould points out, the presence of the definite article before *ktisis* requires the meaning 'the whole creation' (and not AV 'every creature').

Translation: *Go into*, if translated literally, may not be applicable to the context, for in many languages one may only 'go out to' or 'travel around in', when speaking of an extension of territory such as the earth. Otherwise, readers may think that this has some mystic meaning about the souls of people going into the interior of the earth. An equivalent of this expression in some receptor languages is 'go out all over the land' or 'travel everywhere over the earth'.

For *preach* see 1:4 and for *gospel* see 1:1.

In many languages the collective, abstract noun *creation* cannot be translated literally and meaningfully in this context. The equivalent expression is 'among all men' (Zoque) and 'to all who are created' (Ifugao).

16 He who believes and is baptized will be saved; but he who does not believe will be condemned.

Exegesis: *ho pisteusas kai baptistheis* 'he who believes and is baptized': the single definite article governing both participles joins the two verbs together in describing the man who will be saved; the clause could be translated, 'the baptized believer'.

pisteuō 'believe': here and in v. 17 the aorist participle is used absolutely, 'the believer' (in Mark, the present active participle is used absolutely twice, 9:23, 42—never the aorist participle).

baptizō (cf. Mk. 1:5) 'baptize'.

sōthēsetai (cf. Mk. 3:4) 'shall be saved': in the theological sense; in apposition to 'shall be condemned', the reference is eschatological.

ho...apistēsas (cf. v. 11) 'the one who does not believe': the aorist participle is parallel to 'the believer' in the previous clause, and may be translated, 'the unbeliever'.

katakrithēsetai 'shall be condemned': the verb *katakrinō* is not used in Mark (cf. 10:33) in the theological sense, as here. The reference is obviously eschatological: 'he shall be condemned in the Day of Judgment'.

Translation: *Believes* is often translatable only by a transitive verb, requiring an object. In this instance one may use 'the gospel' (or 'the good news') as object.

For *baptize* see 1:4, and for *save* see 10:26.

Condemned is more than 'judged' or 'denounced'. There should be some connotation of judgment for sin, e.g. 'he who does not believe still has his sin', implying a continuing guilt (Tzotzil), 'whom God will cause to find sin', in which only an active form can be used (Zoque), and 'arrive to get words because of sin' (Tzeltal). In some instances condemnation is spoken of in quite idiomatic ways, e.g. 'condemnation will eat in him' (Conob).

17 *And these signs will accompany those who believe: in my name they will cast out demons; they will speak in new tongues;*

Text: *kainais* 'new' is omitted by Westcott and Hort, and Taylor, but included by the great majority of editions of the Greek text.

Exegesis: *sēmeia* (v. 20; cf. Mk. 8:11) 'signs': here, as in Mk. 8:11, the signs are miraculous or supernatural events attesting to the divine origin of the message proclaimed.

tois pisteusasin (cf. v. 16) 'those who believe', 'the believers'.

parakolouthēsei (not in Mark) 'will accompany', 'will follow', 'will attend'.

en tō onomati mou (cf. Mk. 9:38) 'in my name'.

daimonia ekbalousin (cf. v. 9) 'they will expel demons'.

glōssais lalēsousin kainais 'they will speak in new tongues': whether these 'new tongues' are intelligible foreign languages, or ecstatic charismatic utterances, the text does not say. It is to be presumed, however, that the meaning here is the same as that in Acts 2:4-11, rather than that in I Co. 14 (it should be observed, however, that nowhere else is the phrase 'speak in *new* tongues' used: in Acts 2:4 'speak in *other* tongues' is used, while I Co. 14 has simply 'to speak in tongues' or, 'a tongue').

glōssa 'tongue', meaning here 'language' (the word is not used in this sense in Mark—cf. 7:33).

kainē 'new': the meaning here is, presumably, 'new (i.e. strange) to the one speaking it' not necessarily 'new' in the sense of a heretofore unknown language.

Translation: For *signs* see 8:11, but in this context it is difficult to speak of 'signs' as 'accompanying' or 'following'; these are activities restricted to persons, rather than to signs or symbols. Sometimes, however, one can say that 'signs will be present in those who...' or 'signs will be with those who ... ' In other languages the clause must be recast as 'those who believe will show these signs: ...'

For *cast out demons* see 1:26, 32, and 34; and for *in my name* see 9:37.

In most languages one cannot say 'speak in a tongue'. In fact, more often than not one speaks 'with the mouth', not 'with the tongue'. Hence, in this passage one must use 'speak strange languages' or 'speak other languages'. If possible one should leave as ambiguous whether the 'language' in this case is actually a foreign language or ecstatic speech.

18 *they will pick up serpents, and if they drink any deadly thing, it will not hurt them; they will lay their hands on the sick, and they will recover."*

Exegesis: *opheis* (not in Mark) 'snakes', 'serpents'.

thanasimon ti piōsin 'something deadly they may drink': the adjective *thanasimos* 'deadly' (not used elsewhere in the N.T.) probably stands here for 'deadly *poison*'.

ou mē autous blapsē 'it will in no way harm them': the double negative is emphatic.

blaptō (not in Mark) 'harm', 'injure', 'hurt'.

epi arrōstous cheiras epithēsousin 'upon sick people they will lay hands'. For *arrōstos* 'sick', 'feeble' cf. Mk. 6:5; for *epitithenai cheiras* 'lay hands upon' cf. Mk. 5:23.

kalōs hexousin (not elsewhere in the N.T.; cf. *kakōs echein* Mk. 1:32) 'they will get well', 'they will recover'.

Translation: The lack of symmetry and parallelism in the two initial clauses of this verse may cause some trouble, for the first is a statement of actual experience *they will pick up serpents* and the second is a condition *if they drink any deadly thing*. The first clause of this verse may be interpreted merely as a future statement, but it is also possible to relate it to the following clauses in such a way as to understand the passage as a kind of conditional statement, namely, 'if they pick up ..., they will not be hurt.' This requires, however, the interpretation of the third clause as the apodosis of two different 'if' clauses: (1) 'picking up serpents' and (2) 'drinking any deadly thing'. The last two clauses of this verse are similarly related as condition and result, for the first of these two clauses is essentially the condition, 'if they lay their hands on the sick', while the last clause is the result, e.g. 'they will recover'. In languages in which the paratactically related conditional clauses must be more closely attached to the result, one may translate as 'if they pick up serpents and if they drink any deadly thing, they will not suffer harm from these; if they lay their hands on the sick people, these will recover'.

In some languages there are quite different words for serpents, depending upon whether or not they are poisonous. Naturally, the poisonous type is implied in this context.

Deadly thing may be rendered as 'a liquid which would kill them' or 'a drink which kills people'. It is important not to refer exclusively to a kind of poison cup used only in ordeals by which innocence can be proved (a common practice in Africa).

They will lay their hands on the sick and they will recover may be grammatically confusing in languages in which the same subject is understood in two such coordinate clauses unless there is some mark to the contrary. After all, it is not the ones who lay their hands on the sick, but the sick themselves, who recover. Hence, one may be required to recast this sentence as 'they will lay their hands on the sick people, and these people will get well again' or 'if they lay their hands on the sick people, these will get well'.

19 *So then the Lord Jesus, after he had spoken to them, was taken up into heaven, and sat down at the right hand of God.*

Text: *Iēsous* 'Jesus' is omitted by *Textus Receptus*, Tischendorf, and Kilpatrick, but included by the great majority of modern editions of the Greek text.

Exegesis: *ho ... kurios Iēsous* 'the Lord Jesus': this phrase is not found in the Gospels (except, perhaps, in Lk. 24: 3), and *ho kurios* 'the Lord' is not used of Jesus in the Marcan historical narrative (unless it be at 11: 3, which see; cf. 1: 3).

meta to lalēsai autois 'after speaking to them': for the use of *meta* with the infinitive cf. Mk. 1: 14.

anelēmphthē (not in Mark) 'he was taken up'.

ekathisen ek dexiōn tou theou 'he sat at the right hand of God': the language is from Ps. 110: 1, which is quoted in Mk. 12: 36.

Translation: In some languages the construction *the Lord Jesus, after he had spoken to them* is not possible. One must incorporate the subject 'the Lord Jesus' within the dependent clause, 'after the Lord Jesus had spoken to them, he was taken...'

Was taken up must be changed into an active construction in some languages, in which case 'God' may be used as a subject. However, 'taken up' should not be translated in such a way as to imply 'yanked up' or 'hauled up', as in some translations. 'Caused to go up' or 'caused to go up and received' may be employed in some instances.

The right hand may be 'the right side', or as in some languages 'the side of power' or 'the side of strength'.

For *Lord* see 1: 3.

In order that *them* may not be understood as 'the sick' of the preceding verse, it may be necessary to substitute 'disciples'.

20 *And they went forth and preached everywhere, while the Lord worked with them and confirmed the message by the signs that attended it. Amen.*

Text: *Amēn* 'Amen' is included by *Textus Receptus*, Souter (and RSV), but omitted by the great majority of modern editions of the Greek text.

Exegesis: *ekeinoi* (cf. v. 11) 'they', i.e. the disciples.

exelthontes 'going out', 'leaving': presumably, from Jerusalem.

pantachou (cf. Mk. 1:28) 'everywhere'.

tou kuriou sunergountos kai...bebaiountos 'as the Lord worked with (them) and confirmed': 'the Lord' here refers to the ascended and reigning Lord Jesus.

sunergeō (not in Mark) 'work with', 'cooperate'.

bebaioō (not in Mark) 'make firm', 'establish', 'confirm'.

ton logon (cf. Mk. 2:2) 'the (Christian) message', 'the Word'.

dia tōn epakolouthountōn sēmeiōn 'by means of the accompanying signs': for *sēmeia* 'signs' cf. v. 17. It is to be presumed that the signs referred to here are those described in vv. 17-18.

epakoloutheō (not in Mark) 'follow after': it is probable that the force of the verb here is 'authenticate', a meaning which has been found in the papyri (cf. Moulton & Milligan; cf. Milligan *Documents*, 78-79). The signs not only accompanied the preaching of the message, but authenticated it. Cf. Moffatt, 'by the miracles that endorsed it'.

Translation: *They* can usually be translated by a pronoun if in the preceding verse the noun 'disciples' has been employed.

For *preached* see 1:4 and for *signs* see 8:11.

While is used in a somewhat unusual manner in this verse, for the meaning is not that they preached merely while the Lord was working. Rather, *while* implies 'and at the same time', a rendering which must be employed in a number of languages.

Worked with them is in some languages equivalent to 'helped them'.

Confirmed the message may be 'made the message strong' or, as is more often the case, 'showed that what they said was true'. In Tzeltal this expression is idiomatically rendered as 'the signs done by them became a mate for the words'.

There are difficulties in a literal translation of *attended*, for often people cannot speak of 'signs attending' anything. On the other hand, one may be able to say 'by means of the signs which were shown at that time' or 'by the signs which God caused to be done then'.

Amen may be either transliterated (a very common practice) or translated into a form of expression which is closely parallel and customarily used in such contexts, e.g. 'that is just the way it is' (Huichol), 'that's it' (Shilluk), 'may it be thus' (Tzeltal), or 'and so it was'.

THE SHORTER ENDING

The passage that follows is found after Mark 16:8 (and before the Longer Ending, except in the Old Latin manuscript *k*) in the following manuscripts: the Greek Uncial manuscripts *L* (8th century), Ψ (8th or 9th century), 099 (7th century) and 0112 (7th century); the Greek Minuscule manuscripts 274 (marginal reading; 10th century) and 579 (13th century); the Old Latin manuscript *k* (4th or 5th century); in the margin of the Harclean Syriac version (7th century); and in several codices of the Sahidic, Bohairic and Ethiopic versions.

Unlike the Longer Ending, this one was written expressly to provide a suitable ending to the Gospel. It is dated in the 2nd century. (For information on the subject, in addition to the standard commentaries, one may refer to B. H. Streeter *The Four Gospels*, 335-36; Westcott and Hort *The New Testament in the Original Greek, Appendix*, "Notes on Select Readings," 38.)

But they reported briefly to Peter and those with him all that they had been told.

Exegesis: *panta de ta pareggelmena* 'and all (things) that they had been ordered'.

paraggellō (cf. Mk. 6:8) 'command', 'order'.

tois peri ton Petron 'to Peter and his companions': for similar phrases cf. Mk. 4:10, Acts 13:13; cf. Arndt & Gingrich *peri* 2.a.δ.

suntomōs (not in Mark) 'briefly', 'concisely'; Arndt & Gingrich prefer here the meaning 'promptly', 'readily'.

exēggeilan (not in Mark) 'they reported', 'they proclaimed'.

Translation: *They* must refer to the women of 16:1, referred to by pronouns in verse 8.

Briefly may be translated as 'with few words', but the likely meaning of 'promptly' would suggest a better rendering such as 'right away', 'soon', or 'immediately'.

Had been told may be changed to an active form, e.g. 'the young man had told them'.

And after this, Jesus himself sent out by means of them, from east to west, the sacred and imperishable proclamation of eternal salvation.

Exegesis: *meta de tauta* (not in Mark; cf. Longer Ending v. 12) 'and after this'.

apo anatolēs kai achri duseōs 'from the East as far as the West', i.e. 'throughout the whole world' (cf. the similar 'the four winds' in Mk. 13:27). See 'from the east and west' in Mt. 8:11//Lk. 13:29.

anatolē (not in Mark; cf. *anatellō* Mk. 4:6) 'the rising (of the sun)', 'the East'.

achri (not in Mark) 'as far as'.

dusmē (not in Mark) 'the going down (of the sun)', 'the West'.

exapesteilen (not in Mark) 'he sent out', 'he sent forth'.

to hieron kai aphtharton kērugma 'the sacred and incorruptible message'.

hieros (not in Mark; for the substantive *to hieron* 'the Temple', cf. Mk. 11:11) 'sacred', 'holy'.

aphthartos (not in Mark) 'incorruptible', i.e. 'imperishable', 'immortal'.

kērugma (not in Mark; cf. *kērussō* Mk. 1:4) 'message', 'proclamation'.

tēs aiōniou sōtērias 'of the eternal salvation'.

aiōnios (cf. Mk. 3:29) 'eternal'.

sōtēria (not in Mark) 'salvation', 'redemption'.

Translation: *By means of them* must refer to the disciples, not to the women who are the subject of the preceding verse, and might be assumed to be the persons referred to here.

From east to west cannot be translated literally in most languages, for it would mean 'starting from the east and going to the west'. A more accurate rendering in most languages is 'everywhere (or 'all places') both east and west'.

Sent out...the...proclamation is impossible in some languages, since only persons may be sent out 'to proclaim words'. An added problem occurs in this verse, namely, in the adjectives *sacred* and *imperishable* which are attributive to *proclamation*. The only manner in which this may be translated in some languages is 'utter words which are holy and which never will fail'.

Of eternal salvation must be in an objective relationship to 'proclamation' or 'word', e.g. 'word about being saved'. *Salvation* (see 10:26 for *save*) must quite often be rendered as a verb, e.g. 'be saved', 'be rescued', or 'be restored to health', but the addition of the adjective *eternal* tends to create certain problems, since the meaning of eternal must be expressed by some adverbial expression, often a phrase, e.g. 'being saved for ever' or 'being saved for time that will not end'.

ADDITIONAL NOTE
THE ENDING OF THE GOSPEL OF MARK

Only a brief statement of the evidence concerning the ending of the Gospel of Mark will be attempted here.

1. *External Evidence.*

It is not necessary to consider in great detail the manuscript evidence: besides the commentaries, a full account and treatment of the evidence is to be found in Westcott and Hort *The New Testament in the Original Greek, Appendix*, 28-51; B. H. Streeter *The Four Gospels*, 333-60; B. W. Warfield *An Introduction to the Textual Criticism of the New Testament*, 199-204; C. S. C. Williams *Alterations to the Text of the Synoptic Gospels and Acts*, 40-44. The manuscript evidence quoted here is from S. C. E. Legg *Novum Testamentum Graece, Secundum Marcum*.

The Gospel of Mark ends at 16:8 in the two oldest Uncial manuscripts of the New Testament, Codex *B* (*Vaticanus*) and ℵ (*Sinaiticus*), both of the 4th century. In the former the subscription KATA MARKON "according to Mark" follows v. 8, but the next column is left blank, suggesting that the copyist of *B* knew of an ending but did not have it in the manuscript he was copying; in the latter the subscription EUAGGE-LION KATA MARKON "Gospel according to Mark" follows v. 8, after which the Gospel of Luke begins in the next column. The Gospel ends at 16:8 also in the oldest Syriac version of the Gospels, the Sinaitic Syriac (4th or 5th century): at the end of v. 8 there is written in red ink, "Here ends the Gospel of Mark," followed immediately by the beginning of the

Gospel of Luke; and in important codices of the Armenian, Ethiopic and Georgian versions.

Besides the manuscript evidence, there are statements by Eusebius of Caesarea and by Jerome to the effect that vv. 9-20 were missing in Greek manuscripts known to them. Eusebius (c. A.D. 325) stated that "in nearly all the copies of the Gospel according to Mark" the end was at 16:8 (cf. Westcott and Hort, *op. cit.*, 31; Swete, ciii). The same testimony is borne by Jerome (c. A.D. 407) in his letter to Hedibia (cf. Westcott and Hort, *op. cit.*, 33-34).

To these manuscripts and versions must be added the testimony afforded by others. In the Minuscule Greek manuscript 22 (12th century) at the end of 16:8 there is written TELOS "End," followed by a note: "In some of the copies the Evangelist finishes at this point; in many, however, these (words) are current," after which come vv. 9-20 (the "Longer Ending"), followed again by TELOS "End."

Besides these there is also the evidence afforded by those manuscripts and versions which include the Shorter Ending (as well as the Longer Ending), for they also are witnesses to the fact that the Gospel of Mark ends at 16:8. As Warfield *Textual Criticism*, 200, says: "The existence of the shorter conclusion...is *à fortiori* evidence against the longer one. For no one doubts that this shorter conclusion is a spurious invention of the scribes; but it would not have been invented, save to fill the blank." The Shorter Ending stands alone in the Old Latin manuscript *k* (4th or 5th century); it is followed by the Longer Ending in the following: the Greek Uncial manuscript of the Gospels *L* (Codex *Regius*, 8th century), which has a line after v. 8, with the note, "there also are current in some places," followed by the Shorter Ending, and then, without a break, the words "but these also are current after 'for they were afraid'," followed by the Longer Ending in full, after which comes the subscription "According to Mark." In the Greek Uncial manuscript Ψ (8th or 9th century) the Shorter Ending is added to v. 8 without a break or note, after which comes the usual note "but there also are current after 'for they were afraid'," followed by the Longer Ending, and the subscription. The same is true of the Greek Uncial fragments 099 (7th century) and 0112 (7th century).

The Shorter Ending is also found (before the Longer Ending, as usual) in the margin of the Greek Minuscule manucript 274 (10th century) and in 579 (13th century); in the margin of the Harclean Syriac version (7th century), and in several important codices of the Sahidic, Bohairic and Ethiopic versions.

All this documentary evidence raises the question: why were the Longer Ending and the Shorter Ending *added* to the Gospel of Mark? The obvious answer is that the Gospel, ending as it does at v. 8, is incomplete, and these two Endings were added in order to complete the Gospel. They all stand as documentary evidence against what is printed as vv. 9-20 as being genuine: for it is inconceivable that any copyist would have omitted the twelve final verses of the Gospel if they were original. That they should have been added, however, from other sources by copyists who felt that the Gospel, ending at 16:8, was incomplete, is highly reasonable, and is, in fact, the most satisfactory solution of the problem presented by the external evidence.

We may conclude our brief treatment of the external evidence with the words of Hort: "When every item has been taken into account, the conclusion to be drawn from the Documentary evidence alone is that vv. 9-20 are a very early interpolation, early and widely diffused and welcomed" (Westcott and Hort, *op. cit.*, p. 46).

2. *Internal Evidence.*

A consideration of the evidence to be inferred from the nature of the Longer Ending itself should conclusively establish the judgment that it was not written by the author of the Gospel of Mark. In an ascending order of importance, three aspects of the internal evidence will be considered.

(1) *Vocabulary.* The Longer Ending contains (in the Nestle text) 101 different words (the total number of words is 167). Excluding irrelevant words such as proper names, connectives, numerals, prepositions, negative particles and the definite article, there is left a total of 75 different significant words in the section. Of these 75 a total of 15 (including 10 verbs) occur which do not appear in Mark, and 11 others are used in a sense different from that in which they are used in Mark. This means that in the passage slightly over one-third of the significant words used are not "Marcan," that is, either they do not appear in Mark or they are used in a way differing from that in which Mark uses them. One may notice particularly the following: *ekeinos* (vv. 10, 11, 13, 20), *theaomai* (vv. 11, 14), *poreuomai* (vv. 10, 12, 15), *meta tauta* (v. 12), *hoi met' autou genomenoi* (v. 10), *ktisis* (v. 15), *katakrinō* (v. 16), *glōssai k.·inai* (v. 17), *ho kurios Iēsous* (v. 19). In every verse in this passage there is either a word not found in Mark or else a word or phrase used in a non-Marcan manner.

When due allowance is made for the different subject matter, which requires a different vocabulary, it would appear that the marked degree of difference between the vocabulary of 16:9-20 and the Gospel of Mark argues strongly against a single author for both.

(2) *Style.* More cogent than the evidence from the vocabulary is the evidence afforded by the comparison between the literary style of the Gospel of Mark and of the Longer Ending. The beginning of the Longer Ending is most abrupt: the masculine nominative participle *anastas* "having risen," demands for its antecedent "he", (*i.e.* Jesus); the subject of v. 8, however, is the women, as they fled from the tomb. Furthermore, in this section nothing is said concerning the women (one of whom is Mary of Magdala) and their commission to carry the message to the disciples: they disappear entirely from the scene. By all counts, if the evangelist had continued the story after v. 8 he would have related how the women carried the message "to the disciples and Peter" as commanded by the angel (v. 7; unless—which is improbable—we are to suppose that the women kept the story to themselves; in all Gospel accounts of

the command to the women they go immediately and tell it to the disciples: cf. Mt. 28:7-8; Lk. 24:8-11, 22-24). This is exactly what the author of the Shorter Ending has done, in composing an ending to be added on at v. 8. More important still is the fact that twice in the Gospel of Mark (14:28, 16:7) a promise is made of a resurrection appearance to the disciples in Galilee. Surely the evangelist in narrating the appearances of the risen Lord would have included one to the disciples in Galilee. All appearances in vv. 9-20, however, are in Jerusalem and vicinity: to Mary of Magdala (vv. 9-10), to two on their way out of the city "to the country" (v. 12) who return to Jerusalem (v. 13) and tell the rest; and finally to the Eleven as they were eating (vv. 14-18), still in Jerusalem (since there is no indication of a journey of the Eleven to Galilee).

In the same first verse of the Longer Ending (v. 9) Mary Magdalene is referred to as though she had not been mentioned previously in the narrative: yet she is referred to by name three times in the narrative of the crucifixion, burial and resurrection of Jesus (15:40, 47, 16:1).

The whole style of the Longer Ending tells against Marcan authorship: the narrative is concise and barren, lacking the vivid and lifelike details so characteristic of Marcan historical narrative. As Gould says: "It is a mere summarizing of the appearances of our Lord, a manner of narration entirely foreign to this Gospel. Mark is the most vivid and picturesque of the evangelists, abbreviating discourse, but amplifying narration. But this is a mere enumeration" (p. 303).

Clearly vv. 9-20 are "part of an independent composition," is Swete's judgment (p. cx).

(3) *Content*. It is in a consideration of the contents of the Longer Ending, however, that the gravest objections are to be found to the opinion that it is part of the Gospel of Mark. Two items in particular call for examination: (a) the rebuke administered the disciples by Jesus (v. 14) and (b) the signs promised to the believers (vv. 17-18).

The words used in describing the rebuke which Jesus administered the disciples are extremely strong, and inconsistent with the character of Jesus in his relation to the disciples, as revealed in the Gospel of Mark. The verb *oneidizō* "to reproach" is used of the insults flung at Jesus by his enemies (Mk. 15:32), while the nouns *apistia* "unbelief" and *sklērokardia* "hardness of heart" are used in the Gospel to refer to men hostile to Jesus (cf. 6:6 and 10:5).

It is the nature of the "signs" promised to "the believers," however, that raises the strongest objection against receiving vv. 9-20 as part of the Gospel. The bizarre promise of immunity from snakes and poisonous drinks is completely out of character with the Person of Christ as revealed in the Gospel of Mark, the other Gospels, and in the whole of the New Testament. Nowhere did Jesus exempt himself or his followers from the natural laws which govern this life, nor did he ever intimate such exemptions would be given those who believed in him. That such miracles have in fact occasionally taken place is a matter of record; what is to be doubted is that the Lord should have promised them indiscriminately to all believers as part of the blessings which would be bestowed upon them. It is this very "natural" desire for signs which Jesus so strongly rebuked in the Pharisees (Mk. 8:11-13): yet in the Longer Ending he is portrayed as promising the believers "signs" as crassly materialistic and supernatural as any the Pharisees would have asked for!

The conclusion is irresistible: the Longer Ending is not by Mark. Even so conservative a scholar as Lagrange (who is kept by the Biblical Commission of the Roman Catholic Church from concluding that vv. 9-20 are not by Mark) has to distinguish between what he calls "ecclesiastical canonicity" and "literary authenticity," pronouncing in favor of the former, but against the latter. (In adherence to the Commission's verdict, however, he must say, negatively, that the internal evidence "does not necessarily conclude that Mark was not the author of the conclusion.")

Whatever conclusion one reaches as to the reason why the Gospel of Mark ends at 16 : 8, the external evidence of the manuscripts themselves, and the internal evidence of the Longer Ending, as respects vocabulary, style and content, provide cumulative and finally conclusive evidence to the fact that what stands as vv. 9-20 of chapter 16 is not by the author of the Gospel of Mark. As Hort concluded: "vv. 9-20 and the Shorter Conclusion were alike absent from the earliest and purest transmitted text, and alike added at a later time owing to a sense of incompleteness" (Westcott and Hort, op. cit., 51).

3. Canonicity.

There remains to be said a word concerning the Longer Ending, as regards its canonicity. Lagrange, while recognizing its literary inauthenticity, argues from the decision of the Council of Trent to the effect that vv. 9-20 are canonical. "The ending...is a fragment which comes, if not from an apostle, at least from a disciple of the Lord whose authority was recognized. It has been seen that the doubts concerning its literary authenticity cast no suspicion against its canonicity. Everyone agrees that the ending is very ancient, and there is no reason for holding that it does not date from apostolic times" (p. 466).

In the same vein R. H. Lightfoot writes: "It should be borne in mind that, whatever conclusion may be reached about the original ending of St. Mark's gospel, verses 9 to 20 in ch. 16 are part of the canonical scriptures, accepted in and by the universal Church" (The Gospel Message of St. Mark, 116, footnote 3).

Notwithstanding these somewhat dogmatic statements, the problem is not so easily stated nor so simply solved. The principle enunciated by Lagrange and Lightfoot, strictly applied, would mean that the text of the New Testament, as found in the Textus Receptus, is finally and forever the Canon, including all words, phrases, verses and larger sections which the critical study of the text in the last two centuries has shown not to have been part of the original text. Clearly such a position is untenable. Must the Church accept as binding the additions to the text which are clearly of a later origin, betraying, many times, easily recognized human impulses and tendencies on the part of the scribes?

Indeed, as Lightfoot wrote in a letter (dated 12 February 1952), "the attempt to define exactly where canonicity begins or ends, in respect of the individual words of scripture, has not, I believe, ever been attempted; and it would certainly be most difficult." It is not here that the solution to this problem is to be attempted.

It is not difficult, however, to recognize vv. 9-20 as a later addition to the (incomplete) Gospel of Mark which, negatively, contributes nothing to the Church's knowledge of her Lord, and, positively, represents him as speaking in a manner completely foreign to his character, as revealed in the canonical Gospels. The Longer Ending may indeed, as Hort concluded, be founded on some tradition of the apostolic age; however, as he said, "it manifestly cannot claim any apostolic authority" (Westcott and Hort, *op. cit.*, 51).

It would be highly precarious, at the least, for the Church to base her understanding of the events of the post-resurrection period of her Lord's ministry upon such a document as the Longer Ending.

BIBLICAL REFERENCES

Genesis

1: 27	310
2: 24	311
5: 1	310
12: 10	28
18: 14	325
19: 17	266
22: 2	31
22: 3	27
26: 2	28
29: 14	311
29: 21	37
31: 36	61
32: 31	266
37: 27	311
37: 35	28
38: 8	375
38: 9	375
43: 15	28
46: 3	28

Exodus

2: 11	26
3: 2	379
3: 3	379
3: 4	379
3: 5	379
3: 6	379
3: 14	466
12: 8	425
12: 13	425
12: 15	425
12: 16	425
12: 17	425
12: 18	425
12: 19	425
12: 20	425
12: 23	425
12: 27	425
18: 25	112
20: 12	228, 319
20: 13	319
20: 14	319
20: 15	319
20: 16	319
21: 17	228
24: 8	440

Exodus (cont.)

34: 5	415
34: 21	97
36: 1	112

Leviticus

2: 13	304
7: 20	266
7: 21	266
7: 25	266
7: 27	266
12: 6	351
12: 8	351
13	64
14	64
14: 2-32	68
14: 22	68, 251
15: 14	351
15: 25	171
15: 29	351
16: 2	415
16: 29	90
19: 18	384
23: 30	266
24: 5	99
24: 6	99
24: 7	99
24: 8	99
24: 9	99
24: 15	78
24: 16	78

Numbers

11: 25	415
16: 30	28
20: 15	28
23: 7	28
24: 2	28
27: 17	204
31: 19	266
35: 11	266
35: 15	266
35: 30	266

Deuteronomy

4: 32	416
4: 35	385

Deuteronomy (cont.)

5: 16	228, 319
5: 17	319
5: 18	319
5: 19	319
5: 20	319
6: 4	382, 385
6: 5	383, 385
13: 2	412
13: 8	416
16: 5	434
16: 6	434
16: 7	434
21: 23	497
24: 1	309
25: 5f.	375
29: 4	133
30: 4	416

Joshua

3: 16	28
10: 24	389

Judges

3: 10	28
9: 2	311
11: 12	49
11: 29	28
14: 6	28
14: 19	28
15: 14	28
17: 8	96

I Samuel

1: 17	176
10: 6	28
10: 10	28
11: 6	28
16: 13	28
16: 16	28
16: 23	28
18: 10	28
19: 9	28
19: 20	28
19: 23	28
20: 13	471
21: 1	98, 99

524

II Corinthians (cont.)		I Thessalonians		I Peter	
11: 31	465	2: 8	35	1: 3	465
12: 10	31	2: 9	35	2: 6	368
		4: 17	416	2: 7	368
Galatians		5: 3	400	3: 9	336
3: 1	504	5: 15	336	4: 17	35
4: 6	448				
5: 9	253	I Timothy		2 Peter	
		2: 6	337	2: 1-11	11
Ephesians				2: 22	286
1: 3	465	Hebrews			
1: 10	37	3: 2	112	I John	
1: 13	37	3: 11	251	2: 18	11
2: 20	368	4: 3	251	3: 1	396
4: 18	106	4: 5	251	3: 13	498
5: 31	311	6: 1	12		
		12: 16	336		
Philippians				Revelation	
2: 6	509	James		8: 12	45
2: 7	509	3: 9	355		
2: 11	17	4: 15	336		

GREEK WORD LIST

The following Greek words and phrases have been dealt with in greater detail in the passages indicated.

agapētos	1: 11	
aggareuō	15: 21	
agros	5: 14	
akoloutheō	1: 18	
anistēmi	1: 35,	8: 31
aphiēmi	1: 18,	2: 5
apokrinomai	3: 33,	8: 4
apollumi	1: 24	
apoluō	6: 36	
archiereis	8: 31	
baptizō	1: 5	
basileia	1: 15	
didachē	1: 22	
dunamis	5: 30	
egeirō	1: 31	
eggizō	1: 15	
eis	1: 10	
ekballō	1: 12	
embrimaomai	1: 43	
epi tēs gēs	9: 3	
epitimaō	1: 25	
euaggelion	1: 1	
eucharisteō	6: 41	
eulogeō	6: 41	
exomologeō	1: 5	
graphō	1: 2	
hotan	11: 19	
kai egeneto	1: 9	

kalos	4: 8		
katabainō eis	1: 10		
krateō	1: 31		
kurios	1: 3		
lepros	1: 40		
logos	1: 45		
lutron anti	10: 45		
mellō	10: 32		
metanoia	1: 4		
Nazarēnos	14: 67		
parabolē	3: 23		
paradidōmi	1: 14,	3: 19,	4: 29
	14: 10		
peran	3: 8		
perichōros	1: 28		
pherō	1: 32		
pisteuō en	1: 15		
pleroō	1: 15		
pneuma	1: 23,	2: 8	
pneuma hagion	1: 8		
poios	11: 28		
presbuteros	7: 3		
psuchē	3: 4,	8: 35	
sabbata	1: 21		
schizō	1: 10		
skandalizō	4: 17		
sōzō	3: 4		
zēteō	3: 32		

INDEX OF LANGUAGES

Popoluca (Mexico) 32, 56, 67, 107, 140, 183, 195, 196, 199, 216, 225, 229, 264, 316, 348, 360, 389.

Pueblo Aztec (Mexico) 71.

Putu (Liberia) 7, 38, 135, 266, 287, 333, 465, 477.

Quechua (Peru) 4, 21, 23, 45.

Rawang (Burma) 324.

Rincon Zapotec (Mexico) 185, 226, 267.

San Blas (Panama) 4, 7, 10, 13, 19, 30, 36, 39, 41, 47, 54, 74, 106, 137, 183, 184, 199, 202, 220, 225, 226, 229, 235, 282, 298, 302, 324, 369, 417, 482, 486.

Shilluk (Sudan) 13, 32, 35, 56, 65, 71, 78, 80, 83, 107, 117, 121, 123, 125, 133, 140, 142, 147, 154, 159, 164, 168, 172, 176, 180, 181, 204, 216, 242, 330, 372, 515.

Shipibo (Peru) 5, 7, 9, 13, 20, 30, 33, 35, 38, 47, 56, 57, 59, 61, 62, 65, 69, 103, 107, 117, 119, 146, 148, 149, 176, 191, 199, 216, 225, 228, 234, 235, 250, 253, 273, 275, 288, 302, 324, 349, 353, 356, 367, 371, 372, 426, 486, 492, 500.

Sierra Aztec (Mexico) 115, 126, 184, 450.

Sierra Popoloca (Mexico) 184, 191.

South Toradja (Indonesia) 3, 9, 13, 16, 19, 26, 35, 45, 48, 51, 61, 64, 73, 78, 82, 83, 87, 90, 96, 98, 100, 103, 112, 120, 123, 131, 140, 144, 147, 149, 159, 160, 169, 175, 182, 189, 207, 214, 220, 221, 225, 226, 227, 229, 235, 243, 257, 259, 263, 266, 271, 283, 286, 287, 291, 295, 300, 301.

Spanish (Latin America) 1, 2, 18, 45, 164, 195, 225, 238, 243, 248, 275, 302, 323, 336, 370, 394, 418, 428, 433, 449, 482, 485, 491.

Subanen (Philippines) 70, 74, 89, 94, 96, 103, 116, 131, 146, 147, 148, 155, 160, 162, 192, 197, 199, 202, 207, 209, 211, 214, 215, 226, 229, 233, 235, 237, 241, 256, 261, 268, 272, 279, 281, 284, 288, 289, 297, 373, 374, 392, 407, 425, 460, 496.

Tae (Indonesia) 79.

Tagalog (Philippines) 45.

Tarahumara (Mexico) 45, 47, 57, 61, 80, 83, 102, 119, 120, 131, 132, 142,

144, 149, 151, 159, 168, 176, 179, 209, 221, 276, 296, 364, 393, 450, 465, 495.

Tarascan (Mexico) 45, 61, 87, 137, 140, 142, 168, 202, 225, 250.

Taungthu (Burma) 149.

Tchien (Liberia) 433, 441, 448.

Tepehua (Mexico) 225, 462.

Tetelcingo Aztec (Mexico) 133, 147, 159, 225, 266, 269, 441.

Thai (Thailand) 491.

Tiddim (Burma) 324.

Timorese (Indonesia) 38, 58, 79, 137.

Toba Batak (Indonesia) 7, 19, 35, 59, 67, 69, 90, 101, 140, 148, 162, 214, 229, 263, 288, 298, 301.

Tojolabal (Mexico) 166, 172, 204.

Totonac (Mexico) 7, 13, 45, 83, 119, 126, 133, 137, 147, 150, 184, 191, 225, 235, 266, 300, 302, 319, 340.

Trique (Mexico) 13, 16, 38, 92, 94, 101, 106, 107, 113, 115, 119, 127, 147, 162, 164, 166, 172, 192, 195, 197, 214, 216, 229, 247, 258, 266, 323, 328, 348, 406.

Trukese (South Pacific) 225.

Tswa (Mozambique) 13.

Tumbuka (Nyasaland) 143.

Tzeltal (Mexico) 1, 13, 19, 26, 36, 45, 50, 51, 52, 54, 56, 61, 65, 77, 80, 83, 84, 94, 97, 100, 105, 107, 117, 119, 122, 125, 129, 131, 136, 137, 140, 142, 143, 147, 151, 154, 156, 164, 168, 173, 176, 184, 186, 189, 195, 196, 198, 199, 202, 215, 216, 220, 221, 225, 226, 231, 235, 237, 239, 242, 247, 251, 252, 258, 259, 262, 263, 266, 267, 269, 271, 273, 283, 288, 289, 295, 296, 297, 299, 300, 301, 305, 306, 308, 309, 311, 312, 313, 315, 319, 321, 322, 323, 325, 326, 327, 330, 333, 334, 335, 337, 347, 348, 362, 372, 373, 377, 378, 384, 386, 387, 389, 390, 391, 392, 395, 397, 398, 406, 408, 411, 412, 420, 421, 423, 425, 427, 428, 430, 431, 438, 443, 444, 446, 449, 450, 456, 459, 460, 462, 465, 466, 467, 468, 470, 471, 474, 482, 485, 486, 490, 492, 496, 498, 501, 509, 510, 512, 515.

Tzotzil (Mexico) 3, 16, 23, 32, 34, 46, 61, 80, 83, 106, 107, 133, 142, 156,

INDEX OF MAJOR WORKS CITED*

* Not including periodical articles, lexicons, and commentaries on Mark.

533

Richardson, Alan (ed.), *A Theological Word Book* 12, 85, 90.

Robertson, A. T., *Grammar* 26, 27, 29, 50, 53, 193, 336, 354.

Robertson, A. and Plummer, A., *Commentary on I Corinthians* 208.

Robinson, J. A., *Commentary on Ephesians* 79, 106, 191.

Robinson, J. M., *The Problem of History in Mark* 336.

Smith, Morton, *Tannaitic Parallels* 219, 264.

Streeter, B. H., *The Four Gospels* 516, 517.

Taylor, Vincent, *Jesus and His Sacrifice* 336, 337.

Vincent, M. R., *Word Studies* 17, 42, 72, 75, 79, 91, 96, 124, 130, 158, 258, 296, 344, 390, 452.

Warfield, B. W., *An Introduction to Textual Criticism* 517, 518.

Westcott, B. F., *Commentary on Hebrews* 336.

Williams, C. S. C., *Alterations to the Text* 517.